THE BOOK ®

Citroen ZX
Service and Repair Manual

Mark Coombs

Models covered
All Citroën ZX models with petrol engines, including special/limited editions;
Estate; 3 and 5-door Hatchback

(1881-4AF3-352)

1124 cc, 1360 cc, 1580 cc, 1761 cc (8-valve and 16-valve), 1905 cc,
1998 cc (8-valve) and 1998 cc (XU10J4,16-valve)

Does not cover 1998 cc (XU10J4RS, 16-valve) petrol engine, introduced in 1997
Does not cover Diesel engine models

© Haynes Publishing 2002

ABCDE
FGHIJ

A book in the **Haynes Service and Repair Manual Series**

ISBN **1 85960 750 0**

British Library Cataloguing in Publication Data
A catalogue record for this book is available from the British Library.

Printed in the USA

Haynes Publishing
Sparkford, Nr Yeovil, Somerset BA22 7JJ, England

Haynes North America, Inc
861 Lawrence Drive, Newbury Park, California 91320, USA

Editions Haynes
4, Rue de l'Abreuvoir
92415 COURBEVOIE CEDEX, France

Haynes Publishing Nordiska AB
Box 1504, 751 45 UPPSALA, Sverige

Contents

LIVING WITH YOUR CITROEN ZX

Introduction to the Citroen ZX   Page   0•4
Safety first!   Page   0•5

Roadside repairs

Introduction   Page   0•6
If your car won't start   Page   0•6
Jump starting   Page   0•7
Wheel changing   Page   0•8
Identifying leaks   Page   0•9
Towing   Page   0•9

Weekly checks

Introduction   Page   0•10
Underbonnet check points   Page   0•10
Engine oil level   Page   0•11
Power steering fluid level   Page   0•11
Brake fluid level   Page   0•12
Wiper blades   Page   0•12
Coolant level   Page   0•13
Screen/headlamp washer fluid level   Page   0•13
Tyre condition and pressure   Page   0•14
Battery   Page   0•15
Electrical systems   Page   0•15
Lubricants and fluids   Page   0•16
Choosing your engine oil   Page   0•16
Tyre pressures   Page   0•16

MAINTENANCE

Routine maintenance and servicing

Maintenance schedule   Page   1•3
Maintenance procedures   Page   1•5

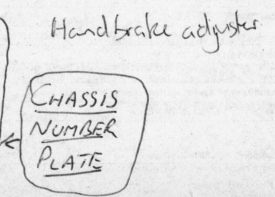

AUTOMOBILES CITROEN
PMAC 0121001V
VF7N2A90007A90731
    1490
    2490
  1-790
  2-740

Handbrake adjuster

CHASSIS NUMBER PLATE

Contents

REPAIRS & OVERHAUL

Engine and associated systems
TU series engine in-car repair procedures   Page 2A•1
XU series engine in-car repair procedures   Page 2B•1
Engine removal and overhaul procedures   Page 2C•1
Cooling, heating and ventilation systems   Page 3•1
Fuel and exhaust systems - carburettor models   Page 4A•1
Fuel and exhaust systems - single-point fuel injection models   Page 4B•1
Fuel and exhaust systems - multi-point fuel injection models   Page 4C•1
Emission control systems   Page 4D•1
Engine electrical systems   Page 5•1

Transmission
Clutch   Page 6•1
Manual transmission   Page 7A•1
Automatic transmission   Page 7B•1
Driveshafts   Page 8•1

Brakes and suspension
Braking system   Page 9•1
Suspension and steering   Page 10•1

Body equipment
Bodywork and fittings   Page 11•1
Body electrical systems   Page 12•1

Wiring diagrams
   Page 12•21

REFERENCE

Dimensions and weights   Page REF•1
Conversion factors   Page REF•2
Buying spare parts   Page REF•3
Vehicle identification   Page REF•3
General repair procedures   Page REF•4
Jacking and vehicle support   Page REF•5
Radio/cassette unit anti-theft system - precaution   Page REF•5
Tools and working facilities   Page REF•6
MOT test checks   Page REF•8
Fault finding   Page REF•12
Glossary of technical terms   Page REF•19

Index
   Page REF•23

The Citroën ZX range was introduced to the UK in June 1991. Originally, the ZX was available with a choice of 1.1 litre (1124 cc), 1.4 litre (1360 cc), 1.6 litre (1580 cc) or 1.9 litre (1905 cc) engines and in five-door Hatchback body configuration. All engines are derived from the well proven TU series (1124 cc and 1360 cc) and XU series (1580 cc and 1905 cc) engines, which have appeared in many Citroën and Peugeot vehicles. Not all engine sizes, however, are available in all markets (the 1.1 litre version is not available in the UK). The engines are of four-cylinder overhead camshaft design, mounted transversely and inclined to the rear, with the transmission mounted on the left-hand side.

In 1992, a three-door Hatchback variant was introduced, together with three new "sports" models, all in three-door Hatchback configuration and equipped with new engines. The new engines were again derived from the XU series and available in 1.8 litre (1761 cc), 2.0 litre (1998 cc - 8-valve) and 2.0 litre (1998 cc - 16-valve) versions.

Further refinements to the range saw the introduction of an Estate model together with various styling and mechanical revisions.

All models are fitted with a five-speed manual transmission as standard, with a four-speed automatic transmission available as an option on certain larger engine models.

Fully-independent front suspension is fitted, with the components attached to a subframe assembly. The rear suspension is semi-independent, with torsion bars and trailing arms.

All models in the range are comprehensively-equipped, and an anti-lock braking system (ABS) and air conditioning system are available as options on certain models (ABS is standard on the 2.0 litre 16-valve).

Provided that regular servicing is carried out in accordance with the manufacturer's recommendations, the Citroën ZX should prove reliable and very economical. The engine compartment is well-designed, and most of the items requiring frequent attention are easily accessible.

Your Citroën ZX Manual

The aim of this Manual is to help you get the best value from your vehicle. It can do so in several ways. It can help you decide what work must be done (even should you choose to get it done by a garage), provide information on routine maintenance and servicing, and give a logical course of action and diagnosis when random faults occur. However, it is hoped that you will use the Manual by tackling the work yourself. On simpler jobs it may even be quicker than booking the car into a garage and going there twice, to leave and collect it. Perhaps most important, a lot of money can be saved by avoiding the costs a garage must charge to cover its labour and overheads.

The Manual has drawings and descriptions to show the function of the various components so that their layout can be understood. Then the tasks are described and photographed in a clear step-by-step sequence.

References to the "left" and "right" of the vehicle are in the sense of a person in the driver's seat facing forward.

Citroën ZX 1.4 Reflex Plus 5-door

Citroën ZX 2.0 16-valve

Acknowledgements

Certain illustrations are the copyright of Citroën Cars Ltd, and are used with their permission. Thanks are also due to Draper Tools Limited, who provided some of the workshop tools, and to all those people at Sparkford who helped in the production of this Manual.

We take great pride in the accuracy of information given in this manual, but vehicle manufacturers make alterations and design changes during the production run of a particular vehicle of which they do not inform us. No liability can be accepted by the authors or publishers for loss, damage or injury caused by any errors in, or omissions from, the information given.

Working on your car can be dangerous. This page shows just some of the potential risks and hazards, with the aim of creating a safety-conscious attitude.

General hazards

Scalding

• Don't remove the radiator or expansion tank cap while the engine is hot.
• Engine oil, automatic transmission fluid or power steering fluid may also be dangerously hot if the engine has recently been running.

Burning

• Beware of burns from the exhaust system and from any part of the engine. Brake discs and drums can also be extremely hot immediately after use.

Crushing

• When working under or near a raised vehicle, always supplement the jack with axle stands, or use drive-on ramps. *Never venture under a car which is only supported by a jack.*
• Take care if loosening or tightening high-torque nuts when the vehicle is on stands. Initial loosening and final tightening should be done with the wheels on the ground.

Fire

• Fuel is highly flammable; fuel vapour is explosive.
• Don't let fuel spill onto a hot engine.
• Do not smoke or allow naked lights (including pilot lights) anywhere near a vehicle being worked on. Also beware of creating sparks (electrically or by use of tools).
• Fuel vapour is heavier than air, so don't work on the fuel system with the vehicle over an inspection pit.
• Another cause of fire is an electrical overload or short-circuit. Take care when repairing or modifying the vehicle wiring.
• Keep a fire extinguisher handy, of a type suitable for use on fuel and electrical fires.

Electric shock

• Ignition HT voltage can be dangerous, especially to people with heart problems or a pacemaker. Don't work on or near the ignition system with the engine running or the ignition switched on.

• Mains voltage is also dangerous. Make sure that any mains-operated equipment is correctly earthed. Mains power points should be protected by a residual current device (RCD) circuit breaker.

Fume or gas intoxication

• Exhaust fumes are poisonous; they often contain carbon monoxide, which is rapidly fatal if inhaled. Never run the engine in a confined space such as a garage with the doors shut.
• Fuel vapour is also poisonous, as are the vapours from some cleaning solvents and paint thinners.

Poisonous or irritant substances

• Avoid skin contact with battery acid and with any fuel, fluid or lubricant, especially antifreeze, brake hydraulic fluid and Diesel fuel. Don't syphon them by mouth. If such a substance is swallowed or gets into the eyes, seek medical advice.
• Prolonged contact with used engine oil can cause skin cancer. Wear gloves or use a barrier cream if necessary. Change out of oil-soaked clothes and do not keep oily rags in your pocket.
• Air conditioning refrigerant forms a poisonous gas if exposed to a naked flame (including a cigarette). It can also cause skin burns on contact.

Asbestos

• Asbestos dust can cause cancer if inhaled or swallowed. Asbestos may be found in gaskets and in brake and clutch linings. When dealing with such components it is safest to assume that they contain asbestos.

Special hazards

Hydrofluoric acid

• This extremely corrosive acid is formed when certain types of synthetic rubber, found in some O-rings, oil seals, fuel hoses etc, are exposed to temperatures above 400°C. The rubber changes into a charred or sticky substance containing the acid. *Once formed, the acid remains dangerous for years. If it gets onto the skin, it may be necessary to amputate the limb concerned.*
• When dealing with a vehicle which has suffered a fire, or with components salvaged from such a vehicle, wear protective gloves and discard them after use.

The battery

• Batteries contain sulphuric acid, which attacks clothing, eyes and skin. Take care when topping-up or carrying the battery.
• The hydrogen gas given off by the battery is highly explosive. Never cause a spark or allow a naked light nearby. Be careful when connecting and disconnecting battery chargers or jump leads.

Air bags

• Air bags can cause injury if they go off accidentally. Take care when removing the steering wheel and/or facia. Special storage instructions may apply.

Diesel injection equipment

• Diesel injection pumps supply fuel at very high pressure. Take care when working on the fuel injectors and fuel pipes.

⚠️ *Warning: Never expose the hands, face or any other part of the body to injector spray; the fuel can penetrate the skin with potentially fatal results.*

Remember...

DO

• Do use eye protection when using power tools, and when working under the vehicle.

• Do wear gloves or use barrier cream to protect your hands when necessary.

• Do get someone to check periodically that all is well when working alone on the vehicle.

• Do keep loose clothing and long hair well out of the way of moving mechanical parts.

• Do remove rings, wristwatch etc, before working on the vehicle – especially the electrical system.

• Do ensure that any lifting or jacking equipment has a safe working load rating adequate for the job.

DON'T

• Don't attempt to lift a heavy component which may be beyond your capability – get assistance.

• Don't rush to finish a job, or take unverified short cuts.

• Don't use ill-fitting tools which may slip and cause injury.

• Don't leave tools or parts lying around where someone can trip over them. Mop up oil and fuel spills at once.

• Don't allow children or pets to play in or near a vehicle being worked on.

The following pages are intended to help in dealing with common roadside emergencies and breakdowns. You will find more detailed fault finding information at the back of the manual, and repair information in the main chapters.

If your car won't start and the starter motor doesn't turn

☐ If it's a model with automatic transmission, make sure the selector is in 'P' or 'N'.
☐ Open the bonnet and make sure that the battery terminals are clean and tight.
☐ Switch on the headlights and try to start the engine. If the headlights go very dim when you're trying to start, the battery is probably flat. Get out of trouble by jump starting (see next page) using a friend's car.

If your car won't start even though the starter motor turns as normal

☐ Is there fuel in the tank?
☐ Is there moisture on electrical components under the bonnet? Switch off the ignition, then wipe off any obvious dampness with a dry cloth. Spray a water-repellent aerosol product (WD-40 or equivalent) on ignition and fuel system electrical connectors like those shown in the photos. On petrol models, pay special attention to the ignition coil wiring connector and HT leads. Diesel engines are not generally as susceptible to damp problems, but all accessible wiring and connectors should still be checked.

A Check the condition and security of the battery connections.

B Check that the spark plug HT leads are securely connected by pushing them onto the spark plugs and ignition coil.

C The throttle potentiometer wiring plug may cause problems if not connected securely.

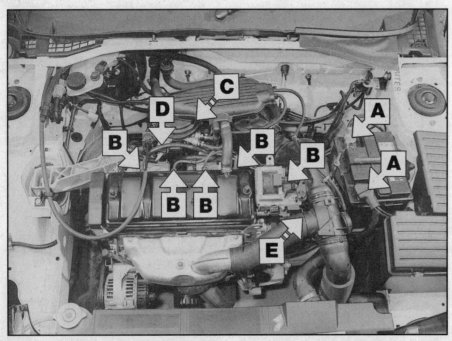

Check that electrical connections are secure (with the ignition switched off) and spray them with a water dispersant spray like WD-40 if you suspect a problem due to damp.

D Check that the idle control stepper motor wiring is secure.

E Check all other engine related wiring plugs for security.

Jump starting

Jump starting will get you out of trouble, but you must correct whatever made the battery go flat in the first place. There are three possibilities:

1 *The battery has been drained by repeated attempts to start, or by leaving the lights on.*

2 *The charging system is not working properly (alternator drivebelt slack or broken, alternator wiring fault or alternator itself faulty).*

3 *The battery itself is at fault (electrolyte low, or battery worn out).*

When jump-starting a car using a booster battery, observe the following precautions:

✔ Before connecting the booster battery, make sure that the ignition is switched off.

✔ Ensure that all electrical equipment (lights, heater, wipers, etc) is switched off.

✔ Take note of any special precautions printed on the battery case.

✔ Make sure that the booster battery is the same voltage as the discharged one in the vehicle.

✔ If the battery is being jump-started from the battery in another vehicle, the two vehicles MUST NOT TOUCH each other.

✔ Make sure that the transmission is in neutral (or PARK, in the case of automatic transmission).

1 Connect one end of the red jump lead to the positive (+) terminal of the flat battery

2 Connect the other end of the red lead to the positive (+) terminal of the booster battery.

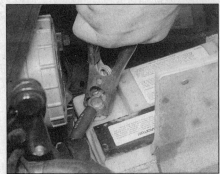

3 Connect one end of the black jump lead to the negative (-) terminal of the booster battery

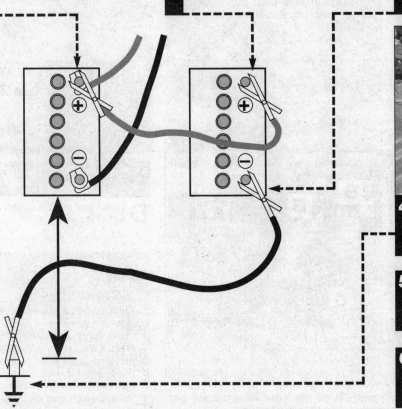

4 Connect the other end of the black jump lead to a bolt or bracket on the engine block, well away from the battery, on the vehicle to be started.

5 Make sure that the jump leads will not come into contact with the fan, drive-belts or other moving parts of the engine.

6 Start the engine using the booster battery and run it at idle speed. Switch on the lights, rear window demister and heater blower motor, then disconnect the jump leads in the reverse order of connection. Turn off the lights etc.

Wheel changing

Some of the details shown here will vary according to model. For instance, the location of the spare wheel and jack is not the same on all cars. However, the basic principles apply to all vehicles.

 Warning: Do not change a wheel in a situation where you risk being hit by other traffic. On busy roads, try to stop in a lay-by or a gateway. Be wary of passing traffic while changing the wheel – it is easy to become distracted by the job in hand.

Preparation

☐ When a puncture occurs, stop as soon as it is safe to do so.
☐ Park on firm level ground, if possible, and well out of the way of other traffic.
☐ Use hazard warning lights if necessary.

☐ If you have one, use a warning triangle to alert other drivers of your presence.
☐ Apply the handbrake and engage first or reverse gear (or "Park" on models with automatic transmission).

☐ Chock the wheel diagonally opposite the one being removed – a couple of large stones will do for this.
☐ If the ground is soft, use a flat piece of wood to spread the load under the jack.

Changing the wheel

1 Location of wheel brace in luggage compartment - Estate shown

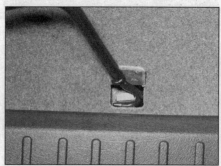

2 Using the wheel brace end to unscrew the spare wheel carrier retaining screw - 10 to 12 turns

3 Lowering the spare wheel carrier - chock is located within wheel

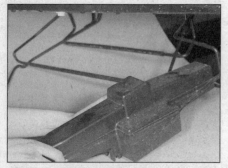

4 Removing the covered jack from the spare wheel carrier

5 Chocking the wheel diagonally opposite the one being changed

6 Using the wheel brace end to detach the wheel trim

7 Using the wheel brace to slightly loosen the wheel bolts

8 Using the jack to raise the vehicle until the wheel is clear of the ground, allowing the wheel bolts and wheel to be removed. Fit the replacement wheel and tighten the nuts to the correct torque

Finally...

☐ Remove the wheel chocks.
☐ Stow the jack and tools in the correct locations in the car.
☐ Check the tyre pressure on the wheel just fitted. If it is low, or you don't have a pressure gauge with you, drive slowly to the nearest garage and inflate the tyre to the right pressure.
☐ Have the damaged tyre or wheel repaired as soon as possible.

Identifying leaks

Puddles on the garage floor or drive, or obvious wetness under the bonnet or underneath the car, suggest a leak that needs investigating. It can sometimes be difficult to decide where the leak is coming from, especially if the engine bay is very dirty already. Leaking oil or fluid can also be blown rearwards by the passage of air under the car, giving a false impression of where the problem lies.

 Warning: Most automotive oils and fluids are poisonous. Wash them off skin, and change out of contaminated clothing, without delay.

 The smell of a fluid leaking from the car may provide a clue to what's leaking. Some fluids are distinctively coloured. It may help to clean the car carefully and to park it over some clean paper overnight as an aid to locating the source of the leak. Remember that some leaks may only occur while the engine is running.

Sump oil

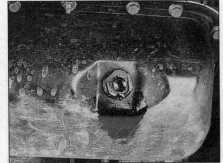

Engine oil may leak from the drain plug...

Oil from filter

...or from the base of the oil filter.

Gearbox oil

Gearbox oil can leak from the seals at the inboard ends of the driveshafts.

Antifreeze

Leaking antifreeze often leaves a crystalline deposit like this.

Brake fluid

A leak occurring at a wheel is almost certainly brake fluid.

Power steering fluid

Power steering fluid may leak from the pipe connectors on the steering rack.

Towing

When all else fails, you may find yourself having to get a tow home – or of course you may be helping somebody else. Long-distance recovery should only be done by a garage or breakdown service. For shorter distances, DIY towing using another car is easy enough, but observe the following points:

☐ Use a proper tow-rope – they are not expensive. The vehicle being towed must display an "ON TOW" sign in its rear window.

☐ Towing eyes are fitted to the front and rear of the vehicle for attachment of the tow rope. On certain models, plastic covers must be unclipped from the bumpers for access to the towing eyes.

☐ Always turn the ignition key to the "on" position when the vehicle is being towed, so that the steering lock is released, and that the direction indicator and brake lights will work.

☐ Before being towed, release the handbrake and select neutral on the transmission.

☐ Note that greater-than-usual pedal pressure will be required to operate the brakes, since the vacuum servo unit is only operational with the engine running.

☐ On models with power steering, greater-than-usual steering effort will also be required.

☐ The driver of the car being towed must keep the tow-rope taut at all times to avoid snatching.

☐ Make sure that both drivers know the route before setting off.

☐ Only drive at moderate speeds and keep the distance towed to a minimum. Drive smoothly and allow plenty of time for slowing down at junctions.

☐ On models with automatic transmission, special precautions apply. If in doubt, do not tow, or transmission damage may result.

Introduction

There are some very simple checks which need only take a few minutes to carry out, but which could save you a lot on inconvenience and expense.

These *"Weekly checks"* require no great skill or special tools, and the small amount of time they take to perform could well prove to be very well spent, for example;

☐ Keeping an eye on tyre condition and pressures, will not only help to stop them wearing out prematurely but could also save your life.

☐ Many breakdowns are caused by electrical problems. Battery-related faults are particularly common and a quick check on a regular basis will often prevent the majority of these.

☐ If your car develops a brake fluid leak, the first time you might know about it is when your brakes don't work properly. Checking the level regularly will give advance warning of this kind of problem.

☐ If the oil or coolant levels run low, the cost of repairing any engine damage will be far greater than fixing the leak.

Underbonnet check points

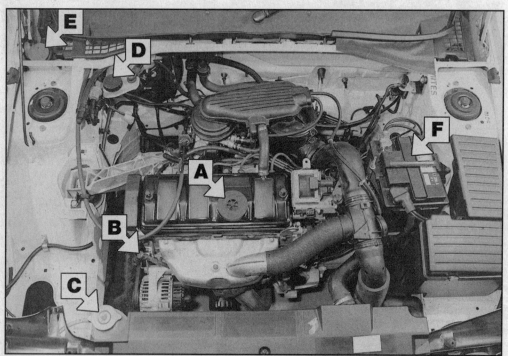

1.4 litre engine

A Engine oil filler cap
B Engine oil level dipstick
C Radiator filler cap
D Brake fluid reservoir
E Screen washer fluid reservoir
F Battery

1.6 litre engine

A Engine oil filler cap
B Engine oil level dipstick
C Radiator filler cap
D Brake fluid reservoir
E Screen washer fluid reservoir
F Battery

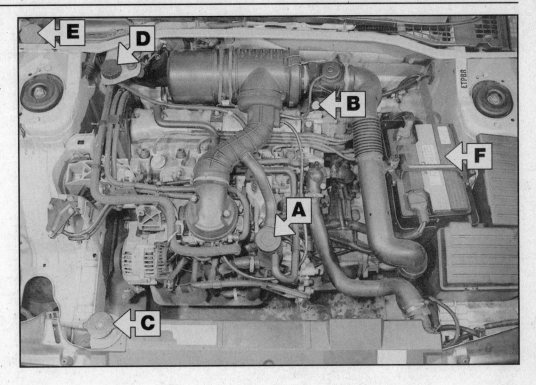

1.8 litre (8-valve) engine

A Engine oil filler cap
B Engine oil level dipstick
C Radiator filler cap
D Brake fluid reservoir
E Screen washer fluid reservoir
F Battery

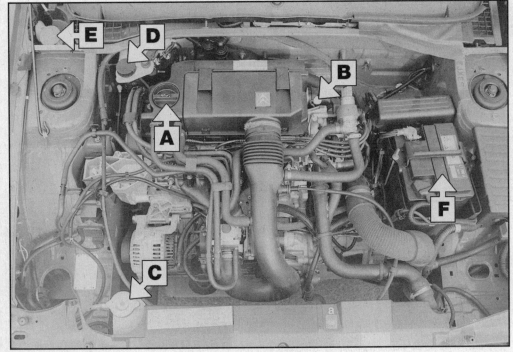

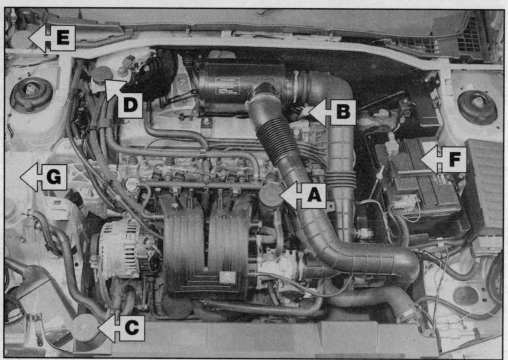

1.9 litre engine

A   Engine oil filler cap
B   Engine oil level dipstick
C   Radiator filler cap
D   Brake fluid reservoir
E   Screen washer fluid reservoir
F   Battery
G   Power steering fluid reservoir

2.0 litre (8-valve) engine

A   Engine oil filler cap
B   Engine oil level dipstick
C   Radiator filler cap
D   Brake fluid reservoir
E   Screen washer fluid reservoir
F   Battery
G   Power steering fluid reservoir

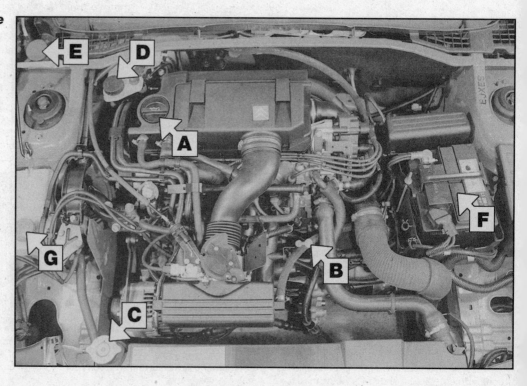

Engine oil level

Before you start

✔ Make sure that the car is on level ground.
✔ Check the oil level before the car is driven, or at least 5 minutes after the engine has been switched off.

 HAYNES HINT *If the oil is checked immediately after driving the vehicle, some of the oil will remain in the upper engine components, resulting in an inaccurate reading on the dipstick!*

The correct oil

Modern engines place great demands on their oil. It is very important that the correct oil for your car is used (see Lubricants and Fluids).

Car Care

● If you have to add oil frequently, you should check whether you have any oil leaks. Place some clean paper under the car overnight, and check for stains in the morning. If there are no leaks, then engine may be burning oil.

● Always maintain the level between the upper and lower dipstick marks. If the level is too low, severe engine damage may occur. Oil seal failure may result if the engine is overfilled by adding too much oil.

1 The dipstick top is usually brightly coloured for easy identification (see *"Underbonnet Check Points"* for exact location). Withdraw the dipstick from its tube.

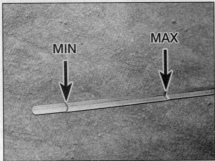

3 Note the oil level on the end of the dipstick, which should be between the upper "MAX" mark and the lower "MIN" mark. Refer to *"Capacities"* in Chapter 1 for how much oil will raise the level from the lower mark to the upper mark.

2 Using a clean rag or paper towel, wipe all oil from the dipstick. Insert the clean dipstick into its tube as far as it will go, then withdraw it again.

4 Oil is added through the filler cap or filler/breather cap orifice. A funnel may help to reduce spillage. Add the oil slowly, checking the level on the dipstick often. Do not overfill.

Power steering fluid level

Before you start:

✔ Make sure that the car is on level ground.
✔ Set the front roadwheels in the straight-ahead position.
✔ The engine must be turned off.

 HAYNES HINT *For the check to be accurate, the steering must not be turned once the engine has been stopped.*

Safety First!

● If the reservoir requires repeated topping-up, there is a fluid leak somewhere in the system which should be investigated immediately.
● If a leak is suspected, the car should not be driven until the power steering system has been checked.

1 The power steering fluid reservoir is mounted forward of the right-hand suspension turret in the engine compartment. "MAX" and "MIN" level marks are indicated on the side of the reservoir and the fluid level should be maintained between these marks at all times.

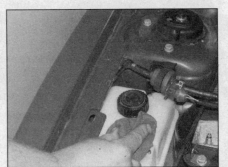

2 If topping-up is necessary, and before removing the filler cap, wipe the surrounding area so that dirt does not enter the reservoir.

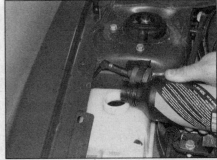

3 Unscrew the cap, top-up the fluid level to the "MAX" mark using the specified type of fluid, then refit and tighten the cap.

Brake fluid level

⚠️ **Warning:**
● **Brake fluid can harm your eyes and damage painted surfaces, so use extreme caution when handling and pouring it.**
● **Do not use fluid that has been standing open for some time, as it absorbs moisture from the air, which can cause a dangerous loss of braking effectiveness.**

 HAYNES HiNT
● **Make sure that your car is on level ground.**
● **The fluid level in the reservoir will drop slightly as the brake pads wear down, but the fluid level must never be allowed to drop below the MIN mark.**

Safety First!
● If the reservoir requires repeated topping-up, this is an indication of a fluid leak somewhere in the system, which should be investigated immediately.
● If a leak is suspected, the car should not be driven until the braking system has been checked. Never take any risks where brakes are concerned.

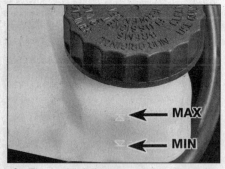

1 The brake fluid reservoir is mounted to the left of the right-hand suspension turret in the engine compartment. "MAX" and "MIN" level marks are indicated on the side of the reservoir and the fluid level should be maintained between these marks at all times.

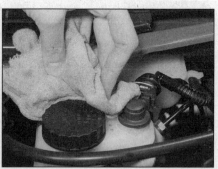

2 If topping-up is necessary, first wipe the area around the filler cap with a clean rag before removing the cap. When adding fluid, it is a good idea to inspect the reservoir for contamination. The system should be drained and refilled if deposits, dirt particles or contamination are seen in the fluid (see Chapter 9).

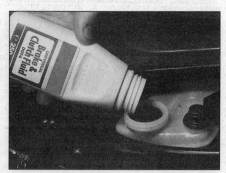

3 Carefully add fluid, avoiding spilling it on surrounding paintwork. Use only the specified brake hydraulic fluid since mixing different types of fluid can cause damage to the system. After filling to the correct level, refit the cap securely and wipe off any spilt fluid

Wiper blades

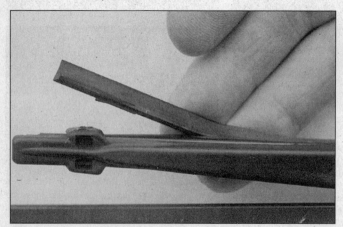

1 Check the condition of the wiper blades. If they are cracked or show any signs of deterioration, or if the glass swept area is smeared, renew them. For maximum clarity of vision, wiper blades should be renewed annually, as a matter of course.

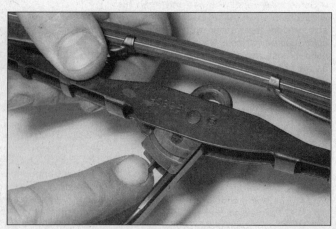

2 To remove a wiper blade, pull the arm fully away from the glass until it locks. Swivel the blade through 90°, press the locking tab with a finger nail and slide the blade out of the arm's hooked end. On refitting, ensure that the blade locks securely into the arm.

Coolant level

Warning: Do not attempt to remove the expansion tank pressure cap when the engine is hot, as there is a very great risk of scalding. Do not leave open containers of coolant about, as it is poisonous.

Car Care

● Adding coolant should not be necessary on a regular basis. If frequent topping-up is required, it is likely there is a leak. Check the radiator, all hoses and joint faces for signs of staining or wetness, and rectify as necessary.

● It is important that antifreeze is used in the cooling system all year round, not just during the winter months. Do not top up with water alone, as the antifreeze will become diluted.

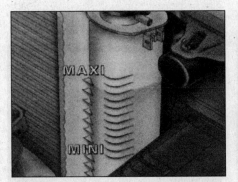

1 The coolant level varies with the temperature of the engine. When the engine is cold, the coolant level should be between the "MAX" and "MIN" marks on the side of the expansion tank, which is incorporated in the right-hand side of the radiator. When the engine is hot, the level may rise slightly.

2 If topping-up is necessary, wait until the engine is cold, then cover the expansion tank with a thick layer of rag and unscrew the filler cap anti-clockwise until it reaches its first stop and a hissing sound is heard. Wait until the hissing ceases, indicating that all pressure is released, then push the cap down and turn it anti-clockwise to the second stop until it can be removed. If more hissing sounds are heard, wait until they have stopped before unscrewing the cap completely. At all times keep well away from the filler opening.

3 Add the recommended mixture of water and antifreeze through the expansion tank filler neck, until the coolant is midway between the "MAX" and "MIN" level marks. Refit the cap, turning it clockwise as far as it will go until it is secure

Screen/headlamp washer fluid level

Car care

✔ Screenwash additives not only keep the windscreen clean during bad weather, they also prevent the washer system freezing in cold weather - which is when you are likely to need it most. Avoid top up using plain water, as the screenwash will become diluted and will freeze in cold weather.
✔ Check the operation of both screen and headlamp washers. Adjust the nozzles using a pin if necessary, aiming the spray to a point slightly above the centre of the swept area.

Warning: On no account use engine coolant antifreeze in the screen washer system - this may damage the paintwork.

1 TThe reservoir for the windscreen/tailgate washer system is located at the rear right-hand corner of the engine compartment. Where fitted, the headlamp washer system reservoir is located under the front right-hand wing and incorporates a filler neck which extends into the engine compartment

2 When topping-up the reservoir(s) a screenwash additive should be added in the quantities recommended on the bottle.

Tyre condition and pressure

It is very important that tyres are in good condition, and at the correct pressure - having a tyre failure at any speed is highly dangerous. Tyre wear is influenced by driving style - harsh braking and acceleration, or fast cornering, will all produce more rapid tyre wear. As a general rule, the front tyres wear out faster than the rears. Interchanging the tyres from front to rear ("rotating" the tyres) may result in more even wear. However, if this is completely effective, you may have the expense of replacing all four tyres at once! Remove any nails or stones embedded in the tread before they penetrate the tyre to cause deflation. If removal of a nail does reveal that the tyre has been punctured, refit the nail so that its point of penetration is marked. Then immediately change the wheel, and have the tyre repaired by a tyre dealer.

Regularly check the tyres for damage in the form of cuts or bulges, especially in the sidewalls. Periodically remove the wheels, and clean any dirt or mud from the inside and outside surfaces. Examine the wheel rims for signs of rusting, corrosion or other damage. Light alloy wheels are easily damaged by "kerbing" whilst parking; steel wheels may also become dented or buckled. A new wheel is very often the only way to overcome severe damage.

New tyres should be balanced when they are fitted, but it may become necessary to re-balance them as they wear, or if the balance weights fitted to the wheel rim should fall off. Unbalanced tyres will wear more quickly, as will the steering and suspension components. Wheel imbalance is normally signified by vibration, particularly at a certain speed (typically around 50 mph). If this vibration is felt only through the steering, then it is likely that just the front wheels need balancing. If, however, the vibration is felt through the whole car, the rear wheels could be out of balance. Wheel balancing should be carried out by a tyre dealer or garage.

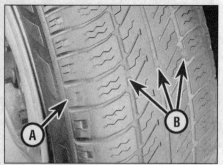

1 *Tread Depth - visual check*
The original tyres have tread wear safety bands (B), which will appear when the tread depth reaches approximately 1.6 mm. The band positions are indicated by a triangular mark on the tyre sidewall (A).

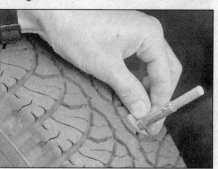

2 *Tread Depth - manual check*
Alternatively, tread wear can be monitored with a simple, inexpensive device known as a tread depth indicator gauge.

3 *Tyre Pressure Check*
Check the tyre pressures regularly with the tyres cold. Do not adjust the tyre pressures immediately after the vehicle has been used, or an inaccurate setting will result. Tyre pressures are shown on page 0•18.

Tyre tread wear patterns

Shoulder Wear

Underinflation (wear on both sides)
Under-inflation will cause overheating of the tyre, because the tyre will flex too much, and the tread will not sit correctly on the road surface. This will cause a loss of grip and excessive wear, not to mention the danger of sudden tyre failure due to heat build-up.
Check and adjust pressures
Incorrect wheel camber (wear on one side)
Repair or renew suspension parts
Hard cornering
Reduce speed!

Centre Wear

Overinflation
Over-inflation will cause rapid wear of the centre part of the tyre tread, coupled with reduced grip, harsher ride, and the danger of shock damage occurring in the tyre casing.
Check and adjust pressures

If you sometimes have to inflate your car's tyres to the higher pressures specified for maximum load or sustained high speed, don't forget to reduce the pressures to normal afterwards.

Uneven Wear

Front tyres may wear unevenly as a result of wheel misalignment. Most tyre dealers and garages can check and adjust the wheel alignment (or "tracking") for a modest charge.
Incorrect camber or castor
Repair or renew suspension parts
Malfunctioning suspension
Repair or renew suspension parts
Unbalanced wheel
Balance tyres
Incorrect toe setting
Adjust front wheel alignment
Note: *The feathered edge of the tread which typifies toe wear is best checked by feel.*

Battery

Caution: *Before carrying out any work on the vehicle battery, read the precautions given in* Safety first! *at the start of this manual.*

✔ Make sure that the battery tray is in good condition, and that the battery retaining clamp is tight. Corrosion on the tray, retaining clamp and the battery itself can be removed with a solution of water and baking soda. Thoroughly rinse all cleaned areas with water. Any metal parts damaged by corrosion should be covered with a zinc-based primer, then painted.

✔ Approximately every 3 months check the charge condition of the battery as described in Chapter 5.

✔ If the battery is flat, and you need to jump start your vehicle, see *Roadside Repairs*.

HAYNES HINT

Battery corrosion can be kept to a minimum by applying a layer of petroleum jelly to the clamps and terminals after they are reconnected.

1 The battery is located in the left-hand side of the engine compartment. The exterior of the battery should be inspected periodically for damage such as a cracked case or cover.

3 If corrosion (white fluffy deposits) is evident, remove the cables from the battery terminals, clean them with a small wire brush, then refit them. Automotive stores sell a useful tool for cleaning the battery posts . . .

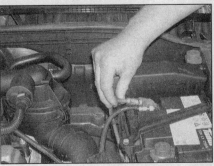

2 Check the tightness of the battery cable clamps to ensure good electrical connections. You should not be able to move them. Also check each cable for cracks and frayed conductors.

4 . . . as well as the battery cable clamps.

Electrical systems

✔ Check all external lights and the horn. Refer to the appropriate Sections of Chapter 12 for details if any of the circuits are found to be inoperative.

✔ Visually check all accessible wiring connectors, harnesses and retaining clips for security, and for signs of chafing or damage.

HAYNES HINT

If you need to check your brake lights and indicators unaided, back up to a wall or garage door and operate the lights. The reflected light should show if they are working properly.

1 If a single indicator light, brake light or headlight has failed, it is likely that a bulb has blown and will need to be replaced. If both brake lights have failed, it is possible that the brake light switch operated by the brake pedal has failed.

2 If more than one indicator light or headlight has failed, it is likely that either a fuse has blown or that there is a fault in the circuit. The main fusebox is located under the facia panel, on the right-hand side. To replace a blown fuse, pull it from position using the plastic tweezers provided. Fit a new fuse of the correct rating (see Chapter 12). If the fuse blows again, it is important to find out why (*see "Electrical fault finding" in Chapter 12*).

3 Additional fuses are located in the engine compartment in a supplementary fusebox mounted adjacent to the battery. The fuses are mounted beneath the small cover inside the supplementary fusebox.

Lubricants and fluids

Engine	Multigrade engine oil, viscosity SAE 10W/30 to 15W/50, to API SG/SH and/or ACEA-A2/A3 *(Duckhams QXR Premium Petrol Engine Oil, or Duckhams Hypergrade Petrol Engine Oil)*
Cooling system	Ethylene glycol-based antifreeze and soft water *(Duckhams Antifreeze and Summer Coolant)*
Manual transmission	Total BV 75/80W gear oil *(Duckhams Hypoid PT 75W-80W)*
Automatic transmission	Dexron type II ATF *(Duckhams ATF Autotrans III)*
Braking system	Hydraulic fluid to SAE J1703F or DOT 4 *(Duckhams Universal Brake and Clutch Fluid)*
Power steering	Dexron type II ATF *(Duckhams ATF Autotrans III)*

Choosing your engine oil

Engines need oil, not only to lubricate moving parts and minimise wear, but also to maximise power output and to improve fuel economy. By introducing a simplified and improved range of engine oils, Duckhams has taken away the confusion and made it easier for you to choose the right oil for your engine.

HOW ENGINE OIL WORKS

• *Beating friction*

Without oil, the moving surfaces inside your engine will rub together, heat up and melt, quickly causing the engine to seize. Engine oil creates a film which separates these moving parts, preventing wear and heat build-up.

• *Cooling hot-spots*

Temperatures inside the engine can exceed 1000° C. The engine oil circulates and acts as a coolant, transferring heat from the hot-spots to the sump.

• *Cleaning the engine internally*

Good quality engine oils clean the inside of your engine, collecting and dispersing combustion deposits and controlling them until they are trapped by the oil filter or flushed out at oil change.

OIL CARE - FOLLOW THE CODE

To handle and dispose of used engine oil safely, always:

• *Avoid skin contact with used engine oil. Repeated or prolonged contact can be harmful.*
• *Dispose of used oil and empty packs in a responsible manner in an authorised disposal site. Call 0800 663366 to find the one nearest to you. Never tip oil down drains or onto the ground.*

OIL BANK LINE
0800 66 33 66
www.oilbankline.org.uk

Tyre pressures (cold)

	Front	Rear
165/70 R 13 tyres		
All models	2.2 bar (32 psi)	2.2 bar (32 psi)
175/65 R 14 tyres*		
Hatchback models	2.2 bar (32 psi)	2.1 bar (30 psi)
Estate models	2.4 bar (35 psi)	2.3 bar (33 psi) - lightly laden
		2.8 bar (41 psi) - fully laden
185/60 R 14 tyres*		
Hatchback models:		
1.8 litre (8-valve) engine models	2.2 bar (32 psi)	2.1 bar (30 psi)
1.8 litre (16-valve) engine models	2.1 bar (30 psi)	2.0 bar (29 psi)
2.0 litre (8-valve) engine models	2.3 bar (33 psi)	2.3 bar (33 psi)
185/65 R 14 tyres*		
Estate models	2.3 bar (33 psi)	2.0 bar (29 psi) - lightly laden
		2.5 bar (36 psi) - fully laden
195/55 R 15 tyres*		
All models	2.2 bar (32 psi)	2.3 bar (33 psi)

* Vehicles equipped with these tyres may have a spare wheel fitted with a smaller size tyre for reasons of space saving. The smaller spare tyre should be inflated to 2.8 bar (41 psi) for 2.0 litre (8-valve) engine models, and 2.5 bar (36 psi) for all other models. Vehicles should not be driven at speeds exceeding 90 mph (144 kmh) with the spare wheel fitted.

Chapter 1
Routine maintenance and servicing

Contents

Air conditioning system refrigerant check 9
Air filter renewal 24
Automatic transmission fluid level check 6
Automatic transmission fluid renewal 22
Auxiliary drivebelt checking and renewal 16
Brake fluid renewal 23
Clutch adjustment check 5
Clutch control mechanism lubrication 17
Coolant renewal 30
Driveshaft gaiter check 8
Emission control systems check 15
Engine oil and filter renewal 3
Front and rear brake pad check 18
Fuel filter renewal - carburettor models 12
Fuel filter renewal - fuel injection models 27
General information 1
Handbrake check and adjustment 20
Hinge and lock lubrication 25
Hose and fluid leak check 4
Idle speed and mixture check and adjustment 14
Ignition system check 13
Manual transmission oil level check 26
Manual transmission oil renewal 29
Rear brake shoe check - models with rear drum brakes 19
Regular maintenance 2
Road test 21
Spark plug renewal 11
Steering and suspension check 7
Timing belt renewal 28
Valve clearance check and adjustment - 1124 cc and
    1360 cc models 10

Degrees of difficulty

| Easy, suitable for novice with little experience | | Fairly easy, suitable for beginner with some experience | | Fairly difficult, suitable for competent DIY mechanic | | Difficult, suitable for experienced DIY mechanic | | Very difficult, suitable for expert DIY or professional | 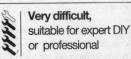 |

Lubricants and fluids

Refer to end of *"Weekly Checks"*

Capacities

Engine oil
Excluding filter:
1124 cc and 1360 cc models	3.2 litres
1580 cc and 1905 cc models	4.5 litres
1761 cc models	4.2 litres
1998 cc (8-valve) models	4.7 litres
1998 cc (16-valve) models	4.0 litres

Including filter:
1124 cc and 1360 cc models	3.5 litres
1580 cc and 1905 cc models	5.0 litres
1761 cc models	4.5 litres
1998 cc (8-valve) models	5.4 litres
1998 cc (16-valve) models	4.3 litres

Difference between "MIN" and "MAX" dipstick marks (approximate):

All except 16-valve models:
Without air conditioning	1.5 litres
With air conditioning	1.3 litres
16-valve models	1.0 litre

Cooling system
1124 cc and 1360 cc models:
Models without air conditioning	6.5 litres
Pre-1993 models with air conditioning	7.5 litres
1993 models onward with air conditioning	6.5 litres

1580 cc and 1905 cc models:
Models with manual transmission	7.5 litres
Models with automatic transmission	8.0 litres
1761 cc models	8.0 litres
1998 cc models	9.0 litres

Transmission
Manual	2.0 litres

Automatic:
From dry	6.2 litres
Drain and refill	2.4 litres

Power steering	1.7 litres
Fuel tank	54.0 litres

Engine

Valve clearances - 1124 cc and 1360 cc models:
Inlet	0.20 mm
Exhaust	0.40 mm

Cooling system

Antifreeze mixture:
28% antifreeze	Protection down to -15°C (5°F)
50% antifreeze	Protection down to -30°C (-22°F)

Note: *Refer to antifreeze manufacturer for latest recommendations.*

Fuel system

Idle speed (all models)	850 ± 50 rpm
Idle mixture CO content:	
Carburettor models	0.8 to 1.2 %
Fuel injection models:	
Without a catalytic converter	1.0 to 2.0 %
With a catalytic converter	Less than 1.0 %

Ignition system

Ignition timing	Refer to Chapter 5	
Spark plugs:	**Type**	**Electrode gap**
1124 cc:		
TU1M L/Z	Bosch FR8LDC	0.9 mm
	Eyquem RFC42LS	0.8 mm
TU1M+ L3	Bosch FR8LDC	0.9 mm
	Eyquem RFC42LZ2E	0.9 mm
1360 cc:		
TU3MC	Bosch FR7LDC	0.8 mm
	Eyquem RFC52LSP	0.9 mm
TU3JP	Bosch F7DCOR	0.8 mm
	Eyquem RFC42LS2E	0.9 mm
1580 cc XU5JPL	Bosch FR8LDC	0.8 mm
	Eyquem RFC42LS2E	0.9 mm
1761 cc:		
XU7JP	Bosch FR8LDC	0.8 mm
	Eyquem RFC42LS2E	0.9 mm
XU7JP4	Bosch FR8LDC	0.9 mm
	Eyquem RFC42LZ2E	0.9 mm
1905 cc XU9JA	Bosch FR7DCO	0.8 mm
1998 cc:		
XU10J2C	Bosch FR8LDC	0.9 mm
	Eyquem RFC42LS2E	0.9 mm
XU10J4D	Eyquem RFC58LS	0.8 mm
XU10J4RS	Eyquem RFC58LZ2E	0.9 mm

Brakes

Brake pad friction material minimum thickness (front and rear)	2.0 mm
Brake shoe friction material minimum thickness	1.5 mm

Tyres

Tyre pressures	See *"Weekly Checks"*

Torque wrench settings

	Nm	lbf ft
Rocker arm adjusting screw locknut - 1124 cc and 1360 cc models	18	13
Spark plugs	25	18
Manual transmission:		
1124 cc and 1360 cc models:		
Filler/level and drain plugs	25	18
1580 cc and larger-engined models:		
Filler/level plug	22	16
Drain plug	35	26
Roadwheel bolts	90	66

1

The maintenance intervals in this manual are provided on the assumption that you, not the dealer, will be carrying out the work. These are the minimum maintenance intervals recommended by the manufacturer for vehicles driven daily. If you wish to keep your vehicle in peak condition at all times, you may wish to perform some of these procedures more often. We encourage frequent maintenance, because it enhances the efficiency, performance and resale value of your vehicle.

If the vehicle is driven in dusty areas, used to tow a trailer, or is driven frequently at slow speeds (idling in traffic) or on short journeys, more frequent maintenance intervals are recommended.

When the vehicle is new, it should be serviced by a factory-authorised dealer service department, in order to preserve the factory warranty.

It should be noted that for the 1994 model year, the service time/mileage intervals were extended by the manufacturer to the periods shown in this schedule. Owners of earlier vehicles may notice a discrepancy between this schedule and the one shown in the Maintenance Guide supplied with the vehicle.

Every 400 km or weekly
☐ Refer to "Weekly Checks".

Every 4500 miles (7500 km) or 6 months - whichever comes first
☐ Renew the engine oil and filter (Section 3).

Note: *Frequent oil and filter changes are good for the engine. We recommend changing the oil at the mileage specified here, or at least twice a year if the mileage covered is a less.*

Every 9000 miles (15 000 km) or 12 months - whichever comes first
☐ Check all components and hoses for fluid leaks (Section 4).
☐ Check/adjust the clutch pedal height (Section 5).
☐ Check the automatic transmission fluid level (Section 6).
☐ Check the steering and suspension components for condition and security (Section 7).
☐ Check the condition of the driveshaft gaiters (Section 8).

Every 18 000 miles (30 000 km)
In addition to all the items listed above, carry out the following:
☐ Check the condition of the air conditioning system refrigerant - where applicable (Section 9).
☐ Check and, if necessary, adjust the valve clearances - 1124 cc and 1360 cc models (Section 10).
☐ Renew the spark plugs - pre-1996 model year vehicles and all 1998 cc 16-valve models (Section 11).
☐ Renew the fuel filter - carburettor models (Section 12).

Every 18 000 miles (30 000 km) (continued)
☐ Check the ignition system and ignition timing (Section 13).
☐ Check the idle speed and mixture adjustment (Section 14).
☐ Check the condition of the emission control system hoses and components (Section 15).
☐ Check the condition of the auxiliary drivebelt, and renew if necessary (Section 16).
☐ Lubricate the clutch control mechanism (Section 17).
☐ Check the condition of the front and rear brake pads, and renew if necessary (Section 18).
☐ Check the condition of the rear brake shoes, and renew if necessary - rear drum brake models (Section 19).
☐ Check the operation of the handbrake (Section 20).
☐ Carry out a road test (Section 21).

Every 27 000 miles (45 000 km)
In addition to all the items listed above, carry out the following:
☐ Renew the automatic transmission fluid (Section 22).

Every 36 000 miles (60 000 km)
In addition to all the items listed above, carry out the following:
☐ Renew the brake fluid (Section 23).
☐ Renew the air filter (Section 24).
☐ Renew the spark plugs - 1996 model year onwards vehicles, except 1998 cc 16-valve models (Section 11).
☐ Lubricate all hinges and locks (Section 25).
☐ Check the manual transmission oil level, and top-up if necessary (Section 26).
☐ Renew the fuel filter - fuel injection models (Section 27).
☐ Renew the timing belt (Section 28) see **Note** below.

Note: *Although the normal interval for timing belt renewal is 72 000 miles (120 000 km), it is strongly recommended that the interval is halved to 36 000 miles (60 000 km) on vehicles which are subjected to intensive use, ie. mainly short journeys or a lot of stop-start driving. The actual belt renewal interval is therefore very much up to the individual owner, but bear in mind that severe engine damage will result if the belt breaks.*

Every 72 000 miles (120 000 km)
In addition to all the items listed above, carry out the following:
☐ Renew the manual transmission oil (Section 29).

Every 2 years (regardless of mileage)
☐ Renew the coolant (Section 30).

Underbonnet view of a 1360 cc fuel injection (KDY engine) model

1 Engine oil filler cap
2 Engine oil dipstick
3 Battery
4 Master cylinder brake fluid reservoir
5 Engine compartment junction box
6 Engine oil filter
7 Radiator filler cap
8 Alternator
9 Windscreen/tailgate washer fluid reservoir filler cap
10 Braking system vacuum servo unit
11 Ignition HT coil
12 Plastic box containing the fuel injection ECU, relay unit and injector resistor
13 Suspension strut upper mounting
14 Air cleaner air temperature control valve
15 Throttle body assembly
16 Evaporative emission control purge valves
17 Ignition timing retard system solenoid valve
18 Air cleaner housing

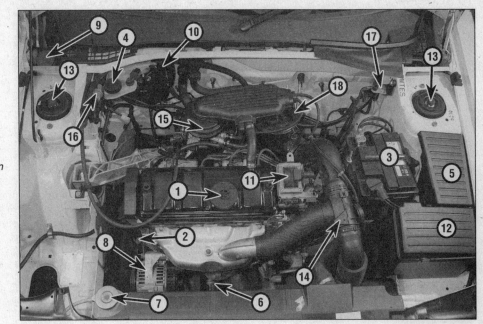

Underbonnet view of a 1580 cc (BDY engine) model

1 Engine oil filler cap
2 Engine oil dipstick
3 Battery
4 Master cylinder brake fluid reservoir
5 Engine compartment junction box
6 Engine oil filter
7 Radiator filler cap
8 Alternator
9 Windscreen/tailgate washer fluid reservoir filler cap
10 Braking system vacuum servo unit
11 Ignition HT coil
12 Plastic box containing the fuel injection ECU and relay unit
13 Suspension strut upper mounting
14 Air cleaner air temperature control valve
15 Throttle body assembly
16 Fuel injection system MAP sensor
17 Thermostat housing
18 Air cleaner housing

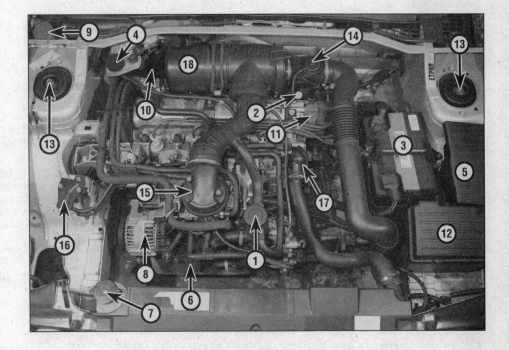

Underbonnet view of a 1761 cc (LFZ engine) model

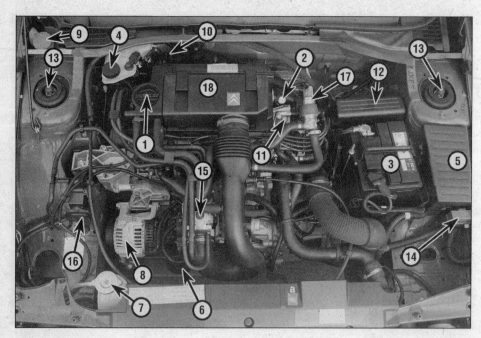

1 Engine oil filler cap
2 Engine oil dipstick
3 Battery
4 Master cylinder brake fluid reservoir
5 Engine compartment junction box
6 Engine oil filter
7 Radiator filler cap
8 Alternator
9 Windscreen/tailgate washer fluid
   reservoir filler cap
10 Braking system vacuum servo unit
11 Ignition HT coil
12 Plastic box containing the fuel injection
   ECU
13 Suspension strut upper mounting
14 Fuel injection system relay unit
15 Throttle housing assembly
16 Fuel injection system MAP sensor
17 Idle speed auxiliary air valve
18 Air cleaner element cover

Underbonnet view of a 1905 cc (D6E engine) model

1 Engine oil filler cap
2 Engine oil dipstick
3 Battery
4 Master cylinder brake fluid reservoir
5 Engine compartment junction box
6 Engine oil filter
7 Radiator filler cap
8 Alternator
9 Windscreen/tailgate washer fluid
   reservoir filler cap
10 Braking system vacuum servo unit
11 Ignition HT coil
12 Fuel injection ECU
13 Suspension strut upper mounting
14 Fuel injection system relay unit
15 Throttle housing assembly
16 Fuel injection system intake air
   temperature sensor
17 Air cleaner housing
18 Power steering fluid reservoir
19 Fuel pressure regulator

Underbonnet view of a 1998 cc 8-valve (RFX engine) model

1 Engine oil filler cap
2 Engine oil dipstick
3 Battery
4 Master cylinder brake fluid reservoir
5 Engine compartment junction box
6 Engine oil filter
7 Radiator filler cap
8 Alternator
9 Windscreen/tailgate washer fluid
   reservoir filler cap
10 Braking system vacuum servo unit
11 Ignition HT coil
12 Plastic box containing the fuel injection
   ECU
13 Suspension strut upper mounting
14 Evaporative emission control system
   purge valve
15 Throttle housing assembly
16 Fuel injection system MAP sensor
17 Air cleaner housing cover
18 Power steering fluid reservoir
19 Fuel pressure regulator

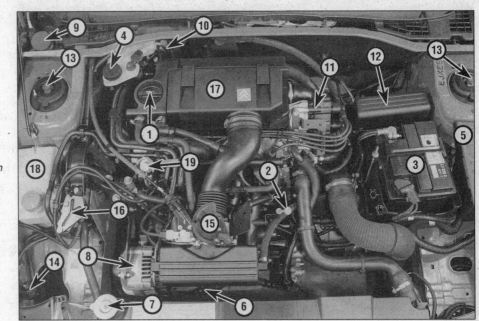

Front underbody view - 1998 cc 16-valve model shown (other models similar)

1 Wiring harness
2 Power steering pump
3 Sump drain plug
4 Oil filter
5 Power steering fluid hose
6 Air filter housing
7 Towing eye
8 Horn
9 Horn compressor
10 Brake caliper
11 Lower suspension arm
12 Track rod balljoint
13 Anti-roll bar
14 Transmission oil drain plug
15 Steering gear assembly
16 Front suspension subframe
17 Driveshaft
18 Engine/transmission rear mounting

Rear underbody view - rear disc brake model shown (drum brake models similar)

1 Fuel tank
2 Fuel tank support bracket
3 Handbrake cables
4 Rear suspension torsion bars
5 Rear suspension tubular crossmember
6 Exhaust heat shield
7 Rear shock absorber
8 Rear suspension trailing arm
9 Brake caliper
10 Rear exhaust box
11 Spare wheel cradle retaining catch
12 Jack case
13 Rear brake pressure-regulating valves

Maintenance procedures

1 General information

This Chapter is designed to help the home mechanic maintain his/her vehicle for safety, economy, long life and peak performance.

The Chapter contains a master maintenance schedule, followed by Sections dealing specifically with each task on the schedule. Visual checks, adjustments, component renewal, and other helpful items are included. Refer to the accompanying illustrations of the engine compartment and of the underside of the vehicle for the locations of the various components.

Servicing your vehicle in accordance with the mileage/time maintenance schedule and the following Sections will provide a planned maintenance programme, which should result in a long and reliable service life. This is a comprehensive plan, so maintaining some items but not others at the specified service intervals, will not produce the same results.

As you service your vehicle, you will discover that many of the procedures can - and should - be grouped together, either because of the particular procedure being performed, or because of the close proximity of two otherwise-unrelated components to one another. For example, if the vehicle is raised for any reason, the exhaust can be inspected at the same time as the suspension and steering components.

The first step in this maintenance programme is to prepare yourself before the actual work begins. Read through all the Sections relevant to the work to be carried out, then make a list of, and gather together, all the parts and tools required. If a problem is encountered, seek advice from a parts specialist, or a dealer service department.

2 Regular maintenance

1 If, from the time the vehicle is new, the routine maintenance schedule is followed closely, and frequent checks are made of fluid levels and high-wear items, as suggested throughout this manual, the engine will be kept in relatively good running condition, and the need for additional work will be minimised.
2 It is possible that there will be times when the engine is running poorly, due to the lack of regular maintenance. This is even more likely if a used vehicle, which has not received regular and frequent maintenance checks, is purchased. In such cases, additional work may need to be carried out, outside of the regular maintenance intervals.
3 If engine wear is suspected, a compression test (Chapter 2, Part A) will provide valuable information regarding the overall performance of the main internal components. Such a test can be used as a basis to decide on the extent of the work to be carried out. If, for example, a compression test indicates serious internal engine wear, the conventional maintenance described in this Chapter will not greatly improve the performance of the engine, and may prove a waste of time and money, unless extensive overhaul work is carried out first.

4 The following series of operations are those most often required to improve the performance of a generally poor-running engine:

Primary operations

(a) Clean, inspect and test the battery (See "Weekly Checks").
(b) Check the levels of all the engine-related fluids (See "Weekly Checks").
(c) Check the condition of all hoses, and check for fluid leaks (Section 4).

(d) Check and if necessary adjust the valve clearances on 1124 cc and 1360 cc models (Section 10).
(e) Renew the spark plugs and clean and inspect the HT leads (Sections 11 and 13).
(f) Check the fuel filter, and renew if necessary (Sections 12 or 27).
(g) Check the condition and tension of the auxiliary drivebelt (Section 16).
(h) Check the condition of the air filter, and renew if necessary (Section 24).
(i) Check and if necessary adjust the idle

speed and mixture settings - where applicable (Section 14).

5 If the above operations do not prove fully effective, carry out the following operations:

Secondary operations

All the items listed under "Primary operations", plus the following:
(a) Check the charging system (Chapter 5).
(b) Check the ignition system (Chapter 5).
(c) Check the fuel system (Chapter 4A, 4B, 4C and 4D).
(e) Renew the ignition HT leads (Section 13).

1

Every 4500 miles (7500 km) or 6 months - whichever comes first

3 Engine oil and filter renewal

Note: *A suitable square-section wrench may be required to undo the sump drain plug on some models. These wrenches can be obtained from most motor factors or Citroën dealers.*

1 Frequent oil and filter changes are the most important preventative maintenance procedures which can be undertaken by the DIY owner. As engine oil ages, it becomes diluted and contaminated, which leads to premature engine wear.

2 Before starting this procedure, gather together all the necessary tools and materials. Also make sure that you have plenty of clean rags and newspapers handy, to mop up any spills. Ideally, the engine oil should be warm, as it will drain better, and more built-up sludge will be removed with it. Take care, however, not to touch the exhaust or any other hot parts of the engine when working under the vehicle. To avoid any possibility of scalding, it is advisable to wear gloves when carrying out this work. This will also protect you from possible skin irritants and other harmful contaminants in used engine oils. Access to the underside of the vehicle will be

greatly improved if it can be raised on a lift, driven onto ramps, or jacked up and supported on axle stands (see *"Jacking and vehicle support"*). Whichever method is chosen, make sure that the vehicle remains level; if it is at an angle, make sure that the oil will flow towards the drain plug.

3 Using a suitable key (typically 8 mm square), slacken the drain plug about half a turn **(see illustration)**. Position a suitable container under the drain plug, then remove the plug completely. If possible, try to keep the plug pressed into the sump while unscrewing it by hand the last couple of turns **(see Haynes Hint)**.

4 Allow some time for the old oil to drain, noting that it may be necessary to reposition the container as the oil flow slows to a trickle.

5 After all the oil has drained, wipe off the drain plug with a clean rag, and renew the sealing washer. Clean the area around the drain plug opening, and refit the plug. Tighten the plug securely.

6 If the filter is also to be renewed, move the container into position under the oil filter, which is located on the front side of the cylinder block, below the inlet manifold.

7 Using an oil filter removal tool, slacken the filter initially, then unscrew it by hand the rest of the way **(see illustration)**. Empty the oil in the old filter into the container.

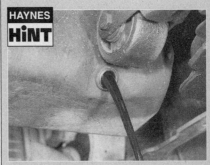

As the drain plug releases from the threads, move it away sharply so the stream of oil issuing from the sump runs into the container, not up your sleeve.

8 Use a clean rag to remove all oil, dirt and sludge from the filter sealing area on the engine. Check the old filter to make sure that the rubber sealing ring hasn't stuck to the engine. If it has, carefully remove it.

9 Apply a light coating of clean engine oil to the sealing ring on the new filter, then screw it into position on the engine **(see illustration)**. Tighten the filter firmly by hand only - do not use any tools. Follow the tightening instructions printed on the filter, if applicable.

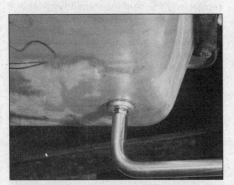

3.3 Slackening the sump drain plug (1905 cc model shown)

3.7 Using an oil filter removal tool to slacken the oil filter (1360 cc model shown)

3.9 Lubricate the oil filter sealing ring before fitting

10 Remove the old oil and all tools from under the car, then (if applicable) lower the car to the ground.
11 Remove the dipstick, then unscrew the oil filler cap from the filler/breather neck or cylinder head cover (as applicable). Fill the engine, using the correct grade and type of oil (refer to *"Lubricants and fluids"*). An oil can spout or funnel may help to reduce spillage. Pour in half the specified quantity of oil first, then wait a few minutes for the oil to run down to the sump. Continue adding oil, a small quantity at a time, until the level is up to the lower mark on the dipstick. Adding a further 1.0 to 1.5 litres (according to model), will bring the level up to the upper mark on the dipstick. Refit the filler cap.
12 Start the engine, and run it for a few minutes, checking for leaks around the oil filter seal and the sump drain plug. Note that there may be a delay of a few seconds before the low oil pressure warning light goes out when the engine is first started. The oil takes time to circulate through the new oil filter and the engine oil galleries before the pressure builds up. Do not rev the engine while the warning light is on.
13 Switch off the engine, and wait a few minutes for the oil to settle in the sump once more. With the new oil circulated and the filter now completely full, recheck the level on the dipstick, and add more oil as necessary.
14 Dispose of the used engine oil and filter safely, with reference to *"General repair procedures"* in the reference Sections of this manual.

Every 9000 miles (15 000 km) or 12 months - whichever comes first

4 Hose and fluid leak check

1 Visually inspect the engine joint faces, gaskets and seals for any signs of water, oil or fuel leaks. Pay particular attention to the areas around the camshaft cover, cylinder head, oil filter and sump joint faces. Bear in mind that, over a period of time, some very slight seepage from these areas is to be expected. What you are really looking for is any indication of a serious leak. Should a leak be found, renew the offending gasket or oil seal by referring to the appropriate Chapters in this manual.
2 Also check the security and condition of all the engine-related pipes and hoses. Ensure that all cable ties or securing clips are in place and in good condition. Clips which are broken or missing can lead to chafing of the hoses, pipes, or wiring, which could cause more serious problems in the future.
3 Carefully check the radiator hoses and heater hoses along their entire length. Renew any hose which is cracked, swollen, or deteriorated. Cracks will show up better if the hose is squeezed. Pay close attention to the hose clips that secure the hoses to the cooling system components. Hose clips can pinch and puncture hoses, resulting in cooling system leaks. If the original Citroën crimped-type hose clips are used, it may be a good idea to replace them with standard worm-drive hose clips.
4 Inspect all the cooling system components (hoses, joint faces, etc.) for leaks **(see Haynes Hint)**. Where any problems of this nature are found on system components, renew the component or gasket with reference to Chapter 3.
5 Where applicable, inspect the automatic transmission fluid cooler hoses for leaks or deterioration.
6 With the vehicle raised, inspect the petrol tank and filler neck for punctures, cracks, and other damage. The connection between the filler neck and tank is especially critical. Sometimes, a rubber filler neck or connecting hose will leak due to loose retaining clamps or deteriorated rubber.
7 Carefully check all rubber hoses and metal fuel lines leading away from the petrol tank. Check for loose connections, deteriorated hoses, crimped lines, and other damage. Pay particular attention to the vent pipes and hoses, which often loop up around the filler neck, and can become blocked or crimped. Follow the lines to the front of the vehicle, carefully inspecting them all the way. Renew damaged sections as necessary.
8 From within the engine compartment, check the security of all fuel hose attachments and pipe unions, and inspect the fuel hoses and vacuum hoses for kinks, chafing and deterioration.
9 Where applicable, check the condition of the power steering fluid hoses and pipes.

5 Clutch adjustment check

1 Check that the clutch pedal moves smoothly and easily through its full travel, and that the clutch itself functions correctly with no trace of slip or drag.
2 If necessary adjust the clutch as described in Chapter 6.

6 Automatic transmission fluid level check

1 Take the vehicle on a short journey to warm the transmission up to normal operating temperature, then park the vehicle on level ground. Leave the engine idling and move the selector lever to the "P" (PARK) position. The fluid level is checked using the dipstick located at the front of the engine compartment, directly in front of the engine/transmission unit.
2 With the engine idling, move the selector lever through all the gear positions, stopping briefly at each position, then return the selector lever to the "P" position. With the selector lever returned to the "P" position, withdraw the dipstick from the tube and wipe all fluid from its end with a clean rag or paper towel. Insert the clean dipstick back into the tube as far as it will go, then withdraw it once more. Note the fluid level on the end of the dipstick. On models with two notches on the dipstick, the level should be between the upper and lower marks **(see illustration)**. On models with three notches on the dipstick, the level should be between the two upper marks (the marks located on either side of the number "80").

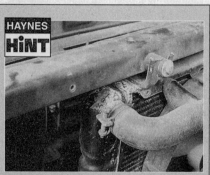
A leak in the cooling system will usually show up as white- or rust-coloured deposits on the area adjoining the leak

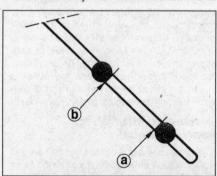
6.2 Automatic transmission fluid dipstick lower (a) and upper (b) fluid level markings

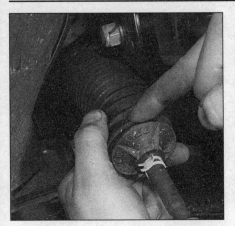

7.2 Checking a steering gear gaiter

7.4 Rocking the roadwheel to check steering/suspension components

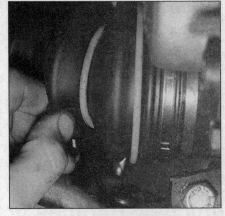

8.1 Checking driveshaft outer constant velocity (CV) joint gaiter

3 If topping-up is necessary, add the required quantity of the specified fluid to the transmission via the dipstick tube. Use a funnel with a fine mesh gauze to avoid spillage and to ensure that no foreign matter enters the transmission. **Note:** *Never overfill the automatic transmission so that the fluid level is above the upper mark on the dipstick.*

4 After topping-up, take the vehicle on a short run to distribute the fresh fluid, then recheck the level again, topping-up if necessary.

5 Always maintain the level between the two dipstick marks. If the level is allowed to fall below the lower mark, fluid starvation may result, which could lead to severe transmission damage.

7 Steering and suspension check

Front suspension and steering check

1 Apply the handbrake, then jack up the front of the car and support it on axle stands (see *"Jacking and vehicle support"*).

2 Visually inspect the balljoint dust covers and the steering rack-and-pinion gaiters for splits, chafing or deterioration **(see illustration)**. Any wear of these components will cause loss of lubricant, together with dirt and water entry, resulting in rapid deterioration of the balljoints or steering gear.

3 On vehicles with power steering, check the fluid hoses for chafing or deterioration, and the pipe and hose unions for fluid leaks. Also check for signs of fluid leakage under pressure from the steering gear rubber gaiters, which would indicate failed fluid seals within the steering gear.

4 Grasp the roadwheel at the 12 o'clock and 6 o'clock positions, and try to rock it **(see illustration)**. Very slight free play may be felt, but if the movement is appreciable, further

investigation is necessary to determine the source. Continue rocking the wheel while an assistant depresses the footbrake. If the movement is now eliminated or significantly reduced, it is likely that the hub bearings are at fault. If the free play is still evident with the footbrake depressed, then there is wear in the suspension joints or mountings.

5 Now grasp the wheel at the 9 o'clock and 3 o'clock positions, and try to rock it as before. Any movement felt now may again be caused by wear in the hub bearings or the steering track-rod balljoints. If the outer balljoint is worn, the visual movement will be obvious. If the inner joint is suspect, it can be felt by placing a hand over the rack-and-pinion rubber gaiter and gripping the track-rod. If the wheel is now rocked, movement will be felt at the inner joint if wear has taken place.

6 Using a large screwdriver or flat bar, check for wear in the suspension mounting bushes by levering between the relevant suspension component and its attachment point. Some movement is to be expected, as the mountings are made of rubber, but excessive wear should be obvious. Also check the condition of any visible rubber bushes, looking for splits, cracks or contamination of the rubber.

7 With the car standing on its wheels, have an assistant turn the steering wheel back and forth, about an eighth of a turn each way. There should be very little, if any, lost movement between the steering wheel and roadwheels. If this is not the case, closely observe the joints and mountings previously described. In addition, check the steering column universal joints for wear, and also check the rack-and-pinion steering gear itself.

Suspension strut/shock absorber check

8 Check for any signs of fluid leakage around the suspension strut/shock absorber body, or from the rubber gaiter around the piston rod. Should any fluid be noticed, the suspension strut/shock absorber is defective internally,

and should be renewed. **Note:** *Suspension struts/shock absorbers should always be renewed in pairs on the same axle.*

9 The efficiency of the suspension strut/shock absorber may be checked by bouncing the vehicle at each corner. Generally speaking, the body will return to its normal position and stop after being depressed. If it rises and returns on a rebound, the suspension strut/shock absorber is probably suspect. Examine also the suspension strut/shock absorber upper and lower mountings for any signs of wear.

8 Driveshaft gaiter check

Driveshaft rubber gaiter and CV joint check

1 With the vehicle raised and securely supported on stands (see *"Jacking and vehicle support"*), turn the steering onto full lock, then slowly rotate the roadwheel. Inspect the condition of the outer constant velocity (CV) joint rubber gaiters, while squeezing the gaiters to open out the folds **(see illustration)**. Check for signs of cracking, splits, or deterioration of the rubber, which may allow the grease to escape, and lead to water and grit entry into the joint. Also check the security and condition of the retaining clips. Repeat these checks on the inner CV joints. If any damage or deterioration is found, the gaiters should be renewed without delay as described in Chapter 8.

2 At the same time, check the general condition of the CV joints themselves, by first holding the driveshaft and attempting to rotate the wheel. Repeat this check by holding the inner joint and attempting to rotate the driveshaft. Any appreciable movement indicates wear in the joints, wear in the driveshaft splines, or a loose driveshaft retaining nut.

Every 18 000 miles (30 000 km)

9 Air conditioning system refrigerant check

⚠ Warning: Do not attempt to open the refrigerant circuit. Refer to the precautions given in Chapter 3.

1 In order to check the condition of the refrigerant, a humidity indicator and a sight glass are provided on top of the drier bottle, which is located at the front right-hand corner of the engine compartment.

Refrigerant humidity check

2 Check the colour of the humidity indicator **(see illustration)**. Blue indicates that the condition of the refrigerant is satisfactory. Red indicates that the refrigerant is saturated with humidity. If the indicator shows red, the system should be drained and recharged, and a new drier bottle should be fitted. **Note:** *The system should be drained and recharged **only** by a Citroën dealer or air conditioning specialist.* **Do not** *attempt to carry out the work yourself.*

Refrigerant flow check

3 Run the engine, and switch on the air conditioning.
4 After a few minutes, inspect the sight glass, and check the fluid flow. Clear fluid should be visible - if not, the following will help to diagnose the problem:
(a) *Clear fluid flow, perhaps with occasional bubbles - the system is functioning correctly.*
(b) *No fluid flow - have the system checked for leaks by a Citroën dealer or air conditioning specialist.*
(c) *Continuous stream of clear air bubbles in fluid - refrigerant level low. Have the system recharged by a Citroën dealer or air-conditioning specialist.*
(d) *Milky air bubbles visible - high humidity (see paragraph 2).*
5 Do not operate the air conditioning system if the refrigerant level is known to be low; damage may result.

10 Valve clearance check and adjustment - 1124 cc and 1360 cc models

Note: *The valve clearances must be checked and adjusted only when the engine is cold.*
Note: *The manufacturer suggests this operation at the first 18 000 mile (30 000 km) service only. After that, checking and adjusting of the valve clearances is not part of the recommended maintenance schedule. The operation should therefore only need to be carried out after engine overhaul, or when investigating noise or power loss which could be attributed to the valve gear.*
1 The importance of having the valve clearances correctly adjusted cannot be overstressed, as they vitally affect the performance of the engine. If the clearances are too big, the engine will be noisy (characteristic rattling or tapping noises) and engine efficiency will be reduced, as the valves open too late and close too early. A more serious problem arises if the clearances are too small, however. If this is the case, the valves may not close fully when the engine is hot, resulting in serious damage to the engine (eg. burnt valve seats and/or cylinder head warping/cracking). The clearances are checked and adjusted as follows.
2 Remove the cylinder head cover as described in Chapter 2A.
3 The engine can now be turned using a suitable socket and extension bar fitted to the crankshaft sprocket/pulley bolt.

HAYNES HiNT *Turning the engine will be easier if the spark plugs are removed*

4 It is important that the clearance of each valve is checked and adjusted only when the valve is fully closed, with the rocker arm resting on the heel of the cam (directly opposite the peak). This can be ensured by carrying out the adjustments in the following sequence, noting that No 1 cylinder is at the transmission end of the engine. The correct valve clearances are given in the Specifications at the end of this Chapter. The valve locations can be determined from the position of the manifolds.

Valve fully open	Adjust valves
No 1 exhaust	No 3 inlet and No 4 exhaust
No 3 exhaust	No 4 inlet and No 2 exhaust
No 4 exhaust	No 2 inlet and No 1 exhaust
No 2 exhaust	No 1 inlet and No 3 exhaust

5 With the relevant valve fully open, check the clearances of the two valves specified. Clearances are checked by inserting a feeler gauge of the correct thickness between the valve stem and the rocker arm adjusting screw. The feeler gauge should be a light, sliding fit. If adjustment is necessary, slacken the adjusting screw locknut, and turn the screw as necessary. Once the correct clearance is obtained, hold the adjusting screw and securely tighten the locknut **(see illustration)**. Recheck the valve clearance, and adjust again if necessary.
6 Rotate the crankshaft until the next valve in the sequence is fully open, and check the clearances of the next two specified valves.
7 Repeat the procedure until all eight valve clearances have been checked (and if necessary, adjusted), then refit the cylinder head cover as described in Chapter 2A.

11 Spark plug renewal

1 The correct functioning of the spark plugs is vital for the correct running and efficiency of the engine. It is essential that the plugs fitted are appropriate for the engine (the suitable type is specified at the start of this Chapter). If this type is used, and the engine is in good condition, the spark plugs should not need attention between scheduled replacement intervals. Spark plug cleaning is rarely necessary, and should not be attempted unless specialised equipment is available, as damage can easily be caused to the firing ends.
2 On 1761 cc (16-valve) engine models, to gain access to the spark plugs, the ignition coil unit fitted in the centre of the cylinder head cover must first be removed. Disconnect the wiring connector at the left-hand end of the coil unit, then undo the six retaining bolts and lift the coil unit upwards, off the spark plugs and from its location in the cylinder head cover. Similarly, on 1998 cc (16-valve) engine models, undo the eight bolts, noting

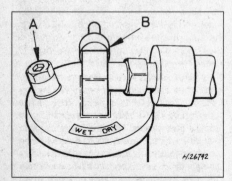

9.2 Air conditioning system refrigerant humidity indicator (A) and sight glass (B)

10.5 Adjusting a valve clearance - 1124 cc and 1360 cc models

11.2 On 1998 cc (16-valve) models, undo the eight bolts (arrowed) and remove the access cover to reach the spark plugs

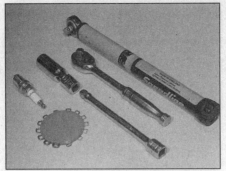

11.7 Tools required for spark plug removal, gap adjustment and refitting

11.12 Measuring the spark plug gap with a feeler gauge

the position of the wiring retaining clip, and remove the spark plug access cover fitted in the centre of the cylinder head (see illustration).

3 On some other models, to improve access to some of the plugs, it may be necessary to remove the air intake duct (refer to Chapter 4 for further information).

4 On 1998 cc (16-valve) engine models, pull the HT coils off the spark plugs. If necessary, to avoid the possibility of the HT coils being connected to the wrong spark plugs on refitting, mark the coils 1 to 4 (No 1 cylinder is at the transmission end of the engine).

5 On all other models, if the marks on the original-equipment spark plug (HT) leads cannot be seen, mark the leads 1 to 4, corresponding to the cylinder the lead serves (No 1 cylinder is at the transmission end of the engine). Pull the leads from the plugs by gripping the end fitting, not the lead, otherwise the lead connection may be fractured.

6 It is advisable to remove the dirt from the spark plug recesses, using a clean brush, vacuum cleaner or compressed air before removing the plugs, to prevent dirt dropping into the cylinders.

7 Unscrew the plugs using a spark plug spanner, suitable box spanner, or a deep socket and extension bar (see illustration). Keep the socket aligned with the spark plug - if it is forcibly moved to one side, the ceramic

insulator may be broken off. As each plug is removed, examine it as follows.

8 Examination of the spark plugs will give a good indication of the condition of the engine. If the insulator nose of the spark plug is clean and white, with no deposits, this is indicative of a weak mixture. It could also indicate that the plug is too "hot" for the engine (a hot plug transfers heat away from the electrode slowly, a cold plug transfers heat away quickly). If this condition is apparent, either correct the mixture setting (where possible), or ensure that the correct grade of plug is fitted.

9 If the tip and insulator nose are covered with hard black-looking deposits, then this is indicative that the mixture is too rich. Should the plug be black and oily, then it is likely that the engine is fairly worn, as well as the mixture being too rich.

10 If the insulator nose is covered with light tan to greyish-brown deposits, then the mixture is correct, and it is likely that the engine is in good condition.

11 The spark plug electrode gap is of considerable importance as, if it is too large or too small, the size of the spark and its efficiency will be seriously impaired. The gap should be set to the value given in the Specifications at the beginning of this Chapter. Note: The plug gap cannot be measured or adjusted on later models fitted with multi-earth electrode spark plugs.

12 To set it, measure the gap with a feeler

gauge. If necessary, bend the outer plug electrode open or closed until the correct gap is achieved (see illustration). The centre electrode should never be bent, as this may crack the insulator and cause plug failure, if nothing worse.

13 Special spark plug electrode gap adjusting tools are available from most motor accessory shops (see illustrations).

14 Before fitting the spark plugs, check that the threaded connector sleeves (on top of the plug) are tight, and that the plug exterior surfaces and threads are clean. Apply a smear of copper-based anti-seize compound to the plug threads (see Haynes Hint).

15 Once the plug begins to screw in correctly, remove the hose, and tighten the plug to the specified torque using the spark plug socket and a torque wrench. Refit the remaining spark plugs in the same manner.

16 On 1761 cc (16-valve) engine models, refit the ignition coil unit to the head cover. Refit the retaining bolts, tightening them securely, then reconnect the coil unit wiring connector.

17 On 1998 cc (16-valve) engine models,

HAYNES HINT

It's often difficult to insert spark plugs into their holes without cross-threading them. To avoid this possibility, fit a short piece of rubber hose over the end of the spark plug. The flexible hose acts as a universal joint, to help align the plug with the plug hole. Should the plug begin to cross-thread, the hose will slip on the spark plug, preventing thread damage

11.13a Measuring the spark plug gap with a wire gauge . . .

11.13b . . . and adjusting the gap using a special adjusting tool

connect the HT coils in their correct order, then refit the access cover to the cylinder head cover. Ensure that the coil wiring is correctly located in the cover recess. Refit the cover bolts, not forgetting the wiring clip, and tighten them securely.

18 On all other models, connect the HT leads in their correct order, and refit any components removed for access.

12 Fuel filter renewal - carburettor models

Warning: Before carrying out the following operation, refer to the precautions given in "Safety first!" at the beginning of this manual, and follow them implicitly. Petrol is a highly-dangerous and volatile liquid, and the precautions necessary when handling it cannot be overstressed.

1 The fuel filter is mounted on the centre of the engine compartment bulkhead, directly behind the engine.

2 To remove the filter, release the retaining clips and disconnect the fuel hoses from the filter. Where the original Citroën crimped-type hose clips are still fitted, cut the clips and discard them; use standard worm-drive hose clips on refitting.

3 Note the direction of the arrow marked on the filter body. Unclip the filter from its retaining bracket, and remove it from the vehicle.

4 Dispose safely of the old filter; it will be highly-inflammable, and may explode if thrown on a fire.

5 Connect the fuel hoses to the new filter. Make sure that the arrow on the filter body is pointing in the direction of the fuel flow, ie. towards the fuel pump **(see illustration)**. Secure the hoses in position by securely tightening the retaining clips, then clip the filter back into position in its retaining bracket.

6 Start the engine, and check the filter hose connections for leaks.

13 Ignition system check

Warning: Voltages produced by an electronic ignition system are considerably higher than those produced by conventional ignition systems. Extreme care must be taken if working on the system with the ignition switched on. Persons with surgically-implanted cardiac pacemaker devices should keep well clear of the ignition circuits, components and test equipment.

1 The ignition system components should be checked for damage or deterioration as described under the relevant sub-heading.

12.5 On carburettor models, ensure that the arrow on the fuel filter body points in the direction of fuel flow

Ignition systems incorporating a distributor

General component check

2 The spark plug (HT) leads should be checked whenever new spark plugs are installed in the engine.

3 Ensure that the leads are numbered before removing them, to avoid confusion when refitting. Pull the leads from the plugs by gripping the end fitting, not the lead, otherwise the lead connection may be fractured.

4 Check inside the end fitting for signs of corrosion, which will look like a white crusty powder. Push the end fitting back onto the spark plug, ensuring that it is a tight fit on the plug. If not, remove the lead again, and use pliers to carefully crimp the metal connector inside the end fitting until it fits securely on the end of the spark plug.

5 Using a clean rag, wipe the entire length of the lead to remove any built-up dirt and grease. Once the lead is clean, check for burns, cracks and other damage. Do not bend the lead excessively, or pull the lead lengthwise - the conductor inside might break.

6 Disconnect the other end of the lead from the distributor cap. Again, pull only on the end fitting. Check for corrosion and a tight fit in the same manner as the spark plug end. If an ohmmeter is available, check the resistance of the lead by connecting the meter between the spark plug end of the lead and the segment inside the distributor cap. Refit the lead securely on completion.

7 Check the remaining leads one at a time, in the same way.

8 If new spark plug (HT) leads are required, purchase a set for your specific car and engine.

9 Remove the distributor cap by unscrewing its retaining screws. Wipe it clean, and carefully inspect it inside and out for signs of cracks, carbon tracks (tracking) and worn, burned or loose contacts; check that the cap's carbon brush is unworn, free to move against spring pressure, and making good contact with the rotor arm. Also inspect the cap seal for signs of wear or damage, and

13.9 The rotor arm is a push fit on the distributor shaft (1360 cc model shown)

renew if necessary. Remove the rotor arm from the distributor shaft and inspect it **(see illustration)**. It is common practice to renew the cap and rotor arm whenever new spark plug (HT) leads are fitted. When fitting a new cap, remove the leads from the old cap one at a time, and fit them to the new cap in the exact same location - do not simultaneously remove all the leads from the old cap, or firing order confusion may occur. On refitting, ensure that the arm is securely pressed onto the shaft, and tighten the cap retaining screws securely.

10 Even with the ignition system in first class condition, some engines may still occasionally experience poor starting, attributable to damp ignition components. A moisture dispersant spray can be very effective.

Ignition timing checking and adjustment

11 Check the ignition timing as described in Chapter 5.

Static (distributorless) ignition systems

General component check

12 On all except 1761 cc and 1998 cc (16-valve) engine models, check the condition of the HT leads as described above in paragraphs 3 to 8. On 16-valve engine models, there are no HT leads, so the only relevant check is that all the primary (LT) circuit wiring connectors are clean and free of corrosion.

Ignition timing check and adjustment

13 Refer to Chapter 5.

14 Idle speed and mixture check and adjustment

1 Before checking the idle speed and mixture setting, always check the following first:

(a) *Check that the ignition timing is accurate (Chapter 5).*

(b) *Check that the spark plugs are in good condition and correctly gapped (Section 11).*

14.4 Adjusting the idle speed - 1360 cc carburettor models

14.7 Adjusting the idle mixture (exhaust gas CO level) - 1360 cc carburettor models

(c) Check that the accelerator cable (and on carburettor models, the choke cable) is correctly adjusted (refer to the relevant Part of Chapter 4).

(d) Check that the crankcase breather hoses are secure, with no leaks or kinks (Section 15).

(e) Check that the air cleaner filter element is clean (Section 24).

(f) Check that the exhaust system is in good condition (refer to the relevant Part of Chapter 4).

(g) If the engine is running very roughly, check the compression pressures as described in Chapter 2.

(h) On fuel injection models, check that the fuel injection/ignition system warning light is not illuminated (refer to the relevant Part of Chapter 4).

2 Take the car on a journey of sufficient length to warm it up to normal operating temperature. **Note:** *Adjustment should ideally be completed within two minutes of return, without stopping the engine. If the radiator electric cooling fan operates, wait for the cooling fan to stop. If adjustment takes longer than stated, regularly clear any excess fuel from the inlet manifold by revving the engine two or three times to between 2000 and 3000 rpm, then allow it to idle again.*

Carburettor models

3 Ensure that all electrical loads are switched off, and that the choke lever is pushed fully in.

If the car does not have a tachometer, connect one following its manufacturer's instructions. Note the idle speed, and compare it with that specified.

4 The idle speed adjusting screw is on the throttle linkage on the right-hand side of the carburettor. On 1124 cc models, the screw is easily accessible from above; on 1360 cc models, the screw is adjusted from behind the carburettor, and access is a little awkward. Using a suitable flat-bladed screwdriver, screw it in (to increase the speed) or out as necessary to obtain the specified speed **(see illustration)**.

5 The idle mixture (exhaust gas CO level) is set at the factory, and should require no further adjustment. If, due to a change in engine characteristics (carbon build-up, bore wear etc) or after a major carburettor overhaul, the mixture becomes incorrect, it can be reset. Note, however, that an exhaust gas analyser (CO meter) will be required to check the mixture, and to set it with the necessary standard of accuracy. If this is not available, the car must be taken to a Citroën dealer for the work to be carried out.

6 If an exhaust gas analyser is available, follow the manufacturer's instructions to check the exhaust gas CO level. If adjustment is required, it is made via mixture adjustment screw. On 1124 cc models, the screw is located on the left-hand side of the carburettor base; on 1360 cc models, it is located at the right-hand rear corner of the

carburettor base. The screw is covered with a tamperproof plug to prevent unnecessary adjustment. To gain access to the screw, use a sharp instrument to hook out the plug.

7 Using a suitable flat-bladed screwdriver, turn the mixture adjustment screw by very small amounts until the level is correct. Screwing it in (clockwise) weakens the idle mixture and reduces the CO level; screwing it out will richen the mixture and increase the CO level **(see illustration)**.

8 When adjustments are complete, disconnect any test equipment, and fit a new tamperproof plug to the mixture adjustment screw. Recheck the idle speed and, if necessary, readjust.

Fuel injection models

1905 cc models

9 Ensure that all electrical loads are switched off. If the car does not have a tachometer, connect one following its manufacturer's instructions. Note the idle speed, and compare it with that specified.

10 The idle speed adjusting screw is situated in the top of the throttle housing. Using a suitable flat-bladed screwdriver, screw it in or out as necessary to obtain the specified speed **(see illustration)**.

11 On models with a catalytic converter (DKZ engine with Motronic M1.3 system) the idle mixture (exhaust gas CO level) is under the control of the engine management ECU, and is not adjustable (see paragraph 18).

12 On models without a catalytic converter (D6E engine with Motronic MP3.1 system), the idle mixture can be adjusted if necessary. The idle mixture is set at the factory, however, and should not normally require adjustment. If, due to a change in engine characteristics (carbon build-up, bore wear etc) or after a major overhaul, the mixture becomes incorrect, it can be reset. An exhaust gas analyser (CO meter) will be required to check the mixture, and to set it with the necessary standard of accuracy. If this is not available, the car must be taken to a Citroën dealer for the work to be carried out.

13 If an exhaust gas analyser is available, follow its manufacturer's instructions to check the exhaust gas CO level. If adjustment is required, it is made using the screw on the mixture adjustment potentiometer. This is mounted on the side of the engine management ECU, in the left-hand rear corner of the engine compartment.

14 Using a suitable flat-bladed screwdriver, turn the screw in very small increments until the level is correct **(see illustration)**.

15 When adjustments are complete, disconnect any test equipment. Recheck the idle speed and, if necessary, readjust.

All other models

16 Experienced home mechanics, with a considerable amount of skill and equipment (including a tachometer and an accurate

1

14.10 Adjusting the idle speed - 1905 cc models

14.14 Adjusting the idle mixture (exhaust gas CO level) - 1905 cc models without a catalytic converter

exhaust gas analyser) may be able to check the exhaust CO level and the idle speed. However, if these are found to be in need of adjustment, the car *must* be taken to a suitably-equipped Citroën dealer.

17 On 1580 cc models, adjustment of the mixture setting (exhaust gas CO level) is possible, but adjustments can only be made by reprogramming the engine management ECU, using special electronic test equipment which is connected to the diagnostic wiring connector (see Chapter 4B).

18 On all other vehicles, adjustments are not possible. If the idle speed or the exhaust gas CO level is incorrect, then there must be a fault in the engine management system; the vehicle should be taken to a Citroën dealer for testing (refer to the relevant Part of Chapter 4).

15 Emission control systems check

1 Details of the emission control system components are given in Chapter 4D.

2 Checking consists simply of a visual check for obvious signs of damaged or leaking hoses and joints.

3 Detailed checking and testing of the evaporative and/or exhaust emission systems (as applicable) should be entrusted to a Citroën dealer.

16 Auxiliary drivebelt checking and renewal

Note: *Citroën specify the use of a special electronic tool (SEEM 4122-T) to correctly set the auxiliary drivebelt tension. If access to this equipment cannot be obtained, an approximate setting can be achieved using the method described below. If the method described is used, the tension must be checked using the special electronic tool at the earliest possible opportunity.*

1 On 1580 cc and 1905 cc models with air conditioning, two auxiliary drivebelts are fitted; one for the air conditioning compressor, and another for the power steering pump and/or alternator (as applicable). On all other models there is only one auxiliary drivebelt.

Checking the auxiliary drivebelt condition

2 Apply the handbrake, then jack up the front of the car and support it on axle stands. Remove the right-hand front roadwheel.

3 From underneath the front of the car, prise out the two retaining clips, and remove the plastic cover from the wing valance to gain access to the crankshaft sprocket/pulley bolt. Where necessary, unclip the coolant hoses from the bracket to improve access further **(see illustrations).**

4 Using a suitable socket and extension bar fitted to the crankshaft sprocket/pulley bolt, rotate the crankshaft so that the entire length of the drivebelt(s) can be examined. Examine the drivebelt(s) for cracks, splitting, fraying or damage. Check also for signs of glazing (shiny patches) and for separation of the belt plies. Renew the belt if worn or damaged.

5 If the condition of the belt is satisfactory, on models where the belt is adjusted manually, check the drivebelt tension as described below. On models with an automatic spring-loaded tensioner, there is no need to check the drivebelt tension.

Auxiliary drivebelt (models with manual adjuster on the alternator lower mounting point) - removal, refitting and tensioning

Removal

6 If not already done, proceed as described in paragraphs 2 and 3. On 1580 cc and 1905 cc models with air conditioning, remove the air conditioning drivebelt as described in paragraphs 40 to 42.

7 Disconnect the battery negative lead.

8 Slacken both the alternator upper and lower mounting nuts/bolts (as applicable).

9 Back off the adjuster bolt(s) to relieve the tension in the drivebelt, then slip the drivebelt from the pulleys **(see illustration).**

Refitting

10 If the belt is being renewed, ensure that the correct type is used. Fit the belt around the pulleys, and take up the slack in the belt by tightening the adjuster bolt.

11 Tension the drivebelt as described in the following paragraphs. On 1580 cc and 1905 cc models, where necessary, refit the air conditioning compressor drivebelt as described in paragraphs 43 to 49.

Tensioning

12 If not already done, proceed as described in paragraphs 2 and 3.

13 Correct tensioning of the drivebelt will ensure that it has a long life. A belt which is too slack will slip and perhaps squeal. Beware, however, of overtightening, as this can cause wear in the alternator bearings.

14 The belt should be tensioned so that, under firm thumb pressure, there is approximately 5.0 mm of free movement at the mid-point between the pulleys on the longest belt run.

15 To adjust, with the upper mounting nut/bolt just holding the alternator firm, and the lower mounting nut/bolt loosened, turn the adjuster bolt until the correct tension is

16.3a Prise out the retaining clips . . .

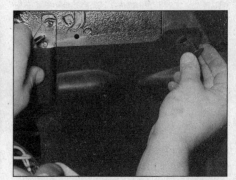

16.3b . . . and remove the plastic cover from underneath the wheel arch

16.3c Where necessary, unclip the coolant hoses to improve access to the crankshaft pulley/sprocket bolt

16.9 Removing the drivebelt - 1360 cc models

16.15 Adjusting the drivebelt tension - drivebelt adjuster on lower alternator mounting point (1905 cc model shown)

achieved **(see illustration)**. Rotate the crankshaft a couple of times, recheck the tension, then securely tighten both the alternator mounting nuts/bolts. Where applicable, also tighten the bolt securing the adjuster strap to its mounting bracket.

16 Reconnect the battery negative lead.

17 Clip the coolant hoses into position (where necessary), then refit the plastic cover to the wing valance. Refit the roadwheel, and lower the vehicle to the ground.

Auxiliary drivebelt (models with a manually-adjusted tensioning pulley) - removal, refitting and tensioning

Note: *For information on the air conditioning compressor drivebelt on 1580 cc and 1905 cc models, refer to paragraphs 40 to 49.*

Removal

18 If not already done, proceed as described in paragraphs 2 and 3.

19 Disconnect the battery negative lead.

20 Slacken the two screws securing the tensioning pulley assembly to the engine **(see illustration)**.

21 Rotate the adjuster bolt to move the tensioner pulley away from the drivebelt until there is sufficient slack for the drivebelt to be removed from the pulleys **(see illustrations)**.

Refitting

22 Fit the drivebelt around the pulleys in the following order:

(a) *Power steering pump and/or air conditioning compressor.*
(b) *Crankshaft.*
(c) *Alternator.*
(d) *Tensioner roller.*

23 Ensure that the ribs on the belt are correctly engaged with the grooves in the pulleys, and that the drivebelt is correctly routed. Take all the slack out of the belt by turning the tensioner pulley adjuster bolt. Tension the belt as follows.

Tensioning

24 If not already done, proceed as described in paragraphs 2 and 3.

25 Correct tensioning of the drivebelt will ensure that it has a long life. A belt which is too slack will slip and perhaps squeal. Beware, however, of overtightening, as this can cause wear in the alternator bearings.

26 The belt should be tensioned so that, under firm thumb pressure, there is approximately 5.0 mm of free movement at the mid-point between the pulleys on the longest belt run.

27 To adjust the tension, with the two tensioner pulley assembly retaining screws slackened, rotate the adjuster bolt until the correct tension is achieved. Once the belt is correctly tensioned, rotate the crankshaft a couple of times and recheck the tension.

28 When the belt is correctly tensioned, securely tighten the tensioner pulley assembly retaining screws, then reconnect the battery negative lead.

29 Clip the coolant hoses into position, then refit the plastic cover to the wing valance. Refit the roadwheel, and lower the vehicle to the ground.

Auxiliary drivebelt (models with an automatic spring-loaded tensioner pulley) - removal, refitting and tensioning

Removal

30 If not already done, proceed as described in paragraphs 2 and 3.

31 Disconnect the battery negative lead.

32 Where necessary, remove the retaining screws from the power steering pump pulley shield, and remove the shield to gain access to the top of the drivebelt.

33 Move the tensioner pulley away from the drivebelt, using a ratchet handle or extension bar with the same size square-section end as the hole in the base of the automatic tensioner arm. Disengage the drivebelt from all the pulleys, noting its correct routing. Remove the drivebelt from the engine, noting that in some cases, it may be necessary to slacken the automatic tensioner mounting bolts to disengage the belt from behind the tensioner pulley.

Refitting and tensioning

34 Fit the drivebelt around the pulleys in the following order:

(a) *Automatic tensioner pulley.*
(b) *Crankshaft.*
(c) *Air conditioning compressor.*
(d) *Power steering pump.*
(e) *Idler pulley.*
(f) *Alternator.*

35 Where necessary, securely tighten the automatic tensioner mounting bolts.

36 Whilst holding the tensioner arm away from the belt, ensure that the ribs on the belt are correctly engaged with the grooves in the pulleys. Release the tensioner arm; the tensioner is spring-loaded, removing the need to manually adjust the belt tension.

37 Refit the power steering pump pulley shield (where removed), and securely tighten its retaining screws.

38 Reconnect the battery negative lead.

39 Clip the coolant hoses into position, then refit the plastic cover to the wing valance. Refit the roadwheel, and lower the vehicle to the ground.

Air conditioning compressor auxiliary drivebelt (1580 cc and 1905 cc models) - removal, refitting and tensioning

Removal

40 If not already done, proceed as described in paragraphs 2 and 3.

16.20 On models with a manually-adjusted tensioner pulley, slacken the two pulley retaining screws (arrowed) . . .

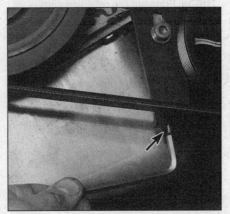

16.21a . . . then slacken the pulley adjuster bolt . . .

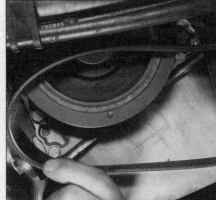

16.21b . . . and slip the drivebelt off its pulleys

41 Disconnect the battery negative lead.
42 Slacken the three bolts securing the tensioner pulley to the sump, to release the drivebelt tension, and unhook the drivebelt from the pulleys.

Refitting

43 Fit the new drivebelt around the pulleys, ensuring that its ribs are correctly located in the pulley grooves.
44 Obtain a suitable ratchet handle or extension bar with the same size square-section end as one of the holes in the tensioner arm. Using this, force the tensioner pulley against the drivebelt to remove the drivebelt slack. Tension the belt as follows.

Tensioning

45 If not already done, proceed as described in paragraphs 2 and 3.
46 Correct tensioning of the drivebelt will ensure that it has a long life. Beware, however, of overtightening, as this can cause wear in the compressor bearings.
47 The belt should be tensioned so that, under firm thumb pressure, there is approximately 5.0 mm of free movement at the mid-point between the pulleys on the top belt run.
48 To adjust the tension, first slacken the three tensioner pulley assembly retaining bolts. Using the ratchet handle or extension bar described in paragraph 44, force the tensioner pulley against the drivebelt until the correct drivebelt tension is obtained. Hold the pulley in this position, and securely tighten its three retaining bolts. Rotate the crankshaft a couple of times, and recheck the tension.
49 When the belt is correctly tensioned, clip the coolant hoses into position, then refit the plastic cover to the wing valance. Refit the roadwheel, and lower the vehicle to the ground.

17 Clutch control mechanism lubrication

1 If excessive effort is required to operate the clutch, check first that the cable is correctly routed and undamaged, then remove the pedal, and make sure that its pivot is properly greased. Refer to Chapter 6 for further information.

18 Front and rear brake pad check

1 Jack up the front and rear of the car and support it securely on axle stands (see *"Jacking and vehicle support"*). Remove the front and rear roadwheels.
2 For a comprehensive check, the brake pads should be removed and cleaned **(see Haynes**

For a quick check, the thickness of friction material remaining on each brake pad can be measured through the aperture in the caliper body

Hint). The operation of the caliper can then also be checked, and the condition of the brake disc itself can be fully examined on both sides. Refer to Chapter 9 for further information.
3 On completion, refit the roadwheels and lower the car to the ground.

19 Rear brake shoe check - models with rear drum brakes

1 Remove the rear brake drums, and check the brake shoes for signs of wear or contamination. At the same time, also inspect the wheel cylinders for signs of leakage, and the brake drum for signs of wear. Refer to the relevant Sections of Chapter 9 for further information.

20 Handbrake check and adjustment

Refer to Chapter 9.

21 Road test

Instruments and electrical equipment

1 Check the operation of all instruments and electrical equipment.
2 Make sure that all instruments read correctly, and switch on all electrical equipment in turn, to check that it functions properly.

Steering and suspension

3 Check for any abnormalities in the steering, suspension, handling or road "feel".

4 Drive the vehicle, and check that there are no unusual vibrations or noises.
5 Check that the steering feels positive, with no excessive "sloppiness", or roughness, and check for any suspension noises when cornering and driving over bumps.

Drivetrain

6 Check the performance of the engine, clutch (where applicable), transmission and driveshafts.
7 Listen for any unusual noises from the engine, clutch and transmission.
8 Make sure that the engine runs smoothly when idling, and that there is no hesitation when accelerating.
9 Check that, where applicable, the clutch action is smooth and progressive, that the drive is taken up smoothly, and that the pedal travel is not excessive. Also listen for any noises when the clutch pedal is depressed.
10 On manual transmission models, check that all gears can be engaged smoothly without noise, and that the gear lever action is not abnormally vague or "notchy".
11 On automatic transmission models, make sure that all gearchanges occur smoothly, without snatching, and without an increase in engine speed between changes. Check that all the gear positions can be selected with the vehicle at rest. If any problems are found, they should be referred to a Citroën dealer.
12 Listen for a metallic clicking sound from the front of the vehicle, as the vehicle is driven slowly in a circle with the steering on full-lock. Carry out this check in both directions. If a clicking noise is heard, this indicates wear in a driveshaft joint, in which case the joint should be renewed.

Check the operation and performance of the braking system

13 Make sure that the vehicle does not pull to one side when braking, and that the wheels do not lock prematurely when braking hard.
14 Check that there is no vibration through the steering when braking.
15 Check that the handbrake operates correctly, without excessive movement of the lever, and that it holds the vehicle stationary on a slope.
16 Test the operation of the brake servo unit as follows. Depress the footbrake four or five times to exhaust the vacuum, then start the engine. As the engine starts, there should be a noticeable "give" in the brake pedal as vacuum builds up. Allow the engine to run for at least two minutes, and then switch it off. If the brake pedal is now depressed again, it should be possible to detect a hiss from the servo as the pedal is depressed. After about four or five applications, no further hissing should be heard, and the pedal should feel considerably harder.

Every 27 000 miles (45 000 km)

22 Automatic transmission fluid renewal

1 Take the vehicle on a short run, to warm the transmission up to normal operating temperature.

2 Park the car on level ground, then switch off the ignition and apply the handbrake firmly. For improved access, jack up the front of the car and support it securely on axle stands. Note that, when refilling and checking the fluid level, the car must be lowered to the ground, and level, to ensure accuracy.

3 Remove the dipstick, then position a suitable container under the transmission. The transmission has two drain plugs: one on the sump, and another on the bottom of the differential housing (see illustration).

4 Unscrew both drain plugs, and allow the fluid to drain completely into the container. Clean the drain plugs, being especially careful to wipe any metallic particles off the magnetic

insert. Discard the original sealing washers; these should be renewed whenever they are disturbed.

⚠ **Warning: If the fluid is hot, take precautions against scalding.**

5 When the fluid has finished draining, clean the drain plug threads and those of the transmission casing. Fit a new sealing washer to each drain plug, and refit the plugs to the transmission, tightening each securely. If the car was raised for the draining operation, now lower it to the ground. Make sure that the car is level (front-to-rear and side-to-side).

6 Refilling the transmission is an awkward operation, adding the specified type of fluid to the transmission a little at a time via the dipstick tube. Use a funnel with a fine mesh gauze, to avoid spillage, and to ensure that no foreign matter enters the transmission. Allow plenty of time for the fluid level to settle properly.

7 Once the level is up to the "MAX" mark on the dipstick (see Section 6), refit the dipstick.

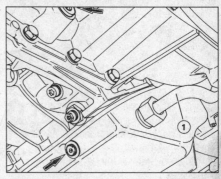

22.3 Automatic transmission fluid drain plugs (arrowed). Transmission is refilled via the dipstick tube (1)

Start the engine, and allow it to idle for a few minutes. Switch the engine off, then recheck the level, topping-up if necessary. Take the car on a short run to fully distribute the new fluid around the transmission, then recheck the fluid level as described in Section 6.

Every 36 000 miles (60 000 km)

23 Brake fluid renewal

⚠ **Warning: Brake hydraulic fluid can harm your eyes, and will damage painted surfaces, so use extreme caution when handling and pouring it. It is also poisonous and highly-inflammable. Do not use fluid that has been standing open for some time, as it absorbs moisture from the air. Excess moisture in the fluid can cause a dangerous loss of braking effectiveness.**

1 The procedure is similar to that for bleeding the hydraulic system, described in Chapter 9. Allowance should be made for all the old fluid to be expelled when bleeding a section of the circuit. The brake fluid reservoir should be emptied by syphoning, using a clean poultry baster or similar, before starting. Take care not to spill fluid onto the surrounding paintwork.

2 Fill the brake fluid reservoir with fresh fluid. Working as described in Chapter 9, open the first bleed nipple in the sequence, and pump the brake pedal gently until the fluid level approaches the "MIN" mark. Do not allow the fluid in the reservoir to fall below this level.

3 Top-up the reservoir to the "MAX" level with new fluid, and continue pumping until new fluid can be seen emerging from the bleed nipple. Old hydraulic fluid is invariably much darker in colour than the new, making it easy

to distinguish the two. Tighten the nipple, and top the reservoir level up to the "MAX" level.

4 Work through all the remaining nipples in the sequence, until new fluid can be seen at all of them. Be careful to keep the master cylinder reservoir topped-up to above the "MIN" level at all times, or air may enter the system and greatly increase the length of the task.

5 When the operation is complete, check that all nipples are securely tightened, and that their dust caps are refitted. Wash off all traces of spilt fluid, and recheck the master cylinder reservoir fluid level.

6 Check the operation of the brakes before taking the car on the road. In particular, check for any "sponginess" felt through the pedal; this would indicate that air has been allowed to enter the system, necessitating further bleeding.

24.1 On 1124 cc and 1360 cc models, disconnect the breather and vacuum hoses from the front of the duct . . .

24 Air filter renewal

1124 cc and 1360 cc models

1 Slacken the retaining clips (where fitted), and disconnect the vacuum hose and breather hose from the front of the air cleaner housing-to-carburettor duct (see illustration). Where the crimped-type Citroën hose clips are fitted, cut the clips and discard them; use standard worm-drive hose clips on refitting.

2 Slacken the retaining clip securing the duct to the carburettor/throttle body. Release the retaining clips securing the lid to the top of the air cleaner housing. Lift the duct and air cleaner lid assembly away, and position it clear of the air cleaner housing (see illustrations).

24.2a . . . then release the air cleaner lid retaining clips, and the duct retaining clip . . .

24.2b . . . and remove the duct, positioning it clear of the air cleaner housing

24.3 Removing the air cleaner element - 1124 cc and 1360 cc models

24.7 On 1580 cc models, slacken the retaining clip and disconnect the air temperature control valve . . .

24.8a . . . then release the retaining clips . . .

24.8b . . . and remove the cover and filter element

24.11 On 1761 cc and 1998 cc (8-valve) models, disconnect the intake duct from the front of the cylinder head cover . . .

3 Lift the air cleaner element out of the housing **(see illustration)**.

4 Fit the new element into the housing, and secure it in position with the retaining clips.

5 Refit the sealing ring to the top of the filter (where fitted), and refit the air cleaner-to-carburettor duct. Ensure that the duct and its sealing rings are correctly seated, and securely tighten the retaining clips.

6 Reconnect the vacuum and breather hoses to the duct, and secure them in position with the retaining clips (where fitted).

1580 cc models

7 Slacken the retaining clip, and disengage the air temperature control valve from the air cleaner housing **(see illustration)**.

8 Release the retaining clips, then remove the

cover from the side of the air cleaner housing. Withdraw the filter element, noting which way round it is fitted **(see illustrations)**.

9 Install the new filter element in the housing, ensuring that it is fitted the correct way round. Refit the cover, securing it in position with the retaining clips.

10 Reconnect the air temperature valve to the filter housing, and securely tighten its retaining clip.

1761 cc and 1998 cc (8-valve) models

11 Slacken the retaining clip, and disconnect the intake duct from the front of the cylinder head cover **(see illustration)**.

12 Slacken and remove the two retaining screws situated at the front of the cylinder

head cover, then release the two air filter cover retaining clips. Remove the filter cover from the cylinder head cover, and withdraw the filter element **(see illustrations)**.

13 Fit the new element in position in the cylinder head cover. Refit the filter cover, securing it in position with its retaining screws and clips.

14 Reconnect the intake duct to the cylinder head cover, and securely tighten its retaining clip.

1761 cc (16-valve) models

15 Slacken the retaining clip and disconnect the inlet duct from the air filter housing lid.

16 Undo the screws securing the lid to the air filter housing body and lift off the lid.

17 Lift out the filter element and wipe clean the housing body and lid.

24.12a . . . then slacken the retaining screws (arrowed) . . .

24.12b . . . and release the retaining clips

24.12c Lift off the filter cover . . .

1

24.12d . . . and withdraw the filter element

24.21a On 1905 cc models, disconnect the intake duct and undo the retaining nuts, remove the end cover . . .

24.21b . . . and withdraw the filter element

18 Place the new element in position in the housing body. Refit the filter housing lid, securing it in position with its retaining screws.
19 Reconnect the inlet duct to the lid, and securely tighten its retaining clip.

1905 cc models

20 Slacken the retaining clip, and disconnect the intake duct from the end of the air cleaner housing.
21 Slacken and remove the two retaining nuts, then remove the cover from the end of the filter housing. Withdraw the filter element, noting which way round it is fitted (see illustrations).
22 Install the new filter element in the housing, ensuring that it is fitted the correct way round. Refit the housing end cover, and securely tighten its retaining nuts.
23 Reconnect the intake duct to the filter housing, and securely tighten its retaining clip.

1998 cc (16-valve) models

24 Firmly apply the handbrake, then jack up the front of the vehicle and support it on axle stands.
25 Working from underneath the vehicle, release the retaining clips and remove the filter housing cover, then lower out the filter element.
26 Install the new element in the filter housing, and refit the housing cover. Secure the cover in position with the retaining clips, then lower the vehicle to the ground.

25 Hinge and lock lubrication

1 Work around the vehicle, and lubricate the hinges of the bonnet, doors and tailgate with a light machine oil.
2 Lightly lubricate the bonnet release mechanism and exposed section of inner cable with a smear of grease.
3 Check carefully the security and operation of all hinges, latches and locks, adjusting them where required. Check the operation of the central locking system (if fitted).
4 Check the condition and operation of the tailgate struts, renewing them if either is leaking or is no longer able to support the tailgate securely when raised.

26 Manual transmission oil level check

Note: *A suitable square-section wrench may be required to undo the transmission filler/level plug on some models. These wrenches can be obtained from most motor factors or your Citroën dealer. A new sealing washer will also be required for the transmission filler/level plug, when refitting.*
1 Park the car on a level surface. Check the oil level before the car is driven, or wait at least 5 minutes after the engine has been switched off. If the oil level is checked immediately after driving the car, some of the oil will remain distributed around the transmission components, resulting in an inaccurate level reading.
2 Prise out the three retaining clips, and remove the small access cover from the left-hand wheel arch liner (see illustration).
3 Wipe clean the area around the filler/level plug, which is the largest bolt among those securing the end cover to the transmission. Unscrew the plug and clean it; discard the sealing washer (see illustration).
4 The oil level should reach the lower edge of the filler/level hole. A certain amount of oil will have gathered behind the filler/level plug, and will trickle out when it is removed; this does *not* necessarily indicate that the level is correct. To ensure that a true level is established, wait until the initial trickle has stopped, then add oil as necessary until a trickle of new oil can be seen emerging. The level will be correct when the flow ceases; use only good-quality oil of the specified type.
5 Refilling the transmission is an awkward operation; above all, allow plenty of time for the oil level to settle properly before checking it. If a large amount had to be added to the transmission, or if a large amount flowed out on checking the level, refit the filler/level plug and take the vehicle on a short journey. With the new oil distributed fully around the transmission components, recheck the level after allowing time for it to settle again (see illustration).

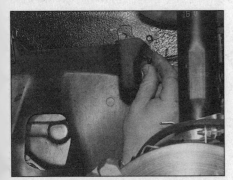

26.2 Removing the access cover from the left-hand wheel arch liner

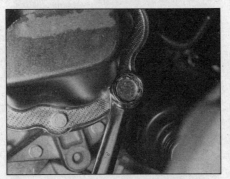

26.3 Removing the manual transmission filler/level plug (1905 cc model shown)

26.5 Topping-up the manual transmission oil

6 If the transmission has been overfilled so that oil flows out as soon as the filler/level plug is removed, first check that the car is completely level (front-to-rear and side-to-side). Allow any surplus oil to drain off into a suitable container.

7 When the level is correct, fit a new sealing washer to the filler/level plug. Tighten the plug to the specified torque wrench setting. Wash off any spilt oil. Refit the access cover to the wheel arch liner, and secure it in position with its retaining clips.

8 Frequent need for topping-up indicates a leak, which should be found and corrected before it becomes serious.

27 Fuel filter renewal - fuel injection models

 Warning: Before carrying out the following operation, refer to the precautions given in "Safety first!" at the beginning of this manual, and follow them implicitly. Petrol is a highly-dangerous and volatile liquid, and the precautions necessary when handling it cannot be overstressed.

1 The fuel filter is situated underneath the rear of the vehicle, mounted on the right-hand side of the fuel tank. To gain access to the filter, chock the front wheels, then jack up the rear of the vehicle and support it on axle stands (see "Jacking and vehicle support").

2 Clamp the fuel hose on the tank side of the filter. Bearing in mind the information given in the relevant Part of Chapter 4 on depressurising the fuel system, release the retaining clips and disconnect the fuel hoses from the filter. Be prepared for fuel spillage.

3 Note the direction of the arrow marked on the filter body. Slacken the retaining clamp screw, then slide the filter out of the clamp, and remove it from underneath the vehicle.

4 Dispose safely of the old filter; it will be highly-inflammable, and may explode if thrown on a fire.

5 Slide the new filter into position in the clamp, ensuring that the arrow on the filter body is pointing in the direction of the fuel flow, ie. towards the throttle body/fuel rail. This can be determined by tracing the fuel hoses back along their length.

6 Connect the fuel hoses to the filter, and secure them in position with their retaining clips. Remove the hose clamp.

7 Start the engine, and check the filter hose connections for leaks. Lower the vehicle to the ground on completion.

28 Timing belt renewal

Refer to the relevant Part of Chapter 2.

Every 72 000 miles (120 000 km)

29 Manual transmission oil renewal

Note: A suitable square-section wrench may be required to undo the transmission filler/level plug on some models. These wrenches can be obtained from most motor factors or your Citroën dealer. A new sealing washer will also be required for the transmission filler/level plug, when refitting.

1 This operation is much quicker and more efficient if the car is first taken on a journey of sufficient length to warm the engine and transmission up to normal operating temperature.

2 Park the car on level ground, then switch off the ignition and apply the handbrake firmly. For improved access, jack up the front of the car and support it securely on axle stands (see "Jacking and vehicle support"). Note that, when refilling and checking the oil level, the car must be lowered to the ground, and level, to ensure accuracy.

3 Prise out the three retaining clips, and remove the small access cover from the left-hand wheel arch liner.

4 Wipe clean the area around the filler/level plug, which is the largest bolt among those securing the end cover to the transmission. Unscrew the filler/level plug, and remove it from the transmission.

5 Position a suitable container under the drain plug (situated at the rear of the transmission) and unscrew the plug. On 1124 cc and 1360 cc models, the plug is on the left-hand side of the differential housing; on 1580 cc and larger-engined models, it is on the base of the differential housing. A square-section wrench (the same as that used for the engine sump drain plug) may be required to undo the drain plug on some models (see illustrations).

6 Allow the oil to drain completely into the container. If the oil is hot, take precautions against scalding. Clean both the filler/level and the drain plugs, being especially careful to wipe any metallic particles off the magnetic inserts. Discard the original sealing washers; they should be renewed whenever they are disturbed.

7 When the oil has finished draining, clean the drain plug threads and those of the transmission casing. Fit a new sealing washer, and refit the drain plug, tightening it to the specified torque wrench setting. If the car was raised for the draining operation, now lower it to the ground. Make sure that the car is level, both front-to-rear and side-to-side.

8 Refilling the transmission is an awkward operation. Above all, allow plenty of time for the oil level to settle properly before checking it.

9 Refill the transmission with the exact amount of the specified type of oil, then check the oil level as described in Section 26. If the correct amount was poured into the transmission, and a large amount flows out on checking the level, refit the filler/level plug and take the car on a short journey. With the new oil distributed fully around the transmission components, recheck the level after allowing time for it to settle again.

10 Once the level is correct, refit the access cover to the wheel arch liner, securing it in position with its retaining clips.

29.5a Removing the manual transmission drain plug (arrowed) - 1124 cc and 1360 cc models

29.5b Removing the manual transmission drain plug - 1580 cc and larger-engined models

Every 2 years (regardless of mileage)

30 Coolant renewal

Cooling system draining

Warning: Wait until the engine is cold before starting this procedure. Do not allow antifreeze to come in contact with your skin, or with the painted surfaces of the vehicle. Rinse off spills immediately with plenty of water. Never leave antifreeze lying around in an open container, or in a puddle in the driveway or on the garage floor. Children and pets are attracted by its sweet smell, but antifreeze can be fatal if ingested.

1 To drain the cooling system, remove the expansion tank filler cap. Turn the cap anti-clockwise until it reaches the first stop. Wait until any pressure remaining in the system is released, then push the cap down, turn it anti-clockwise to the second stop, and lift off.

2 Position a suitable container beneath the coolant drain outlet at the lower left-hand side of the radiator. If desired, a suitable length of tubing can be attached to the outlet, to direct the flow of coolant (see illustration).

3 Loosen the drain plug (there is no need to remove it completely), and allow the coolant to drain into the container.

4 To assist draining, open the cooling system bleed screws, which are located as follows:

1124 cc and 1360 cc models

(a) At the top left-hand corner of the radiator (see illustration).
(b) In the top of the coolant outlet housing mounted on the left-hand end of the cylinder head.
(c) In the heater outlet hose connection (to improve access, this bleed screw may be located in the end of an extension hose joined to the connection).
(d) In the top of the cooling system de-aeration chamber mounted on the right-hand rear corner of the cylinder block - pre-1993 models without air conditioning (see illustration).

1580 cc and larger-engined models

(a) At the top left-hand corner of the radiator.
(b) In the top of the thermostat housing cover.
(c) In the heater outlet hose connection (to improve access, this bleed screw may be located in the end of an extension hose joined to the connection) (see illustration).

(d) In the coolant hose located directly above the thermostat housing cover - all except 1998 cc 16-valve models (see illustration).
(e) One on the front coolant hose connection, and one on the rear coolant hose connection to the coolant outlet housing mounted on the left-hand end of the cylinder head - 1998 cc 16-valve models.

5 When the flow of coolant stops, reposition the container below the cylinder block drain plug. On 1998 cc models, the drain plug is located at the rear of the cylinder block; on all other models, the plug is located on the front of the block.

6 Remove the drain plug, and allow the coolant to drain into the container (see illustration).

7 If the coolant has been drained for a reason other than for renewal, then provided it is clean and less than two years old, it can be re-used.

Cooling system flushing

Note: A new sealing ring will be required when refitting the radiator bottom hose.

8 If coolant renewal has been neglected, or if the antifreeze mixture has become diluted, then in time, the cooling system may gradually

30.4a Removing the radiator bleed screw

30.4b Cooling system de-aeration chamber bleed screw (arrowed) - pre-1993 1124 cc and 1360 cc models without air conditioning

30.2 Tubing (1) attached to radiator coolant drain outlet. Note drain plug (2)

30.4c Removing the heater outlet hose bleed screw (screw located in extension hose)

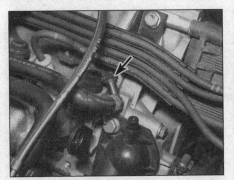
30.4d Thermostat housing coolant hose bleed screw (arrowed) - 1580 cc model

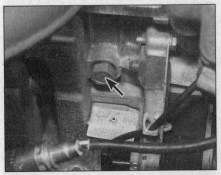
30.6 Cylinder block drain plug (arrowed) - 1124 cc and 1360 cc models

30.21 A "header tank" arrangement will be required to refill the cooling system. Note the O-ring seal (1) and the clamped breather hose (2)

lose efficiency. The coolant passages will eventually become restricted due to rust, scale deposits, and other sediment. This situation can be remedied by flushing the system clean.

9 The radiator should be flushed independently of the engine, to avoid unnecessary contamination.

Radiator flushing

10 To flush the radiator, first tighten the radiator drain plug and the radiator bleed screw.

11 Disconnect the top and bottom hoses from the radiator (it is only necessary to disconnect the larger radiator bottom hose), as described in Chapter 3.

12 Insert a garden hose into the radiator top inlet. Direct a flow of clean water through the radiator, and continue flushing until clean water emerges from the radiator bottom outlet.

13 If, after a reasonable period, the water still does not run clear, the radiator can be flushed with a good proprietary cleaning agent. It is important that the cleaning agent manufacturer's instructions are followed carefully. If the contamination is particularly bad, insert the hose in the radiator bottom outlet, and flush the radiator in the reverse direction to normal flow.

Engine flushing

14 To flush the engine, first refit the cylinder block drain plug, and tighten the cooling system bleed screws.

15 Remove the thermostat as described in Chapter 3, then temporarily refit the thermostat cover.

16 With the top and bottom hoses disconnected from the radiator, insert a garden hose into the radiator top hose. Direct a clean flow of water through the engine, and continue flushing until clean water emerges from the radiator bottom hose.

17 On completion of flushing, refit the thermostat and reconnect the hoses with reference to Chapter 3. Note that a new sealing ring should be used when reconnecting the radiator bottom hose.

Cooling system filling

18 Before attempting to fill the cooling system, make sure that all hoses and clips are in good condition, and that the clips are tight. Note that antifreeze must be used all year round, to prevent corrosion of the engine components (refer to the following sub-Section). Also check that the radiator and cylinder block drain plugs are in place and tight.

19 Remove the expansion tank filler cap.

20 Open all the cooling system bleed screws (see paragraph 4).

21 Some of the cooling system hoses are positioned at a higher level than the top of the radiator expansion tank. It is therefore necessary to use a "header tank" when refilling the cooling system, to reduce the possibility of air being trapped in the upper parts of the system. Although Citroën dealers use a special header tank, the same effect can be achieved by using a suitable bottle, with a seal, between the bottle and the expansion tank **(see illustration)**.

22 Clamp the expansion tank breather hose, then fit the "header tank" to the expansion tank, and slowly fill the system. Coolant will emerge from each of the bleed screws in turn, starting with the lowest screw. As soon as coolant free from air bubbles emerges from the lowest screw, tighten that screw, and watch the next bleed screw in the system. Repeat the procedure until the coolant is emerging from the highest bleed screw in the cooling system, then tighten all bleed screws securely.

23 Start the engine, and run it at a fast idle speed (do not exceed 2000 rpm) until the cooling fans cut in.

24 Remove the "header tank", taking great care not to scald yourself with the hot coolant, then fit the expansion tank cap. Unclamp the expansion tank breather hose.

25 Stop the engine, and allow it to cool.

26 Check the coolant level, which should be up to the "MAX" mark on the side of the expansion tank. Top-up the level if necessary.

Antifreeze mixture

27 The antifreeze should always be renewed at the specified intervals. This is necessary not only to maintain the antifreeze properties, but also to prevent corrosion which would otherwise occur as the corrosion inhibitors become progressively less effective.

28 Always use an ethylene-glycol-based antifreeze which is suitable for use in mixed-metal cooling systems. The quantity of antifreeze required, and the levels of protection, are indicated in the Specifications.

29 Before adding antifreeze, the system should be drained, preferably flushed, and all hoses checked for condition and security.

30 After filling with antifreeze, a label should be attached to the expansion tank, stating the type and concentration of antifreeze used, and the date installed. Any subsequent topping-up should be made with the same type and concentration of antifreeze.

31 Do not use engine antifreeze in the windscreen/tailgate washer system, as it will cause damage to the vehicle paintwork. A screenwash additive should be added to the washer system in its manufacturer's recommended quantities.

Chapter 2 Part A:
TU series engine in-car repair procedures

Contents

Camshaft and rocker arms - removal, inspection and refitting 9
Camshaft oil seal - renewal 8
Compression test - description and interpretation 2
Crankshaft oil seals - renewal 13
Cylinder head - removal and refitting 10
Cylinder head cover - removal and refitting 4
Engine assembly/valve timing holes - general information and usage 3
Engine oil and filter renewal ....See Chapter 1
Engine oil level check ....See "Weekly checks"
Engine/transmission mountings - inspection and renewal 15
Flywheel - removal, inspection and refitting 14
General engine checks .... See Chapter 1
General information 1
Oil pump - removal, inspection and refitting 12
Sump - removal and refitting 11
Timing belt - general information, removal and refitting 6
Timing belt covers - removal and refitting 5
Timing belt tensioner and sprockets - removal, inspection and
  refitting 7
Valve clearances - checking and adjustment .... See Chapter 1

Degrees of difficulty

Easy, suitable for novice with little experience	Fairly easy, suitable for beginner with some experience	Fairly difficult, suitable for competent DIY mechanic	Difficult, suitable for experienced DIY mechanic	Very difficult, suitable for expert DIY or professional

Specifications

Engine (general)
Engine codes*:
1124 cc carburettor engine	H1A (TU1K)
1124 cc fuel injection engine:	
Up to mid-1996	HDZ (TU1M L/Z)
Mid-1996 onward	HDZ (TU1M+ L3)
1360 cc carburettor engine	K2D (TU3.2K)
1360 cc fuel injection engine with a distributor	KDY (TU3M L/Z)
1360 cc fuel injection engine with a static ignition system:	
Up to mid-1996	KDX (TU3MC L/Z)
Mid-1996 onward	KFX (TU3JP)

Bore:
1124 cc engine	72.00 mm
1360 cc engine	75.00 mm

Stroke:
1124 cc engine	69.00 mm
1360 cc engine	77.00 mm
Direction of crankshaft rotation	Clockwise (viewed from right-hand side of vehicle)
No 1 cylinder location	At transmission end of block

Compression ratio:
1124 cc engine	9.4 : 1
1360 cc engine	9.3 : 1

*The engine code is stamped on a plate attached to the front left-hand end of the cylinder block; this is the code most often used by Citroën. The full code given in brackets is the factory identification number, and is not often referred to by Citroën or this manual.

Lubrication system
Oil pump type	Gear-type, chain-driven off the crankshaft
Minimum oil pressure at 90°C	4 bars at 4000 rpm
Oil pressure warning switch operating pressure	0.5 bars

Camshaft

Drive	Toothed belt
Number of bearings	5

Cam lift:
1124 cc engine	8.2 mm
1360 cc engine	9.4 mm

Camshaft bearing journal diameter (outside diameter):
No 1	36.950 to 36.925 mm
No 2	40.650 to 40.625 mm
No 3	41.250 to 41.225 mm
No 4	41.850 to 41.825 mm
No 5	42.450 to 42.425 mm

Cylinder head bearing journal diameter (inside diameter):
No 1	37.000 to 37.039 mm
No 2	40.700 to 47.739 mm
No 3	41.300 to 41.339 mm
No 4	41.900 to 41.939 mm
No 5	42.500 to 42.539 mm

Torque wrench settings

	Nm	lbf ft
Cylinder head cover nuts	16	12
Timing belt cover bolts	8	6
Crankshaft pulley retaining bolts	8	6
Timing belt tensioner pulley nut	23	17
Camshaft sprocket retaining bolt	80	59
Crankshaft sprocket retaining bolt	110	81
Camshaft thrust fork retaining bolt	16	12
Cylinder head bolts:		
Stage 1	20	15
Stage 2	Angle-tighten through 240°	Angle-tighten through 240°
Sump drain plug	30	22
Sump retaining nuts and bolts	8	6
Oil pump retaining bolts	8	6
Flywheel retaining bolts	65	48
Big-end bearing cap nuts	40	30
Main bearing ladder casting:		
11 mm bolts:		
Stage 1	20	15
Stage 2	Angle-tighten through 45°	Angle-tighten through 45°
6 mm bolts	8	6
Engine/transmission right-hand mounting:		
Mounting bracket retaining nuts	45	33
Engine/transmission left-hand mounting:		
Mounting bracket-to-transmission nuts	18	13
Mounting bracket-to-body bolts	25	18
Centre nut	38	28
Engine/transmission rear mounting:		
Mounting assembly-to-block bolts	40	30
Mounting bracket-to-mounting bolt	70	52
Mounting bracket-to-subframe bolt	95	70

1 General information

How to use this Chapter

This Part of Chapter 2 describes those repair procedures that can reasonably be carried out on the TU series engine (1124 cc and 1360 cc models) while it remains in the car. If the engine has been removed from the car and is being dismantled as described in Part C, any preliminary dismantling pro-cedures can be ignored. Refer to Part B for information on the XU series engine (1580 cc and larger-engined models).

Note that, while it may be possible physically to overhaul items such as the piston/connecting rod assemblies while the engine is in the car, such tasks are not normally carried out as separate operations. Usually, several additional procedures (not to mention the cleaning of components and of oilways) have to be carried out. For this reason, all such tasks are classed as major overhaul procedures, and are described in Part C of this Chapter.

Part C describes the removal of the engine/transmission unit from the vehicle, and the full overhaul procedures that can then be carried out.

TU series engine description

The TU series engine is a well-proven engine which has been fitted to many previous Citroën and Peugeot vehicles. The engine is of the in-line four-cylinder, overhead camshaft (OHC) type, mounted transversely at the front of the car (see illustration). The clutch and transmission are attached to its left-hand end. The ZX range is fitted with both 1124 cc (not available in the UK) and 1360 cc versions of the engine; carburettor and fuel-injected versions are available.

The crankshaft runs in five main bearings. Thrustwashers are fitted to No 2 main bearing (upper half) to control crankshaft endfloat.

1.4 Cutaway view of the TU series engine

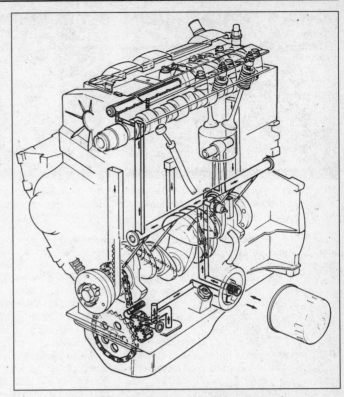

1.11 Lubrication system of the TU series engine

The connecting rods rotate on horizontally-split bearing shells at their big-ends. The pistons are attached to the connecting rods by gudgeon pins, which are an interference fit in the connecting rod small-end eyes. The aluminium-alloy pistons are fitted with three piston rings - two compression rings and an oil control ring.

The cylinder bores have replaceable wet liners. Sealing O-rings are fitted at the base of each liner, to prevent the escape of coolant into the sump.

The inlet and exhaust valves are each closed by coil springs, and operate in guides pressed into the cylinder head; the valve seat inserts are also pressed into the cylinder head, and can be renewed separately if worn.

The camshaft is driven by a toothed timing belt, and operates the eight valves via rocker arms. Valve clearances are adjusted by a screw-and-locknut arrangement. The camshaft rotates in bearings that are line-bored through the cylinder head. The timing belt also drives the coolant pump.

Lubrication is by means of an oil pump, which is driven (via a chain and sprocket) off the right-hand end of the crankshaft. It draws oil through a strainer located in the sump, and then forces it through an externally-mounted filter into galleries in the cylinder block/crankcase. From there, the oil is distributed to the crankshaft (main bearings) and camshaft. The big-end bearings are supplied with oil via internal drillings in the crankshaft, while the camshaft bearings also receive a pressurised

supply. The camshaft lobes and valves are lubricated by splash, as are all other engine components **(see illustration)**.

Throughout this manual, it is often necessary to identify the engines not only by their capacity, but also by their engine code. The engine code, which consists of three letters (eg. KDY), is stamped on a plate attached to the front left-hand end of the cylinder block **(see illustration)**.

Repair operations possible with the engine in the car

The following work can be carried out with the engine in the car:

(a) Compression pressure - testing.
(b) Cylinder head cover - removal and refitting.
(c) Timing belt covers - removal and refitting.
(d) Timing belt - removal, refitting and adjustment.
(e) Timing belt tensioner and sprockets - removal and refitting.
(f) Camshaft oil seal(s) - renewal.
(g) Camshaft and rocker arms - removal, inspection and refitting.*
(h) Cylinder head - removal and refitting.
(i) Cylinder head and pistons - decarbonising.
(j) Sump - removal and refitting.
(k) Oil pump - removal, overhaul and refitting.
(l) Crankshaft oil seals - renewal.
(m) Engine/transmission mountings - inspection and renewal.
(n) Flywheel - removal, inspection and refitting.

1.12 Engine code is stamped on a plate (arrowed) attached to the front of the cylinder block - viewed from above

The cylinder head must be removed for the successful completion of this work. Refer to Section 9 for details.

2 Compression test - description and interpretation

1 When engine performance is down, or if misfiring occurs which cannot be attributed to the ignition or fuel systems, a compression test can provide diagnostic clues as to the engine's condition. If the test is performed regularly, it can give warning of trouble before any other symptoms become apparent.
2 The engine must be fully warmed-up to normal operating temperature, the battery

3.4 Insert a 6 mm bolt (arrowed) through hole in cylinder block flange and into timing hole in the flywheel . . .

3.5 . . . then insert a 10 mm bolt through the cam sprocket timing hole, and locate it in the cylinder head

4.3 Disconnect the breather hose from the cylinder head cover . . .

must be fully charged, and all the spark plugs must be removed (Chapter 1). The aid of an assistant will also be required.

3 On models with an ignition system incorporating a distributor, disable the ignition system by disconnecting the ignition HT coil lead from the distributor cap and earthing it on the cylinder block. Use a jumper lead or similar wire to make a good connection.

4 On models with a static (distributorless) ignition system, disable the ignition system by disconnecting the LT wiring connector from the ignition HT coil(s), referring to Chapter 5 for further information.

5 Fit a compression tester to the No 1 cylinder spark plug hole - the type of tester which screws into the plug thread is to be preferred.

6 Have the assistant hold the throttle wide open, and crank the engine on the starter motor; after one or two revolutions, the compression pressure should build up to a maximum figure, and then stabilise. Record the highest reading obtained.

7 Repeat the test on the remaining cylinders, recording the pressure in each.

8 All cylinders should produce very similar pressures; a difference of more than 2 bars between any two cylinders indicates a fault. Note that the compression should build up quickly in a healthy engine; low compression on the first stroke, followed by gradually-increasing pressure on successive strokes, indicates worn piston rings. A low compression reading on the first stroke, which does not build up during successive strokes, indicates leaking valves or a blown head gasket (a cracked head could also be the cause). Deposits on the undersides of the valve heads can also cause low compression.

9 Although Citroën do not specify exact compression pressures, as a guide, any cylinder pressure of below 10 bars can be considered as less than healthy. Refer to a Citroën dealer or other specialist if in doubt as to whether a particular pressure reading is acceptable.

10 If the pressure in any cylinder is low, carry out the following test to isolate the cause. Introduce a teaspoonful of clean oil into that

cylinder through its spark plug hole, and repeat the test.

11 If the addition of oil temporarily improves the compression pressure, this indicates that bore or piston wear is responsible for the pressure loss. No improvement suggests that leaking or burnt valves, or a blown head gasket, may be to blame.

12 A low reading from two adjacent cylinders is almost certainly due to the head gasket having blown between them; the presence of coolant in the engine oil will confirm this.

13 If one cylinder is about 20 percent lower than the others and the engine has a slightly rough idle, a worn camshaft lobe could be the cause.

14 If the compression reading is unusually high, the combustion chambers are probably coated with carbon deposits. If this is the case, the cylinder head should be removed and decarbonised.

15 On completion of the test, refit the spark plugs and reconnect the ignition system.

3 Engine assembly/valve timing holes - general information and usage

Note: *Do not attempt to rotate the engine whilst the crankshaft/camshaft are locked in position. If the engine is to be left in this state for a long period of time, it is a good idea to place warning notices inside the vehicle, and in the engine compartment. This will reduce the possibility of the engine being accidentally cranked on the starter motor, which is likely to cause damage with the locking pins in place.*

1 On all models, timing holes are drilled in the camshaft sprocket and in the rear of the flywheel. The holes are used to ensure that the crankshaft and camshaft are correctly positioned when assembling the engine (to prevent the possibility of the valves contacting the pistons when refitting the cylinder head), or refitting the timing belt. When the timing holes are aligned with access holes in the cylinder head and the front of the cylinder block, suitable diameter pins can be inserted to lock both the camshaft and crankshaft in

position, preventing them from rotating. Proceed as follows.

2 Remove the timing belt upper cover as described in Section 5.

3 The crankshaft must now be turned until the timing hole in the camshaft sprocket is aligned with the corresponding hole in the cylinder head. The holes are aligned when the camshaft sprocket hole is in the 2 o'clock position, when viewed from the right-hand end of the engine. The crankshaft can be turned by using a spanner on the crankshaft sprocket bolt, noting that it should always be rotated in a clockwise direction (viewed from the right-hand end of the engine).

4 With the camshaft sprocket hole correctly positioned, insert a 6 mm diameter bolt or drill through the hole in the front, left-hand flange of the cylinder block, and locate it in the timing hole in the rear of the flywheel **(see illustration)**. Note that it may be necessary to rotate the crankshaft slightly, to get the holes to align.

5 With the flywheel correctly positioned, insert a 10 mm diameter bolt or a drill through the timing hole in the camshaft sprocket, and locate it in the hole in the cylinder head **(see illustration)**.

6 The crankshaft and camshaft are now locked in position, preventing unnecessary rotation.

4 Cylinder head cover - removal and refitting

Removal

1 Disconnect the battery negative lead.

2 Where necessary, undo the bolts securing the HT lead retaining clips to the rear of the cylinder head cover, and position the clips clear of the cover.

3 Slacken the retaining clip, and disconnect the breather hose from the left-hand end of the cylinder head cover **(see illustration)**. Where the original crimped-type Citroën hose clip is still fitted, cut it off and discard it. Use a standard worm-drive clip on refitting.

4 Undo the two retaining nuts, and remove

4.4 . . . then slacken and remove the cover retaining nuts and washers (arrowed) . . .

4.5 . . . and lift off the cylinder head cover

4.6a Lift off the spacers (second one arrowed) . . .

the washer from each of the cylinder head cover studs **(see illustration)**.

5 Lift off the cylinder head cover, and remove it along with its rubber seal **(see illustration)**. Examine the seal for signs of damage and deterioration, and if necessary, renew it.

6 Remove the spacer from each stud, and lift off the oil baffle plate **(see illustrations)**.

Refitting

7 Carefully clean the cylinder head and cover mating surfaces, and remove all traces of oil.

8 Fit the rubber seal over the edge of the cylinder head cover, ensuring that it is correctly located along its entire length **(see illustration)**.

9 Refit the oil baffle plate to the engine, and locate the spacers in their recesses in the baffle plate.

10 Carefully refit the cylinder head cover to the engine, taking great care not to displace the rubber seal.

11 Check that the seal is correctly located, then refit the washers and cover retaining nuts, and tighten them to the specified torque.

12 Where necessary, refit the HT lead clips to the rear of the head cover, and securely tighten their retaining bolts.

13 Reconnect the breather hose to the cylinder head cover, securely tightening its retaining clip, and reconnect the battery negative lead.

4.6b . . . and remove the oil baffle plate

4.8 On refitting, ensure the rubber seal is correctly located on the cylinder head cover

5.1a Undo the two retaining bolts (arrowed) . . .

5.1b . . . and remove the upper timing belt cover

5 Timing belt covers - removal and refitting

Removal

Upper cover

1 Slacken and remove the two retaining bolts (one at the front and one at the rear), and remove the upper timing cover from the cylinder head **(see illustrations)**.

Centre cover

Note: *On later engines, the centre cover is combined with the lower cover and is not a separate component.*

2 Remove the upper cover as described in paragraph 1, then free the wiring from its retaining clips on the centre cover **(see illustration)**.

5.2 Free the wiring loom from its retaining clip . . .

3 Slacken and remove the three retaining bolts (one at the rear of the cover, beneath the engine mounting plate, and two directly above

5.3 . . . then undo the three retaining bolts (locations arrowed) and remove the centre timing belt cover

the crankshaft pulley), and manoeuvre the centre cover out from the engine compartment **(see illustration)**.

5.6a Undo the three retaining bolts (arrowed) . . .

5.6b . . . and remove the crankshaft pulley

5.7 Undo the retaining bolt and remove the lower timing belt cover

Lower cover

4 Remove the auxiliary drivebelt as described in Chapter 1.

5 Remove the upper and centre covers as described in paragraphs 1 to 3.

6 Undo the three crankshaft pulley retaining bolts and remove the pulley, noting which way round it is fitted **(see illustrations)**.

7 Slacken and remove the single retaining bolt, and slide the lower cover off the end of the crankshaft **(see illustration)**.

Refitting

Upper cover

8 Refit the cover, ensuring it is correctly located with the centre cover, and tighten its retaining bolts.

Centre cover

9 Manoeuvre the centre cover back into position, ensuring it is correctly located with the lower cover, and tighten its retaining bolts.

10 Clip the wiring loom into its retaining clips on the front of the centre cover, then refit the upper cover as described in paragraph 8.

Lower cover

10 Locate the lower cover over the timing belt sprocket, and tighten its retaining bolt.

11 Fit the pulley to the end of the crankshaft, ensuring it is fitted the correct way round, and tighten its retaining bolts to the specified torque.

12 Refit the centre and upper covers as described above, then refit and tension the auxiliary drivebelt as described in Chapter 1.

---

6 Timing belt - general information, removal and refitting

Note: *Citroën specify the use of a special electronic tool (SEEM belt tensioning measuring tool) to correctly set the timing belt tension. If access to this equipment cannot be obtained, an approximate setting can be achieved using the method described below. If the method described is used, the tension must be checked using the special electronic tool at the earliest possible opportunity. Do not drive the vehicle over large distances, or use high engine speeds, until the belt tension*

is known to be correct. Refer to a Citroën dealer for advice.

General information

1 The timing belt drives the camshaft and coolant pump from a toothed sprocket on the front of the crankshaft. If the belt breaks or slips in service, the pistons are likely to hit the valve heads, resulting in extensive (and expensive) damage.

2 The timing belt should be renewed at the specified intervals (see Chapter 1), or earlier if it is contaminated with oil, or if it is at all noisy in operation (a "scraping" noise due to uneven wear).

3 If the timing belt is being removed, it is a wise precaution to check the condition of the coolant pump at the same time (check for signs of coolant leakage). This may avoid the need to remove the timing belt again at a later stage, should the coolant pump fail.

Removal

4 Disconnect the battery negative terminal.

5 Align the engine assembly/valve timing holes as described in Section 3, and lock both the camshaft sprocket and the flywheel in position. *Do not* attempt to rotate the engine whilst the locking pins are in position.

6 Remove the timing belt centre and lower covers as described in Section 5.

7 Loosen the timing belt tensioner pulley retaining nut. Pivot the pulley in a clockwise direction, using a square-section key fitted to the hole in the pulley hub, then retighten the retaining nut.

6.8 Mark the direction of rotation on the belt, if it is to be re-used

8 If the timing belt is to be re-used, use white paint or similar to mark the direction of rotation on the belt (if markings do not already exist) **(see illustration)**. Slip the belt off the sprockets.

9 Check the timing belt carefully for any signs of uneven wear, splitting, or oil contamination. Pay particular attention to the roots of the teeth. Renew the belt if there is the slightest doubt about its condition. If the engine is undergoing an overhaul, and has covered more than 24 000 miles (40 000 km) with the existing belt fitted, renew the belt as a matter of course, regardless of its apparent condition. The cost of a new belt is nothing when compared to the cost of repairs, should the belt break in service. If signs of oil contamination are found, trace the source of the oil leak, and rectify it. Wash down the engine timing belt area and all related components, to remove all traces of oil.

Refitting

10 Prior to refitting, thoroughly clean the timing belt sprockets. Check that the tensioner pulley rotates freely, without any sign of roughness. If necessary, renew the tensioner pulley as described in Section 7. Make sure that the locking pins are still in place, as described in Section 3.

11 Manoeuvre the timing belt into position, ensuring that the arrows on the belt are pointing in the direction of rotation (clockwise when viewed from the right-hand end of the engine).

12 Do not twist the timing belt sharply while refitting it. Fit the belt over the crankshaft and camshaft sprockets. Make sure that the "front run" of the belt is taut - ie, ensure that any slack is on the tensioner pulley side of the belt. Fit the belt over the water pump sprocket and tensioner pulley. Ensure that the belt teeth are seated centrally in the sprockets.

13 Loosen the tensioner pulley retaining nut. Pivot the pulley anti-clockwise to remove all free play from the timing belt, then retighten the nut.

Tensioning without the special electronic measuring tool

Note: *If this method is used, ensure that the belt tension is checked by a Citroën dealer at the earliest possible opportunity.*

2A

6.14 Using the Citroën special tool to tension the timing belt

14 Citroën dealers use a special tool to tension the timing belt **(see illustration)**. A similar tool may be fabricated using a suitable square-section bar attached to an arm; a hole should be drilled in the arm at a distance of 80 mm from the centre of the square-section bar. Fit the tool to the hole in the tensioner pulley, keeping the tool arm as close to the horizontal as possible, and hang a 1.5 kg (3.3 lb) weight from the hole in the tool. In the absence of an object of the specified weight, a spring balance can be used to exert the required force, ensuring that the spring balance is held at 90° to the tool arm. Slacken the pulley retaining nut, allowing the weight or force exerted (as applicable) to push the tensioner pulley against the belt, then retighten the pulley nut.

15 If the special tool is not available, an approximate setting may be achieved as follows. Slacken the pulley retaining nut, and pivot the tensioner pulley anti-clockwise until it is just possible to turn the timing belt through 90° by finger and thumb, midway between the crankshaft and camshaft sprockets. The square hole in the tensioner pulley hub should be directly below the retaining nut, and the deflection of the belt at the mid-point between the sprockets should be approximately 6.0 mm. If this method is used, the belt tension should be checked by a Citroën dealer at the earliest possible opportunity.

16 Remove the locking pins from the camshaft sprocket and flywheel.

17 Using a suitable socket and extension bar on the crankshaft sprocket bolt, rotate the crankshaft through four complete rotations in a clockwise direction (viewed from the right-hand end of the engine). *Do not* at any time rotate the crankshaft anti-clockwise.

18 Slacken the tensioner pulley nut, re-tension the belt using one of the methods just described, then tighten the tensioner pulley nut to the specified torque.

19 Rotate the crankshaft through a further two turns clockwise, and check that both the camshaft sprocket and flywheel timing holes are still correctly aligned.

20 If all is well, refit the timing belt covers as described in Section 5, and reconnect the battery negative terminal.

Tensioning using the special electronic measuring tool

21 Fit the special belt tensioning measuring equipment to the "front run" of the timing belt, approximately midway between the camshaft and crankshaft sprockets. Fit an 8mm square key to the hole in the front face of the tensioner pulley. Turn the tensioner so that the timing belt is tensioned to a setting of 45 units, then retighten its retaining nut.

22 Remove the locking tools from the camshaft sprocket and flywheel, and remove the measuring tool from the belt.

23 Using a suitable socket and extension bar on the crankshaft sprocket bolt, rotate the crankshaft through four complete rotations in a clockwise direction (viewed from the right-hand end of the engine). *Do not* at any time rotate the crankshaft anti-clockwise.

24 Slacken the tensioner pulley retaining nut, and refit the measuring tool to the belt. If a "new" belt is being fitted, tension it to a setting of 40 units. If an "old" belt is being re-used, tighten it to a setting of 36 units. **Note:** *Citroën state that a belt becomes "old" after 1 hour's use.* With the belt correctly tensioned, tighten the pulley retaining nut to the specified torque.

25 Remove the measuring tool from the belt, then rotate the crankshaft through another two complete rotations in a clockwise direction, so that both the camshaft sprocket and flywheel timing holes are realigned. *Do not* at any time rotate the crankshaft anti-clockwise. Fit the measuring tool to the belt, and check the belt tension. A "new" belt should give a reading of 51 ± 3 units; an "old" belt should be 45 ± 3 units.

26 If the belt tension is incorrect, repeat the procedures in paragraphs 24 and 25.

27 With the belt tension correctly set, refit the timing belt covers as described in Section 5, and reconnect the battery negative terminal.

7 Timing belt tensioner and sprockets - removal, inspection and refitting

Note: *This Section describes the removal and refitting of the components concerned as individual operations. If more than one of them is to be removed at the same time, start by removing the timing belt as described in Section 6; remove the actual component as described below, ignoring the preliminary dismantling steps.*

Removal

1 Disconnect the battery negative terminal.

2 Position the engine assembly/valve timing holes as described in Section 3, and lock both the camshaft sprocket and flywheel in position. *Do not* attempt to rotate the engine whilst the pins are in position.

Camshaft sprocket

3 Remove the centre timing belt cover as described in Section 5.

4 Loosen the timing belt tensioner pulley retaining nut. Rotate the pulley in a clockwise direction, using a suitable square-section key fitted to the hole in the pulley hub, then retighten the retaining nut.

5 Disengage the timing belt from the sprocket, and move the belt clear, taking care not to bend or twist it sharply. Remove the locking pin from the camshaft sprocket.

6 Slacken the camshaft sprocket retaining bolt and remove it, along with its washer. To prevent the camshaft rotating as the bolt is slackened, a sprocket-holding tool will be required. *Do not* attempt to use the sprocket locking pin to prevent the sprocket from rotating whilst the bolt is slackened.

TOOL TiP

To prevent the camshaft sprocket from rotating, use two lengths of steel strip (one long, the other short), and three nuts and bolts; one nut and bolt forms the pivot of a forked tool, with the remaining two nuts and bolts at the tips of the "forks" to engage with the sprocket spokes.

7 With the retaining bolt removed, slide the sprocket off the end of the camshaft. If the locating peg is a loose fit in the rear of the sprocket, remove it for safe-keeping. Examine the camshaft oil seal for signs of oil leakage and, if necessary, renew it as described in Section 8.

Crankshaft sprocket

8 Remove the centre and lower timing belt covers as described in Section 5.

9 Loosen the timing belt tensioner pulley retaining nut. Rotate the pulley in a clockwise direction, using a suitable square-section key fitted to the hole in the pulley hub, then retighten the retaining nut.

10 To prevent crankshaft rotation whilst the sprocket retaining bolt is slackened, select

7.10 Use the fabricated tool shown to lock flywheel ring gear and prevent the crankshaft rotating

7.11a Remove the crankshaft sprocket retaining bolt . . .

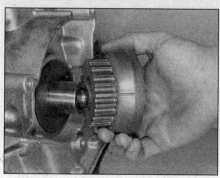

7.11b . . . then slide off the sprocket

top gear, and have an assistant apply the brakes firmly. If the engine has been removed from the vehicle, lock the flywheel ring gear, using an arrangement similar to that shown **(see illustration)**. *Do not* be tempted to use the flywheel locking pin to prevent the crankshaft from rotating; temporarily remove the locking pin from the rear of the flywheel prior to slackening the pulley bolt, then refit it once the bolt has been slackened. Disengage the timing belt from the sprocket, and move the belt clear, taking care not to bend or twist it sharply.

11 Unscrew the retaining bolt and washer, then slide the sprocket off the end of the crankshaft **(see illustrations)**. Refit the locating pin to the rear of the timing hole in the rear of the flywheel.

12 If the Woodruff key is a loose fit in the crankshaft, remove it and store it with the sprocket for safe-keeping. If necessary, also slide the flanged spacer off the end of the crankshaft **(see illustration)**. Examine the crankshaft oil seal for signs of oil leakage and, if necessary, renew as described in Section 13.

Tensioner pulley

13 Remove the centre timing belt cover as described in Section 5.
14 Slacken and remove the timing belt tensioner pulley retaining nut, and slide the pulley off its mounting stud. Examine the mounting stud for signs of damage and, if necessary, renew it.

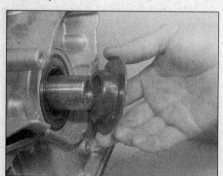

7.12 Remove the flanged spacer if necessary

Inspection

15 Clean the sprockets thoroughly, and renew any that show signs of wear, damage or cracks.
16 Clean the tensioner assembly, but do not use any strong solvent which may enter the pulley bearing. Check that the pulley rotates freely about its hub, with no sign of stiffness or of free play. Renew the tensioner pulley if there is any doubt about its condition, or if there are any obvious signs of wear or damage.

Refitting
Camshaft sprocket

17 Refit the locating peg (where removed) to the rear of the sprocket, then locate the sprocket on the end of the camshaft. Ensure that the locating peg is correctly engaged with the cutout in the camshaft end.
18 Refit the sprocket retaining bolt and washer. Tighten the bolt to the specified torque, whilst retaining the sprocket with the tool used on removal.
19 Realign the timing hole in the camshaft sprocket (see Section 3) with the corresponding hole in the cylinder head, and refit the locking pin.
20 Refit the timing belt to the camshaft sprocket. Ensure that the "front run" of the belt is taut - ie, ensure that any slack is on the tensioner pulley side of the belt. Do not twist the belt sharply while refitting it, and ensure that the belt teeth are seated centrally in the sprockets.
21 Loosen the tensioner pulley retaining nut. Rotate the pulley anti-clockwise to remove all free play from the timing belt, then retighten the nut.
22 Tension the belt as described in paragraphs 14 to 19 of Section 6.
23 Refit the timing belt covers as described in Section 5.

Crankshaft sprocket

24 Where removed, locate the Woodruff key in the crankshaft end, then slide on the flanged spacer, aligning its slot with the Woodruff key.
25 Align the crankshaft sprocket slot with the Woodruff key, and slide it onto the end of the crankshaft.

26 Temporarily remove the locking pin from the rear of the flywheel, then refit the crankshaft sprocket retaining bolt and washer. Tighten the bolt to the specified torque, whilst preventing crankshaft rotation using the method employed on removal. Refit the locking pin to the rear of the flywheel.
27 Relocate the timing belt on the crankshaft sprocket. Ensure that the "front run" of the belt is taut - ie, ensure that any slack is on the tensioner pulley side of the belt. Do not twist the belt sharply while refitting it, and ensure that the belt teeth are seated centrally in the sprockets.
28 Loosen the tensioner pulley retaining nut. Rotate the pulley anti-clockwise to remove all free play from the timing belt, then retighten the nut.
29 Tension the belt as described in paragraphs 14 to 19 of Section 6.
30 Refit the timing belt covers as described in Section 5.

Tensioner pulley

31 Refit the tensioner pulley to its mounting stud, and fit the retaining nut.
32 Ensure that the "front run" of the belt is taut - ie, ensure that any slack is on the pulley side of the belt. Check that the belt is centrally located on all its sprockets. Rotate the pulley anti-clockwise to remove all free play from the timing belt, then tighten the pulley retaining nut securely.
33 Tension the belt as described in paragraphs 14 to 19 of Section 6.
34 Refit the timing belt covers as described in Section 5.

8 Camshaft oil seal - renewal

Note: *If the camshaft oil seal is to be renewed with the timing belt still in place, check first that the belt is free from oil contamination. (Renew the belt as a matter of course if signs of oil contamination are found; see Section 6.) Cover the belt to protect it from oil contamination while work is in progress. Ensure that all traces of oil are removed from the area before the belt is refitted.*

9.4 Remove the circlip, and slide the components off the end of the rocker arm

9.5a To remove the left-hand pedestal, lock two nuts together and unscrew the stud . . .

9.5b . . . then remove the grub screw

2A

1 Remove the camshaft sprocket as described in Section 7.
2 Punch or drill two small holes opposite each other in the oil seal. Screw a self-tapping screw into each, and pull on the screws with pliers to extract the seal.
3 Clean the seal housing, and polish off any burrs or raised edges, which may have caused the seal to fail in the first place.
4 Lubricate the lips of the new seal with clean engine oil, and drive it into position until it seats on its locating shoulder. Use a suitable tubular drift, such as a socket, which bears only on the hard outer edge of the seal. Take care not to damage the seal lips during fitting. Note that the seal lips should face inwards.
5 Refit the camshaft sprocket as described in Section 7.

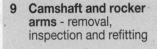

9 Camshaft and rocker arms - removal, inspection and refitting

General information

1 The rocker arm assembly is secured to the top of the cylinder head by the cylinder head bolts. Although in theory it is possible to undo the head bolts and remove the rocker arm assembly without removing the head, in practice, this is not recommended. Once the bolts have been removed, the head gasket will be disturbed, and the gasket will almost certainly leak or blow after refitting. For this reason, removal of the rocker arm assembly

cannot be done without removing the cylinder head and renewing the head gasket.
2 The camshaft is slid out of the right-hand end of the cylinder head, and therefore cannot be removed without first removing the cylinder head, due to a lack of clearance.

Removal
Rocker arm assembly

3 Remove the cylinder head as described in Section 10.
4 To dismantle the rocker arm assembly, carefully prise off the circlip from the right-hand end of the rocker shaft; retain the rocker pedestal, to prevent it being sprung off the end of the shaft. Slide the various components off the end of the shaft, keeping all components in their correct fitted order. Make a note of each component's correct fitted position/orientation as it is removed, to ensure it is fitted correctly on reassembly (see illustration).
5 To separate the left-hand pedestal and shaft, first unscrew the cylinder head cover retaining stud from the top of the pedestal; this can be achieved using a stud extractor, or two nuts locked together. With the stud removed, unscrew the grub screw from the top of the pedestal, and withdraw the rocker shaft (see illustrations).

Camshaft

6 Remove the cylinder head as described in Section 10.
7 With the head on a bench, remove the locating pin, then remove the camshaft

sprocket as described in paragraphs 6 and 7 of Section 7.
8 Undo the retaining bolt, and remove the camshaft thrust fork from the left-hand end of the cylinder head (see illustration).
9 Using a large flat-bladed screwdriver, carefully prise the oil seal out of the right-hand end of the cylinder head, then slide out the camshaft (see illustrations). Discard the seal - a new one must be used on refitting.

Inspection
Rocker arm assembly

10 Examine the rocker arm bearing surfaces which contact the camshaft lobes for wear ridges and scoring. Renew any rocker arms on which these conditions are apparent. If a rocker arm bearing surface is badly scored, also examine the corresponding lobe on the camshaft for wear, as it is likely that both will be worn. Renew worn components as necessary. The rocker arm assembly can be dismantled as described in paragraphs 4 and 5.
11 Inspect the ends of the (valve clearance) adjusting screws for signs of wear or damage, and renew as required.
12 If the rocker arm assembly has been dismantled, examine the rocker arm and shaft bearing surfaces for wear ridges and scoring. If there are obvious signs of wear, the relevant rocker arm(s) and/or the shaft must be renewed.
Camshaft
13 Examine the camshaft bearing surfaces and cam lobes for signs of wear ridges and scoring. Renew the camshaft if any of these

9.8 Undo the retaining bolt, and remove the camshaft thrust fork (arrowed) . . .

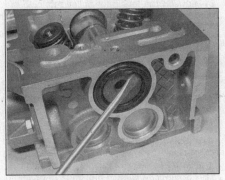

9.9a . . . prise out the oil seal . . .

9.9b . . . and slide out the camshaft

conditions are apparent. Examine the condition of the bearing surfaces, both on the camshaft journals and in the cylinder head. If the head bearing surfaces are worn excessively, the cylinder head will need to be renewed. If the necessary measuring equipment is available, camshaft bearing journal wear can be checked by direct measurement, noting that No 1 journal is at the transmission end of the head.

14 Examine the thrust fork for signs of wear or scoring, and renew as necessary.

Refitting

Rocker arm assembly

15 If the rocker arm assembly was dismantled, refit the rocker shaft to the left-hand pedestal, aligning its locating hole with the pedestal threaded hole. Refit the grub screw, and tighten it securely. With the grub screw in position, refit the cylinder head cover mounting stud to the pedestal, and tighten it securely. Apply a smear of clean engine oil to the shaft, then slide on all removed components, ensuring each is correctly fitted in its original position. Once all components are in position on the shaft, compress the right-hand pedestal and refit the circlip. Ensure that the circlip is correctly located in its groove on the shaft.

16 Refit the cylinder head and rocker arm assembly as described in Section 10.

Camshaft

17 Ensure that the cylinder head and camshaft bearing surfaces are clean, then liberally oil the camshaft bearings and lobes. Slide the camshaft back into position in the cylinder head. On carburettor engines, take care that the fuel pump operating lever is not trapped by the camshaft as it is slid into position.

18 Locate the thrust fork with the left-hand end of the camshaft. Refit the fork retaining bolt, tightening it to the specified torque setting.

19 Lubricate the lips of the new seal with clean engine oil, then drive it into position until it seats on its locating shoulder. Use a suitable tubular drift, such as a socket, which bears only on the hard outer edge of the seal. Take care not to damage the seal lips during fitting. Note that the seal lips should face inwards.

20 Refit the camshaft sprocket as described in paragraphs 17 to 19 of Section 7.

21 Refit the cylinder head as described in Section 10.

10 Cylinder head - removal and refitting

Removal

1 Disconnect the battery negative lead.
2 Drain the cooling system as described in Chapter 1.

3 Remove the cylinder head cover as described in Section 4.

4 Align the engine assembly/valve timing holes as described in Section 3, and lock both the camshaft sprocket and flywheel in position. *Do not* attempt to rotate the engine whilst the tools are in position.

5 Note that the following text assumes that the cylinder head will be removed with both inlet and exhaust manifolds attached; this is easier, but makes it a bulky and heavy assembly to handle. If it is wished to remove the manifolds first, proceed as described in the relevant Part of Chapter 4.

6 Working as described in the relevant Part of Chapter 4, disconnect the exhaust system front pipe from the manifold. Where fitted, disconnect or release the lambda sensor wiring, so that it is not strained by the weight of the exhaust.

7 Remove the air cleaner housing and inlet duct assembly as described in the relevant Part of Chapter 4.

8 On carburettor engines, disconnect the following from the carburettor and inlet manifold as described in Chapter 4A:
(a) *Fuel feed hose from the pump and the return hose from the anti-percolation chamber (plug all openings, to prevent loss of fuel and the entry of dirt into the system).*
(b) *Accelerator cable.*
(c) *Choke cable.*
(d) *Carburettor coolant hoses - 1124 cc models.*
(e) *Carburettor heating element and idle cut-off solenoid wiring connector(s) - 1360 cc models.*
(f) *Vacuum servo unit vacuum hose, coolant hose and all other relevant breather/vacuum hoses from the manifold.*

9 On fuel injection engines, carry out the following operations as described in the relevant Part of Chapter 4:
(a) *Depressurise the fuel system, and disconnect the fuel feed and return hoses from the throttle body/fuel rail (plug all openings, to prevent loss of fuel and entry of dirt into the fuel system).*
(b) *Disconnect the accelerator cable.*
(c) *On single-point injection models, disconnect the relevant electrical connectors from the throttle body.*
(d) *On multi-point injection models, disconnect the relevant electrical connectors from the throttle housing, fuel injectors and (where necessary) the idle speed auxiliary air valve/stepper motor.*
(e) *Disconnect the vacuum servo unit hose, coolant hose(s) and all the other relevant/breather hoses from the manifold.*

10 On engines with a three-piece timing belt cover arrangement, remove the upper and centre covers as described in Section 5. On engines with a two-piece cover arrangement, remove both covers.

11 Loosen the timing belt tensioner pulley retaining nut. Pivot the pulley in a clockwise direction, using a suitable square-section key

fitted to the hole in the pulley hub, then retighten the retaining nut.

12 Disengage the timing belt from the camshaft sprocket, and position the belt clear of the sprocket. Ensure that the belt is not bent or twisted sharply.

13 Slacken the retaining clips, and disconnect the coolant hoses from the thermostat housing (on the left-hand end of the cylinder head).

14 Depress the retaining clip(s), and disconnect the wiring connector(s) from the electrical switch and/or sensor(s) which are screwed into the thermostat housing/cylinder head (as appropriate). Also where necessary release the TDC connector from its support on the distributor bracket on the left-hand end of the cylinder head.

Models with a distributor

15 Disconnect the LT wiring connectors from the distributor and HT coil. Release the TDC sensor wiring connector from the side of the coil mounting bracket, and disconnect the vacuum pipe from the distributor vacuum diaphragm unit. If the cylinder head is to be dismantled for overhaul, remove the distributor and ignition HT coil as described in Chapter 5. If the cylinder numbers are not already marked on the HT leads, number each lead, to avoid the possibility of the leads being incorrectly connected on refitting. Disconnect the HT leads from the spark plugs, and remove the distributor cap and lead assembly.

Models with a distributorless ignition system

16 Disconnect the wiring connector from the ignition HT coil. If the cylinder head is to be dismantled for overhaul, remove the ignition HT coil as described in Chapter 5. If the cylinder numbers are not already marked on the HT leads, number each lead, to avoid the possibility of the leads being incorrectly connected on refitting. Note that the HT leads should be disconnected from the spark plugs instead of the coil, and the coil and leads removed as an assembly.

All models

17 Slacken and remove the bolt securing the engine oil dipstick tube to the cylinder head.
18 If it is necessary to remove the engine mounting, place a jack beneath the engine with a block of wood on the jack head. Raise the jack until it is supporting the weight of the engine.
19 Slacken and remove the three nuts securing the right-hand engine/transmission mounting bracket to the engine. Remove the single nut securing the bracket to the mounting rubber, and lift off the bracket.
20 Working in the *reverse* of the sequence shown in illustration 10.40a, progressively slacken the ten cylinder head bolts by half a turn at a time, until all bolts can be unscrewed by hand.
21 With all the cylinder head bolts removed, lift the rocker arm assembly off the cylinder head. Note the locating pins which are fitted to the base of each rocker arm pedestal. If

2A

any pin is a loose fit in the head or pedestal, remove it for safe-keeping.

22 The joint between the cylinder head and gasket and the cylinder block/crankcase must now be broken without disturbing the wet liners. To break the joint, obtain two L-shaped metal bars which fit into the cylinder head bolt holes. Gently "rock" the cylinder head free towards the front of the car **(see illustration)**. Do not try to swivel the head on the cylinder block/crankcase; it is located by dowels, as well as by the tops of the liners. **Note:** *If care is not taken and the liners are moved, there is also a possibility of the bottom seals being disturbed, causing leakage after refitting the head.* When the joint is broken, lift the cylinder head away; seek assistance if possible, as it is a heavy assembly, especially if it is being removed complete with the manifolds. Remove the gasket from the top of the block, noting the two locating dowels. If the locating dowels are a loose fit, remove them and store them with the head for safe-keeping. Do not discard the gasket - it will be needed for identification purposes (see paragraphs 28 and 29).

23 Do not attempt to rotate the crankshaft with the cylinder head removed, otherwise the wet liners may be displaced. Operations that require the rotation of the crankshaft (eg cleaning the piston crowns), should only be carried out once the cylinder liners are firmly clamped in position. In the absence of the special Citroën liner clamps, the liners can be clamped in position using large flat washers positioned underneath suitable-length bolts. Alternatively, the original head bolts could be temporarily refitted, with suitable spacers fitted to their shanks.

24 If the cylinder head is to be dismantled for overhaul, remove the camshaft as described in Section 9, then refer to Part C of this Chapter.

Preparation for refitting

25 The mating faces of the cylinder head and cylinder block/crankcase must be perfectly clean before refitting the head. Use a hard plastic or wood scraper to remove all traces of gasket and carbon; also clean the piston crowns. Refer to paragraph 23 before turning the crankshaft. Take particular care during the cleaning operations, as aluminium alloy is easily damaged. Also, make sure that the carbon is not allowed to enter the oil and water passages - this is particularly important for the lubrication system, as carbon could block the oil supply to the engine's components. Using adhesive tape and paper, seal the water, oil and bolt holes in the cylinder block/crankcase. To prevent carbon entering the gap between the pistons and bores, smear a little grease in the gap. After cleaning each piston, use a small brush to remove all traces of grease and carbon from the gap, then wipe away the remainder with a clean rag. Clean all the pistons in the same way.

26 Check the mating surfaces of the cylinder block/crankcase and the cylinder head for nicks, deep scratches and other damage. If slight, they may be removed carefully with a

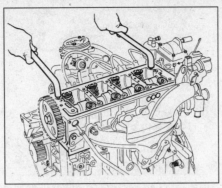

10.22 Using two angled metal rods to free the cylinder head from the block

file, but if excessive, machining may be the only alternative to renewal.

27 If warpage of the cylinder head gasket surface is suspected, use a straight-edge to check it for distortion. Refer to Part C of this Chapter if necessary.

28 When purchasing a new cylinder head gasket, it is essential that a gasket of the correct thickness is obtained. On some models only one thickness of gasket is available, so this is not a problem. However on certain other models, there are two different thicknesses available - the standard gasket which is fitted at the factory, and a slightly thicker "repair" gasket (+ 0.2 mm), for use once the head gasket face has been machined. If the cylinder head has been machined, it should have the letter "R" stamped adjacent to the No 3 exhaust port, and the gasket should also have the letter "R" stamped adjacent to No 3 cylinder on its front upper face. The gaskets can also be identified as described in the following paragraph, using the cut-outs on the left-hand end of the gasket.

29 With the gasket fitted the correct way up on the cylinder block, there will be a single cut-out, or no cut-out at all, at the rear of the left-hand side of the gasket identifying the engine type (ie. TU engine). In the centre of the gasket there will likely be another series of between 0 and 4 cut-outs, identifying the manufacturer of the gasket and whether or not it contains asbestos (these cut-outs are of little importance). The important cut-out location is at the front of the gasket; on the standard gasket there will be no cut-out in this position, whereas on the thicker "repair" gasket there will be a single cut-out **(see illustration)**. Identify the gasket type, and ensure that the new gasket obtained is of the correct thickness. If there is any doubt as to which gasket is fitted, take the old gasket along to your Citroën dealer, and have him confirm the gasket type. Note that on engines manufactured from approximately mid-1996 onward, there are even more variations of gasket type. This is due to various changes that have been made to the cylinder head to meet the latest exhaust emission requirements, and vary according to specific engine type. If working on a post-1995 model it is essential that the engine type, code and serial numbers are taken to a Citroën dealer to ensure that the correct gasket is obtained.

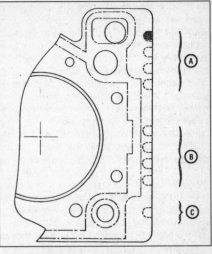

10.29 TU engine series gasket markings

A Engine type identification cutouts
B Gasket manufacturer identification cutouts
C Gasket thickness identification cutout

30 Check the condition of the cylinder head bolts, and particularly their threads, whenever they are removed. Wash the bolts in suitable solvent, and wipe them dry. Check each for any sign of visible wear or damage, renewing any bolt if necessary. Measure the length of each bolt, from the end of the thread to the underside of the bolt head, to check for stretching. If the length of any bolt exceeds 175.5 mm it must be renewed. It is strongly recommended that the bolts should be renewed as a complete set whenever they are disturbed.

31 Prior to refitting the cylinder head, check the cylinder liner protrusion as described in Part C of this Chapter.

Refitting

32 Wipe clean the mating surfaces of the cylinder head and cylinder block/crankcase. Check that the two locating dowels are in position at each end of the cylinder block/crankcase surface and, if necessary, remove the cylinder liner clamps.

33 Position a new gasket on the cylinder block/crankcase surface, ensuring that its identification cut-outs are at the left-hand end of the gasket **(see illustration)**.

10.33 Locate the cylinder head gasket on the block . . .

34 Check that the flywheel and camshaft sprocket are still correctly locked in position with their respective tools then, with the aid of an assistant, carefully refit the cylinder head assembly to the block, aligning it with the locating dowels **(see illustration)**.

35 Ensure that the locating pins are in position in the base of each rocker pedestal, then refit the rocker arm assembly to the cylinder head **(see illustration)**.

36 Apply a smear of grease to the threads, and to the underside of the heads, of the cylinder head bolts. Citroën specify Molykote G Rapid Plus grease (available from your Citroën dealer - a sachet is supplied with the top-end gasket set); in the absence of the specified grease, a good-quality high-melting-point grease may be used.

37 Carefully enter each bolt into its relevant hole (*do not drop them in*) and screw in, by hand only, until finger-tight.

38 Working progressively and in the sequence shown, tighten the cylinder head bolts to their Stage 1 torque setting, using a torque wrench and suitable socket **(see illustrations)**.

39 Once all the bolts have been tightened to their Stage 1 setting, working again in the given sequence, angle-tighten the bolts through the specified Stage 2 angle, using a socket and extension bar. It is recommended that an angle-measuring gauge is used during this stage of the tightening, to ensure accuracy **(see illustration)**. If a gauge is not available, use white paint to make alignment marks between the bolt head and cylinder head prior to tightening; the marks can then be used to check that the bolt has been rotated through the correct angle during tightening.

40 With the cylinder head bolts correctly tightened, refit the right-hand engine mounting bracket, and tighten its retaining nuts to the specified torque. The jack can then be removed from underneath the engine.

41 Refit the dipstick tube retaining bolt and tighten it securely.

42 Refit the timing belt to the camshaft sprocket. Ensure that the "front run" of the belt is taut - ie, ensure that any slack is on the tensioner pulley side of the belt. Do not twist the belt sharply while refitting it, and ensure that the belt teeth are seated centrally in the sprockets.

43 Loosen the tensioner pulley retaining nut. Pivot the pulley anti-clockwise to remove all free play from the timing belt, then retighten the nut.

10.34 . . . then lower the cylinder head into position . . .

44 Tension the belt as described under the relevant sub-heading in Section 6, then refit the timing belt covers as described in Section 5.

Models with a distributor

45 If the head was stripped for overhaul, refit the distributor and HT coil as described in Chapter 5, ensuring that the HT leads are correctly reconnected. If the head was not stripped, reconnect the wiring connector and vacuum pipe to the distributor, and the HT lead to the coil; clip the TDC sensor wiring connector onto the coil bracket.

Models with a distributorless ignition system

46 If the head was stripped for overhaul, refit the ignition HT coil and leads as described in Chapter 5, ensuring that the leads are correctly reconnected. If the head was not stripped, simply reconnect the wiring connector to the HT coil.

All models

47 Reconnect the wiring connector(s) to the coolant switch/sensor(s) on the left-hand end of the head.

48 Reconnect the coolant hoses to the thermostat housing, securely tightening their retaining clips.

49 Working as described in the relevant Part of Chapter 4, carry out the following tasks:

(a) Refit all disturbed wiring, hoses and control cable(s) to the inlet manifold and fuel system components.

10.35 . . . and refit the rocker arm assembly

(b) On carburettor models, reconnect and adjust the choke and accelerator cables.
(c) On fuel injection models, reconnect and adjust the accelerator cable.
(d) Reconnect the exhaust system front pipe to the manifold. If applicable, reconnect the lambda sensor wiring connector.
(e) Refit the air cleaner and inlet duct.

50 Check and, if necessary, adjust the valve clearances as described in Chapter 1.

51 On completion, reconnect the battery, and refill the cooling system as described in Chapter 1.

11 Sump - removal and refitting

Removal

1 Firmly apply the handbrake, then jack up the front of the vehicle and support it on axle stands. Disconnect the battery negative lead.

2 Drain the engine oil, then clean and refit the engine oil drain plug, tightening it to the specified torque. If the engine is nearing its service interval when the oil and filter are due for renewal, it is recommended that the filter is also removed, and a new one fitted. After reassembly, the engine can then be refilled with fresh oil. Refer to Chapter 1 for further information.

3 Remove the exhaust system front pipe as described in Chapter 4.

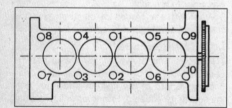
10.38a Cylinder head bolt tightening sequence

10.38b Working in the sequence shown, tighten the head bolts first to the stage 1 torque setting . . .

10.39 . . . then through the angle specified for stage 2

4 Progressively slacken and remove all the sump retaining nuts and bolts **(see illustration)**.
5 Break the joint by striking the sump with the palm of your hand, then lower the sump and withdraw it from underneath the vehicle **(see illustration)**.
6 While the sump is removed, take the opportunity to check the oil pump pick-up/strainer for signs of clogging or splitting. If necessary, remove the pump as described in Section 12, and clean or renew the strainer.

Refitting

7 Clean all traces of sealant from the mating surfaces of the cylinder block/crankcase and sump, then use a clean rag to wipe out the sump and the engine's interior.
8 Ensure that the sump and cylinder block/crankcase mating surfaces are clean and dry, then apply a coating of suitable sealant to the sump mating surface. Citroën recommend the use of Auto-Joint E10 sealant (available from your Citroën dealer); in the absence of the specified sealant, any good-quality sealant may be used.
9 Offer up the sump, locating it on its retaining studs, and refit its retaining nuts and bolts. Tighten the nuts and bolts evenly and progressively to the specified torque.
10 Refit the exhaust front pipe as described in Chapter 4.
11 Replenish the engine oil as described in Chapter 1.

12 Oil pump - removal, inspection and refitting

Removal

1 Remove the sump as described in Section 11.
2 Slacken and remove the three bolts securing the oil pump to the base of the main bearing ladder **(see illustration)**. Disengage the pump sprocket from the chain, and remove the oil pump. If the pump locating dowel is a loose fit, remove and store it with the retaining bolts for safe-keeping.

Inspection

3 Examine the oil pump sprocket for signs of

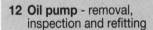

12.2 Oil pump is retained by three bolts

11.4 Slacken and remove the sump retaining nuts and bolts . . .

damage and wear, such as chipped or missing teeth. If the sprocket is worn, the pump assembly must be renewed, since the sprocket is not available separately. It is also recommended that the chain and drive sprocket, fitted to the crankshaft, be renewed at the same time. Renewal of the chain and drive sprocket is an operation requiring the removal of the main bearing ladder, and cannot therefore be carried out with the engine still fitted to the vehicle. Refer to Part C for further information.
4 Slacken and remove the five bolts securing the strainer cover to the pump body, then lift off the strainer cover. Remove the relief valve piston and spring, noting which way round they are fitted.
5 Examine the pump rotors and body for signs of wear ridges and scoring. If worn, the complete pump assembly must be renewed.
6 Examine the relief valve piston for signs of wear or damage, and renew if necessary. The condition of the relief valve spring can only be measured by comparing it with a new one; if there is any doubt about its condition, it should also be renewed. Both the piston and spring are available individually.
7 Thoroughly clean the oil pump strainer with a suitable solvent, and check it for signs of clogging or splitting. If the strainer is damaged, the strainer and cover assembly must be renewed.
8 Locate the relief valve spring and piston in the strainer cover, then refit the cover to the pump body. Align the relief valve piston with its bore in the pump. Refit the five cover retaining bolts, tightening them securely.

13.2 Using a screwdriver to lever out the crankshaft front oil seal

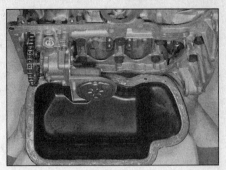

11.5 . . . then remove the sump from the engine

Refitting

9 Ensure that the locating dowel is in position, then locate the pump sprocket with its drive chain. Seat the pump on the main bearing ladder. Refit the pump retaining bolts, and tighten them to the specified torque setting.
10 Refit the sump as described in Section 11.

13 Crankshaft oil seals - renewal

Right-hand oil seal

1 Remove the crankshaft sprocket and flanged spacer as described in Section 7. Secure the timing belt clear of the working area, so that it cannot be contaminated with oil. Make a note of the correct fitted depth of the seal in its housing.
2 Punch or drill two small holes opposite each other in the seal. Screw a self-tapping screw into each, and pull on the screws with pliers to extract the seal. Alternatively, the seal can be levered out of position using a suitable flat-bladed screwdriver, taking great care not to damage the crankshaft shoulder or seal housing **(see illustration)**.
3 Clean the seal housing, and polish off any burrs or raised edges, which may have caused the seal to fail in the first place.
4 Lubricate the lips of the new seal with clean engine oil, and carefully locate the seal on the end of crankshaft. Note that its sealing lip must face inwards. Take care not to damage the seal lips during fitting.
5 Using a suitable tubular drift (such as a socket) which bears only on the hard outer edge of the seal, tap the seal into position, to the same depth in the housing as the original was prior to removal.
6 Wash off any traces of oil, then refit the crankshaft sprocket as described in Section 7.

Left-hand oil seal

7 Remove the flywheel as described in Section 14.
8 Make a note of the correct fitted depth of the seal in its housing. Punch or drill two small holes opposite each other in the seal. Screw a self-tapping screw into each, and pull on the screws with pliers to extract the seal.

2A

9 Clean the seal housing, and polish off any burrs or raised edges, which may have caused the seal to fail in the first place.

10 Lubricate the lips of the new seal with clean engine oil, and carefully locate the seal on the end of the crankshaft.

11 Using a suitable tubular drift, which bears only on the hard outer edge of the seal, drive the seal into position, to the same depth in the housing as the original was prior to removal.

12 Wash off any traces of oil, then refit the flywheel as described in Section 14.

14 Flywheel - removal, inspection and refitting

Removal

1 Remove the transmission as described in Chapter 7, then remove the clutch assembly as described in Chapter 6.

2 Prevent the flywheel from turning by locking the ring gear teeth with a similar arrangement to that shown in illustration 7.10 (Section 7). Alternatively, bolt a strap between the flywheel and the cylinder block/crankcase. *Do not* attempt to lock the flywheel in position using the locking pin described in Section 3.

3 Slacken and remove the flywheel retaining bolts, and discard them; they must be renewed whenever they are disturbed.

4 Remove the flywheel. Do not drop it, as it is very heavy. If the locating dowel is a loose fit in the crankshaft end, remove and store it with the flywheel for safe-keeping.

Inspection

5 If the flywheel's clutch mating surface is deeply scored, cracked or otherwise damaged, the flywheel must be renewed. However, it may be possible to have it surface-ground; seek the advice of a Citroën dealer or engine reconditioning specialist.

6 If the ring gear is badly worn or has missing teeth, it must be renewed. This job is best left to a Citroën dealer or engine reconditioning specialist. The temperature to which the new ring gear must be heated for installation is critical and, if not done accurately, the hardness of the teeth will be destroyed.

Refitting

7 Clean the mating surfaces of the flywheel and crankshaft. Remove any remaining locking compound from the threads of the crankshaft holes, using the correct-size tap, if available.

8 If the new flywheel retaining bolts are not supplied with their threads already pre-coated, apply a suitable thread-locking compound to the threads of each bolt. Citroën recommend the use of Frenetanch E3 (available from your Citroën dealer); in the absence of this, ensure that a good-quality locking compound is used.

9 Ensure that the locating dowel is in position. Offer up the flywheel, locating it on the dowel, and fit the new retaining bolts.

10 Lock the flywheel using the method employed on dismantling, and tighten the retaining bolts to the specified torque.

11 Refit the clutch as described in Chapter 6. Remove the locking tool, and refit the transmission as described in Chapter 7.

15 Engine/transmission mountings - inspection and renewal

Inspection

1 If improved access is required, raise the front of the car and support it securely on axle stands.

2 Check the mounting rubber to see if it is cracked, hardened or separated from the metal at any point; renew the mounting if any such damage or deterioration is evident.

3 Check that all the mounting's fasteners are securely tightened; use a torque wrench to check if possible.

4 Using a large screwdriver or a crowbar, check for wear in the mounting by carefully levering against it to check for free play. Where this is not possible, enlist the aid of an assistant to move the engine/transmission unit back and forth, or from side to side, while you watch the mounting. While some free play is to be expected even from new components, excessive wear should be obvious. If excessive free play is found, check first that the fasteners are correctly secured, then renew any worn components as described below.

Renewal
Right-hand mounting

5 Disconnect the battery negative lead.

6 Place a jack beneath the engine, with a block of wood on the jack head. Raise the jack until it is supporting the weight of the engine.

7 Slacken and remove the three nuts securing the right-hand engine/transmission mounting bracket to the engine. Remove the single nut securing the bracket to the mounting rubber, and lift off the bracket.

8 Lift the rubber buffer plate off the mounting rubber stud, then unscrew the mounting rubber from the body and remove it from the vehicle.

9 Check carefully for signs of wear or damage on all components, and renew them where necessary.

10 On reassembly, screw the mounting rubber into the vehicle body, and tighten it securely.

11 Refit the rubber buffer plate to the mounting rubber stud, and install the mounting bracket.

12 Tighten the mounting bracket retaining nuts to the specified torque setting.

13 Remove the jack from underneath the engine, and reconnect the battery negative terminal.

Left-hand mounting

14 Remove the battery and the battery tray, as described in Chapter 5. Slacken and

remove the battery support plate mounting bolts. Release the wiring from its retaining clip on the plate, and remove the plate from the engine compartment.

15 Place a jack beneath the transmission, with a block of wood on the jack head. Raise the jack until it is supporting the weight of the transmission.

16 Slacken and remove the mounting rubber centre nut, and the two nuts securing it to the bracket. Lift the mounting rubber off its centre stud.

17 Where necessary, slacken and remove the two mounting bolts (situated underneath the bracket) securing the mounting bracket to the body, and remove the bracket from the engine compartment. The transmission bracket can then be removed, once its three mounting nuts have been undone.

18 Check carefully for signs of wear or damage on all components, and renew them where necessary.

19 Where necessary, refit the bracket to the top of the transmission housing, tightening its mounting nuts to the specified torque. Refit the bracket to the body, and tighten its retaining bolts to the specified torque.

20 Locate the mounting rubber on the mounting stud, and refit its two mounting nuts, tightening them securely. Refit the mounting centre nut and tighten to the specified torque. Remove the jack from underneath the transmission.

21 Refit the battery support plate, tightening its retaining bolts securely. Refit the battery and its tray as described in Chapter 5.

Rear mounting

22 If not already done, firmly apply the handbrake, then jack up the front of the vehicle and support it securely on axle stands.

23 Slacken and remove the nuts and bolts securing the mounting bracket to the rear mounting assembly and the subframe, and manoeuvre the bracket out of position.

24 To remove the rear mounting assembly, it is first necessary to remove the right-hand driveshaft as described in Chapter 8.

25 With the driveshaft removed, undo the four bolts securing the mounting assembly to the rear of the cylinder block, and remove it from underneath the vehicle.

26 Check carefully for signs of wear or damage on all components, and renew them where necessary. Note that it is not possible to renew the mounting rubber separately, if the rubber is damaged, the complete rear mounting assembly must be renewed.

27 On reassembly, fit the rear mounting assembly to the rear of the cylinder block, and tighten its retaining bolts to the specified torque. Refit the driveshaft as described in Chapter 8.

28 Manoeuvre the mounting bracket into position, and refit the bolts securing it to the mounting and subframe. Tighten each bolt to its respective torque setting, then lower the vehicle to the ground.

Chapter 2 Part B:
XU series engine in-car repair procedures

Contents

Camshaft oil seal(s) - renewal 9
Camshaft(s) and followers - removal, inspection and refitting 10
Compression test - description and interpretation 2
Crankshaft oil seals - renewal 16
Crankshaft pulley - removal and refitting 5
Cylinder head - removal and refitting 12
Cylinder head cover - removal and refitting 4
Engine assembly/valve timing holes - general information and
    usage 3
Engine oil and filter renewal . . . . See Chapter 1
Engine oil level check . . . . .See "Weekly checks"
Engine/transmission mountings - inspection and renewal 18
Flywheel/driveplate - removal, inspection and refitting 17
General engine checks . . . . See Chapter 1
General information 1
Oil cooler - removal and refitting 15
Oil pump - removal, inspection and refitting 14
Sump - removal and refitting . . '. 13
Timing belt - general information, removal and refitting 7
Timing belt covers - removal and refitting 6
Timing belt tensioner and sprockets - removal, inspection
    and refitting 8
Valve clearances - checking and adjustment 11

2B

Degrees of difficulty

Easy, suitable for novice with little experience	**Fairly easy,** suitable for beginner with some experience	**Fairly difficult,** suitable for competent DIY mechanic 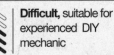	**Difficult,** suitable for experienced DIY mechanic	**Very difficult,** suitable for expert DIY or professional

Specifications

Engine (general)

Designation:
    1580 cc engine XU5
    1761 cc engine XU7
    1905 cc engine XU9
    1998 cc engines XU10
Engine codes*:
    1580 cc engine without a catalytic converter . . . . B4A (XU5M 2K, XU5M 3K or XU5M 4K)
    1580 cc engine with a catalytic converter . . . . BDY (XU5M 3/LZ) or BFZ (XU5JP/LZ)
    1761 cc (8-valve) engine . . . . LFZ (XU7JP/LZ) or L6A (XU7JP/K)
    1761 cc (16-valve) engine . . . . LFY (XU7JP4)
    1905 cc engine without a catalytic converter . . . . D6E (XU9JA K)
    1905 cc engine with a catalytic converter . . . . DKZ (XU9JA Z)
    1998 cc (8-valve) engine . . . . RFX (XU10J2C/LZ)
    1998 cc (16-valve) engine . . . . RFY (XU10J4D/LZ), RFT (XU10J4D/LZ)
Bore:
    1580 cc, 1761 cc and 1905 cc engines . . . . 83.00 mm
    1998 cc engines . . . . 86.00 mm
Stroke:
    1580 cc engine . . . . 73.00 mm
    1761 cc engine . . . . 81.00 mm
    1905 cc engine . . . . 88.00 mm
    1998 cc engines . . . . 86.00 mm
Direction of crankshaft rotation . . . . Clockwise (viewed from the right-hand side of vehicle)
No 1 cylinder location . . . . At the transmission end of block
Compression ratio:
    1580 cc engine . . . . 8.95 : 1
    1761 cc (8-valve) engine . . . . 9.25 : 1
    1761 cc (16-valve) engine . . . . 10.4 : 1
    1905 cc engine . . . . 9.2 : 1
    1998 cc (8-valve) engine . . . . 9.5 : 1
    1998 cc (16-valve) engine . . . . 10.4 : 1

*The engine code is either stamped on a plate attached to the front right-hand end of the cylinder block (next to the engine mounting), or stamped directly onto the front face of the cylinder block (just to the left of the oil filter). This is the code most often used by Citroën. The full code given in brackets is the factory identification number, and is not often referred to by Citroën or this manual.

Camshaft

Drive	Toothed belt
No of bearings	5

Cam lift:

1580 cc engine	9.7 mm
1905 cc engine	11.5 mm
1761 and 1998 cc engines	Not available

Camshaft bearing journal diameter (outside diameter):

1580 cc and 1905 cc models:

No 1	26.980 to 26.959 mm
No 2	27.480 to 27.459 mm
No 3	27.980 to 27.959 mm
No 4	28.480 to 28.459 mm
No 5	35.975 to 35.950 mm
1761 cc and 1998 cc models	Not available

Cylinder head bearing journal diameter (inside diameter):

1580 cc and 1905 cc models:

No 1	27.000 to 27.033 mm
No 2	27.500 to 27.533 mm
No 3	28.000 to 28.033 mm
No 4	28.500 to 28.533 mm
No 5	36.000 to 36.039 mm
1761 cc and 1998 cc models	Not available

Note: *At the time of writing, no camshaft specifications were available for the 1761 cc and 1998 cc models.*

Valve clearances

Inlet	0.20 mm
Exhaust	0.40 mm

Lubrication system

Oil pump type	Gear-type, chain-driven off the crankshaft right-hand end
Minimum oil pressure at 90°C	4.5 bars at 4000 rpm
Oil pressure warning switch operating pressure	0.8 bars

Torque wrench settings

	Nm	lbf ft
1580 cc, 1761 cc (8-valve) and 1905 cc engines		
Big-end bearing cap nuts:		
Stage 1	40	30
Fully slacken all nuts, then tighten to:		
Stage 2	20	15
Stage 3	Angle-tighten through 70°	
Camshaft bearing cap nuts	16	12
Camshaft sprocket retaining bolt	35	26
Crankshaft pulley retaining bolt	110	81
Cylinder head bolts:		
Stage 1	60	44
Fully slacken each bolt in sequence, then tighten to:		
Stage 2	20	15
Stage 3	Angle-tighten through 300°	
Cylinder head cover nuts/bolts	10	7
Engine/transmission right-hand mounting:		
Mounting bracket retaining nuts	45	33
Engine/transmission left-hand mounting:		
Mounting bracket-to-body bolts	25	18
Mounting stud	50	37
Centre nut	80	59
Engine/transmission rear mounting:		
Mounting assembly-to-block bolts	45	33
Mounting bracket-to-mounting bolt	50	37
Mounting bracket-to-subframe bolt	50	37
Flywheel/driveplate retaining bolts	50	37
Front oil seal carrier bolts	16	12
Main bearing cap nuts/bolts:		
Retaining nuts/bolts	54	40
Centre bearing cap side bolts	23	17
Oil pump retaining bolts	13	10

	Nm	lbf ft
1580 cc, 1761 cc (8-valve) and 1905 cc engines (continued)		
Sump retaining bolts	16	12
Timing belt cover bolts	8	6
Timing belt tensioner:		
Semi-automatic timing belt tensioner:		
Retaining nuts	16	12
Cam spindle nut	13	10
Manually-adjusted tensioner pulley bolt	20	15
1761 cc (16-valve) engine		
Big-end bearing cap nuts:*		
Stage 1	20	15
Stage 2	Angle-tighten through 70°	
Camshaft bearing housings:		
Stage 1	5	4
Stage 2	10	7
Camshaft sprocket-to-hub retaining bolts	10	7
Camshaft sprocket hub-to-camshaft retaining bolts	75	55
Crankshaft pulley retaining bolt*	130	96
Cylinder head bolts:		
Stage 1	60	44
Fully slacken each bolt in sequence, then tighten to:		
Stage 2	20	15
Stage 3	Angle-tighten through 300°	
Cylinder head cover fasteners	10	7
Dipstick guide tube bolt	10	7
Engine-to-transmission fixing bolts	45	33
Flywheel/driveplate retaining bolts	50	37
Front oil seal carrier bolts	16	12
Ignition coil unit retaining bolts	10	7
Left-hand engine/transmission mounting:		
Mounting bracket-to-body bolts	25	18
Mounting stud	50	37
Centre nut	80	59
Main bearing cap bolts:		
Bearing bolts	54	40
Side securing bolts	23	17
Oil pump retaining bolts	16	12
Piston oil jet spray tube bolt	10	7
Right-hand engine/transmission mounting:		
Mounting bracket-to-engine nuts	45	33
Mounting bracket-to-engine bolts	60	44
Mounting bracket-to-rubber mounting nut	45	33
Rubber mounting-to-body nut	40	30
Sump retaining bolts	16	12
Timing belt cover bolts	8	6
Timing belt idler pulley bolt	37	27
Timing belt tensioner pulley bolt	21	16
1998 cc (8-valve and 16-valve) engines		
Big-end bearing cap nuts:*		
Stage 1	40	30
Fully slacken all nuts, then tighten to:		
Stage 2	20	15
Stage 3	Angle-tighten a further 70°	
Camshaft bearing cap nuts/bolts:		
8-valve engine	16	12
16-valve engine	10	7
Camshaft sprocket retaining bolt:		
8-valve engine	35	26
16-valve engine	45	33
Crankshaft pulley retaining bolt(s):		
8-valve engine	110	81
16-valve engine	27	20
Crankshaft sprocket retaining bolt - 16-valve engine	110	81
Cylinder head bolts:*		
Stage 1	40	30
Stage 2	75	55
Stage 3	Angle-tighten a further 165°	

Torque wrench settings (continued)

	Nm	lbf ft
1998 cc (8-valve and 16-valve) engines (continued)		
Cylinder head cover nuts/bolts	10	7
Engine/transmission left-hand mounting:		
Mounting bracket-to-body bolts	25	18
Mounting stud	50	37
Centre nut	80	59
Engine/transmission rear mounting:		
Mounting assembly-to-block bolts	45	33
Mounting bracket-to-mounting bolt	50	37
Mounting bracket-to-subframe bolt	70	52
Engine/transmission right-hand mounting:		
Mounting bracket retaining nuts/bolts	45	33
Curved retaining plate	20	15
Flywheel/driveplate retaining bolts	50	37
Front oil seal carrier bolts	16	12
Main bearing cap bolts	70	52
Oil pump retaining bolts	13	10
Piston oil jet spray tube bolt	10	7
Sump retaining bolts	16	12
Timing belt cover bolts	8	6
Timing belt tensioner:		
8-valve engine	20	15
16-valve engine (both pulley bolt and backplate bolts)	20	15

*New nuts must be used

1 General information

How to use this Chapter

This Part of Chapter 2 describes those repair procedures that can reasonably be carried out on the XU series engine (1580 cc and larger), while it remains in the car. If the engine has been removed from the car and is being dismantled as described in Part C, any preliminary dismantling procedures can be ignored. Refer to Part A for information on the TU series engine (1124 cc and 1360 cc).

Note that, while it may be possible physically to overhaul items such as the piston/connecting rod assemblies while the engine is in the car, such tasks are not usually carried out as separate operations. Usually, several additional procedures (not to mention the cleaning of components and of oilways) have to be carried out. For this reason, all such tasks are classed as major overhaul procedures, and are described in Part C of this Chapter.

Part C describes the removal of the engine/transmission unit from the vehicle, and the full overhaul procedures that can then be carried out.

XU series engine description

The XU series engine is a well-proven engine which has been fitted to many previous Citroën and Peugeot vehicles. The engine is of the in-line four-cylinder type, mounted transversely at the front of the car. The clutch and transmission are attached to its left-hand end. The 1761 cc and 1998 cc 16-valve engines are of the DOHC (double overhead camshaft) type; all others are SOHC (single overhead camshaft) engines.

The crankshaft runs in five main bearings. Thrustwashers are fitted to No 2 main bearing cap, to control crankshaft endfloat.

The connecting rods rotate on horizontally-split bearing shells at their big-ends. The pistons are attached to the connecting rods by gudgeon pins. On 1998 cc 16-valve engines, the gudgeon pins are a sliding fit in the connecting rods and are secured in position with circlips. On all other engines, the gudgeon pins are an interference fit in the connecting rod small-end eyes. The aluminium alloy pistons are fitted with three piston rings - two compression rings and an oil control ring.

On 1580 cc, 1761 cc (8-valve), and 1905 cc engines, the cylinder block is of the "wet-liner" type. The cylinder block is cast in aluminium alloy, and the bores have replaceable cast-iron liners that are located from the top of the cylinder block. Sealing O-rings are fitted at the base of each liner, to prevent the escape of coolant into the sump.

On the 1761 cc (16-valve) and all 1998 cc engines, the engine is of the conventional "dry-liner" type. The cylinder block is cast in iron, and no separate bore liners are fitted.

On the 8-valve engines, the camshaft is driven by a toothed timing belt, and it operates the valves via followers located beneath each cam lobe. The valve clearances are adjusted by shims, positioned between the followers and the tip of the valve stem.

The camshafts on 16-valve engines are also driven by a common toothed timing belt; the front camshaft operates the inlet valves, and the rear camshaft operates the exhaust valves. The valve clearances are self-adjusting by means of hydraulic tappets.

Each camshaft runs in bearing caps which are bolted to the top of the cylinder head. The inlet and exhaust valves are each closed by coil springs, and operate in guides pressed into the cylinder head. Both the valve seats and guides can be renewed separately if worn.

The water pump is driven by the timing belt, and is located in the right-hand end of the cylinder block.

Lubrication is by means of an oil pump which is driven (via a chain and sprocket) off the crankshaft right-hand end. It draws oil through a strainer located in the sump, and then forces it through an externally-mounted filter into galleries in the cylinder block/crankcase. From there, the oil is distributed to the crankshaft (main bearings) and camshaft. The big-end bearings are supplied with oil via internal drillings in the crankshaft; the camshaft bearings also receive a pressurised supply. The camshaft lobes and valves are lubricated by splash, as are all other engine components. An oil cooler is fitted to some models to keep the oil temperature constant under severe operating conditions - it is mounted behind the oil filter. The oil cooler is supplied with coolant from the engine cooling system.

Throughout the manual, it is often necessary to identify the engines not only by their cubic capacity, but also by their engine code. The engine code consists of three letters (eg. LFZ). The code is stamped on a plate attached to the front, right-hand end of the cylinder block, or alternatively, it is stamped directly onto the front face of the cylinder block, on the machined surface located just to the left of the oil filter (next to the crankcase vent hose union).

Repair operations possible with the engine in the car

The following work can be carried out with the engine in the car:

(a) *Compression pressure - testing.*
(b) *Cylinder head cover - removal and refitting.*
(c) *Crankshaft pulley - removal and refitting.*
(d) *Timing belt covers - removal and refitting.*
(e) *Timing belt - removal, refitting and adjustment.*
(f) *Timing belt tensioner and sprockets - removal and refitting.*
(g) *Camshaft oil seal(s) - renewal.*
(h) *Camshaft(s) and followers - removal, inspection and refitting.*
(i) *Valve clearances - checking and adjustment.*
(j) *Cylinder head - removal and refitting.*
(k) *Cylinder head and pistons - decarbonising.*
(l) *Sump - removal and refitting.*
(m) *Oil pump - removal, overhaul and refitting.*
(n) *Crankshaft oil seals - renewal.*
(o) *Engine/transmission mountings - inspection and renewal.*
(p) *Flywheel/driveplate - removal, inspection and refitting.*
(q) *Oil cooler (1998 cc 16-valve models) - removal and refitting.*

2 Compression test - description and interpretation

Refer to Part A, Section 2.

3 Engine assembly/valve timing holes - general information and usage

Note: *Do not attempt to rotate the engine whilst the crankshaft/camshaft are locked in position. If the engine is to be left in this state for a long period of time, it is a good idea to place suitable warning notices inside the vehicle, and in the engine compartment. This will reduce the possibility of the engine being accidentally cranked on the starter motor, which is likely to cause damage with the locking pins in place.*

1 On all models, timing holes are drilled in the camshaft sprocket(s) and crankshaft pulley. The holes are used to align the crankshaft and camshaft(s), to prevent the possibility of the valves contacting the pistons when refitting the cylinder head, or when refitting the timing belt. When the holes are aligned with their corresponding holes in the cylinder head and cylinder block (as appropriate), suitable diameter pins can be inserted to lock both the camshaft and crankshaft in position, preventing them rotating unnecessarily. Proceed as follows.

2 Remove the timing belt upper cover as described in Section 6.
3 Apply the handbrake, jack up the front of the car and support it on axle stands. Remove the right-hand front roadwheel.
4 From underneath the front of the car, prise out the two retaining clips and remove the plastic cover from the wing valance, to gain access to the crankshaft pulley bolt. Where necessary, unclip the coolant hoses from the bracket, to improve access further. The crankshaft can then be turned using a suitable socket and extension bar fitted to the pulley bolt. Note that the crankshaft must always be turned in a clockwise direction (viewed from the right-hand side of vehicle).

1761 cc 16-valve models

5 Rotate the crankshaft pulley until the timing holes in both camshafts are aligned with their corresponding holes in the cylinder head. The holes are aligned when the inlet camshaft sprocket hole is in approximately the 5 o'clock position and the exhaust camshaft sprocket hole is in approximately the 7 o'clock position, when viewed from the right-hand end of the engine.
6 With the camshaft sprocket holes correctly positioned, insert a 6 mm diameter bolt or drill through the timing hole in the crankshaft pulley, and locate it in the corresponding hole in the end of the engine. Note that the hole size may vary according to the type of pulley fitted and auxiliary drivebelt arrangement. If the bolt or drill is not a snug fit, try a larger size until a good fit is achieved in both the pulley and cylinder block.
7 With the crankshaft locked in position, insert a suitable bolt or drill through the timing hole in each camshaft sprocket and locate it in the cylinder head **(see illustration)**.
8 The crankshaft and camshafts are now locked in position, preventing rotation.

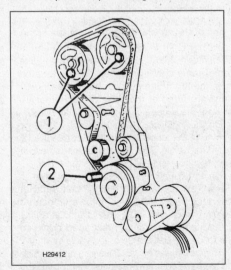

3.7 Camshaft sprocket timing hole (1) and crankshaft pulley timing hole (2) locked with suitable timing pins - 1761 cc 16-valve models

1998 cc 16-valve models

9 Rotate the crankshaft pulley until the timing holes in both camshafts are aligned with their corresponding holes in the cylinder head. The holes are aligned when the inlet camshaft sprocket hole is in the 8 o'clock position, and the exhaust camshaft sprocket is in the 6 o'clock position, when viewed from the right-hand end of the engine.
10 With the camshaft sprocket holes correctly positioned, insert a 6 mm diameter bolt (or a drill of suitable size), through the timing hole in the crankshaft pulley, and locate it in the corresponding hole in the end of the cylinder block. Note that it may be necessary to rotate the crankshaft slightly, to get the holes to align.
11 With the crankshaft pulley locked in position, insert a 6 mm diameter bolt (or a drill) through the timing hole in each camshaft sprocket, and locate it in the cylinder head. Note that the special Citroën locking pins are actually 8 mm in diameter, with only their ends stepped down to 6 mm to locate in the cylinder head **(see illustration)**. To simulate this, wrap insulation tape around the outer end of the bolt or drill, to build it up until it is a snug fit in the camshaft hole.
12 The crankshaft and camshafts are now locked in position, preventing unnecessary rotation.

All other models

13 Rotate the crankshaft pulley until the timing hole in the camshaft sprocket is aligned with its corresponding hole in the cylinder head. Note that the hole is aligned when the sprocket hole is in the 8 o'clock position, when viewed from the right-hand end of the engine.
14 On early 1580 cc and 1905 cc models having a semi-automatic timing belt tensioner, a 10 mm diameter bolt (or a drill of suitable size) will be required to lock the crankshaft pulley in position.
15 On later 1580 cc and 1905 cc models, and all 1761 and 1998 cc 8-valve models (which have a manually-adjusted timing belt tensioner pulley) the pulley can be locked in position with an 8 mm diameter bolt or drill. The special Citroën locking pin is actually

3.11 Camshaft sprocket locking pins in position (arrowed) - 1998 cc 16-valve models

3.17 Camshaft sprocket and crankshaft pulley locking pins in position (1580 cc model shown)

4.4 Where original Citroën hose clips are still fitted, cut them off and discard them

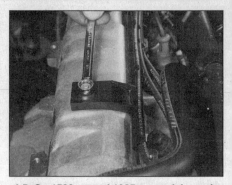

4.5 On 1580 cc and 1905 cc models, undo the retaining bolts/nuts and position the HT lead retaining clips clear of the head cover

10 mm in diameter, with only its end stepped down to 8 mm to locate in the cylinder block. To simulate this, wrap insulation tape around the outer end of the bolt/drill, to build it up until it is a snug fit in the pulley hole.

16 With the camshaft sprocket holes correctly positioned, insert the required bolt or drill through the timing hole in the crankshaft pulley, and locate it in the corresponding hole in the end of the cylinder block. Note that it may be necessary to rotate the crankshaft slightly, to get the holes to align.

17 With the crankshaft pulley locked in position, insert the appropriate bolt or drill through the timing hole in the camshaft sprocket and locate it in the cylinder head (see illustration).

18 The crankshaft and camshaft are now locked in position, preventing unnecessary rotation.

4 Cylinder head cover - removal and refitting

Removal

1 Disconnect the battery negative lead.

1580 cc and 1905 cc models

2 On 1580 cc models, remove the air cleaner-to-throttle body duct, and the air cleaner housing, as described in Chapter 4.

3 On 1905 cc models, remove the air cleaner housing as described in Chapter 4, and position the intake duct clear of the cylinder head cover.

4 On all models, slacken the retaining clip and disconnect the breather hose from the top of the cylinder head cover. Where the original crimped-type Citroën hose clip is still fitted, cut it off and discard it. Replace it with a standard worm-drive hose clip on refitting (see illustration).

5 Undo the two nuts/bolts securing the HT lead retaining bracket to the cylinder head, and position the bracket clear of the head cover (see illustration).

6 Slacken and remove the two remaining cylinder head cover retaining bolts, along with their sealing washers.

7 Lift off the cylinder head cover, and remove it along with its rubber seal. Examine the seal for signs of damage and deterioration, and if necessary, renew it. Also examine the retaining bolt sealing washers for signs of damage, and renew if required.

1761 cc and 1998 cc 8-valve models

8 Slacken the retaining clips, and disconnect the breather hoses from the front right-hand end of the cover. Where the original crimped-type Citroën hose clips are still fitted, cut them off and discard them; use standard worm-drive hose clips on refitting.

9 Slacken the retaining clip, and disconnect the air cleaner-to-throttle housing duct from

the front of the cylinder head cover. Also remove the intake duct from the left-hand side of the head cover.

10 Release the two retaining clips, then undo the two retaining screws located at the front, and remove the air cleaner element cover from the cylinder head cover. Remove the air cleaner element, and store it with the cover.

11 Slacken and remove the ten cylinder head cover retaining nuts, lift off the cylinder head cover, and remove it along with its rubber seal (see illustration). Examine the seal for signs of damage and deterioration, and if necessary, renew it.

1761 cc 16-valve models

Note: *Certain later models may be fitted with plastic cylinder head covers, rather than aluminium alloy as before. The procedure given below is not greatly affected by this change, except that the number of retaining bolts for each cover increases, and the bolts are located around the edge of each cover.*

12 Referring to Chapter 1, Section 11, if necessary, disconnect the wiring connector at the left-hand end of the ignition coil unit, located in the centre of the cylinder head covers. Undo the six retaining bolts and lift the coil unit upwards, off the spark plugs and from its location between the covers (see illustration).

13 Remove the Allen bolts from the fuel pipe cover, and remove the cover (see illustrations).

4.11 Cylinder head cover retaining nuts (arrowed) - 1761 cc and 1998 cc 8-valve models

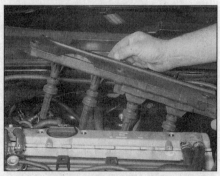

4.12 Removing the ignition coil unit - 1761 cc 16-valve models

4.13a Remove the two Allen bolts . . .

4.13b . . . and lift off the fuel pipe cover - 1761 cc 16-valve models

4.14a Disconnect the fuel supply pipe from the fuel pressure regulator . . .

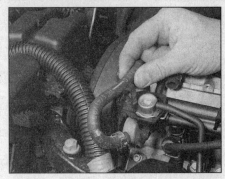

4.14b . . . and the return pipe, releasing it from the plastic clip - 1761 cc 16-valve models

2B

14 Refer to the relevant Part of Chapter 4 and depressurise the fuel system. Taking suitable precautions against fuel spillage, disconnect the fuel pipes from the fuel pressure regulator as necessary. Detach the fuel supply and return pipes from the carrier bracket fitted across the cylinder head covers. Unscrew the retaining nuts and remove the fuel pipe carrier bracket **(see illustrations)**.

15 Slacken the retaining clips, and disconnect the breather hoses from the front left-hand side of the front cover **(see illustration)**. Where the original crimped-type hose clips are still fitted, cut them off and discard them; use standard worm-drive hose clips on refitting.

16 Working in a spiral sequence starting from the outside and working inwards, progressively slacken, then remove the retaining studs and bolts from each cylinder head cover.

17 Lift off each cover in turn and remove it. The cover seal should remain attached as the cover is removed - do not try to remove it, unless it is obviously damaged.

1998 cc 16-valve models

18 Refer to the information given in Chapter 4 on depressurising the fuel system. Slacken the retaining clips, and disconnect the fuel feed and return hoses from their unions at the front of the head cover. Where the original crimped-type Citroën hose clips are still fitted,

cut them off and discard them; use standard worm-drive hose clips on refitting. Plug both the hose and fuel rail ends, to prevent the possible entry of dirt into the fuel system. Mop up any spilt fuel.

19 Undo the retaining nut and bolt securing the fuel hose retaining clips to the top of the cylinder head cover, and remove both clips. Position both fuel hoses clear of the head cover, so that they do not hinder the removal procedure.

20 Slacken and remove the remaining seven retaining bolts, and lift the spark plug access cover off the cylinder head cover.

21 Pull each ignition HT coil off its spark plug. Trace the coil wiring back to its connector on the left-hand end of the cylinder head. Rotate the locking ring anti-clockwise, disconnect it from the main wiring loom, and remove the wiring and coils as an assembly.

22 Disconnect the breather hose from the left-hand end of the cylinder head. Any original crimped-type hose clips can be discarded, as already mentioned.

23 Slacken and remove the twelve cylinder head cover retaining bolts, noting the correct fitted positions of any brackets or clips. Note that the bolts are of four different lengths, and it is important that each is refitted in the correct position. To avoid confusion on refitting, remove each bolt in turn, and store it in its correct fitted position by pushing it

through a clearly-marked cardboard template.

24 Lift off the cylinder head cover, and remove it along with its rubber seal. Recover the four spark plug hole sealing rings from the cylinder head. Examine all seals for signs of damage and deterioration, and renew as necessary.

Refitting

1580 cc and 1905 cc models

25 Carefully clean the cylinder head and cover mating surfaces, and remove all traces of oil.

26 Fit the rubber seal over the edge of the cylinder head cover, ensuring that it is correctly located along its entire length.

27 Carefully refit the cylinder head cover to the engine, taking great care not to displace the rubber seal.

28 Check that the seal is correctly located, then refit the cover retaining bolts and sealing washers (not forgetting to position the HT lead bracket under the centre bolt head), and tighten them to the specified torque.

29 Refit the remaining HT lead bracket retaining bolt, and tighten it securely.

30 Reconnect the breather hose to the cylinder head cover, and securely tighten its retaining clip.

31 Refit the air cleaner housing and duct as described in Chapter 4, and reconnect the battery negative terminal.

4.15c Unscrew the retaining nuts . . .

4.14d . . . and remove the fuel pipe carrier bracket - 1761 cc 16-valve models

4.15 Disconnect the breather hoses from the front cylinder head cover - 1761 cc 16-valve models

1761 cc and 1998 cc 8-valve models

32 Clean the cylinder head and cover mating surfaces, and remove all traces of oil.

33 Locate the rubber seal in the cover groove, ensuring that it is correctly located along its entire length.

34 Carefully refit the cylinder head cover to the engine, taking great care not to displace the rubber seal.

35 Check that the seal is correctly located, then refit the cover retaining nuts, and tighten them evenly and progressively to the specified torque.

36 Refit the air cleaner element, and install the element cover. Securely tighten the cover retaining screws, and secure it in position with the retaining clips.

37 Reconnect the breather hoses, intake duct and throttle housing duct to the cover, tightening their retaining clips securely. Reconnect the battery.

1761 cc 16-valve models

Note: *Certain later models may be fitted with plastic cylinder head covers, rather than aluminium alloy as before. No tightening sequence for the plastic cover bolts is quoted by Citroën.*

38 Clean the cylinder head and cover mating surfaces, and remove all traces of oil.

39 Check the condition of the rubber seal attached to each cover. The seal is designed to be re-usable, and so should not automatically be replaced unless its condition is suspect. If the seal is broken, it can be repaired using a bead of suitable sealant.

40 Carefully refit the cylinder head covers to the engine.

41 Refit the cover retaining bolts and studs and, working in the sequence shown (where applicable), tighten them evenly and progressively to the specified torque **(see illustration)**.

42 Reconnect the breather hoses to the front cover, and securely tighten the retaining clips.

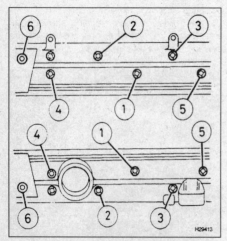

4.41 Alloy cylinder head cover fasteners tightening sequence - 1761 cc 16-valve models

43 Refit the ignition coil unit between the two covers. Refit the retaining bolts, tightening them securely, then reconnect the coil unit wiring connector.

44 Refit the fuel pipe carrier bracket to the covers, then refit the fuel pipes to their locations and secure with the fuel pipe cover.

45 Reconnect the battery negative terminal. On completion, start the engine and check the fuel hose unions for signs of leakage.

1998 cc 16-valve models

46 Carry out the operations described in paragraphs 32 to 34. Fit the four spark plug hole seals to the recesses in the cylinder head.

47 Check that the seal is correctly located, then refit the cover retaining bolts. Ensure that each bolt is refitted in its correct location, and that all retaining clips/brackets are correctly positioned. Tighten the cylinder head cover retaining bolts evenly and progressively to the specified torque.

48 Reconnect the breather hose to the end of the cover, and securely tighten its retaining clip.

49 Connect the HT coil wiring loom to its wiring connector, and secure it in position by rotating the locking ring. Ensuring that the wiring is correctly routed, reconnect the HT coils to the tops of the spark plugs.

50 Refit the spark plug access cover to the head cover, and refit its retaining bolts (not forgetting the fuel hose retaining clip). Ensure that the HT coil wiring is correctly located in the cover cutout, and that the fuel hoses are positioned under the retaining clip, then securely tighten the retaining bolts.

51 Fit the rear fuel hose retaining clip, and securely tighten its retaining nut.

52 Reconnect the feed and return hoses to their respective fuel rail unions, ensuring their retaining clips are securely tightened.

53 Reconnect the battery negative terminal. On completion, start the engine and check the fuel hose unions for signs of leakage.

---

5 Crankshaft pulley - removal and refitting

Removal

1 Remove the auxiliary drivebelt as described in Chapter 1.

1998 cc 16-valve models

2 Undo the four pulley retaining bolts and remove the pulley from the end of the crankshaft, noting which way around it is fitted. If the pulley locating roll pin is a loose fit, remove it and store it with the pulley for safe-keeping. If necessary, the pulley can be prevented from rotating as described in paragraph 3.

5.3 Use a fabricated tool like this one to lock the flywheel ring gear and prevent crankshaft rotation

All other models

3 To prevent crankshaft turning whilst the pulley retaining bolt is being slackened, select top gear and have an assistant apply the brakes firmly. If the engine has been removed from the vehicle, lock the flywheel ring gear using the arrangement shown **(see illustration)**. *Do not* attempt to lock the pulley by inserting a bolt/drill through the pulley timing hole.

4 Unscrew the retaining bolt and washer, then slide the pulley off the end of the crankshaft. If the pulley locating roll pin or Woodruff key (as applicable) is a loose fit, remove it and store it with the pulley for safe-keeping.

Refitting

1998 cc 16-valve models

5 Ensure that the locating roll pin is in position in the crankshaft. Offer up the pulley, ensuring that it is the correct way around. Locate the pulley on the roll pin, then refit the retaining bolts and tighten them to the specified torque. If necessary, prevent the pulley from rotating as described in paragraph 3.

6 Refit and tension the auxiliary drivebelt as described in Chapter 1.

All other models

7 Ensure that the Woodruff key is correctly located in its crankshaft groove, or that the roll pin is in position (as applicable). Refit the pulley to the end of the crankshaft, aligning its locating groove or hole with the Woodruff key or pin.

8 Thoroughly clean the threads of the pulley retaining bolt, then apply a coat of locking compound to the bolt threads. Citroën recommend the use of Frenbloc E6 (available from your Citroën dealer); in the absence of this, any good-quality locking compound may be used.

9 Refit the crankshaft pulley retaining bolt and washer. Tighten the bolt to the specified torque, preventing the crankshaft from turning using the method employed on removal.

10 Refit and tension the auxiliary drivebelt as described in Chapter 1.

6 Timing belt covers - removal and refitting

1580 cc and 1905 cc models

Upper cover

1 Release the retaining clips, and free the fuel hoses from the top of the cover.
2 Undo the two cover retaining bolts (situated at the base of the cover), and remove the cover from the engine compartment.

Centre cover - early (pre-1992) models with a semi-automatic belt tensioner

3 Slacken and remove the four cover retaining nuts and bolts (two directly below the mounting bracket, and two at the base of the cover), then manoeuvre the cover upwards out of the engine compartment.

Centre cover - later (1992-on) models with a manually-adjusted belt tensioner pulley

4 Slacken and remove the two cover retaining bolts (located directly beneath the mounting bracket). Move the cover upwards to free it from the two locating pins situated at the base of the cover, and remove it from the engine compartment.

Lower cover

5 Remove the crankshaft pulley as described in Section 5.
6 Remove the centre cover as described above.
7 On early models, undo the three lower cover retaining bolts and remove the cover from the engine.
8 On later models, undo the two cover retaining bolts and remove the cover from the engine.

Lower (inner) cover - early (pre-1992) models with a semi-automatic belt tensioner

9 Remove the timing belt as described in Section 7.
10 Slacken and remove the remaining bolts, noting their correct fitted positions, and remove the cover from the end of the cylinder block.

1761 cc 8-valve models

Upper cover

11 Proceed as described in paragraphs 1 and 2.

Centre cover

12 Proceed as described in paragraph 4.

Lower cover

13 Remove the crankshaft pulley as described in Section 5.
14 Remove the centre cover as described in paragraph 4.
15 Undo the two cover retaining bolts, and remove the cover from the engine.

1761 cc 16-valve models

Upper (outer) cover

16 Unclip the wiring harness from its location in the shaped top of the engine right-hand mounting, and from the inlet manifold bracket. Where applicable, release the air conditioning hose which runs between the timing belt cover and the engine mounting. Move the hose and wiring harness to one side (do NOT attempt to disconnect the air conditioning hose).
17 Prise out the clips and remove the trim cover from the top of the engine right-hand mounting.
18 Where applicable, lift the tab provided in the centre of the timing belt cover upwards to release the centre locating pegs.
19 Unscrew and remove the three upper retaining screws, and withdraw the timing belt cover. Recover the rubber pads from the centre locating pegs, where applicable.

Lower cover

20 Remove the crankshaft pulley (Section 5).
21 Slacken and remove the retaining bolts, then remove the lower timing belt cover from the engine. Note that on some models it may be necessary to unbolt the auxiliary drivebelt tensioner assembly and remove it from the engine in order to allow the cover to be removed.

Upper (inner) cover

22 Remove the timing belt as described in Section 7.
23 Remove both camshaft sprockets as described in Section 8.
24 Remove the six bolts securing the cover to the side of the cylinder head, and remove the cover from the engine.

1998 cc 8-valve models

Upper cover

25 Release the retaining clip, and free the fuel hoses from the top of the timing belt cover.
26 Slacken and remove the two cover retaining bolts, then lift the upper cover upwards and out of the engine compartment.

Lower cover

27 Remove the crankshaft pulley as described in Section 5.
28 Slacken and remove the three retaining bolts, then remove the lower timing belt cover from the engine.

1998 cc 16-valve models

Upper (outer) cover

29 Undo the two upper retaining bolts securing the outer cover to the inner cover. Slide the cover retaining clip upwards to release it from its fasteners **(see illustration)**.
30 Ease the outer cover away from the engine. Lift it upwards, freeing it from its locating bolts at the base of the cover, and out of the engine compartment.

6.29 Timing belt upper (outer) cover retaining clip (arrowed) - 1998 cc 16-valve models

Lower cover

31 Remove the crankshaft pulley as described in Section 5.
32 Remove the upper (outer) cover as described above.
33 Slacken and remove the two upper cover lower locating bolts, along with their spacers. Undo the two lower cover retaining bolts, and remove the cover from the engine.

Upper (inner) cover

34 Remove the timing belt as described in Section 7.
35 Remove both camshaft sprockets as described in Section 8.
36 Undo the six bolts securing the cover to the side of the cylinder head, and remove the cover from the engine.

Refitting

37 Refitting is a reversal of the relevant removal procedure, ensuring that each cover section is correctly located, and that the cover retaining nuts and/or bolts are securely tightened (to the specified torque, where given).

7 Timing belt - general information, removal and refitting

General information

1 The timing belt drives the camshaft(s) and coolant pump from a toothed sprocket on the front of the crankshaft. If the belt breaks or slips in service, the pistons are likely to hit the valve heads, resulting in extensive (and expensive) damage.
2 The timing belt should be renewed at the specified intervals (see Chapter 1), or earlier if it is contaminated with oil, or if it is at all noisy in operation (a "scraping" noise due to uneven wear).
3 If the timing belt is being removed, it is a wise precaution to check the condition of the coolant pump at the same time (check for signs of coolant leakage). This may avoid the need to remove the timing belt again at a later stage, should the coolant pump fail.

2B

7.7 On early 1580 cc and 1905 cc models, slacken the tensioner assembly retaining nuts . . .

7.8 . . . and the spindle locknut, then release the belt tension by turning the tensioner cam spindle using an open-ended spanner

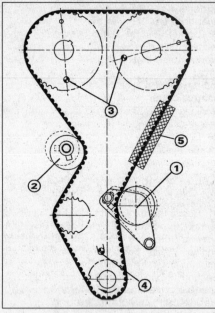

7.22 Timing belt arrangement - 1998 cc 16-valve models

1 *Front tensioner assembly*
2 *Rear tensioner pulley*
3 *Camshaft sprocket timing holes*
4 *Crankshaft pulley timing hole*
5 *Belt tension measuring area (using Citroën special tool)*

Removal

Early (pre-1992) 1580 cc and 1905 cc models with a semi-automatic belt tensioner

4 Disconnect the battery negative terminal.
5 Align the engine assembly/valve timing holes as described in Section 3, and lock the camshaft sprocket and crankshaft pulley in position. *Do not* attempt to rotate the engine whilst the pins are in position.
6 Remove the centre and lower timing belt covers as described in Section 6.
7 Slacken (but do not remove) the two nuts securing the tensioner assembly to the end of the cylinder block **(see illustration)**. Loosen the tensioner cam spindle locknut, located on the rear of cylinder block flange.
8 Using a suitable open-ended spanner on the square-section end of the tensioner cam spindle, rotate the cam until the tensioner spring is fully compressed and the belt tension is relieved **(see illustration)**. Hold the cam in this position, and securely tighten the locknut.
9 Place a jack beneath the engine, with a block of wood on the jack head. Raise the jack until it is supporting the weight of the engine.
10 Slacken and remove the three nuts securing the engine/transmission right-hand mounting bracket to the engine bracket. Remove the single nut securing the bracket to the mounting rubber, and lift off the bracket. Undo the three bolts securing the engine bracket to the end of the cylinder head/block, and remove the bracket.
11 If the timing belt is to be re-used, use white paint or chalk to mark the direction of rotation on the belt (if markings do not already exist), then slip the belt off the sprockets. Note that the crankshaft must not be rotated whilst the belt is removed.
12 Check the timing belt carefully for any signs of uneven wear, splitting, or oil contamination. Pay particular attention to the roots of the teeth. Renew it if there is the slightest doubt about its condition. If the engine is undergoing an overhaul, and has covered more than 24 000 miles (40 000 km)

with the existing belt fitted, renew the belt as a matter of course, regardless of its apparent condition. The cost of a new belt is nothing compared with the cost of repairs, should the belt break in service. If signs of oil contamination are found, trace the source of the oil leak and rectify it. Wash down the engine timing belt area and all related components, to remove all traces of oil.

Later (1992-on) 1580 cc and 1905 cc models with a manually-adjusted belt tensioner pulley, and all 1761 cc and 1998 cc 8-valve models

13 Disconnect the battery negative terminal.
14 Align the engine assembly/valve timing holes as described in Section 3, and lock the camshaft sprocket and crankshaft pulley in position. *Do not* attempt to rotate the engine whilst the pins are in position.
15 Remove the centre and/or lower timing belt cover(s) as described in Section 6 (as applicable).
16 Loosen the timing belt tensioner pulley retaining bolt. Pivot the pulley in a clockwise direction, using a suitable square-section key fitted to the hole in the pulley hub, then securely retighten the retaining bolt.
17 On 1580 cc, 1761 cc and 1905 cc models, dismantle the engine right-hand mounting as described above in paragraphs 9 and 10.
18 On all models, remove and inspect the timing belt as described in paragraphs 11 and 12.

1761 cc and 1998 cc 16-valve models

19 Disconnect the battery negative terminal.
20 Align the engine assembly/valve timing holes as described in Section 3, and lock the camshaft sprocket(s) in position. *Do not* attempt to rotate the engine whilst the pins are in position.
21 Remove the timing belt upper (outer) and lower covers with reference to Section 6. To improve access, refer to Section 18 and remove the engine right-hand mounting. This is not essential, but it does make several of the timing belt components much easier to remove with the engine in the car.
22 Loosen the timing belt rear tensioner

pulley retaining bolt. Pivot the pulley in a clockwise direction, using a suitable square-section key fitted to the hole in the pulley hub, then securely retighten the retaining bolt.
23 On 1998 cc models, loosen the two front tensioner assembly retaining bolts. Move the tensioner pulley away from the belt using the square-section key.
24 Refit the crankshaft pulley, and tighten the bolt moderately, holding the engine against rotation as for removal. Fit the locking tool through the crankshaft pulley, to prevent rotation. Check that the camshaft sprocket locking pins are still in position then remove and inspect the timing belt as described in paragraphs 11 and 12.

Refitting

Early (pre-1992) 1580 cc and 1905 cc models with a semi-automatic belt tensioner

25 Before refitting, thoroughly clean the timing belt sprockets. Check that the tensioner pulley rotates freely, without any sign of roughness. If necessary, renew the tensioner pulley as described in Section 8.
26 Ensure that the camshaft sprocket locking pin is still in position. Temporarily refit the crankshaft pulley, and insert the locking pin through the pulley timing hole to ensure that the crankshaft is still correctly positioned.
27 Remove the crankshaft pulley. Manoeuvre the timing belt into position, ensuring that any arrows on the belt are pointing in the direction

of rotation (clockwise when viewed from the right-hand end of the engine).

28 Do not twist the timing belt sharply while refitting it. Fit the belt over the crankshaft and camshaft sprockets. Ensure that the belt "front run" is taut - ie, any slack should be on the tensioner pulley side of the belt. Fit the belt over the water pump sprocket and tensioner pulley. Ensure that the belt teeth are seated centrally in the sprockets.

29 Slacken the tensioner cam spindle locknut, and check that the tensioner pulley is forced against the timing belt by spring pressure.

30 Refit the crankshaft pulley, tightening its retaining bolt by hand only.

31 Rotate the crankshaft through at least two complete rotations in a clockwise direction (viewed from the right-hand end of the engine). Realign the camshaft and crankshaft engine assembly/valve timing holes (see Section 3). *Do not* at any time rotate the crankshaft anti-clockwise. Both camshaft and crankshaft timing holes should be aligned so that the locking pins can be easily inserted. This indicates that the valve timing is correct.

32 If the timing holes are not correctly positioned, release the tensioner assembly as described in paragraph 8, and disengage the belt from the camshaft sprocket. Rotate the camshaft and crankshaft slightly as required until both locking pins are in position. Relocate the timing belt on the camshaft sprocket. Ensure that the belt "front run" is taut - ie, that any slack is on the tensioner pulley side of the belt. Slacken the tensioner locknut, then remove the locking pins and repeat the procedure described in paragraph 31.

33 Once both timing holes are correctly aligned, tighten the two tensioner assembly retaining nuts to the specified torque. Tighten the tensioner cam spindle locknut to its specified torque.

34 With the belt correctly installed and tensioned, refit the engine bracket to the side of the cylinder head/block, and securely tighten its retaining bolts. Refit the right-hand mounting bracket, and tighten its retaining nuts to the specified torque. The jack can then be removed from underneath the engine.

35 Remove the crankshaft pulley, then refit the timing belt covers as described in Section 6.

36 Install the crankshaft pulley as described in Section 5, and reconnect the battery negative terminal.

Later (1992-on) 1580 cc and 1905 cc models with a manually-adjusted belt tensioner pulley, and all 1761 cc and 1998 cc 8-valve models

Note: *Citroën specify the use of a special electronic tool (SEEM belt tension measuring tool) to correctly set the timing belt tension. If this equipment is not available, an approximate setting can be achieved using the method described below. If this method is used, however, the belt tension must be checked using the special electronic tool at the earliest possible opportunity. Do not drive the vehicle over large distances, or use high engine speeds, until the belt tension is known to be correct. Refer to a Citroën dealer for advice.*

37 Install the timing belt as described above in paragraphs 25 to 28.

38 Loosen the tensioner pulley retaining bolt. Using the square-section key, pivot the pulley anti-clockwise to remove all free play from the timing belt.

39 If the special belt tension measuring equipment is available, it should be fitted to the "front run" of the timing belt. The tensioner roller should be adjusted so that the initial belt tension is 16 ± 2 units on 1998 cc 8-valve models, and 30 ± 2 units on all other models.

40 Tighten the pulley retaining bolt to the specified torque. Refit the crankshaft pulley again, tightening its retaining bolt by hand only.

41 Carry out the operations described in paragraph 31 (and where necessary, paragraph 32, ignoring the information about the tensioner) to ensure that both timing holes are correctly aligned and the valve timing is correct.

42 If the tension is being set without using the special measuring tool, proceed as follows. Check that, under moderate pressure from the thumb and forefinger, the belt can just be twisted through 90° at the mid-point of the "front run" of the belt. Note that this method is only an initial setting, and the belt tension *must* checked at the earliest available opportunity using the special measuring tool. Failure to do so could lead to the belt breaking (through over-tightening) or slipping (through slackness), resulting in serious engine damage. If necessary, readjust the tensioner pulley position as required. Tighten its retaining bolt to the specified torque on completion.

43 If the special measuring tool is being used, the belt tension on the "front run" of the belt on all models should be 44 ± 2 units. Readjust the tensioner pulley position as required, then retighten the retaining bolt to the specified torque. Rotate the crankshaft through a further two rotations clockwise, and recheck the tension. Repeat this procedure as necessary until the correct tension reading is obtained after rotating the crankshaft.

44 With the belt tension correctly set, on 1580 cc, 1761 cc and 1905 cc models, refit the engine bracket to the side of the cylinder head/block, and securely tighten its retaining bolts. Refit the right-hand engine mounting bracket, and tighten its retaining nuts to the specified torque. The jack can then be removed from underneath the engine.

45 On all models, remove the crankshaft pulley, then refit the timing belt cover(s) as described in Section 6.

46 Refit the crankshaft pulley as described in Section 5, and reconnect the battery negative terminal.

1761 cc 16-valve models

Note: *Citroën specify the use of a special electronic tool (SEEM belt tensioning measuring tool) to correctly set the timing belt tension. If this equipment is not available, an approximate setting can be achieved using the method described below. If this method is used, however, the tension must be checked using the special electronic tool at the earliest possible opportunity. Do not drive the vehicle over large distances, or use high engine speeds, until the belt tension is known to be correct. Refer to a Citroën dealer for advice.*

47 Before refitting, thoroughly clean the timing belt sprockets. Check that the tensioner and idler pulleys rotate freely, without any sign of roughness. If necessary, renew the pulleys as described in Section 8.

48 Ensure that the camshaft sprocket locking pins are still in position. Temporarily refit the crankshaft pulley (if removed), and insert the locking pin through the pulley timing hole to ensure that the crankshaft is still correctly positioned.

49 Without removing the locking pins, slacken the six camshaft sprocket retaining bolts (three on each sprocket). Check that both sprockets are free to turn within the limits of their elongated bolt holes.

50 Tighten the camshaft sprocket retaining bolts finger-tight, then slacken them all by one sixth of a turn.

51 Again without removing the locking pins, turn each camshaft sprocket clockwise to the ends of their retaining bolt slots.

52 Remove the crankshaft pulley. Manoeuvre the timing belt into position on the crankshaft sprocket, ensuring that any arrows on the belt are pointing in the direction of rotation (clockwise when viewed from the right-hand end of the engine).

53 Refit the timing belt lower cover and the crankshaft pulley (Sections 6 and 5).

54 With the timing belt engaged with the crankshaft sprocket, keep it tight on its right-hand run and engage it with the front idler pulley then up and into engagement with the inlet camshaft sprocket.

55 Keeping the belt tight and rotating the inlet camshaft sprocket anti-clockwise as necessary, feed the belt over the exhaust camshaft sprocket, taking care not to let the belt jump a tooth on the crankshaft sprocket as it is being fitted.

56 While still keeping the belt tight, feed it over the rear tensioner pulley and finally around the coolant pump.

57 If the special belt tension measuring equipment is available, proceed as described in paragraphs 58 to 68, and then from paragraph 75 onwards. If the tension is being set without the use of the special measuring equipment, proceed to paragraph 69.

58 If the special belt tension measuring equipment is available, it should be fitted to the "front run" of the timing belt. The tensioner pulley should be adjusted, by turning it anti-

2B

clockwise to give a belt pre-tensioning setting of 45 units. Hold the tensioner pulley in this position and tighten the retaining bolt to the specified torque.

59 Check that the sprockets have not been turned so far that the retaining bolts are at the end of their slots. If they are, repeat the refitting operation. If all is satisfactory, tighten the sprocket retaining bolts to the specified torque.

60 Remove the locking pins, then rotate the crankshaft through two complete rotations in a clockwise direction (viewed from the right-hand end of the engine). Realign the crankshaft engine assembly/valve timing hole and refit the locking pin to the crankshaft pulley.

61 Slacken the camshaft sprocket retaining bolts, retighten them finger-tight, then slacken them all by one sixth of a turn.

62 Refit the camshaft sprocket locking pins, then slacken the tensioner pulley retaining bolt once more. Refit the belt tension measuring equipment to the front run of the belt, and turn the tensioner pulley to give a setting of 26 units on the tensioning gauge. Hold the tensioner pulley in this position and tighten the retaining bolt to the specified torque.

63 Retighten all sprocket retaining bolts to the specified torque.

64 The belt tension must now be checked as follows. Remove the locking pins, then rotate the crankshaft once again through two complete rotations in a clockwise direction. Realign the crankshaft engine assembly/valve timing hole, and refit the locking pin to the crankshaft pulley.

65 Slacken the camshaft sprocket retaining bolts, retighten them finger-tight, then slacken them all by one sixth of a turn.

66 Refit the camshaft sprocket locking pins, turning the sprockets slightly if required. Tighten the camshaft sprocket retaining bolts to the specified torque.

67 Remove the camshaft and crankshaft locking tools. Turn the crankshaft approximately one quarter of a turn in the normal direction of rotation, until the locking tool hole in the crankshaft pulley is aligned with the timing belt lower cover front retaining bolt. It is important that this position is achieved ONLY by turning the belt forwards - if the belt is turned back at all to achieve alignment, the belt tension check will not be valid.

68 In this position, refit the tension measuring equipment to the front run of the belt, and check that the reading is between 32 and 40 units. If not, the entire belt tensioning procedure must be repeated from the start.

69 If the tension is being set without the use of the special measuring equipment, the tensioner pulley should be adjusted, by turning it anti-clockwise, until all free play is removed from the belt. Hold the tensioner pulley in this position and tighten the retaining bolt to the specified torque.

70 Carry out the check described in paragraph 59. If all is satisfactory, tighten all sprocket retaining bolts to the specified torque.

71 Remove the locking pins, then rotate the crankshaft through two complete rotations in a clockwise direction (viewed from the right-hand end of the engine). Realign the crankshaft engine assembly/valve timing hole, and refit the locking pin to the crankshaft pulley.

72 Slacken the camshaft sprocket retaining bolts, retighten them finger-tight, then slacken them all by one sixth of a turn.

73 Refit the camshaft sprocket locking pins, then slacken the tensioner pulley retaining bolt once more. Turn the tensioner pulley to tension the belt until, under moderate pressure from the thumb and forefinger, the belt can just be twisted through 45° at the mid-point between the inlet camshaft sprocket and the idler pulley. Note that this method is only a provisional setting, and the belt tension must be checked at the earliest opportunity using the special belt tensioning equipment. Failure to do this could lead to the belt breaking (through over-tightening) or slipping (through slackness), resulting in serious engine damage. With the tension set, hold the tensioner pulley in this position, and tighten the retaining bolt to the specified torque.

74 Retighten all sprocket retaining bolts to the specified torque.

75 Once the belt tension has been correctly set, refit the engine right-hand mounting components as described in Section 18.

76 Refit the timing belt upper, centre and lower covers (as applicable) as described in Section 6, and reconnect the battery negative terminal.

1998 cc 16-valve models

Note: *Citroën specify the use of a special electronic tool (SEEM belt tension measuring tool) to correctly set the timing belt tension. If this equipment is not available, an approximate setting can be achieved using the method described below. If this method is used, however, the tension must be checked using the special electronic tool at the earliest possible opportunity. Do not drive the vehicle over large distances, or use high engine speeds, until the belt tension is known to be correct. Refer to a Citroën dealer for advice.*

77 Before refitting, thoroughly clean the timing belt sprockets. Check that each tensioner pulley rotates freely, without any sign of roughness. If necessary, renew the tensioner pulley(s) as described in Section 8.

78 Ensure that the camshaft and crankshaft sprocket locking pins are still in position. Slacken both tensioner mounting bolts so that they are free to pivot easily.

79 Manoeuvre the timing belt into position, ensuring that any arrows on the belt are pointing in the direction of rotation (clockwise when viewed from the right-hand end of the engine).

80 Note that there are also timing marks on the belt, in the form of yellow lines, to ensure it is correctly positioned on both camshaft sprockets and the crankshaft sprocket. The two single-line timing marks should be aligned with the timing dot (directly opposite the sprocket timing hole) on each camshaft sprocket. The double-line timing mark should be aligned with the crankshaft sprocket, where it will be directly opposite the sprocket Woodruff key slot. Citroën state that the use of these timing marks is optional, but they are useful in helping to ensure that the valve timing is correctly set at the first attempt.

81 With the three locking pins in position, move both the front and rear tensioner pulleys towards the timing belt until both pulleys are contacting the belt. Securely tighten the rear tensioner retaining bolt.

82 If the tension is being set without the use of the special measuring tool, proceed as follows. Using the square-section key fitted to the hole in the tensioner backplate, move the front tensioner pulley against the belt until all free play is removed from the belt. Hold the tensioner in this position, and tighten the pulley retaining bolts to the specified torque.

83 If the special belt tension measuring equipment is available, it should be fitted to the "front run" of the timing belt, between the front tensioner and the camshaft sprocket. Move the tensioner pulley backplate so that the belt is initially over-tensioned to a setting of 45 units, then back the tensioner off until the belt tension is 22 ± 2 units. Hold the backplate in this position, and tighten both tensioner pulley retaining bolts to the specified torque.

84 Slacken the rear tensioner pulley retaining bolt. Using the square-section key, pivot the pulley anti-clockwise until all free play is removed from the belt. If the belt tension measuring equipment is being used, set the tensioner pulley so that the belt tension on the "front run" is 32 ± 2 units. Hold the tensioner in position, and tighten its retaining bolt to the specified torque setting.

85 Remove the locking pins from the camshaft and crankshaft sprockets and, where fitted, the tensioning measuring device from the belt.

86 Rotate the crankshaft through at least two complete rotations in a clockwise direction (viewed from the right-hand end of the engine). Realign the camshaft and crankshaft engine assembly/valve timing holes (see Section 3). *Do not* at any time rotate the crankshaft anti-clockwise. Both camshaft timing holes and the crankshaft timing hole should be correctly positioned so that the locking pins can be easily inserted, indicating that the valve timing is correct.

87 If the timing holes are not correctly positioned, slacken the tensioner assembly retaining bolts, and disengage the belt from the camshaft sprockets. Rotate the camshafts and crankshaft slightly as required until all

2B

locking pins are in position, then relocate the timing belt on the camshaft sprocket. Ensure that the belt "top run" and "front run" are taut - ie, ensure that any slack is on the rear tensioner pulley and water pump side of the belt. Repeat the tensioning procedure described in paragraphs 81 to 86 until the valve timing is correct.

88 Once the valve timing is correctly set, remove the locking pins and recheck the belt tension.

89 If the tension is being set without the special measuring tool, proceed as follows. Check that, under moderate pressure from the thumb and forefinger, the belt can just be twisted through 45°, at the mid-point between the camshaft sprocket and tensioner pulley on the "front run" of the belt. Note that this method is only an initial setting, and the belt tension *must* checked at the earliest available opportunity using the special measuring tool. Failure to do so could lead to the belt breaking (through over-tightening) or slipping (through slackness), resulting in serious engine damage. If necessary, readjust the rear tensioner pulley position as required, and tighten its retaining bolt to the specified torque.

90 If the special measuring tool is being used, the final belt tension on the "front run" of the belt, between the camshaft sprocket and tensioner pulley, should be 53 ± 2 units. Readjust the rear tensioner pulley position as required, then retighten the retaining bolt to the specified torque. Rotate the crankshaft through a further two rotations clockwise, and recheck the tension. Repeat this procedure as necessary, until the correct tension reading is obtained after the crankshaft has been rotated.

91 Once the belt tension is correctly set, refit the timing belt covers as described in Section 6. Refit the crankshaft pulley as described in Section 5, and reconnect the battery negative terminal

8 Timing belt tensioner and sprockets - removal, inspection and refitting

Note: *This Section describes the removal and refitting of the components concerned as individual operations - if more than one is to be removed at the same time, start by removing the timing belt as described in Section 7; remove the actual component as described below, ignoring the preliminary dismantling steps.*

Removal

1 Disconnect the battery negative lead.
2 Align the engine assembly/valve timing holes as described in Section 3, locking the camshaft sprocket(s) and the crankshaft pulley in position, and proceed as described under the relevant sub-heading. *Do not attempt to rotate the engine whilst the pins are in position.*

Camshaft sprocket - early (pre-1992) 1580 cc and 1905 cc models with a semi-automatic belt tensioner

3 Remove the centre timing belt cover as described in Section 6.
4 Slacken (but do not remove) the two nuts securing the tensioner assembly to the end of the cylinder block. Loosen the tensioner cam spindle locknut, located on the rear of cylinder block flange.
5 Using a suitable open-ended spanner on the square-section end of the tensioner cam spindle, rotate the cam until the tensioner spring is fully compressed and the belt tension is relieved. Hold the cam in this position, and securely tighten the locknut.
6 Remove the locking pin from the camshaft sprocket. Disengage the timing belt from the sprocket and position it clear, taking care not to bend or twist the belt sharply.
7 Slacken the camshaft sprocket retaining bolt and remove it, along with its washer. To prevent the camshaft rotating as the bolt is slackened, a sprocket holding tool will be required. *Do not* attempt to use the sprocket locking pin to prevent the sprocket from rotating whilst the bolt is slackened

 To prevent the camshaft sprocket from rotating, use two lengths of steel strip (one long, the other short), and three nuts and bolts; one nut and bolt forms the pivot of a forked tool, with the remaining two nuts and bolts at the tips of the "forks" to engage with the sprocket spokes as shown in illustration 8.51.

8 With the retaining bolt removed, slide the sprocket off the end of the camshaft. If the locating peg is a loose fit in the rear of the sprocket, remove it for safe-keeping. Examine the camshaft oil seal for signs of oil leakage and, if necessary, renew it as described in Section 9.

Camshaft sprocket - later (1992-on) 1580 cc and 1905 cc models with a manually-adjusted belt tensioner pulley, and all 1761 cc and 1998 cc 8-valve models

9 On all except 1998 cc 8-valve models, remove the centre timing belt cover as described in Section 6.
10 Loosen the timing belt tensioner pulley retaining bolt. Rotate the pulley in a clockwise direction, using a suitable square-section key fitted to the hole in the pulley hub, then retighten the retaining bolt.
11 Remove the camshaft sprocket as described above in paragraphs 6 to 8.

Camshaft sprocket(s) - 1761 cc 16-valve models

12 Remove the timing belt upper (outer) and lower covers as described in Section 6.

13 For improved access, support the engine on a jack, and remove the right-hand engine mounting components as described in Section 18.
14 Loosen the timing belt tensioner pulley retaining bolt and pivot the pulley in a clockwise direction, using a suitable square-section key fitted to the hole in the pulley hub, then retighten the retaining bolt.
15 Check that the camshaft sprocket locking pins are still in position, then disengage the timing belt from the camshaft sprockets and position it clear, taking care not to bend or twist the belt sharply.
16 If the sprockets are to be removed without their hubs, undo the three retaining bolts and remove the relevant sprocket. Suitably mark the sprockets "inlet" or "exhaust" as they are removed.
17 If both the sprockets and the hubs are to be removed, remove the sprocket locking pins, then slacken the sprocket hub centre retaining bolt. To prevent the sprockets rotating as the bolt is slackened, a sprocket holding tool will be required. In the absence of the special Citroën tool, an acceptable substitute can be fabricated at home **(see Tool Tip)**. *Do not* attempt to use the sprocket locking pin to prevent the sprocket from rotating whilst the bolt is slackened.
18 Undo the retaining bolt(s) and remove the relevant sprocket. Remove the previously-slackened hub retaining bolt, and withdraw the hub from the end of the camshaft. Note that the hubs are marked for identification with a single digit on their front face. The inlet hub is marked "1" and the exhaust hub is marked "2".

Camshaft sprocket(s) - 1998 cc 16-valve models

19 Loosen the timing belt rear tensioner pulley retaining bolt. Pivot the pulley in a clockwise direction, using a suitable square-section key fitted to the hole in the pulley hub, then securely retighten the retaining bolt.
20 Loosen the two front tensioner assembly retaining bolts. Move the tensioner pulley away from the belt, using the same square-section key on the pulley backplate.
21 Remove the camshaft sprocket retaining bolt as described above in paragraphs 6 and 7.
22 Slide the sprocket off the end of the camshaft. If the Woodruff key is a loose fit in the camshaft, remove it and store it with the sprocket for safe-keeping. Examine the camshaft oil seal for signs of oil leakage and, if necessary, renew it as described in Section 9.

Crankshaft sprocket - 1580 cc, 1761 cc, 1905 cc and 1998 cc 8-valve models

23 Remove the centre and/or lower timing belt cover(s) (as applicable) as described in Section 6.
24 On early (pre-1992) 1580 cc and 1905 cc models with a semi-automatic belt tensioner, release the timing belt tensioner as described above in paragraphs 4 and 5.

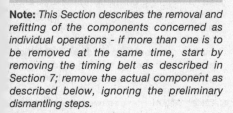

25 On later (1992-on) 1580 cc and 1905 cc models with a manually-adjusted belt tensioner pulley, and all 1761 cc and 1998 cc 8-valve models, release the timing belt tensioner as described in paragraph 10.

26 Disengage the timing belt from the crankshaft sprocket, and slide the sprocket off the end of the crankshaft. Remove the Woodruff key from the crankshaft, and store it with the sprocket for safe-keeping. Where necessary, also slide the flanged spacer (where fitted) off the end of the crankshaft.

27 Examine the crankshaft oil seal for signs of oil leakage and, if necessary, renew it as described in Section 16.

Crankshaft sprocket - 1998 cc 16-valve models

28 Remove the lower timing belt cover as described in Section 6.

29 Release the timing belt tensioners as described above in paragraphs 19 and 20. Disengage the timing belt from the crankshaft sprocket, and remove the locking pin.

30 To prevent the crankshaft turning whilst the sprocket retaining bolt is being slackened, select top gear, and have an assistant apply the brakes firmly. If the engine has been removed from the vehicle, lock the flywheel ring gear using the arrangement shown in illustration 5.3 (Section 5). *Do not* be tempted to use the locking pin to prevent the crankshaft from rotating.

31 Unscrew the retaining bolt and washer, then slide the sprocket off the end of the crankshaft. If the Woodruff key is a loose fit in the crankshaft, remove it and store it with the sprocket for safe-keeping.

32 Where necessary, slide the flanged spacer (where fitted) off the end of the crankshaft.

33 Examine the crankshaft oil seal for signs of oil leakage and, if necessary, renew it as described in Section 16.

Tensioner assembly - early (pre-1992) 1580 cc and 1905 cc models with a semi-automatic belt tensioner

34 Remove the centre timing belt cover as described in Section 6.

35 Slacken and remove the two nuts and washers securing the tensioner assembly to the end of the cylinder block. Carefully ease the spring cover off its studs, taking care not to allow the spring to fly out as the cover is withdrawn. Remove the spring and cover from the engine **(see illustration)**.

36 Slacken and remove the tensioner cam spindle locknut and washer, located on the rear of cylinder block flange, and withdraw the cam spindle.

37 The tensioner pulley and backplate assembly can then be manoeuvred out from behind the timing belt.

Tensioner pulley - later (1992-on) 1580 cc and 1905 cc models with a manually-adjusted belt tensioner pulley, and all 1761 cc and 1998 cc 8-valve models

38 On all except 1998 cc 8-valve models, remove the centre timing belt cover as described in Section 6.

39 Slacken and remove the timing belt tensioner pulley retaining bolt, and slide the pulley off its mounting stud. Examine the mounting stud for signs of damage and if necessary, renew it.

Tensioner and idler pulleys - 1761 cc 16-valve models

40 Remove the timing belt upper (outer) and lower covers as described in Section 6.

41 For improved access, support the engine on a jack, and remove the right-hand engine mounting components as described in Section 18.

42 Loosen the timing belt tensioner pulley retaining bolt, and pivot the pulley in a clockwise direction, using a suitable square-section key fitted to the hole in the pulley hub, then retighten the retaining bolt.

43 Check that the camshaft sprocket locking pins are still in position, then disengage the timing belt from the camshaft sprockets and position it clear, taking care not to bend or twist the belt sharply.

44 Undo the tensioner and idler pulley retaining bolts, and remove the pulleys from the engine.

Tensioner pulleys - 1998 cc 16-valve models

45 The rear tensioner pulley is removed as described above in paragraph 32.

46 To remove the front tensioner pulley, slacken and remove the two bolts securing the pulley backplate to the cylinder block, and remove the assembly from the engine unit.

Inspection

47 Clean the camshaft/crankshaft sprockets thoroughly, and renew any that show signs of wear, damage or cracks.

48 Clean the tensioner assembly, but do not use any strong solvent which may enter the pulley bearing. Check that the pulley rotates freely on the backplate, with no sign of stiffness or free play. Renew the assembly if there is any doubt about its condition, or if there are any obvious signs of wear or damage.

49 On early 1580 cc and 1905 cc models, the tensioner spring should also be carefully checked, as its condition is critical for the correct tensioning of the timing belt. The only way of checking the spring tension is to compare it with a new one; if there is any doubt as to its condition, the spring should be renewed.

Refitting

Camshaft sprocket - early (pre-1992) 1580 cc and 1905 cc models with a semi-automatic belt tensioner

50 Refit the locating peg (where removed) to the rear of the sprocket. Locate the sprocket on the end of the camshaft, ensuring that the locating peg is correctly engaged with the cutout in the camshaft end.

51 Refit the sprocket retaining bolt and washer, and tighten it to the specified torque. Retain the sprocket with the tool used on removal **(see illustration)**.

52 Realign the hole in the camshaft sprocket with the corresponding hole in the cylinder head, and refit the locking pin. Check that the crankshaft pulley locking pin is still in position.

53 Refit the timing belt to the camshaft sprocket. Ensure that the "front run" of the belt is taut - ie, that any slack is on the tensioner pulley side of the belt. Do not twist the belt sharply while refitting it, and ensure that the belt teeth are seated centrally in the sprockets.

54 Release the tensioner cam spindle locknut, and check that the tensioner pulley is forced against the timing belt under spring pressure.

55 Tension the timing belt as described in paragraphs 31 to 33 of Section 7.

56 With the belt correctly tensioned, and the tensioner retaining nuts and locknut tightened to the specified torque setting, refit the timing belt covers as described in Section 6. Reconnect the battery on completion.

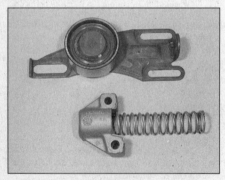

8.35 Timing belt tensioner assembly components - early 1580 cc and 1905 cc models

8.51 Using a home-made tool to retaining the camshaft sprocket whilst the sprocket retaining bolt is tightened (TU engine shown)

Camshaft sprocket - later (1992-on) 1580 cc and 1905 cc models with a manually-adjusted belt tensioner pulley, and all 1761 cc and 1998 cc 8-valve models

57 Refit the camshaft sprocket as described above in paragraphs 50 to 53.

58 With the timing belt correctly engaged on the sprockets, tension the belt as described in paragraphs 38 to 43 of Section 7.

59 Once the belt is correctly tensioned, refit the timing belt covers as described in Section 6.

Camshaft sprocket(s) - 1761 cc 16-valve models

60 If both the sprockets and the hubs have been removed, engage the sprocket hub with the camshaft. Ensure that the correct hub is fitted to the relevant camshaft by observing the hub identification markings described in paragraph 18.

61 Refit the sprocket retaining bolt and washer, and tighten it to the specified torque. Temporarily refit the sprockets, to allow the hub to be held stationary with the tool as the bolt is tightened.

62 Turn the hub so that the locking pin can be engaged.

63 If the sprockets have been removed, leaving the hubs in place, position the sprocket on its hub, and refit the three bolts finger-tight only at this stage. Ensure that the correct sprocket is fitted to the relevant camshaft according to the identification made on removal.

64 Relocate and tension the timing belt as described in Section 7. If removed, refit the engine right-hand mounting as described in Section 18.

Camshaft sprocket(s) - 1998 cc 16-valve models

65 Refit the Woodruff key to its slot in the camshaft end. Slide on the sprocket, aligning its slot with the Woodruff key.

66 Refit the sprocket retaining bolt and washer. Tighten the bolt to the specified torque, whilst retaining the sprocket with the tool used on removal.

67 Realign the hole in the camshaft sprocket with the corresponding hole in the cylinder head, and refit the locking pin.

68 Relocate the timing belt on the camshaft sprocket(s), and tension the timing belt as described in paragraphs 80 to 90 of Section 7.

69 Once the belt is correctly tensioned, refit the timing belt cover as described in Section 6.

Crankshaft sprocket - 1580 cc, 1761 cc, 1905 cc and 1998 cc 8-valve models

70 Slide on the flanged spacer (where fitted), and refit the Woodruff key to its slot in the crankshaft end.

71 Slide on the crankshaft sprocket, aligning its slot with the Woodruff key.

72 Ensure that the camshaft sprocket locking pin is still in position. Temporarily refit the crankshaft pulley, and insert the locking pin through the pulley timing hole, to ensure that the crankshaft is still correctly positioned.

73 Remove the crankshaft pulley. Engage the timing belt with the crankshaft sprocket. Ensure that the belt "front run" is taut - ie, that any slack is on the tensioner pulley side of the belt. Fit the belt over the water pump sprocket and tensioner pulley. Do not twist the belt sharply while refitting it, and ensure that the belt teeth are seated centrally in the sprockets.

74 On early (pre-1992) 1580 cc and 1905 cc models with a semi-automatic tensioner, release the tensioner cam spindle locknut, checking that the tensioner pulley is forced against the timing belt under spring pressure. Tension the timing belt as described in paragraphs 30 to 33 of Section 7.

75 On later (1992-on) 1580 cc and 1905 cc models with a manually-adjusted belt tensioner pulley, and all 1761 cc and 1998 cc 8-valve models, tension the timing belt as described in 38 to 43 of Section 7.

76 On all models, remove the crankshaft pulley, then refit the timing belt cover(s) as described in Section 6.

77 Refit the crankshaft pulley as described in Section 5, and reconnect the battery negative terminal.

Crankshaft sprocket - 1998 cc 16-valve models

78 Slide on the flanged spacer (where fitted), and refit the Woodruff key to its slot in the crankshaft end.

79 Slide on the crankshaft sprocket, aligning its slot with the Woodruff key.

80 Thoroughly clean the threads of the sprocket retaining bolt, then apply a coat of locking compound to the threads of the bolt. Citroën recommend the use of Frenbloc E6 (available from your Citroën dealer); in the absence of this, any good-quality locking compound may be used.

81 Refit the crankshaft sprocket retaining bolt and washer. Tighten the bolt to the specified torque, whilst preventing crankshaft rotation using the method employed on removal.

82 Refit the locking pin to the crankshaft sprocket, and check that both the camshaft sprocket locking pins are still in position.

83 Relocate the timing belt on the crankshaft sprocket, and tension the timing belt as described in paragraphs 80 to 90 of Section 7.

84 Once the belt is correctly tensioned, refit the timing belt cover as described in Section 6.

Tensioner assembly - early (pre-1992) 1580 cc and 1905 cc models with a semi-automatic belt tensioner

85 Manoeuvre the tensioner pulley and backplate assembly into position behind the timing belt, and locate it on the mounting studs.

86 Insert the tensioner cam spindle through the backplate from the front of the block, and refit its washer and locknut, tightening it by hand only at this stage.

87 Fit the spring to the inside of the spring cover. Compress the spring, and slide the spring cover onto the two mounting studs, ensuring that the spring end is correctly located behind the backplate tang.

88 Refit the tensioner mounting nuts and washers, tightening them by hand only. Check that the tensioner is forced against the timing belt by spring pressure, and is free to move smoothly and easily.

89 Ensure that the "front run" of the belt is taut - ie, that any slack is on the pulley side of the belt. Check that the belt is centrally located on all its sprockets, then release the tensioner assembly and allow it to tension the belt.

90 Tension the timing belt, and check the valve timing as described in paragraphs 31 to 33 of Section 7.

91 With the belt correctly tensioned, and the tensioner retaining nuts and locknut tightened to the specified torque setting, refit the timing belt covers as described in Section 6. Reconnect the battery on completion.

Tensioner pulley - later (1992-on) 1580 cc and 1905 cc models with a manually-adjusted belt tensioner pulley, and all 1761 cc and 1998 cc 8-valve models

92 Refit the tensioner pulley to its mounting stud, and fit the retaining bolt.

93 Ensure that the "front run" of the belt is taut - ie, that any slack is on the pulley side of the belt. Check that the belt is centrally located on all its sprockets. Rotate the pulley anti-clockwise to remove all free play from the timing belt, and securely tighten the pulley retaining nut.

94 Tension the belt as described in 38 to 43 of Section 7.

95 Once the belt is correctly tensioned, refit the timing belt covers as described in Section 6.

Tensioner and idler pulleys - 1761 cc 16-valve models

96 Refit the tensioner and idler pulleys and secure with the retaining bolts.

97 Relocate and tension the timing belt as described in Section 7. If removed, refit the engine right-hand mounting as described in Section 18.

Tensioner pulleys - 1998 cc 16-valve models

98 Refit the rear tensioner pulley to its mounting stud, and fit the retaining bolt. Align the front pulley backplate with its holes, and refit both its retaining bolts. Tighten all retaining bolts finger-tight only, so that both tensioners are free to pivot.

99 Tension the timing belt as described in paragraphs 81 to 90 of Section 7.

100 Once the belt is correctly tensioned, refit the timing belt cover as described in Section 6.

9 Camshaft oil seal(s) - renewal

Note: *If the camshaft oil seal is to be renewed with the timing belt still in place, check first that the belt is free from oil contamination. (Renew the belt as a matter of course if signs of oil contamination are found; see Section 7.) Cover the belt, to protect it from contamination by oil while work is in progress. If the timing belt is removed, ensure that all traces of oil are removed from the area before the belt is refitted.*

1 Remove the camshaft sprocket(s) as described in Section 8.

2 Punch or drill two small holes opposite each other in the oil seal. Screw a self-tapping screw into each, and pull on the screws with pliers to extract the seal.

3 Clean the seal housing, and polish off any burrs or raised edges, which may have caused the seal to fail in the first place.

4 Lubricate the lips of the new seal with clean engine oil, and drive it into position until it seats on its locating shoulder. Use a suitable tubular drift, such as a socket, which bears only on the hard outer edge of the seal. Take care not to damage the seal lips during fitting. Note that the seal lips should face inwards.

5 Refit the camshaft sprocket(s) as described in Section 8.

10 Camshaft(s) and followers - removal, inspection and refitting

Removal

1 Disconnect the battery negative terminal, and remove the cylinder head cover as described in Section 4. Proceed as described under the relevant sub-heading.

1761 cc 16-valve models

2 Refer to Section 8 and remove both camshaft sprockets together with their hubs, and also remove the timing belt tensioner pulley.

3 Remove the timing belt upper (inner) cover as described in Section 6.

4 Progressively slacken, a little at a time, the twelve bolts securing each camshaft bearing housing to the cylinder head. Release the bearing housings from their dowels and cylinder head locations. When each housing is free, remove the bolts and washers completely, and lift off the bearing housings.

5 As both camshafts are identical, suitably mark them "inlet" and "exhaust", or "front" and "rear" before removal.

6 Tilt the camshafts by pressing them down at their transmission end to release the centralising bearing at the timing belt end.

10.23 Working as described in the text, unscrew the retaining nuts . . .

Carefully lift the camshafts up and out of their locations, and slide the oil seal off each camshaft end.

7 Obtain sixteen small, clean plastic containers, and number them inlet 1 to 8 and exhaust 1 to 8; alternatively, divide a larger container into sixteen compartments, and number each compartment accordingly. Using a rubber sucker, withdraw each hydraulic tappet in turn, and place it in its respective container. Do not interchange the tappets, or the rate of wear will be much-increased.

1998 cc 16-valve models

8 Remove the vacuum pump from the left-hand end of the cylinder head, as described in Chapter 9.

9 Remove both camshaft sprockets as described in Section 8.

10 Undo the six bolts securing the inner timing belt cover to the side of the cylinder head, and remove the cover from the engine.

11 Carefully ease the oil supply pipe out from the top of the camshaft bearing caps, and remove it. Note the O-ring seals fitted to each of the pipe unions.

12 The camshaft bearing caps should be numbered 1 to 5, number 1 being at the transmission end of the engine. If not, make identification marks on the caps, using white paint or a suitable marker pen.

13 Working in the *reverse* of the sequence shown in illustration 10.45, evenly and progressively slacken the camshaft bearing cap retaining screws by one turn at a time. This will relieve the valve spring pressure on the bearing caps gradually and evenly. Once the pressure has been relieved, the bolts can be fully unscrewed and removed.

14 Lift off the bearing caps, noting the correct fitted location of the locating dowels. If the dowels are a loose fit, remove them and store them with the bearing caps for safe-keeping.

15 Lift the camshafts out of the cylinder head, and slide the oil seals off the camshaft ends. The inlet camshaft can be identified by the braking system vacuum pump drive slot in its left-hand end; therefore, there is no need to mark the camshafts for identification.

10.24 . . . and remove the camshaft bearing caps . . .

16 Obtain sixteen small, clean plastic containers, and number them 1 to 16. Using a rubber sucker, withdraw each cam follower in turn, invert it to prevent oil loss, and place it in its respective container. The container should then be filled with clean engine oil. Do not interchange the cam followers, or the rate of wear will be much-increased. Do not allow them to lose oil, or the hydraulic tappet mechanism will take a long time to refill with oil on restarting the engine, resulting in incorrect valve clearances.

All other models

17 Remove the camshaft sprocket as described in Section 8.

18 On models with a distributor, remove the distributor as described in Chapter 5.

19 On models with a static (distributorless) ignition system, remove the ignition HT coil as described in Chapter 5.

20 With the distributor or coil removed (as applicable), slacken the upper bolt securing the thermostat housing to the left-hand end of the cylinder head. Remove the bolt, along with its sealing washer. This is necessary since the bolt screws into the left-hand (No 1) camshaft bearing cap.

21 Carefully ease the oil supply pipe out from the top of the camshaft bearing caps, and remove it. Note the O-ring seals fitted to each of the pipe unions.

22 The camshaft bearing caps should be numbered 1 to 5, number 1 being at the transmission end of the engine. If not, make identification marks on the caps, using white paint or a suitable marker pen. Also mark each cap in some way to indicate its correct fitted orientation. This will avoid the possibility of installing the caps the wrong way around on refitting.

23 Evenly and progressively slacken the camshaft bearing cap retaining nuts by one turn at a time. This will relieve the valve spring pressure on the bearing caps gradually and evenly. Once the pressure has been relieved, the nuts can be fully unscrewed and removed **(see illustration)**.

24 Note the correct fitted orientation of the bearing caps, then remove them from cylinder head **(see illustration)**.

25 Lift the camshaft away from the cylinder

2B

10.25 . . . then lift the camshaft away from the cylinder head

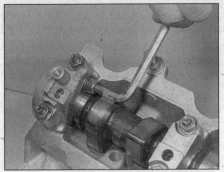

10.30a On early 1580 cc and 1905 cc models, slacken the retaining bolt . . .

10.30b . . . and remove the camshaft thrust fork from the bearing cap

head, and slide the oil seal off the camshaft end **(see illustration)**.

26 Obtain eight small, clean plastic containers, and number them 1 to 8; alternatively, divide a larger container into eight compartments. Using a rubber sucker, withdraw each follower in turn, and place it in its respective container. Do not interchange the cam followers, or the rate of wear will be much-increased. If necessary, also remove the shim from the top of the valve stem, and store it with its respective follower. Note that the shim may stick to the inside of the follower as it is withdrawn. If this happens, take care not to allow it to drop out as the follower is removed.

Inspection

27 Examine the camshaft bearing surfaces and cam lobes for signs of wear ridges and scoring. Renew the camshaft if any of these conditions are apparent. Examine the condition of the bearing surfaces, both on the camshaft journals and in the cylinder head/bearing caps. If the head bearing surfaces are worn excessively, the cylinder head will need to be renewed. If suitable measuring equipment is available, camshaft bearing journal wear can be checked by direct measurement (where the necessary specifications have been quoted by Citroën), noting that No 1 journal is at the transmission end of the head.

28 Examine the cam follower bearing surfaces which contact the camshaft lobes for wear ridges and scoring. Renew any follower on which these conditions are apparent. If a follower bearing surface is badly scored, also examine the corresponding lobe on the camshaft for wear, as it is likely that both will be worn. Renew worn components as necessary.

29 On 16-valve models, if the engine's valve clearances have sounded noisy, particularly if the noise persists after initial start-up from cold, there is reason to suspect a faulty hydraulic tappet mechanism. Only a good mechanic experienced in these engines can tell whether the noise level is typical, or if renewal of one or more of the tappets is warranted. If a faulty hydraulic tappet is diagnosed and the engine's service history is

unknown, it is always worth trying the effect of renewing the engine oil and filter before going to the expense of renewing any of the cam followers. Use only *good-quality* engine oil of the recommended viscosity and specification (Chapter 1). It is not possible to overhaul the hydraulic tappet mechanism, so if any tappet's operation is faulty, it must be renewed.

30 On earlier 1580 cc and 1905 cc models, inspect the camshaft thrust fork (fitted to the side of No 5 camshaft bearing cap) for signs of wear or scoring, and if necessary renew it **(see illustrations)**. The fork is retained by a single bolt; on refitting, ensure that the bolt is securely tightened. On later models, the thrust fork is no longer fitted, and the camshaft endfloat is controlled by the camshaft bearing cap.

Refitting

1761 cc 16-valve models

31 Before refitting, remove all traces of oil from the bearing housing retaining bolt holes in the cylinder head, using a clean rag. Also ensure that both the cylinder head and bearing housing mating faces are clean and free from oil.

32 Liberally oil the cylinder head hydraulic tappet bores and the tappets. Carefully refit the tappets to the cylinder head, ensuring that each tappet is refitted to its original bore. Some care will be required to enter the tappets squarely into their bores. Check that each tappet rotates freely in its bore.

33 Liberally oil the camshaft bearings in the cylinder head and the camshaft lobes, then refit the camshafts to the cylinder head. Turn the camshafts so that the groove at the timing belt end of each camshaft is positioned as follows:

Exhaust camshaft groove positioned at 12 o'clock (vertical).
Inlet camshaft groove at 11 o'clock (opposite locking tool hole).

34 Ensure that the four locating dowels are in position, one at each corner of the cylinder head.

35 Apply a bead of silicone-based jointing compound around the perimeter of the mating

faces and around the retaining bolt hole locations.

36 Liberally oil the camshaft bearings, and carefully locate the bearing housings over the camshafts. Refit the retaining bolts, ensuring that each has a washer under its head.

37 Working in the order shown, progressively tighten the bearing housing retaining bolts to the Stage 1 torque setting, then to the Stage 2 setting **(see illustration)**.

38 Refit the timing belt upper (inner) cover as described in Section 6.

39 Refit the timing belt tensioner pulley as described in Section 8.

40 Refit the camshaft covers as described in Section 4.

41 Fit a new camshaft oil seal(s), using the information given in Section 9, then refit the camshaft sprocket(s) and hub(s) as described in Section 8.

1998 cc 16-valve models

42 Liberally oil the cylinder head cam follower bores and the followers. Note that, if new followers are being fitted, they must be charged with oil before installation by placing them in a bath of clean engine oil and "working" them. Carefully refit the followers to the cylinder head, ensuring that each follower

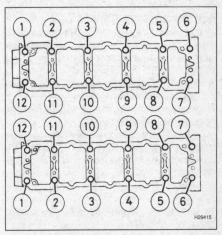

10.37 Camshaft bearing housing retaining bolt tightening sequence - 1761 cc 16-valve models

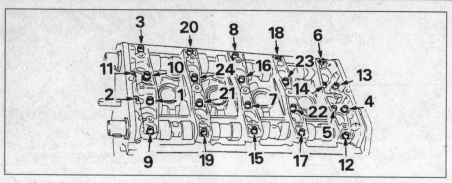

10.45 Camshaft bearing cap bolt tightening sequence - 1998 cc 16-valve models

10.46 Take care not to displace the O-rings when refitting the oil supply pipe to the camshaft bearing caps

is refitted to its original bore, where applicable. Some care will be required to enter the followers squarely into their bores.

43 Liberally oil the camshaft bearings and lobes, then refit the camshafts to the cylinder head. Temporarily refit the Woodruff keys and sprockets to the end of each camshaft. Set each camshaft so that its sprocket timing hole is aligned with the corresponding cutout in the cylinder head. Also ensure that the crankshaft is still locked in position (see Section 3).

44 Ensure that the bearing cap locating dowels are pressed firmly into their recesses. Check that the mating surfaces are completely clean, unmarked and free from oil. Refit the bearing caps, using the identification marks noted on removal to ensure that each is installed correctly and in its original location.

45 Working in the sequence shown, progressively tighten the camshaft bearing cap bolts by one turn at a time, until the caps touch the cylinder head evenly. Go round again, working in the same sequence, and tighten all the bolts to the specified torque setting **(see illustration)**. Work only as described, to impose the pressure of the valve springs gradually and evenly on the bearing caps.

46 Examine the oil supply pipe union O-rings for signs of damage or deterioration, and renew as necessary. Check that the supply pipe oil spray holes are clear, unblocking them with a pin if necessary. Apply a smear of clean engine oil to the O-rings. Ease the pipe assembly into position in the top of the bearing caps, taking great care not to displace the O-rings **(see illustration)**.

47 Refit the inner timing belt cover to the side of the cylinder head, and tighten its retaining bolts to the specified torque.

48 Fit two new camshaft oil seals using the information given in Section 7, then refit the camshaft sprockets as described in Section 8.

49 Refit the vacuum pump as described in Chapter 9.

50 Refit the cylinder head cover as described in Section 4, and reconnect the battery negative terminal.

All other models

51 Where removed, refit each shim to the top of its original valve stem. *Do not* interchange

the shims, as this will upset the valve clearances (see Section 11).

52 Liberally oil the cylinder head cam follower bores and the followers. Carefully refit the followers to the cylinder head, ensuring that each follower is refitted to its original bore. Some care will be required to enter the followers squarely into their bores.

53 Liberally oil the camshaft bearings and lobes, then refit the camshaft to the cylinder head. Temporarily refit the sprocket to the end of the shaft, and position it so that the sprocket timing hole is aligned with the corresponding cutout in the cylinder head. Also ensure that the crankshaft is still locked in position (see Section 3).

54 Ensure that the bearing cap and head mating surfaces are completely clean, unmarked, and free from oil. Refit the bearing caps, using the identification marks noted on removal to ensure that each is installed correctly and in its original location.

55 Evenly and progressively tighten the camshaft bearing cap nuts by one turn at a time until the caps touch the cylinder head. Then go round again and tighten all the nuts to the specified torque setting. Work only as described, to impose the pressure of the valve springs gradually and evenly on the bearing caps.

56 Examine the oil supply pipe union O-rings for signs of damage or deterioration, and renew as necessary. Apply a smear of clean engine oil to the O-rings. Ease the pipe into position in the top of the bearing caps, taking great care not to displace the O-rings.

57 Examine the sealing washer for signs of damage or deterioration, and renew it if necessary. Refit the upper retaining bolt to the thermostat housing, tightening it to the specified torque setting.

58 On models with a distributor, refit the distributor as described in Chapter 5.

59 On models with a static (distributorless) ignition system, refit the ignition HT coil as described in Chapter 5.

60 Fit a new camshaft oil seal, using the information given in Section 7, then refit the camshaft sprocket as described in Section 8.

61 Refit the cylinder head cover as described in Section 4, and reconnect the battery negative terminal.

11 Valve clearances - checking and adjustment

Checking

16-valve models

1 On 1998 cc 16-valve models, the valve clearances are automatically adjusted by the hydraulic tappet mechanism fitted to each cam follower. Therefore it is not necessary, or indeed possible, to check or adjust the valve clearances manually. If the valve gear has become noisy, a faulty tappet mechanism should be suspected. Refer to paragraph 29 of Section 10 for further information.

All other models

2 On these models, the importance of having the valve clearances correctly adjusted cannot be overstressed, as they vitally affect the performance of the engine. Checking should not be regarded as a routine operation, however. It should only be necessary when the valve gear has become noisy, after engine overhaul, or when trying to trace the cause of power loss. The clearances are checked as follows. The engine must be cold for the check to be accurate.

3 Apply the handbrake, then jack up the front of the car and support it on axle stands. Remove the right-hand front roadwheel.

4 From underneath the front of the car, prise out the two retaining clips, and remove the plastic cover from the wing valance to gain access to the crankshaft sprocket bolt. Where necessary, unclip the coolant hoses from the bracket to improve access further.

5 The engine can now be turned over using a suitable socket and extension bar fitted to the crankshaft pulley bolt.

6 Remove the cylinder head cover as described in Section 4.

7 Draw the outline of the engine on a piece of paper, numbering the cylinders 1 to 4, with No 1 cylinder at the transmission end of the engine. Show the position of each valve, together with the specified valve clearance (see paragraph 11). Above each valve, draw

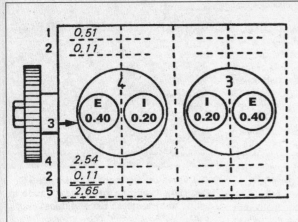

11.7 Example of valve shim thickness calculation

I Inlet
E Exhaust
1 Measured clearance
2 Difference between 1 and 3
3 Specified clearance
4 Thickness of original shim fitted
5 Thickness of new shim required

11.9 Measuring a valve clearance using a feeler gauge

2B

two lines for noting (1) the actual clearance and (2) the amount of adjustment required **(see illustration)**.

8 Turn the crankshaft until the inlet valve of No 1 cylinder (nearest the transmission end) is fully closed, with the tip of the cam facing directly away from the cam follower.

9 Using feeler gauges, measure the clearance between the base of the cam and the follower **(see illustration)**. Record the clearance on line (1).

10 Repeat the measurement for the other seven valves, turning the crankshaft as necessary so that the cam lobe in question is always facing directly away from the relevant follower.

11 Calculate the difference between each measured clearance and the desired value, and record it on line (2). Since the clearance is different for inlet and exhaust valves, make sure that you are aware which valve you are dealing with. The valve sequence from either end of the engine is:

Ex - In - In - Ex - Ex - In - In - Ex

12 If all the clearances are within tolerance, refit the cylinder head cover with reference to Section 4. Clip the coolant hoses into position (if removed) and refit the plastic cover to the wing valance.

13 Refit the roadwheel, and lower the vehicle to the ground.

14 If any clearance measured is outside the specified tolerance, adjustment must be carried out as described in the following paragraphs.

Adjustment

15 Remove the camshaft as described in Section 10.

16 Withdraw the first follower from the cylinder head, and recover the shim from the top of the valve stem. Note that the shim may stick to the inside of the follower as it is withdrawn. If this happens, take care not to allow it to drop out as the follower is removed. Remove all traces of oil from the shim, and measure its thickness with a micrometer **(see illustrations)**. The shims usually carry

thickness markings, but wear may have reduced the original thickness.

17 Refer to the clearance recorded for the valve concerned. If the clearance was more than that specified, the shim thickness must be *increased* by the difference recorded (2). If the clearance was less than that specified, the thickness of the shim must be *decreased* by the difference recorded (2).

18 Draw three more lines beneath each valve on the calculation paper, as shown in **illustration 11.7**. On line (4), note the measured thickness of the shim, then add or deduct the difference from line (2) to give the final shim thickness required on line (5).

19 Shims are available in thicknesses between 2.225 mm and 3.550 mm, in steps of 0.025 mm. Clean new shims before measuring or fitting them.

20 Repeat the procedure given in paragraphs 16 to 18 on the remaining valves, keeping each follower identified for position.

21 When reassembling, oil the shim, and fit it on the valve stem with the size marking face downwards. Oil the follower, and lower it onto the shim. Do not raise the follower after fitting, as the shim may become dislodged.

22 When all the followers are in position, complete with their shims, refit the camshaft as described in Section 10. Recheck the valve

clearances before refitting the cylinder head cover, to make sure they are correct.

12 Cylinder head - removal and refitting

Removal

1 Disconnect the battery negative lead.

2 Drain the cooling system as described in Chapter 1.

3 Align the engine assembly/valve timing holes as described in Section 3, locking both the camshaft sprocket and crankshaft pulley in position, and proceed as described under the relevant sub-heading. *Do not* attempt to rotate the engine whilst the pins are in position.

1580 cc and 1905 cc models

4 Remove the cylinder head cover as described in Section 4, and remove the air cleaner mounting bracket from the rear of cylinder head.

5 Note that the following text assumes that the cylinder head will be removed with both inlet and exhaust manifolds attached; this is easier, but makes it a bulky and heavy assembly to handle. If it is wished first to

11.16a Lift out the follower and remove the shim (arrowed)

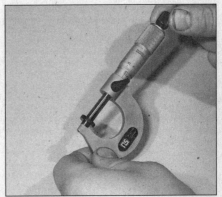

11.16b Using a micrometer to measure shim thickness

remove the manifolds, proceed as described in Chapter 4.

6 Working as described in Chapter 4, disconnect the exhaust system front pipe from the manifold. Where necessary, disconnect or release the lambda sensor wiring, so that it is not strained by the weight of the exhaust.

7 Disconnect the following from the throttle body/housing and inlet manifold, as described in Chapter 4:

(a) *Depressurise the fuel system, and disconnect the fuel feed and return hoses. Plug all openings, to prevent loss of fuel and the entry of dirt into the system.*

(b) *Disconnect the accelerator cable.*

(c) *Disconnect the vacuum servo unit vacuum hose, coolant hose and all the other relevant vacuum/breather hoses, from the inlet manifold and throttle body/housing.*

(d) *Undo the retaining nut, and position the oil filler neck clear of the inlet manifold.*

(e) *On 1580 cc models, disconnect the three electrical connector plugs from the throttle body.*

(f) *On 1905 cc models, disconnect the wiring connectors from the throttle potentiometer and the fuel injectors, and free the wiring loom from the manifold.*

8 Slacken the retaining clips, and disconnect the coolant hoses from the thermostat housing (on the left-hand end of the cylinder head).

9 Depress the retaining clip(s), and disconnect the wiring connector(s) from the electrical switch(es) and/or sensor(s) which are screwed into the thermostat housing, or into the left-hand end of the cylinder head (as appropriate).

10 Slacken and remove the bolt securing the engine oil dipstick to the rear of the cylinder head, and withdraw the tube from the cylinder block.

11 On early (pre-1992) models with a semi-automatic timing belt tensioner, release the tensioner and disengage the timing belt from the camshaft sprocket as described in paragraphs 3 to 6 of Section 8.

12 On later (1992-on) models with a manually-adjusted tensioner pulley, release the tensioner and disengage the timing belt from the camshaft sprocket as described in paragraphs 9 and 10 of Section 8.

13 Place a jack beneath the engine, with a block of wood on the jack head. Raise the jack until it is supporting the weight of the engine.

14 Slacken and remove the three nuts securing the engine/transmission right-hand mounting bracket to the engine bracket. Remove the single nut securing the bracket to the mounting rubber, and lift off the bracket. Undo the three bolts securing the engine bracket to the end of the cylinder head/block, and remove the bracket.

15 On 1905 cc models with a distributor, disconnect the wiring connector from the ignition HT coil. If the cylinder head is to be dismantled for overhaul, remove the distributor as described in the relevant Sections of Chapter 5. Disconnect the HT leads from the spark plugs, and remove the distributor cap and lead assembly. If the cylinder numbers are not already marked on the HT leads, number each lead, to avoid the possibility of the leads being incorrectly connected on refitting.

16 On models with a static (distributorless) ignition system, disconnect the wiring connector from the ignition HT coil. If the cylinder head is to be dismantled for overhaul, remove the ignition HT coil as described in Chapter 5. Note that the HT leads should be disconnected from the spark plugs instead of the coil, and the coil and leads removed as an assembly. If the cylinder numbers are not already marked on the HT leads, number each lead, to avoid the possibility of the leads being incorrectly connected on refitting.

17 Working in the *reverse* of the sequence shown in illustration 12.71, progressively slacken the ten cylinder head bolts by half a turn at a time, until all bolts can be unscrewed by hand. Remove the bolts along with their washers, noting the correct location of the spacer fitted to the right-hand rear bolt (as viewed from the driver's seat - bolt 10 in illustration 12.71).

18 With all the cylinder head bolts removed, the joint between the cylinder head and gasket and the cylinder block/crankcase must now be broken without disturbing the wet liners. Although these liners are better-located and sealed than some wet-liner engines, there is still a risk of coolant and foreign matter leaking into the sump if the cylinder head is lifted carelessly. If care is not taken and the liners are moved, there is also a possibility of the bottom seals being disturbed, causing leakage after refitting the head.

19 To break the joint, obtain two L-shaped metal bars which fit into the cylinder head bolt holes, and gently "rock" the cylinder head free towards the front of the car (see Part A, Section 10, illustration 10.23). *Do not* try to swivel the head on the cylinder block/crankcase; it is located by dowels, as well as by the tops of the liners.

20 When the joint is broken, lift the cylinder head away. Seek assistance if possible, as it is a heavy assembly, especially if it is complete with the manifolds. Remove the gasket from the top of the block, noting the two locating dowels. If the locating dowels are a loose fit, remove them and store them with the head for safe-keeping. Do not discard the gasket; it will be needed for identification purposes (see paragraphs 63 and 64).

21 *Do not* attempt to turn the crankshaft with the cylinder head removed, otherwise the wet liners may be displaced. Operations that require the crankshaft to be turned (eg cleaning the piston crowns), should only be carried out once the cylinder liners are firmly clamped in position.

TOOL TiP

Cylinder liners can be clamped in position using large flat washers positioned underneath suitable-length bolts. Alternatively, the original head bolts could be temporarily refitted, with suitable spacers fitted to their shanks.

22 If the cylinder head is to be dismantled for overhaul, remove the camshaft as described in Section 10, then refer to Part C of this Chapter.

1761 cc 8-valve models

23 Remove the cylinder head cover as described in Section 4.

24 Remove the air cleaner-to-throttle housing duct as described in Chapter 4.

25 Note that the following text assumes that the cylinder head will be removed with both inlet and exhaust manifolds attached; this is easier, but makes it a bulky and heavy assembly to handle. If it is wished first to remove the manifolds, proceed as described in Chapter 4.

26 Working as described in Chapter 4, disconnect the exhaust system front pipe from the manifold. Where necessary, disconnect or release the lambda sensor wiring, so that it is not strained by the weight of the exhaust.

27 Carry out the following operations as described in Chapter 4:

(a) *Depressurise the fuel system, and disconnect the fuel feed and return hoses. Plug all openings, to prevent loss of fuel and the entry of dirt into the system.*

(b) *Disconnect the accelerator cable.*

(c) *Disconnect the vacuum servo unit vacuum hose, and all the other relevant vacuum/breather hoses, from the inlet manifold and throttle housing. Release the hoses from the retaining clips on the manifold.*

(d) *Disconnect all the electrical connector plugs from the throttle housing.*

(e) *Disconnect the wiring connectors from the fuel injectors, and free the wiring loom from the manifold.*

(f) *Remove the idle speed auxiliary air valve.*

28 Slacken the retaining clips, and disconnect the coolant hoses from the thermostat housing (on the left-hand end of the cylinder head).

29 Depress the retaining clip(s), and disconnect the wiring connector(s) from the electrical switch(es) and/or sensor(s) which are screwed into the thermostat housing, or into the left-hand end of the cylinder head (as appropriate).

30 Slacken and remove the bolt securing the engine oil dipstick tube to the left-hand end of the cylinder head, and withdraw the tube from the cylinder block.

31 Disconnect the wiring connector from the ignition HT coil. If the cylinder head is to be dismantled for overhaul, remove the ignition HT coil as described in Chapter 5. Note that the HT leads should be disconnected from the spark plugs instead of the coil, and the coil and leads removed as an assembly. If the cylinder numbers are not already marked on the HT leads, number each lead, to avoid the possibility of the leads being incorrectly connected on refitting.

32 Remove the cylinder head as described above in paragraphs 17 to 22.

1761 cc 16-valve models

33 Remove the air cleaner assembly and inlet ducting as described in Chapter 4.

34 Remove the cylinder head covers as described in Section 4.

35 Remove the inlet manifold as described in Chapter 4.

36 Working as described in Chapter 4, disconnect the exhaust downpipe from the manifold. Where necessary, disconnect or release the lambda sensor wiring, so that it is not strained by the weight of the exhaust.

37 Lift out the wire clip and disconnect the radiator hose from the coolant outlet elbow.

38 Disconnect all remaining vacuum/breather hoses, electrical connector plugs and wiring from the cylinder head.

39 Release the timing belt tensioner and disengage the timing belt from the camshaft sprockets as described in Section 8.

40 Working in the *reverse* of the tightening sequence, progressively slacken the ten cylinder head bolts by half a turn at a time, until all bolts can be unscrewed by hand.

41 Remove all the bolts, along with their washers, from the cylinder head.

42 With all the cylinder head bolts removed, lift the cylinder head away. Seek assistance if possible, as it is a heavy assembly.

43 Remove the gasket from the top of the block, noting the two locating dowels. If the locating dowels are a loose fit, remove them and store them with the head for safe-keeping.

44 If the cylinder head is to be dismantled for overhaul, remove the camshafts as described in Section 10, then refer to the relevant Sections of Part C of this Chapter.

1998 cc 8-valve models

45 Carry out the operations described in paragraphs 23 to 31. Note that there is no idle speed auxiliary air valve, and that the dipstick tube is mounted onto the side of the inlet manifold.

46 Working in the *reverse* of the sequence shown in illustration 12.71, progressively slacken the ten cylinder head bolts by half a turn at a time, until all bolts can be unscrewed by hand.

47 Remove all the bolts, along with their

washers, and discard them; the bolts and washers must be renewed as a matter of course.

48 With all the cylinder head bolts removed, lift the cylinder head away. Seek assistance if possible, as it is a heavy assembly.

49 Remove the gasket from the top of the block, noting the two locating dowels. If the locating dowels are a loose fit, remove them and store them with the head for safe-keeping.

50 If the cylinder head is to be dismantled for overhaul, remove the camshaft as described in Section 10, then refer to the relevant Sections of Part C of this Chapter.

1998 cc 16-valve models

51 Remove the camshafts as described in Section 10.

52 Remove the exhaust manifold, and the inlet manifold and ACAV assembly, as described in Chapter 4.

53 Slacken the retaining clips, and disconnect the coolant hoses from the thermostat housing (on the left-hand end of the cylinder head).

54 Depress the retaining clip(s), and disconnect the wiring connector(s) from the electrical switch(es) and/or sensor(s) which are screwed into the coolant outlet housing on the left-hand end of the cylinder head.

55 Slacken and remove the bolt securing the engine oil dipstick tube to the rear of the cylinder head, and withdraw the tube from the cylinder block.

56 Working in the *reverse* of the sequence shown in illustration 12.71, progressively slacken the ten cylinder head bolts by half a turn at a time, until all bolts can be unscrewed by hand. Remove all the bolts, along with their washers, and discard them; the bolts and washers must be renewed as a matter of course.

57 With all the cylinder head bolts removed, lift the cylinder head away. Seek assistance if possible, as it is a heavy assembly. Note that, on right-hand drive models, there is limited clearance between the top of the head and the braking system master cylinder, so take care not to damage the master cylinder reservoir as the head is lifted clear.

58 Remove the gasket from the top of the block, noting the two locating dowels. If the locating dowels are a loose fit, remove them and store them with the head for safe-keeping.

59 Refer to Part C of this Chapter for cylinder head overhaul information.

Preparation for refitting

60 The mating faces of the cylinder head and cylinder block/crankcase must be perfectly clean before refitting the head. Use a hard plastic or wooden scraper to remove all traces of gasket and carbon; also clean the piston crowns. On 1580 cc, 1761 cc and 1905 cc engines, refer to paragraph 21 before turning the engine. Take particular care on these

models, as the soft aluminium alloy is easily damaged. On all models, make sure that the carbon is not allowed to enter the oil and water passages - this is particularly important for the lubrication system, as carbon could block the oil supply to the engine's components. Using adhesive tape and paper, seal the water, oil and bolt holes in the cylinder block/crankcase. To prevent carbon entering the gap between the pistons and bores, smear a little grease in the gap. After cleaning each piston, use a small brush to remove all traces of grease and carbon from the gap, then wipe away the remainder with a clean rag. Clean all the pistons in the same way.

61 Check the mating surfaces of the cylinder block/crankcase and the cylinder head for nicks, deep scratches and other damage. If slight, they may be removed carefully with a file, but if excessive, machining may be the only alternative to renewal. If warpage of the cylinder head gasket surface is suspected, use a straight-edge to check it for distortion. Refer to Part C of this Chapter if necessary.

62 On 1580 cc, 1761 cc and 1905 cc models, check the cylinder liner protrusion as described in Part C of this Chapter, Section 12.

Cylinder head gasket and head bolt information

63 When purchasing a new cylinder head gasket, it is essential that a gasket of the correct thickness is obtained. On some models only one thickness of gasket is available, so this is not a problem. However on other models, there are two different thicknesses available - the standard gasket which is fitted at the factory, and a slightly thicker "repair" gasket (+ 0.2 mm), for use once the head gasket face has been machined. If the cylinder head has been machined, it should have the letter "R" stamped adjacent to the No 3 exhaust port, and the gasket should also have the letter "R" stamped adjacent to No 3 cylinder on its front upper face. The gaskets can also be identified as described in the following paragraph, using the cut-outs on the left-hand end of the gasket.

64 With the gasket fitted the correct way up on the cylinder block, there will be either a single hole, or a series of holes, punched in the tab on the left-hand end of the gasket. The standard (1.2 mm) gasket has only one hole punched in it; the slightly thicker (1.4 mm) gasket has either two or three holes punched in it, depending on its manufacturer. Identify the gasket type, and ensure the new gasket obtained is of the correct thickness. If there is any doubt as to which gasket is fitted, take the old gasket along to your Citroën dealer, and have the dealer confirm the gasket type.

65 Check the condition of the cylinder head bolts, and particularly their threads, whenever they are removed. Wash the bolts in a suitable solvent, and wipe them dry. Check each bolt for any sign of visible wear or damage,

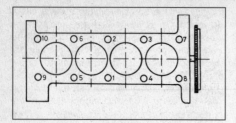

12.71 Cylinder head bolt tightening sequence

renewing them if necessary. Measure the length of each bolt (without the washer fitted, where applicable) from the underside of its head to the end of the bolt, to check for stretching (although this is not a conclusive test, in the event that all ten bolts have stretched by the same amount). On 1998 cc 8-valve and 16-valve engines, the cylinder head bolts must be renewed whenever they are disturbed. On 1761 cc 16-valve engines, the bolts may be re-used providing their maximum length does not exceed 160.0 mm. On all other engines a maximum length dimension is not specified by Citroën, however, considering the stress which the cylinder head bolts are under, it is recommended that they are renewed, regardless of their apparent condition.

Refitting

66 Wipe clean the mating surfaces of the cylinder head and cylinder block/crankcase. Check that the two locating dowels are in position at each end of the cylinder block/crankcase surface. Where applicable, remove the cylinder liner clamps.

67 Position a new gasket on the cylinder block/crankcase surface, ensuring that its identification holes are at the left-hand end of the gasket.

1580 cc and 1905 cc models

68 Check that the crankshaft pulley and camshaft sprocket are still locked in position with their respective pins. With the aid of an assistant, carefully refit the cylinder head assembly to the block, aligning it with the locating dowels.

69 Apply a smear of grease to the threads, and to the underside of the heads, of the cylinder head bolts. Citroën recommend the use of Molykote G10 grease (available from your Citroën dealer); in the absence of the specified grease, any good-quality high-melting-point grease may be used.

70 Carefully enter each bolt and washer into its relevant hole (*do not drop it in*) and screw it in finger-tight, not forgetting to fit the spacer to the right-hand rear bolt.

71 Working progressively and in the sequence shown, tighten the cylinder head bolts to their stage 1 torque setting, using a torque wrench and suitable socket **(see illustration)**.

72 Once all the bolts have been tightened to their stage 1 torque setting, fully slacken all

the head bolts, working in the reverse of the tightening sequence. Once the bolts are loose, tighten all bolts to their stage 2 specified torque setting, again following the specified sequence.

73 With all the bolts tightened to their stage 2 setting, working again in the specified sequence, angle-tighten the bolts through the specified stage 3 angle, using a socket and extension bar. It is recommended that an angle-measuring gauge is used during this stage of tightening, to ensure accuracy. If a gauge is not available, use white paint to make alignment marks between the bolt head and cylinder head prior to tightening; the marks can then be used to check that the bolt has rotated sufficiently.

74 Once the cylinder head bolts are correctly tightened, reconnect the wiring connector to the ignition HT coil. Otherwise, if the head was stripped for overhaul, refit the HT coil or distributor (as applicable), as described in Chapter 5.

75 Fit the timing belt over the camshaft sprocket. Refit the mounting bracket to the end of the cylinder head, and securely tighten its retaining bolts. Refit the engine right-hand mounting bracket, and tighten its retaining nuts to the specified torque. The jack can then be removed from underneath the engine.

76 On early (pre-1992) models with a semi-automatic timing belt tensioner, refit and tension the timing belt as described in paragraphs 52 to 56 of Section 8.

77 On later (1992-on) models with a manually-adjusted belt tensioner pulley, refit the belt to the camshaft sprocket as described in paragraphs 52 and 53 of Section 8. Tension the belt as described in paragraphs 38 to 43 of Section 7.

78 The remainder of the refitting procedure is a reversal of removal, noting the following points:

(a) *Ensure that all wiring is correctly routed, and that all connectors are securely reconnected to the correct components.*

(b) *Ensure that the coolant hoses are correctly reconnected, and that their retaining clips are securely tightened.*

(c) *Ensure that all vacuum/breather hoses are correctly reconnected.*

(d) *Refit the cylinder head cover as described in Section 4.*

(e) *Reconnect the exhaust system to the manifold, refit the air cleaner housing and ducts, and adjust the accelerator cable, as described in Chapter 4. If the manifolds were removed, refit these as described in Chapter 4.*

(f) *On completion, refill the cooling system as described in Chapter 1, and reconnect the battery.*

1761 cc 8-valve models

79 Refit the cylinder head as described above in paragraphs 68 to 75.

80 Refit the timing belt to the camshaft sprocket as described in paragraphs 52

and 53 of Section 8, and tension the belt as described in paragraphs 38 to 43 of Section 7.

81 The remainder of the refitting procedure is a reversal of removal, noting the points made in paragraph 68.

1761 cc 16-valve models

82 Check that the crankshaft pulley and camshaft sprocket are still locked in position with their respective pins. With the aid of an assistant, carefully refit the cylinder head assembly to the block, aligning it with the locating dowels.

83 Apply a smear of grease to the threads, and to the underside of the heads, of the cylinder head bolts. Citroën recommend the use of Molykoté G Rapid Plus (available from your Citroën dealer); in the absence of the specified grease, any good-quality high-melting-point grease may be used.

84 Carefully enter each bolt and washer into its relevant hole (*do not drop it in*) and screw it in finger-tight.

85 Working progressively and in the sequence shown, tighten the cylinder head bolts to their Stage 1 torque setting, using a torque wrench and a suitable socket **(see illustration 12.71)**.

86 Once all the bolts have been tightened to their Stage 1 torque setting, fully slacken all the head bolts, working in the reverse of the tightening sequence. Once the bolts are loose, tighten all the bolts to their Stage 2 specified torque setting, again following the specified sequence.

87 With all the bolts tightened to their Stage 2 setting, working again in the specified sequence, angle-tighten the bolts through the specified Stage 3 angle, using a socket and extension bar. It is recommended that an angle-measuring gauge is used during this stage of tightening, to ensure accuracy. If a gauge is not available, use white paint to make alignment marks between the bolt head and cylinder head prior to tightening; the marks can then be used to check that the bolt has rotated sufficiently.

88 Once the cylinder head bolts are correctly tightened, refit the removed components in the reverse order of removal, noting the following points:

(a) *Fit the timing belt loosely over the sprockets. Refit the mounting bracket to the end of the cylinder head, and securely tighten its retaining bolts. Refit the engine right-hand mounting bracket, and tighten its retaining nuts to the specified torque. The jack can then be removed from underneath the engine.*

(b) *Refit the timing belt as described in Section 8, and tension the belt as described in Section 7.*

(c) *Refit the inlet manifold as described in Chapter 4.*

(d) *Ensure that all wiring is correctly routed, and that all connectors are securely reconnected to the correct components.*

(e) *Ensure that the coolant hoses are*

correctly reconnected, and that their retaining clips are securely tightened.

(f) Ensure that all vacuum/breather hoses are correctly reconnected.

(g) Refit the camshaft cover(s) as described in Section 4, and refit and reconnect the HT coil unit.

(h) Reconnect the exhaust system to the manifold, refit the air cleaner housing and ducts, and adjust the accelerator cable, as described in Chapter 4.

(i) On completion, refill the cooling system as described in Chapter 1 and reconnect the battery.

1998 cc 8-valve models

89 Refit the cylinder head as described above in paragraphs 68 to 70, noting the following points:

(a) Ensure that new head bolts and washers are used.

(b) Ignore the remark about the spacer fitted to the right-hand rear bolt.

90 Working progressively and in the sequence shown in illustration 12.71, tighten the cylinder head bolts to their stage 1 torque setting, using a torque wrench and suitable socket.

91 Once all the bolts are tightened to their stage 1 torque setting, tighten all bolts to their stage 2 specified torque setting, again following the specified sequence.

92 Working in the specified sequence, angle-tighten the bolts through the specified stage 3 angle, using a socket and extension bar, referring to the information given in paragraph 73.

93 Once the cylinder head bolts are correctly tightened, reconnect the wiring connector to the ignition HT coil. Otherwise, if the head was stripped for overhaul, refit the HT coil or distributor (as applicable), as described in Chapter 5.

94 Refit the timing belt to the camshaft sprocket as described in paragraphs 52 and 53 of Section 8, and tension the belt as described in paragraphs 38 to 43 of Section 7.

95 The remainder of the refitting procedure is a reversal of removal, noting the points made in paragraph 78.

1998 cc 16-valve models

96 Refit the cylinder head using the information given in paragraphs 89 to 92.

97 Refit the camshafts as described in Section 10.

98 The remainder of the refitting procedure is a direct reversal of removal, noting the relevant points made in paragraph 78.

13 Sump - removal and refitting

Removal

1 Disconnect the battery negative lead.

2 Drain the engine oil, then clean and refit the engine oil drain plug, tightening it securely. If

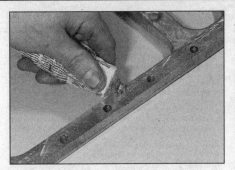

13.10a Where a sump spacer plate is fitted, apply a coat of suitable sealant to the plate upper surface . . .

the engine is nearing its service interval when the oil and filter are due for renewal, it is recommended that the filter is also removed, and a new one fitted. After reassembly, the engine can then be refilled with fresh oil. Refer to Chapter 1 for further information.

3 Apply the handbrake, jack up the front of the vehicle and support it on axle stands.

4 On models with air conditioning, where the compressor is mounted onto the side of the sump, remove the drivebelt as described in Chapter 1. Unbolt the compressor, and position it clear of the sump. Support the weight of the compressor by tying it to the vehicle, to prevent any excess strain being placed on the compressor lines. Do not disconnect the refrigerant lines from the compressor (refer to the warnings given in Chapter 3).

5 Where necessary, disconnect the wiring connector from the oil temperature sender unit, which is screwed into the sump.

6 Progressively slacken and remove all the sump retaining bolts. Since the sump bolts vary in length, remove each bolt in turn, and store it in its correct fitted order by pushing it through a clearly-marked cardboard template. This will avoid the possibility of installing the bolts in the wrong locations on refitting.

7 Break the joint by striking the sump with the palm of your hand. Lower the sump, and withdraw it from underneath the vehicle. Remove the gasket (where fitted), and discard it; a new one must be used on refitting.

8 While the sump is removed, take the opportunity to check the oil pump pick-up/strainer for signs of clogging or splitting. If necessary, remove the pump as described in Section 14, and clean or renew the strainer.

9 On some models, a large spacer plate is fitted between the sump and the base of the cylinder block/crankcase. If this plate is fitted, undo the two retaining screws from diagonally-opposite corners of the plate. Remove the plate from the base of the engine, noting which way round it is fitted.

Refitting

9 Clean all traces of sealant/gasket from the mating surfaces of the cylinder block/crankcase and sump, then use a clean rag to wipe out the sump and the engine's interior.

13.10b . . . then refit the plate to the base of the cylinder block/crankcase

10 Where a spacer plate is fitted, remove all traces of sealant/gasket from the spacer plate, then apply a thin coating of suitable sealant (see paragraph 11) to the plate upper mating surface (see illustration). Offer up the plate to the base of the cylinder block/crankcase, and securely tighten its retaining screws.

11 On models where the sump was fitted without a gasket (cast-aluminium sump), ensure that the sump mating surfaces are clean and dry, then apply a thin coating of suitable sealant to the sump mating surface. Citroën recommend the use of Auto-Joint E10 sealant (available from your Citroën dealer); in the absence of the specified sealant, any good-quality sealant may be used.

12 On models where the sump was fitted with a gasket (pressed-steel sump), ensure that all traces of the old gasket have been removed, and that the sump mating surfaces are clean and dry. Position the new gasket on the top of the sump, using a dab of grease to hold it in position.

13 Offer up the sump to the cylinder block/crankcase. Refit its retaining bolts, ensuring that each is screwed into its original location. Tighten the bolts evenly and progressively to the specified torque setting.

14 Where necessary, align the air conditioning compressor with its mountings on the sump, and insert the retaining bolts. Securely tighten the compressor retaining bolts, then refit the drivebelt as described in Chapter 1.

15 Reconnect the wiring connector to the oil temperature sensor (where fitted).

16 Lower the vehicle to the ground, then refill the engine with oil as described in Chapter 1.

14 Oil pump - removal, inspection and refitting

Removal

1 Remove the sump as described in Section 13.

2 Where necessary, undo the two retaining screws, and slide the sprocket cover off the front of the oil pump.

3 Slacken and remove the three bolts securing the oil pump to the base of the cylinder block/crankcase. Disengage the

14.3 Removing the oil pump

14.5a Remove the oil pump cover retaining bolts . . .

14.5b . . . then lift off the cover and remove the spring . . .

pump sprocket from the chain, and remove the oil pump **(see illustration)**. Where necessary, also remove the spacer plate which is fitted behind the oil pump.

Inspection

4 Examine the oil pump sprocket for signs of damage and wear, such as chipped or missing teeth. If the sprocket is worn, the pump assembly must be renewed, since the sprocket is not available separately. It is also recommended that the chain and drive sprocket, fitted to the crankshaft, be renewed at the same time. To renew the chain and drive sprocket, first remove the crankshaft timing belt sprocket as described in Section 8. Unbolt the oil seal carrier from the cylinder block. The sprocket and chain can then be slid off the end of the crankshaft. Refer to Part C for further information.

5 Slacken and remove the bolts (along with the baffle plate, where fitted) securing the strainer cover to the pump body. Lift off the strainer cover, and take off the relief valve piston and spring, noting which way round they are fitted **(see illustrations)**.

6 Examine the pump rotors and body for signs of wear ridges or scoring. If worn, the complete pump assembly must be renewed.

7 Examine the relief valve piston for signs of wear or damage, and renew if necessary. The condition of the relief valve spring can only be measured by comparing it with a new one; if there is any doubt about its condition, it should also be renewed. Both the piston and spring are available individually.

8 Thoroughly clean the oil pump strainer with a suitable solvent, and check it for signs of clogging or splitting. If the strainer is damaged, the strainer and cover assembly must be renewed.

9 Locate the relief valve spring and piston in the strainer cover. Refit the cover to the pump body, aligning the relief valve piston with its bore in the pump. Refit the baffle plate (where fitted) and the cover retaining bolts, and tighten them securely.

Refitting

10 Offer up the spacer plate (where fitted), then locate the pump sprocket with its drive chain. Seat the pump on the base of the cylinder block/crankcase. Refit the pump retaining bolts, and tighten them to the specified torque setting.

11 Where necessary, slide the sprocket cover into position on the pump. Refit its retaining bolts, tightening them securely.

12 Refit the sump as described in Section 13.

15 Oil cooler - removal and refitting

Removal

1 Firmly apply the handbrake, then jack up the front of the vehicle and support it on axle stands.

2 Drain the cooling system as described in

Chapter 1. Alternatively, clamp the oil cooler coolant hoses directly above the cooler, and be prepared for some coolant loss as the hoses are disconnected.

3 Position a suitable container beneath the oil filter. Unscrew the filter using an oil filter removal tool if necessary, and drain the oil into the container. If the oil filter is damaged or distorted during removal, it must be renewed. Given the low cost of a new oil filter relative to the cost of repairing the damage which could result if a re-used filter springs a leak, it is probably a good idea to renew the filter in any case.

4 Release the hose clips, and disconnect the coolant hoses from the oil cooler.

5 Unscrew the oil cooler/oil filter mounting bolt from the cylinder block, and withdraw the cooler. Note the locating notch in the cooler flange, which fits over the lug on the cylinder block **(see illustration)**. Discard the oil cooler sealing ring; a new one must be used on refitting.

Refitting

6 Fit a new sealing ring to the recess in the rear of the cooler, then offer the cooler to the cylinder block.

7 Ensure that the locating notch in the cooler flange is correctly engaged with the lug on the cylinder block, then refit the mounting bolt and tighten it securely.

8 Fit the oil filter, then lower the vehicle to the ground. Top-up the engine oil level as described in *"Weekly checks"*.

9 Refill or top-up the cooling system as described in *"Weekly checks"* (as applicable). Start the engine, and check the oil cooler for signs of leakage.

16 Crankshaft oil seals - renewal

Right-hand oil seal

1 Remove the crankshaft sprocket and flanged spacer as described in Section 8. Secure the timing belt clear of the working area, so that it cannot be contaminated with oil. Make a note of the correct fitted depth of the seal in its housing.

14.5c . . . and relief valve piston, noting which way round it is fitted

15.5 Oil cooler/oil filter mounting bolt (A) and locating notch (B)

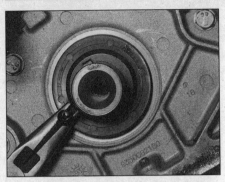

16.2 Using a self-tapping screw and pliers to remove the crankshaft oil seal

2 Punch or drill two small holes opposite each other in the seal. Screw a self-tapping screw into each, and pull on the screws with pliers to extract the seal (see illustration). Alternatively, the seal can be levered out of position. Use a flat-bladed screwdriver, and take great care not to damage the crankshaft shoulder or seal housing.
3 Clean the seal housing, and polish off any burrs or raised edges, which may have caused the seal to fail in the first place.
4 Lubricate the lips of the new seal with clean engine oil, and carefully locate the seal on the end of crankshaft. Note that its sealing lip must be facing inwards. Take care not to damage the seal lips during fitting.
5 Fit the new seal using a suitable tubular drift, such as a socket, which bears only on the hard outer edge of the seal. Tap the seal into position, to the same depth in the housing as the original was prior to removal.
6 Wash off any traces of oil, then refit the crankshaft sprocket as described in Section 8.

Left-hand oil seal

7 Remove the flywheel/driveplate as described in Section 17. Make a note of the correct fitted depth of the seal in its housing.
8 Punch or drill two small holes opposite each other in the seal. Screw a self-tapping screw into each, and pull on the screws with pliers to extract the seal.

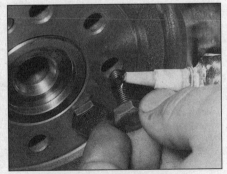

17.10 If the new flywheel bolt threads are not supplied with their threads pre-coated, apply a suitable locking compound to them . . .

9 Clean the seal housing, and polish off any burrs or raised edges, which may have caused the seal to fail in the first place.
10 Lubricate the lips of the new seal with clean engine oil, and carefully locate the seal on the end of the crankshaft.
11 Fit the new seal using a suitable tubular drift, which bears only on the hard outer edge of the seal. Drive the seal into position, to the same depth in the housing as the original was prior to removal.
12 Wash off any traces of oil, then refit the flywheel/driveplate as described in Section 17.

17 Flywheel/driveplate - removal, inspection and refitting

Removal

Flywheel (models with manual transmission)

1 Remove the transmission as described in Chapter 7A, then remove the clutch assembly as described in Chapter 6.
2 Prevent the flywheel from turning by locking the ring gear teeth with a similar arrangement to that shown in illustration 5.3 (Section 5). Alternatively, bolt a strap between the flywheel and the cylinder block/crankcase. *Do not* attempt to lock the flywheel in position using the crankshaft pulley locking pin described in Section 3.
3 Slacken and remove the flywheel retaining bolts, and remove the flywheel from the end of the crankshaft. Be careful not to drop it; it is heavy. If the flywheel locating dowel is a loose fit in the crankshaft end, remove it and store it with the flywheel for safe-keeping. Discard the flywheel bolts; new ones must be used on refitting.

Driveplate (models with automatic transmission)

4 Remove the transmission as described in Chapter 7B. Lock the driveplate as described in paragraph 2. Mark the relationship between the torque converter plate and the driveplate, and slacken all the driveplate retaining bolts.

17.12 . . . then refit the flywheel, and tighten the bolts to the specified torque

5 Remove the retaining bolts, along with the torque converter plate and the two shims (one fitted on each side of the torque converter plate). Note that the shims are of different thickness, the thicker one being on the outside of the torque converter plate. Discard the driveplate retaining bolts; new ones must be used on refitting.
6 Remove the driveplate from the end of the crankshaft. If the locating dowel is a loose fit in the crankshaft end, remove it and store it with the driveplate for safe-keeping.

Inspection

7 On models with manual transmission, examine the flywheel for scoring of the clutch face, and for wear or chipping of the ring gear teeth. If the clutch face is scored, the flywheel may be surface-ground, but renewal is preferable. Seek the advice of a Citroën dealer or engine reconditioning specialist to see if machining is possible. If the ring gear is worn or damaged, the flywheel must be renewed, as it is not possible to renew the ring gear separately.
8 On models with automatic transmission, check the torque converter driveplate carefully for signs of distortion. Look for any hairline cracks around the bolt holes or radiating outwards from the centre, and inspect the ring gear teeth for signs of wear or chipping. If any sign of wear or damage is found, the driveplate must be renewed.

Refitting

Flywheel - models with manual transmission

9 Clean the mating surfaces of the flywheel and crankshaft. Remove any remaining locking compound from the threads of the crankshaft holes, using the correct-size tap, if available.
10 If the new flywheel retaining bolts are not supplied with their threads already pre-coated, apply a suitable thread-locking compound to the threads of each bolt. Citroën recommend the use of Frenetanch E3 (available from your Citroën dealer); in the absence of this, any good-quality locking compound may be used (see illustration).
11 Ensure the locating dowel is in position. Offer up the flywheel, locating it on the dowel, and fit the new retaining bolts.
12 Lock the flywheel using the method employed on dismantling, and tighten the retaining bolts to the specified torque (see illustration).
13 Refit the clutch as described in Chapter 6. Remove the flywheel locking tool, and refit the transmission as described in Chapter 7A.

Driveplate - models with automatic transmission

14 Carry out the operations described above in paragraphs 9 and 10, substituting "driveplate" for all references to the flywheel.
15 Locate the driveplate on its locating dowel.

2B

16 Offer up the torque converter plate, with the thinner shim positioned behind the plate and the thicker shim on the outside, and align the marks made prior to removal.

17 Fit the new retaining bolts, then lock the driveplate using the method employed on dismantling. Tighten the retaining bolts to the specified torque wrench setting.

18 Remove the driveplate locking tool, and refit the transmission as described in Chapter 7B.

18 Engine/transmission mountings -
inspection and renewal

Inspection

1 If improved access is required, raise the front of the car and support it securely on axle stands.

2 Check the mounting rubber to see if it is cracked, hardened or separated from the metal at any point; renew the mounting if any such damage or deterioration is evident.

3 Check that all the mounting's fasteners are securely tightened; use a torque wrench to check if possible.

4 Using a large screwdriver or a crowbar, check for wear in the mounting by carefully levering against it to check for free play. Where this is not possible, enlist the aid of an assistant to move the engine/transmission unit back and forth, or from side to side, while you watch the mounting. While some free play is to be expected even from new components, excessive wear should be obvious. If excessive free play is found, check first that the fasteners are correctly secured, then renew any worn components as described below.

Renewal

Right-hand mounting - 1580 cc, 1761 cc 8-valve and 1905 cc models

5 Disconnect the battery negative lead. Release all the relevant hoses and wiring from their retaining clips, and position clear of the mounting so that they do not hinder the removal procedure.

6 Place a jack beneath the engine, with a block of wood on the jack head. Raise the jack until it is supporting the weight of the engine.

7 Slacken and remove the three nuts securing the right-hand mounting bracket to the engine unit. Remove the single nut securing the bracket to the mounting rubber, and lift off the bracket.

8 Lift the rubber buffer plate off the mounting rubber stud, then unscrew the mounting rubber from the body and remove it from the vehicle. If necessary, the mounting bracket can be unbolted and removed from the side of the cylinder head.

9 Check all components carefully for signs of wear or damage, and renew them where necessary.

10 On reassembly, screw the mounting rubber into the vehicle body, and tighten it securely. Where removed, refit the mounting bracket to the side of the cylinder head, and securely tighten its retaining bolts.

11 Refit the rubber buffer plate to the mounting rubber stud, and install the mounting bracket.

12 Tighten the mounting bracket retaining nuts to the specified torque setting.

13 Remove the jack from underneath the engine, and reconnect the battery negative terminal.

Right-hand mounting - 1761 cc 16-valve models

14 Disconnect the battery negative lead. Release all the relevant hoses and wiring from their retaining clips, and position clear of the mounting so that they do not hinder the removal procedure.

15 Place a jack beneath the engine, with a block of wood on the jack head. Raise the jack until it is supporting the weight of the engine.

16 Slacken and remove the nuts and bolts securing the right-hand mounting bracket to the engine. Remove the single nut securing the bracket to the mounting rubber, and lift off the bracket.

17 Lift the rubber buffer plate off the mounting rubber stud, then unscrew the mounting rubber from the body and remove it from the vehicle.

18 Check all components carefully for signs of wear or damage, and renew them where necessary.

19 On reassembly, screw the mounting rubber into the vehicle body, and tighten it securely.

20 Refit the rubber buffer plate to the mounting rubber stud, and install the mounting bracket.

21 Tighten the mounting bracket retaining nuts/bolts to the specified torque setting.

22 Remove the jack from below the engine, and reconnect the battery negative lead.

Right-hand mounting - 1998 cc 8-valve and 16-valve models

23 Disconnect the battery negative lead. Release all the relevant hoses and wiring from their retaining clips. Place the hoses/wiring clear of the mounting so that the removal procedure is not hindered.

24 Place a jack beneath the engine, with a block of wood on the jack head. Raise the jack until it is supporting the weight of the engine.

25 Undo the two bolts securing the curved mounting retaining plate to the body. Lift off the plate, and withdraw the rubber damper from the top of the mounting bracket.

26 Slacken and remove the two nuts and two bolts securing the right-hand engine/transmission mounting bracket to the engine. Remove the single nut securing the bracket

to the mounting rubber, and lift off the bracket.

27 Lift the rubber buffer plate off the mounting rubber stud, then unscrew the mounting rubber from the body and remove it from the vehicle. If necessary, the mounting bracket can be unbolted and removed from the front of the cylinder block.

28 Check all components carefully for signs of wear or damage, and renew as necessary.

29 On reassembly, screw the mounting rubber into the vehicle body, and tighten it securely. Where removed, refit the mounting bracket to the front of the cylinder block, and securely tighten its retaining bolts.

30 Refit the rubber buffer plate to the mounting rubber stud, and install the mounting bracket.

31 Tighten the mounting bracket retaining nuts to the specified torque setting, and remove the jack from underneath the engine.

32 Refit the rubber damper to the top of the mounting bracket, and refit the curved retaining plate. Tighten the retaining plate bolts to the specified torque, and reconnect the battery.

Left-hand mounting

33 Remove the battery and battery tray, as described in Chapter 5. Slacken and remove the battery support plate mounting bolts. Release the wiring from its retaining clip on the plate, and remove the plate from the engine compartment.

34 Place a jack beneath the transmission, with a block of wood on the jack head. Raise the jack until it is supporting the weight of the transmission.

35 Slacken and remove the centre nut and washer from the left-hand mounting. Undo the two bolts securing the mounting bracket assembly to the vehicle body, and remove the assembly from the mounting stud.

36 Slide the spacer off the mounting stud, then unscrew the stud from the top of the transmission housing, and remove it along with its washer. If the mounting stud is tight, a universal stud extractor can be used to unscrew it.

37 Check all components carefully for signs of wear or damage, and renew as necessary.

38 Clean the threads of the mounting stud, and apply a coat of thread-locking compound to its threads. Refit the stud and washer to the top of the transmission, and tighten it to the specified torque setting.

39 Slide the spacer onto the mounting stud, then refit the mounting bracket assembly. Tighten both the mounting bracket-to-body bolts and the mounting centre nut to their specified torque settings, and remove the jack from underneath the transmission.

40 Refit the battery support plate, tightening its retaining bolts securely, then refit the battery as described in Chapter 5.

Rear mounting

41 Refer to Part A of this Chapter, Section 15.

Chapter 2 Part C:
Engine removal and general overhaul procedures

Contents

Crankshaft - inspection 14	Engine overhaul - dismantling sequence 6
Crankshaft - refitting and main bearing running clearance check . . . 18	Engine overhaul - general information 2
Crankshaft - removal 11	Engine overhaul - reassembly sequence 16
Cylinder block/crankcase - cleaning and inspection 12	Engine/transmission removal - methods and precautions 3
Cylinder head - dismantling 7	General information 1
Cylinder head - reassembly 9	Main and big-end bearings - inspection 15
Cylinder head and valves - cleaning and inspection 8	Piston/connecting rod assembly - inspection 13
Engine - initial start-up after overhaul 20	Piston/connecting rod assembly - refitting and big-end bearing
Engine and automatic transmission - removal, separation and	running clearance check 19
refitting 5	Piston/connecting rod assembly - removal 10
Engine and manual transmission - removal, separation and	Piston rings - refitting 17
refitting 4	

Degrees of difficulty

Easy, suitable for novice with little experience	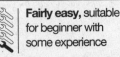	Fairly easy, suitable for beginner with some experience		Fairly difficult, suitable for competent DIY mechanic	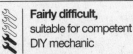	Difficult, suitable for experienced DIY mechanic		Very difficult, suitable for expert DIY or professional	

Specifications

Note: *At the time of writing, many specifications for the 1761 cc and 1998 cc engines were not available. Where the relevant specifications are not given here, refer to your Citroën dealer for further information.*

Cylinder head
Maximum gasket face distortion	0.05 mm
Cylinder head height:	
Standard:	
1124 cc and 1360 cc engines	111.2 ± 0.08 mm
1580 cc, 1761 cc, 1905 cc and 1998 cc 8-valve engines	141.0 ± 0.05 mm
1761 cc 16-valve engine	137.0 ± 0.05 mm
1998 cc 16-valve engine	132.0 ± 0.15 mm
Minimum after refinishing:	
1124 cc and 1360 cc engines	111.0 mm
1580 cc, 1761 cc, 1905 cc and 1998 cc 8-valve engines	140.8 mm
1761 cc 16-valve engine	Not available
1998 cc 16-valve engine	131.8 mm

Pistons
Piston diameter:	
1124 cc engine:	
Size group A	71.940 ± 0.010 mm
Size group B	71.950 ± 0.010 mm
Size group C	71.960 ± 0.010 mm
1360 cc engine:	
Size group A	74.950 ± 0.010 mm
Size group B	74.960 ± 0.010 mm
Size group C	74.970 ± 0.010 mm
1580 cc, 1761 cc and 1905 cc engines:	
Size group A	82.960 ± 0.007 mm
Size group B	82.970 ± 0.007 mm
Size group C	82.980 ± 0.007 mm
1998 cc engines	Not available

Cylinder block

Cylinder bore diameter:
  1124 cc engine:
    Size group A .... 72.000 to 72.010 mm
    Size group B .... 72.010 to 72.020 mm
    Size group C .... 72.020 to 72.030 mm
  1360 cc engine:
    Size group A .... 75.000 to 75.010 mm
    Size group B .... 75.010 to 75.020 mm
    Size group C .... 75.020 to 75.030 mm
  1580 cc, 1761 cc and 1905 cc engines:
    Size group A .... 83.000 to 83.010 mm
    Size group B .... 83.010 to 83.020 mm
    Size group C .... 83.020 to 83.030 mm
  1998 cc engines .... Not available (86 mm nominal)
Liner protrusion above block mating surface - aluminium-block engine only:
  Standard .... 0.03 to 0.10 mm
  Maximum difference between any two liners .... 0.05 mm

Crankshaft

Endfloat .... 0.07 to 0.32 mm
Main bearing journal diameter:
  1124 cc and 1360 cc engines:
    Standard .... 49.965 to 49.981 mm
    Undersize .... 49.665 to 49.681 mm
  1580 cc and 1905 cc engines:
    Standard .... 59.981 to 60.000 mm
    Undersize .... 59.681 to 59.700 mm
  1761 cc and 1998 cc engines .... Not available
Big-end bearing journal diameter:
  1124 cc and 1360 cc engines:
    Standard .... 44.975 to 45.000 mm
    Undersize .... 44.675 to 44.700 mm
  1580 cc and 1905 cc engines:
    Standard .... 49.984 to 50.000 mm
    Undersize .... 49.684 to 49.700 mm
  1761 cc and 1998 cc engines .... Not available
Maximum bearing journal out-of-round (all models) .... 0.007 mm
Main bearing running clearance:
  1124 cc and 1360 cc models*:
    Pre-February 1992 models .... 0.023 to 0.083 mm
    February 1992-on models .... 0.023 to 0.048 mm
  1580 cc, 1761 cc and
  1905 cc engines** .... 0.025 to 0.050 mm
  1998 cc engines .... 0.038 to 0.069 mm
Big-end bearing running clearance - all models** .... 0.025 to 0.050 mm

*On 1124 cc and 1360 cc models, the main bearing shells were modified in February 1992, resulting in a reduction in the specified running clearance - see text for further information.
**These are suggested figures, typical for this type of engine - no exact values are stated by Citroën.

Piston rings

End gaps:
  Top compression ring:
    1124 cc engine .... 0.25 to 0.45 mm
    1360 cc engine .... 0.3 to 0.5 mm
    1580 cc engine .... 0.4 to 0.6 mm
    1905 cc engine .... 0.2 to 0.4 mm
    1761 cc and 1998 cc engines* .... 0.3 to 0.5 mm
  Second compression ring:
    1124 cc engine .... 0.25 to 0.45 mm
    1360 cc engine .... 0.3 to 0.5 mm
    1580 cc and 1905 cc engines .... 0.15 to 0.35 mm
    1761 cc and 1998 cc engines* .... 0.3 to 0.5 mm
  Oil control ring:
    1124 cc engine .... 0.20 to 0.45 mm
    All other models* .... 0.3 to 0.5 mm

*These are suggested figures, typical for this type of engine - no exact values are stated by Citroën.

Connecting rods

Maximum weight difference between any two piston/connecting rod assemblies:
1124 cc and 1360 cc engines	5.0 g
1580 cc, 1761 cc and 1905 cc engines	13.0 g
1998 cc engines	7.0 g

Valves

Valve head diameter:

Inlet:
1124 cc and 1360 cc engines	36.8 mm
1580 cc engine	41.6 mm
1761 cc engine	Not available
1905 cc engine	41.8 mm
1998 cc 8-valve engine	42.6 mm
1998 cc 16-valve engine	34.7 mm

Exhaust:
1124 cc and 1360 cc engines	29.4 mm
1580 cc and 1905 cc engines	34.7 mm
1761 cc engine	Not available
1998 cc 8-valve engine	34.5 mm
1998 cc 16-valve engine	29.7 mm

Valve stem diameter:

Inlet:
1124 cc and 1360 cc engines	6.84 to 6.99 mm
1580 cc and 1905 cc engines	7.83 to 7.98 mm
1761 cc and 1998 cc engines	Not available

Exhaust:
1124 cc and 1360 cc engines	6.83 to 6.98 mm
1580 cc and 1905 cc engines	7.83 to 7.98 mm
1761 cc and 1998 cc engines	Not available

Overall length:

Inlet:
1124 cc and 1360 cc engines	112.76 ± 0.25 mm
1580 cc and 1905 cc engines	108.79 ± 0.1 mm
1761 cc and 1998 cc engines	Not available

Exhaust:
1124 cc and 1360 cc engines	112.56 ± 0.25 mm
1580 cc and 1905 cc engines	108.37 ± 0.1 mm
1761 cc and 1998 cc engines	Not available

Torque wrench settings

TU series engine - 1124 cc and 1360 cc
Refer to Chapter 2 Part A Specifications

XU series engine - 1580 cc and larger
Refer to Chapter 2 Part B Specifications

1 General information

Included in this Part of Chapter 2 are details of removing the engine/transmission from the car and general overhaul procedures for the cylinder head, cylinder block/crankcase and all other engine internal components.

The information given ranges from advice concerning preparation for an overhaul and the purchase of replacement parts, to detailed step-by-step procedures covering removal, inspection, renovation and refitting of engine internal components.

After Section 6, all instructions are based on the assumption that the engine has been removed from the car. For information concerning in-car engine repair, as well as the removal and refitting of those external components necessary for full overhaul, refer to Part A or B of this Chapter (as applicable) and to Section 6. Ignore any preliminary dismantling operations described in Part A (1124 cc and 1360 cc models) or Part B (1580 cc and larger models) that are no longer relevant once the engine has been removed from the car.

Apart from torque wrench settings, which are given at the beginning of Part A or Part B, all specifications relating to engine overhaul are at the beginning of this Part of Chapter 2

2 Engine overhaul - general information

It is not always easy to determine when, or if, an engine should be completely overhauled, as a number of factors must be considered.

High mileage is not necessarily an indication that an overhaul is needed, while low mileage does not preclude the need for an overhaul. Frequency of servicing is probably the most important consideration. An engine which has had regular and frequent oil and filter changes, as well as other required maintenance, should give many thousands of miles of reliable service. Conversely, a neglected engine may require an overhaul very early in its life.

Excessive oil consumption is an indication that piston rings, valve seals and/or valve guides are in need of attention. Make sure that oil leaks are not responsible before deciding that the rings and/or guides are worn. Perform a compression test, as described in Part A of this Chapter, to determine the likely cause of the problem.

Check the oil pressure with a gauge fitted in place of the oil pressure switch, and compare it with that specified. If it is extremely low, the main and big-end bearings, and/or the oil pump, are probably worn out.

Loss of power, rough running, knocking or metallic engine noises, excessive valve gear noise, and high fuel consumption may also point to the need for an overhaul, especially if they are all present at the same time. If a complete service does not remedy the situation, major mechanical work is the only solution.

An engine overhaul involves restoring all internal parts to the specification of a new engine. During an overhaul, the cylinder liners (where applicable), the pistons and the piston rings are renewed. New main and big-end bearings are generally fitted; if necessary, the crankshaft may be renewed, to restore the journals. The valves are also serviced as well, since they are usually in less-than-perfect condition at this point. While the engine is being overhauled, other components, such as the distributor, starter and alternator, can be overhauled as well. The end result should be an as-new engine that will give many trouble-free miles.

Note: *Critical cooling system components such as the hoses, thermostat and water pump should be renewed when an engine is overhauled. The radiator should be checked carefully, to ensure that it is not clogged or leaking. Also, it is a good idea to renew the oil pump whenever the engine is overhauled.*

Before beginning the engine overhaul, read through the entire procedure, to familiarise yourself with the scope and requirements of the job. Overhauling an engine is not difficult if you follow carefully all of the instructions, have the necessary tools and equipment, and pay close attention to all specifications. It can, however, be time-consuming. Plan on the car being off the road for a minimum of two weeks, especially if parts must be taken to an engineering works for repair or reconditioning. Check on the availability of parts and make sure that any necessary special tools and equipment are obtained in advance. Most work can be done with typical hand tools, although a number of precision measuring tools are required for inspecting parts to determine if they must be renewed. Often the engineering works will handle the inspection of parts and offer advice concerning reconditioning and renewal.

Note: *Always wait until the engine has been completely dismantled, and until all components (especially the cylinder block/crankcase and the crankshaft) have been inspected, before deciding what service and repair operations must be performed by an engineering works. The condition of these components will be the major factor to consider when determining whether to overhaul the original engine, or to buy a reconditioned unit. Do not, therefore, purchase parts or have overhaul work done on other components until they have been thoroughly inspected. As a general rule, time*

is the primary cost of an overhaul, so it does not pay to fit worn or sub-standard parts.

As a final note, to ensure maximum life and minimum trouble from a reconditioned engine, everything must be assembled with care, in a spotlessly-clean environment.

3 Engine/transmission removal - methods and precautions

1 If you have decided that the engine must be removed for overhaul or major repair work, several preliminary steps should be taken.
2 Locating a suitable place to work is extremely important. Adequate work space, along with storage space for the car, will be needed. If a workshop or garage is not available, at the very least, a flat, level, clean work surface is required.
3 Cleaning the engine compartment and engine/transmission before beginning the removal procedure will help keep tools clean and organized.
4 An engine hoist or A-frame will also be necessary. Make sure the equipment is rated in excess of the combined weight of the engine and transmission. Safety is of primary importance, considering the potential hazards involved in lifting the engine/transmission out of the car.
5 If this is the first time you have removed an engine, an assistant should ideally be available. Advice and aid from someone more experienced would also be helpful. There are many instances when one person cannot simultaneously perform all of the operations required when lifting the engine out of the vehicle.
6 Plan the operation ahead of time. Before starting work, arrange for the hire of or obtain all of the tools and equipment you will need. Some of the equipment necessary to perform engine/transmission removal and installation safely and with relative ease (in addition to an engine hoist) is as follows: a heavy duty trolley jack, complete sets of spanners and sockets as described in the front of this manual, wooden blocks, and plenty of rags and cleaning solvent for mopping up spilled oil, coolant and fuel. If the hoist must be hired,

make sure that you arrange for it in advance, and perform all of the operations possible without it beforehand. This will save you money and time.
7 Plan for the car to be out of use for quite a while. An engineering works will be required to perform some of the work which the do-it-yourselfer cannot accomplish without special equipment. These places often have a busy schedule, so it would be a good idea to consult them before removing the engine, in order to accurately estimate the amount of time required to rebuild or repair components that may need work.
8 Always be extremely careful when removing and refitting the engine/transmission. Serious injury can result from careless actions. Plan ahead and take your time, and a job of this nature, although major, can be accomplished successfully.

4 Engine and manual transmission - removal, separation and refitting

Removal

Note: *The engine can be removed from the car only as a complete unit with the transmission; the two are then separated for overhaul.*
1 Park the vehicle on firm, level ground. Chock the rear wheels, then firmly apply the handbrake. Jack up the front of the vehicle, and securely support it on axle stands. Remove both front roadwheels.
2 Set the bonnet in the upright position, and remove the battery and battery tray as described in Chapter 5. Slacken and remove the battery support plate retaining bolts. Free the wiring from its retaining clips on the edge of the plate, and remove the plate.
3 Remove the complete air cleaner housing and duct assembly, as described in the relevant Part of Chapter 4 **(see illustrations)**.
4 If the engine is to be dismantled, working as described in Chapter 1, first drain the oil and remove the oil filter. Clean and refit the drain plug, tightening it securely.
5 Drain the transmission oil as described in

4.3a Remove the air cleaner housing . . .

4.3b . . . and intake duct - 1360 cc model shown

Chapter 1. Refit the drain and filler plugs, and tighten them to their specified torque settings.
6 Remove the alternator as described in Chapter 5.
7 Where applicable, remove the power steering pump as described in Chapter 10.
8 On models with air conditioning, unbolt the compressor, and position it clear of the engine unit. Support the weight of the compressor by tying it to the vehicle body, to prevent any excess strain being placed on the compressor lines whilst the engine is removed. *Do not disconnect the refrigerant lines from the compressor (refer to the warnings given in Chapter 3).*
9 Drain the cooling system (see Chapter 1), saving the coolant if it is fit for re-use. Although not essential, it may also be worth removing the radiator (Chapter 3), which is easily damaged during engine removal.

1124 cc and 1360 cc models

10 On carburettor models, carry out the following operations, using the information given in Chapter 4:
(a) *Disconnect the fuel feed hose from the anti-percolation chamber.*
(b) *Disconnect the accelerator and choke cables from the carburettor.*
(c) *Disconnect the braking system servo vacuum hose from the inlet manifold.*
(d) *Remove the exhaust system front pipe.*
11 On fuel injection models, carry out the following operations, using the information given in Chapter 4:
(a) *Depressurise the fuel system, and disconnect the fuel feed and return hoses from the throttle body.*
(b) *Disconnect the accelerator cable from the throttle body.*
(c) *Disconnect the wiring connectors from the throttle body.*
(d) *Disconnect the purge valve and/or braking system servo vacuum hoses from the inlet manifold (as applicable).*
(e) *Remove the exhaust system front pipe.*
12 Slacken the retaining clips, then disconnect the radiator top hose from the thermostat housing, and the radiator bottom hose from the water pump housing. Trace both coolant hoses back from the heater matrix union on the engine compartment bulkhead, and disconnect them from the engine. Position all hoses clear of the engine, so that they do not hinder the removal procedure.
13 Working as described in Chapter 6, disconnect the clutch cable from the transmission, and position it clear of the working area.
14 Carry out the following operations, using the information given in Chapter 7:
(a) *Disconnect the gearchange selector rod from the transmission.*
(b) *Disconnect the speedometer cable from the speedometer drive.*
(c) *Release the power steering pipe from the underside of the transmission.*

(d) *Disconnect the wiring connector(s) from the reversing light switch and speedometer drive (as applicable).*
15 Remove the right-hand driveshaft as described in Chapter 8.
16 Free the left-hand driveshaft inner end from the transmission, as described in Chapter 7, Part A, Section 4.
17 Disconnect the wiring connectors from the components listed below. To aid refitting, label each connector as it is disconnected. This will prevent connectors being wrongly connected on refitting, and will also prove helpful when re-routing the loom around the engine compartment.
(a) *Oil pressure switch on cylinder block front face.*
(b) *Coolant temperature switch/senders screwed into the thermostat housing/left-hand end of cylinder head.*
(c) *Distributor (where fitted) or ignition HT coil.*
(d) *TDC sensor.*
(e) *Starter motor (see Chapter 5).*
18 Check that all necessary wiring connectors have been disconnected from the engine, then free the wiring loom from its retaining clips. Free the loom from the engine, noting its correct routing, and position it so that it will not hinder the engine/transmission lifting procedure.
19 Manoeuvre the engine hoist into position, and attach it to the lifting brackets bolted onto the cylinder head. Raise the hoist until it is supporting the weight of the engine.
20 Slacken and remove the centre nut and washer from the engine/transmission left-hand mounting. Undo the two bolts securing the mounting bracket assembly to the vehicle body, and remove the mounting bracket assembly.
21 From underneath the vehicle, slacken and remove the nuts and bolts securing the rear mounting bracket to the mounting assembly and subframe, and remove the bracket.
22 Undo the three nuts securing the engine/transmission right-hand mounting bracket to the engine. Remove the single nut securing the bracket to its mounting rubber, and remove the bracket **(see illustration)**.
23 Make a final check that any components which would prevent the removal of the engine/transmission from the car have been removed or disconnected. Ensure that components such as the gearchange selector rod are secured so that they cannot be damaged on removal.
24 Lift the engine/transmission out of the car, ensuring that nothing is trapped or damaged. Enlist the help of an assistant during this procedure, as it will be necessary to tilt the assembly slightly to clear the body panels. Great care must also be taken to ensure that the radiator (if not removed) and, on right-hand drive models, the braking system master cylinder reservoir, are not damaged during the removal procedure.
25 Once the engine is high enough, lift it out

over the front of the body, and lower the unit to the ground.

1580 cc models

26 Carry out the following operations, using the information given in Chapter 4:
(a) *Depressurise the fuel system. Disconnect the fuel feed and return hoses from the throttle body, and free the hoses from any relevant retaining clips.*
(b) *Disconnect the accelerator cable from the throttle body.*
(c) *Disconnect the wiring connectors from the throttle body and intake air temperature sensor.*
(d) *Disconnect the purge valve and braking system servo vacuum hoses from the inlet manifold.*
(e) *Disconnect the exhaust system front pipe from the manifold.*
(f) *Remove the auxiliary air valve (where fitted).*
27 Slacken the retaining clips, then disconnect the radiator top hose from the thermostat housing, and the radiator bottom hose from the water pump housing. Trace both coolant hoses back from the heater matrix union on the engine compartment bulkhead, and disconnect them from the engine. Also trace the small-bore coolant hose back from the right-hand side of the radiator to the engine, and disconnect these from the engine. Position all hoses clear of the engine, so that they do not hinder the removal procedure.
28 Working as described in Chapter 6, disconnect the clutch cable from the transmission, and position it clear of the working area.
29 Carry out the following operations, using the information given in Chapter 7:
(a) *Disconnect the gearchange mechanism link rods from the transmission.*
(b) *Disconnect the speedometer cable from the speedometer drive.*
(c) *Release the power steering pipe from the underside of the transmission.*
(d) *Disconnect the wiring connector(s) from the reversing light switch and speedometer drive (as applicable).*
30 Remove the right-hand driveshaft as described in Chapter 8.

4.22 Engine/transmission right-hand bracket retaining nuts (arrowed)

2C

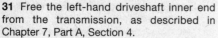

4.35a On 1761 cc models, disconnect the wiring connectors (arrowed) from the throttle housing . . .

31 Free the left-hand driveshaft inner end from the transmission, as described in Chapter 7, Part A, Section 4.
32 Disconnect the wiring connectors from the components listed below. To aid refitting, label each connector as it is disconnected. This will prevent connectors being wrongly connected on refitting, and will also prove helpful when re-routing the loom around the engine compartment.
(a) Oil pressure switch, oil level sender and/or oil temperature switch (as applicable - see Chapter 5).
(b) Coolant temperature switch/senders screwed into the thermostat housing/left-hand end of cylinder head.
(c) Ignition HT coil.
(d) TDC sensor.
(e) Starter motor (see Chapter 5).
33 Check that all necessary wiring connectors have been disconnected from the engine, then free the wiring loom from all its relevant retaining clips. Free the loom from the engine, noting its correct routing, and position it so that it will not hinder the engine/transmission lifting procedure.
34 The engine and transmission can then be removed as described above in paragraphs 19 to 25.

1761 cc models

35 Carry out the following operations, using the information given in Chapter 4:

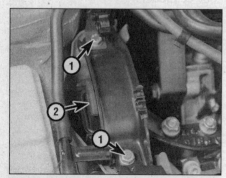

4.41a Right-hand mounting curved retaining plate retaining bolts (1), rubber damper (2) . . .

4.35b . . . and remove the auxiliary air valve

(a) Depressurise the fuel system. Disconnect the fuel feed and return hoses from the fuel rail, and free the hoses from any relevant retaining clips.
(b) Disconnect the accelerator cable from the throttle housing.
(c) Disconnect the wiring connectors from the throttle housing and fuel injectors **(see illustration)**.
(d) Disconnect the purge valve and braking system servo vacuum hoses from the inlet manifold.
(e) Disconnect the exhaust system front pipe from the manifold.
(f) Remove the auxiliary air valve **(see illustration)**.
(g) Remove the ECU and its protective plastic box.
36 The engine and transmission can then be removed as described above in paragraphs 27 to 34.

1905 cc models

37 Carry out the following operations, using the information given in Chapter 4:
(a) Depressurise the fuel system. Disconnect the fuel feed and return hoses from the fuel rail, and free the hoses from any relevant retaining clips.
(b) Disconnect the accelerator cable from the throttle housing.
(c) Disconnect the wiring connectors from the throttle potentiometer and fuel injectors.

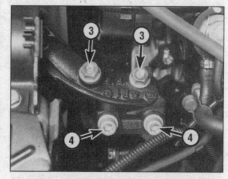

4.41b . . . mounting bracket retaining nuts (3) and bolts (4) - 1998 cc models

(d) Disconnect the purge valve and/or braking system servo vacuum hoses from the inlet manifold (as applicable).
(e) Disconnect the exhaust system front pipe from the manifold.
(f) On models with a catalytic converter, remove the airflow meter.
38 The engine and transmission can then be removed as described above in paragraphs 27 to 34.

1998 cc 8-valve models

39 Carry out the following operations, using the information given in Chapter 4:
(a) Depressurise the fuel system. Disconnect the fuel feed and return hoses from the fuel rail, and free the hoses from any relevant retaining clips.
(b) Disconnect the accelerator cable from the throttle housing.
(c) Disconnect the wiring connectors from the throttle housing, knock sensor, and the fuel injectors.
(d) Disconnect the purge valve and braking system servo vacuum hoses from the inlet manifold.
(e) Disconnect the exhaust system front pipe from the manifold.
(f) Remove the ECU and its protective plastic box.
40 The engine and transmission can then be removed as described above in paragraphs 27 to 34; note, however, that the engine right-hand mounting is dismantled as follows.
41 Undo the two bolts securing the curved mounting retaining plate to the body. Lift off the plate, and withdraw the rubber damper from the top of the mounting bracket. Slacken and remove the two nuts and two bolts securing the right-hand mounting bracket to the engine. Remove the single nut securing the bracket to the mounting rubber, and lift off the bracket **(see illustrations)**.

1998 cc 16-valve models

42 Carry out the following operations, using the information given in Chapter 4:
(a) Depressurise the fuel system. Disconnect the fuel feed and return hoses from their fuel rail unions, and free the hoses from the retaining clips on the cylinder head cover.
(b) Remove the inlet manifold.
(c) Disconnect the wiring connectors from the camshaft position sensor, knock sensor, and the fuel injectors.
(d) Disconnect the exhaust system front pipe from the manifold.
(e) Remove the ECU and its protective plastic box.
43 Locate the ignition HT coil wiring connector (on the left-hand end of the cylinder head). Rotate the locking ring anti-clockwise, and disconnect the connector from the main wiring loom.
44 Disconnect the braking system servo vacuum hose from its union just to the rear of the vacuum pump.

45 The engine and transmission can then be removed as described above in paragraphs 27 to 34; note, however, that the engine right-hand mounting is dismantled as follows.

46 Undo the two bolts securing the curved mounting retaining plate to the body. Lift off the plate, and withdraw the rubber damper from the top of the mounting bracket. Slacken and remove the two nuts and two bolts securing the right-hand mounting bracket to the engine. Remove the single nut securing the bracket to the mounting rubber, and lift off the bracket.

Separation

47 With the engine/transmission assembly removed, support the assembly on suitable blocks of wood, on a workbench (or failing that, on a clean area of the workshop floor).

48 Undo the retaining bolts, and remove the flywheel lower cover plate (where fitted) from the transmission.

49 On models with a "pull-type" clutch release mechanism (see Chapter 6 for further information), tap out the retaining pin or unscrew the retaining bolt (as applicable), and remove the clutch release lever from the top of the release fork shaft. This is necessary to allow the fork shaft to rotate freely, so that it disengages from the release bearing as the transmission is pulled away from the engine. Make an alignment mark across the centre of the clutch release fork shaft, using a scriber, paint or similar, and mark its relative position on the transmission housing (see Chapter 7, Part A, Section 7 for further information).

50 Slacken and remove the retaining bolts, and remove the starter motor from the transmission.

51 Ensure that both engine and transmission are adequately supported, then slacken and remove the remaining bolts securing the transmission housing to the engine. Note the correct fitted positions of each bolt (and the relevant brackets) as they are removed, to use as a reference on refitting.

52 Carefully withdraw the transmission from the engine, ensuring that the weight of the transmission is not allowed to hang on the input shaft while it is engaged with the clutch friction disc.

53 If they are loose, remove the locating dowels from the engine or transmission, and keep them in a safe place.

54 On models with a "pull-type" clutch, make a second alignment mark on the transmission housing, marking the relative position of the release fork mark after removal. This should indicate the angle at which the release fork is positioned. The mark can then be used to position the release fork prior to installation, to ensure that the fork correctly engages with the clutch release bearing as the transmission is installed.

Refitting

55 If the engine and transmission have been separated, perform the operations described below in paragraphs 56 to 64. If not, proceed as described from paragraph 65 onwards.

56 Apply a smear of high-melting-point grease to the splines of the transmission input shaft. Do not apply too much, otherwise there is a possibility of the grease contaminating the clutch friction plate.

57 Ensure that the locating dowels are correctly positioned in the engine or transmission.

58 On models with a "pull-type" clutch, position the clutch release bearing so that its "HAUT" mark is at the top, and the "BAS" mark is at the bottom. Align the release fork shaft mark with the second mark made on the transmission housing. This will ensure that the release fork and bearing will engage correctly as the transmission is refitted to the engine.

59 Carefully offer the transmission to the engine, until the locating dowels are engaged. Ensure that the weight of the transmission is not allowed to hang on the input shaft as it is engaged with the clutch friction disc.

60 On models with a "pull-type" clutch, with the transmission fully engaged with the engine, check that the release fork and bearing are correctly engaged. If the release fork and bearing are correctly engaged, the mark on the release fork should be aligned with the original mark made on the transmission housing (see Chapter 7, Part A, Section 7 for further information).

61 Refit the transmission housing-to-engine bolts, ensuring that all the necessary brackets are correctly positioned, and tighten them to the specified torque setting.

62 Refit the starter motor, and securely tighten its retaining bolts.

63 On models with a "pull-type" clutch release mechanism, refit the clutch release lever to the top of the release fork shaft, securing it in position with its retaining pin or bolt (as applicable).

64 Where necessary, refit the lower flywheel cover plate to the transmission, and securely tighten its retaining bolts.

65 Reconnect the hoist and lifting tackle to the engine lifting brackets. With the aid of an assistant, lift the assembly over the engine compartment.

66 The assembly should be tilted as necessary to clear the surrounding components, as during removal; lower the assembly into position in the engine compartment, manipulating the hoist and lifting tackle as necessary.

67 With the engine/transmission in position, refit the right-hand engine/transmission mounting bracket, tightening its retaining nuts and bolts (as applicable) by hand only at this stage.

68 Refit the left-hand engine/transmission mounting bracket assembly to the vehicle, and tighten its retaining bolts to the specified torque. Refit the centre nut and washer to the left-hand mounting, tightening it to the specified torque setting. Tighten the right-hand mounting bracket retaining nuts and

bolts (as applicable) to their specified torque setting.

69 On 1998 cc 8-valve and 16-valve models, refit the rubber damper to the top of the right-hand mounting bracket. Refit the curved retaining plate, and tighten its retaining bolts to the specified torque.

70 On all models, from underneath the vehicle, refit the rear mounting bracket, and tighten both its retaining bolts to the specified torque. The hoist can then be detached from the engine and removed.

71 The remainder of the refitting procedure is a direct reversal of the removal sequence, noting the following points:

(a) *Ensure that the wiring loom is correctly routed and retained by all the relevant retaining clips; all connectors should be correctly and securely reconnected.*

(b) *Prior to refitting the driveshafts to the transmission, renew the driveshaft oil seals as described in Chapter 7.*

(c) *Ensure that all coolant hoses are correctly reconnected, and securely retained by their retaining clips.*

(d) *Adjust the clutch cable as described in Chapter 6.*

(e) *Adjust the choke cable and/or accelerator cable (as applicable) as described in Chapter 4.*

(f) *Refill the engine and transmission with correct quantity and type of lubricant, as described in Chapter 1.*

(g) *Refill the cooling system as described in Chapter 1.*

5 Engine and automatic transmission - removal, separation and refitting

Removal

Note: *The engine can be removed from the car only as a complete unit with the transmission; the two are then separated for overhaul.*

1 Carry out the operations described in paragraphs 1 to 9 of Section 4.

1580 cc models

2 Carry out the following operations, using the information given in Chapter 4:

(a) *Depressurise the fuel system. Disconnect the fuel feed and return hoses from the throttle body, and free the hoses from any relevant retaining clips.*

(b) *Disconnect the accelerator cable from the throttle body.*

(c) *Disconnect the wiring connectors from the throttle body and intake air temperature sensor.*

(d) *Disconnect the purge valve and braking system servo vacuum hoses from the inlet manifold.*

(e) *Disconnect the exhaust system front pipe from the manifold.*

(f) *Remove the auxiliary air valve (where fitted).*

1761 cc models

3 Carry out the following operations, using the information given in Chapter 4:
(a) *Depressurise the fuel system. Disconnect the fuel feed and return hoses from the fuel rail, and free the hoses from any relevant retaining clips.*
(b) *Disconnect the accelerator cable from the throttle housing.*
(c) *Disconnect the wiring connectors from the throttle housing and fuel injectors.*
(d) *Disconnect the purge valve and braking system servo vacuum hoses from the inlet manifold.*
(e) *Disconnect the exhaust system front pipe from the manifold.*
(f) *Remove the auxiliary air valve.*
(g) *Remove the ECU and its protective plastic box.*

1905 cc models

4 Carry out the following operations, using the information given in Chapter 4:
(a) *Depressurise the fuel system. Disconnect the fuel feed and return hoses from the fuel rail, and free the hoses from any relevant retaining clips.*
(b) *Disconnect the accelerator cable from the throttle housing.*
(c) *Disconnect the wiring connectors from the throttle potentiometer and fuel injectors.*
(d) *Disconnect the purge valve and/or braking system servo vacuum hoses from the inlet manifold (as applicable).*
(e) *Disconnect the exhaust system front pipe from the manifold.*
(f) *On models with a catalytic converter, remove the airflow meter.*

All models

5 Slacken the retaining clips, then disconnect the radiator top hose from the thermostat housing, and the radiator bottom hose from the water pump housing. Trace both coolant hoses back from the heater matrix union on the engine compartment bulkhead, and disconnect them from the engine. Also trace the small-bore coolant hoses back from the left-hand right-hand side of the radiator to the engine/transmission, and disconnect these from the engine and transmission fluid cooler. Position all hoses clear of the engine, so that they do not hinder the removal procedure.
6 Carry out the following operations, using the information given in Chapter 7:
(a) *Remove the transmission dipstick tube.*
(b) *Disconnect the wiring from the starter inhibitor/reversing light switch and the speedometer drive housing. Release the earth strap(s) from the top of the transmission housing.*
(c) *Disconnect the selector cable.*
(d) *Release the power steering pipe from the underside of the transmission.*
(e) *Disconnect the speedometer cable.*
7 Remove the right-hand driveshaft as described in Chapter 8.

8 Free the left-hand driveshaft inner end from the transmission, as described in Chapter 7, Part A, Section 4.
9 Disconnect the wiring connectors from the components listed below. To aid refitting, label each connector as it is disconnected. This will prevent connectors being wrongly connected on refitting, and will also prove helpful when re-routing the loom around the engine compartment.
(a) *Oil pressure switch, oil level sender and/or oil temperature switch (as applicable - see Chapter 5).*
(b) *Coolant temperature switch/senders screwed into the thermostat housing/left-hand end of cylinder head.*
(c) *Ignition HT coil.*
(d) *TDC sensor.*
(e) *Starter motor (see Chapter 5).*
10 Check that all necessary wiring connectors have been disconnected from the engine, then free the wiring loom from its retaining clips. Free the loom from the engine, noting its correct routing, and position it so that it will not hinder the engine/transmission lifting procedure.
11 Manoeuvre the engine hoist into position, and attach it to the lifting brackets bolted onto the cylinder head. Raise the hoist until it is supporting the weight of the engine.
12 Slacken and remove the centre nut and washer from the engine/transmission left-hand mounting. Undo the two bolts securing the mounting bracket assembly to the vehicle body, and remove the mounting bracket assembly.
13 From underneath the vehicle, slacken and remove the nuts and bolts securing the rear mounting bracket to the mounting assembly and subframe, and remove the bracket.
14 Undo the three nuts securing the engine/transmission right-hand mounting bracket to the engine. Remove the single nut securing the bracket to its mounting rubber, and remove the bracket.
15 Make a final check that all components that will prevent the removal of the engine/transmission from the car have been removed or disconnected. Ensure that all components are secured so that they cannot be damaged on removal.
16 Lift the engine/transmission out of the car, ensuring that nothing is trapped or damaged. Enlist the help of an assistant during this procedure, as it will be necessary to tilt the assembly slightly to clear the body panels. Great care must also be taken to ensure that the radiator (if not removed) and, on right-hand drive models, the braking system master cylinder reservoir, are not damaged during the removal procedure.
17 Once the engine is high enough, lift it out over the front of the body, and lower the unit to the ground.

Separation

18 With the engine/transmission assembly removed, support the assembly on suitable

blocks of wood, on a workbench (or failing that, on a clean area of the workshop floor).
19 Detach the kickdown cable from the throttle cam. Work back along the cable, freeing it from any retaining clips, and noting its correct routing.
20 Undo the retaining bolts and remove the driveplate lower cover plate from the transmission, to gain access to the torque converter retaining bolts. Slacken and remove the visible bolt. Rotate the crankshaft using a socket and extension bar on the pulley bolt, and undo the remaining bolts securing the torque converter to the driveplate as they become accessible. There are three bolts in total.
21 Slacken and remove the retaining bolts, and remove the starter motor from the transmission.
22 To ensure that the torque converter does not fall out as the transmission is removed, secure it in position using a length of metal strip bolted to one of the starter motor bolt holes.
23 Ensure that both the engine and transmission are adequately supported, then slacken and remove the remaining bolts securing the transmission housing to the engine. Note the correct fitted positions of each bolt (and any relevant brackets) as they are removed, to use as a reference on refitting.
24 Carefully withdraw the transmission from the engine. If the locating dowels are a loose fit in the engine/transmission, remove them and keep them in a safe place.

Refitting

25 If the engine and transmission have been separated, perform the operations described below in paragraphs 26 to 32. If not, proceed as described from paragraph 33 onwards.
26 Ensure that the bush fitted to the centre of the crankshaft is in good condition. Apply a little Molykote G1 grease (available from your Citroën dealer) to the torque converter centring pin. Do not apply too much, otherwise there is a possibility of the grease contaminating the torque converter.
27 Ensure that the locating dowels are correctly positioned in the engine or transmission.
28 Carefully offer the transmission to the engine, until the locating dowels are engaged.
29 Refit the transmission housing-to-engine bolts, ensuring that all the necessary brackets are correctly positioned, and tighten them to the specified torque setting.
30 Remove the torque converter retaining strap installed prior to removal. Align the torque converter threaded holes with the retaining plate, and refit the three retaining bolts.
31 Tighten the torque converter retaining bolts to the specified torque setting, then refit the driveplate lower cover.
32 Refit the starter motor, and securely tighten its retaining bolts.

33 Reconnect the hoist and lifting tackle to the engine lifting brackets. With the aid of an assistant, lift the assembly over the engine compartment.

34 The assembly should be tilted as necessary to clear surrounding components, as during removal; lower the assembly into position in the engine compartment, manipulating the hoist and lifting tackle as necessary.

35 With the engine/transmission in position, refit the engine/transmission right-hand mounting bracket, tightening its retaining nuts by hand only at this stage.

36 Refit the engine/transmission left-hand mounting bracket assembly to the vehicle, and tighten its retaining bolts to the specified torque. Refit the centre nut and washer to the left-hand mounting, tightening it to the specified torque setting. Tighten the right-hand mounting bracket retaining nuts to their specified torque setting.

37 From underneath the vehicle, refit the rear mounting bracket, and tighten both its retaining bolts to the specified torque. The hoist can then be detached from the engine and removed.

38 The remainder of the refitting procedure is a reversal of the removal sequence, noting the following points:
(a) *Ensure that the wiring loom is correctly routed, and retained by all the relevant retaining clips; all connectors should be correctly and securely reconnected.*
(b) *Prior to refitting the driveshafts to the transmission, renew the driveshaft oil seals as described in Chapter 7.*
(c) *Ensure that all coolant hoses are correctly reconnected, and securely retained by their retaining clips.*
(d) *Adjust the selector cable and kickdown cable as described in Chapter 7, Part B.*
(e) *Adjust the accelerator cable as described in Chapter 4.*
(f) *Refill the engine and transmission with correct quantity and type of lubricant, as described in Chapter 1.*
(g) *Refill the cooling system as described in Chapter 1.*

6 Engine overhaul - dismantling sequence

1 It is much easier to dismantle and work on the engine if it is mounted on a portable engine stand. These stands can often be hired from a tool hire shop. Before the engine is mounted on a stand, the flywheel/driveplate should be removed, so that the stand bolts can be tightened into the end of the cylinder block/crankcase.

2 If a stand is not available, it is possible to dismantle the engine with it blocked up on a sturdy workbench, or on the floor. Be extra-careful not to tip or drop the engine when working without a stand.

3 If you are going to obtain a reconditioned

engine, all the external components must be removed first, to be transferred to the replacement engine (just as they will if you are doing a complete engine overhaul yourself). These components include the following:
(a) *Alternator mounting brackets (Chapter 5).*
(b) *Power steering pump and air conditioning compressor brackets (where fitted) (Chapters 3 and 10).*
(c) *Distributor, HT leads and spark plugs (as applicable) (Chapters 1 and 5).*
(d) *Thermostat and housing, and coolant outlet chamber/elbow (Chapter 3).*
(e) *Dipstick tube.*
(f) *Carburettor/fuel injection system components (Chapter 4).*
(g) *All electrical switches and sensors.*
(h) *Inlet and exhaust manifolds (Chapter 4).*
(i) *ACAV assembly - 1998 cc 16-valve engines only (Chapter 4).*
(j) *Oil filter (Chapter 1).*
(k) *Fuel pump - carburettor engines only (Chapter 4).*
(l) *Engine mountings (Part A or B of this Chapter).*
(m) *Flywheel/driveplate (Part A or B of this Chapter).*

Note: *When removing the external components from the engine, pay close attention to details that may be helpful or important during refitting. Note the fitted position of gaskets, seals, spacers, pins, washers, bolts, and other small items.*

4 If you are obtaining a "short" engine (which consists of the engine cylinder block/crank-case, crankshaft, pistons and connecting rods all assembled), then the cylinder head, sump, oil pump, and timing belt will have to be removed also.

5 If you are planning a complete overhaul, the engine can be dismantled, and the internal components removed, in the order given below, referring to Part A or B of this Chapter unless otherwise stated.
(a) *Inlet and exhaust manifolds (Chapter 4).*
(b) *ACAV assembly - 1998 cc 16-valve engines only (Chapter 4).*
(c) *Timing belt, sprockets and tensioner(s).*
(d) *Cylinder head.*
(e) *Flywheel.*
(f) *Sump.*
(g) *Oil pump.*

7.3b . . . then extract the collets and release the spring compressor

(h) *Piston/connecting rod assemblies (Section 10).*
(i) *Crankshaft (Section 11).*

6 Before beginning the dismantling and overhaul procedures, make sure that you have all of the correct tools necessary. Refer to *"Tools and working facilities"* at the end of this manual for further information.

7 Cylinder head - dismantling

Note: *New and reconditioned cylinder heads are available from the manufacturer, and from engine overhaul specialists. Be aware that some specialist tools are required for the dismantling and inspection procedures, and new components may not be readily available. It may therefore be more practical and economical for the home mechanic to purchase a reconditioned head, rather than dismantle, inspect and recondition the original head.*

1 Remove the cylinder head as described in Part A or B of this Chapter (as applicable).

2 Remove the camshaft(s), followers and shims (as applicable) as described in Part A or B of this Chapter.

3 Using a valve spring compressor, compress each valve spring in turn until the split collets can be removed. Release the compressor, and lift off the spring retainer, spring and spring seat. Using a pair of pliers, carefully extract the valve stem seal from the top of the guide **(see illustrations)**.

7.3a Compress the valve spring using a spring compressor . . .

7.3c Remove the spring retainer . . .

2C

7.3d ... followed by the valve spring ...

7.3e ... and the spring seat

7.3f Remove the valve stem oil seal using a pair of pliers

4 If, when the valve spring compressor is screwed down, the spring retainer refuses to free and expose the split collets, gently tap the top of the tool, directly over the retainer, with a light hammer. This will free the retainer.

5 Withdraw the valve through the combustion chamber.

6 It is essential that each valve is stored together with its collets, retainer, spring, and spring seat. The valves should also be kept in their correct sequence, unless they are so badly worn that they are to be renewed. Note that No 1 valve is nearest to the transmission (flywheel/driveplate) end of the engine.

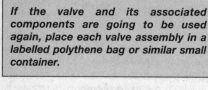

If the valve and its associated components are going to be used again, place each valve assembly in a labelled polythene bag or similar small container.

---

8 Cylinder head and valves -
cleaning and inspection

1 Thorough cleaning of the cylinder head and valve components, followed by a detailed inspection, will enable you to decide how much valve service work must be carried out during the engine overhaul. **Note:** *If the engine has been severely overheated, it is best to assume that the cylinder head is warped - check carefully for signs of this.*

Cleaning

2 Scrape away all traces of old gasket material and sealing compound from the cylinder head.

3 Scrape away the carbon from the combustion chambers and ports, then wash the cylinder head thoroughly with paraffin or a suitable solvent.

4 Scrape off any heavy carbon deposits that may have formed on the valves, then use a power-operated wire brush to remove deposits from the valve heads and stems.

Inspection

Note: *Be sure to perform all the following inspection procedures before concluding that the services of a machine shop or engine overhaul specialist are required. Make a list of all items that require attention.*

Cylinder head

5 Inspect the head very carefully for cracks, evidence of coolant leakage, and other damage. If cracks are found, a new cylinder head should be obtained.

6 Use a straight-edge and feeler gauge blade to check that the cylinder head surface is not distorted **(see illustration)**. If it is, it may be possible to have it machined, provided that the cylinder head is not reduced to less than the specified height. The cylinder head height is measured from the centre of the cylinder head camshaft bore to the cylinder head gasket face. **Note:** *Cylinder heads that have had their gasket surface refaced by Citroën will be stamped with an "R" somewhere on* the left-hand end of the cylinder head, around the thermostat housing area. These heads have had 0.2 mm machined off the gasket face. When fitting to the engine, a slightly thicker head gasket should be used (see Part A or B for further information).

7 Examine the valve seats in each of the combustion chambers. If they are severely pitted, cracked, or burned, they will need to be renewed or re-cut by an engine overhaul specialist. If they are only slightly pitted, this can be removed by grinding-in the valve heads and seats with fine valve-grinding compound, as described below. **Note:** *It is not possible to renew the valve seats on the 1998 cc 16-valve engine.*

8 Check the valve guides for wear by inserting the relevant valve, and checking for side-to-side motion of the valve. A very small amount of movement is acceptable. If the movement seems excessive, remove the valve. Measure the valve stem diameter (see below), and renew the valve if it is worn. If the valve stem is not worn, the wear must be in the valve guide, and the guide must be renewed. The renewal of valve guides is best carried out by a Citroën dealer or engine overhaul specialist, who will have the necessary tools available. Where no valve stem diameter is specified, seek the advice of a Citroën dealer on the best course of action.

9 If the valve seats are to be re-cut or re-ground, this must be done only *after* the guides have been renewed.

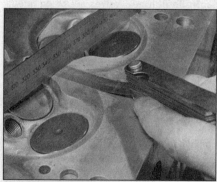

8.6 Checking the cylinder head gasket surface for distortion

8.11 Measuring a valve stem diameter

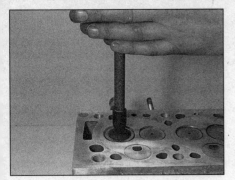

8.14 Grinding-in a valve

9.1 Lubricate the valve stems prior to refitting

9.2 Fitting a valve stem oil seal using a socket

2C

Valves

10 Examine the head of each valve for pitting, burning, cracks, and general wear. Check the valve stem for scoring and wear ridges. Rotate the valve, and check for any obvious indication that it is bent. Look for pits and excessive wear on the tip of each valve stem. Renew any valve that shows any such signs of wear or damage.

11 If the valve appears satisfactory at this stage, measure the valve stem diameter at several points using a micrometer **(see illustration)**. Any significant difference in the readings obtained indicates wear of the valve stem. Should any of these conditions be apparent, the valve(s) must be renewed.

12 If the valves are in satisfactory condition, they should be ground (lapped) into their respective seats, to ensure a smooth, gas-tight seal. If the seat is only lightly pitted, or if it has been re-cut, fine grinding compound *only* should be used to produce the required finish. Coarse valve-grinding compound should *not* be used unless a seat is badly burned or deeply pitted. If this is the case, the cylinder head and valves should be inspected by an expert, to decide whether seat re-cutting, or even the renewal of the valve or seat insert (where possible) is required.

13 Valve grinding is carried out as follows. Place the cylinder head upside-down on a bench.

14 Smear a trace of (the appropriate grade of) valve-grinding compound on the seat face, and press a suction grinding tool onto the valve head. With a semi-rotary action, grind the valve head to its seat, lifting the valve occasionally to redistribute the grinding compound **(see illustration)**.

 A light spring placed under the valve head will greatly ease the grinding operation.

15 If coarse grinding compound is being used, work only until a dull, matt even surface is produced on both the valve seat and the valve, then wipe off the used compound, and repeat the process with fine compound. When a smooth unbroken ring of light grey matt

finish is produced on both the valve and seat, the grinding operation is complete. *Do not* grind-in the valves any further than absolutely necessary, or the seat will be prematurely sunk into the cylinder head.

16 To check that the seat has not been over-ground, measure the valve stem installed height, as described in paragraph 7 above.

17 When all the valves have been ground-in, carefully wash off *all* traces of grinding compound using paraffin or a suitable solvent, before reassembling the cylinder head.

Valve components

18 Examine the valve springs for signs of damage and discoloration. No minimum free length is specified by Citroën, so the only way of judging valve spring wear is by comparison with a new component.

19 Stand each spring on a flat surface, and check it for squareness. If any of the springs are damaged, distorted or have lost their tension, obtain a complete new set of springs. It is normal to renew the valve springs as a matter of course if a major overhaul is being carried out.

20 Renew the valve stem oil seals regardless of their apparent condition.

9 Cylinder head - reassembly

1 Lubricate the stems of the valves, and insert them into their original locations **(see illustration)**. If new valves are being fitted, insert them into the locations to which they have been ground.

2 Refit the spring seat then, working on the first valve, dip the new valve stem seal in fresh engine oil. Carefully locate it over the valve and onto the guide. Take care not to damage the seal as it is passed over the valve stem. Use a suitable socket or metal tube to press the seal firmly onto the guide **(see illustration)**.

3 Locate the valve spring on top of its seat, then refit the spring retainer.

4 Compress the valve spring, and locate the split collets in the recess in the valve stem. Use a little grease to hold the collets in place. Release the compressor, then repeat the procedure on the remaining valves.

9.6 Refitting a cam follower - 1905 cc model. Note the shim (arrowed)

5 With all the valves installed, place the cylinder head flat on the bench and, using a hammer and interposed block of wood, tap the end of each valve stem to settle the components.

6 Refit the shims (where fitted), cam followers and camshaft(s) as described in Part A or B (as applicable) **(see illustration)**.

10 Piston/connecting rod assembly - removal

1 Remove the cylinder head, sump and oil pump as described in Part A or B of this Chapter (as applicable)

2 If there is a pronounced wear ridge at the top of any bore, it may be necessary to remove it with a scraper or ridge reamer, to avoid piston damage during removal. Such a ridge indicates excessive wear of the cylinder bore.

3 Using a hammer and centre-punch, paint or similar, mark each connecting rod big-end bearing cap with its respective cylinder number on the flat machined surface provided; if the engine has been dismantled before, note carefully any identifying marks made previously **(see illustration)**. Note that No 1 cylinder is at the transmission (flywheel/driveplate) end of the engine.

4 Turn the crankshaft to bring pistons 1 and 4 to BDC (bottom dead centre).

5 Unscrew the nuts from No 1 piston big-end bearing cap. Take off the cap, and recover the

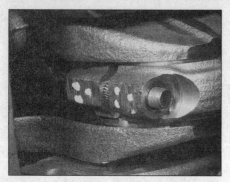

10.3 Connecting rod and big-end bearing cap marked for identification (No 3 cylinder shown)

10.5 Removing a big-end bearing cap and shell

10.6 To protect the crankshaft journals, tape over the connecting rod stud threads prior to removal

bottom half bearing shell **(see illustration)**. If the bearing shells are to be re-used, tape the cap and the shell together.

6 To prevent the possibility of damage to the crankshaft bearing journals, tape over the connecting rod stud threads **(see illustration)**.

7 Using a hammer handle, push the piston up through the bore, and remove it from the top of the cylinder block. Recover the bearing shell, and tape it to the connecting rod for safe-keeping.

8 Loosely refit the big-end cap to the connecting rod, and secure with the nuts - this will help to keep the components in their correct order.

9 Remove No 4 piston assembly in the same way.

11.9 Removing the oil seal carrier from the front of the cylinder block - XU series engine

10 Turn the crankshaft through 180° to bring pistons 2 and 3 to BDC (bottom dead centre), and remove them in the same way.

11 Crankshaft - removal

1 Remove the crankshaft sprocket and the oil pump as described in Part A or B of this Chapter (as applicable).

2 Remove the pistons and connecting rods, as described in Section 10. If no work is to be done on the pistons and connecting rods, there is no need to remove the cylinder head, or to push the pistons out of the cylinder bores. The pistons should just be pushed far enough up the bores that they are positioned clear of the crankshaft journals.

3 Check the crankshaft endfloat as described in Section 14, then proceed as follows.

TU series engine - 1124 cc and 1360 cc

4 Work around the outside of the cylinder block, and unscrew all the small (6 mm) bolts securing the main bearing ladder to the base of the cylinder block. Note the correct fitted depth of both the front and rear crankshaft oil seals in the cylinder block/main bearing ladder.

5 Working in a diagonal sequence, evenly and progressively slacken the ten large (11 mm) main bearing ladder retaining bolts by a

turn at a time. Once all the bolts are loose, remove them from the ladder.

6 With all the retaining bolts removed, carefully lift the main bearing ladder casting away from the base of the cylinder block. Recover the lower main bearing shells, and tape them to their respective locations in the casting. If the two locating dowels are a loose fit, remove them and store them with the casting for safe-keeping.

7 Lift out the crankshaft, and discard both the oil seals. Remove the oil pump drive chain from the end of the crankshaft. Where necessary, slide off the drive sprocket, and recover the Woodruff key.

8 Recover the upper main bearing shells, and store them along with the relevant lower bearing shell. Also recover the two thrustwashers (one fitted either side of No 2 main bearing) from the cylinder block.

XU series engine - 1580 cc and larger

9 Slacken and remove the retaining bolts, and remove the oil seal carrier from the front (timing belt) end of the cylinder block, along with its gasket **(see illustration)**.

10 Remove the oil pump drive chain, and slide the drive sprocket off the end of the crankshaft. Remove the Woodruff key, and store it with the sprocket for safe-keeping **(see illustrations)**.

11 The main bearing caps should be numbered 1 to 5, starting from the transmission (flywheel/driveplate) end of the engine

11.10a Remove the oil pump drive chain . . .

11.10b . . . then slide off the drive sprocket . . .

11.10c . . . and remove the Woodruff key from the crankshaft

(see illustration). If not, mark them accordingly using a centre-punch. Also note the correct fitted depth of the rear crankshaft oil seal in the bearing cap.

12 On 1580 cc, 1761 cc and 1905 cc engines, undo the two bolts (one at the front of the block, and one at the rear) securing the centre main bearing cap to the block. Remove the bolts, along with their sealing washers.

13 On all engines, slacken and remove the main bearing cap retaining bolts/nuts, and lift off each bearing cap. Recover the lower bearing shells, and tape them to their respective caps for safe-keeping. Also recover the lower thrustwasher halves from the side of No 2 main bearing cap (see illustration). Remove the rubber sealing strips from the sides of No 1 main bearing cap, and discard them.

14 Lift out the crankshaft, and discard the rear oil seal (see illustration).

15 Recover the upper bearing shells from the cylinder block, and tape them to their respective caps for safe-keeping (see illustration). Remove the upper thrustwasher halves from the side of No 2 main bearing, and store them with the lower halves.

11.13 Removing No 2 main bearing cap. Note the thrustwasher (arrowed)

11.11 Main bearing cap identification markings (arrowed)

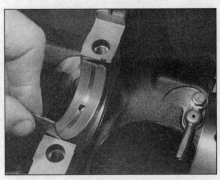
11.15 Remove the upper main bearing shells from the cylinder block/crankcase, and store them with their lower shells

11.14 Lifting out the crankshaft - XU series engine

12 Cylinder block/crankcase - cleaning and inspection

Cleaning

1 Remove all external components and electrical switches/sensors from the block. For complete cleaning, the core plugs should ideally be removed (see illustration). Drill a small hole in the plugs, then insert a self-tapping screw into the hole. Pull out the plugs by pulling on the screw with a pair of grips, or by using a slide hammer.

2 On aluminium block engines with wet liners (all engines except 1998 cc), remove the liners as described in paragraph 16.

3 On 1998 cc 16-valve engines, undo the retaining bolt and remove the piston oil jet spray tube from inside the cylinder block.

4 Scrape all traces of gasket from the cylinder block/crankcase, and from the main bearing ladder (where fitted), taking care not to damage the gasket/sealing surfaces.

5 Remove all oil gallery plugs (where fitted). The plugs are usually very tight - they may have to be drilled out, and the holes re-tapped. Use new plugs when the engine is reassembled.

6 If any of the castings are extremely dirty, all should be steam-cleaned.

7 After the castings are returned, clean all oil holes and oil galleries one more time. Flush all internal passages with warm water until the water runs clear. Dry thoroughly, and apply a light film of oil to all mating surfaces, to prevent rusting. On 1998 cc engines, also oil the cylinder bores. If you have access to compressed air, use it to speed up the drying process, and to blow out all the oil holes and galleries.

⚠ **Warning: Wear eye protection when using compressed air!**

8 If the castings are not very dirty, you can do an adequate cleaning job with hot (as hot as you can stand!), soapy water and a stiff brush. Take plenty of time, and do a thorough job. Regardless of the cleaning method used, be sure to clean all oil holes and galleries very thoroughly, and to dry all components well. On 1998 cc engines, protect the cylinder bores as described above, to prevent rusting.

9 All threaded holes must be clean, to ensure accurate torque readings during reassembly. To clean the threads, run the correct-size tap into each of the holes to remove rust, corrosion, thread sealant or sludge, and to

restore damaged threads (see illustration). If possible, use compressed air to clear the holes of debris produced by this operation. A good alternative is to inject aerosol-applied water-dispersant lubricant into each hole, using the long spout usually supplied.

⚠ **Warning: Wear eye protection when cleaning out these holes in this way!**

10 Apply suitable sealant to the new oil gallery plugs, and insert them into the holes in the block. Tighten them securely.

11 On 1998 cc 16-valve engines, clean the threads of the piston oil jet retaining bolt, and apply a drop of thread-locking compound to the bolt threads. Citroën recommend the use of Frenbloc E6 (available from your Citroën

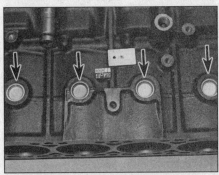
12.1 Cylinder block core plugs (arrowed)

12.9 Cleaning a cylinder block threaded hole using a suitable tap

12.16a On aluminium block engines, remove each liner . . .

12.16b . . . and recover the bottom O-ring seal (arrowed)

13.2 Removing a piston ring with the aid of a feeler gauge

dealer); in the absence of this, any suitable good-quality locking compound may be used. Refit the piston oil jet spray tube to the cylinder block, and tighten its retaining bolt to the specified torque setting.

12 If the engine is not going to be reassembled right away, cover it with a large plastic bag to keep it clean; protect all mating surfaces and the cylinder bores as described above, to prevent rusting.

Inspection

Cast-iron cylinder block

13 Visually check the castings for cracks and corrosion. Look for stripped threads in the threaded holes. If there has been any history of internal water leakage, it may be worthwhile having an engine overhaul specialist check the cylinder block/crankcase with special equipment. If defects are found, have them repaired if possible, or renew the assembly.

14 Check the each cylinder bore for scuffing and scoring. Check for signs of a wear ridge at the top of the cylinder, indicating that the bore is excessively worn.

15 Since Citroën do not state any specific wear limits for the cylinder bores or pistons, it is not possible to assess the amount of wear by direct measurement. If there is any doubt about the condition of the cylinder bores, seek the advice of a Citroën dealer or engine reconditioning specialist. At the time of writing, oversize pistons were not available, so therefore it is not advisable to rebore the cylinders. Consult your Citroën dealer for piston availability; if oversize pistons are not available, and the bores are worn, renewal of the block seems to be the only option.

Aluminium cylinder block with wet liners

16 Remove the liner clamps (where used), then use a hard wood drift to tap out each liner from inside the cylinder block. When all the liners are released, tip the cylinder block/crankcase on its side and remove each liner from the top of the block. As each liner is removed, stick masking tape on its left-hand (transmission side) face, and write the cylinder number on the tape. No 1 cylinder is at the transmission (flywheel/driveplate) end of the

engine. Remove the O-ring from the base of each liner, and discard **(see illustrations)**.

17 Check each cylinder liner for scuffing and scoring. Check for signs of a wear ridge at the top of the liner, indicating that the bore is excessively worn.

18 If the necessary measuring equipment is available, measure the bore diameter of each cylinder liner at the top (just under the wear ridge), centre, and bottom of the cylinder bore, parallel to the crankshaft axis.

19 Next, measure the bore diameter at the same three locations, at right-angles to the crankshaft axis. Compare the results with the figures given in the Specifications.

20 Repeat the procedure for the remaining cylinder liners.

21 If the liner wear exceeds the permitted tolerances at any point, or if the cylinder liner walls are badly scored or scuffed, then renewal of the relevant liner assembly will be necessary. If there is any doubt about the condition of the cylinder bores, seek the advice of a Citroën dealer or engine reconditioning specialist.

22 If renewal is necessary, new liners, complete with pistons and piston rings, can be purchased from a Citroën dealer. Note that it is not possible to buy liners individually - they are supplied only as a matched assembly complete with piston and rings.

23 To allow for manufacturing tolerances, pistons and liners are separated into three size groups. The size group of each piston is indicated by a letter (A, B or C) stamped onto its crown, and the size group of each liner is indicated by a series of 1 to 3 notches on the upper lip of the liner; a single notch for group A, two notches for group B, and three notches for group C. Ensure that each piston and its respective liner are both of the same size group. It is permissible to have different size group piston and liner assemblies fitted to the same engine, but never fit a piston of one size group to a liner in a different group.

24 Prior to installing the liners, thoroughly clean the liner mating surfaces in the cylinder block, and use fine abrasive paper to polish away any burrs or sharp edges which might damage the liner O-rings. Clean the liners and wipe dry, then fit a new O-ring to the base of

each liner. To aid installation, apply a smear of oil to each O-ring and to the base of the liner.

25 If the original liners are being refitted, use the marks made on removal to ensure that each is refitted the correct way round, and is inserted into its original bore. Insert each liner into the cylinder block, taking care not to damage the O-ring, and press it home as far as possible by hand. Using a hammer and a block of wood, tap each liner lightly but fully onto its locating shoulder. Wipe clean, then lightly oil, all exposed liner surfaces, to prevent rusting.

26 With all four liners correctly installed, use a dial gauge (or a straight-edge and feeler blade) to check that the protrusion of each liner above the upper surface of the cylinder block is within the limits given in the Specifications. The maximum difference between any two liners must not be exceeded.

27 If new liners are being fitted, it is permissible to interchange them to bring the difference in protrusion within limits. Remember to keep each piston with its respective liner.

28 If liner protrusion cannot be brought within limits, seek the advice of a Citroën dealer or engine reconditioning specialist before proceeding with the engine rebuild.

13 Piston/connecting rod assembly - inspection

1 Before the inspection process can begin, the piston/connecting rod assemblies must be cleaned, and the original piston rings removed from the pistons.

2 Carefully expand the old rings over the top of the pistons. The use of two or three old feeler blades will be helpful in preventing the rings dropping into empty grooves **(see illustration)**. Be careful not to scratch the piston with the ends of the ring. The rings are brittle, and will snap if they are spread too far. They're also very sharp - protect your hands and fingers. Note that the third ring incorporates an expander. Always remove the rings from the top of the piston. Keep each set

13.15a On 1998 cc 16-valve models, prise out the circlip . . .

13.15b . . . withdraw the gudgeon pin . . .

13.15c . . . and separate the piston from the connecting rod

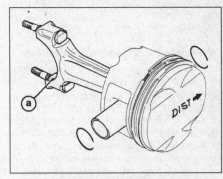

13.19 On 1998 cc 16-valve models, on refitting ensure that the piston arrow is positioned as shown, in relation to the connecting rod bearing shell cutout (a)

of rings with its piston if the old rings are to be re-used.

3 Scrape away all traces of carbon from the top of the piston. A hand-held wire brush (or a piece of fine emery cloth) can be used, once the majority of the deposits have been scraped away.

4 Remove the carbon from the ring grooves in the piston, using an old ring. Break the ring in half to do this (be careful not to cut your fingers - piston rings are sharp). Be careful to remove only the carbon deposits - do not remove any metal, and do not nick or scratch the sides of the ring grooves.

5 Once the deposits have been removed, clean the piston/connecting rod assembly with paraffin or a suitable solvent, and dry thoroughly. Make sure that the oil return holes in the ring grooves are clear.

6 If the pistons and cylinder bores are not damaged or worn excessively, and if the cylinder block does not need to be rebored, the original pistons can be refitted. Normal piston wear shows up as even vertical wear on the piston thrust surfaces, and slight looseness of the top ring in its groove. New piston rings should always be used when the engine is reassembled.

7 Carefully inspect each piston for cracks around the skirt, around the gudgeon pin holes, and at the piston ring "lands" (between the ring grooves).

8 Look for scoring and scuffing on the piston skirt, holes in the piston crown, and burned areas at the edge of the crown. If the skirt is scored or scuffed, the engine may have been suffering from overheating, and/or abnormal combustion which caused excessively high operating temperatures. The cooling and lubrication systems should be checked thoroughly. Scorch marks on the sides of the pistons show that blow-by has occurred. A hole in the piston crown, or burned areas at the edge of the piston crown, indicates that abnormal combustion (pre-ignition, knocking, or detonation) has been occurring. If any of the above problems exist, the causes must be investigated and corrected, or the damage will occur again. The causes may include incorrect ignition timing, or a faulty injector.

9 Corrosion of the piston, in the form of pitting, indicates that coolant has been leaking into the combustion chamber and/or the crankcase. Again, the cause must be corrected, or the problem may persist in the rebuilt engine.

10 On aluminium-block engines with wet liners, it is not possible to renew the pistons separately; pistons are only supplied with piston rings and a liner, as a part of a matched assembly (see Section 12). On iron-block engines, pistons can be purchased from a Citroën dealer.

11 Examine each connecting rod carefully for signs of damage, such as cracks around the big-end and small-end bearings. Check that the rod is not bent or distorted. Damage is highly unlikely, unless the engine has been seized or badly overheated. Detailed checking of the connecting rod assembly can only be carried out by a Citroën dealer or engine repair specialist with the necessary equipment.

12 On XU series (1580 cc and larger) engines, due to the tightening procedure for the connecting rod big-end cap retaining nuts, it is highly recommended that the big-end cap nuts and bolts are renewed as a complete set prior to refitting.

13 On all engines except the 1998 cc 16-valve engine, the gudgeon pins are an interference fit in the connecting rod small-end bearing. Therefore, piston and/or connecting rod renewal should be entrusted to a Citroën dealer or engine repair specialist, who will have the necessary tooling to remove and install the gudgeon pins.

14 On 1998 cc 16-valve engines, the gudgeon pins are of the floating type, secured in position by two circlips. On these engines, the pistons and connecting rods can be separated as follows.

15 Using a small flat-bladed screwdriver, prise out the circlips, and push out the gudgeon pin **(see illustrations)**. Hand pressure should be sufficient to remove the pin. Identify the piston and rod to ensure correct reassembly. Discard the circlips - new ones *must* be used on refitting.

16 Examine the gudgeon pin and connecting rod small-end bearing for signs of wear or damage. Wear can be cured by renewing both the pin and bush. Bush renewal, however, is a specialist job - press facilities are required, and the new bush must be reamed accurately.

17 The connecting rods themselves should not be in need of renewal, unless seizure or some other major mechanical failure has occurred. Check the alignment of the connecting rods visually, and if the rods are not straight, take them to an engine overhaul specialist for a more detailed check.

18 Examine all components, and obtain any new parts from your Citroën dealer. If new pistons are purchased, they will be supplied complete with gudgeon pins and circlips. Circlips can also be purchased individually.

19 Position the piston so that the arrow on the piston crown is positioned as shown in illustration 13.19, in relation to the connecting rod big-end bearing shell cutouts **(see illustration)**. Apply a smear of clean engine oil to the gudgeon pin. Slide it into the piston and through the connecting rod small-end. Check that the piston pivots freely on the rod, then secure the gudgeon pin in position with two new circlips. Ensure that each circlip is correctly located in its groove in the piston.

14.2 Checking crankshaft endfloat using a dial gauge

14.3 Checking crankshaft endfloat using feeler gauges

14.10 Measuring a crankshaft big-end journal diameter

14 Crankshaft - inspection

Checking crankshaft endfloat

1 If the crankshaft endfloat is to be checked, this must be done when the crankshaft is still installed in the cylinder block/crankcase, but is free to move (see Section 11).

2 Check the endfloat using a dial gauge in contact with the end of the crankshaft. Push the crankshaft fully one way, and then zero the gauge. Push the crankshaft fully the other way, and check the endfloat. The result can be compared with the specified amount, and will give an indication as to whether new thrustwashers are required **(see illustration)**.

3 If a dial gauge is not available, feeler gauges can be used. First push the crankshaft fully towards the flywheel end of the engine, then use feeler gauges to measure the gap between the web of No 2 crankpin and the thrustwasher **(see illustration)**.

Inspection

4 Clean the crankshaft using paraffin or a suitable solvent, and dry it, preferably with compressed air if available.

⚠ *Warning: Wear eye protection when using compressed air! Be sure to clean the oil holes with a pipe cleaner or similar probe, to ensure that they are not obstructed.*

5 Check the main and big-end bearing journals for uneven wear, scoring, pitting and cracking.

6 Big-end bearing wear is accompanied by distinct metallic knocking when the engine is running (particularly noticeable when the engine is pulling from low speed) and some loss of oil pressure.

7 Main bearing wear is accompanied by severe engine vibration and rumble - getting progressively worse as engine speed increases - and again by loss of oil pressure.

8 Check the bearing journal for roughness by running a finger lightly over the bearing surface. Any roughness (which will be accompanied by obvious bearing wear)

indicates that the crankshaft requires regrinding (where possible) or renewal.

9 If the crankshaft has been reground, check for burrs around the crankshaft oil holes (the holes are usually chamfered, so burrs should not be a problem unless regrinding has been carried out carelessly). Remove any burrs with a fine file or scraper, and thoroughly clean the oil holes as described previously.

10 Using a micrometer, measure the diameter of the main and big-end bearing journals, and compare the results with the Specifications **(see illustration)**. By measuring the diameter at a number of points around each journal's circumference, you will be able to determine whether or not the journal is out-of-round. Take the measurement at each end of the journal, near the webs, to determine if the journal is tapered. Compare the results obtained with those given in the Specifications. Where no specified journal diameters are quoted, seek the advice of a Citroën dealer.

11 Check the oil seal contact surfaces at each end of the crankshaft for wear and damage. If the seal has worn a deep groove in the surface of the crankshaft, consult an engine overhaul specialist; repair may be possible, but otherwise a new crankshaft will be required.

TU series engines (1124 cc and 1360 cc)

12 Note that Citroën produce a set of oversize bearing shells for both the main bearings and big-end bearings. If the crankshaft has worn beyond the specified limits, and the crankshaft journals have not already been reground, it may be possible to have the crankshaft reconditioned, and to fit the oversize shells. Seek the advice of your Citroën dealer or engine specialist on the best course of action.

XU series engines (1580 cc and larger)

13 At the time of writing, it is not clear whether Citroën produce oversize bearing shells for all of these engines. On some engines, if the crankshaft journals have not already been reground, it may be possible to have the crankshaft reconditioned, and to fit oversize shells. If no oversize shells are

available and the crankshaft has worn beyond the specified limits, it will have to be renewed. Consult your Citroën dealer or engine specialist for further information on parts availability.

15 Main and big-end bearings - inspection

1 Even though the main and big-end bearings should be renewed during the engine overhaul, the old bearings should be retained for close examination, as they may reveal valuable information about the condition of the engine. The bearing shells are graded by thickness, the grade of each shell being indicated by the colour code marked on it.

2 Bearing failure can occur due to lack of lubrication, the presence of dirt or other foreign particles, overloading the engine, or corrosion **(see illustration)**. Regardless of the cause of bearing failure, the cause must be corrected (where applicable) before the

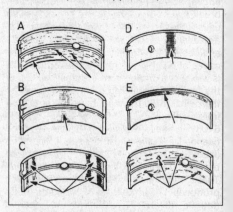

15.2 Typical bearing failures

A   Scratched by dirt; dirt embedded in bearing material
B   Lack of oil; overlay wiped out
C   Improper seating; bright (polished) sections
D   Tapered journal; overlay gone from entire surface
E   Radius ride
F   Fatigue failure; craters or pockets

engine is reassembled, to prevent it from happening again.

3 When examining the bearing shells, remove them from the cylinder block/crankcase, the main bearing ladder/caps (as appropriate), the connecting rods and the connecting rod big-end bearing caps. Lay them out on a clean surface in the same general position as their location in the engine. This will enable you to match any bearing problems with the corresponding crankshaft journal. *Do not* touch any shell's bearing surface with your fingers while checking it, or the delicate surface may be scratched.

4 Dirt and other foreign matter gets into the engine in a variety of ways. It may be left in the engine during assembly, or it may pass through filters or the crankcase ventilation system. It may get into the oil, and from there into the bearings. Metal chips from machining operations and normal engine wear are often present. Abrasives are sometimes left in engine components after reconditioning, especially when parts are not thoroughly cleaned using the proper cleaning methods. Whatever the source, these foreign objects often end up embedded in the soft bearing material, and are easily recognized. Large particles will not embed in the bearing, and will score or gouge the bearing and journal. The best prevention for this cause of bearing failure is to clean all parts thoroughly, and keep everything spotlessly-clean during engine assembly. Frequent and regular engine oil and filter changes are also recommended.

5 Lack of lubrication (or lubrication breakdown) has a number of interrelated causes. Excessive heat (which thins the oil), overloading (which squeezes the oil from the bearing face) and oil leakage (from excessive bearing clearances, worn oil pump or high engine speeds) all contribute to lubrication breakdown. Blocked oil passages, which usually are the result of misaligned oil holes in a bearing shell, will also oil-starve a bearing, and destroy it. When lack of lubrication is the cause of bearing failure, the bearing material is wiped or extruded from the steel backing of the bearing. Temperatures may increase to the point where the steel backing turns blue from overheating.

6 Driving habits can have a definite effect on bearing life. Full-throttle, low-speed operation (labouring the engine) puts very high loads on bearings, tending to squeeze out the oil film. These loads cause the bearings to flex, which produces fine cracks in the bearing face (fatigue failure). Eventually, the bearing material will loosen in pieces, and tear away from the steel backing.

7 Short-distance driving leads to corrosion of bearings, because insufficient engine heat is produced to drive off the condensed water and corrosive gases. These products collect in the engine oil, forming acid and sludge. As the oil is carried to the engine bearings, the acid attacks and corrodes the bearing material.

8 Incorrect bearing installation during engine assembly will lead to bearing failure as well. Tight-fitting bearings leave insufficient bearing running clearance, and will result in oil starvation. Dirt or foreign particles trapped behind a bearing shell result in high spots on the bearing, which lead to failure.

9 *Do not* touch any shell's bearing surface with your fingers during reassembly; there is a risk of scratching the delicate surface, or of depositing particles of dirt on it.

10 As mentioned at the beginning of this Section, the bearing shells should be renewed as a matter of course during engine overhaul; to do otherwise is false economy. Refer to Section 18 for details of bearing shell selection.

16 Engine overhaul - reassembly sequence

1 Before reassembly begins, ensure that all new parts have been obtained, and that all necessary tools are available. Read through the entire procedure to familiarise yourself with the work involved, and to ensure that all items necessary for reassembly of the engine are at hand. In addition to all normal tools and materials, thread-locking compound will be needed. A suitable tube of liquid sealant will also be required for the joint faces that are fitted without gaskets. It is recommended that Citroën's own product(s) are used, which are specially formulated for this purpose; the relevant product names are quoted in the text of each Section where they are required.

2 In order to save time and avoid problems, engine reassembly can be carried out in the following order:

(a) *Crankshaft (Section 18).*
(b) *Piston/connecting rod assemblies (Section 19).*
(c) *Oil pump.*
(d) *Sump (See Part A or B - as applicable).*
(e) *Flywheel (See Part A or B - as applicable).*
(f) *Cylinder head (See Part A or B - as applicable).*
(g) *Timing belt inner cover, tensioner and sprockets, and timing belt (See Part A or B - as applicable).*
(h) *Engine external components.*

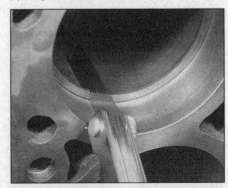

17.5 Measuring a piston ring end gap

3 At this stage, all engine components should be absolutely clean and dry, with all faults repaired. The components should be laid out (or in individual containers) on a completely clean work surface.

17 Piston rings - refitting

1 Before fitting new piston rings, the ring end gaps must be checked as follows.

2 Lay out the piston/connecting rod assemblies and the new piston ring sets, so that the ring sets will be matched with the same piston and cylinder during the end gap measurement and subsequent engine reassembly.

3 Insert the top ring into the first cylinder, and push it down the bore using the top of the piston. This will ensure that the ring remains square with the cylinder walls. Position the ring near the bottom of the cylinder bore, at the lower limit of ring travel. Note that the top and second compression rings are different. The second ring is easily identified by the step on its lower surface, and by the fact that its outer face is tapered.

4 Measure the end gap using feeler gauges.

5 Repeat the procedure with the ring at the top of the cylinder bore, at the upper limit of its travel, and compare the measurements with the figures given in the Specifications **(see illustration)**.

6 If the gap is too small (unlikely if genuine Citroën parts are used), it must be enlarged, or the ring ends may contact each other during engine operation, causing serious damage. Ideally, new piston rings providing the correct end gap should be fitted. As a last resort, the end gap can be increased by filing the ring ends very carefully with a fine file. Mount the file in a vice equipped with soft jaws, slip the ring over the file with the ends contacting the file face, and slowly move the ring to remove material from the ends. Take care, as piston rings are sharp, and are easily broken.

7 With new piston rings, it is unlikely that the end gap will be too large. If the gaps are too large, check that you have the correct rings for your engine and for the particular cylinder bore size.

8 Repeat the checking procedure for each ring in the first cylinder, and then for the rings in the remaining cylinders. Remember to keep rings, pistons and cylinders matched up.

9 Once the ring end gaps have been checked and if necessary corrected, the rings can be fitted to the pistons.

10 Fit the piston rings using the same technique as for removal. Fit the bottom (oil control) ring first, and work up. When fitting the oil control ring, first insert the expander, then fit the ring with its gap positioned 180° from the expander gap. Ensure that the second compression ring is fitted the correct way up, with its identification mark (either a

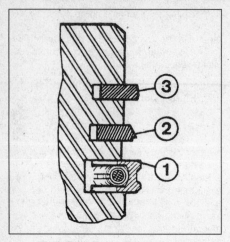

17.10 Piston ring fitting diagram

1 Oil control ring
2 Second compression ring
3 Top compression ring

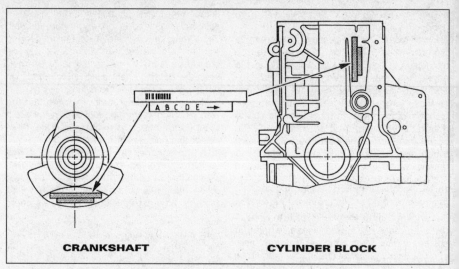

CRANKSHAFT   **CYLINDER BLOCK**

18.5 Cylinder block and crankshaft main bearing reference marking locations - February 1992-on TU series engines

dot of paint or the word "TOP" stamped on the ring surface) at the top, and the stepped surface at the bottom **(see illustration)**. Arrange the gaps of the top and second compression rings 120° either side of the oil control ring gap. **Note:** *Always follow any instructions supplied with the new piston ring sets - different manufacturers may specify different procedures. Do not mix up the top and second compression rings, as they have different cross-sections.*

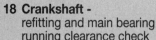

18 Crankshaft -
refitting and main bearing running clearance check

Selection of new bearing shells

TU series engine - 1124 cc and 1360 cc

1 On early engines, both upper and lower main bearing shells were of the same thickness, with only two sizes of bearing shells being available; a standard size for use with the standard crankshaft, and a set of oversize bearing shells for use once the crankshaft bearing journals have been reground.

2 However, since February 1992, the specified main bearing running clearance has been significantly reduced. This has been achieved by the introduction of three different grades of bearing shell, in both standard sizes and oversizes. The grades are indicated by a colour-coding marked on the edge of each shell, which denotes the shell's thickness, as listed in the following table. The upper shell on all bearings is of the same size (class B, colour code black), and the running clearance is controlled by fitting a lower bearing shell of the required thickness. This arrangement has been fitted to all engines produced since February 1992 and, if possible, should also be

fitted to earlier engines during overhaul. Seek the advice of your Citroën dealer on parts availability and the best course of action when ordering new bearing shells.

Bearing colour code	Thickness (mm)	
	Standard	Oversize
Blue (class A)	1.823	1.973
Black (class B)	1.835	1.985
Green (class C)	1.848	1.998

3 On early engines, the correct size of bearing shell must be selected by measuring the running clearance as described under the sub-heading below.

4 On engines produced since February 1992, when the new bearing shell sizes were introduced, the crankshaft and cylinder block/crankcase have reference marks on them, to identify the size of the journals and bearing bores.

5 The cylinder block reference marks are on the right-hand (timing belt) end of the block, and the crankshaft reference marks are on the right-hand (timing belt) end of the crankshaft, on the right-hand web of No 4 crankpin **(see illustration)**. These marks can be used to select bearing shells of the required thickness as follows.

6 On both the crankshaft and block there are two lines of identification: a bar code, which is used by Citroën during production, and a row of five letters. The first letter in the sequence refers to the size of No 1 bearing (at the flywheel/driveplate end). The last letter in the sequence (which is followed by an arrow) refers to the size of No 5 main bearing. These marks can be used to select the required bearing shell grade as follows.

7 Obtain the identification letter of both the relevant crankshaft journal and the cylinder block bearing bore. Noting that the cylinder block letters are listed across the top of the chart, and the crankshaft letters down the side, trace a vertical line down from the relevant cylinder block letter, and a horizontal

line across from the relevant crankshaft letter, and find the point at which both lines cross. This crossover point will indicate the grade of lower bearing shell required to give the correct main bearing running clearance. For example, the illustration shows cylinder block reference G, and crankshaft reference T, crossing at a point within the area of Class A, indicating that a blue-coded (Class A) lower bearing shell is required to give the correct main bearing running clearance **(see illustration)**.

8 Repeat this procedure so that the required bearing shell grade is obtained for each of the five main bearing journals.

XU series engine - 1580 cc and larger

9 On early engines in the range, both upper and lower main bearing shells were of the same thickness, with only two sizes of bearing shells being available; a standard size for use with the standard crankshaft, and a set of oversize bearing shells for use once the crankshaft bearing journals have been reground.

10 On later engines, the upper main bearing shells are all of one size grade, and the main bearing running clearance is controlled by

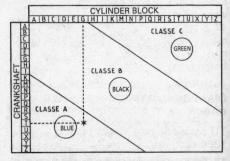

18.7 Main bearing shell selection chart, for use with later TU series engines - see text for further information

18.15 On TU series engines, note that the grooved bearing shells are fitted to Nos 2 and 4 main bearing journals

18.19 Plastigage in place on a crankshaft main bearing journal

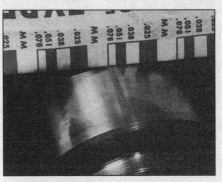

18.22 Measuring the width of the deformed Plastigage using the scale on the card provided

fitting lower bearings of the required grade. Four different grades of lower bearing shell are available, the grades being indicated by a colour-coding marked on the edge of each shell, which denotes the shell's thickness as follows.

1580 cc, 1761 cc and 1905 cc engines

Bearing colour	Thickness (mm)
Upper bearing:	
Yellow	1.856
Lower bearing:	
Blue	1.836
Black	1.848
Grey or green	1.859
Red	1.870

1998 cc engines

Bearing colour	Thickness (mm)
Upper bearing:	
Black	1.847
Lower bearing:	
Blue	1.844
Black	1.857
Green	1.866
Red	1.877

Note: On all XU series engines, upper shells are easily distinguished from lower shells, by their grooved bearing surface; the lower shells have a plain surface.

11 It is not clear at the time of writing whether oversize bearing shells are available for later engines. On early engines, if possible, it is recommended that the later bearing shell arrangement is fitted during overhaul. Seek the advice of your Citroën dealer on parts availability, and on the best course of action when ordering new bearing shells.

12 Since there are no bearing identification marks, the relevant main bearing shell grade must be selected by measuring the main bearing running clearance.

Main bearing running clearance check

TU series engine - 1124 cc and 1360 cc

13 On early engines, if the modified bearing shells are to be fitted, obtain a set of new black (Class B) upper bearing shells and new blue (Class A) lower bearing shells. On later

(February 1992-on) engines where the modified bearing shells are already fitted, the running clearance check can be carried out using the original bearing shells. However, it is preferable to use a new set, since the results obtained will be more conclusive.

14 Clean the backs of the bearing shells, and the bearing locations in both the cylinder block/crankcase and the main bearing ladder.

15 Press the bearing shells into their locations, ensuring that the tab on each shell engages in the notch in the cylinder block/crankcase or main bearing ladder location. Take care not to touch any shell's bearing surface with your fingers. Note that the grooved bearing shells, both upper and lower, are fitted to Nos 2 and 4 main bearings (see illustration). If the original bearing shells are being used for the check, ensure that they are refitted in their original locations. The clearance can be checked in either of two ways.

16 One method (which will be difficult to achieve without a range of internal micrometers or internal/external expanding calipers) is to refit the main bearing ladder casting to the cylinder block/crankcase, with the bearing shells in place. With the casting retaining bolts correctly tightened, measure the internal diameter of each assembled pair of bearing shells. If the diameter of each corresponding crankshaft journal is measured and then subtracted from the bearing internal diameter, the result will be the main bearing running clearance.

17 The second (and more accurate) method is to use an American product known as "Plastigage". This consists of a fine thread of perfectly-round plastic, which is compressed between the bearing shell and the journal. When the shell is removed, the plastic is deformed, and can be measured with a special card gauge supplied with the kit. The running clearance is determined from this gauge. Plastigage should be available from your Citroën dealer (reference number OUT 30 4133 T); otherwise, enquiries at one of the larger specialist motor factors should produce the name of a stockist in your area. The procedure for using Plastigage is as follows.

18 With the main bearing upper shells in place, carefully lay the crankshaft in position. Do not use any lubricant; the crankshaft journals and bearing shells must be perfectly clean and dry.

19 Cut several lengths of the appropriate-size Plastigage (they should be slightly shorter than the width of the main bearings), and place one length on each crankshaft journal axis (see illustration).

20 With the main bearing lower shells in position, refit the main bearing ladder casting, tightening its retaining bolts as described in paragraph 40. Take care not to disturb the Plastigage, and do not rotate the crankshaft at any time during this operation.

21 Remove the main bearing ladder casting, again taking great care not to disturb the Plastigage or rotate the crankshaft.

22 Compare the width of the crushed Plastigage on each journal to the scale printed on the Plastigage envelope, to obtain the main bearing running clearance (see illustration). Compare the clearance measured with that given in the Specifications at the start of this Chapter.

23 If the clearance is significantly different from that expected, the bearing shells may be the wrong size (or excessively worn, if the original shells are being re-used). Before deciding that different-size shells are required, make sure that no dirt or oil was trapped between the bearing shells and the caps or block when the clearance was measured. If the Plastigage was wider at one end than at the other, the crankshaft journal may be tapered.

24 If the clearance is not as specified, use the reading obtained, along with the shell thicknesses quoted above, to calculate the necessary grade of bearing shells required. When calculating the bearing clearance required, bear in mind that it is always better to have the running clearance towards the lower end of the specified range, to allow for wear in use.

25 Where necessary, obtain the required grades of bearing shell, and repeat the running clearance checking procedure as described above.

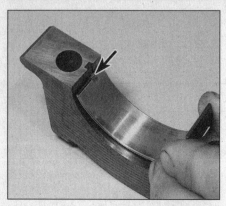

18.29 On XU series engines, all the lower shells have a plain bearing surface. Ensure that the tab (arrowed) is correctly located in the cap

18.35 Refitting a crankshaft thrustwasher - TU series engine

18.36 Ensure each bearing shell tab (arrowed) is correctly located, and lubricate the shell with clean engine oil

26 On completion, carefully scrape away all traces of the Plastigage material from the crankshaft and bearing shells. Use your fingernail, or a wooden or plastic scraper which is unlikely to score the bearing surfaces.

XU series engine - 1580 cc and larger

27 On early engines, if the modified bearing shells are to be fitted, obtain a set of new upper bearing shells, and new green or grey (as applicable) lower bearing shells (see paragraph 10). On later engines where the modified bearing shells are already fitted, the running clearance check can be carried out using the original bearing shells. However, it is preferable to use a new set, since the results obtained will be more conclusive.
28 Clean the backs of the bearing shells, and the bearing locations in both the cylinder block/crankcase and the main bearing caps.
29 Press the bearing shells into their locations, ensuring that the tab on each shell engages in the notch in the cylinder block/crankcase or bearing cap. Take care not to touch any shell's bearing surface with your fingers. Note that the upper bearing shells all have a grooved bearing surface,

whereas the lower shells have a plain bearing surface (see illustration). If the original bearing shells are being used for the check, ensure that they are refitted in their original locations.
30 The clearance can be checked in either of two ways.
31 One method (which will be difficult to achieve without a range of internal micrometers or internal/external expanding calipers) is to refit the main bearing caps to the cylinder block/crankcase, with bearing shells in place. With the cap retaining bolts tightened to the specified torque, measure the internal diameter of each assembled pair of bearing shells. If the diameter of each corresponding crankshaft journal is measured and then subtracted from the bearing internal diameter, the result will be the main bearing running clearance.
32 The second, and more accurate, method is to use Plastigage. The method is as described above in paragraphs 17 to 26, substituting "main bearing caps" for all references to the main bearing ladder casting.
33 Note that Citroën do not specify a main bearing running clearance for the 1580 cc, 1761 cc, or 1905 cc engines. The figure given

in the Specifications is a guide figure which is typical for this type of engine. On these engines, therefore, always refer to your Citroën dealer for details of the exact running clearance before condemning the components concerned.

Final crankshaft refitting

TU series engine - 1124 cc and 1360 cc

34 Carefully lift the crankshaft out of the cylinder block once more.
35 Using a little grease, stick the upper thrustwashers to each side of the No 2 main bearing upper location; ensure that the oilway grooves on each thrustwasher face outwards (away from the cylinder block) (see illustration).
36 Place the bearing shells in their locations as described above in paragraphs 14 and 15. If new shells are being fitted, ensure that all traces of protective grease are cleaned off using paraffin. Wipe dry the shells and connecting rods with a lint-free cloth. Liberally lubricate each bearing shell in the cylinder block/crankcase with clean engine oil (see illustration).
37 Refit the Woodruff key, then slide on the oil pump drive sprocket, and locate the drive chain on the sprocket (see illustration). Lower the crankshaft into position so that Nos 2 and 3 cylinder crankpins are at TDC. Check the crankshaft endfloat as described in Section 14.
38 Thoroughly degrease the mating surfaces of the cylinder block/crankcase and the main bearing ladder. Apply a thin bead of suitable sealant to the cylinder block/crankcase mating surface of the main bearing ladder casting, then spread to an even film (see illustration). Citroën recommend the use of Auto Joint E10 sealant (available from your Citroën dealer); in the absence of the specified sealant, any suitable good-quality sealant may be used.
39 Lubricate the lower bearing shells with clean engine oil, then refit the main bearing

18.37 Refitting the oil pump drive chain and sprocket - TU series engine

18.38 Apply a thin film of suitable sealant to the cylinder block/crankcase mating surface . . .

18.39 . . . then lower the main bearing ladder into position

18.40a Tighten the ten 11 mm main bearing bolts to the stage 1 torque setting . . .

18.40b . . . then angle-tighten them through the specified stage 2 angle

2C

ladder, ensuring that the shells are not displaced, and that the locating dowels engage correctly **(see illustration)**.

40 Install the ten 11 mm main bearing ladder retaining bolts, and tighten them all by hand only. Working progressively outwards from the centre bolts, tighten the ten bolts, by a turn at a time, to the specified stage 1 torque wrench setting. Once all the bolts have been tightened to the stage 1 setting, angle-tighten the bolts through the specified stage 2 setting using a socket and extension bar. It is recommended that an angle-measuring gauge is used during this stage of the tightening, to ensure accuracy **(see illustrations)**.

HAYNES HiNT *If an angle-measuring gauge is not available, use a dab of white paint to make alignment marks between the bolt head and casting prior to tightening; the marks can then be used to check that the bolt has been rotated sufficiently during tightening.*

41 Refit all the 6 mm bolts securing the main bearing ladder to the base of the cylinder block, and tighten them to the specified

torque. Check that the crankshaft rotates freely.

42 Refit the piston/connecting rod assemblies to the crankshaft as described in Section 19.

43 Ensuring that the drive chain is correctly located on the sprocket, refit the oil pump and sump as described in Part A of this Chapter.

44 Fit two new crankshaft oil seals as described in Part A. Where removed, refit the cylinder head as described in Part A.

XU series engine - 1580 cc and larger

45 Carefully lift the crankshaft out of the cylinder block once more.

46 Using a little grease, stick the upper thrustwashers to each side of the No 2 main bearing upper location; ensure that the oilway grooves on each thrustwasher face outwards (away from the cylinder block) **(see illustration)**.

47 Place the bearing shells in their locations as described above in paragraphs 28 and 29. If new shells are being fitted, ensure that all traces of protective grease are cleaned off using paraffin. Wipe dry the shells and connecting rods with a lint-free cloth.

48 Liberally lubricate each bearing shell in the cylinder block/crankcase with clean engine oil. Lower the crankshaft into position, ensuring that the bearing shells and thrustwashers remain correctly seated.

49 Using a little grease, stick the lower thrustwashers to each side of the No 2 main bearing cap location; ensure that the oilway grooves on each thrustwasher face outwards (away from the cap).

50 Before fitting the bearing caps, check the crankshaft endfloat as described in Section 14.

51 Fit main bearing caps Nos 2 to 5 to their correct locations, ensuring that they are fitted the correct way round (the bearing shell tab recesses in the block and caps must be on the same side). Insert the bolts/nuts, tightening them only loosely at this stage.

52 Apply a small amount of sealant to the No 1 main bearing cap face mating on the cylinder block, around the sealing strip holes **(see illustration)**.

53 Locate the tab of each sealing strip over the pins on the base of No 1 bearing cap, and press the strips into the bearing cap grooves. It is now necessary to obtain two thin metal strips, of 0.25 mm thickness or less, in order to prevent the strips moving when the cap is being fitted. Citroën garages use the tool shown, which acts as a clamp. Metal strips (such as old feeler blades) can be used, provided all burrs which may damage the sealing strips are first removed **(see illustrations)**.

18.46 Fitting a thrustwasher to No 2 main bearing upper location - XU series engine

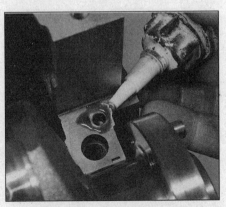

18.52 Applying sealant to the cylinder block No 1 main bearing cap mating face

18.53a Fitting a sealing strip to No 1 main bearing cap

18.53b Using the Citroën special tool to fit No 1 main bearing cap

18.54a Fitting No 1 main bearing cap, using metal strips to retain the side seals

18.54b Removing a metal strip from No 1 main bearing cap using a pair of pliers

54 Where applicable, oil both sides of the metal strips, and hold them on the sealing strips. Fit the No 1 main bearing cap, insert the bolts loosely, then carefully pull out the metal strips in a horizontal direction, using a pair of pliers (see illustrations).

55 Tighten all the main bearing cap bolts/nuts evenly to the specified torque. Using a sharp knife, trim off the ends of the No 1 bearing cap sealing strips, so that they protrude above the cylinder block/crankcase mating surface by approximately 1 mm (see illustrations).

56 On 1580 cc, 1761 cc and 1905 cc engines, refit the centre main bearing side retaining bolts and sealing washers (one at the front of the block, and one at the rear) and tighten them both to the specified torque.

57 Fit a new crankshaft rear oil seal as described in Part B of this Chapter.

58 Refit the piston/connecting rod assemblies to the crankshaft as described in Section 19.

59 Refit the Woodruff key, then slide on the oil pump drive sprocket, and locate the drive chain on the sprocket.

60 Ensure that the mating surfaces of the front oil seal carrier and cylinder block are clean and dry. Note the correct fitted depth of the oil seal then, using a large flat-bladed screwdriver, lever the old seal out of the housing.

61 Apply a smear of suitable sealant to the oil seal carrier mating surface. Citroën recommend the use of Formajoint E7 sealant (available from your Citroën dealer); in the absence of the specified sealant, any suitable good-quality sealant may be used.

62 Ensure that the locating dowels are in position, then slide the carrier over the end of the crankshaft and into position on the cylinder block. Tighten the carrier retaining bolts to the specified torque.

63 Fit a new crankshaft front oil seal as described in Part B of this Chapter.

64 Ensuring that the drive chain is correctly located on the sprocket, refit the oil pump and sump as described in Part B of this Chapter.

65 Where removed, refit the cylinder head as described in Part B.

19 Piston/connecting rod assembly - refitting and big-end bearing running clearance check

Selection of bearing shells

1 On TU series (1124 cc and 1360 cc) engines, there are two sizes of big-end bearing shell produced by Citroën; a standard size for use with the standard crankshaft, and an oversize for use once the crankshaft

journals have been reground. When ordering shells, quote the diameter of the crankshaft big-end crankpins, to ensure that the correct set of shells are purchased.

2 On XU series (1580 cc and larger) engines, at the time of writing, it is not clear if oversize bearing shells (for use with a reground crankshaft) are available for all engines. On some engines, there appears only to be one size of big-end bearing shell available from Citroën. Consult your Citroën dealer for the latest information on parts availability. To be safe, always quote the diameter of the crankshaft big-end crankpins when ordering bearing shells.

3 Prior to refitting the piston/connecting rod assemblies, it is recommended that the big-end bearing running clearance is checked as follows.

Big-end bearing running clearance check

4 Clean the backs of the bearing shells, and the bearing locations in both the connecting rod and bearing cap.

5 Press the bearing shells into their locations, ensuring that the tab on each shell engages in the notch in the connecting rod and cap. Take care not to touch any shell's bearing surface with your fingers (see illustration). If the original bearing shells are being used for the

18.55a With all bearing caps correctly installed, tighten their retaining nuts and bolts to the specified torque . . .

18.55b . . . then trim the ends of No 1 bearing cap sealing strips, so that they protrude above the cylinder block mating surface by approximately 1 mm

19.5 Fitting a bearing shell to a connecting rod - ensure that the tab (arrowed) engages with the recess in the connecting rod

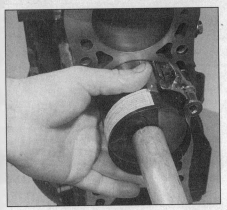

19.19 Tap the piston into the bore using a hammer handle

19.22a On XU series engines, tighten the big-end bearing cap nuts to the stage 1 specified torque, then fully slacken them and tighten them to the stage 2 torque . . .

19.22b . . . then through the angle specified for stage 3

2C

check, ensure they are refitted in their original locations. The clearance can be checked in either of two ways.

6 One method is to refit the big-end bearing cap to the connecting rod, ensuring they are fitted the correct way round (see paragraph 20), with the bearing shells in place. With the cap retaining nuts correctly tightened, use an internal micrometer or vernier caliper to measure the internal diameter of each assembled pair of bearing shells. If the diameter of each corresponding crankshaft journal is measured and then subtracted from the bearing internal diameter, the result will be the big-end bearing running clearance.

7 The second, and more accurate, method is to use Plastigage (see Section 18).

8 Ensure that the bearing shells are correctly fitted. Place a strand of Plastigage on each (cleaned) crankpin journal.

9 Refit the (clean) piston/connecting rod assemblies to the crankshaft, and refit the big-end bearing caps, using the marks made or noted on removal to ensure they are fitted the correct way around.

10 Tighten the bearing cap nuts as described below in paragraph 21 or 22 (as applicable). Take care not to disturb the Plastigage or rotate the connecting rod during the tightening sequence.

11 Dismantle the assemblies without rotating the connecting rods. Use the scale printed on the Plastigage envelope to obtain the big-end bearing running clearance.

12 If the clearance is significantly different from that expected, the bearing shells may be the wrong size (or excessively worn, if the original shells are being re-used). Make sure that no dirt or oil was trapped between the bearing shells and the caps or connecting rod when the clearance was measured. If the Plastigage was wider at one end than at the other, the crankpins may be tapered.

13 Note that Citroën do not specify a recommended big-end bearing running

clearance. The figure given in the Specifications is a guide figure, which is typical for this type of engine. Before condemning the components concerned, refer to your Citroën dealer or engine reconditioning specialist for further information on the specified running clearance. Their advice on the best course of action to be taken can then also be obtained.

14 On completion, carefully scrape away all traces of the Plastigage material from the crankshaft and bearing shells. Use your fingernail, or some other object which is unlikely to score the bearing surfaces.

Final piston/connecting rod refitting

15 Note that the following procedure assumes that the cylinder liners (where fitted) are in position in the cylinder block/crankcase as described in Section 12, and that the crankshaft and main bearing ladder/caps are in place (see Section 18).

16 Ensure that the bearing shells are correctly fitted as described above in paragraphs 4 and 5. If new shells are being fitted, ensure that all traces of the protective grease are cleaned off using paraffin. Wipe dry the shells and connecting rods with a lint-free cloth.

17 Lubricate the cylinder bores, the pistons, and piston rings, then lay out each piston/connecting rod assembly in its respective position.

18 Start with assembly No 1. Make sure that the piston rings are still spaced as described in Section 17, then clamp them in position with a piston ring compressor.

19 Insert the piston/connecting rod assembly into the top of cylinder/liner No 1. Ensure that the arrow on the piston crown is pointing towards the timing belt end of the engine. Using a block of wood or hammer handle against the piston crown, tap the assembly into the cylinder/liner until the piston crown is

flush with the top of the cylinder/liner **(see illustration)**.

20 Ensure that the bearing shell is still correctly installed. Liberally lubricate the crankpin and both bearing shells. Taking care not to mark the cylinder/liner bores, pull the piston/connecting rod assembly down the bore and onto the crankpin. Refit the big-end bearing cap, tightening its retaining nuts finger-tight at first. Note that the faces with the identification marks must match (which means that the bearing shell locating tabs abut each other).

21 On TU series (1124 cc and 1360 cc) engines, tighten the bearing cap retaining nuts evenly and progressively to the specified torque setting.

22 On XU series (1580 cc and larger) engines except 1761 cc 16-valve models, tighten the bearing cap retaining nuts evenly and progressively to the Stage 1 torque setting. Fully slacken both nuts, then tighten them to the Stage 2 torque setting. Once both nuts have been tightened to the Stage 2 setting, angle-tighten them through the specified Stage 3 angle, using a socket and extension bar. It is recommended that an angle-measuring gauge is used during this stage of the tightening to ensure accuracy **(see illustrations)**. On 1761 cc 16-valve engines, tighten the bearing cap retaining nuts evenly and progressively to the Stage 1 torque setting, then angle-tighten them through the Stage 2 angle, using a socket, extension bar and angle-measuring gauge.

23 On all engines, once the bearing cap retaining nuts have been correctly tightened, rotate the crankshaft. Check that it turns freely; some stiffness is to be expected if new components have been fitted, but there should be no signs of binding or tight spots.

24 Refit the remaining three piston/connecting rod assemblies in the same way.

25 Refit the cylinder head and oil pump as described in Part A or B of this Chapter (as applicable).

20 Engine -
initial start-up after overhaul

1 With the engine refitted in the car, double-check the engine oil and coolant levels. Make a final check that everything has been reconnected, and that there are no tools or rags left in the engine compartment.
2 Remove the spark plugs. On models with a distributor, disable the ignition system by disconnecting the ignition HT coil lead from the distributor cap, and earthing it on the cylinder block. Use a jumper lead or similar wire to make a good connection. On models with a static (distributorless) ignition system, disable the ignition system by disconnecting the LT wiring connector from the ignition HT coil(s), referring to Chapter 5 for further information.
3 Turn the engine on the starter until the oil pressure warning light goes out. Refit the spark plugs, and reconnect the spark plug (HT) leads, referring to Chapter 1 for further information. Reconnect any HT leads or wiring which was disconnected in paragraph 2.
4 Start the engine, noting that this may take a little longer than usual, due to the fuel system components being empty.
5 While the engine is idling, check for fuel, water and oil leaks. Don't be alarmed if there are some odd smells and smoke from parts getting hot and burning off oil deposits. On 1998 cc 16-valve engines, some valvegear noise may be heard at first; this should disappear as the oil circulates fully around the engine, and normal pressure is restored in the hydraulic tappet mechanisms.
6 Assuming all is well, keep the engine idling until hot water is felt circulating through the top hose. Check the ignition timing and idle speed and mixture (as appropriate), then switch the engine off.
7 After a few minutes, recheck the oil and coolant levels as described in Chapter 1, and top-up as necessary.
8 If they were tightened as described, there is no need to re-tighten the cylinder head bolts once the engine has first run after reassembly.
9 If new pistons, rings or crankshaft bearings have been fitted, the engine must be treated as new and run-in for the first 500 miles (800 km). *Do not* operate the engine at full-throttle, or allow it to labour at low engine speeds in any gear. It is recommended that the oil and filter be changed at the end of this period.

Chapter 3
Cooling, heating and ventilation systems

Contents

Air conditioning compressor (auxiliary) drivebelt -
checking and renewal .... See Chapter 1
Air conditioning system - general information and precautions 11
Air conditioning system components - removal and refitting 12
Air conditioning system refrigerant check .... See Chapter 1
Antifreeze mixture .... See Chapter 1
Coolant level check .... See "Weekly checks"
Coolant pump - removal and refitting 7
Cooling system - draining .... See Chapter 1
Cooling system - filling .... See Chapter 1
Cooling system - flushing .... See Chapter 1

Cooling system electrical switches and sensors - testing,
removal and refitting 6
Cooling system hoses - disconnection and renewal 2
Electric cooling fan(s) - testing, removal and refitting 5
General information and precautions 1
Heating and ventilation system - general information 8
Heater/ventilation components - removal and refitting 9
Heater vents - removal and refitting 10
Radiator - removal, inspection and refitting 3
Thermostat - removal, testing and refitting 4

Degrees of difficulty

Easy, suitable for novice with little experience	Fairly easy, suitable for beginner with some experience	Fairly difficult, suitable for competent DIY mechanic 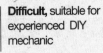	Difficult, suitable for experienced DIY mechanic	Very difficult, suitable for expert DIY or professional

Specifications

General
Maximum system pressure .... 1.4 bars

Thermostat
Opening temperatures:
Starts to open .... 89°C
Fully-open .... 101°C

Electric cooling fan(s)
Cooling fan(s) cut in:
Single-speed cooling fan:
1998 cc 8-valve models .... 95°C
All other models .... 97°C
Twin-speed cooling fan(s):*
Slow speed .... 97°C
Fast speed .... 101°C
Cooling fan(s) cut out:
Single-speed cooling fan:
1998 cc 8-valve models .... 86°C
All other models .... 92°C
Twin-speed cooling fan(s):*
Slow speed .... 92°C
Fast speed .... 96°C

*Twin-speed cooling fans are fitted to all models with air conditioning, and to models supplied to countries with a hot climate.

Torque wrench settings	Nm	lbf ft
Coolant pump bolts:		
1124 cc and 1360 cc models:		
Lower bolt	7	5
Upper bolt	16	12
1580 cc and larger-engined models	15	11
Temperature switches/sensors:		
Screwed into radiator	35	26
Screwed into cylinder head/coolant outlet housing	18	13

1 General information and precautions

General information

The cooling system is of pressurised type, comprising a coolant pump driven by the timing belt, an aluminium crossflow radiator with integral expansion tank, electric cooling fan(s), a thermostat, heater matrix, and all associated hoses and switches.

The system functions as follows. Cold coolant in the bottom of the radiator passes through the bottom hose to the coolant pump, where it is pumped around the cylinder block and head passages, and through the oil cooler(s) (where fitted). After cooling the cylinder bores, combustion surfaces and valve seats, the coolant reaches the underside of the thermostat, which is initially closed. The coolant passes through the heater, and is returned via the cylinder block to the coolant pump.

When the engine is cold, the coolant circulates only through the cylinder block, cylinder head, and heater. When the coolant reaches a predetermined temperature, the thermostat opens, and the coolant passes through the top hose to the radiator. As the coolant circulates through the radiator, it is cooled by the inrush of air when the car is in forward motion. The airflow is supplemented by the action of the electric cooling fan(s) when necessary. Upon reaching the bottom of the radiator, the coolant has now cooled, and the cycle is repeated.

When the engine is at normal operating temperature, the coolant expands, and some of it is displaced into the expansion tank. Coolant collects in the tank, and is returned to the radiator when the system cools.

On models with automatic transmission, a proportion of the coolant is recirculated from the bottom of the radiator through the transmission fluid cooler mounted on the transmission. On 16-valve models, the coolant is also passed through the engine oil cooler.

The electric cooling fan(s) mounted in front of the radiator are controlled by a thermostatic switch. At a predetermined coolant temperature, the switch/sensor actuates the fan.

Precautions

⚠️ **Warning: Do not attempt to remove the expansion tank filler cap, or to disturb any part of the cooling system, while the engine is hot, as there is a high risk of scalding. If the expansion tank filler cap must be removed before the engine and radiator have fully cooled (even though this is not recommended), the pressure in the cooling system must first be relieved. Cover the cap with a thick layer of cloth, to avoid scalding, and slowly unscrew the filler cap until a hissing sound is heard. When the hissing has stopped, indicating that the pressure has reduced, slowly unscrew the filler cap until it can be removed; if more hissing sounds are heard, wait until they have stopped before unscrewing the cap completely. At all times, keep well away from the filler cap opening, and protect your hands.**

⚠️ **Warning: Do not allow antifreeze to come into contact with your skin, or with the painted surfaces of the vehicle. Rinse off spills immediately, with plenty of water. Never leave antifreeze lying around in an open container, or in a puddle in the driveway or on the garage floor. Children and pets are attracted by its sweet smell, but antifreeze can be fatal if ingested.**

⚠️ **Warning: If the engine is hot, the electric cooling fan may start rotating even if the engine is not running. Be careful to keep your hands, hair, and any loose clothing well clear when working in the engine compartment.**

⚠️ **Warning: Refer to Section 11 for precautions to be observed when working on models equipped with air conditioning.**

2 Cooling system hoses - disconnection and renewal

Note: *Refer to the warnings given in Section 1 of this Chapter before proceeding. Hoses should only be disconnected once the engine has cooled sufficiently to avoid scalding.*

1 If the checks described in Chapter 1 reveal a faulty hose, it must be renewed as follows.

2 First drain the cooling system (see Chapter 1). If the coolant is not due for renewal, it may be re-used, providing it is collected in a clean container.

3 To disconnect a hose, proceed as follows, according to the type of hose connection.

Conventional hose connections - general instructions

4 On conventional connections, the clips used to secure the hoses in position may be either standard worm-drive clips or disposable crimped types. The crimped type of clip is not designed to be re-used and should be replaced with a worm drive type on reassembly.

5 To disconnect a hose, use a screwdriver to slacken or release the clips, then move them along the hose, clear of the relevant inlet/outlet. Carefully work the hose free **(see illustration)**. The hoses can be removed with relative ease when new - on an older car, they may have stuck.

6 If a hose proves to be difficult to remove, try to release it by rotating its ends before attempting to free it. Gently prise the end of the hose with a blunt instrument (such as a flat-bladed screwdriver), but do not apply too much force, and take care not to damage the pipe stubs or hoses. Note in particular that the radiator inlet stub is fragile; do not use excessive force when attempting to remove the hose.

> **HAYNES HiNT** *If all else fails, cut the hose with a sharp knife, then slit it so that it can be peeled off in two pieces. Although this may prove expensive if the hose is otherwise undamaged, it is preferable to buying a new radiator. Check first, however, that a new hose is readily available.*

7 When fitting a hose, first slide the clips onto the hose, then work the hose into position. If crimped-type clips were originally fitted, use standard worm-drive clips when refitting the hose. If the hose is stiff, use a little soapy water as a lubricant, or soften the hose by soaking it in hot water. Do not use oil or grease, which may attack the rubber.

8 Work the hose into position, checking that it is correctly routed, then slide each clip back along the hose until it passes over the flared end of the relevant inlet/outlet, before tightening the clip securely.

9 Refill the cooling system with reference to Chapter 1.

10 Check thoroughly for leaks as soon as possible after disturbing any part of the cooling system.

Radiator bottom hose

Removal

11 Turn the locking ring ("2") anti-clockwise until it contacts the stop ("1") **(see illustration)**.

12 Press the connector away from the hose, to ensure that the two retaining lugs are free **(see illustration)**.

13 Pull the hose, complete with the connector, from the radiator.

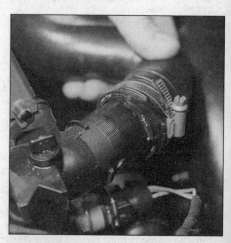

2.5 Disconnecting the radiator top hose

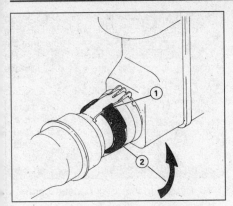

2.11 To release the radiator bottom hose connection, turn the locking ring (2) until it contacts the stop (1)

14 Recover the O-ring from the connector, and discard it; a new one must be used on refitting.

Refitting

15 Wipe the connector and the stub on the radiator thoroughly with a clean, lint-free cloth.

16 Fit a new O-ring to the male half of the connector, ensuring that it is correctly seated **(see illustration)**.

17 Turn the locking ring clockwise until it clicks.

18 Offer the hose to the stub on the radiator, with the locating cut-out in the male part of the connector located at the bottom **(see illustration)**.

19 Push the connector into the stub until both the retaining lugs click into position. Make sure that the O-ring is not trapped.

20 Pull the connector rearwards (away from the stub) to adjust the position of the retaining lugs if necessary.

21 Refill the cooling system with reference to Chapter 1.

22 Check thoroughly for leaks as soon as possible after disturbing any part of the cooling system.

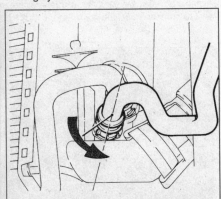

2.24 To release the radiator bypass hose, turn the connector on the end of the hose anti-clockwise

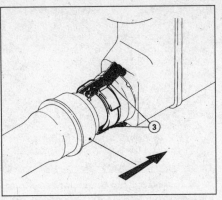

2.12 Press the connector away from the hose, to ensure that the two retaining lugs (3) are free

Radiator bypass hose connection

Removal

23 The hose is secured by means of a bayonet-fit connector.

24 Turn the connector on the end of the hose anti-clockwise as far as it will go **(see illustration)**.

25 Rock the connector back and forth to release it from the radiator outlet. Remove the O-ring, and discard it; a new must be used on refitting.

Refitting

26 Wipe the connector and the stub on the radiator thoroughly with a clean, lint-free cloth.

27 Fit a new O-ring to the male half of the connector.

28 Offer the connector to the outlet on the radiator, and twist anti-clockwise to engage

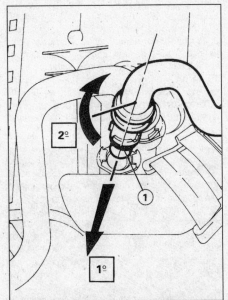

2.28 On refitting, engage the guide rails (1) with the lugs on the radiator, then twist the hose end in a clockwise direction

2.16 On refitting, fit a new O-ring (arrowed) to the hose union

2.18 Offer the hose to the radiator, with the cut-out (arrowed) at the bottom

the guide rails on the connector with the lugs on the radiator **(see illustration)**.

29 Push the connector fully home to compress the O-ring.

30 Turn the connector clockwise as far as the stop.

31 Refill the cooling system with reference to Chapter 1.

32 Check thoroughly for leaks as soon as possible after disturbing any part of the cooling system.

Heater matrix hose connections

Removal

33 The two hoses are connected to the matrix by means of a single connector.

34 Prise the metal retaining clip from the top of the connector **(see illustration)**.

2.34 Remove the metal clip from the top of the heater matrix connector on the engine compartment bulkhead . . .

3

2.35 . . . then release the plastic retaining clip . . .

2.36 . . . and pull the connector away from the bulkhead - recover the O-rings (arrowed)

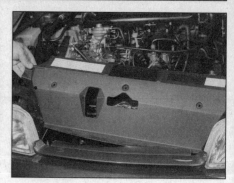

3.3 Removing the cover panel from the radiator

35 Release the plastic retaining clip by pushing it towards the left-hand hose connection **(see illustration)**.
36 Pull the connector assembly from the heater matrix. Recover the O-ring seals from the connector, and discard them; new ones should be used on refitting **(see illustration)**.

Refitting

37 Refitting is a reversal of the removal procedure, using new O-rings.
38 Refill the cooling system with reference to Chapter 1.
39 Check thoroughly for leaks as soon as possible after disturbing any part of the cooling system.

| 3 | Radiator - removal, inspection and refitting |

Note: *New sealing rings must be used when reconnecting the radiator lower hoses - see Section 2. If leakage is the reason for removing the radiator, bear in mind that minor leaks can often be cured using a radiator sealant with the radiator in situ.*

Removal

1 Disconnect the battery negative lead.
2 Drain the cooling system as described in Chapter 1.
3 Undo the three retaining screws, and

remove the plastic cover panel from above the radiator **(see illustration)**.
4 Disconnect the wiring plug from the cooling fan switch (where fitted) on the left-hand side of the radiator **(see illustration)**.
5 Disconnect the radiator upper hose(s) (left-hand side), and the lower hoses (right-hand side), with reference to Section 2.
6 Depress the two retaining clips, located at the top ends of the radiator, then carefully lift the radiator from the vehicle. Note the locating lugs at the bottom of the radiator, which locate in the mounting rubbers in the lower body panel **(see illustrations)**.

Inspection

7 If the radiator has been removed due to suspected blockage, reverse-flush it as described in Chapter 1. Clean dirt and debris from the radiator fins, using an air line (in which case, wear eye protection) or a soft brush. Be careful, as the fins are sharp, and easily damaged.
8 If necessary, a radiator specialist can perform a "flow test" on the radiator, to establish whether an internal blockage exists.
9 A leaking radiator must be referred to a specialist for permanent repair. Do not attempt to weld or solder a leaking radiator, as damage to the plastic components may result.
10 In an emergency, minor leaks from the radiator can be cured by using a suitable radiator sealant, in accordance with its manufacturer's instructions, with the radiator in situ.

11 If the radiator is to be sent for repair or renewed, remove all hoses, and the cooling fan switch (where fitted).
12 Inspect the condition of the radiator mounting rubbers, and renew them if necessary.

Refitting

13 Refitting is a reversal of removal, bearing in mind the following points:
(a) *Ensure that the lower lugs on the radiator are correctly engaged with the mounting rubbers in the body panel.*
(b) *Reconnect the hoses with reference to Section 2, using new O-rings where applicable.*
(c) *On completion, refill the cooling system as described in Chapter 1.*

| 4 | Thermostat - removal, testing and refitting |

Removal

1 Disconnect the battery negative lead.
2 Drain the cooling system as described in Chapter 1.
3 Where necessary, release any relevant wiring and hoses from the retaining clips, and position clear of the thermostat housing to improve access. On 1905 cc models, access is also improved if the air cleaner duct is removed (see Chapter 4).

3.4 Disconnecting the cooling fan switch wiring plug

3.6a Depress the retaining clips . . .

3.6b . . . and withdraw the radiator

4.4a Thermostat housing cover retaining bolts (arrowed) - 1360 cc models

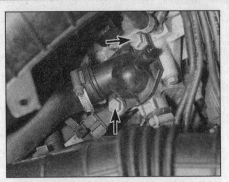

4.4b Thermostat housing cover retaining bolts (arrowed) - 1905 cc models

4.5 Removing the sealing ring from the thermostat flange

4 Unscrew the retaining bolts, and carefully withdraw the thermostat housing cover to expose the thermostat. Take care not to strain the coolant hoses connected to the cover **(see illustrations)**.

5 Lift the thermostat from the housing, and recover the sealing ring(s) **(see illustration)**.

Testing

6 A rough test of the thermostat may be made by suspending it with a piece of string in a container full of water. Heat the water to bring it to the boil - the thermostat must open by the time the water boils. If not, renew it.

7 If a thermometer is available, the precise opening temperature of the thermostat may be determined; compare with the figures given in the Specifications. The opening temperature is also marked on the thermostat.

8 A thermostat which fails to close as the water cools must also be renewed.

Refitting

9 Refitting is a reversal of removal, bearing in mind the following points:
(a) Examine the sealing ring(s) for signs of damage or deterioration, and if necessary, renew.
(b) Ensure that the thermostat is fitted the correct way round, with the spring(s) facing into the housing.
(c) On completion, refill the cooling system as described in Chapter 1.

5.6 Disconnecting the wiring plug from a cooling fan

5 Electric cooling fan(s) - testing, removal and refitting

Testing

1 Current supply to the cooling fan(s) is via the ignition switch (see Chapter 5) and a fuse (see Chapter 12). The circuit is completed by the cooling fan thermostatic switch, which (on most models) is mounted in the left-hand side of the radiator. On models with air conditioning, the cooling fans are controlled by the "Bitron" sensor - see Section 6.

2 If a fan does not appear to work, run the engine until normal operating temperature is reached, then allow it to idle. The fan should cut in within a few minutes (before the temperature gauge needle enters the red section, or before the coolant temperature warning light comes on). If not, switch off the ignition and disconnect the wiring plug from the cooling fan switch. Bridge the two contacts in the wiring plug using a length of spare wire, and switch on the ignition. If the fan now operates, the switch is probably faulty, and should be renewed.

3 If the fan still fails to operate, check that battery voltage is available at the feed wire to the switch; if not, then there is a fault in the feed wire (possibly due to a fault in the fan motor, or a blown fuse). If there is no problem with the feed, check that there is continuity

5.7 Withdrawing a cooling fan motor assembly - twin-fan arrangement

between the switch earth terminal and a good earth point on the body; if not, then the earth connection is faulty, and must be re-made.

4 If the switch and the wiring are in good condition, the fault must lie in the motor itself. The motor can be checked by disconnecting it from the wiring loom, and connecting a 12-volt supply directly to it.

Removal

5 Remove the radiator as described in Section 3.

6 Disconnect the wiring plug from the rear of the motor **(see illustration)**.

7 On models with a plastic radiator shroud (both single- and twin-fan arrangements), unscrew the three motor retaining nuts, rotating the fan blades as necessary so that the bolts can be counterheld from the front as the nuts are unscrewed. Withdraw the motor assembly, complete with the fan, from the front of the vehicle **(see illustration)**.

8 On models with a single cooling fan where the motor is secured to the body by a metal frame, undo the retaining bolts, then remove the motor and mounting frame from the vehicle.

9 If desired, the fan blades can be removed from the motor shaft, after its retaining screw or clip (as applicable) has been removed.

10 If the motor is faulty, the complete unit must be renewed, as no spares are available.

Refitting

11 Refitting is a reversal of removal. Refit the radiator as described in Section 3.

6 Cooling system electrical switches and sensors - testing, removal and refitting

Electric cooling fan thermostatic switch - models without air conditioning

Testing

1 Testing of the switch is described in Section 5, as part of the electric cooling fan test procedure.

6.2 Electric cooling fan thermostatic switch - models without air conditioning

6.12 Coolant temperature gauge/temperature warning light sender (arrowed) - 1360 cc models

Removal

2 The switch is located in the left-hand side of the radiator **(see illustration)**. The engine and radiator should be cold before removing the switch.

3 Disconnect the battery negative lead.

4 Partially drain the cooling system to just below the level of the switch (as described in Chapter 1). Alternatively, have ready a suitable bung to plug the switch aperture in the radiator when the switch is removed. If this method is used, take great care not to damage the radiator, and do not use anything which will allow foreign matter to enter the radiator.

5 Disconnect the wiring plug from the switch.

6 Carefully unscrew the switch from the radiator, and recover the sealing ring (where applicable). If the system has not been drained, plug the switch aperture to prevent further coolant loss.

Refitting

7 If the switch was originally fitted using sealing compound, clean the switch threads thoroughly, and coat them with fresh sealing compound.

8 If the switch was originally fitted using a sealing ring, use a new sealing ring on refitting.

9 Refitting is a reversal of removal. Tighten the switch to the specified torque, and refill (or top-up) the cooling system as described in Chapter 1.

10 On completion, start the engine and run it until it reaches normal operating temperature. Continue to run the engine, and check that the cooling fan cuts in and out correctly.

Electric cooling fan thermostatic switch - models with air conditioning

11 The cooling fans are controlled by the "Bitron" sensor. This is located in the thermostat housing, which is bolted onto the left-hand end of the cylinder head - see paragraphs 20 to 22.

Coolant temperature gauge/temperature warning light sender

Testing

Note: *On models with air conditioning, the sender provides a signal to the gauge only. The coolant temperature warning light is operated by the "Bitron" temperature sensor described later in this Section.*

12 The coolant temperature gauge/warning light sender is screwed into the thermostat housing, which is bolted onto the left-hand end of the cylinder head. The sender can be identified by its blue wiring connector **(see illustration)**.

13 The temperature gauge (where fitted) is fed with a stabilised voltage from the instrument panel feed (via the ignition switch and a fuse). The gauge earth is controlled by the sender. The sender contains a thermistor - an electronic component whose electrical resistance decreases at a predetermined rate as its temperature rises. When the coolant is cold, the sender resistance is high, current flow through the gauge is reduced, and the gauge needle points towards the blue (cold) end of the scale. As the coolant temperature rises and the sender resistance falls, current flow increases, and the gauge needle moves towards the upper end of the scale. If the sender is faulty, it must be renewed.

14 On models with a temperature warning light, the light is fed with a voltage from the instrument panel. The light earth is controlled by the sender. The sender is effectively a switch, which operates at a predetermined temperature to earth the light and complete the circuit. If the light is fitted in addition to a gauge, the senders for the gauge and light are incorporated in a single unit, with two wires, one each for the light and gauge earths. On models with air conditioning, the light is operated via the "Bitron" sensor - see paragraphs 20 to 22.

15 If the gauge develops a fault, first check the other instruments; if they do not work at all, check the instrument panel electrical feed. If the readings are erratic, there may be a fault in the voltage stabiliser, which will necessitate renewal of the stabiliser (the stabiliser is integral with the instrument panel printed circuit board - see Chapter 12). If the fault lies in the temperature gauge alone, check it as follows.

16 If the gauge needle remains at the "cold" end of the scale when the engine is hot, disconnect the sender wiring plug, and earth the relevant wire to the cylinder head. If the needle then deflects when the ignition is switched on, the sender unit is proved faulty, and should be renewed. If the needle still does not move, remove the instrument panel (Chapter 12) and check the continuity of the wire between the sender unit and the gauge, and the feed to the gauge unit. If continuity is shown, and the fault still exists, then the gauge is faulty, and the gauge unit should be renewed.

17 If the gauge needle remains at the "hot" end of the scale when the engine is cold, disconnect the sender wire. If the needle then returns to the "cold" end of the scale when the ignition is switched on, the sender unit is proved faulty, and should be renewed. If the needle still does not move, check the remainder of the circuit as described previously.

18 The same basic principles apply to testing the warning light. The light should illuminate when the relevant sender wire is earthed.

Removal and refitting

19 The procedure is similar to that described previously in this Section for the electric cooling fan thermostatic switch. On some models, access to the switch is very poor, and other components may need to be removed before the sender unit can be reached.

"Bitron" temperature sensor - models with air conditioning

Testing

20 The sensor forms part of the air conditioning "Bitron" control system (see Section 11). Testing of the sensor should be entrusted to a Citroën dealer.

Removal and refitting

21 The "Bitron" temperature sensor is screwed into the thermostat housing, which is bolted onto the left-hand end of the cylinder head. The sensor can be identified by its brown wiring connector.

22 The procedure is similar to that described previously in this Section for the electric cooling fan thermostatic switch. On some models, access to the switch is very poor, and other components may need to be removed before the sender unit can be reached.

Coolant temperature sensor - fuel injection models

Testing

23 The fuel injection system coolant temperature sensor is screwed into the thermostat housing, which is bolted onto the left-hand end of the cylinder head. The sensor can be identified by its green wiring connector.

24 The sensor is a thermistor (see paragraph 13). The fuel injection/engine management ECU supplies the sensor with a

7.3a On 1580 cc and larger-engined models, unscrew the retaining bolts (arrowed) . . .

7.3b . . . and remove the coolant pump

set voltage and then, by measuring the current flowing in the sensor circuit, it determines the engine's temperature. This information is then used, in conjunction with other inputs, to control the injector opening time (pulse width). On some models, the idle speed and/or ignition timing settings are also temperature-dependent.

25 If the sensor circuit should fail to provide adequate information, the ECU's back-up facility will override the sensor signal. In this event, the ECU assumes a predetermined setting which will allow the fuel injection/engine management system to run, albeit at reduced efficiency. When this occurs, the warning light on the instrument panel will come on, and the advice of a Citroën dealer should be sought. The sensor itself can only be tested using special Citroën diagnostic equipment. *Do not* attempt to test the circuit using any other equipment, as there is a high risk of damaging the ECU.

Removal and refitting

26 The procedure is similar to that described previously in this Section for the electric cooling fan thermostatic switch. On some models, access to the switch is very poor, and certain components may need to be removed before the sensor can be reached.

7 Coolant pump - removal and refitting

Removal

1 Drain the cooling system as described in Chapter 1.
2 Remove the timing belt as described in Chapter 2.
3 Slacken and remove the retaining bolts, and withdraw the pump from the cylinder block (see illustrations). Recover the pump O-ring (1124 cc and 1360 cc models) or gasket (1580 cc and larger-engined models). A new O-ring or gasket should be used on refitting.

Refitting

4 Ensure that the mating surfaces of the

pump and the cylinder block are clean and dry.
5 On 1124 cc and 1360 cc models, fit a new O-ring to the rear of the pump. Refit the pump to the engine, and tighten its retaining bolts to the specified torque.
6 On 1580 cc and larger-engined models, position a new gasket on the rear of the pump. Offer the pump to the engine, ensuring that the gasket remains correctly positioned. Install the pump retaining bolts, and tighten them to the specified torque.
7 Refit the timing belt as described in Chapter 2.
8 Refill the cooling system as described in Chapter 1.

8 Heating and ventilation system - general information

1 The heating/ventilation system consists of a four-speed blower motor (housed behind the facia), face level vents in the centre and at each end of the facia, and air ducts to the front footwells.
2 The control unit is located in the facia, and the controls operate flap valves to deflect and mix the air flowing through the various parts of the heating/ventilation system. The flap valves

9.3a Undo the two retaining screws (arrowed) . . .

are contained in the air distribution housing, which acts as a central distribution unit, passing air to the various ducts and vents.
3 Cold air enters the system through the grille at the rear of the engine compartment. If required, the airflow is boosted by the blower, and then flows through the various ducts, according to the settings of the controls. Stale air is expelled through ducts at the rear of the vehicle. If warm air is required, the cold air is passed over the heater matrix, which is heated by the engine coolant.
4 On models fitted with air conditioning, a recirculation switch enables the outside air supply to be closed off, while the air inside the vehicle is recirculated. This can be useful to prevent unpleasant odours entering from outside the vehicle, but should only be used briefly, as the recirculated air inside the vehicle will soon become stale.

9 Heater/ventilation components - removal and refitting

Heater/ventilation control unit

Removal

1 Disconnect the battery negative lead.
2 Remove the centre console as described in Chapter 11. On lower-specification models where no centre console is fitted, undo the retaining screws and remove the heater duct cover (where fitted) from the centre of the facia assembly.
3 Where a radio/cassette player is fitted, remove it as described in Chapter 12, then undo the two retaining screws and remove the mounting bracket from the radio aperture (see illustrations). Where no radio/cassette player is fitted, carefully prise out the storage box from the centre of the facia panel.
4 Undo the four centre vent panel retaining screws (two located above the heater controls, and two directly below), then unclip the panel and withdraw it from the facia. Disconnect the wiring connectors from the cigarette lighter and ashtray illumination bulb,

9.3b . . . and remove the mounting bracket from the radio aperture

3

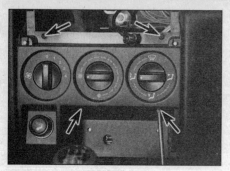

9.4a Undo the four centre vent panel retaining screws (arrowed) . . .

9.4b . . . and withdraw the panel from the facia

9.5 Undo the heater panel retaining screws, and release the clip (arrowed)

and remove the centre vent panel assembly from the vehicle (see illustrations).

5 Undo the two heater control panel retaining screws, then release the lower panel retaining clip and manoeuvre the panel out from the centre of the facia (see illustration).

9.9 Control cable connection (1) and retaining clip (2) at heater assembly

6 Disconnect the control cables and the wiring connector(s) from the rear of the heater control panel, noting their locations, and withdraw the panel from the vehicle.

Refitting

7 Refitting is reversal of removal, bearing in mind the following points:
(a) Ensure that the control cables are correctly reconnected to the control panel, as noted before removal.
(b) Refit the radio/cassette player with reference to Chapter 12.

Heater/ventilation control cables

Removal

8 Remove the complete heater assembly as described later in this Section.

9 The cables can now be disconnected from the heater assembly and the heater control panel (see illustration). Note the locations of the cables before disconnecting them.

Refitting

10 Refitting is a reversal of removal.

Heater matrix

Removal

11 Remove the facia assembly as described in Chapter 11.

12 Remove the retaining screws, and release the wiring retaining brackets from the top of the heater unit, noting their locations (see illustration).

13 Working inside the vehicle, disconnect the wiring plug from the right-hand side of the heater unit (see illustration).

14 Remove the heater assembly lower retaining bolt (see illustration).

15 Working in the engine compartment, remove the two heater unit retaining nuts from the bulkhead (below the heater matrix hose connector), and recover the washers (see illustration).

16 Drain the cooling system as described in

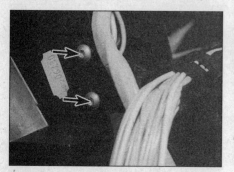

9.12 Heater unit wiring bracket retaining screws (arrowed)

9.13 Disconnect the wiring plug from the right-hand side of the heater

9.14 Heater assembly lower retaining bolt (arrowed)

9.15 Heater unit retaining nut on engine compartment bulkhead

9.17a Remove the two retaining screws (arrowed) . . .

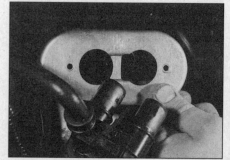

9.17b . . . and withdraw the retaining plate from the bulkhead

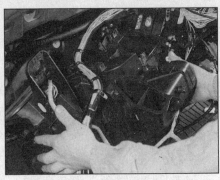

9.18 Withdrawing the heater unit

9.19 Withdrawing the heater matrix from the heater assembly

9.20a Undo the retaining bolts . . .

Chapter 1. Disconnect the heater hose connector from the heater matrix, with reference to Section 2.

17 Remove the two retaining screws, and withdraw the retaining plate from the heater matrix hose connector **(see illustrations)**.

18 Working inside the vehicle, withdraw the heater unit, complete with the control panel **(see illustration)**. Be careful not to spill coolant inside the car.

19 Remove the retaining screws, where applicable, then release the clips and withdraw the heater matrix from the heater assembly **(see illustration)**.

Refitting

20 Refitting is a reversal of the removal procedure, bearing in mind the following points:

(a) If a new matrix is to be fitted, unbolt the hose connector elbow from the old matrix, and fit it to the new matrix using new O-rings **(see illustrations)**.

(b) Reconnect the heater hoses to the matrix with reference to Section 2.

(c) Refit the facia assembly as described in Chapter 11.

(d) Refill the cooling system as described in Chapter 1.

Heater blower motor

Removal

21 Working inside the vehicle, remove the facia felt undercover and the driver's side lower facia panel (left-hand-drive models) or the glovebox (right-hand-drive models), as applicable, with reference to Chapter 11.

22 Unscrew the three blower motor retaining screws, and lower the assembly from the facia **(see illustration)**.

23 Pull off the cover and disconnect the two wiring plugs, then withdraw the assembly from the vehicle **(see illustration)**.

Refitting

24 Refitting is a reversal of removal.

Heater blower motor resistor

Removal

25 Disconnect the battery negative lead.

26 Remove the wiper arm as described in Chapter 12.

27 Open the bonnet, and remove the six wiper motor cover/vent panel retaining screws. Carefully ease the cover out from behind the windscreen sealing strip. Disengage its front locating pegs, and manoeuvre the panel away from the vehicle.

28 Remove the plastic cover from the heater blower motor intake duct.

29 Twist the resistor anti-clockwise to release it from the bracket, then disconnect the wiring plug and withdraw the unit **(see illustrations)**. Tie a piece of string to the wiring connector, to prevent it falling back out of the duct.

Refitting

30 Refitting is a reversal of removal, refitting the wiper arm with reference to Chapter 12.

3

9.20b . . . and remove the hose connector elbow from the old heater matrix

9.20c Fit the elbow to the new matrix, using new O-rings

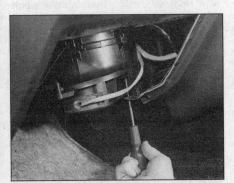

9.22 Unscrewing a heater blower motor retaining screw

9.23 Pull off the cover (arrowed) and disconnect the wiring plugs

9.29a To remove the heater blower motor resistor . . .

9.29b . . . twist the unit anti-clockwise and disconnect the wiring plug

10.1 Withdrawing a facia side vent

Complete heater assembly

Removal

31 Removal of the complete heater assembly is described in paragraphs 11 to 18, as part of the heater matrix removal and refitting procedure.

Refitting

32 Refitting is a reversal of removal, with reference to paragraph 20.

10 Heater vents - removal and refitting

Facia side vents

Removal

1 Carefully release the relevant vent from the facia, using a screwdriver (with a piece of card under the blade to avoid damage to the facia trim), then withdraw the vent (see illustration).

Refitting

2 Simply push the nozzle into its housing in the facia, ensuring that it is correctly engaged with the heater duct, until the retaining lugs click into place.

Facia centre vents

Removal

3 Remove the centre vent panel from the facia as described in Section 9, paragraphs 1 to 4.
4 Working at the rear of the centre vent panel, remove the retaining screws, then withdraw the vent assembly from the panel.

Refitting

5 Refitting is a reversal of removal.

11 Air conditioning system - general information and precautions

General information

1 An air conditioning system is available on certain models (see illustration). It enables the temperature of incoming air to be lowered, and also dehumidifies the air, which makes for rapid demisting and increased comfort.
2 The cooling side of the system works in the same way as a domestic refrigerator. Refrigerant gas is drawn into a belt-driven compressor, and passes into a condenser mounted on the front of the radiator, where it loses heat and becomes liquid. The liquid passes through an expansion valve to an evaporator, where it changes from liquid under high pressure to gas under low pressure. This change is accompanied by a drop in temperature, which cools the evaporator. The refrigerant returns to the compressor, and the cycle begins again.
3 Air blown through the evaporator passes to the air distribution unit, where it is blown through the heater matrix to achieve the desired temperature in the passenger compartment.
4 The heating side of the system works in the same way as on models without air conditioning (see Section 8).
5 The operation of the system is controlled electronically by the "Bitron" control unit, which controls the electric cooling fan(s), the compressor, and the facia-mounted warning light. Any problems with the system should be referred to a Citroën dealer.

Precautions

6 When an air conditioning system is fitted, it is necessary to observe special precautions whenever dealing with any part of the system, or its associated components. If for any reason the system must be disconnected, entrust this task to your Citroën dealer or a refrigeration engineer.

⚠️ Warning: The refrigeration circuit contains a liquid refrigerant (Freon), and it is therefore dangerous to disconnect any part of the system without specialised knowledge and equipment.

7 The refrigerant is potentially dangerous, and should only be handled by qualified persons. If it is splashed onto the skin, it can cause frostbite. It is not itself poisonous, but in the presence of a naked flame (including a cigarette) it forms a poisonous gas. Uncontrolled discharging of the refrigerant is dangerous, and potentially damaging to the environment.
8 Do not operate the air conditioning system if it is known to be short of refrigerant, as this may damage the compressor.

12 Air conditioning system components - removal and refitting

⚠️ Warning: Do not attempt to open the refrigerant circuit. Refer to the precautions given in Section 11.

1 The only operation which can be carried out easily without discharging the refrigerant is renewal of the compressor drivebelt. This is described in Chapter 1, Section 21. (The "Bitron" temperature sensor may be renewed using the information in Section 6.) All other operations must be referred to a Citroën dealer or an air conditioning specialist.
2 If necessary, the compressor can be unbolted and moved aside, without disconnecting its flexible hoses, after removing the drivebelt.

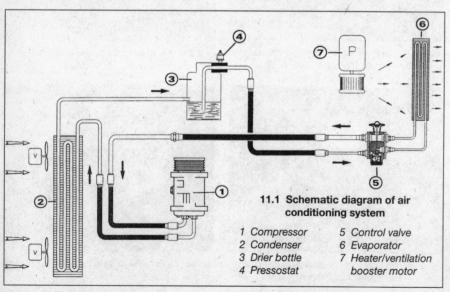

11.1 Schematic diagram of air conditioning system

1 Compressor	5 Control valve
2 Condenser	6 Evaporator
3 Drier bottle	7 Heater/ventilation
4 Pressostat	booster motor

Chapter 4 Part A:
Fuel and exhaust systems - carburettor engines

Contents

Accelerator cable - removal, refitting and adjustment 7
Accelerator pedal - removal and refitting 8
Air cleaner air temperature control system - general
    information and component renewal 3
Air cleaner assembly - removal and refitting 2
Air cleaner filter element renewal . . . . See Chapter 1
Carburettor - general information 11
Carburettor - removal and refitting 12
Choke cable - removal, refitting and adjustment 9
Exhaust manifold - removal and refitting 16
Exhaust system - general information, removal and refitting 17
Fuel filter - renewal . . . . See Chapter 1

Fuel gauge sender unit - removal and refitting 5
Fuel pump - testing, removal and refitting 4
Fuel tank - removal and refitting 6
General fuel system checks . . . . See Chapter 1
General information and precautions 1
Idle speed and mixture adjustment . . . . See Chapter 1
Inlet manifold - removal and refitting 15
Solex 32 PBISA carburettor (1124 cc models) - fault
    finding, overhaul and adjustments 13
Solex 32-34 Z2 carburettor (1360 cc models) - fault
    finding, overhaul and adjustments 14
Unleaded petrol - general information and usage 10

4A

Degrees of difficulty

Easy, suitable for novice with little experience	Fairly easy, suitable for beginner with some experience	Fairly difficult, suitable for competent DIY mechanic	Difficult, suitable for experienced DIY mechanic	Very difficult, suitable for expert DIY or professional

Specifications

Fuel pump

Type . . . .   Mechanical, driven by eccentric on camshaft

Carburettor

Type:
    1124 cc models . . . .   Solex 32 PBISA 16
    1360 cc models . . . .   Solex 32-34 Z2
Designation:
    1124 cc models . . . .   32 PBISA 16 - 411
    1360 cc models . . . .   32-34 Z2 - 528
Choke type (both carburettors) . . . .   Manual, cable-operated

Solex 32 PBISA carburettor data - 1124 cc models

Venturi diameter . . . .   25 mm
Main jet 127.5
Idle jet   48
Air correction jet   175
Emulsion tube . . . .   EM
Enrichment jet   50
Accelerator pump   40
Needle valve 1.5
Float height setting . . . .   See text
Throttle valve fast idle setting . . . .   0.6 mm
Choke pull-down setting . . . .   2.8 mm
Idle speed . . . .   850 ± 50 rpm
Idle mixture CO content . . . .   0.8 to 1.2 %

Solex 32-34 Z2 carburettor data - 1360 cc models

	Primary	Secondary
Venturi diameter	24 mm	25 mm
Main jet	115	120
Idle jet	40	-
Air correction jet/emulsion tube	155	160
Bypass jet	-	50
Econostat jet	-	80
Accelerator pump	35	
Pneumatic enrichment device	45	
Needle valve	1.6	
Float height setting	35 mm	
Throttle valve fast idle setting	0.5 mm	
Choke pull-down setting	3.0 mm	
Idle speed	850 ± 50 rpm	
Idle mixture CO content	0.8 to 1.2 %	

Recommended fuel
Recommended fuel .... 95 RON unleaded (UK unleaded premium)

Torque wrench settings

	Nm	lbf ft
Fuel pump retaining bolts	16	12
Inlet manifold retaining nuts	8	6
Exhaust manifold retaining nuts	16	12
Exhaust system fasteners:		
Front pipe-to-manifold nuts	30	22
Front pipe mounting bolt	35	26
Front pipe-to-intermediate pipe nuts	10	7
Clamping ring nuts	20	15

1 General information and precautions

The fuel system consists of a fuel tank mounted under the rear of the car, a mechanical fuel pump, and a carburettor. The fuel pump is operated by an eccentric on the camshaft, and. is mounted on the rear of the cylinder head. The air cleaner contains a disposable paper filter element, and incorporates a flap valve air temperature control system; this allows cold air from the outside of the car, and warm air from the exhaust manifold, to enter the air cleaner in the correct proportions.

The fuel pump lifts fuel from the fuel tank via a filter, which is mounted on the engine compartment bulkhead, and supplies it to the carburettor via an anti-percolation chamber. The anti-percolation chamber ensures that the supply of fuel to the carburettor is kept at a constant pressure, and is free of air bubbles. Excess fuel is returned from the anti-percolation chamber to the fuel tank.

On 1124 cc models, a Solex 32 PBISA single-choke carburettor is fitted; 1360 cc models have a Solex 32-34 Z2 twin-choke carburettor. On both carburettors, mixture enrichment for cold starting is by a cable-operated choke control.

The exhaust system consists of three sections; the front pipe, the intermediate pipe and silencer box, and the tailpipe and main silencer box. The system is suspended throughout its entire length by rubber mountings.

Warning: Many of the procedures in this Chapter require the removal of fuel lines and connections, which may result in some fuel spillage. Before carrying out any operation on the fuel system, refer to the precautions given in "Safety first!" at the beginning of this manual, and follow them implicitly. Petrol is a highly-dangerous and volatile liquid, and the precautions necessary when handling it cannot be overstressed.

2 Air cleaner assembly - removal and refitting

Removal

1 Slacken the retaining clips (where fitted), and disconnect the vacuum hose and breather hose from the front of the air cleaner housing-to-carburettor duct **(see illustration)**. Where the crimped-type Citroën hose clips are fitted, cut the clips and discard them; use standard worm-drive hose clips on refitting.

2 Slacken the retaining clips, then lift the duct off the top of the carburettor and air cleaner housing. Disconnect the air temperature control valve hose from the end of the duct, and remove the duct from the engine compartment **(see illustrations)**. Recover the rubber sealing ring(s) from the top of the carburettor and/or air cleaner housing (as applicable).

3 Disconnect the intake duct from the front of the air cleaner housing, and remove the air cleaner housing from the engine compartment.

4 To remove the intake duct assembly, undo the retaining nut(s) securing the duct to the left-hand wing valance, then release the.

2.1 Disconnect the vacuum and breather hoses (arrowed) from the front of the duct ...

2.2a ... slacken the retaining clips ...

2.2b . . . and remove the duct, disconnecting the air temperature control valve hose (arrowed)

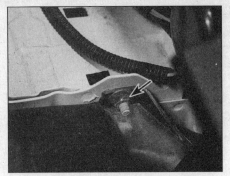

2.4a Undo the intake duct front retaining nut (arrowed) . . .

2.4b . . . then release the rear fastener, and remove the duct and hose assembly

fastener securing the rear of the duct to the cylinder head (see illustrations). Disconnect the hot-air intake hose from the exhaust manifold, and remove the duct and hose assembly from the engine compartment.

Refitting

5 Refitting is a reversal of the removal procedure, noting the following points:
(a) Examine the rubber sealing ring(s) for signs of damage or deterioration, and if necessary renew. Note that, on some models, the carburettor seal is fitted with an O-ring; this should also be renewed if it is damaged.
(b) Ensure the air cleaner housing locating peg is correctly engaged with its mounting on the top of the transmission (see illustration).
(c) Prior to tightening the air cleaner-to-carburettor duct retaining clips, ensure the duct is correctly seated on both the air cleaner housing and carburettor flanges.

3 Air cleaner air temperature control system - general information and component renewal

General information

1 The system is controlled by a heat-sensitive vacuum switch, mounted in the end of the air cleaner housing-to-carburettor duct. When the engine is started from cold, the switch is open, allowing inlet manifold depression to act on the air temperature control valve diaphragm in the intake duct. This vacuum causes the diaphragm to rise, drawing a flap valve across the cold-air intake, thus allowing only (warmed) air from the exhaust manifold to enter the air cleaner.
2 As the temperature of the exhaust-warmed air in the air cleaner-to-carburettor duct rises, the wax capsule in the vacuum switch deforms and closes the switch, cutting off the vacuum supply to the air temperature control valve assembly. As the vacuum supply is cut,

the flap is gradually lowered across the hot-air intake until, when the engine is fully warmed-up to normal operating temperature, only cold air from the front of the car is entering the air cleaner.
3 To check the system, allow the engine to cool down completely, then slacken the retaining clip and disconnect the intake duct from the front of the control valve assembly; the flap valve in the duct should be securely seated across the hot-air intake. Start the engine; the flap should immediately rise to close off the cold-air intake, and should then lower steadily as the engine warms up, until it is eventually seated across the hot-air intake again.
4 To check the vacuum switch, disconnect the vacuum pipe from the control valve when the engine is running, and place a finger over the pipe end. When the engine is cold, full inlet manifold vacuum should be present in the pipe, and when the engine is at normal operating temperature, there should be no vacuum in the pipe.
5 To check the air temperature control valve assembly, slacken the retaining clip and disconnect the intake duct from the front of the valve assembly; the flap valve should be securely seated across the hot-air intake. Disconnect the vacuum pipe, and suck hard at the control valve stub; the flap should rise to shut off the cold-air intake.
6 If either component is faulty, it must be renewed.

3.8a Remove the retaining clip . . .

2.5 On refitting, ensure the air cleaner housing peg is correctly located in its mounting rubber (arrowed)

Vacuum switch - renewal

7 Remove the air cleaner housing-to-carburettor duct, as described in paragraphs 1 and 2 of Section 2.
8 Bend up the tangs on the switch retaining clip, then remove the clip, along with its seal, and withdraw the switch from inside the duct (see illustrations). Examine the seal for signs of damage or deterioration, and renew if necessary.
9 On refitting, ensure the switch and duct mating surfaces are clean and dry, and position the switch inside of the duct.
10 Fit the seal over the switch unions, and refit the retaining clip. Ensure the switch is pressed firmly against the duct, and secure it

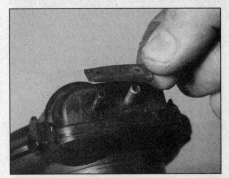

3.8b . . . and seal . . .

4A

3.8c ... then withdraw the vacuum switch from inside the duct

3.12 Air temperature control valve assembly

4.3 Arrows on fuel pump unions indicate the direction of fuel flow

in position by bending down the retaining clip tangs.

11 Refit the duct as described in Section 2.

Air temperature control valve - renewal

12 Disconnect the vacuum pipe from the air temperature control valve, then slacken the retaining clips securing the intake ducts to the valve (see illustration).

13 Disconnect both intake ducts and the hot-air intake hose from the control valve assembly, and remove it from the vehicle.

14 Refitting is the reverse of the removal procedure, noting that the air temperature control valve assembly can only be renewed as a complete unit.

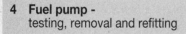

4 Fuel pump - testing, removal and refitting

Note: *Refer to the warning note in Section 1 before proceeding.*

Testing

1 To test the fuel pump on the engine, disconnect the outlet pipe which leads to the carburettor. Hold a wad of rag by the pump outlet while an assistant spins the engine on the starter. *Keep your hands away from the electric cooling fan.* Regular spurts of fuel should be ejected as the engine turns. Be

careful not to spill fuel onto hot engine components.

2 The pump can also be tested by removing it. With the pump outlet pipe disconnected but the inlet pipe still connected, hold the wad of rag by the outlet. Operate the pump lever by hand, moving it in and out; if the pump is in a satisfactory condition, the lever should move and return smoothly, and a strong jet of fuel should be ejected.

Removal

3 Identify the pump inlet and outlet hoses, and slacken both retaining clips (see illustration). Where the crimped-type Citroën hose clips are fitted, cut the clips and discard them; use standard worm-drive hose clips on refitting. Place wads of rag beneath the hose unions to catch any spilled fuel, then disconnect both hoses from the pump; plug the hose ends to minimise fuel loss.

4 Remove the insulating cover from the fuel pump, then slacken and remove the bolts securing the pump to the rear of the cylinder head. Remove the pump along with its insulating block. Discard the insulating block: a new one must be used on refitting.

Refitting

5 Ensure the pump and cylinder head mating surfaces are clean and dry, then offer up the new insulating block and refit the pump to the cylinder head. Tighten the pump retaining bolts to the specified torque, then refit the pump insulating cover.

6 Reconnect the inlet and outlet hoses to the relevant pump unions, and securely tighten their retaining clips.

5 Fuel gauge sender unit - removal and refitting

Note: *Refer to the warning note in Section 1 before proceeding.*

Removal

1 Disconnect the battery negative lead.

2 For access to the sender unit, tilt or remove the rear seats as described in Chapter 11.

3 Using a screwdriver, carefully prise the plastic access cover from the floor to expose the sender unit. It is located under the left-hand cover (see illustration).

4 Disconnect the wiring connector from the sender unit, and tape the connector to the vehicle body to prevent it disappearing behind the tank (see illustration).

5 Mark the hoses for identification purposes, then slacken the feed and return hose retaining clips. Where the crimped-type Citroën hose clips are fitted, cut the clips and discard them; use standard worm-drive hose clips on refitting. Disconnect both hoses from the top of the sender unit, and plug the hose ends.

6 Noting the alignment marks on the tank, sender unit and the locking ring, unscrew the ring and remove it from the tank. This is best

5.3 Remove the plastic access cover ...

5.4 ... and disconnect the wiring connector from the fuel gauge sender unit (fuel-injected model shown)

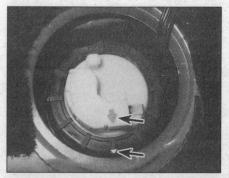

5.6a Note the position of the alignment marks (arrowed) on the sender unit and locking ring ...

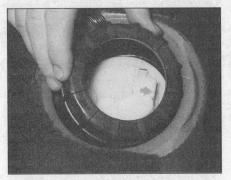

5.6b ... then unscrew the locking ring

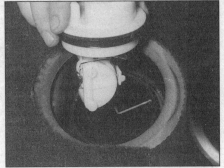

5.7a Withdraw the sender unit from the tank ...

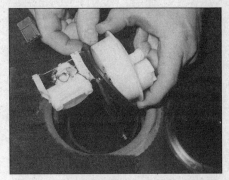

5.7b ... and remove the rubber sealing ring

accomplished by using a screwdriver on the raised ribs of the locking ring, as follows. Carefully tap the screwdriver to turn the ring anti-clockwise until it can be unscrewed by hand **(see illustrations)**.

7 Carefully lift the sender unit from the top of the fuel tank, taking great care not to bend the sender unit float arm, or to spill fuel onto the interior of the vehicle. Recover the rubber sealing ring and discard it - a new one must be used on refitting **(see illustrations)**.

Refitting

8 Refitting is a reversal of the removal procedure, noting the following points:

(a) *Prior to refitting, fit a new rubber sealing ring to the sender unit.*

(b) *Refit the sender unit to the tank, aligning its arrow with the centre of the three alignment marks on the fuel tank. Secure the sender in position with the locking ring, and check that the locking ring, sender unit and fuel tank marks are all correctly aligned.*

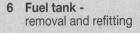

6 Fuel tank - removal and refitting

Note: *Refer to the warning note in Section 1 before proceeding.*

Removal

1 Before removing the fuel tank, all fuel must

be drained from the tank. Since a fuel tank drain plug is not provided, it is therefore preferable to carry out the removal operation when the tank is nearly empty. Before proceeding, disconnect the battery negative lead, and syphon or hand-pump the remaining fuel from the tank.

2 Remove the exhaust system and relevant heat shield(s) as described in Section 17.

3 Disconnect the two handbrake cables from the handbrake lever, as described in Chapter 9.

4 From underneath the vehicle, remove the retaining clips, and release each handbrake cable from its guides on the underside of the fuel tank **(see illustration)**. Position both cables clear of the tank, so that they will not hinder the removal procedure.

5 Disconnect the wiring connector from the fuel gauge sender unit, as described in Section 5.

6 Working at the right-hand side of the fuel tank, slacken the retaining clips, then disconnect the vent pipes from the base of the filler neck, and the main filler neck hose from the fuel tank. Where the original crimped-type Citroën hose clips are fitted, cut the clips and discard them; use standard worm-drive hose clips on refitting.

7 Trace the fuel feed and return hoses back from the right-hand side of the tank to their union with the fuel pipes. Slacken the retaining clips and disconnect both hoses from the fuel pipes, noting the point made above about the crimped-type hose clips.

6.4 Handbrake cable-to-fuel tank retaining clip (arrowed)

Plug the hose and pipe ends, to prevent the entry of dirt into the system.

8 Place a trolley jack with an interposed block of wood beneath the tank, then raise the jack until it is supporting the weight of the tank.

9 Slacken and remove the retaining nut and bolts, then remove the two support rods from the underside of the tank **(see illustrations)**.

10 Slowly lower the fuel tank out of position, disconnecting any other relevant vent pipes as they become accessible (where necessary), and remove the tank from underneath the vehicle.

11 If the tank is contaminated with sediment or water, remove the sender unit (Section 5), and swill the tank out with clean fuel. The tank is injection-moulded from a synthetic material - if seriously damaged, it should be renewed. However, in certain cases, it may be possible

4A

6.9a Fuel tank front left-hand retaining bolt

6.9b Fuel tank support rod retaining nut ...

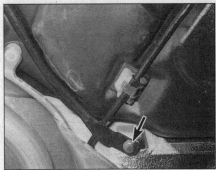

6.9c ... and retaining bolt

to have small leaks or minor damage repaired. Seek the advice of a specialist before attempting to repair the fuel tank.

Refitting

12 Refitting is the reverse of the removal procedure, noting the following points:
(a) When lifting the tank back into position, take care to ensure that none of the hoses become trapped between the tank and vehicle body.
(b) Ensure all pipes and hoses are correctly routed, and securely held in position with their retaining clips.
(c) Reconnect the handbrake cables and adjust the handbrake as described in Chapter 9.
(d) On completion, refill the tank with a small amount of fuel, and check for signs of leakage prior to taking the vehicle out on the road.

7 Accelerator cable - removal, refitting and adjustment

Removal

1 Working in the engine compartment, free the accelerator inner cable from the carburettor throttle cam, then pull the outer cable out from its mounting bracket rubber grommet. Slide the flat washer off the end of the cable, and remove the spring clip.
2 Working back along the length of the cable, free it from any retaining clips or ties, noting its correct routing.
3 Working from inside the vehicle, release the fasteners by rotating them through a quarter of a turn anti-clockwise, and remove the driver's side lower facia panel.
4 Release the retaining clips, and remove the felt undercover from underneath the driver's side of the facia panel.
5 Release the retaining clip, and detach the inner cable from the top of the accelerator pedal.
6 Release the outer cable from its retainer on the pedal mounting bracket, then tie a length of string to the end of the cable.
7 Return to the engine compartment, and withdraw the cable from the bulkhead. When

the end of the cable appears, untie the string and leave it in position - it can then be used to draw the cable back into position on refitting.

Refitting

8 Tie the string to the end of the cable, then use the string to draw the cable into position through the bulkhead. Once the cable end is visible, untie the string, then clip the outer cable into its pedal bracket retainer, and clip the inner cable into position in the pedal end.
9 Check that the cable is securely retained, then refit the felt undercover and driver's side lower facia panel.
10 From within the engine compartment, ensure the outer cable is correctly seated in the bulkhead grommet, then work along the cable, securing it in position with the retaining clips and ties, and ensuring that the cable is correctly routed.
11 Slide the flat washer onto the cable end, and refit the spring clip.
12 Pass the outer cable through its carburettor mounting bracket grommet, and reconnect the inner cable to the throttle cam. Adjust the cable as described below.

Adjustment

13 Remove the spring clip from the accelerator outer cable. Ensuring that the throttle cam is fully against its stop, gently pull the cable out of its grommet until all free play is removed from the inner cable.
14 With the cable held in this position, refit the spring clip to the last exposed outer cable groove in front of the rubber grommet and washer. When the clip is refitted and the outer cable is released, there should be only a small amount of free play in the inner cable (see illustration).
15 Have an assistant depress the accelerator pedal, and check that the throttle cam opens fully and returns smoothly to its stop.

8 Accelerator pedal - removal and refitting

Removal

1 Disconnect the accelerator cable from the pedal as described in paragraphs 3 to 5 of Section 7.

Right-hand drive models

2 Unscrew the nut from the end of the pedal pivot shaft, whilst retaining the pivot shaft with an open-ended spanner on the flats provided.
3 Pull the pedal and pivot shaft assembly from the support bracket.
4 Examine the pivot shaft for signs of wear or damage and, if necessary, renew it. The pivot shaft is a screw fit in the pedal.

Left-hand drive models

5 Slacken and remove the two nuts securing the pedal mounting bracket to the bulkhead. Slide off the outer part of the mounting clamp, then withdraw the pedal from behind the facia, and slide off the inner part of the clamp.
6 Examine the mounting bracket and pedal pivot points for signs of wear, and renew as necessary.

Refitting

7 Refitting is a reversal of the removal procedure, applying a little multi-purpose grease to the pedal pivot point. On completion, adjust the accelerator cable as described in Section 7.

9 Choke cable - removal, refitting and adjustment

Removal

1 Working in the engine compartment, free the choke inner cable from the carburettor linkage, then slacken and remove the retaining bolt and remove the outer cable retaining clamp (see illustration).
2 Slacken the retaining clip securing the rubber collar to the outer cable, and slide the collar off the cable. Where the original crimped-type Citroën hose clip is still fitted, cut the clip and discard it; use a standard worm-drive hose clip on refitting.
3 Working back along the length of the cable, free it from any retaining clips or ties, noting its correct routing. Tie a length of string to the end of the choke inner cable.
4 Working from inside the vehicle, pull the choke lever fully out, to gain access to the retaining screw (see illustration). Slacken and remove the retaining screw, then

7.14 Adjusting the accelerator cable

9.1 Undo the retaining bolt and remove the choke cable retaining clip

9.4 Choke lever retaining screw (arrowed)

9.9 Choke cable-to-rubber collar retaining clip (arrowed)

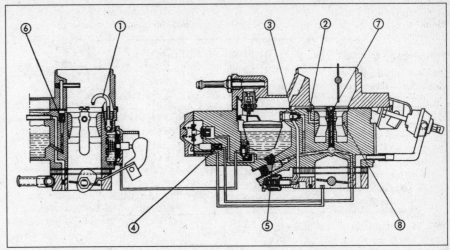

11.1 Sectional view of the Solex 32 PBISA carburettor fitted to 1124 cc models

1 Accelerator pump tube	4 Enrichment jet	7 Air correction jet
2 Idle ventilator	5 Main jet	8 Venturi
3 Idle jet	6 Fuel econostat	

withdraw the lever and cable assembly from the facia, disconnecting the wiring from the lever switch (where fitted) as it becomes accessible. Once the end of the cable appears through the lever aperture, untie the string and leave it in position in the vehicle - it can then be used to draw the cable back into position on refitting.

Refitting

5 Tie the string the end of the choke cable, then use the sting to draw the cable into position through the bulkhead into the engine compartment. Once the cable end is fully in position, untie the string.

6 Reconnect the wiring connector (where fitted), and locate the choke lever in its facia panel aperture. Refit the lever retaining screw, tightening it securely.

7 From within the engine compartment, ensure the outer cable is correctly seated in the bulkhead grommet. Work along the cable, securing it in position with all the relevant retaining clips and ties, and ensuring that the cable is correctly routed.

8 Slide the rubber collar and retaining clip onto the end of the cable, then engage the inner end of the cable with carburettor linkage. Align the rubber collar with the carburettor bracket, then refit the retaining clip and securely tighten its retaining bolt. Adjust the cable as described below.

Adjustment

9 If not already done, slacken the retaining clip securing the rubber collar to the outer cable. Where the crimped-type Citroën hose clip is still fitted, cut the clip and discard it; use a standard worm-drive hose clip on refitting **(see illustration)**.

10 Ensuring that the choke lever is flush with the facia panel and the carburettor linkage is fully against its stop, move the outer cable in the rubber collar until the position is found where there is only a small amount of free play present in the inner cable. Hold the outer cable in this position, and securely tighten the clip securing the rubber collar to the outer cable.

11 Have an assistant operate the choke lever, and check that the choke linkage closes fully and returns smoothly to its stop. If necessary, repeat the adjustment procedure.

10 Unleaded petrol - general information and usage

Note: *The information given in this Chapter is correct at the time of writing. If updated information is thought to be required, check with a Citroën dealer. If travelling abroad, consult one of the motoring organisations (or a similar authority) for advice on the fuel available.*

1 The fuel recommended by Citroën is given in the Specifications Section of this Chapter, followed by the equivalent petrol currently on sale in the UK.

2 All Citroën ZX carburettor models are designed to run on 95 octane unleaded petrol. Super unleaded (98 octane) petrol can also be used if wished, though there is no advantage in doing so.

11 Carburettor - general information

Solex 32 PBISA carburettor - 1124 cc models

1 The Solex PBISA carburettor is a downdraught single-venturi instrument, with a manually-controlled choke **(see illustration)**. The carburettor consists of three main components - the upper body, the main body, and the throttle body (which contains the throttle valve assembly). An insulating block placed between the carburettor body and throttle body prevents excess heat transfer from the manifold to the main body.

2 The throttle body contains a drilling through which the engine coolant runs. The engine coolant warms the carburettor body quickly on cold starts, improving atomisation of the fuel/air mixture and preventing carburettor icing, during warm-up.

3 During slow running and at idle, fuel from the float chamber passes into the idle channel through a metered idle jet. Here it is mixed with a small amount of air from a calibrated air bleed. The resulting mixture is drawn through a channel, to be discharged from the idle orifice under the throttle valve. A tapered mixture screw is used to vary the outlet, and this ensures fine control of the idle mixture.

4 A progression slot provides extra enrichment as it is uncovered by the opening of the throttle valve during initial acceleration.

5 Under normal operating conditions, fuel is drawn through a calibrated main jet, into the base of the auxiliary venturi. An emulsion tube is placed in the auxiliary venturi, capped with an air correction jet. The fuel is mixed with air, drawn in through the holes in the emulsion tube. The resulting mixture is discharged into the main airstream via four orifices, spaced at 90° apart, in the upper part of the auxiliary venturi.

6 The carburettor also has an accelerator pump, to provide an initial spurt of extra fuel during sudden acceleration. The accelerator pump is controlled by a diaphragm, and is mechanically operated by a lever and rod which is connected to the throttle linkage.

7 The idle speed is set by an adjustable screw. The adjustable mixture screw is sealed during production with a tamperproof plug, to prevent unnecessary or inexpert adjustment.

Solex 32-34 Z2 carburettor - 1360 cc models

8 The Solex 32-34 Z2 carburettor is a downdraught progressive twin-venturi

4A

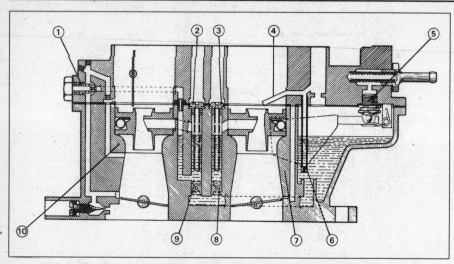

11.8 Sectional view of the Solex 32-34 Z2 carburettor fitted to 1360 cc models

1 Idle jet
2 Primary air correction jet/emulsion tube
3 Secondary air correction jet/emulsion tube
4 Secondary fuel jet
5 Needle valve
6 Bypass jet
7 Secondary venturi
8 Secondary main jet
9 Primary main jet
10 Primary venturi

instrument **(see illustration)**. The throttle linkages are arranged so that the secondary throttle valve will not start to open until the primary valve is about two-thirds open, but at full throttle both valves are fully open. The choke control is manual.

9 An electrical heating element is fitted to the base of the throttle body. The heater warms the carburettor body quickly on cold starts, improving atomisation of the fuel/air mixture and preventing carburettor icing during warm-up. The heater is fed directly from the ignition switch, and functions on the PTC (Positive Temperature Coefficient) principle; ie. as the heater temperature rises, so does its resistance.

10 During slow running and at idle, fuel from the float chamber passes into the idle channel through a metered idle jet. Here it is mixed with a small amount of air from a calibrated air bleed. The resulting mixture is drawn through a channel, to be discharged from the idle orifice under the primary throttle plate. A tapered mixture screw is used to vary the

outlet, and this ensures fine control of the idle mixture.

11 On some models, an idle cut-off valve is used to prevent run-on when the engine is switched off. The valve uses a solenoid plunger to block the idle jet when the ignition is switched off.

12 A progression slot provides extra enrichment as it is uncovered by the opening of the throttle valve during initial acceleration.

13 Under normal operating conditions, the amount of fuel discharged into the airstream is controlled by a calibrated main jet. Fuel is drawn through the main jet, into the base of a vertical well which dips down into the fuel in the float chamber; an emulsion tube is placed in the well. The fuel is then mixed with air, drawn in through the air correction jet and through the holes in the emulsion tube. The resulting mixture is discharged from the main orifice through an auxiliary vent.

14 The carburettor also has an accelerator pump to provide an initial spurt of extra fuel during sudden acceleration. The accelerator

pump is mechanically operated by a lever and cam which is attached to the primary throttle linkage. During acceleration, fuel is pumped through a ball valve located in the pump injector, and is discharged into both the primary and secondary venturis. The inlet ball valve is located in a channel from the float chamber; excess fuel/air mixture is returned to the float chamber through a separate channel.

15 The idle speed is set by an adjustable screw. The adjustable mixture screw is sealed during production with a tamperproof plug, to prevent unnecessary or inexpert adjustment.

12 Carburettor - removal and refitting

Note: *Refer to the warning note in Section 1 before proceeding. Where original crimped-type Citroën hose clips are still fitted, the clips should be cut and discarded; obtain some standard worm-drive hose clips for refitting.*

Removal

1 Disconnect the battery negative terminal.
2 Remove the air cleaner-to-carburettor duct as described in paragraphs 1 and 2 of Section 2.
3 Free the accelerator inner cable from the throttle cam, then pull the outer cable out from its mounting bracket rubber grommet, along with its flat washer and spring clip.
4 Disconnect the choke inner cable from the carburettor linkage, then undo the retaining bolt and remove the retaining clamp. Position the cable clear of the carburettor.
5 On 1124 cc models, slacken the retaining clips and disconnect the coolant hoses from the base of the carburettor. Plug the hose ends to minimise coolant loss, and mop up any spilt coolant immediately.
6 On 1360 cc models, disconnect the wiring connector from the carburettor heating element and, where fitted, from the idle cut-off solenoid **(see illustration)**.
7 Slacken the retaining clip, and disconnect the fuel feed hose from the carburettor. Place wads of rag around the union to catch any spilled fuel, and plug the hose as soon as it is disconnected, to minimise fuel loss **(see illustration)**.

12.6 Disconnecting the carburettor wiring connector - 1360 cc models

12.7 Carburettor fuel hose union - 1360 cc models

12.9 Carburettor retaining nuts (two of four arrowed) - 1360 cc models

8 Make a note of the correct fitted positions of all the relevant vacuum pipes and breather hoses, to ensure they are correctly positioned on refitting, then release the retaining clips (where fitted) and disconnect them from the carburettor.

9 Unscrew the two (1124 cc models) or four (1360 cc models) nuts and washers securing the carburettor to the inlet manifold. Remove the carburettor assembly from the car **(see illustration)**. Remove the insulating spacer and/or gasket(s). Discard the gasket(s); new ones must be used on refitting. Plug the inlet manifold port with a wad of clean cloth, to prevent the possible entry of foreign matter.

Refitting

10 Refitting is the reverse of the removal procedure, noting the following points:

(a) *Ensure the carburettor and inlet manifold sealing faces are clean and flat. Fit a new gasket, and securely tighten the carburettor retaining nuts.*

(b) *Use the notes made on dismantling to ensure all hoses are refitted to their original positions and, where necessary, are securely held by their retaining clips.*

(c) *Where the original crimped-type Citroën hose clips were fitted, discard them; use standard worm-drive hose clips when refitting.*

(d) *Refit and adjust the choke and accelerator cables as described in Sections 7 and 9.*

(e) *Refit the air cleaner duct as described in Section 2.*

(f) *On completion, check and, if necessary, adjust the idle speed and mixture settings as described in Chapter 1.*

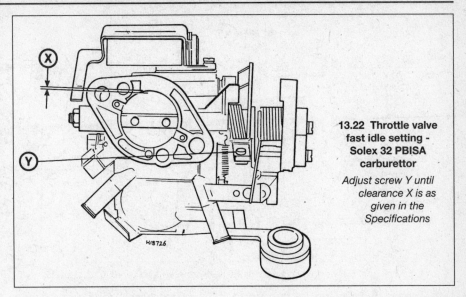

13.22 Throttle valve fast idle setting - Solex 32 PBISA carburettor

Adjust screw Y until clearance X is as given in the Specifications

---

13 Solex 32 PBISA carburettor (1124 cc models) - fault finding, overhaul and adjustments

Fault finding

1 If a carburettor fault is suspected, always check first that the ignition timing is correctly set, that the spark plugs are in good condition and correctly gapped, that the accelerator and choke cables are correctly adjusted, and that the air cleaner filter element is clean; refer to the relevant Sections of Chapter 1, Chapter 5 or this Chapter. If the engine is running very roughly, first check the valve clearances as described in Chapter 1, then check the compression pressures as described in Chapter 2.

2 If careful checking of all the above produces no improvement, the carburettor must be removed for cleaning and overhaul.

3 Note that in the rare event of a complete carburettor overhaul being necessary, it may prove more economical to renew the carburettor as a complete unit. Check the price and availability of a new carburettor and

of its component parts before starting work; note that most sealing washers, screws and gaskets are available in kits, as are some of the major sub-assemblies. In most cases, it will be sufficient to dismantle the carburettor and to clean the jets and passages.

Overhaul

Note: *Refer to the warning note in Section 1 before proceeding.*

4 Remove the carburettor from the vehicle as described in Section 12.

5 Disconnect the vacuum hose from the choke pull-down diaphragm.

6 Disconnect the choke spring (where necessary), then undo the six screws and lift off the carburettor upper body.

7 Tap out the float pivot pin, and remove the float assembly, needle valve, and float chamber gasket. Check that the needle valve anti-vibration ball is free in the valve end, then examine the needle valve tip and seat for wear or damage. Examine the float assembly and pivot pin for signs of wear and damage. The float assembly must be renewed if it appears to be leaking - shake the float to detect the presence of fuel inside.

8 Unscrew the fuel inlet union and inspect the fuel filter. Clean the filter housing of debris and dirt, and renew the filter if it is blocked.

9 Undo the four screws, detach the accelerator pump cover, and remove the pump diaphragm and spring, noting which way around they are fitted. Examine the diaphragm for signs of damage and deterioration, and renew if necessary.

10 Unscrew the idle jet from the main body.

11 Unscrew the main jet from the float chamber. Note that it may be necessary to remove a plug in the float chamber body, to expose an opening through which the main jet can be withdrawn.

12 Remove the combined air correction jet and emulsion tube from the auxiliary venturi.

13 Remove the two screws, separate the carburettor main body and throttle body

assemblies, and recover the insulating spacer. Examine the throttle valve spindle and throttle bore for signs of wear or damage and, if necessary, renew the throttle body assembly.

14 Remove the idle mixture adjustment screw tamperproof cap. Screw the screw in until it seats lightly, counting the *exact* number of turns required to do this, then unscrew it. On refitting, screw the screw in until it seats lightly, then back the screw off by the number of turns noted on removal, to return the screw to its original position.

15 Clean the jets, carburettor body assemblies, float chamber and internal drillings. An air line may be used to clear the internal passages once the carburettor is fully dismantled.

> ⚠ **Warning: If high pressure air is directed into drillings and passages where a diaphragm is fitted, the diaphragm is likely to be damaged.**

> **HAYNES HINT** *Aerosol cans of carburettor cleaner are widely available, and can prove very useful in helping to clear internal passages of stubborn obstructions.*

16 Use a straight edge to check all carburettor body assembly mating surfaces for distortion.

17 On reassembly, renew any worn components, and fit a complete set of new gaskets and seals. A jet kit and a gasket and seal kit are available from your Citroën dealer.

18 Reassembly is a reversal of the dismantling procedure. Ensure that all jets are securely locked in position, but take great care not to overtighten them. Ensure all mating surfaces are clean and dry, and that all body sections are correctly assembled with

4A

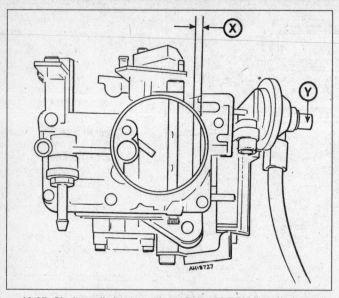

13.25 Choke pull-down setting - Solex 32 PBISA carburettor

Adjust screw Y until clearance X is as given in the Specifications

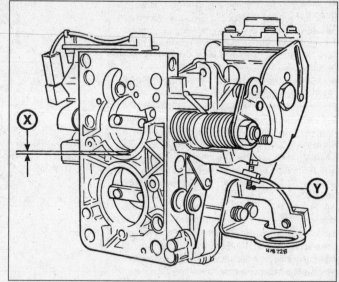

14.19 Throttle valve fast idle setting - Solex 32-34 Z2 carburettor

Adjust screw Y until clearance X is as given in the Specifications

their fuel and air passages correctly aligned. Before refitting the carburettor to the vehicle, set the throttle valve fast idle and choke pull-down settings as described below.

Adjustments

Idle speed and mixture

19 Refer to Chapter 1.

Float height setting

20 To accurately check the float height setting, a special float height checking gauge is required. Therefore, this task must be entrusted to a Citroën dealer. As a guide, with the carburettor body inverted, so that the float is at the top and the needle valve is depressed, the distance between the upper edge of the float and the sealing face of the upper body (with its gasket fitted) should be approximately 38 mm. To adjust the float height setting, *carefully* bend the pivot arm.

Throttle valve fast idle setting

21 Invert the carburettor, and operate the carburettor choke linkage to fully close the choke valve. The fast idle screw will butt against the fast idle cam, and force the throttle valve open slightly.

22 Using the shank of a twist drill, measure the clearance between the edge of the throttle valve and bore, and compare this to the clearance given in the Specifications. If necessary, adjust by turning the fast idle adjustment screw in the appropriate direction until the specified clearance is obtained **(see illustration)**.

Choke pull-down setting

23 Operate the carburettor choke linkage to fully close the choke valve, and hold the linkage in this position.

24 Attach a hand-held vacuum pump to the choke pull-down diaphragm, and apply a vacuum to the diaphragm so that the diaphragm rod is pulled fully into the diaphragm body. In the absence of a vacuum pump, the rod can be pushed into the diaphragm using a small screwdriver.

25 With the rod fully retracted, use the shank of a twist drill to measure the clearance between the edge of the choke valve and bore, and compare this to the clearance given in the Specifications **(see illustration)**. If necessary, remove the plug from the diaphragm cover, and adjust by turning the adjustment screw. Once the pull-down setting is correctly adjusted, refit the plug to the diaphragm cover, and remove the vacuum pump (where used).

14 Solex 32-34 Z2 carburettor (1360 cc models) - fault finding, overhaul and adjustments

Fault finding

1 Refer to Section 13.

Overhaul

Note: *Refer to the warning note in Section 1 before proceeding.*

2 Remove the carburettor from the vehicle as described in Section 12.

3 Unscrew the idle cut-off solenoid (where fitted) from the carburettor body, and remove it along with its plunger and spring. To test the solenoid, connect a 12-volt battery to it (positive terminal to the solenoid terminal, negative terminal to the solenoid body), and check that the plunger is retracted fully into the body. Disconnect the battery, and check that the plunger is pushed out by spring pressure. If the valve does not perform as expected, and cleaning does not improve

the situation, the solenoid valve must be renewed.

4 Remove the five screws, and lift off the carburettor upper body.

5 Tap out the float pivot pin, and remove the float assembly, needle valve, and float chamber gasket. Check that the needle valve anti-vibration ball is free in the valve end, then examine the needle valve tip and seat for wear or damage. Examine the float assembly and pivot pin for signs of wear and damage. The float assembly must be renewed if it appears to be leaking - shake the float to detect the presence of fuel inside.

6 Unscrew the fuel inlet union and inspect the fuel filter. Clean the filter housing of debris and dirt, and renew the filter if it is blocked.

7 Undo the four screws, detach the accelerator pump cover, and remove the pump diaphragm and spring, noting which way around they are fitted. Examine the diaphragm for signs of damage and deterioration, and renew if necessary. Remove the choke pull-down diaphragm and part-load enrichment diaphragms, and examine them in the same way.

8 Unscrew the idle jet from the upper body.

9 Unscrew both the primary and secondary combined air correction jets and emulsion tubes.

10 Using a long thin screwdriver, unscrew the main jets from the bottom of the emulsion tube drillings. Invert the carburettor, and catch the jets as they fall out of the drillings.

11 Remove the idle mixture adjustment screw tamperproof cap. Screw the screw in until it seats lightly, counting the *exact* number of turns required to do this, then unscrew it. On refitting, screw the screw in until it seats lightly, then back the screw off by the number of turns noted on removal, to return the screw to its original position.

12 Examine the carburettor components as described in paragraphs 15 to 17 of Section 13.

13 To test the carburettor heating element, connect a multimeter, set to the resistance function, between the heater wiring terminal and the carburettor body. A resistance reading of approximately 0.25 to 0.5 ohms should be obtained. If an open-circuit is present, or an extremely high resistance reading is obtained, it is likely that the heating element is faulty. Seek the advice of your Citroën dealer before condemning the heater. The dealer will also be able to advise whether or not the heating element is available separately.

14 Reassembly is a reversal of the dismantling procedure. Ensure that all jets are securely locked in position, but take great care not to overtighten them. Ensure all mating surfaces are clean and dry, and that all body sections are correctly assembled with their fuel and air passages correctly aligned. Prior to refitting the carburettor to the vehicle, set the float height, throttle valve fast idle and choke pull-down settings as described below.

Adjustments

Idle speed and mixture

15 Refer to Chapter 1.

Float height setting

16 Invert the carburettor body, so the float is at the top and the needle valve is depressed. Measure the distance between the upper edge of the float and the sealing face of the upper body (with its gasket fitted). This measurement should be as given in the Specifications at the start of this Chapter.

17 If necessary, the float height can be adjusted by *carefully* bending the small tang on the float arm which contacts the needle valve.

Throttle valve fast idle setting

18 Invert the carburettor, and pull the carburettor choke linkage to fully close the choke valve. The fast idle screw will butt against the fast idle cam, and force the throttle valve open slightly.

19 Using the shank of a twist drill, measure the clearance between the edge of the throttle valve and bore, and compare this to the clearance given in the Specifications at the start of this Chapter. If necessary, adjust by turning the fast idle adjustment screw in the appropriate direction until the specified clearance is obtained **(see illustration)**.

Choke pull-down setting

20 Pull the carburettor choke linkage to fully close the choke valve, and hold the linkage in this position.

21 Attach a hand-held vacuum pump to the choke pull-down diaphragm, and apply a vacuum to the diaphragm so that the diaphragm rod is pulled fully into the diaphragm body. In the absence of a vacuum

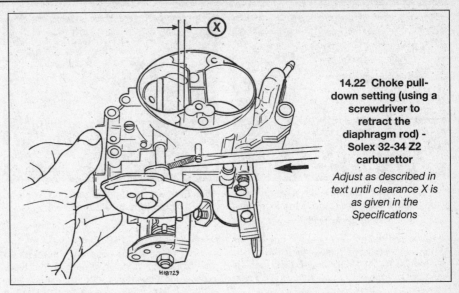

14.22 Choke pull-down setting (using a screwdriver to retract the diaphragm rod) - Solex 32-34 Z2 carburettor

Adjust as described in text until clearance X is as given in the Specifications

pump, the rod can be pushed into the diaphragm with a small screwdriver.

22 With the rod fully retracted, use the shank of a twist drill to measure the clearance between the edge of the choke valve and bore, and compare this to the clearance given in the Specifications **(see illustration)**. If necessary, remove the plug from the diaphragm cover, and adjust by turning the adjustment screw. Once the pull-down setting is correctly adjusted, refit the plug to the diaphragm cover, and remove the vacuum pump (where used).

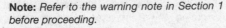

15 Inlet manifold - removal and refitting

Note: *Refer to the warning note in Section 1 before proceeding.*

Removal

1 Remove the carburettor as described in Section 12.

2 Drain the cooling system as described in Chapter 1.

3 Undo the bolt(s) securing the anti-percolation chamber mounting bracket to the manifold, and position the chamber clear of the manifold so that it does not hinder removal.

4 Slacken the retaining clips, then disconnect the vacuum servo unit hose from the left-hand side of the manifold, and the coolant hose from the base of the manifold.

5 Make a final check that all the necessary vacuum/breather hoses have been disconnected from the manifold.

6 Unscrew the six retaining nuts, then manoeuvre the manifold away from the head and out of the engine compartment. Note that there is no manifold gasket.

Refitting

7 Refitting is the reverse of the removal procedure, noting the following points:

(a) Ensure that the manifold and cylinder head mating surfaces are clean and dry, and apply a thin coating of suitable sealing compound to the manifold mating surface. Install the manifold, and tighten its retaining nuts to the specified torque setting.

(b) Ensure all relevant hoses are reconnected to their original positions, and are securely held (where necessary) by their retaining clips.

(c) Refit the carburettor as described in Section 12.

(d) On completion, refill the cooling system as described in Chapter 1.

16 Exhaust manifold - removal and refitting

Removal

1 Disconnect the hot-air intake hose from the manifold shroud, and remove it from the vehicle **(see illustration)**.

2 Slacken and remove the three retaining

16.1 Remove the hot-air intake hose . . .

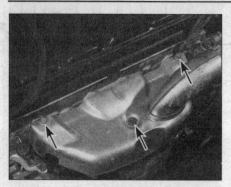

16.2 . . . then undo the three retaining bolts (arrowed) and remove the exhaust manifold shroud

16.5 Exhaust manifold is retained by eight nuts (upper four arrowed)

screws, and remove the shroud from the top of the exhaust manifold (see illustration).

3 Firmly apply the handbrake, then jack up the front of the vehicle and support it on axle stands.

4 Undo the nuts securing the exhaust front pipe to the manifold, then remove the bolt securing the front pipe to its mounting bracket. Disconnect the front pipe from the manifold, and recover the gasket.

5 Undo the eight retaining nuts securing the manifold to the head (see illustration). Manoeuvre the manifold out of the engine compartment, and discard the manifold gaskets.

Refitting

6 Refitting is the reverse of the removal procedure, noting the following points:

(a) Examine all the exhaust manifold studs for signs of damage and corrosion; remove all traces of corrosion, and repair or renew any damaged studs.

(b) Ensure that the manifold and cylinder head sealing faces are clean and flat, and fit the new manifold gaskets. Tighten the manifold retaining nuts to the specified torque.

(c) Reconnect the front pipe to the manifold using the information given in Section 17.

17 Exhaust system - general information, removal and refitting

General information

1 The exhaust system consists of three sections; the front pipe, the intermediate pipe and silencer box, and the tailpipe and main silencer box. All exhaust sections are joined by flanged joints. The front pipe joints are secured by nuts and bolts, the intermediate pipe joint being of the spring-loaded ball type, to allow for movement in the exhaust system, and the intermediate pipe-to-silencer joint is secured by a clamping ring.

2 The system is suspended throughout its entire length by rubber mountings.

Removal

3 Each exhaust section can be removed individually, or alternatively, the complete system can be removed as a unit. Even if only one part of the system needs attention, it is often easier to remove the whole system and separate the sections on the bench.

4 To remove the system or part of the system, first jack up the front or rear of the car, and support it on axle stands. Alternatively, position the car over an inspection pit, or on car ramps.

Front pipe

5 Undo the nuts securing the front pipe flange joint to the manifold, and the single bolt securing the front pipe to its mounting bracket. Separate the flange joint, and collect the gasket.

6 Slacken and remove the two nuts securing the front pipe flange joint to the intermediate pipe, and recover the spring cups and springs. Remove the bolts, then withdraw the front pipe from underneath the vehicle, and recover the wire-mesh gasket.

Intermediate pipe

7 Undo the two nuts securing the front pipe flange joint to the intermediate pipe. Recover the springs and spring cups, and withdraw the bolts.

8 Slacken the intermediate pipe-to-tailpipe clamping ring bolts, and disengage the clamp from the flange joint.

9 Free the intermediate pipe from its mounting rubbers, withdraw it from underneath the vehicle, and recover the wire-mesh gasket from the front pipe joint.

Tailpipe

10 Slacken the intermediate pipe-to-tailpipe clamping ring bolts, and disengage the clamp from the flange joint.

11 Unhook the tailpipe from its mounting rubbers, and remove it from the vehicle.

Complete system

12 Undo the nuts securing the front pipe flange joint to the manifold, and the single bolt securing the front pipe to its mounting bracket. Separate the flange joint, and collect the gasket. Free the system from all its mounting rubbers, and lower it from under the vehicle.

Heat shield(s)

13 The heat shields are secured to the underside of the body by various nuts and bolts. Each shield can be removed once the relevant exhaust section has been removed. If a shield is being removed to gain access to a component located behind it, it may prove sufficient in some cases to remove the retaining nuts and/or bolts, and simply lower the shield, without disturbing the exhaust system.

Refitting

14 Each section is refitted by reversing the removal sequence, noting the following points:

(a) Ensure that all traces of corrosion have been removed from the flanges, and renew all necessary gaskets.

(b) Inspect the rubber mountings for signs of damage or deterioration, and renew as necessary.

(c) Prior to assembling the front pipe-to-intermediate pipe joint, a smear of high-temperature grease should be applied to the joint mating surfaces. Citroën recommend the use of Gripcott AF G2 grease (available from your Citroën dealer).

(d) In the case of the intermediate pipe-to-tailpipe joint, apply a smear of exhaust system jointing paste to the flange joint, to ensure a gas-tight seal. Tighten the clamping ring nuts evenly and progressively to the specified torque setting, so that the clearance between the clamp halves is equal on either side.

(e) Prior to tightening the exhaust system fasteners, ensure that all rubber mountings are correctly located, and that there is adequate clearance between the exhaust system and vehicle underbody.

Chapter 4 Part B: Fuel and exhaust systems – single-point fuel injection models

Contents

Accelerator cable - removal, refitting and adjustment 4
Accelerator pedal - removal and refitting 5
Air cleaner air temperature control system - general
   information and component renewal 3
Air cleaner assembly and intake ducts - removal and refitting 2
Air cleaner filter element renewal . . . . See Chapter 1
Bosch Monopoint system components - removal and refitting 14
Exhaust manifold - removal and refitting 17
Exhaust system - general information, removal and refitting 18
Fuel filter - renewal . . . . See Chapter 1
Fuel gauge sender unit - removal and refitting 10
Fuel injection system - depressurisation 8
Fuel injection system - testing and adjustment 13
Fuel injection systems - general information 7
Fuel pump - removal and refitting 9
Fuel tank - removal and refitting 11
General fuel system checks . . . . See Chapter 1
General information and precautions 1
Idle speed and mixture adjustment . . . . See Chapter 1
Inlet manifold - removal and refitting 16
Magneti Marelli system components - removal and refitting 15
Throttle body - removal and refitting 12
Unleaded petrol - general information and usage 6

Degrees of difficulty

| Easy, suitable for novice with little experience | | Fairly easy, suitable for beginner with some experience | | Fairly difficult, suitable for competent DIY mechanic | | Difficult, suitable for experienced DIY mechanic | | Very difficult, suitable for expert DIY or professional | |
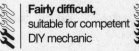

Specifications

System type
1124 cc (H1A engine) models . . . . Bosch Monopoint A2.2
1124 cc (HDZ engine) models:
   Up to mid-1996 . . . . Bosch Monopoint A2.2 or MA3.0
   Mid-1996 onward . . . . Bosch Monopoint MA3.1
1360 cc (KDY engine) models . . . . Bosch Monopoint A2.2
1360 cc (KDX engine) models . . . . Bosch Monopoint MA3.0
1580 cc (B4A engine) models . . . . Magneti Marelli G5.S2 or G6.12
1580 cc (BDY engine) models . . . . Magneti Marelli G6.10
Note: *Refer to the relevant part of Chapter 2 for further information on engine code identification*

Fuel system data
Fuel pump type . . . . Electric, immersed in tank
Fuel pump regulated constant pressure:
   Bosch system . . . . 1.0 bar
   Magneti Marelli system . . . . 0.8 ± 0.1 bar
Specified idle speed (not adjustable) . . . . 850 ± 50 rpm (controlled by ECU)
Idle mixture CO content:
   Bosch system (not adjustable) . . . . Less than 1.0 % (controlled by ECU)
   Magneti Marelli system*:
      1580 cc (B4A engine) models . . . . 1.0 to 2.0 %
      1580 cc (BDY engine) models . . . . Less than 1.0 % (controlled by ECU)
On the Magneti Marelli system, idle mixture adjustment is possible, but only using special electronic equipment - see text

Recommended fuel . . . . 95 RON unleaded (UK unleaded premium)

Torque wrench settings

	Nm	lbf ft
Inlet manifold nuts:		
1124 cc and 1360 cc models	8	6
1580 cc models	22	16
Exhaust manifold nuts:		
1124 cc and 1360 cc models	16	12
1580 cc models	22	16
Exhaust system fasteners:		
1124 cc and 1360 cc models:		
Front pipe-to-manifold nuts	30	22
Front pipe mounting bolt	35	26
Front pipe-to-intermediate pipe nuts	10	7
Clamping ring nuts	20	15
1580 cc models:		
Front pipe-to-manifold nuts	10	7
Clamping ring nuts	20	15

1 General information and precautions

The fuel system consists of a fuel tank (which is mounted under the rear of the car, with an electric fuel pump immersed in it), a fuel filter, fuel feed and return lines, and the throttle body assembly (which incorporates the single fuel injector and the fuel pressure regulator). In addition, there is an Electronic Control Unit (ECU) and various sensors, electrical components and related wiring. The air cleaner contains a disposable paper filter element, and incorporates a flap valve air temperature control system. This allows cold air from the outside of the car and warm air from around the exhaust manifold to enter the air cleaner in the correct proportions.

Refer to Section 7 for further information on the operation of each fuel injection system, and to Section 18 for information on the exhaust system.

Throughout this Section, it is occasionally necessary to identify vehicles by their engine codes rather than by engine capacity. Refer to the relevant Part of Chapter 2 for further information on engine code identification.

 Warning: Many of the procedures in this Chapter require the removal of fuel lines and connections, which may result in some fuel spillage. Before *carrying out any operation on the fuel system, refer to the precautions given in "Safety first!" at the beginning of this manual, and follow them implicitly. Petrol is a highly-dangerous and volatile liquid, and the precautions necessary when handling it cannot be overstressed.*

Note: *Residual pressure will remain in the fuel lines long after the vehicle was last used. When disconnecting any fuel line, first depressurise the fuel system as described in Section 8.*

2 Air cleaner assembly and intake ducts - removal and refitting

1124 cc and 1360 cc models

1 Refer to Chapter 4A, Section 2, substituting "throttle body" for all references to the carburettor.

1580 cc models
Removal

2 Slacken the retaining clip, and disconnect the air cleaner housing-to-throttle body duct from the front of the air cleaner housing.
3 Slacken the retaining clip, and disconnect the air cleaner air temperature control valve assembly from the end of the air cleaner housing.
4 Free the air cleaner housing retaining strap from its retaining clip, then lift the air cleaner housing away from its mounting bracket. If necessary, the mounting bracket can then be unbolted and removed from the engine compartment **(see illustrations)**.
5 To remove the intake duct, first disconnect the vacuum hose from the air temperature control valve diaphragm. If not already done, slacken the retaining clip securing the control valve to the air cleaner housing. Undo the nut(s) securing the front of the duct to the vehicle body, then release the fastener securing the rear of the duct in position. Disconnect the hot-air intake hose from the manifold shroud, and remove the duct and hose assembly from the engine compartment **(see illustration)**.

2.4a On 1580 cc models, release the rubber retaining strap . . .

2.4b . . . and lift the air cleaner housing out of the engine compartment

2.4c Air cleaner mounting bracket retaining bolts (arrowed) - 1580 cc models

2.5 Removing the intake duct and hose assembly - 1580 cc models

6 To remove the air cleaner housing-to-throttle body duct, disconnect the breather hose from the side of the duct, then disconnect the vacuum hoses from the air temperature control system vacuum valve, noting their correct fitted positions. Slacken the retaining clip securing the duct to the air cleaner housing, then slacken and remove the two nuts and washers securing the duct to the throttle body. Remove the duct from engine compartment. On early models, it will be necessary to disconnect the auxiliary air valve hose from the duct, and to recover the rubber sealing ring from the top of the throttle body **(see illustrations)**.

Refitting

7 Refitting is a reversal of the removal procedure, ensuring that all hoses are properly reconnected, and that all ducts are correctly seated and securely held by their retaining clips.

3 Air cleaner air temperature control system - general information and component renewal

1124 cc and 1360 cc models

1 Refer to Chapter 4A, Section 3, substituting "throttle body" for all references to the carburettor.

1580 cc models

General information

2 Refer to Chapter 4A, Section 3, substituting "throttle body" for all references to the carburettor.

Vacuum switch - renewal

3 Remove the air cleaner-to-throttle body duct as described in paragraph 6 of Section 2.
4 Bend up the tangs on the switch retaining clip, then remove the clip and withdraw the switch from inside the duct.
5 On refitting, ensure the switch and duct mating surfaces are clean and dry, and position the switch on the inside of the duct. Refit the retaining clip, then press the switch firmly against the duct, securing it in position by bending down the retaining clip tangs.
6 Refit the duct as described in Section 2.

Air temperature control valve - renewal

7 Disconnect the vacuum pipe from the air temperature control valve, then slacken the retaining clips securing the valve to the air cleaner housing, hot-air intake hose, and the intake duct.
8 Disconnect the intake duct and hose from the control valve, then free the valve from the air cleaner assembly and remove it from the vehicle.
9 Refitting is the reverse of the removal procedure, noting that the air temperature control valve assembly can only be renewed as a complete unit.

2.6a Undo the two retaining nuts . . .

2.6b . . . then detach the duct from the throttle body, and recover the sealing ring

4 Accelerator cable - removal, refitting and adjustment

1 Refer to Chapter 4A, Section 7, substituting "throttle body" for all references to the carburettor. On automatic transmission models, once the accelerator cable is correctly adjusted, check the kickdown cable adjustment as described in Chapter 7B.

5 Accelerator pedal - removal and refitting

Refer to Chapter 4A, Section 8.

6 Unleaded petrol - general information and usage

Note: *The information given in this Chapter is correct at the time of writing. If updated information is thought to be required, check with a Citroën dealer. If travelling abroad, consult one of the motoring organisations (or a similar authority) for advice on the fuel available.*

1 The fuel recommended by Citroën is given in the Specifications Section of this Chapter, followed by the equivalent petrol currently on sale in the UK.
2 All Citroën ZX single-point injection models are designed to run on unleaded fuel with a minimum octane rating of 95 (RON).
3 Super unleaded petrol (98 octane) can also be used in all models if wished, though there is no advantage in doing so.

7 Fuel injection systems - general information

Bosch Monopoint A2.2 system

1 The Bosch Monopoint A2.2 fuel injection system is fitted to certain 1124 cc fuel-injected models, and to early fuel-injected 1360 cc (KDY engine) models. The system incorporates a closed-loop catalytic converter and an evaporative emission control system, and complies with the latest emission control standards. The system operates as follows.

2 The fuel pump, immersed in the fuel tank, pumps fuel from the fuel tank to the fuel injector, via a filter mounted underneath the rear of the vehicle. Fuel supply pressure is controlled by the pressure regulator in the throttle body assembly. The regulator operates by allowing excess fuel to return to the tank.

3 The electrical control system consists of the ECU, along with the following sensors.

(a) Throttle potentiometer - informs the ECU of the throttle position, and the rate of throttle opening or closing.
(b) Coolant temperature sensor - informs the ECU of engine temperature.
(c) Intake air temperature sensor - informs the ECU of the temperature of the air passing through the throttle body.
(d) Lambda sensor - informs the ECU of the oxygen content of the exhaust gases (explained in greater detail in Part D of this Chapter).
(e) Microswitch (built into idle speed stepper motor) - informs the ECU when the throttle valve is closed (ie when the accelerator pedal is released).
(f) Ignition HT coil - ECU monitors the coil low tension (LT) circuit to determine the engine speed.

4 All the above information is analysed by the ECU and, based on this, the ECU determines the appropriate fuelling requirements for the engine. The ECU controls the fuel injector by varying its pulse width - the length of time the injector is held open - to provide a richer or weaker mixture, as appropriate. The mixture is constantly varied by the ECU, to provide the best setting for cranking, starting (with either a hot or cold engine), warm-up, idle, cruising, and acceleration.

5 The ECU also has full control over the engine idle speed, via a stepper motor which is fitted to the throttle body. The motor pushrod rests against a cam on the throttle

4B

valve spindle. When the throttle valve is closed (accelerator pedal released), the ECU uses the motor to vary the opening of the throttle valve and so control the idle speed.

6 The ECU also controls the exhaust and evaporative emission control systems, which are described in detail in Part D of this Chapter.

7 If there is an abnormality in any of the readings obtained from either the coolant temperature sensor, the intake air temperature sensor or the lambda sensor, the ECU enters its back-up mode. In this event, the ECU ignores the abnormal sensor signal, and assumes a pre-programmed value which will allow the engine to continue running (albeit at reduced efficiency). If the ECU enters this back-up mode, the warning light on the instrument panel will come on, and the relevant fault code will be stored in the ECU memory.

8 If the warning light comes on, the vehicle should be taken to a Citroën dealer at the earliest opportunity. A complete test of the engine management system can then be carried out, using a special electronic diagnostic test unit which is simply plugged into the system's diagnostic connector.

Bosch Monopoint MA3.0 and MA3.1 systems

9 The Bosch Monopoint MA3.0 engine management (fuel injection/ignition) system is fitted to early 1124 cc (HDZ engine) models and 1360 cc (KDX engine) models, and the upgraded, but similar, MA3.1 system is fitted to later 1124 cc (HDZ engine) models. The MA3.0 and 3.1 systems differ from the earlier A2.2 system in that they are full engine management systems controlling both the fuel injection and ignition system, rather than purely the fuel injection system. Refer to Chapter 5 for information on the ignition side of the system.

10 The fuel injection side of the system is very similar to the A2.2 system described above, the only difference being that a couple of additional sensors are incorporated into the system. A crankshaft sensor is fitted to the engine, to inform the ECU of engine speed and crankshaft position, and a vehicle speed sensor is fitted to the gearbox, to inform the ECU of the road speed.

11 The crankshaft sensor is needed since the ECU also controls the ignition side of the system, and cannot use the ignition low tension (LT) circuit to calculate engine speed. The sensor works in conjunction with a reluctor ring fixed to the rear of the flywheel. The reluctor ring originally has a total of sixty teeth, which are equally-spaced at intervals of 6°. Of these sixty teeth, two adjacent teeth are removed, to leave a gap of 18°. The ECU uses this gap to establish where TDC is, and calculates engine speed from the frequency of teeth passing the crankshaft sensor.

Magneti Marelli system

12 On 1580 cc models, a Magneti Marelli engine management (fuel injection/ignition) system is fitted. There are three versions of the system, all of which differ slightly, but operate on the same principle. The differences are as follows.

13 Early models with the B4A (XU5M 2K) engine are fitted with the **G5.S2 system**. This system differs from later models in that it uses an auxiliary air valve to control the engine idle speed.

14 Later models with the B4A (XU5M 2K or 3K) engine are fitted with the **G6.12 system**. On this system, a stepper motor is fitted to the throttle body assembly to control the engine idle speed.

15 Later models with the BDY engine are fitted with the **G6.10 system**. This system is a development of the G6.12 system, incorporating a catalytic converter and an evaporative emission control system.

16 The fuel injection side of the system operates as described in the following paragraphs. Refer to Chapter 5 for information on the ignition side of the system.

17 The fuel pump, immersed in the fuel tank, pumps fuel from the fuel tank to the fuel injector, via a filter. Fuel supply pressure is controlled by the pressure regulator in the throttle body assembly. The regulator operates by allowing excess fuel to return to the tank. To reduce emissions and to improve driveability when the engine is cold, engine coolant is passed through the manifold and around the throttle body assembly.

18 The electrical control system consists of the ECU, along with the following sensors.

(a) *Manifold absolute pressure (MAP) sensor - informs the ECU of the load on the engine (expressed in terms of inlet manifold vacuum).*

(b) *Crankshaft sensor - informs the ECU of crankshaft position and engine speed.*

(c) *Throttle potentiometer - informs the ECU of the throttle position, and the rate of throttle opening/closing.*

(d) *Coolant temperature sensor - informs the ECU of engine temperature.*

(e) *Fuel/air mixture temperature sensor - informs the ECU of the temperature of the fuel/air mixture charge entering the cylinders.*

(f) *Lambda (oxygen) sensor - informs the ECU of the oxygen content of the exhaust gases (explained in greater detail in Part D of this Chapter).*

19 In addition, the ECU senses battery voltage (adjusting the injector pulse width to suit, and using the stepper motor to increase the idle speed and, therefore, the alternator output if the voltage is too low). Short-circuit protection and diagnostic capabilities are incorporated into the ECU, and it can both receive and transmit information via the engine management circuit diagnostic connector, thus permitting engine diagnosis and tuning by special diagnostic equipment.

20 All the above signals are compared by the ECU, using digital techniques, with set values pre-programmed (mapped) into its memory. Based on this information, the ECU selects the response appropriate to those values, and controls the ignition HT coil (see Chapter 5), and the fuel injector (varying its pulse width - the length of time the injector is held open - to provide a richer or weaker mixture, as appropriate). The mixture, idle speed and ignition timing are constantly varied by the ECU, to provide the best settings for cranking, starting (with either a hot or cold engine), warm-up, idle, cruising, and acceleration.

21 On the G5.S2 system, the ECU controls the idle speed via an auxiliary air valve. The air valve is connected to the air intake duct and to the throttle body, downstream of the throttle valve. When the throttle valve is closed, the ECU controls the opening of the valve, which in turn regulates the amount of air entering the manifold, and so controls the idle speed.

22 On the G6.12 and G6.10 systems, the ECU regulates the engine idle speed via a stepper motor which is fitted to the throttle body. The motor has a pushrod controlling the opening of an air passage which bypasses the throttle valve. When the throttle valve is closed, the ECU controls the movement of the motor pushrod, which regulates the amount of air which flows through the throttle body passage, and so controls the idle speed. The bypass passage is also used as an additional air supply during cold starting.

23 On the G6.10 system, the ECU also controls the exhaust and evaporative emission control systems, which are described in detail in Part D of this Chapter.

24 If there is an abnormality in any of the readings obtained from any of engine management circuit sensors, the ECU enters its back-up mode. In this event, the ECU ignores the abnormal sensor signal, and assumes a pre-programmed value which will allow the engine to continue running (albeit at reduced efficiency). On entering this back-up mode, the engine management warning light in the instrument panel will come on, informing the driver of the fault, and the relevant fault code will be stored in the ECU memory.

25 If the warning light comes on, the vehicle should be taken to a Citroën dealer at the earliest opportunity. A complete test of the engine management system can then be carried out, using a special electronic diagnostic test unit which is simply plugged into the system's diagnostic connector.

8 Fuel injection system - depressurisation

Note: *Refer to the warning note in Section 1 before proceeding.*

⚠ *Warning: The following procedure will merely relieve the pressure in the fuel system - remember that fuel will still be present in the system components, and take precautions accordingly before disconnecting any of them.*

1 The fuel system referred to in this Section is defined as the tank-mounted fuel pump, the fuel filter, the fuel injector and the pressure regulator in the injector housing, and the metal pipes and flexible hoses of the fuel lines between these components. All these contain fuel which will be under pressure while the engine is running, and/or while the ignition is switched on. The pressure will remain for some time after the ignition has been switched off, and it must be relieved in a controlled fashion when any of these components are disturbed for servicing work.

2 Disconnect the battery negative terminal.

3 Place a suitable container beneath the connection or union to be disconnected, and have a large rag ready to soak up any escaping fuel not being caught by the container.

4 Slowly loosen the connection or union nut to avoid a sudden release of pressure, and position the rag around the connection, to catch any fuel spray which may be expelled. Once the pressure is released, disconnect the fuel line. Plug the pipe ends, to minimise fuel loss and prevent the entry of dirt into the fuel system.

9 Fuel pump - removal and refitting

Note: *Refer to the warning note in Section 1 before proceeding.*

Removal

Note: *1997 models onward are fitted with a single hole fuel tank in which the fuel pump and fuel gauge sender unit are combined in one assembly. The following procedures are applicable to the later arrangement, but note that the fuel lines now incorporate quick-fit connectors instead of crimped-type hose clips.*

1 Disconnect the battery negative lead.

2 For access to the fuel pump, tilt or remove the rear seats as described in Chapter 11.

3 Using a screwdriver, carefully prise the plastic access cover from the floor to expose the fuel pump. The pump is located under the right-hand cover.

4 Disconnect the wiring connector from the fuel pump, and tape the connector to the vehicle body, to prevent it disappearing behind the tank.

5 Mark the hoses for identification purposes, then slacken the feed and return hose retaining clips. Where the crimped-type Citroën hose clips are fitted, cut the clips and discard them; use standard worm-drive hose clips on refitting. Disconnect both hoses from the top of the pump, and plug the hose ends.

6 Noting the alignment marks on the tank, pump cover and the locking ring, unscrew the ring and remove it from the tank. This is best accomplished by using a screwdriver on the raised ribs of the locking ring. Carefully tap the screwdriver to turn the ring anti-clockwise until it can be unscrewed by hand.

7 Displace the pump cover, then reach into the tank and unclip the pump from the tank base. Lift the fuel pump assembly out of the fuel tank, taking great care not to damage the filter, or to spill fuel onto the interior of the vehicle. Recover the rubber sealing ring and discard it - a new one must be used on refitting.

8 Note that the fuel pump is only available as a complete assembly - no components are available separately.

Refitting

9 Ensure the fuel pump pick-up filter is clean and free of debris. Fit the new sealing ring to the top of the fuel tank.

10 Carefully manoeuvre the pump assembly into the fuel tank, and clip it into position in the base of the tank.

11 Align the mark on the fuel pump cover with the centre of the three alignment marks on the fuel tank, then refit the locking ring. Securely tighten the locking ring, then check that the locking ring, pump cover and tank marks are all correctly aligned.

12 Reconnect the feed and return hoses to the top of the fuel pump, using the marks made on removal to ensure that they are correctly reconnected, and securely tighten their retaining clips.

13 Reconnect the pump wiring connector.

14 Reconnect the battery negative terminal, and start the engine. Check the fuel pump feed and return hoses unions for signs of leakage.

15 If all is well, refit the plastic access cover. Tilt or refit the rear seat as described in Chapter 11 (as applicable).

10 Fuel gauge sender unit - removal and refitting

On pre-1997 models, refer to Chapter 4A, Section 5, noting that there are no fuel pipe connections to the sender unit. On later models, the sender unit and fuel pump are combined in one assembly; refer to Section 9 of this Chapter.

11 Fuel tank - removal and refitting

Refer to Chapter 4A, Section 6, noting that it will be necessary to depressurise the fuel system as the feed and return hoses are disconnected (see Section 8). It will also be necessary to disconnect the wiring connector from the fuel pump before lowering the tank out of position.

12 Throttle body - removal and refitting

4B

Note: *Refer to the warning note in Section 1 before proceeding.*

Removal

1 Disconnect the battery negative terminal.

2 On 1124 cc and 1360 cc models, remove the air cleaner housing-to-throttle body duct, using the information given in Section 2.

3 On 1580 cc models, relieve any pressure in the cooling system by unscrewing the filler cap. Undo the two nuts securing the intake duct to the throttle body, and position the duct clear of the body along with its rubber sealing ring. Working quickly to minimise coolant loss, disconnect the two coolant hoses from the rear of the throttle body assembly, and plug the hose ends with a suitable bolt or screw **(see illustration)**.

12.3 Throttle body coolant hoses (arrowed) - 1580 cc models

12.4a On 1124 cc and 1360 cc models, disconnect the wiring connectors from the throttle potentiometer . . .

12.4b . . . the idle control stepper motor and the injector wiring loom (arrowed)

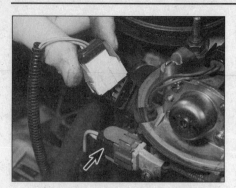

12.4c Disconnecting the throttle potentiometer wiring connector - 1580 cc models (injector wiring connector arrowed)

4 Depress the retaining clips and disconnect the wiring connectors from the throttle potentiometer, the idle control stepper motor (where fitted), and the injector wiring loom connector which is situated on the side of the throttle body **(see illustrations)**.
5 Bearing in mind the information given in Section 8 about depressurising the fuel system, release the retaining clips and disconnect the fuel feed and return hoses from the throttle body assembly. If the original crimped-type Citroën clips are still fitted, cut the clips and discard them; use standard worm-drive hose clips on refitting **(see illustration)**.

12.6b . . . then free the outer cable from its bracket, and recover the flat washer and spring clip (arrowed) - 1360 cc model shown

12.5 Throttle body fuel feed and return hose unions (1360 cc model shown)

6 Disconnect the accelerator inner cable from the throttle cam, then withdraw the outer cable from the mounting bracket, along with its flat washer and spring clip **(see illustrations)**.
7 Disconnect the distributor vacuum hose, idle control auxiliary air valve and/or purge valve hose from the throttle body (as applicable) **(see illustration)**.
8 Slacken and remove the bolts securing the throttle body assembly to the inlet manifold, then remove the assembly along with its gasket and/or insulating spacer **(see illustrations)**.
9 If necessary, with the throttle body removed, undo the retaining screws and separate the upper and lower sections, noting the gasket which is fitted between the two.

Refitting

10 Refitting is a reverse of the removal procedure, bearing in mind the following points:
(a) Where applicable, ensure the mating surfaces of the upper and lower throttle body sections are clean and dry. Fit a new gasket and reassemble the two sections, tightening the retaining screws securely.
(b) Ensure the mating surfaces of the manifold and throttle body are clean and dry, then fit a new gasket. Securely tighten the throttle body retaining bolts.
(c) Ensure all hoses are correctly reconnected and, where necessary, that their retaining clips are securely tightened.

12.6a Disconnect the accelerator inner cable from the throttle cam . . .

(d) On completion, adjust the accelerator cable using the information given in Section 4.
(e) On 1580 cc models, check and, if necessary, top-up the cooling system as described in Chapter 1.

13 Fuel injection system - testing and adjustment

Testing

1 If a fault appears in the fuel injection system, first ensure that all the system wiring connectors are securely connected and free of corrosion. Ensure that the fault is not due to poor maintenance; ie, check that the air cleaner filter element is clean, the spark plugs are in good condition and correctly gapped, the valve clearances are correctly adjusted, the cylinder compression pressures are correct, the ignition timing is correct, and that the engine breather hoses are clear and undamaged, referring to Chapters 1, 2 and 5 for further information.
2 If these checks fail to reveal the cause of the problem, the vehicle should be taken to a suitably-equipped Citroën dealer for testing. A wiring block connector is incorporated in the engine management circuit, into which a special electronic diagnostic tester can be plugged. The connector is located inside either the engine compartment junction box or

12.7 Disconnecting the purge valve hose from the throttle body - 1360 cc model

12.8a Throttle body retaining bolts (arrowed) - 1360 cc model

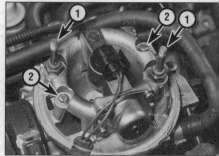

12.8b Throttle body retaining bolts/ studs (1) and upper body retaining screws (2) - 1580 cc model

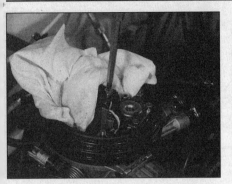

14.3a Undo the injector cap retaining screw, noting the use of a rag to catch any fuel spray . . .

14.3b . . . then lift off the cap and withdraw the injector

14.4 On refitting, ensure that the cap terminals are correctly aligned with the injector pins (arrowed)

the ECU plastic box. The tester will locate the fault quickly and simply, alleviating the need to test all the system components individually, which is a time-consuming operation that also carries a risk of damaging the ECU.

Adjustment

3 Experienced home mechanics with a considerable amount of skill and equipment (including a tachometer and an accurately calibrated exhaust gas analyser) may be able to check the exhaust CO level and the idle speed. However, if these are found to be in need of adjustment, the car *must* be taken to a suitably-equipped Citroën dealer for further testing.

4 On the Bosch Monopoint system, no adjustment is possible. Should the idle speed or exhaust gas CO level be incorrect, then a fault must be present in the fuel injection system.

5 On the Magneti Marelli system, it is possible to adjust the mixture setting (exhaust gas CO level) and ignition timing. However, adjustments can be made only by re-programming the ECU, using special diagnostic equipment connected to the system via the diagnostic connector.

14 Bosch Monopoint system components - removal and refitting

Note: *On later 1360 cc models with the MA3.0 system, the throttle body is effectively a sealed unit, with no components available separately. This means that, if any of the throttle body components (including the idle control stepper motor) become faulty, the complete assembly must be renewed.*

Fuel injector

Note: *Refer to the warning note in Section 1 before proceeding. If a faulty injector is suspected, before condemning the injector, it is worth trying the effect of one of the proprietary injector-cleaning treatments.*

On models with the MA3.0 or MA3.1 system, at the time of writing, neither the fuel injector or its seals are available separately. If the injector is faulty, the complete throttle body assembly must be renewed. Refer to

your Citroën dealer for the latest information. Although the unit can be dismantled for cleaning, if required, it should not be disturbed unless absolutely necessary.

1 Disconnect the battery negative terminal.
2 Remove the air cleaner-to-throttle body duct, using the information given in Section 2.
3 Undo the injector cap retaining screw, then lift off the cap and withdraw the injector from the housing, noting the sealing ring and O-ring. As the cap screw is slackened and the injector is withdrawn, place a clean rag over the injector, to catch any fuel spray which may be released (see illustrations).
4 Refitting is a reversal of the removal procedure, ensuring that the injector sealing ring(s) and injector cap O-ring are in good condition. When refitting the injector cap, ensure that the injector pins are correctly aligned with the cap terminals - the terminals are marked "+" and "-" for identification (see illustration).

Fuel pressure regulator

Note: *Refer to the warning note in Section 1 before proceeding. At the time of writing, the fuel pressure regulator assembly was not available separately from the throttle body assembly. Refer to a Citroën dealer for the latest information. Although the unit can be dismantled for cleaning, if required, it should not be disturbed unless absolutely necessary.*
5 Disconnect the battery negative terminal.
6 Remove the air cleaner-to-throttle

body duct, using the information given in Section 2.
7 Using a marker pen, make alignment marks between the regulator cover and throttle body, then slacken and remove the cover retaining screws (see illustration). As the screws are slackened, place a clean rag over the cover, to catch any fuel spray which may be released.
8 Lift off the cover, then remove the spring and withdraw the diaphragm, noting its correct fitted orientation. Remove all traces of dirt, and examine the diaphragm for signs of splitting. If damage is found, it will probably be necessary to renew the throttle body assembly.
9 Refitting is a reverse of the removal procedure, ensuring that the diaphragm and cover are fitted the correct way round, and that the retaining screws are securely tightened.

Idle control stepper motor

Note: *On models with the MA3.0 or MA3.1 system, at the time of writing, the idle control stepper motor was not available separately. If the motor is faulty, the complete throttle body assembly must be renewed. Refer to your Citroën dealer for the latest information.*
10 Disconnect the battery negative terminal.
11 Depress the retaining clip, and disconnect the wiring connector from the idle control stepper motor.
12 Undo the retaining screws, and remove the motor from the front of the throttle body (see illustration).

14.7 Fuel pressure regulator retaining screws (arrowed)

14.12 Idle control stepper motor retaining screws (arrowed)

4B

14.15 Intake air temperature sensor (arrowed) is an integral part of the injector cap

14.18 Circular plastic cover (where fitted) is retained by three nuts

14.19 Injector cap wiring connector is a push fit in the throttle body

13 Refitting is a reverse of the removal procedure, ensuring that the motor retaining screws are securely tightened.

Throttle potentiometer

14 The throttle potentiometer is a sealed unit, and *under no circumstances* should it be disturbed. For this reason, on some models, it is secured to the throttle body assembly by tamperproof screws. If the throttle potentiometer is faulty, the complete throttle body assembly must be renewed - refer to your Citroën dealer for the latest information.

Intake air temperature sensor

Note: *Refer to the warning note in Section 1 before proceeding. On models with the MA3.0 or MA3.1 system, at the time of writing, the intake air temperature sensor was not available separately. If the sensor is faulty, the complete throttle body assembly must be renewed. Refer to your Citroën dealer for the latest information.*

15 The intake air temperature sensor is an integral part of the throttle body injector cap **(see illustration)**. To remove the cap, first disconnect the battery negative terminal, then remove the air cleaner-to-throttle body duct, using the information given in Section 2.

16 Depress the retaining clip, and disconnect the wiring connector from the front of the throttle body.

17 Place a clean rag over the injector cap, to catch any fuel spray which may be released. Undo the injector cap retaining screw, and lift off the cap along with its O-ring.

18 Where necessary, undo the three retaining nuts and remove the circular plastic cover from the top of the throttle body **(see illustration)**.

19 Release the injector cap connector from the throttle body, and remove the injector cap assembly **(see illustration)**.

20 Refitting is a reversal of the removal procedure, ensuring that the injector cap O-ring is in good condition. Take care to ensure that the cap terminals are correctly aligned with the injector pin, and securely tighten the cap retaining screw.

Coolant temperature sensor

21 Refer to Chapter 3.

Electronic control unit (ECU)

22 The ECU is located inside the plastic box which is situated directly in front of the battery.

23 To remove the ECU, first disconnect the battery.

24 Unclip the lid from the box, and slide out the ECU and mounting plate. Disconnect the wiring connector(s) from the ECU, slacken and remove the bolts securing it to the mounting plate, and remove it from the vehicle **(see illustrations)**.

25 Refitting is a reverse of the removal procedure, ensuring that the wiring connectors are securely reconnected.

Fuel injection system relay unit

26 The relay unit is inside the plastic box which is situated directly in front of the battery.

27 To remove the relay unit, first disconnect the battery.

28 Unclip the lid from the box, then unclip the relay unit from the mounting plate, disconnect the wiring connector and remove it from the vehicle **(see illustration)**.

29 Refitting is the reverse of removal, ensuring that the relay unit is securely held in position by its retaining clip.

Injector resistor

30 The injector resistor is inside the plastic box which is situated directly in front of the battery.

31 To remove the resistor, first disconnect the battery.

32 Unclip the lid from the box, then slide out the mounting plate and undo the resistor retaining bolt. Disconnect the wiring connector, and remove the resistor from the vehicle **(see illustration)**.

33 Refitting is a reversal of the removal procedure.

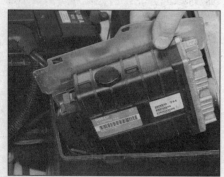

14.24a Slide out the mounting plate . . .

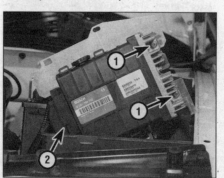

14.24b . . . then undo the retaining bolts (1), disconnect the wiring connector (2), and remove the ECU

14.28 Removing the fuel injection system relay unit

14.32 Injector resistor is mounted on the rear of the ECU mounting plate

15.3 Disconnecting the injector wiring connector. Injector retaining clip screw (arrowed)

15.7 Fuel pressure regulator is retained by four screws (arrowed)

4B

Crankshaft sensor (MA3.0 and MA3.1 system)

34 The crankshaft sensor is situated on the front face of the transmission (clutch) housing.
35 To remove the sensor, first disconnect the battery negative terminal.
36 Trace the wiring back from the sensor to the wiring connector, and disconnect it from the main harness.
37 Prise out the rubber grommet, then undo the retaining bolt and withdraw the sensor from the transmission.
38 Refitting is a reverse of the removal procedure. Ensure that the sensor retaining bolt is securely tightened, and that the grommet is correctly seated in the transmission housing.

Vehicle speed sensor (MA3.0 and MA3.1system)

39 The vehicle speed sensor is an integral part of the speedometer drive housing. Refer to Chapter 7A, Section 6 for removal and refitting details.

15 Magneti Marelli system components - removal and refitting

Fuel injector

Note: *Refer to the warning note at the start of this Section before proceeding. If a faulty injector is suspected, before condemning the injector, it is worth trying the effect of one of the proprietary injector-cleaning treatments. If this fails, the vehicle should be taken to a Citroën dealer for testing using the appropriate specialist equipment. At the time of writing, it appears that the fuel injector is not available separately and, if faulty, the complete upper throttle body assembly must be renewed. Refer to a Citroën dealer for the latest information.*

1 Disconnect the battery negative terminal.
2 Slacken and remove the two nuts and washers securing the intake duct to the throttle body, and move the duct out of the

way. Remove the rubber sealing ring from the top of the throttle body.
3 Release the retaining tangs, and disconnect the injector wiring connector (see illustration).
4 Undo the retaining screw, then remove the retaining clip and lift the injector out of the housing, noting its sealing ring. As the screw is slackened, place a clean rag over the injector, to catch any fuel spray which may be released.
5 Refitting is a reverse of the removal procedure, ensuring that the injector sealing ring is in good condition.

Fuel pressure regulator

Note: *Refer to the warning note in Section 1 before proceeding. At the time of writing, the fuel pressure regulator assembly was not available separately from the throttle body assembly. Refer to a Citroën dealer for the latest information. Although the unit can be dismantled for cleaning, if required, it should not be disturbed unless absolutely necessary.*

6 Slacken and remove the two nuts and washers securing the intake duct to the throttle body, and move the duct out of the way, along with its rubber sealing ring. Disconnect the battery negative terminal.
7 Using a marker pen, make alignment marks between the regulator cover and throttle body, then undo the four retaining screws (see illustration). As the screws are slackened, place a clean rag over the cover, to catch any fuel spray which may be released.
8 Lift off the cover, then remove the spring and withdraw the diaphragm, noting its correct fitted orientation. Remove all traces of dirt, and examine the diaphragm for signs of splitting. If damage is found, it will apparently be necessary to renew the complete upper throttle body assembly, as described earlier in this Section.
9 Refitting is a reverse of the removal procedure, ensuring that the diaphragm and cover are fitted the correct way around, and that the retaining screws are securely tightened.

15.15 Disconnecting the stepper motor wiring connector

Idle control auxiliary air valve - G5.S2 system

10 The idle control auxiliary air valve is situated directly behind the throttle body, mounted onto the cylinder head.
11 To remove the valve, first disconnect the battery.
12 Slacken the retaining clips, and disconnect the two hoses from the side of the valve. Mark the hoses to ensure they are correctly reconnected on refitting.
13 Disconnect the wiring connector, then undo the two retaining nuts and remove the auxiliary air valve from the engine compartment.
14 Refitting is a reverse of the removal procedure.

Idle control stepper motor - G6.12 and G6.10 systems

Note: *At the time of writing, it appears that the stepper motor is not available separately and, if faulty, the complete lower throttle body assembly must be renewed as described earlier in this Section. Refer to your Citroën dealer for the latest information.*

15 To remove the stepper motor, depress the retaining tabs and disconnect the wiring connector (see illustration). Undo the two retaining screws, and withdraw the motor from the rear of the throttle body assembly.
16 Refitting is a reverse of removal.

15.18 Throttle potentiometer is secured to the throttle body by two screws (arrowed)

15.20 The fuel/air mixture temperature sensor (arrowed) is screwed into the right-hand side of the inlet manifold

15.26a Undo the three retaining bolts . . .

Throttle potentiometer

17 Disconnect the battery negative terminal, then depress the retaining tabs and disconnect the wiring connector from the throttle potentiometer.

18 Undo the two retaining screws, and remove the throttle potentiometer from the right-hand side of the throttle body assembly (see illustration).

19 Refitting is a reversal of the removal procedure, ensuring that the throttle potentiometer tang is correctly engaged with the throttle spindle.

Fuel/air mixture temperature sensor

20 The fuel/air mixture temperature sensor is screwed into the right-hand side of the inlet manifold, and is removed as follows (see illustration).

21 To remove the sensor, first disconnect the battery negative terminal.

22 Disconnect the wiring connector, then unscrew the fuel/air mixture temperature sensor from the inlet manifold.

23 Refitting is a reverse of the removal procedure, ensuring that the switch is securely tightened.

Manifold absolute pressure (MAP) sensor

24 The MAP sensor is mounted on a bracket

situated on the right-hand side of the engine compartment, next to the alternator.

25 To remove the sensor, first disconnect the battery negative terminal.

26 Slacken and remove the three retaining nuts and bolts, then free the MAP sensor from the bracket. Disconnect the wiring connector and vacuum hose, and remove the sensor from the engine compartment (see illustrations).

27 Refitting is a reverse of the removal procedure.

Coolant temperature sensor

28 Refer to Chapter 3, Section 6.

Crankshaft sensor

29 The crankshaft sensor is fitted to the top of the transmission housing, beside the left-hand end of the cylinder block.

30 To remove the sensor, first disconnect the battery negative terminal.

31 Trace the wiring back from the sensor to its wiring connector, then depress the retaining tabs and disconnect it from the main wiring harness. Release the wiring connector from any relevant retaining clips (see illustration).

32 To gain access to the sensor, it is necessary to remove the metal plate from the top of the transmission housing. The plate is retained by one of the engine-to-transmission

bolts, and by a second bolt securing the plate to the top of the transmission.

33 With the plate removed, undo the bolt securing the sensor to the transmission housing, and remove the sensor from the vehicle.

34 Refitting is a reverse of removal, ensuring that the sensor retaining bolt is securely tightened.

Electronic control unit (ECU)

35 Refer to paragraphs 22 to 25 of Section 14.

Fuel injection system relay unit

36 Refer to paragraphs 26 to 29 of Section 14.

16 Inlet manifold - removal and refitting

Removal

1124 cc and 1360 cc models

1 Remove the throttle body as described in Section 12.

2 Drain the cooling system as described in Chapter 1.

3 Slacken the retaining clip, and disconnect the coolant hose(s) from the manifold.

4 Slacken the retaining clip, and disconnect the vacuum servo unit hose from the left-hand side of the manifold.

5 Make a final check that all the necessary vacuum/breather hoses have been disconnected from the manifold.

6 Unscrew the six retaining nuts, then manoeuvre the manifold away from the head and out of the engine compartment. Note that there is no manifold gasket.

1580 cc models

7 Remove the throttle body as described in Section 12.

8 Drain the cooling system as described in Chapter 1.

9 Disconnect the wiring connector from the fuel/air mixture temperature sensor, which is situated on the right-hand side of the manifold.

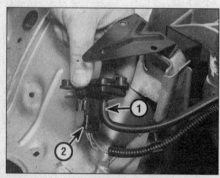

15.26b . . . then release the MAP sensor from its mounting bracket, and disconnect the vacuum hose (1) and wiring connector (2)

15.31 The crankshaft sensor wiring connector (arrowed) is situated on top of the transmission housing

16.10 Oil filler/breather retaining nut (arrowed) - 1580 cc models

16.12 Inlet manifold coolant hose and MAP sensor hose (arrowed) - 1580 cc models

10 Undo the nut securing the oil filler/breather to the side of the manifold, then release the assembly from its retaining stud, and position it clear of the manifold (see illustration).
11 Undo the bolt securing the wiring/hose support bracket to the top of the manifold, and position the bracket clear of the manifold.
12 Disconnect the coolant hose and the MAP sensor vacuum hose from the front of the manifold (see illustration).
13 Undo and remove the six manifold retaining nuts and washers, and remove the manifold from the engine. Remove the gasket and discard it - a new one should be used on refitting.

Refitting
1124 cc and 1360 cc models
14 Refitting is the reverse of the removal procedure, noting the following points:
(a) Ensure that the manifold and cylinder head mating surfaces are clean and dry, and apply a thin coating of suitable sealing compound to the manifold mating surface. Refit the manifold, and tighten its retaining nuts to the specified torque.
(b) Ensure that all relevant hoses are reconnected to their original positions, and are securely held (where necessary) by their retaining clips.
(c) Refit the throttle body as described in Section 12.
(d) On completion, refill the cooling system as described in Chapter 1.

1580 cc models
15 Refitting is a reverse of the removal procedure, noting the following points:
(a) Ensure that the manifold and cylinder head mating surfaces are clean and dry, and fit a new manifold gasket. Refit the manifold, and tighten its retaining nuts to the specified torque.
(b) Ensure that all relevant hoses are reconnected to their original positions, and are securely held (where necessary) by the retaining clips.
(c) Refit the throttle body as described in Section 12.

(d) On completion, refill the cooling system as described in Chapter 1.

17 Exhaust manifold - removal and refitting

Removal
1124 cc and 1360 cc models
1 Refer to Chapter 4A, Section 16, noting that the lambda (oxygen) sensor wiring connectors should be disconnected. Alternatively, care must be taken to support the front pipe, to avoid any strain being placed on the sensor wiring.

1580 cc models
2 Remove the air cleaner housing and mounting bracket, as described in Section 2.
3 Slacken the clip securing the hot-air intake hose to the bottom of the air temperature control valve, then disconnect the hose from the manifold shroud and remove it from the engine compartment.
4 Undo the remaining manifold shroud retaining bolts, and remove the shroud.
5 Firmly apply the handbrake, then jack up the front of the vehicle and support it on axle stands.
6 Slacken and remove the two nuts securing the front pipe flange joint to the manifold, and recover the springs. Remove the bolts, then free the front pipe from the manifold, and recover the wire-mesh sealing ring. Either support the front pipe to avoid placing any strain on the lambda sensor wiring (where fitted), or disconnect the wiring connectors.
7 Undo the eight retaining nuts securing the manifold to the head. Manoeuvre the manifold out of the engine compartment, and discard the manifold gaskets.

Refitting (all models)
8 Refitting is the reverse of the removal procedure, noting the following points:
(a) Examine all the exhaust manifold studs for signs of damage and corrosion; remove all traces of corrosion, and repair or renew any damaged studs.

(b) Ensure that the manifold and cylinder head sealing faces are clean and flat, and fit the new manifold gaskets. Tighten the manifold retaining nuts to the specified torque.
(c) Reconnect the front pipe to the manifold using the information given in Section 18.
(d) On 1580 cc models, refit the disturbed air cleaner components as described in Section 2.

18 Exhaust system - general information, removal and refitting

General information
1 On 1124 cc and 1360 cc models, the exhaust system consists of four sections; the front pipe, the catalytic converter, the intermediate pipe, and the tailpipe and main silencer box. All exhaust sections are joined by a flanged joint. The front pipe joints are secured by nuts and bolts, the catalytic converter joint being of the spring-loaded ball type, to allow for movement in the exhaust system. The catalytic converter-to-intermediate pipe joint and the intermediate pipe-to-silencer joint are secured by a clamping ring.
2 On 1580 cc models without a catalytic converter, the exhaust system consists of two sections; the front pipe and intermediate silencer box, and the tailpipe and main silencer box. On 1580 cc models with a catalytic converter, the system consists of three sections; the front pipe and catalytic converter, the intermediate pipe and silencer box, and the tailpipe and main silencer box. The front pipe-to-manifold joint is of the spring-loaded ball type, to allow for movement in the exhaust system, the other joint(s) being secured by a clamping ring.
3 The system is suspended throughout its entire length by rubber mountings.

Removal
4 Each exhaust section can be removed individually, or alternatively, the complete system can be removed as a unit. Even if only one part of the system needs attention, it is often easier to remove the whole system and separate the sections on the bench.
5 To remove the system or part of the system, first jack up the front or rear of the car, and support it on axle stands. Alternatively, position the car over an inspection pit, or on car ramps.
Front pipe - 1124 cc and 1360 cc models
6 Trace the wiring back from the lambda (oxygen) sensor to its wiring connectors, and disconnect it from the main wiring harness.
7 Undo the nuts securing the front pipe flange joint to the manifold, and the single bolt

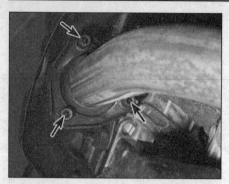

18.7a Front pipe-to-manifold retaining nuts (arrowed) . . .

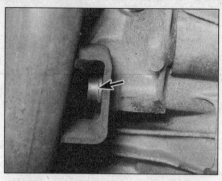

18.7b . . . and front pipe mounting bolt (arrowed) - 1124 cc and 1360 cc models (viewed from underneath)

18.8 Front pipe-to-catalytic converter joint - 1124 cc and 1360 cc models

18.10 Typical exhaust system clamping ring

securing the front pipe to its mounting bracket (see illustrations). Separate the flange joint, and collect the gasket.

8 Slacken and remove the two nuts securing the front pipe to the catalytic converter, and recover the spring cups and springs (see illustration). Remove the bolts, then withdraw the front pipe from underneath the vehicle, taking care not to damage the lambda sensor, and recover the wire-mesh gasket from the joint.

Front pipe assembly - 1580 cc models without a catalytic converter

9 Slacken and remove the two nuts securing the front pipe to the manifold, and recover the spring cups and springs. Remove the bolts, then release the front pipe from the manifold, and recover the wire-mesh gasket from the joint.

10 Slacken the front pipe-to-tailpipe clamping ring bolts, and disengage the clamp from the flange joint (see illustration).

11 Free the front pipe assembly from its mounting rubbers, and withdraw it from underneath the vehicle.

Front pipe assembly - 1580 cc models with a catalytic converter

12 Trace the wiring back from the lambda (oxygen) sensor to its wiring connectors, and disconnect it from the main wiring harness.

13 Disconnect the front pipe from the manifold and intermediate pipe as described

above in paragraphs 9 and 10, then remove the front pipe assembly from underneath the vehicle. Be careful not to drop it - the catalytic converter is fragile.

Catalytic converter - 1124 cc and 1360 cc models

14 Undo the two nuts securing the front pipe flange joint to the catalytic converter. Recover the springs and spring cups, and withdraw the bolts.

15 Slacken the catalytic converter-to-intermediate pipe clamping ring bolts, and disengage the clamp from the flange joint.

16 Free the catalytic converter from the intermediate pipe, then withdraw it from underneath the vehicle. Be careful not to drop it - it is fragile. Recover the wire-mesh gasket from the front pipe joint.

Intermediate pipe - 1124 cc and 1360 cc models

17 Slacken the clamping ring bolts, and disengage the clamps from both the intermediate pipe flange joints.

18 Free the intermediate pipe from its mounting rubbers, then disengage it first from the tailpipe and then from the catalytic converter. Remove the intermediate pipe from underneath the vehicle.

Intermediate pipe - 1580 cc models with a catalytic converter

19 Slacken the clamping ring bolts, and

disengage the clamps from both the intermediate pipe flange joints.

20 Free the intermediate pipe from its mounting rubbers, then disengage it first from the tailpipe and then from the front pipe. Remove the intermediate pipe from underneath the vehicle.

Tailpipe - all models

21 Slacken the intermediate pipe-to-tailpipe clamping ring bolts, and disengage the clamp from the flange joint.

22 Unhook the tailpipe from its mounting rubbers, and remove it from the vehicle.

Complete system - all models

23 Using the information given under the relevant sub-heading above, unbolt the front pipe from the manifold, removing the bolt securing the front pipe to its mounting bracket and/or disconnecting the lambda sensor wiring (as applicable). Free the system from all its mounting rubbers, and withdraw it from under the vehicle.

Heat shield(s) - all models

24 The heat shields are secured to the underside of the body by various nuts and bolts. Each shield can be removed once the appropriate exhaust section has been removed. If the shield is being removed to gain access to a component located behind it, it may prove sufficient in some cases to remove the retaining nuts and bolts, and simply lower the shield, without disturbing the exhaust system.

Refitting

25 Each section is refitted by reversing the removal procedure, noting the following points:

(a) *Ensure that all traces of corrosion have been removed from the flanges, and renew all necessary gaskets.*

(b) *Inspect the rubber mountings for signs of damage or deterioration, and renew as necessary.*

(c) *Prior to assembling a spring-loaded ball type joint, a smear of high-temperature grease should be applied to the joint mating surfaces. Citroën recommend the use of Gripcott AF G2 grease (available from your Citroën dealer).*

(d) *On joints which are secured by clamping rings, apply a smear of exhaust system jointing paste to the joint mating surfaces, to ensure an gas-tight seal. Tighten the clamping ring nuts evenly and progressively to the specified torque, so that the clearance between the clamp halves is equal on either side.*

(e) *Before tightening the exhaust system fasteners, ensure that all rubber mountings are correctly located, and that there is adequate clearance between the exhaust system and vehicle underbody.*

Chapter 4 Part C: Fuel and exhaust systems – multi-point fuel injection models

Contents

ACAV intake system (1998 cc 16-valve models) -
  general information, removal and refitting 20
Accelerator cable - removal, refitting and adjustment 3
Accelerator pedal - removal and refitting 4
Air cleaner assembly and intake ducts - removal and refitting 2
Air cleaner filter element renewal . . . . See Chapter 1
Bosch Motronic M1.3 system components - removal and refitting . . . 17
Bosch Motronic MP3.1 system components - removal and refitting . . 16
Bosch Motronic MP3.2 system components - removal and refitting . . 18
Bosch Motronic MP5.1 and MP5.2 system components -
  removal and refitting 15
Exhaust manifold - removal and refitting 21
Exhaust system - general information, removal and refitting 22
Fuel filter - renewal . . . . See Chapter 1
Fuel gauge sender unit - removal and refitting 9

Fuel injection system - depressurisation 7
Fuel injection system - testing and adjustment 11
Fuel injection systems - general information 6
Fuel pump - removal and refitting 8
Fuel tank - removal and refitting 10
General fuel system checks . . . . See Chapter 1
General information and precautions 1
Idle speed and mixture adjustment . . . . See Chapter 1
Inlet manifold - removal and refitting 19
Magneti Marelli 1AP system components - removal and refitting . . . 13
Magneti Marelli 8P and Sagem/Lucas 4GJ system components -
  removal and refitting 14
Throttle housing - removal and refitting 12
Unleaded petrol - general information and usage 5

Degrees of difficulty

Easy, suitable for novice with little experience	**Fairly easy,** suitable for beginner with some experience	**Fairly difficult,** suitable for competent DIY mechanic 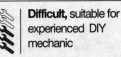	**Difficult,** suitable for experienced DIY mechanic	**Very difficult,** suitable for expert DIY or professional

Specifications

System type

1360 cc (KFX engine) models	Magneti Marelli 1AP.40
1580 cc (BFZ engine) models	Magneti Marelli 8P or Sagem/Lucas 4GJ
1761 cc 8-valve (LFZ engine) models	Magneti Marelli 8P
1761 cc 8-valve (L6A engine) models	Bosch Motronic MP5.1
1761 cc 16-valve (LFY engine) models	Bosch Motronic MP5.2
1905 cc (D6E engine) models	Bosch Motronic MP3.1
1905 cc (DKZ engine) models	Bosch Motronic M1.3
1998 cc 8-valve (RFX engine) models	Magneti Marelli 8P
1998 cc 16-valve (RFY and RFT engine) models	Bosch Motronic MP3.2

Fuel system data

Fuel pump type	Electric, immersed in tank
Fuel pump regulated constant pressure (at specified idle speed):	
Bosch Motronic and Sagem/Lucas systems	2.5 to 3.0 bars (depending on system)
Magneti Marelli systems	2.0 bars

Recommended fuel

95 RON unleaded (UK unleaded premium)

Torque wrench settings

	Nm	lbf ft
Inlet manifold nuts/bolts:		
1360 cc models	10	7
All other models	22	16
Exhaust manifold nuts	22	16
Exhaust system fasteners:		
Front pipe-to-manifold nuts	10	7
Clamping ring nut(s):		
Clamps secured with one bolt	25	18
Clamps secured with two bolts	20	15

1 General information and precautions

The fuel supply system consists of a fuel tank (which is mounted under the rear of the car, with an electric fuel pump immersed in it), a fuel filter, fuel feed and return lines. The fuel pump supplies fuel to the fuel rail, which acts as a reservoir for the four fuel injectors which inject fuel into the inlet tracts. The fuel filter incorporated in the feed line from the pump to the fuel rail ensures that the fuel supplied to the injectors is clean.

Refer to Section 6 for further information on the operation of each fuel injection system, and to Section 21 for information on the exhaust system. Throughout this Section, it is also occasionally necessary to identify vehicles by their engine codes rather than by engine capacity alone. Refer to the relevant Part of Chapter 2 for further information on engine code identification.

⚠️ **Warning: Many of the procedures in this Chapter require the removal of fuel lines and connections, which may result in some fuel spillage. Before carrying out any operation on the fuel system, refer to the precautions given in "Safety first!" at the beginning of this manual, and follow them implicitly.**

Petrol is a highly-dangerous and volatile liquid, and the precautions necessary when handling it cannot be overstressed.
Note: *Residual pressure will remain in the fuel lines long after the vehicle was last used. When disconnecting any fuel line, first depressurise the fuel system as described in Section 7.*

2 Air cleaner assembly and intake ducts - removal and refitting

Removal

1360 cc models

1 Slacken the retaining clips (where fitted) and disconnect the vacuum and breather hoses from the top of the air cleaner housing. Where crimped-type hose clips or ties are fitted, cut and discard them; replace them with standard worm-drive hose clips or new cable-ties when refitting.

2 Slacken the retaining clips or ties, and free the throttle housing duct from the top of the air cleaner housing. Also remove the inlet duct from the side of the housing. If necessary, free the duct from the throttle housing and remove it, along with its sealing ring.

3 Lift the air cleaner housing assembly out of the engine compartment.

4 To remove the inlet duct assembly, drill out the rivets securing the duct to the crossmember, then release the fastener

securing the rear of the duct to the cylinder head, and remove the duct and hose assembly from the engine compartment.

1580 cc, 1761 cc and 1998 cc 8-valve models

5 Slacken the retaining clip, and disconnect the breather hose(s) from the side of the air cleaner-to-throttle housing duct. Slacken the duct retaining clips, then disconnect it from the air cleaner and throttle housing, and remove it from the vehicle **(see illustrations)**. Where necessary, recover the rubber sealing ring from the throttle housing.

6 Release the two retaining clips, then slacken and remove the two retaining screws from the front of the cylinder head cover, and remove the air cleaner element cover from the head. Withdraw the air cleaner element.

7 To remove the intake duct, undo the bolt securing the rear section of the duct to the end of the cylinder head, then slacken the retaining clip and disconnect the duct from the cylinder head cover. Undo the nut securing the front of the duct to the left-hand wing valance, and manoeuvre the duct out of the engine compartment **(see illustration)**.

1761 cc 16-valve models

8 Slacken the retaining clips and disconnect the inlet duct from the throttle housing and air cleaner housing lid.

9 Undo the screws securing the lid to the air cleaner housing body. Lift off the lid and take out the filter element.

10 Lift the housing body upward to disengage it from the lower locating lugs. On some models, as the housing is lifted up, it will be necessary to disengage a small plastic retaining tag at the front securing the housing to the cold air inlet duct underneath.

11 To remove the cold air inlet duct, undo the air cleaner housing mounting bracket bolts and withdraw the bracket. Release the cold air inlet from the bracket as it is removed.

12 Release the other end of the cold air inlet from its body attachments and manipulate the duct from the car.

1905 cc models

13 Slacken the retaining clips, and disconnect the intake duct and throttle housing duct from the air cleaner **(see illustration)**.

2.5a On 1761 cc and 1998 cc 8-valve models, slacken the clips and disconnect the hose(s) from the air cleaner-to-throttle body duct . . .

2.5b . . . then slacken the duct retaining clips . . .

2.5c . . . and remove the duct from the engine compartment

2.7 Intake duct front retaining nut

2.13 On 1905 cc models, slacken the retaining clips and disconnect the intake and throttle housing ducts from the air cleaner . . .

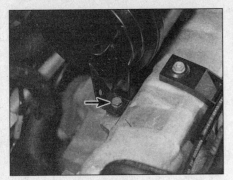

2.14a ... then undo the retaining bolt (arrowed) ...

2.14b ... and the two retaining nuts (locations arrowed), then remove the air cleaner housing

14 Slacken and remove the bolt securing the air cleaner right-hand mounting bracket to the rear of the cylinder head, and the two nuts securing the housing to its left-hand mounting bracket. Lift the air cleaner housing out of the engine compartment **(see illustrations)**.

15 To remove the intake duct, undo the nut(s) securing the front of the duct to the left-hand wing valance, then undo the nut securing the duct to its mounting bracket (where fitted). Disconnect the duct from the air cleaner housing, if not already having done so, and remove it from the vehicle.

16 On models without a catalytic converter (Bosch Motronic MP3.1 system), to remove the air cleaner-to-throttle housing duct, first disconnect the wiring connector from the intake air temperature sensor. Slacken the retaining clip, and disconnect the vacuum pipe from the front of the duct. Slacken the clips, disconnect the duct from the air cleaner and throttle housings, and remove the duct. Recover the rubber sealing ring from the throttle housing.

17 On models with a catalytic converter (Bosch Motronic M1.3 system), the air cleaner-to-throttle housing duct is in two sections, with the airflow meter situated in the middle. Each section can be removed once its retaining clips have been slackened, noting that, in the case of the front duct section, it will also be necessary to disconnect the vacuum pipe.

1998 cc 16-valve models

18 Slacken the retaining clip, and disconnect the air cleaner-to-throttle housing duct from the throttle housing. Recover the rubber sealing ring. Release the retaining clips, and disconnect the breather hose(s) from the duct.

19 Apply the handbrake, then jack up the front of the vehicle and support it on axle stands.

20 From underneath the vehicle, slacken and remove the retaining nuts securing the resonator chamber to the side of the air cleaner housing, and remove the chamber.

21 Undo the air cleaner housing retaining bolt(s), and remove the housing and duct assembly from underneath the vehicle.

Refitting

22 Refitting is a reversal of the removal procedure, ensuring that all hoses are properly reconnected, and that all ducts are correctly seated and securely held by their retaining clips.

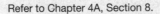

3 Accelerator cable - removal, refitting and adjustment

1 Refer to Chapter 4A, Section 7, substituting "throttle housing" for all references to the carburettor. On models with automatic transmission, once the accelerator cable is correctly adjusted, check the kickdown cable adjustment as described in Chapter 7B.

4 Accelerator pedal - removal and refitting

Refer to Chapter 4A, Section 8.

5 Unleaded petrol - general information and usage

Note: *The information given in this Chapter is correct at the time of writing. If updated information is thought to be required, check with a Citroën dealer. If travelling abroad, consult one of the motoring organisations (or a similar authority) for advice on the fuel available.*

1 The fuel recommended by Citroën is given in the Specifications Section of this Chapter, followed by the equivalent petrol currently on sale in the UK.

2 All Citroën ZX multi-point injection models are designed to run on unleaded fuel with a minimum octane rating of 95 (RON).

3 Super unleaded petrol (98 octane) can also be used in all models if wished, though there is no advantage in doing so.

6 Fuel injection systems - general information

Note: *The fuel injection ECU is of the "self-learning" type, meaning that as it operates, it also monitors and stores the settings which give optimum engine performance under all operating conditions. When the battery is disconnected, these settings are lost and the ECU reverts to the base settings programmed into its memory at the factory. On restarting, this may lead to the engine running/idling roughly for a short while, until the ECU has re-learned the optimum settings. This process is best accomplished by taking the vehicle on a road test (for approximately 15 minutes), covering all engine speeds and loads, concentrating mainly in the 2500 to 3500 rpm region.*

Magneti Marelli 1AP system

1 The Magneti Marelli 1AP engine management (fuel injection/ignition) system is fitted to 1360 cc (KFX engine) models from mid 1996 onward. The system incorporates a closed-loop catalytic converter and an evaporative emission control system, and complies with the very latest emission control standards. Refer to Chapter 5 for information on the ignition side of the system; the fuel side of the system operates as follows.

2 The fuel pump supplies fuel from the tank to the fuel rail, via a replaceable cartridge filter mounted underneath the rear of the vehicle. The pump itself is mounted inside the fuel tank, the pump motor is permanently immersed in fuel, to keep it cool. The fuel rail is mounted directly above the fuel injectors and acts as a fuel reservoir.

3 Fuel rail supply pressure is controlled by the pressure regulator, mounted at the end of the fuel rail. The regulator contains a spring-loaded valve, which lifts to allow excess fuel to return to the tank when the optimum operating pressure of the fuel system is exceeded (eg during low speed, light load cruising). The regulator also contains a diaphragm which is supplied with vacuum from the inlet manifold. This allows the regulator to reduce the fuel supply pressure during light load, high manifold depression conditions (eg during idling or deceleration) to prevent excess fuel being "sucked" through the open injectors. Note that on later models, a fuel pressure regulator is not fitted; a fuel pressure monitoring point is provided at the left hand end of the fuel rails

4 The fuel injectors are electromagnetic pintle valves, which spray atomised fuel into the combustion chambers under the control of the engine management system ECU. There are four injectors, one per cylinder, mounted in the inlet manifold close to the cylinder head. Each injector is mounted at an angle that allows it to spray fuel directly onto the back of the inlet valve(s).

5 The ECU controls the volume of fuel injected by varying the length of time for which each injector is held open.

6 The fuel injection system is of the semi-sequential type, whereby fuel is injected into each cylinder's inlet tract twice per engine cycle; once during the power stroke and once during the induction stroke.

7 The electrical control system consists of the ECU, along with the following sensors:

(a) *Throttle potentiometer - informs the ECU of the throttle valve position, and the rate of throttle opening/closing.*

(b) *Coolant temperature sensor - informs the ECU of engine temperature.*

(c) *Intake air temperature sensor - informs the ECU of the temperature of the air passing through the throttle housing.*

(d) *Lambda sensor - informs the ECU of the oxygen content of the exhaust gases (explained in greater detail in Part D of this Chapter).*

(e) *Manifold Absolute Pressure (MAP) sensor - informs the ECU of the load on the engine (expressed in terms of inlet manifold vacuum).*

(f) *Crankshaft sensor - informs the ECU of engine speed and crankshaft angular position.*

(g) *Vehicle speed sensor - informs the ECU of the vehicle speed.*

(h) *Knock sensor - informs the ECU of pre-ignition (detonation) within the cylinders.*

8 Signals from each of the sensors are compared by the ECU and, based on this information, the ECU selects the response appropriate to those values, and controls the fuel injectors (varying the pulse width - the length of time the injectors are held open - to provide a richer or weaker air/fuel mixture, as appropriate). The air/fuel mixture is constantly varied by the ECU, to provide the best settings for cranking, starting (with either a hot or cold engine) and engine warm-up, idle, cruising and acceleration.

9 The ECU also has full control over the engine idle speed, via a stepper motor fitted to the throttle body. The stepper motor pushrod controls the amount of air passing through a by-pass drilling at the side of the throttle. When the throttle valve is closed (accelerator pedal released), the ECU uses the motor to alter the position of the pushrod, controlling the amount of air bypassing the throttle valve and so controlling the idle speed. The ECU also carries out "fine tuning" of the idle speed by varying the ignition timing to increase or reduce the torque of the engine as it is idling. This helps to stabilise the idle speed when electrical or mechanical loads (such as headlights, air conditioning, etc) are switched on and off.

10 On certain models, the throttle housing is fitted with an electric heating element. The heater is supplied with current by the ECU, warming the throttle body on cold starts to help prevent icing of the throttle valve.

11 The exhaust and evaporative loss emission control systems are described in more detail in Chapter 4 Part D.

12 If there is any abnormality in any of the readings obtained from either the coolant temperature sensor, the intake air temperature sensor or the lambda sensor, the ECU enters its "back-up" mode. If this happens, the erroneous sensor signal is overridden, and the ECU assumes a pre-programmed "back-up" value, which will allow the engine to continue running, albeit at reduced efficiency. If the ECU enters this mode, the warning lamp on the instrument panel will be illuminated, and the relevant fault code will be stored in the ECU memory.

13 If the warning light illuminates, the vehicle should be taken to a Peugeot dealer at the earliest opportunity. Once there, a complete test of the engine management system can be carried out, using a special electronic diagnostic test unit, which is plugged into the system's diagnostic connector.

Magneti Marelli 8P and Sagem/Lucas 4GJ systems

14 The Magneti Marelli 8P or Sagem/Lucas 4GJ engine management (fuel injection/ignition) systems are fitted to 1580 cc (BFZ engine) models, 1761 cc, 8-valve (LFZ engine) models and 1998 cc (RFX engine) models. Both systems are very similar in operation to the Magneti Marelli 1AP system described previously but in addition, the throttle housing may be fitted with an electric heating element. The heater is supplied with current by the ECU, warming the throttle body on cold starts to help prevent icing of the throttle valve.

Bosch Motronic MP5.1 and MP 5.2 systems

15 1761 cc, 8-valve (L6A engine) models and 1761 cc, 16-valve (LFY engine) models are equipped with the Bosch Motronic engine management (fuel injection/ignition) system. Both systems are very similar in operation to the Magneti Marelli 1AP system described previously, but with the following differences.

16 The Bosch Motronic systems employ "banked" fuel injection, where all four injectors are activated simultaneously. Fuel is injected into each cylinder's inlet tract on every engine stroke and is then drawn into the combustion chamber during the induction stroke.

17 On the MP5.1 system, ECU control of the engine idle speed is by means of an auxiliary air valve which bypasses the throttle valve. When the throttle valve is closed, the ECU controls the opening of the air valve, which in turn regulates the amount of air entering the manifold, and so controls the idle speed.

18 On both Motronic systems the throttle housing is fitted with an electric heating element. The heater is supplied with current by the ECU, warming the throttle body on cold starts to help prevent icing of the throttle valve.

19 The MP5.1 system is not fitted with a knock sensor.

Bosch Motronic MP3.1 system

20 The Bosch Motronic MP3.1 engine management (fuel injection/ignition) system is fitted to all 1905 cc models without a catalytic converter (D6E engine). Refer to Chapter 5 for information on the ignition side of the system.

21 The MP3.1 system is very similar in operation to the systems described above, noting the following differences:

(a) *On the MP3.1 system, there is no lambda (oxygen) sensor or vehicle speed sensor. The idle mixture (exhaust gas CO content) can be manually adjusted via the mixture adjustment potentiometer.*

(b) *The ECU has no control over the engine idle speed; the idle speed is manually set using a screw on the throttle housing. An auxiliary air valve (not to be confused with the idle speed control valve on the MP5.1 system) is incorporated in the system, but this is used purely as an additional air supply on cold starts and during the warm-up period.*

(c) *There is no heating element fitted to the throttle housing. The engine coolant is circulated around the housing, to warm the housing after cold starts.*

(d) *There is no evaporative emission control system.*

Bosch Motronic M1.3 system

22 The Bosch Motronic M1.3 engine management (fuel injection/ignition) system is fitted to all 1905 cc models with a catalytic converter (DKZ engine). Refer to Chapter 5 for information on the ignition side of the system.

23 The M1.3 system is very similar in operation to the systems described above, noting the following differences:

(a) *On the M1.3 system, there is no vehicle speed sensor or MAP sensor. In place of the MAP sensor, an airflow meter is fitted to the throttle housing intake duct, to inform the ECU of the volume of air passing through the duct and entering the throttle housing.*

(b) *The ECU has no control over the engine idle speed; the idle speed is manually set using a screw on the throttle housing. An auxiliary air valve (not to be confused with the idle speed control valve on the MP5.1 system) is incorporated in the system, but this is used purely as an additional air supply on cold starts and during the warm-up period.*

(c) *There is no heating element fitted to the throttle housing. The engine coolant is circulated around the housing, to warm the housing after cold starts.*

Bosch Motronic MP3.2 system

24 The Bosch Motronic MP3.2 engine management (fuel injection/ignition) system is fitted to all 1998 cc 16-valve models. Refer to Chapter 5 for information on the ignition side of the system.

25 The MP3.2 system is very similar in operation to the systems described above, noting that, in addition to the sensors listed, a camshaft position sensor is incorporated into the system. The camshaft position sensor is fitted to the left-hand end of the cylinder head, directly over the top of the inlet camshaft, and informs the ECU when No 1 cylinder is at Top Dead Centre (TDC).

26 The MP3.2 system differs from all the other fuel injection systems in that it is a "sequential" system. This means that each of the four fuel injectors is triggered individually, just before the inlet valve on that particular cylinder opens. This is in contrast to all other systems, on which all four injectors are triggered simultaneously; this happens once for every revolution of the crankshaft.

7 Fuel system - depressurisation

Note: *Refer to the warning note in Section 1 before proceeding.*

⚠️ **Warning: The following procedure will merely relieve the pressure in the fuel system - remember that fuel will still be present in the system components and take precautions accordingly before disconnecting any of them.**

1 The fuel system referred to in this Section is defined as the tank-mounted fuel pump, the fuel filter, the fuel injectors, the fuel rail and the pressure regulator, and the metal pipes and flexible hoses of the fuel lines between these components. All these contain fuel which will be under pressure while the engine is running, and/or while the ignition is switched on. The pressure will remain for some time after the ignition has been switched off, and it must be relieved in a controlled fashion when any of these components are disturbed for servicing work.

2 Disconnect the battery negative terminal.

3 Place a container beneath the connection/ union to be disconnected, and have a large rag ready to soak up any escaping fuel not being caught by the container.

4 Slowly loosen the connection or union nut to avoid a sudden release of pressure, and position the rag around the connection, to catch any fuel spray which may be expelled. Once the pressure is released, disconnect the fuel line. Plug the pipe ends, to minimise fuel loss and prevent the entry of dirt into the fuel system.

8 Fuel pump - removal and refitting

Note: *Refer to the warning note in Section 1 before proceeding.*

Removal

Note: *1997 models onward are fitted with a single hole fuel tank in which the fuel pump and fuel gauge sender unit are combined in one assembly. The following procedures are applicable to the later arrangement, but note that the fuel lines now incorporate quick-fit connectors instead of crimped-type hose clips.*

1 Disconnect the battery negative lead.

2 For access to the fuel pump, tilt or remove the rear seats, as described in Chapter 11.

3 Using a screwdriver, carefully prise the plastic access cover from the floor, to expose the fuel pump (located under the right-hand cover).

4 Disconnect the wiring connector from the fuel pump, and tape the connector to the vehicle body, to prevent it disappearing behind the tank.

5 Mark the hoses for identification purposes, then slacken the feed and return hose retaining clips. Where the original crimped-type Citroën hose clips are fitted, cut the clips and discard them; use standard worm-drive hose clips on refitting. Disconnect both hoses from the top of the pump, and plug the hose ends.

6 Noting the alignment marks on the tank, pump cover and the locking ring, unscrew the ring and remove it from the tank. This is best accomplished by using a screwdriver on the raised ribs of the locking ring, as follows. Carefully tap the screwdriver to turn the ring anti-clockwise until it can be unscrewed by hand.

7 Displace the pump cover, then reach into the tank and unclip the pump from the tank base. Carefully lift the fuel pump assembly out of the fuel tank, taking care not to damage the filter, or to spill fuel onto the interior of the vehicle. Recover the rubber sealing ring and discard it - a new one must be used on refitting.

8 Note that the fuel pump is only available as a complete assembly - no components are available separately.

Refitting

9 Ensure the fuel pump pick-up filter is clean and free of debris. Fit the new sealing ring to the top of the fuel tank.

10 Carefully manoeuvre the pump assembly into the fuel tank, and clip it into position in the base of the tank.

11 Align the mark on the fuel pump cover with the centre of the three alignment marks on the fuel tank, then refit the locking ring. Securely tighten the locking ring, and check that the locking ring, pump cover and tank marks are all correctly aligned.

12 Reconnect the feed and return hoses to the top of the fuel pump, using the marks made on removal to ensure they correctly reconnected, and securely tighten their retaining clips.

13 Reconnect the pump wiring connector.

14 Reconnect the battery negative terminal, and start the engine. Check the fuel pump feed and return hoses unions for signs of leakage.

15 If all is well, refit the plastic access cover, and tilt or refit the rear seat as described in Chapter 11 (as applicable).

9 Fuel gauge sender unit - removal and refitting

On pre-1997 models, refer to Chapter 4A, Section 5, noting that there are no fuel pipe connections to the sender unit. On later models, the sender unit and fuel pump are combined in one assembly; refer to Section 8 of this Chapter.

10 Fuel tank - removal and refitting

Refer to Chapter 4A, Section 6, noting that it will be necessary to depressurise the fuel system as the feed and return hoses are disconnected (see Section 7). It will also be necessary to disconnect the wiring connector from the fuel pump before lowering the tank out of position (see Section 8).

11 Fuel injection system - testing and adjustment

Testing

1 If a fault appears in the fuel injection system, first ensure that all the system wiring connectors are securely connected and free of corrosion. Ensure that the fault is not due to poor maintenance; ie, check that the air cleaner filter element is clean, the spark plugs are in good condition and correctly gapped, the cylinder compression pressures are correct, the ignition timing is correct, and that the engine breather hoses are clear and undamaged, referring to Chapters 1, 2 and 5 for further information.

2 If these checks fail to reveal the cause of the problem, the vehicle should be taken to a suitably-equipped Citroën dealer for testing. A wiring block connector is incorporated in the engine management circuit, into which a special electronic diagnostic tester can be plugged; the connector is located inside either

4C

11.2 Diagnostic wiring connector located in the engine compartment junction box

the engine compartment junction box, or directly in front of the box (see illustration). The tester will locate the fault quickly and simply, alleviating the need to test all the system components individually, which is a time-consuming operation that carries a risk of damaging the ECU.

Adjustment

3 On 1905 cc models without a catalytic converter (Motronic MP3.1 system), both the idle speed and idle mixture (exhaust gas CO level) are adjustable. On 1905 cc models with a catalytic converter (Motronic M1.3 system), only the idle speed is adjustable (mixture adjustment is not possible). Refer to Chapter 1 for information on adjustment procedures.

4 On all other models, experienced home mechanics with a considerable amount of skill and equipment (including a tachometer and an accurately calibrated exhaust gas analyser) may be able to check the exhaust CO level and the idle speed. However, if these are found to be in need of adjustment, the car *must* be taken to a suitably-equipped Citroën dealer for further testing. Neither the mixture adjustment (exhaust gas CO level) nor the idle speed are adjustable, and should either be incorrect, a fault must be present in the fuel injection system.

12 Throttle housing - removal and refitting

Removal

1 Disconnect the battery negative terminal.

1360 cc models

2 Slacken the retaining clip, then disconnect the inlet duct from the throttle housing and recover the sealing ring. Where a crimped-type hose clip or tie is fitted, cut and discard it; replace it with a standard worm-drive hose clip or new cable-tie on refitting.

3 Disconnect the accelerator inner cable from the throttle cam, then withdraw the outer cable from the mounting bracket, along with its rubber washer and spring clip.

4 Depress the retaining clip and disconnect the wiring connector(s) from the throttle potentiometer, and, where necessary, from the electric heating element, the air temperature sensor, and/or the stepper motor (as applicable).

5 Slacken and remove the retaining screws, and remove the throttle housing from the inlet manifold. Recover the O-ring from manifold (where fitted) and discard it; a new one must be used when refitting.

1580 cc models

6 Remove the air cleaner-to-throttle housing duct as described in Section 2.

7 Disconnect the accelerator inner cable from the throttle cam, then withdraw the outer cable from the mounting bracket, along with its flat washer and spring clip. On automatic transmission models, also disconnect the kickdown cable as described in Chapter 7B.

8 On models with an idle speed control stepper motor, disconnect the air hoses, labelling them if necessary for refitting.

9 Depress the retaining clips, and disconnect the wiring connectors from the throttle potentiometer, the electric heating element,

the air temperature sensor and idle control stepper motor (as applicable).

10 Release the retaining clips (where fitted), and disconnect all the relevant vacuum and breather hoses from the throttle housing. Make identification marks on the hoses, to ensure that they are connected correctly on refitting.

11 Slacken and remove the retaining screws, and remove the throttle housing from the inlet manifold. Remove the O-ring from the manifold, and discard it - a new one must be used on refitting.

1761 cc and 1998 cc 8-valve models

12 Remove the air cleaner-to-throttle housing duct as described in Section 2.

13 Disconnect the accelerator inner cable from the throttle cam, then withdraw the outer cable from the mounting bracket, along with its flat washer and spring clip (see illustration).

14 Depress the retaining clips, and disconnect the wiring connectors from the throttle potentiometer, the electric heating element, the air temperature sensor and idle control stepper motor (as applicable) (see illustration).

15 Release the retaining clips (where fitted), and disconnect all the relevant vacuum and breather hoses from the throttle housing (see illustration). Make identification marks on the hoses, to ensure they are connected correctly on refitting.

16 Slacken and remove the three retaining screws, and remove the throttle housing from the inlet manifold. Remove the O-ring from the manifold, and discard it - a new one must be used on refitting.

1905 cc models

17 Slacken the retaining clip, disconnect the intake duct from the end of the throttle housing, and recover the rubber sealing ring (where fitted) (see illustrations).

18 Disconnect the accelerator inner cable from the throttle cam. Slacken and remove the bolt and nut securing the outer cable

12.13 Disconnecting the accelerator cable - 1998 cc 8-valve model

12.14 Throttle housing wiring connectors (arrowed) - 1761 cc model

12.15 Throttle housing vacuum hoses (arrowed) - 1761 cc model

12.17a On 1905 cc models, slacken the retaining clip . . .

12.17b . . . then disconnect the duct and recover the rubber sealing ring

12.18a Disconnect the accelerator cable from the throttle cam . . .

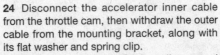

mounting bracket to the manifold, then withdraw the bracket. Remove the flat washer from the end of the cable for safekeeping **(see illustrations)**. On models with automatic transmission, free the kickdown cable from the throttle cam.

19 Depress the retaining clip, and disconnect the wiring connector from the throttle potentiometer **(see illustration)**.

20 Relieve any pressure in the cooling system by unscrewing the filler cap. Slacken the retaining clips, and disconnect the two coolant hoses from the base of the throttle housing. Plug the hose ends, working quickly to minimise coolant loss.

21 Release the retaining clips (where fitted), and disconnect all the relevant vacuum and breather hose(s) from the throttle housing **(see illustration)**. Make identification marks on the hoses, to ensure they are correctly reconnected on refitting.

22 Undo the remaining two retaining nuts, and remove the throttle housing from the manifold. On early models, it will also be necessary to remove the nut and bolt securing the base of the housing to its support bracket **(see illustration)**. Remove the O-ring from the manifold, and discard it - a new one must be used on refitting.

1998 cc 16-valve models

23 Slacken the retaining clip, disconnect the intake duct from the end of the throttle housing, and recover the rubber sealing ring (where fitted).

24 Disconnect the accelerator inner cable from the throttle cam, then withdraw the outer cable from the mounting bracket, along with its flat washer and spring clip.

25 Depress the retaining clips, and disconnect the wiring connectors from the throttle potentiometer, the electric heating element, and the air temperature sensor.

26 Slacken the retaining clips (where fitted), and disconnect all the relevant vacuum and breather hoses from the throttle housing. Make identification marks on the hoses, to ensure they are connected correctly on refitting.

27 Slacken the nut securing the throttle housing lower mounting bracket to the transmission housing.

28 Slacken and remove the housing retaining screws, then remove the throttle housing from the inlet manifold. Remove the O-ring from the manifold, and discard it - a new one must be used on refitting.

Refitting

29 Refitting is a reversal of the removal procedure, noting the following points:

(a) *Fit a new O-ring to the manifold, then refit the throttle housing and securely tighten its retaining nuts or screws (as applicable).*

(b) *Ensure all hoses are correctly reconnected and, where necessary, are securely held in position by the retaining clips.*

12.18b . . . then undo the retaining nut and bolt (arrowed) . . .

12.18c . . . and remove the bracket. Remove the flat washer (arrowed) for safekeeping

4C

12.19 Disconnect the throttle potentiometer wiring connector . . .

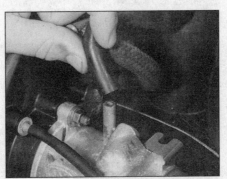

12.21 . . . and the breather hose from the throttle housing

12.22 Undo the two remaining nuts, and remove the throttle housing

(c) *Ensure all wiring is correctly routed, and that the connectors are securely reconnected.*

(d) *On completion, adjust the accelerator cable as described in Section 3.*

(e) *On 1905 cc models, check the coolant level and top up if necessary (Chapter 1).*

13 Magneti Marelli 1AP system components - removal and refitting

Fuel rail and injectors

Note: *Refer to the warning note in Section 1 before proceeding.*

Note: *If a faulty injector is suspected, before condemning the injector, it is worth trying the effect of one of the proprietary injector-cleaning treatments.*

1 Disconnect the battery negative cable and position it away from the terminal, then depressurise the fuel system, with reference to Section 7.

2 Disconnect the vacuum pipe from the port at the top of the fuel pressure regulator.

3 Bearing in mind the information given in Section 7, slacken the retaining clips and disconnect the fuel feed and return hoses from the fuel rail. Where the original crimped-type Citroën hose clips are still fitted, cut them off and discard; replace them with standard worm-drive hose clips on refitting.

4 Depress the retaining tangs and disconnect the wiring connectors from the four injectors.

5 Slacken and remove the fuel rail retaining bolts nuts, then carefully ease the fuel rail and injector assembly out from the inlet manifold and remove it from the vehicle. Remove the O-rings from the lower end of each injector, and discard them; they must be renewed whenever they are disturbed.

6 Slide out the retaining clip(s) and remove the relevant injector(s) from the fuel rail. Remove the upper O-ring from each disturbed injector and discard; any O-rings which are disturbed during removal must be renewed.

7 Refitting is a reversal of the removal procedure, noting the following points:

(a) *Fit new O-rings to all injector unions disturbed on removal.*

(b) *Apply a smear of engine oil to the O-rings to aid installation, then ease the injectors and fuel rail into position, ensuring that none of the O-rings are displaced.*

(c) *On completion, start the engine and check for fuel leaks.*

Fuel pressure regulator

Note: *Later models are not fitted with a fuel pressure regulator.*

Caution: Refer to the warning note in Section 1 before proceeding.

8 Disconnect the vacuum pipe from the regulator.

9 Place a wad of rag under and around the regulator, to catch any fuel spray which may

be released, then remove the retaining clip and ease the regulator out from the fuel rail.

10 Refitting is a reversal of the removal procedure. Examine the regulator seal for signs of damage or deterioration, and renew if necessary.

Throttle potentiometer

11 Disconnect the battery negative terminal.

12 Depress the retaining clip and disconnect the wiring connector from the throttle potentiometer.

13 Slacken and remove the two retaining screws, then disengage the potentiometer from the throttle valve spindle and remove it from the vehicle.

14 Refitting is a reverse of the removal procedure, ensuring that the potentiometer is correctly engaged with the throttle valve spindle.

Electronic control unit (ECU)

15 The ECU is situated inside its own protective plastic box, located directly behind the battery. To remove the ECU, first disconnect the battery negative terminal.

16 Unclip the lid from the plastic box, and slide the ECU and mounting plate out of position.

17 Disconnect the wiring connector from the ECU, then undo the retaining screws and remove the ECU from the engine compartment.

18 Refitting is the reverse of removal, ensuring that the wiring connector is securely connected.

Idle speed control stepper motor

19 The idle speed control stepper motor is located on the side of the throttle housing assembly. To remove the motor, first disconnect the battery negative terminal.

20 Release the retaining clip, and disconnect the wiring connector from the motor.

21 Slacken and remove the two retaining screws, and withdraw the motor from the throttle housing.

22 Refitting is a reversal of the removal procedure.

Manifold absolute pressure (MAP) sensor

23 On early models, the sensor is mounted on a bracket on the bulkhead at the rear of the engine compartment bulkhead. On later models, the manifold pressure sensor is mounted directly on the inlet manifold casting. To remove it, first ensure that the ignition is switched off.

24 Release the locking tab and unplug the wiring from the sensor connector.

25 On early models, disconnect the vacuum hose, then remove the screws and withdraw

the sensor from the mounting bracket. On later models, remove the securing screws and withdraw the sensor from the manifold, recovering the sealing ring.

26 Refitting is a reversal of removal.

Coolant temperature sensor

27 The coolant temperature sensor is threaded into the thermostat housing, at the left-hand end of the cylinder head. Do not confuse it with the other sensors in the thermostat housing - refer to the information given in Chapter 3, Section 6 for location and identification details.

28 Allow the engine to cool completely, then partially drain the cooling system with reference to Chapter 1.

29 Ensure that the ignition is switched off then unplug the wiring from the sensor connector.

30 Carefully unscrew the sensor from the thermostat housing - be prepared for some coolant spillage. Recover the sensor sealing ring.

31 Refitting is a reversal of removal. Ensure that the sensor wiring is securely reconnected, and top-up the cooling system with reference to "Weekly checks".

Intake air temperature sensor

32 The sensor is threaded into the underside of the throttle body. Before removing the sensor, first ensure that the ignition is switched off.

33 Unplug the wiring from the sensor connector, then unscrew the sensor and remove it from the vehicle. Recover the sealing ring, where applicable.

34 Refitting is the reverse of removal.

Crankshaft/TDC sensor

35 The crankshaft/TDC sensor is situated on the front face of the transmission clutch housing.

36 To remove the sensor, first ensure that the ignition is switched off.

37 Trace the wiring back from the sensor to the wiring connector, and disconnect it from the main harness.

38 Prise out the rubber grommet, then undo the retaining bolt and withdraw the sensor from the transmission.

39 Refitting is reverse of the removal procedure, ensuring that the sensor retaining bolt is securely tightened and the grommet is correctly seated in the transmission housing.

Knock sensor

40 The knock sensor is screwed onto the rear face of the cylinder block.

41 To gain access to the sensor, firmly apply the handbrake, then jack up the front of the vehicle and support it on axle stands (see "Jacking and vehicle support"). Access to the sensor can then be gained from underneath the vehicle.

42 Trace the wiring back from the sensor to

its wiring connector, and disconnect it from the main loom.

43 Slacken and remove the bolt securing the sensor to the cylinder block, and remove it from underneath the vehicle.

44 Refitting is a reversal of the removal procedure, ensuring that the sensor wiring is correctly routed.

Throttle housing heating element

45 The throttle housing heating element is fitted to the side of the throttle housing. To remove the element, first disconnect the battery negative cable and position it away from the terminal.

46 To improve access, disconnect the accelerator inner cable from the throttle cam, then withdraw the outer cable from the mounting bracket, along with its flat washer and spring clip.

47 Disconnect the element wiring connector, then undo the retaining screw, and free the wiring connector from the throttle housing.

48 Undo the screws securing the accelerator cable bracket to the side of the throttle housing. Carefully remove the bracket, and recover the spring from the top of the heating element.

49 Ease the heating element out from the throttle housing. Examine the O-ring for signs of damage or deterioration, and renew if necessary.

50 Refitting is a reversal of the removal procedure; where necessary, use a new O-ring.

Vehicle speed sensor

51 The vehicle speed sensor is an integral part of the speedometer drive housing. Refer to Chapter 7A or B, as applicable, for removal and refitting details.

Lambda sensor

52 Refer to the information given in Chapter 4D.

14 Magneti Marelli 8P and Sagem/Lucas 4GJ system components - removal and refitting

1580 cc and 1761 cc 8-valve models

Fuel injectors

Note: *Refer to the warning note in Section 1 before proceeding. If a faulty injector is suspected, before condemning the injector, it is worth trying the effect of one of the proprietary injector-cleaning treatments.*

1 Disconnect the battery negative terminal.

2 Remove the air cleaner-to-throttle housing duct as described in Section 2.

3 Undo the two bolts securing the wiring tray to the top of the manifold, and position the tray clear of the injectors.

4 Depress the retaining clip(s), and disconnect the wiring connector(s) from the injector(s).

5 Slacken the retaining screw, and remove the injector retaining plate; Nos 1 and 2 injectors are retained by one plate, Nos 3 and 4 by another.

6 Place a wad of clean rag over the injector, to catch any fuel spray which may be released, then carefully ease the relevant injector(s) out of the manifold. Remove the O-rings from the end of each disturbed injector, and discard them - these must be renewed whenever they are disturbed.

7 On refitting the injectors, fit a new O-rings to the end of each injector. Apply a smear of engine oil to the O-ring, to aid installation, then ease the injector(s) back into position in the manifold.

8 Ensure each injector connector is correctly positioned, then refit the retaining plate and securely tighten its screw. Reconnect the wiring connector(s) to the injector(s).

9 Refit the wiring tray to the top of the manifold, and securely tighten its retaining bolts.

10 Refit the air cleaner-to-throttle body duct, and reconnect the battery negative lead. Start the engine, and check the injectors for signs of leakage.

Fuel pressure regulator

Note: *Refer to the warning and note in Section 1 before proceeding.*

11 As applicable, disconnect the fuel hoses from the regulator, taking precautions against fuel spillage. Depending on model, access to the regulator may be poor with the fuel rail in position - if necessary, remove the fuel rail as described earlier, then remove the regulator.

12 Disconnect the vacuum pipe from the regulator.

13 Place some rag below the regulator to catch any spilt fuel. Remove the retaining clip and ease the regulator out from the fuel rail.

14 Refitting is a reversal of the removal procedure. Examine the regulator seal for signs of damage or deterioration, and renew if necessary.

Throttle potentiometer

15 The throttle potentiometer is fitted to the right-hand side of the throttle housing. To remove the potentiometer, first disconnect the battery negative terminal.

16 Depress the retaining clip, and disconnect the potentiometer wiring connector.

17 Slacken and remove the two retaining screws, and remove the potentiometer from the throttle housing.

18 Refitting is the reverse of removal, ensuring that the potentiometer is correctly engaged with the throttle valve spindle.

Electronic Control Unit (ECU)

19 Refer to Section 13.

Idle speed control stepper motor

20 Refer to Section 13.

Manifold absolute pressure (MAP) sensor

21 Refer to Section 13.

Coolant temperature sensor

22 Refer to Chapter 3.

Intake air temperature sensor

23 The intake air temperature sensor is located in the throttle housing.

24 To remove the sensor, first remove the throttle potentiometer.

25 Depress the retaining clip, and disconnect the wiring from the air temperature sensor.

26 Remove the screw securing the sensor connector to the top of the throttle housing, then carefully ease the sensor out of position and remove it from the throttle housing. Examine the sensor O-ring for damage or deterioration, and renew if necessary.

27 Refitting is a reversal of removal, using a new O-ring where necessary, and ensuring that the throttle potentiometer is correctly engaged with the throttle valve spindle.

Crankshaft sensor

28 Refer to Section 13.

Throttle housing heating element

29 The throttle housing heating element is fitted to the top of the throttle housing. To remove the element, first disconnect the battery negative terminal.

30 Depress the retaining tangs, and disconnect the wiring connector from the heating element.

31 Undo the screw(s) securing the wiring connector to the throttle housing, then displace the connector and carefully withdraw the heating element from the throttle housing. Examine the O-ring (where fitted) for damage or deterioration, and renew if necessary.

32 Refitting is a reversal of the removal procedure, taking great care to ensure that the element wiring does not become trapped as the wiring connector bolt(s) are tightened.

1998 cc 8-valve models

Fuel rail and injectors

Note: *Refer to the warning note in Section 1 before proceeding. If a faulty injector is suspected, before condemning the injector, it is worth trying the effect of one of the proprietary injector-cleaning treatments.*

33 Disconnect the battery negative terminal.

34 Remove the air cleaner-to-throttle housing duct, referring to Section 2.

35 Disconnect the vacuum pipe from the fuel pressure regulator.

36 Release the retaining clip, and free the various hoses from the top of the fuel rail.

37 Bearing in mind the information given in Section 7, slacken the retaining clip, and disconnect the fuel feed and return hoses from the ends of the fuel rail. Where the original crimped-type Citroën hose clips are still fitted, cut them off and discard them; use

4C

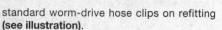

14.37 Fuel feed hose connection (1), injector wiring connectors (2) and (two of the three) fuel rail retaining bolts (3) - 1998 cc 8-valve models

14.48 Unclip the lid from the plastic box to gain access to the ECU

14.53 Idle speed control stepper motor is retained by two screws (arrowed) - 1998 cc 8-valve models

standard worm-drive hose clips on refitting (see illustration).

38 Depress the retaining clips, and unplug the wiring connectors from the four injectors.

39 Slacken and remove the three fuel rail retaining bolts, then carefully ease the fuel rail and injector assembly out from the inlet manifold, and remove it from the vehicle. Remove the O-rings from the end of each injector, and discard them; these must be renewed whenever they are disturbed.

40 Slide out the retaining clip(s), and remove the relevant injector(s) from the fuel rail. Remove the upper O-ring from each injector as it is removed, and discard it; all O-rings must be renewed once they have been disturbed.

41 Refitting is a reversal of the removal procedure, noting the following points:
(a) Fit new O-rings to all disturbed injectors.
(b) Apply a smear of engine oil to the O-rings to aid installation, then ease the injectors and fuel rail into position, ensuring that none of the O-rings are displaced.
(c) On completion, start the engine and check for fuel leaks.

Fuel pressure regulator

42 Refer to Section 13.

Throttle potentiometer

43 Remove the throttle housing (Section 12).
44 Disconnect the wiring then undo the two

retaining screws, and remove the potentiometer from the throttle housing.
45 On refitting, ensure that the potentiometer is correctly engaged with the throttle valve spindle, and securely tighten its screws.
46 Refit the throttle housing (see Section 12).

Electronic control unit (ECU)

47 The ECU is situated inside its own protective plastic box, located directly behind the battery. To remove the ECU, first disconnect the battery negative terminal.
48 Unclip the lid from the plastic box, and slide the ECU and mounting plate out of position (see illustration).
49 Disconnect the wiring connector from the ECU, then undo the retaining screws and remove the ECU from the engine compartment.
50 Refitting is the reverse of removal, ensuring that the wiring connector is securely connected.

Idle speed control stepper motor

51 The idle speed control stepper motor is located on the right-hand side of the throttle housing assembly. To remove the motor, first disconnect the battery negative terminal.
52 Release the retaining clip, and disconnect the wiring connector from the motor.
53 Slacken and remove the two retaining screws, and withdraw the motor from the throttle housing (see illustration).

54 Refitting is a reversal of the removal procedure.

Manifold absolute pressure (MAP) sensor

55 The MAP sensor is situated on the right-hand side of the engine compartment, mounted on the front of the engine/transmission mounting (see illustration). To remove the sensor, first disconnect the battery negative terminal.
56 Undo the three nuts, and free the sensor from the underside of the mounting bracket.
57 Depress the retaining clip, disconnect the wiring connector and vacuum hose from the sensor, and remove the sensor from the engine compartment.
58 Refitting is a reversal of removal.

Coolant temperature sensor

59 Refer to Chapter 3.

Intake air temperature sensor

60 The intake air temperature sensor is located in the base of the throttle housing (see illustration).
61 To remove the sensor, first remove the throttle housing as described in Section 12, then undo the two retaining screws and remove the throttle potentiometer from the base of the housing.
62 Trace the wiring back from the sensor to its wiring connector, and remove the screw securing the connector to the throttle housing.
63 Carefully ease the sensor out of position, and remove it from the throttle housing. Examine the sensor O-ring for damage or deterioration, and renew if necessary.
64 Refitting is a reversal of removal, using a new O-ring where necessary.

Crankshaft sensor

65 Refer to Section 13.

Throttle housing heating element

66 The throttle housing heating element is fitted to the top of the throttle housing. To remove the element, first disconnect the battery negative terminal.
67 Depress the retaining tangs, and disconnect the wiring connector from the

14.55 MAP sensor location - 1998 cc 8-valve models

14.60 On 1998 cc 8-valve models, the intake air temperature sensor (arrowed) is located in the base of the throttle housing

14.67 Disconnecting the wiring connector from the throttle housing heating element - 1998 cc 8-valve models

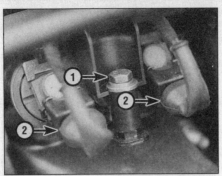

15.3 Wiring tray retaining bolt (1) and injector wiring connectors (2) - 1761 cc model

15.22 Idle speed auxiliary air valve - 1761 cc model

heating element, which is located on the right-hand side of the throttle housing cam **(see illustration)**.

68 Undo the two screws securing the wiring connector to the throttle housing, then displace the connector and carefully withdraw the heating element from the throttle housing. Examine the O-ring (where fitted) for damage or deterioration, and renew if necessary.

69 Refitting is a reversal of the removal procedure, taking great care to ensure that the element wiring does not become trapped as the wiring connector screws are tightened.

Vehicle speed sensor

70 The vehicle speed sensor is an integral part of the transmission speedometer drive assembly. Refer to Chapter 7A for removal and refitting details.

Knock sensor

71 The knock sensor is screwed onto the rear face of the cylinder block.

72 To gain access to the sensor, chock the rear wheels, then jack up the front of the vehicle and support it on axle stands (see "*Jacking and vehicle support*"). Access to the sensor can then be gained from underneath the vehicle.

73 Trace the wiring back from the sensor to its wiring connector, and disconnect it from the main loom.

74 Slacken and remove the bolt securing the sensor to the cylinder block, and remove it from underneath the vehicle.

75 Refitting is a reversal of the removal procedure, ensuring the sensor wiring is correctly routed and the retaining bolt securely tightened.

---

15 Bosch Motronic MP5.1 and MP5.2 system components - removal and refitting

---

1761 cc 8-valve models
Fuel rail and injectors

Note: *Refer to the warning and note in Section 1 before proceeding. If a faulty injector is suspected, before condemning the injector, it is worth trying the effect of one of the proprietary injector-cleaning treatments.*

1 Disconnect the battery negative terminal.
2 Remove the air cleaner-to-throttle housing duct as described in Section 2.
3 Undo the two bolts securing the wiring tray to the top of the manifold, and position tray clear of the injectors **(see illustration)**.
4 Depress the retaining clip(s) and disconnect the wiring connector(s) from the injector(s).
5 Slacken the retaining screw and remove the injector retaining plate; Nos 1 and 2 injectors are retained by one plate, Nos 3 and 4 by another.
6 Place a wad of clean rag over the injector to catch any fuel spray which may be released, then carefully ease the relevant injector(s) out of the manifold. Remove the O-ring from the end of each disturbed injector and discard it - these must be renewed whenever they are disturbed.
7 On refitting the injectors, fit a new O-ring to the end of each injector. Apply a smear of engine oil to the O-ring, to aid installation, then ease the injector(s) back into position in the manifold.
8 Ensure each injector connector is pointing upwards, then refit the retaining plate and securely tighten its retaining screw. Reconnect the wiring connector(s) to the injector(s).
9 Refit the wiring tray to the top of the manifold, and securely tighten its retaining bolts.
10 Refit the air cleaner-to-throttle housing duct, and reconnect the battery. Start the engine and check the injectors for signs of leakage.

Fuel pressure regulator

Note: *Refer to the warning and note in Section 1 before proceeding.*
11 Disconnect the vacuum pipe from the regulator.
12 Place a wad of clean rag over the regulator to catch any fuel spray which may be released. Remove the retaining clip and slide the regulator out of the end of the fuel rail.
13 Refitting is a reversal of the removal procedure. Examine the regulator seal for signs of damage or deterioration, and renew if necessary.

Throttle potentiometer

14 The throttle potentiometer is fitted to the right-hand side of the throttle housing. To remove the potentiometer, first disconnect the battery negative terminal.
15 Depress the retaining clip, and disconnect the potentiometer wiring connector.
16 Slacken and remove the two retaining screws, and remove the potentiometer from the throttle housing.
17 Refitting is the reverse of removal, ensuring that the potentiometer is correctly engaged with the throttle valve spindle.

Electronic control unit (ECU)

18 The ECU is situated inside its own protective plastic box, located directly behind the battery. To remove the ECU, first disconnect the battery negative terminal.
19 Unclip the lid from the plastic box, and slide the ECU and mounting plate out of position.
20 Disconnect the wiring connector from the ECU, then undo the retaining screws and remove the ECU from the engine compartment.
21 Refitting is the reverse of removal, ensuring that the wiring connector is securely connected.

Idle speed auxiliary air valve

22 The auxiliary air valve is mounted on the left-hand end of the cylinder head, directly above the ignition HT coil **(see illustration)**. To remove the valve, first disconnect the battery negative terminal.
23 Depress the retaining clip, and disconnect the wiring connector from the top of the valve.
24 Slacken the retaining clip(s), and disconnect the two hoses from the valve. Slide the valve rubber retaining clip off its pegs, and remove the valve from the engine compartment.
25 Refitting is a reversal of the removal procedure, ensuring that the hoses are securely connected.

Manifold absolute pressure (MAP) sensor

26 The MAP sensor is situated on the right-hand side of the engine compartment,

4C

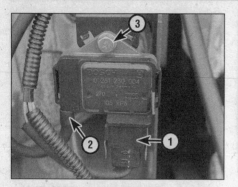

15.27 MAP sensor wiring connector (1), vacuum hose (2) and retaining nut (3) - 1761 cc model

15.31 On 1761 cc models, the intake air temperature sensor (arrowed) is situated behind the throttle potentiometer

attached to the engine/transmission mounting point. To remove the sensor, first disconnect the battery negative terminal.

27 Depress the retaining clip and disconnect the wiring connector from the sensor, then disconnect the vacuum hose **(see illustration)**.

28 Undo the retaining bolt and remove the sensor from the engine compartment.

29 Refitting is a reversal of removal.

Coolant temperature sensor

30 Refer to Chapter 3.

Intake air temperature sensor

31 The intake air temperature sensor is located in the throttle housing **(see illustration)**.

32 To remove the sensor, first remove the throttle potentiometer as described previously.

33 Depress the retaining clip and disconnect the wiring connector from the air temperature sensor.

34 Remove the screw securing the sensor connector to the top of the throttle housing, then carefully ease the sensor out of position, and remove it from the throttle housing. Examine the sensor O-ring for damage or deterioration, and renew if necessary.

35 Refitting is a reversal of removal, using a new O-ring where necessary and ensuring that the throttle potentiometer is correctly engaged with the throttle valve spindle.

Crankshaft sensor

36 The crankshaft sensor is mounted on top of the transmission housing, next to the left-hand end of the cylinder block. To remove the sensor, first disconnect the battery negative terminal.

37 Access to the sensor is poor, and it will be necessary to remove the battery and battery tray (see Chapter 5) and/or the intake duct assembly (see Section 2) to improve access (depending on model and specification). On some models, it will also be necessary to remove the metal plate from the top of the transmission housing; the plate is retained by one of the engine-to-transmission bolts, and by a second bolt securing the plate to the top of the transmission.

38 Trace the wiring back from the sensor to

the wiring connector, and disconnect it from the main harness. Undo the retaining bolt and remove the sensor from the top of the transmission housing.

39 Refitting is reverse of the removal procedure, ensuring that the sensor wiring is correctly routed.

Throttle housing heating element

40 The throttle housing heating element is fitted to the top of the throttle housing. To remove the element, first disconnect the battery negative terminal.

41 Depress the retaining tangs, and disconnect the wiring connector from the heating element, which is located on the right-hand side of the throttle housing cam.

42 Undo the two screws securing the wiring connector to the throttle housing, then displace the connector and carefully withdraw the heating element from the throttle housing. Examine the O-ring (where fitted) for damage or deterioration, and renew if necessary.

43 Refitting is a reversal of the removal procedure, taking great care to ensure that the element wiring does not become trapped as the wiring connector screws are tightened.

1761 cc 16-valve models

Fuel rail and injectors

Note: *Refer to the warning and note in Section 1 before proceeding. If a faulty injector is suspected, before condemning the injector, it is worth trying the effect of one of the proprietary injector-cleaning treatments.*

44 Disconnect the battery negative terminal.

45 Disconnect the vacuum pipe from the fuel pressure regulator. Where applicable, slacken and remove the retaining nut and bolt, and release the wiring/hose retaining clip from the end of the fuel rail.

46 Bearing in mind the information given in Section 7, slacken the retaining clips and disconnect the fuel feed and return hoses from the fuel rail or fuel pressure regulator, as applicable. Where the original crimped-type Citroën hose clips are still fitted, cut them and discard; replace them with standard worm-type hose clips on refitting.

47 Disconnect the wiring harness connector along the front of the fuel rail then depress the

retaining tangs and disconnect the wiring connectors from the four fuel injectors.

48 Slacken and remove the fuel rail retaining bolts, then carefully ease the fuel rail and injector assembly out from the inlet manifold and remove it from the vehicle. Remove the O-rings from the end of each injector and discard them; they must be renewed whenever they are disturbed.

49 Slide out the retaining clip(s) and remove the relevant injector(s) from the fuel rail. Remove the upper O-ring from each disturbed injector and discard; all disturbed O-rings must be renewed.

50 Refitting is a reversal of the removal procedure, noting the following points.

(a) Fit new O-rings to all disturbed injector unions.

(b) Apply a smear of engine oil to the O-rings to aid installation then ease the injectors and fuel rail into position, ensuring that none of the O-rings are displaced.

(c) On completion, start the engine and check for fuel leaks.

Fuel pressure regulator

Note: *Refer to the warning and note in Section 1 before proceeding.*

51 As applicable, disconnect the fuel hoses from the regulator, taking precautions against fuel spillage. Depending on model, access to the regulator may be poor with the fuel rail in position - if necessary, remove the fuel rail as described earlier, then remove the regulator.

52 Disconnect the vacuum pipe from the regulator.

53 Place some rag below the regulator to catch any spilt fuel. Remove the retaining clip and ease the regulator out from the fuel rail.

54 Refitting is a reversal of the removal procedure. Examine the regulator seal for signs of damage or deterioration, and renew if necessary.

Throttle potentiometer

55 Disconnect the battery negative terminal. Depress the retaining clip and disconnect the wiring connector from the throttle potentiometer.

56 Slacken and remove the two retaining screws, then disengage the potentiometer from the throttle valve spindle, and remove it from the vehicle.

57 Refitting is a reverse of the removal procedure ensuring that the potentiometer is correctly engaged with the throttle valve spindle.

Electronic control unit (ECU)

58 Refer to paragraphs 18 to 21.

Idle speed stepper motor

59 The idle speed stepper motor is located on the side of the throttle housing assembly. To remove the motor, first disconnect the battery negative terminal.

60 Release the retaining clip, and disconnect the wiring connector from the motor.

61 Slacken and remove the two retaining screws, and withdraw the motor from the throttle housing.

62 Refitting is a reversal of removal.

Manifold absolute pressure (MAP) sensor

63 The MAP sensor is situated on the inlet manifold. To remove it, first disconnect the battery negative terminal.

64 Disconnect the wiring connector and vacuum hose and remove the MAP sensor from the manifold.

65 Refitting is a reversal of removal.

Coolant temperature sensor

66 Refer to Chapter 3.

Intake air temperature sensor

67 The intake air temperature sensor is fitted to the throttle housing. To remove the sensor, first disconnect the battery negative terminal.

68 Loosen the worm-drive clip, and release the inlet air duct from the throttle housing. The intake air temperature sensor is visible in the top of the housing.

69 Trace the wiring back from the sensor to its wiring connector on the throttle housing, and unplug the connector.

70 The sensor itself can be pressed out of the throttle housing. Note that it is sealed in place with sealant, to prevent air leaks; a suitable sealant will be required for refitting.

71 Refitting is the reverse of removal.

Crankshaft sensor

72 The crankshaft sensor is situated on the front face of the transmission clutch housing.

73 To remove the sensor, first disconnect the battery negative terminal.

74 Trace the wiring back from the sensor to the wiring connector, and disconnect it from the main harness.

75 Prise out the rubber grommet, then undo the retaining bolt and withdraw the sensor from the transmission.

76 Refitting is reverse of the removal procedure, ensuring that the sensor retaining bolt is securely tightened and the grommet is correctly seated in the transmission housing.

Vehicle speed sensor

77 The vehicle speed sensor is an integral part of the transmission speedometer drive assembly. Refer to Chapter 7A for removal and refitting details.

Knock sensor

78 The knock sensor is screwed onto the rear face of the cylinder block.

79 To gain access to the sensor, chock the rear wheels, then jack up the front of the vehicle and support it on axle stands (see "*Jacking and vehicle support*"). Access to the sensor can then be gained from underneath the vehicle.

80 Trace the wiring back from the sensor to its wiring connector, and disconnect it from the main loom.

81 Slacken and remove the bolt securing the sensor to the cylinder block, and remove it from underneath the vehicle.

82 Refitting is a reversal of the removal procedure, ensuring the sensor wiring is correctly routed and the securing bolt securely tightened.

---

16 Bosch Motronic MP3.1 system components - removal and refitting

Note: *Check parts availability with a Citroën dealer prior to removing individual components. At the time of writing, certain components are only available as part of a larger assembly - eg the throttle potentiometer is only available as part of the throttle housing assembly.*

Fuel rail and injectors

Note: *Refer to the warning note in Section 1 before proceeding. If a faulty injector is suspected, before condemning the injector, it is worth trying the effect of one of the proprietary injector-cleaning treatments.*

1 Disconnect the battery negative terminal.

2 Disconnect the vacuum pipe from the fuel pressure regulator.

3 Bearing in mind the information given in Section 7, slacken the retaining clips, and disconnect the fuel feed and return hoses from the either end of the fuel rail. Where the original crimped-type Citroën hose clips are still fitted, cut them off and discard them; use standard worm-drive hose clips on refitting **(see illustration).**

4 Depress the retaining tangs, and

16.3 Where original crimped-type Citroën hose clips are fitted, cut them and discard

disconnect the wiring connectors from the four injectors **(see illustration).**

5 Slacken and remove the two fuel rail retaining bolts, then carefully ease the fuel rail and injector assembly out from the inlet manifold and remove it from the vehicle **(see illustration).** Remove the O-rings from the end of each injector, and discard them; these must be renewed whenever they are disturbed.

6 Slide out the retaining clip(s), and remove the relevant injector(s) from the fuel rail. Remove the upper O-ring from each injector as it is removed, and discard it; all O-rings must be renewed once they have been disturbed.

7 Refitting is a reversal of the removal procedure, noting the following points:

(a) Fit new O-rings to all disturbed injectors.

(b) Apply a smear of engine oil to the O-rings to aid installation, then ease the injectors and fuel rail into position, ensuring that none of the O-rings are displaced.

(c) On completion, start the engine and check for fuel leaks.

Fuel pressure regulator

Note: *Refer to the warning note in Section 1 before proceeding.*

8 Disconnect the vacuum pipe from the regulator.

9 Place a wad of clean rag over the regulator, to catch any fuel spray which may be released. Remove the retaining clip, and slide the regulator out of the end of the fuel rail **(see illustration).**

16.4 Disconnecting the injector wiring connectors - 1905 cc model

16.5 On 1905 cc models, the fuel rail is retained by two bolts (arrowed)

16.9 Fuel pressure regulator retaining clip (arrowed) can be prised out of position using a flat-bladed screwdriver

4C

16.13 Throttle potentiometer is secured to the throttle housing by two screws

16.14 On refitting, ensure that the potentiometer is correctly engaged with the throttle valve spindle (arrowed)

16.17a Undo the ECU upper retaining bolt . . .

16.17b . . . and loosen its lower mounting nut. The lower mounting is slotted to ease removal

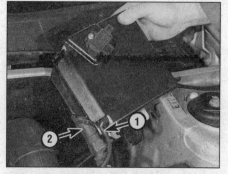

16.17c Remove the ECU, disconnecting its vacuum hose (1) and wiring connector (2) as they become accessible

10 Refitting is a reversal of the removal procedure. Examine the regulator seal for signs of damage or deterioration, and renew if necessary.

Throttle potentiometer

11 Disconnect the battery negative terminal.
12 Depress the retaining clip, and disconnect the wiring connector from the throttle potentiometer.
13 Slacken and remove the two retaining screws, then disengage the potentiometer from the throttle valve spindle and remove it from the vehicle (see illustration).
14 Refitting is a reverse of the removal procedure, ensuring that the potentiometer is correctly engaged with the throttle valve spindle (see illustration).

Electronic Control Unit (ECU)

15 The ECU is located in the rear left-hand corner of the engine compartment. To remove the ECU, first disconnect the battery negative terminal.
16 Depress the retaining clip, and disconnect the wiring connector from the idle mixture adjustment potentiometer.
17 Slacken and remove the upper bolt securing the ECU mounting bracket to the wing valance, then loosen the lower bolt (there is no need to remove the lower bolt, as the mounting is slotted). Withdraw the bracket and ECU assembly from the engine

compartment, disconnecting the wiring connector and vacuum pipe from the ECU as they become accessible (see illustrations).
18 With the assembly on the bench, undo the bolts securing the ECU to the bracket, and separate the two components.
19 Refitting is a reversal of the removal procedure, ensuring that the wiring connector and vacuum pipe are securely reconnected.

Idle speed mixture adjustment potentiometer

20 The idle speed mixture adjustment potentiometer is situated in the rear left-hand corner of the engine compartment, mounted onto the ECU bracket. To remove it, first disconnect the battery negative terminal.
21 Depress the retaining tangs and disconnect the wiring connector, then undo the retaining screw and remove the potentiometer from the vehicle (see illustrations).
22 Refitting is the reverse of removal. On completion, check and, if necessary, adjust the idle mixture setting (exhaust gas CO level) as described in Chapter 1.

Auxiliary air valve

23 The auxiliary air valve is mounted on the left-hand end of the cylinder head, directly beneath the ignition HT coil (see illustration).
24 To improve access to the valve, remove the ignition HT coil as described in Chapter 5.
25 Depress the retaining clip, and disconnect the wiring connector from the air valve.
26 Slacken the retaining clips, and

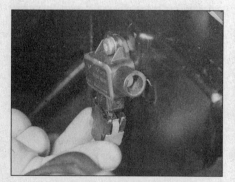

16.21a Disconnect the wiring connector . . .

16.21b . . . then undo the retaining screw and remove the idle speed mixture potentiometer

16.23 Auxiliary air valve location - wiring connector arrowed

16.31 Disconnecting the wiring connector from the intake air temperature sensor

16.39a Disconnect the wiring connector . . .

16.39b . . . then undo the retaining bolt, and remove the fuel injection relay unit from the front of the junction box

4C

disconnect the vacuum hoses from either end of the auxiliary air valve.

27 Undo the two retaining bolts, and remove the auxiliary air valve from the engine compartment.

28 Refitting is a reversal of the removal procedure.

Manifold absolute pressure (MAP) sensor

29 The MAP sensor is an integral part of the electronic control unit (ECU). Refer to paragraphs 15 to 19 for removal and refitting details.

Coolant temperature sensor

30 Refer to Chapter 3, Section 6.

Intake air temperature sensor

31 The intake air temperature sensor is located in the air cleaner-to-throttle housing duct **(see illustration)**. To remove the sensor, first disconnect the battery negative terminal.

32 Disconnect the wiring connector, then unscrew the sensor from the intake duct and remove it from the vehicle.

33 Refitting is the reverse of removal.

Crankshaft sensor

34 The crankshaft sensor is mounted on top of the transmission housing, next to the left-hand end of the cylinder block. To remove the sensor, first disconnect the battery negative terminal.

35 Access to the sensor is poor, and it will be necessary to remove the battery and battery tray (see Chapter 5) and/or the intake duct assembly (see Section 2) to improve access (depending on model and specification). On some models, it will also be necessary to remove the metal plate from the top of the transmission housing; the plate is retained by one of the engine-to-transmission bolts, and by a second bolt securing the plate to the top of the transmission.

36 Trace the wiring back from the sensor to its wiring connector, and disconnect it from the main wiring harness. Undo the retaining bolt, and remove the sensor from the top of the transmission housing.

37 Refitting is a reversal of the removal procedure, ensuring that the sensor wiring is correctly routed.

Fuel injection system relay unit

38 The fuel injection system relay unit is mounted on the front of the engine compartment junction box. To remove the relay unit, first disconnect the battery negative terminal.

39 Open up the junction box lid, then slacken and remove the relay mounting nut and washer. Release the retaining clip, then disconnect the wiring connector and remove the relay unit from the engine compartment **(see illustrations)**.

40 Refitting is the reverse of removal.

17 Bosch Motronic M1.3 system components - removal and refitting

Note: *Check parts availability with a Citroën dealer prior to removing individual components. At the time of writing, certain components are only available as part of a larger assembly, eg the throttle switch is only available as part of the throttle housing assembly.*

Fuel rail and injectors

1 The fuel rail and injectors can be removed as described in Section 16, noting that it will first be necessary to remove the ignition HT coil as described in Chapter 5.

Fuel pressure regulator

2 Refer to Section 16.

Throttle switch

3 Disconnect the battery negative terminal.

4 Depress the retaining clip, and disconnect the wiring connector from the throttle potentiometer.

5 Slacken and remove the two retaining screws, then disengage the potentiometer from the throttle valve spindle and remove it from the vehicle.

6 When refitting the switch, ensure it is

correctly engaged with the throttle valve spindle, and lightly tighten its retaining screws. Slowly operate the throttle valve whilst listening to the switch; the switch should click as soon as the throttle valve starts to open, and again just before it is fully closed. Position the switch until this is so, then securely tighten its retaining screws.

7 Reconnect the wiring connector, and reconnect the battery.

Electronic Control Unit (ECU)

8 Refer to the information given in Section 16, noting that there is no idle mixture adjustment potentiometer to disconnect.

Airflow meter

9 Disconnect the battery negative terminal.

10 Depress the retaining clip, and disconnect the wiring connector from the airflow meter.

11 Slacken the retaining clips, and disconnect the intake ducts from either end of the airflow meter.

12 Slacken and remove the retaining nuts and bolts, and remove the airflow meter from the engine compartment.

13 Refitting is a reverse of the removal procedure.

Auxiliary air valve

14 The auxiliary air valve is mounted on the left-hand end of the cylinder head, directly beneath the airflow meter.

15 To improve access to the valve, remove the airflow meter as described above.

16 Depress the retaining clip, and disconnect the wiring connector from the air valve.

17 Slacken the retaining clips, and disconnect the vacuum hoses from either end of the auxiliary air valve.

18 Undo the two retaining bolts, and remove the auxiliary air valve from the engine compartment.

19 Refitting is a reversal of the removal procedure.

Manifold absolute pressure (MAP) sensor

20 Refer to Section 16.

Coolant temperature sensor

21 Refer to Chapter 3.

Intake air temperature sensor

22 The intake air temperature sensor is an integral part of the airflow meter, and is not available separately. Refer to paragraphs 9 to 13 for airflow meter removal and refitting details.

Crankshaft sensor

23 Refer to Section 16.

Fuel injection system relay unit

24 Refer to Section 16.

18 Bosch Motronic MP3.2 system components - removal and refitting

Note: *Check parts availability with a Citroën dealer prior to removing individual components. At the time of writing, certain components are only available as part of a larger assembly, eg the throttle potentiometer is only available as part of the throttle housing assembly.*

Fuel rail and injectors

Note: *Refer to the warning note in Section 1 before proceeding. If a faulty injector is suspected, before condemning the injector, it is worth trying the effect of one of the proprietary injector-cleaning treatments.*

1 Disconnect the battery negative terminal.
2 Disconnect the vacuum pipe from the fuel pressure regulator.
3 Bearing in mind the information given in Section 7, slacken the retaining clips, and disconnect the fuel feed and return hoses from the right-hand end of the fuel rail. Where the original crimped-type Citroën hose clips are still fitted, cut them off and discard them; use standard worm-drive hose clips on refitting.
4 Depress the retaining tangs, and disconnect the wiring connectors from the four injectors. To avoid the possibility of the wiring connectors being incorrectly reconnected on refitting, mark each connector with its cylinder number (No 1 is at the transmission end of the engine).
5 Slacken and remove the two fuel rail

retaining bolts, then carefully ease the fuel rail and injector assembly out from the inlet manifold, and remove it from the vehicle. Remove the O-rings from the end of each injector, and discard them; these must be renewed whenever they are disturbed.
6 Slide out the retaining clip(s), and remove the relevant injector(s) from the fuel rail. Remove the upper O-ring from each injector as it is removed, and discard it; all O-rings must be renewed once they have been disturbed.
7 Refitting is a reversal of the removal procedure, noting the following points:
(a) Fit new O-rings to all disturbed injectors.
(b) Apply a smear of engine oil to the O-rings to aid installation, then ease the injectors and fuel rail into position, ensuring that none of the O-rings are displaced.
(c) Using the marks made on removal, ensure that all the injector wiring connectors are correctly reconnected.
(d) On completion, start the engine and check for fuel leaks.

Fuel pressure regulator

8 Refer to Section 16 **(see illustration)**.

Throttle potentiometer

9 The throttle potentiometer is fitted to the rear of the throttle housing.
10 To improve access to the potentiometer, remove the throttle housing as described in Section 12.
11 Undo the two retaining screws, and remove the potentiometer from the base of the throttle housing.
12 On refitting, ensure that the potentiometer is correctly engaged with the throttle valve spindle, and securely tighten its retaining screws.
13 Refit the throttle housing as described in Section 12.

Electronic Control Unit (ECU)

14 Refer to Section 14.

Idle speed auxiliary air valve

15 The idle speed auxiliary air valve is mounted on the left-hand end of the inlet manifold, directly in front of the braking

system vacuum pump. To remove the valve, first disconnect the battery negative terminal.
16 Depress the retaining clip, and disconnect the wiring connector from the top of the valve **(see illustration)**.
17 Free the valve from its mounting rubber, then disconnect the two hoses from the base of the valve and manoeuvre the valve out from the engine compartment.
18 Refitting is a reverse of the removal sequence, ensuring that the hoses are securely reconnected.

Manifold absolute pressure (MAP) sensor

19 The MAP sensor is an integral part of the electronic control unit (ECU). Refer to Section 14 for ECU removal and refitting details.

Coolant temperature sensor

20 Refer to Chapter 3.

Intake air temperature sensor

21 The intake air temperature sensor is located in the throttle housing.
22 To remove the sensor, first remove the throttle potentiometer as described in paragraphs 9 to 11.
23 Trace the wiring back from the sensor to its wiring connector, and remove the screw securing the connector to the top of the throttle housing.
24 Carefully ease the sensor out of position, and remove it from the throttle housing. Examine the sensor O-ring for signs of damage or deterioration, and renew if necessary.
25 Refitting is a reversal of the removal procedure, using a new O-ring where necessary. Refit the potentiometer as described in paragraphs 12 and 13.

Camshaft position sensor

26 The camshaft position sensor is located on the left-hand end of the cylinder head, directly over the end of the inlet camshaft. To remove the sensor, first disconnect the battery negative terminal.
27 Depress the retaining clip, and disconnect the wiring connector from the sensor **(see illustration)**.

18.8 Fuel pressure regulator location - 1998 cc 16-valve models

18.16 Disconnecting the wiring connector from the idle speed auxiliary air valve - 1998 cc 16-valve models

18.27 Disconnecting the wiring connector from the camshaft position sensor - 1998 cc 16-valve models

28 Undo the retaining screw, and withdraw the sensor from the end of the cylinder head. Examine its O-ring for signs of damage or deterioration, and renew if necessary.
29 Refitting is a reversal of the removal procedure, using a new O-ring where necessary.

Crankshaft sensor

30 Refer to Section 16.

Fuel injection system relay unit

31 Refer to Section 16.

Vehicle speed sensor

32 The vehicle speed sensor is an integral part of the transmission speedometer drive assembly. Refer to Chapter 7A for removal and refitting details.

Knock sensor

33 The knock sensor is screwed onto the rear face of the cylinder block.
34 To gain access to the sensor, firmly apply the handbrake, then jack up the front of the vehicle and support it on axle stands. Access to the sensor can then be gained from underneath the vehicle.
35 Trace the wiring back from the sensor to its wiring connector, and disconnect it from the main loom.
36 Slacken and remove the bolt securing the sensor to the cylinder block, and remove it from underneath the vehicle.
37 Refitting is a reversal of the removal procedure, ensuring that the sensor wiring is correctly routed and its retaining bolt securely tightened.

Throttle housing heating element

38 The throttle housing heating element is fitted to the top of the throttle housing, and is an integral part of the throttle housing. At the time of writing, no information is available on element removal and refitting. Refer to your Citroën dealer for further information.

19 Inlet manifold - removal and refitting

Removal

1 Remove the throttle housing as described in Section 12.

1360 cc models

2 Unplug the wiring connector from the manifold absolute pressure sensor, with reference to Section 13.
3 Release the retaining clips (where fitted), and disconnect all the relevant vacuum and breather hoses from the manifold. Make identification marks on the hoses, to ensure that they are connected correctly on refitting.
4 Bearing in mind the information given in Section 7, slacken the retaining clips and disconnect the fuel feed and return hoses

from the fuel rail. Where the original crimped-type Citroën hose clips are still fitted, cut them off and discard; replace them with standard worm-drive hose clips on refitting.
5 Depress the retaining tangs, and disconnect the wiring connectors from the four injectors. Free the wiring from any relevant retaining clips, and position it clear of the manifold.
6 Where applicable, undo the retaining bolts and remove the support bracket from the underside of the manifold.
7 Undo the manifold retaining nuts, and withdraw the manifold from the engine compartment. Recover the four manifold seals, and discard them; new ones must be used on refitting.

1580 cc and 1761 cc 8-valve models

8 Undo the two bolts securing the wiring tray to the top of the manifold, and position the tray, and its associated wiring and hoses, clear of the manifold so that it does not hinder removal.
9 Depress the retaining clips, and disconnect the wiring connectors from the four injectors.
10 Bearing in mind the information given in Section 7, slacken the retaining clips, and disconnect the fuel feed and return hoses from the either side of the manifold. Where the original crimped-type Citroën hose clips are still fitted, cut them off and discard them; use standard worm-drive hose clips on refitting.
11 Slacken the retaining clip(s), and disconnect the braking system vacuum servo unit hose, and all the relevant vacuum/breather hoses, from the top of the manifold. Where necessary, make identification marks on the hoses, to ensure that they are correctly reconnected on refitting.
12 Undo the manifold retaining nuts, and withdraw the manifold from the engine compartment. Recover the two manifold seals, and discard them - new ones must be used on refitting.

1761 cc 16-valve models

13 Remove the fuel rail and injectors as described in Section 15.
14 Slacken the retaining clip(s), and disconnect the braking system vacuum servo unit hose, and all the relevant

vacuum/breather hoses, from the manifold. Where necessary, make identification marks on the hoses, to ensure that they are correctly reconnected on refitting.
15 Slacken and remove the bolt securing the dipstick tube to the rear of the manifold.
16 Release the wiring loom from the retaining clips and brackets at the rear and at the timing belt end of the engine.
17 Undo the nuts and bolts securing the manifold to the cylinder head, and move the manifold away from the engine. As it is withdrawn, disconnect the wiring plug from the MAP sensor on the base of the manifold. Remove the manifold from the engine compartment.
18 Recover the manifold seals from the recesses in the manifold, and discard them - new ones must be used on refitting.

1905 cc models

19 On models with a catalytic converter, remove the ignition HT coil as described in Chapter 5.
20 Depress the retaining tangs, and disconnect the wiring connectors from the four injectors. Free the wiring from any relevant retaining clips, and position it clear of the manifold.
21 Bearing in mind the information given in Section 7, slacken the retaining clips, and disconnect the fuel feed and return hoses from the either side of the manifold. Where the original crimped-type Citroën hose clips are still fitted, cut them off and discard them; use standard worm-drive hose clips on refitting.
22 Slacken the retaining clip(s), and disconnect the braking system vacuum servo unit hose, and all the relevant vacuum/breather hoses, from the top of the manifold (see illustration). Where necessary, make identification marks on the hoses, to ensure that they are correctly reconnected on refitting.
23 Slacken or cut the retaining clip (as applicable), and disconnect the breather hose from the top of the cylinder head cover.
24 Slacken and remove the bolt securing the support stay to the underside of the manifold, and the bolt securing the oil filler/breather neck to the left-hand side of the manifold (see illustration).

19.22 Disconnecting the braking system vacuum servo unit hose from the manifold - 1905 cc models

19.24 On 1905 cc models, undo the bolt (arrowed) securing the oil filler/breather neck to the manifold

4C

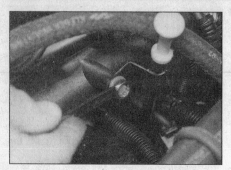

19.28 Removing the dipstick tube retaining bolt - 1998 cc 8-valve models

19.29 Manifold retaining nut and bolt locations (arrowed) - 1998 cc 8-valve models

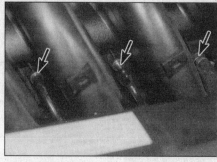

19.31 On 1998 cc 16-valve models, disconnect the vacuum and breather hoses (arrowed) from the front of the inlet manifold . . .

25 Undo the five manifold retaining nuts, and withdraw the manifold from the engine compartment. Recover the manifold gasket(s), and discard them - new ones must be used on refitting.

1998 cc 8-valve models

26 Carry out the operations described in paragraphs 20 to 22.
27 Release the retaining clip, and free all the disconnected hoses from the clip on the top of the fuel rail.
28 Slacken and remove the bolt securing the dipstick tube to the side of the manifold (see illustration).
29 Undo the six nuts and bolts securing the manifold to the cylinder head, and remove the manifold from the engine compartment (see illustration). Recover the manifold seals, and discard them - new ones must be used on refitting.

1998 cc 16-valve models

30 Slacken the retaining clip and disconnect the large breather hose from the front of the oil filler neck.
31 Slacken the retaining clip(s), and disconnect the vacuum/breather hoses, from the front of the manifold (see illustration). Where necessary, make identification marks on the hoses, to ensure that they are correctly reconnected on refitting.
32 Undo the three retaining screws and lift

off the cover from the top of the inlet manifold-to-ACAV valve assembly joint. Free the wiring loom and position it clear of the manifold (see illustration).
33 Slacken and remove the screws securing the inlet manifold to the ACAV butterfly valve housing, then manoeuvre the inlet manifold out of the engine compartment. Recover the four intake tract sealing rings from the manifold, and discard them - new ones must be used on refitting.

Refitting

34 Refitting is a reverse of the relevant removal procedure, noting the following points:
(a) Ensure that the manifold and cylinder head mating surfaces are clean and dry.
(b) Locate the new seals in their recesses in the manifold, or fit new manifold gasket(s) over the studs, as applicable. Refit the manifold and tighten its retaining nuts to the specified torque.
(c) Ensure that all relevant hoses are reconnected to their original positions, and are securely held (where necessary) by the retaining clips.
(d) Refit the throttle housing as described in Section 12.

20 ACAV intake system (1998 cc 16-valve models) - general information, removal and refitting

General information

1 To ensure optimum efficiency at high engine speeds, and maximum torque at lower engine speeds, 16-valve models have an inlet manifold with a variable intake tract system. Citroën call this system ACAV (variable acoustic characteristic induction) (see illustration).
2 The inlet manifold is divided into two tracts of different length and diameter; a long tract (for low-speed torque) which is 650 mm long, diameter 36 mm, and a short tract (for high-speed power) which is 370 mm long, diameter 45 mm.
3 Situated between the manifold and the cylinder head is a line of four butterfly valves, mounted in an alloy housing. Mounted on either end of the housing is a vacuum diaphragm assembly. Each diaphragm is connected to the butterfly valve spindles via a pushrod. The vacuum diaphragms are connected to an electrically-operated solenoid valve, which is in turn connected to the braking system vacuum pump. The pump

19.32 . . . then undo the three retaining screws (arrowed) and remove the cover from the top of the manifold

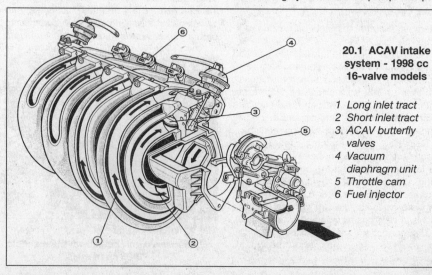

20.1 ACAV intake system - 1998 cc 16-valve models

1 Long inlet tract
2 Short inlet tract
3 ACAV butterfly valves
4 Vacuum diaphragm unit
5 Throttle cam
6 Fuel injector

is mounted on the end of the cylinder head, and is driven off the left-hand end of the inlet camshaft.

4 At engine speeds below 1800 rpm and above 5080 rpm, the ECU closes the solenoid valve, shutting off the vacuum supply to the diaphragms, and the butterfly valves are closed. With the valves closed, the short intake tracts are closed, and the incoming air flows only through the long intake tract, boosting the torque output.

5 At engine speeds between 1800 rpm and 5080 rpm, the ECU opens the solenoid valve. The vacuum present in the pump is then allowed to act on the vacuum diaphragms, which draws the pushrods into the diaphragm bodies, and opens up the four butterfly valves. With the valves open, the incoming air is allowed to flow through both the short and long intake tracts, for maximum power.

6 To check the system, start the engine and allow it to idle. Slowly increase the engine speed, whilst observing the vacuum diaphragm pushrods. At approximately 1800 rpm, the pushrods should be drawn into the diaphragm bodies (valves open). Release the throttle cam, and allow the engine to idle again; the pushrods should extend from the diaphragms (valves closed).

7 To check the operation of the solenoid valve, disconnect the vacuum pipe from the diaphragm. Start the engine, and allow it to idle. Place your finger over the end of the pipe; no vacuum should be present in the pipe. Slowly increase the engine speed; at approximately 1800 rpm, vacuum should be felt in the pipe. Allow the engine to idle again, and check that the vacuum supply is switched off. If this is not the case, either the solenoid valve or its supply voltage is at fault.

8 To check the operation of either vacuum diaphragm assembly, disconnect the vacuum pipe, and suck hard at the control valve stub; the pushrod should be drawn into the diaphragm body, and the valve should open. If this is not the case, the vacuum diaphragm is faulty.

Removal and refitting
ACAV valve assembly

9 Remove the inlet manifold as described in Section 19.
10 Bearing in mind the information given in Section 7, slacken the retaining clip, and disconnect the fuel feed and return hoses from their unions on the fuel rail. Where the original crimped-type Citroën hose clips are still fitted, cut them off and discard them; use standard worm-drive hose clips on refitting.
11 Depress the retaining tangs, and disconnect the wiring connectors from the four injectors. To avoid the possibility of the wiring connectors being incorrectly reconnected on refitting, mark each connector with its relevant cylinder number (No 1 is at the transmission end of the engine).
12 Disconnect the vacuum hoses from the fuel pressure regulator and the ACAV diaphragm hose T-piece.

20.16 ACAV vacuum diaphragm unit - 1998 cc 16-valve models

13 Slacken and remove the nuts and three bolts securing the valve assembly to the cylinder head, then slide the assembly off its mounting studs and remove it from the engine compartment. Remove the valve assembly gasket from the head, and discard it - a new one must be used on refitting.
14 Examine the assembly, checking that the butterfly valves open freely and close smoothly. If not, the assembly must be renewed. The only components available separately are the vacuum diaphragm units - if either one is faulty, it must be renewed as described below.
15 Refitting is a reverse of the removal procedure, noting the following points:
(a) Ensure that the valve assembly and cylinder head mating surfaces are clean and dry, and fit the new manifold gasket over the studs. Refit the valve assembly, and securely tighten its retaining nuts and bolts.
(b) Ensure all relevant hoses are reconnected to their original positions, and are securely held (where necessary) by the retaining clips.
(c) Refit the inlet manifold as described in Section 19.
(d) On completion, check the operation of the ACAV system as described above.

Vacuum diaphragm unit

16 Disconnect the vacuum hose from the diaphragm unit. Using a suitable flat-bladed screwdriver, carefully lever the unit pushrod off the valve linkage balljoint **(see illustration)**.
17 Slacken and remove the two bolts securing the diaphragm unit mounting bracket to the valve assembly, and remove the diaphragm from the engine.
18 Refitting is a reversal of the removal

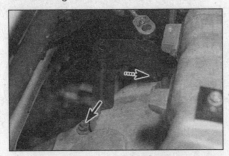
21.2a On 1905 cc models, undo the two retaining bolts (arrowed) . . .

20.19 ACAV solenoid valve retaining nut (1), wiring connector (2) and hose connections (3) - 1998 cc 16-valve models

procedure, ensuring that the diaphragm pushrod is clipped firmly onto the linkage balljoint.

Solenoid valve

19 The solenoid control valve is mounted on the left-hand end of the cylinder head **(see illustration)**. To remove the valve, first disconnect the battery negative terminal.
20 Depress the retaining clip, and disconnect the wiring connector from the valve.
21 Undo the nut securing the valve to the cylinder head, then withdraw the valve, disconnecting its vacuum hoses as they become accessible.
22 Refitting is a reversal of the removal procedure. Test the system on completion, as described above.

21 Exhaust manifold - removal and refitting

Removal

1 Firmly apply the handbrake, then jack up the front of the vehicle and support it on axle stands.
2 On 1905 cc models, to improve access to the manifold from above, remove the air cleaner housing as described in Section 2, then undo the two mounting bracket retaining bolts, and remove the bracket from the top of the exhaust manifold **(see illustrations)**.
3 On all models, undo the bolts securing the shroud to the top of the manifold, and remove the shroud from the manifold **(see illustration)**.
4 Slacken and remove the two nuts securing

21.2b . . . and remove the air cleaner mounting bracket from the top of exhaust manifold

4C

21.3 Undo the retaining bolts and remove the exhaust manifold shroud (1905 cc model shown)

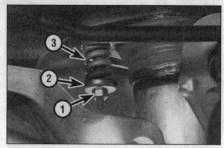

22.6a Exhaust front pipe-to-manifold joint securing nut (1), spring cup (2) and spring (3) - viewed from underneath

22.6b Exhaust front pipe-to-manifold joint bolts (arrowed) - viewed from above

the front pipe flange joint to the manifold, and recover the springs. Remove the bolts, then free the front pipe from the manifold, and recover the wire-mesh sealing ring. Either support the front pipe, to avoid placing any strain on the lambda sensor wiring (where fitted), or disconnect the lambda sensor wiring connectors.

5 Undo the retaining nuts securing the manifold to the head. Manoeuvre the manifold out of the engine compartment, and discard the manifold gasket(s) - new ones should be obtained for refitting.

Refitting

6 Refitting is the reverse of the removal procedure, noting the following points:

(a) Examine all the exhaust manifold studs for signs of damage and corrosion; remove all traces of corrosion, and repair or renew any damaged studs.

(b) Ensure that the manifold and cylinder head sealing faces are clean and flat, and fit the new manifold gaskets. Tighten the manifold retaining nuts to the specified torque.

(c) Reconnect the front pipe to the manifold, using the information given in Section 22.

22 Exhaust system - general information, removal and refitting

General information

1 On 1905 cc models without a catalytic converter, the exhaust system consists of two sections: the front pipe and intermediate silencer box, and the tailpipe and main silencer box. The front pipe-to-manifold joint is of the spring-loaded ball type, to allow for movement in the exhaust system, and the front pipe-to-silencer joint is secured by a clamping ring.

2 On all other models, the exhaust system consists of three sections: the front pipe and catalytic converter, the intermediate pipe and silencer box, and the tailpipe and main silencer box. All exhaust sections are joined by flanged joints. The front pipe-to-manifold joint is of the spring-loaded ball type, to allow for movement in the exhaust system, and the front pipe-to-intermediate pipe and intermediate pipe-to-silencer joints are secured by clamping rings.

3 On all models, the system is suspended

throughout its entire length by rubber mountings.

Removal

4 Each exhaust section can be removed individually, or alternatively, the complete system can be removed as a unit. Even if only one part of the system needs attention, it is often easier to remove the whole system and separate the sections on the bench.

5 To remove the system or part of the system, first jack up the front or rear of the car, and support it on axle stands. Alternatively, position the car over an inspection pit, or on car ramps.

Front pipe - 1905 cc models without a catalytic converter

6 Slacken and remove the two nuts securing the front pipe to the manifold, and recover the spring cups and springs. Remove the bolts, then release the front pipe from the manifold, and recover the wire-mesh gasket from the joint **(see illustrations)**.

7 Slacken the front pipe-to-tailpipe clamping ring bolt(s), and disengage the clamp from the flange joint.

8 Free the front pipe from its mounting rubbers, and withdraw it from underneath the vehicle.

Front pipe - all models with a catalytic converter

9 Trace the wiring back from the lambda (oxygen) sensor to its wiring connectors, and disconnect it from the main wiring harness.

10 Disconnect the front pipe from the manifold and intermediate pipe as described above in paragraphs 6 and 7, then remove the front pipe from underneath the vehicle. Be careful not to damage the catalytic converter - it is fragile.

Intermediate pipe - all models with a catalytic converter

11 Slacken the intermediate pipe clamping ring bolts, and disengage the clamps from both the flange joints.

12 Free the intermediate pipe from its mounting rubbers, and withdraw it from underneath the vehicle.

Tailpipe - all models

13 Slacken the intermediate pipe-to-tailpipe clamping ring bolt(s), and disengage the clamp from the flange joint.

14 Unhook the tailpipe from its mounting rubbers, and remove it from the vehicle.

Complete system - all models

15 Using the information given under the relevant sub-heading above, unbolt the front pipe from the manifold, and disconnect the lambda sensor wiring (where applicable). Free the system from all its mounting rubbers, and withdraw it from under the vehicle.

Heat shield(s) - all models

16 The heat shields are secured to the underside of the body by various nuts and bolts. Each shield can be removed once the relevant exhaust section has been removed. If the shield is being removed to gain access to a component located behind it, it may prove sufficient in some cases to remove the retaining nuts and/or bolts, and simply lower the shield, without disturbing the exhaust system.

Refitting

17 Each section is refitted by a reverse of the removal sequence, noting the following points:

(a) Clamping rings which are secured by a single bolt (fitted to all 1998 cc models, and to some others) should be renewed as a matter of course. They are designed to deform on tightening, and cannot be re-used.

(b) Ensure that all traces of corrosion have been removed from the flanges, and renew all necessary gaskets.

(c) Inspect the rubber mountings for signs of damage or deterioration, and renew as necessary.

(d) Prior to assembling the spring-loaded ball type joint, a smear of high-temperature grease should be applied to the joint mating surfaces. Citroën recommend the use of Gripcott AF G2 grease (available from your Citroën dealer).

(e) On joints which are secured by clamping rings, apply a smear of exhaust system jointing paste to the joint mating surfaces, to ensure an gas-tight seal.

(f) Prior to tightening the exhaust system fasteners, ensure all rubber mountings are correctly located, and that there is adequate clearance between the exhaust system and vehicle underbody.

(g) On models with clamping rings which are secured by two bolts, tighten the clamping ring nuts evenly and progressively to the specified torque, to ensure that the clearance between the clamp halves is equal on either side.

Chapter 4 Part D: Emission control systems

Contents

Catalytic converter - general information and precautions 3
Emission control system components - testing and renewal 2
General information 1

Degrees of difficulty

Easy, suitable for novice with little experience		Fairly easy, suitable for beginner with some experience		Fairly difficult, suitable for competent DIY mechanic		Difficult, suitable for experienced DIY mechanic		Very difficult, suitable for expert DIY or professional

1 General information

Apart from their ability to use unleaded petrol, and the various built-in fuel system features which help to minimise emissions, all models have at least the crankcase emission-control system described below. Models with a catalytic converter are also fitted with the exhaust and evaporative emission control systems (refer to Part B or C of this Chapter for further information).

Crankcase emission control

To reduce the emission of unburned hydrocarbons from the crankcase into the atmosphere, the engine is sealed, and the blow-by gases and oil vapour are drawn from the crankcase, through a wire-mesh oil separator, into the inlet tract, to be burned by the engine during normal combustion.

Under conditions of high manifold depression (idling, deceleration) the gases will be sucked positively out of the crankcase. Under conditions of low manifold depression (acceleration, full-throttle running) the gases are forced out of the crankcase by the (relatively) higher crankcase pressure; if the engine is worn, the raised crankcase pressure (due to increased blow-by) will cause some of the flow to return under all manifold conditions.

Evaporative emission control

To minimise the escape into the atmosphere of unburned hydrocarbons, an evaporative emissions control system is fitted to models equipped with a catalytic converter. The fuel tank filler cap is sealed, and a charcoal canister, mounted underneath the right-hand wing, collects the petrol vapours generated in the tank when the car is parked. The canister stores them until they can be cleared from the canister (under the control of the fuel injection/ignition system ECU) via the purge solenoid valve(s). When the valve is opened, the fuel vapours pass into the inlet tract, to be burned by the engine during normal combustion.

To ensure that the engine runs correctly when it is cold and/or idling, and to protect the catalytic converter from the effects of an over-rich mixture, the ECU does not open the purge control valve(s) until the engine has warmed up and is under load; the valve solenoid is then modulated on and off, to allow the stored vapour to pass into the inlet tract.

Exhaust emission control

To minimise the amount of pollutants which escape into the atmosphere, some models are fitted with a catalytic converter in the exhaust system. On all models where a catalytic converter is fitted, the system is of the "closed-loop" type; a lambda (oxygen) sensor in the exhaust system provides the fuel injection/ignition system ECU with constant feedback, enabling the ECU to adjust the mixture to provide the best possible conditions for the converter to operate.

The lambda sensor has a built-in heating element, controlled by the ECU through the lambda sensor relay, to quickly bring the sensor's tip to an efficient operating temperature. The sensor's tip is sensitive to oxygen, and sends the ECU a varying voltage depending on the amount of oxygen in the exhaust gases. If the intake air/fuel mixture is too rich, the exhaust gases are low in oxygen, so the sensor sends a low-voltage signal. The voltage rises as the mixture weakens and the amount of oxygen in the exhaust gases rises. Peak conversion efficiency of all major pollutants occurs if the intake air/fuel mixture is maintained at the chemically-correct ratio for the complete combustion of petrol - 14.7 parts (by weight) of air to 1 part of fuel (the "stoichiometric" ratio). The sensor output voltage alters in a large step at this point, the ECU using the signal change as a reference point, and correcting the intake air/fuel mixture accordingly by altering the fuel injector pulse width (the length of time that the injector is open).

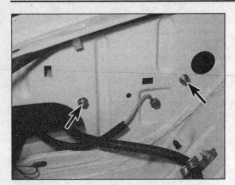

2.3 Charcoal canister is secured to the right-hand wing valance by two nuts (arrowed)

2.5 Peel back the wheel arch liner to gain access to the charcoal canister from underneath the wing

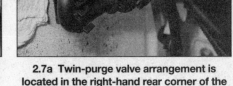

2.7a Twin-purge valve arrangement is located in the right-hand rear corner of the engine compartment - 1360 cc model shown

2 Emission control system components - testing and renewal

Crankcase emission control

1 The components of this system require no routine attention, other than to check that the hose(s) are clear and undamaged at regular intervals.

Evaporative emission control

Testing

2 If the system is thought to be faulty, disconnect the hoses from the charcoal canister and purge control valve, and check that they are clear by blowing through them. If the purge control valve(s) or charcoal canister are thought to be faulty, they must be renewed.

Charcoal canister - renewal

3 From within the engine compartment, slacken and remove the two nuts securing the charcoal canister to the right-hand wing valance (see illustration).
4 Slacken and remove the lower bolt securing the right-hand wheel arch liner to the bumper, then prise out the front liner retaining clips.
5 Peel the liner away from the wing to gain access to the canister, then disconnect both upper and lower hoses from the canister and

manoeuvre the canister out from underneath the wing (see illustration). Store or dispose of the canister carefully - it may contain fuel vapour.
6 Refitting is a reverse of the removal procedure, ensuring that the hoses are correctly refitted.

Purge valve(s) - renewal

7 Either a single- or a twin-purge valve arrangement is fitted, depending on model. The purge valve(s) is/are mounted on the right-hand side of the engine compartment (see illustrations).
8 To renew a purge valve, first disconnect the battery negative terminal. Depress the retaining clip, and disconnect the wiring connector from the valve.
9 Disconnect the hoses from either end of the valve, then release the valve from its retaining clip and remove it from the engine compartment, noting which way round it is fitted.
10 Refitting is a reversal of the removal procedure, ensuring that the valve is fitted the correct way round and that the hoses are securely connected.

Exhaust emission control

Testing

11 The performance of the catalytic converter can be checked only by measuring the idle mixture setting (exhaust gas CO

content) using an accurately calibrated exhaust gas analyser, as described in Chapter 1.
12 If the CO level at the tailpipe is too high, the vehicle should be taken to a Citroën dealer so that the complete fuel injection and ignition systems, including the lambda sensor, can be thoroughly checked using the special diagnostic equipment.
13 Once this has been done, any fault must lie in the catalytic converter, which should be renewed as described in Part B or C of this Chapter (as applicable).

Catalytic converter - renewal

14 Refer to Part B or C of this Chapter (as applicable).

Lambda sensor - renewal

Note: *The lambda sensor is fragile, and will not work if it is dropped or knocked, if its power supply is disrupted, or if any cleaning materials are used on it.*

15 On 1124 cc and 1360 cc models, the lambda sensor is screwed into the top of the exhaust front pipe. Trace the wiring back from the sensor to the engine compartment junction box (see illustrations). Open the junction box, then unclip the relay plate and withdraw it from the box, to gain access to the sensor wiring connectors. Disconnect both wiring connectors, and withdraw the wiring from the bottom of the box.

2.7b Single purge valve is located in the front right-hand corner of the engine compartment - 1998 cc 16-valve model shown

2.15a On 1124 cc and 1360 cc models, the lambda sensor is screwed into the top of the exhaust front pipe . . .

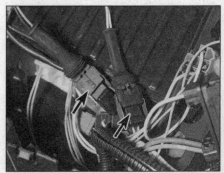

2.15b . . . and the wiring connectors (arrowed) are located inside the junction box

2.16 On 1580 cc and larger models, the lambda sensor wiring connectors are clipped onto the back of the battery/ECU box

16 On 1580 cc and larger-engined models, the lambda sensor is screwed into the base of the exhaust front pipe. Firmly apply the handbrake, then jack up the front of the car and support it on axle stands. Trace the wiring back from the lambda sensor to the engine compartment. Release the wiring connectors from the rear of the battery/ECU box, and disconnect them from the main wiring loom **(see illustration)**.

17 Unscrew the sensor from the exhaust system front pipe, and remove it along with its sealing washer.

18 Refitting is a reverse of the removal procedure, using a new sealing washer. Ensure that the sensor is securely tightened. Check that the wiring is correctly routed, and in no danger of contacting either the exhaust system or the engine.

3 Catalytic converter - general information and precautions

The catalytic converter is a reliable and simple device, which needs no maintenance in itself, but there are some facts of which an owner should be aware, if the converter is to function properly for its full service life.

(a) DO NOT use leaded (UK "4-star") petrol in a car equipped with a catalytic converter - the lead will coat the precious metals, reducing their converting efficiency, and will eventually destroy the converter.

(b) Always keep the ignition and fuel systems well-maintained in accordance with the manufacturer's schedule, as given in Chapter 1. In particular, ensure that the air cleaner filter element, the fuel filter (where fitted) and the spark plugs are renewed at the correct interval. If the intake air/fuel mixture is allowed to become too rich due to neglect, unburned fuel will enter the catalytic converter, overheating the element and eventually destroying the converter.

(c) If the engine develops a misfire, do not drive the car at all (or at least as little as possible) until the fault is cured - the misfire will allow unburned fuel to enter the converter, which will result in its overheating, as noted above.

(d) DO NOT push- or tow-start the car - this will soak the catalytic converter in unburned fuel, causing it to overheat when the engine does start - see (b) or (c) above.

(e) DO NOT switch off the ignition at high engine speeds - ie do not "blip" the throttle immediately before switching off the engine. If the ignition is switched off at anything above idle speed, unburned fuel will enter the (very hot) catalytic converter, with the possible risk of its igniting on the element and damaging the converter.

(f) DO NOT use fuel or engine oil additives - these may contain substances harmful to the catalytic converter.

(g) DO NOT continue to use the car if the engine burns oil to the extent of leaving a visible trail of blue smoke - the unburned carbon deposits will clog the converter passages, and reduce its efficiency; in severe cases, the element will overheat.

(h) Remember that the catalytic converter operates at very high temperatures - hence the heat shields on the car's underbody - and the casing will become hot enough to ignite combustible materials which brush against it. DO NOT, therefore, park the car in dry undergrowth, or over long grass or piles of dead leaves.

(i) Remember that the catalytic converter is FRAGILE - do not strike it with tools during servicing work, and take great care when working on the exhaust system. Ensure that the converter is well clear of any jacks or other lifting gear used to raise the car, and do not drive the car over rough ground, road humps, etc, in such a way as to "ground" the exhaust system.

(j) In some cases, particularly when the car is new and/or is used for stop/start driving, a sulphurous smell (like that of rotten eggs) may be noticed from the exhaust. This is common to many catalytic converter-equipped cars, and seems to be due to the small amount of sulphur found in some petrols reacting with hydrogen in the exhaust, to produce hydrogen sulphide (H_2S) gas; while this gas is toxic, it is not produced in sufficient amounts to be a problem. Once the car has covered a few thousand miles, the problem should disappear - in the meanwhile, a change of driving style, or of the brand of petrol used, may effect a solution.

(k) The catalytic converter, used on a well-maintained car, should last for between 50 000 and 100 000 miles - from this point on, the CO level should be carefully checked at all specified service intervals, to ensure that the converter is still operating efficiently. If the converter is no longer effective, it must be renewed.

4D

Notes

Chapter 5 Engine electrical systems

Contents

Alternator - removal and refitting 13	Ignition switch - removal and refitting 18
Alternator brushes and regulator - inspection and renewal 14	Ignition system - general information 5
Alternator drivebelt - removal, refitting and tensioning 12	Ignition system - testing 6
Battery - removal and refitting 4	Ignition system amplifier unit(s) - removal and refitting 9
Battery - testing and charging 3	Ignition timing - checking and adjustment 10
Battery check ....See "Weekly checks"	Oil level sensor - removal and refitting 20
Charging system - testing 11	Oil pressure warning light switch - removal and refitting 19
Distributor - removal and refitting 8	Oil temperature sensor - removal and refitting 21
Electrical fault finding - general information 2	Starter motor - brush renewal 17
Electrical system check .... See Chapter 1	Starter motor - removal and refitting 16
General information and precautions 1	Starting system - testing 15
Ignition HT coil(s) - removal, testing and refitting 7	

Degrees of difficulty

Easy, suitable for novice with little experience	**Fairly easy,** suitable for beginner with some experience	**Fairly difficult,** suitable for competent DIY mechanic	**Difficult,** suitable for experienced DIY mechanic	**Very difficult,** suitable for expert DIY or professional

5

Specifications

System type .... 12-volt, negative earth

Battery

Type .... Lead acid
Make .... Fulmen, Delco or Steco
Charge condition:
  Poor .... 12.5 volts
  Normal .... 12.6 volts
  Good .... 12.7 volts

Ignition system

System type*:
1124 cc (H1A engine) models .... Breakerless electronic, with distributor
1124 cc (HDZ engine) models, up to mid-1996 .... Breakerless electronic, with distributor
1124 cc (HDZ engine) models, mid-1996 onwards .... Static (distributorless) system controlled by engine management ECU
1360 cc (K2D and KDY engine) models .... Breakerless electronic, with distributor
1360 cc (KDX and KFX engine) models .... Static (distributorless) system controlled by engine management ECU
1580 cc, 1761 cc, 1905 cc (D6E engine) and 1998 cc models ..... Static (distributorless) system controlled by engine management ECU
1905 cc (DKZ engine) models .... Distributor-type system, controlled by engine management ECU

*Refer to text for further information on each system

Ignition system (continued)

Firing order . . . .   1-3-4-2 (No 1 cylinder at transmission end of engine)
Ignition timing:
   1124 cc and 1360 cc models with a distributor . . . .   8° BTDC @ idling speed
   All other models . . . .   Controlled by ECU - see text
Ignition HT coil resistances*:
   1124 cc and 1360 cc models with a distributor:
      Primary windings . . . .   0.8 ohms
      Secondary windings . . . .   6500 ohms
   1124 cc and 1360 cc models with distributorless system:
      Primary windings . . . .   0.6 to 0.8 ohms
      Secondary windings . . . .   19 000 ohms
   1580 cc and 1905 cc models:
      Primary windings . . . .   0.8 ohms
      Secondary windings - Bosch coil . . . .   14 000 ohms
      Secondary windings - Sagem coil . . . .   7 000 ohms
      Secondary windings - Valeo coil . . . .   8 600 ohms
   1761 cc models . . . .   N/A
   1998 cc models:
      Primary windings . . . .   0.6 to 0.8 ohms
      Secondary windings . . . .   N/A
*Values given are only accurate when the coil is at 20°C. Where no values are quoted, refer to a Citroën dealer for advice.

Alternator

Type . . . .   Valeo, Bosch or Mitsubishi

Starter motor

Type . . . .   Valeo or Bosch

---

1 General information and precautions

General information

The engine electrical system includes all charging, starting and ignition system components. Because of their engine-related functions, these components are covered separately from the body electrical devices such as the lights, instruments, etc (which are covered in Chapter 12).

The electrical system is of the 12-volt negative earth type.

The battery is of the low-maintenance or "maintenance-free" ("sealed for life") type, and is charged by the alternator, which is belt-driven from the crankshaft pulley.

The starter motor is of the pre-engaged type, incorporating an integral solenoid. On starting, the solenoid moves the drive pinion into engagement with the flywheel ring gear before the starter motor is energised. Once the engine has started, a one-way clutch prevents the motor armature being driven by the engine until the pinion disengages from the flywheel.

Refer to Section 5 for further information on the various ignition systems.

Precautions

Further details of the various systems are given in the relevant Sections of this Chapter. While some repair procedures are given, the usual course of action is to renew the component concerned. The owner whose interest extends beyond mere component renewal should obtain a copy of the "Automobile Electrical & Electronic Systems Manual", available from the publishers of this manual.

It is necessary to take extra care when working on the electrical system, to avoid damage to semi-conductor devices (diodes and transistors), and to avoid the risk of personal injury. In addition to the precautions given in "Safety first!" at the beginning of this manual, observe the following when working on the system.

Always remove rings, watches, etc before working on the electrical system. Even with the battery disconnected, capacitive discharge could occur if a component's live terminal is earthed through a metal object. This could cause a shock or nasty burn.

Do not reverse the battery connections. Components such as the alternator, fuel injection electronic control unit, or any other components having semi-conductor circuitry, could be irreparably damaged.

If the engine is being started using jump leads and a slave battery, connect the batteries positive-to-positive and negative-to-negative (see "Booster battery (jump) starting"). This also applies when connecting a battery charger.

Never disconnect the battery terminals, the alternator, any electrical wiring or any test instruments when the engine is running.

Do not allow the engine to turn the alternator when the alternator is not connected.

Never "test" for alternator output by "flashing" the output lead to earth.

Never use an ohmmeter of the type incorporating a hand-cranked generator for circuit or continuity testing.

Always ensure that the battery negative lead is disconnected when working on the electrical system.

Before using electric-arc welding equipment on the car, disconnect the battery, alternator and components such as the fuel injection/ignition electronic control unit, to protect them from the risk of damage.

The radio/cassette unit fitted as standard equipment by Citroën is equipped with a built-in security code, to deter thieves. If the power source to the unit is cut, the anti-theft system will activate. Even if the power source is immediately reconnected, the radio/cassette unit will not function until the correct security code has been entered. Therefore, if you do not know the correct security code for the radio/cassette unit, do not disconnect the battery negative terminal of the battery, or remove the radio/cassette unit from the vehicle. Refer to "Radio/cassette unit anti-theft system precaution" Section at the beginning of this manual for details of how to enter the security code.

2 Electrical fault finding - general information

Refer to Chapter 12, Section 2.

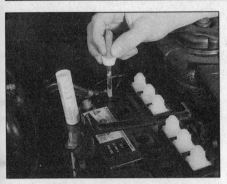

3.1 Using a hydrometer to check the battery electrolyte specific gravity

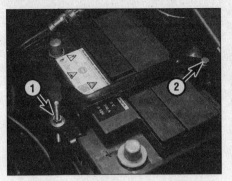

4.4 Battery clamp plate securing nut (1) and bolt (2)

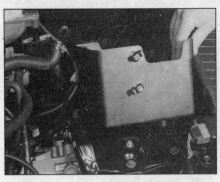

4.6 Removing the plastic battery tray

3 Battery - testing and charging

Standard and low-maintenance battery - testing

1 If the vehicle covers a small annual mileage, it is worthwhile checking the specific gravity of the electrolyte every three months, to determine the state of charge of the battery. Use a hydrometer (these are readily-available from motor accessory outlets) to make the check, and compare the results with the following table (see illustration). Note that the specific gravity readings assume an electrolyte temperature of 15°C (60°F); for every 10°C (18°F) below 15°C (60°F), subtract 0.007. For every 10°C (18°F) above 15°C (60°F), add 0.007.

	Ambient temperature above 25°C (77°F)	Ambient temperature below 25°C (77°F)
Fully-charged	1.210 to 1.230	1.270 to 1.290
70% charged	1.170 to 1.190	1.230 to 1.250
Fully-discharged	1.050 to 1.070	1.110 to 1.130

2 If the battery condition is suspect, first check the specific gravity of electrolyte in each cell. A variation of 0.040 or more between any cells indicates loss of electrolyte or deterioration of the internal plates.
3 If the specific gravity variation is 0.040 or more, the battery should be renewed. If the cell variation is satisfactory but the battery is discharged, it should be charged as described later in this Section.

Maintenance-free battery - testing

4 In cases where a "sealed for life" maintenance-free battery is fitted, topping-up and testing of the electrolyte in each cell is not possible. The condition of the battery can therefore only be tested using a battery condition indicator or a voltmeter.
5 Certain models my be fitted with a "Delco" type maintenance-free battery, with a built-in charge condition indicator. The indicator is located in the top of the battery casing, and indicates the condition of the battery by its colour. If the indicator shows green, then the battery is in a good state of charge. If the indicator turns darker, eventually to black, then the battery requires charging, as described later in this Section. If the indicator shows clear/yellow, then the electrolyte level in the battery is too low to allow further use, and the battery should be renewed. *Do not* attempt to charge, load or jump-start a battery when the indicator shows clear/yellow.
6 If testing the battery using a voltmeter, connect the voltmeter across the battery, and compare the result with those given in the Specifications under "charge condition". The test is only accurate if the battery has not been subjected to any kind of charge for the previous six hours. If this is not the case, switch on the headlights for 30 seconds, then switch them off and wait four to five minutes before testing the battery. All other electrical circuits must be switched off, so check that the doors and tailgate are fully shut when making the test.
7 Voltage readings corresponding to the various states of charge are given in the Specifications.
8 If the battery is to be charged, remove it from the vehicle (Section 4) and charge it as described later in this Section.

Standard and low-maintenance battery - charging

Note: *The following is intended as a guide only. Always refer to the manufacturer's recommendations (often printed on a label attached to the battery) before charging a battery.*
9 Charge the battery at a rate of 3.5 to 4 amps, and continue to charge the battery at this rate until no further rise in specific gravity is noted over a four-hour period.
10 Alternatively, a trickle charger, charging at the rate of 1.5 amps, can safely be used overnight.
11 Special rapid "boost" charges, which are claimed to restore the power of the battery in 1 to 2 hours, are not recommended, as they can cause serious damage to the battery plates through overheating.
12 While charging the battery, note that the temperature of the electrolyte should never exceed 37.8°C (100°F).

Maintenance-free battery - charging

Note: *The following is intended as a guide only. Always refer to the battery manufacturer's recommendations (often printed on a label attached to the battery) before charging.*
13 This battery type takes considerably longer to fully recharge than the standard type, the time taken being dependent on the extent of discharge, but it can take anything up to three days.
14 A constant-voltage type charger is required, to be set, when connected, to 13.9 to 14.9 volts with a charger current below 25 amps. Using this method, the battery should be useable within three hours, giving a voltage reading of 12.5 volts, but this is for a partially-discharged battery; as mentioned, full charging can take considerably longer.
15 If the battery is to be charged from a fully-discharged state (condition reading less than 12.2 volts), have it recharged by your Citroën dealer or local automotive electrician, as the charge rate is higher, and constant supervision during charging is necessary.

4 Battery - removal and refitting

Removal

1 The battery is located on the left-hand side of the engine compartment.
2 Disconnect the lead(s) at the negative (earth) terminal, by unscrewing the retaining nut and removing the terminal clamp.
3 Disconnect the positive terminal lead(s) in the same way.
4 Unscrew the nut and the bolt securing the battery clamp plate, then lift the clamp plate from the top of the battery (see illustration).
5 Lift the battery from the plastic tray.
6 If desired, the plastic tray can be lifted from the metal support plate, after unclipping any relevant hoses and wiring from its sides (see illustration).

5

Refitting

7 Refitting is a reversal of removal, but smear petroleum jelly on the terminals when reconnecting the leads, and always reconnect the positive lead first, and the negative lead last.

5 Ignition system - general information

1124 cc and 1360 cc carburettor models

1 On 1124 cc and 1360 cc carburettor models, a breakerless electronic ignition system is used. The system basically comprises the HT ignition coil and the distributor, both of which are mounted on the left-hand end of the cylinder head, the distributor being driven off the end of the camshaft.

2 The distributor contains a reluctor mounted onto its shaft, and a magnet and stator fixed to its body. The ignition amplifier unit is also mounted onto the side of the distributor body. The system operates as follows.

3 When the ignition is switched on but the engine is stationary, the transistors in the amplifier unit prevent current flowing through the ignition system primary (LT) circuit.

4 As the crankshaft rotates, the reluctor moves through the magnetic field created by the stator. When the reluctor teeth are in alignment with the stator projections, a small AC voltage is created. The amplifier unit uses this voltage to switch the transistors in the unit and complete the ignition system primary (LT) circuit.

5 As the reluctor teeth move out of alignment with the stator projections, the AC voltage changes, and the transistors in the amplifier unit are switched again to interrupt the primary (LT) circuit. This causes a high voltage to be induced in the coil secondary (HT) windings, which then travels down the HT lead to the distributor and onto the relevant spark plug.

6 A TDC sensor is fitted to the rear of the flywheel, but the sensor is not part of the ignition system; it is for diagnostic purposes only.

Early 1124 cc and 1360 cc fuel injected models

7 On 1124 cc and 1360 cc fuel-injected models equipped with the Bosch Monopoint A2.2 fuel injection system, a breakerless electronic ignition system is fitted. This operates in the same way as that described above for the carburettor models.

8 In addition to the system components described above, the system is equipped with an ignition timing retard system. This limits the nitrous oxide (Nox) content of the exhaust gases by reducing the ignition advance at certain engine temperatures. The system is controlled by the fuel injection electronic control unit (ECU). The ECU has control over an electrically-operated solenoid valve, mounted in the left-hand rear corner of the engine compartment, which is fitted in the vacuum pipe linking the distributor vacuum diaphragm unit to the inlet manifold **(see illustration)**. At certain engine temperatures, the ECU switches off the solenoid valve, which then cuts off the vacuum supply to the distributor vacuum diaphragm, thereby reducing the ignition advance.

9 A TDC sensor is fitted to the rear of the flywheel, but the sensor is not part of the ignition system; it is for diagnostic purposes only.

Later 1124 cc and 1360 cc fuel injected models, and all 1580 cc and 1761 cc 8-valve models

10 On these models, the ignition system is integrated with the fuel injection system, to form a combined engine management system under the control of one ECU (refer to Chapter 4 for further information).

11 The ignition side of the system is of the static (distributorless) type, consisting simply of a four-output ignition coil. The ignition coil actually consists of two separate HT coils, which supply two cylinders each (one coil supplies cylinders 1 and 4, the other cylin-ders 2 and 3). Under the control of the ECU, the ignition coil operates on the "wasted-spark" principle. The spark plugs are fired in two pairs, twice for every complete cycle of the engine. One plug of each pair will fire on a compression stroke, and one on an exhaust stroke; the spark on the exhaust stroke has no effect on the running of the engine, and is therefore "wasted". The ECU uses the inputs from the various sensors to calculate the required ignition advance setting and coil charging time.

1761 cc 16-valve models

12 On 1761 cc 16-valve engine models, the ignition side of the system is also of the static (distributorless) type, and consists primarily of four ignition coils located in an ignition coil unit fitted to the centre of the cylinder head cover. The coils are integral with the spark plug caps and are pushed directly onto the spark plugs, one for each plug. This removes the need for any HT leads connecting the coils to the plugs. The ECU uses the inputs from the various sensors to calculate the required ignition advance setting and calculate the coil charging time.

1905 cc models

13 On 1905 cc models, the ignition system is integrated with the fuel injection system, to form a combined engine management system under the control of one ECU via the ignition amplifier module. (Refer to Chapter 4 for further information.) However, two different ignition set-ups are used, depending on engine type.

14 On models not equipped with a catalytic converter (D6E engine with Bosch Motronic MP3.1 system), the ignition system is of the static (distributorless) type, with a four-output ignition coil. The system functions as described above, in paragraph 11.

15 On models with a catalytic converter (DKZ engine with Bosch Motronic M1.3

5.8 Ignition timing retard system solenoid valve - 1124 cc and early 1360 cc fuel-injected models

system), the ignition system uses a conventional HT coil and distributor to distribute the HT voltage to the relevant spark plug.

1998 cc 8-valve models

16 On 1998 cc 8-valve models, the ignition system is as described above for later 1360 cc, 1580 cc and 1761 cc models, but with the addition of a knock sensor incorporated into the ignition system. The knock sensor is mounted onto the cylinder head, and operates as described below for 1998 cc 16-valve models.

1998 cc 16-valve models

17 The ignition system on 1998 cc 16-valve models is of the static (distributorless) type. However, the system differs from the other static systems in that it is a "sequential" system, with each plug sparking individually once every cycle of the engine, rather than operating on the "wasted-spark" principle where the plugs spark in pairs, firing twice for every cycle of the engine.

18 The ignition system components consist of two amplifier modules, four ignition HT coils, and a knock sensor. The ignition system is integrated with the fuel injection system, to form a combined engine management system under the control of one ECU via the ignition amplifier modules. Refer to Chapter 4 for further information.

19 Each ignition amplifier module operates two HT coils; the ignition HT coils are integral with the plug caps, and are pushed directly onto the spark plugs, one for each plug. This removes the need for any HT leads connecting the coils to the plugs. The ECU uses the inputs from the various sensors to calculate the required ignition advance setting and coil charging time.

20 The knock sensor is mounted onto the cylinder head, and prevents the engine "pinking" under load. The sensor detects abnormal vibration, and is thus able to detect the knocking which occurs when the engine starts to "pink" (pre-ignite). The knock sensor sends an electrical signal to the ECU, which in turn retards the ignition advance setting until the "pinking" ceases.

6 Ignition system - testing

Ignition systems with a distributor

Note: *Refer to the precautions given in Section 1 of this Chapter before starting work. Always switch off the ignition before disconnecting or connecting any component, and when using a multi-meter to check resistances.*

General

1 The components of electronic ignition systems are normally very reliable; most faults are far more likely to be due to loose or dirty connections, or to "tracking" of HT voltage due to dirt, dampness or damaged insulation, than to the failure of any of the system's components. *Always* check all wiring thoroughly before condemning an electrical component, and work methodically to eliminate all other possibilities before deciding that a particular component is faulty.

2 The old practice of checking for a spark by holding the live end of an HT lead a short distance away from the engine is *not* recommended; not only is there a high risk of a powerful electric shock, but the HT coil or amplifier unit will be damaged. Similarly, *never* try to "diagnose" misfires by pulling off one HT lead at a time.

Engine will not start

3 If the engine either will not turn at all, or only turns very slowly, check the battery and starter motor. Connect a voltmeter across the battery terminals (meter positive probe to battery positive terminal), disconnect the ignition coil HT lead from the distributor cap and earth it, then note the voltage reading obtained while turning the engine on the starter for (no more than) ten seconds. If the reading obtained is less than approximately 9.5 volts, first check the battery, starter motor and charging system as described in the relevant Sections of this Chapter.

4 If the engine turns at normal speed but will not start, check the HT circuit by connecting a timing light (following the equipment manufacturer's instructions) and turning the engine on the starter motor. If the light flashes, voltage is reaching the spark plugs, so these should be checked first. If the light does not flash, check the HT leads themselves, followed by the distributor cap, carbon brush and rotor arm, using the information given in Chapter 1.

5 If there is a spark, check the fuel system for faults, referring to the relevant Part of Chapter 4 for further information.

6 If there is still no spark, check the voltage at the ignition HT coil "+" terminal; it should be the same as the battery voltage (ie, at least 11.7 volts). If the voltage at the coil is less than battery voltage by 1 volt or more, check the feed back through the fusebox and ignition switch to the battery and its earth, until the fault is found.

7 If the feed to the HT coil is sound, check the coil's primary and secondary winding resistance as described later in this Section. Renew the coil if faulty, but be check carefully the condition of the LT connections themselves before doing so, to ensure that the fault is not due to dirty or poorly-fastened connectors.

8 If the HT coil is in good condition, the fault is probably within the amplifier unit or distributor stator assembly (1124 cc and 1360 cc models) or the engine management ECU (1905 cc models). Testing of these components should be entrusted to a Citroën dealer.

Engine misfires

9 An irregular misfire suggests either a loose connection or intermittent fault on the primary circuit, or an HT fault on the coil side of the rotor arm.

10 With the ignition switched off, check carefully through the system, ensuring that all connections are clean and securely fastened. If the equipment is available, check the LT circuit as described above.

11 Check that the HT coil, the distributor cap and the HT leads are clean and dry. Check the leads themselves and the spark plugs (by substitution, if necessary), then check the distributor cap, carbon brush and rotor arm as described in Chapter 1.

12 Regular misfiring is almost certainly due to a fault in the distributor cap, HT leads or spark plugs. Use a timing light (paragraph 4 above) to check whether HT voltage is present at all leads.

13 If HT voltage is not present on any particular lead, the fault will be in that lead, or in the distributor cap. If HT is present on all leads, the fault will be in the spark plugs; check and renew them if there is any doubt about their condition.

14 If no HT voltage is present, check the HT coil; its secondary windings may be breaking down under load.

Static (distributorless) ignition systems

15 If a fault appears in the engine management (fuel injection/ignition) system, first ensure that the fault is not due to a poor electrical connection, or to poor maintenance; ie, check that the air cleaner filter element is clean, that the spark plugs are in good condition and correctly gapped, and that the engine breather hoses are clear and undamaged. Refer to Chapter 1 for further information. Also check that the accelerator cable is correctly adjusted, as described in Chapter 4. If the engine is running very roughly, check the compression pressures as described in Chapter 2, and the valve clearances as described in Chapter 1.

16 If these checks fail to reveal the cause of the problem, the vehicle should be taken to a suitably-equipped Citroën dealer for testing. A wiring block connector is incorporated in the engine management circuit, into which a special electronic diagnostic tester can be plugged. The tester will locate the fault quickly and simply, alleviating the need to test all the system components individually, which is a time-consuming operation that carries a high risk of damaging the ECU.

17 The only ignition system checks which can be carried out by the home mechanic are those described in Chapter 1 relating to the spark plugs, and also the ignition coil test described in this Chapter. If necessary, the system wiring and wiring connectors can be checked as described in Chapter 12, ensuring that the ECU wiring connector(s) have first been disconnected.

7 Ignition HT coil(s) - removal, testing and refitting

Removal

1124 cc and 1360 cc models with a distributor

1 Disconnect the battery negative terminal.

2 Disconnect the hot-air intake hose from the exhaust manifold shroud and air temperature control valve, and remove it from the engine. Release the intake duct fastener, and position the duct clear of the coil.

3 Disconnect the wiring connector from the capacitor mounted on the coil mounting bracket, and release the TDC sensor wiring connector from the front of the bracket **(see illustration)**.

4 Disconnect the HT lead from the coil, then

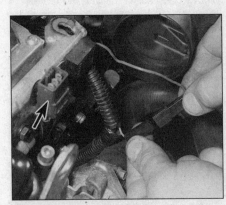

7.3 On 1124 cc and 1360 cc models, disconnect the capacitor wiring connector, and release the TDC sensor connector (arrowed) . . .

7.4a . . . then disconnect the HT lead . . .

7.4b . . . and wiring connector (arrowed) from the ignition HT coil

7.5a Undo the two retaining bolts (arrowed) . . .

depress the retaining clip and disconnect the coil wiring connector **(see illustrations)**.
5 Slacken and remove the two retaining bolts, and remove the coil and mounting bracket from the cylinder head **(see illustrations)**. Where necessary, slacken and remove the four screws and nuts, and separate the HT coil and mounting bracket.

1905 cc models with a distributor

6 Disconnect the battery negative terminal.
7 Depress the retaining clip, and disconnect the wiring connector from the ignition HT coil.
8 Disconnect the HT lead from the coil.
9 Slacken and remove the four HT coil retaining screws, and remove the coil from the top of the inlet manifold.

1124 cc, 1360 cc and 1905 cc models (distributorless system), and all 1580 cc, 1761 cc and 1998 cc 8-valve models

10 Disconnect the battery negative terminal. The ignition HT coil is mounted on the left-hand end of the cylinder head.
11 Depress the retaining clip, and disconnect the wiring connector from the HT coil **(see illustration)**.
12 Make a note of the correct fitted positions of the HT leads, then disconnect them from the coil terminals. Note that, on genuine Citroën leads, each HT lead is marked with its cylinder number, indicated by blocks printed near the end of the lead; the coil terminals are also numbered for identification.

13 Undo the four retaining screws securing the coil to its mounting bracket, and remove it from the engine compartment.

1761 cc 16-valve models

14 Disconnect the battery negative terminal. There are four separate ignition HT coils, one on the top of each spark plug.
15 Disconnect the wiring connector at the left-hand end of the coil unit.
16 Undo the six Allen bolts and lift the coil unit upwards, off the spark plugs and from its location between the camshaft covers. The individual coils can now be removed as required.

1998 cc 16-valve models

17 Disconnect the battery negative terminal. There are four separate ignition HT coils, one on the top of each spark plug.
18 To gain access to the coils, undo the eight retaining bolts, noting the correct fitted position of the wiring clip, and remove the access cover from the centre of the cylinder head cover.
19 To remove an HT coil, depress the retaining clip and disconnect the wiring connector, then pull the coil off the spark plug and remove it along with its rubber seal.

Testing

20 Testing the coil involves using a multimeter set to its resistance function, to check the primary (LT "+" to "-" terminals) and secondary (LT "+" to HT lead terminal) windings for continuity. Bear in mind that on the four-output,

static type HT coil, there are two sets of each windings. Compare the results obtained to those given in the Specifications at the start of this Chapter, where available. Note that the resistance of the coil windings will vary slightly according to the coil temperature; the results in the Specifications are approximate values, and are accurate only when the coil is at 20°C. Where no values are quoted, refer to your Citroën dealer for advice.
21 Check that there is no continuity between the HT lead terminal and the coil body/mounting bracket.
22 If the coil is thought to be faulty, have your findings confirmed by a Citroën dealer or other specialist before renewing the coil.

Refitting

23 Refitting is a reversal of the removal procedure, ensuring that the wiring connectors are securely reconnected and, where necessary, that the HT leads are correctly connected.

8 Distributor - removal and refitting

Removal

1124 cc and 1360 cc models

1 Disconnect the battery negative terminal. If necessary, to improve access to the distributor, remove the ignition HT coil as

7.5b . . . and remove the coil and mounting bracket from the engine

7.11 Disconnecting the wiring connector (A) from the ignition HT coil - 1580 cc engine shown. Note the HT lead markings (arrowed)

8.2a Peel back the waterproof cover . . .

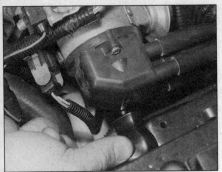

8.2b . . . then undo the retaining screws . . .

8.2c . . . and remove the cap from the end of the distributor

8.3a Disconnect the distributor wiring connector . . .

described in Section 7, and the air intake duct as described in Chapter 4 (as appropriate).

2 Peel back the waterproof cover, slacken and remove the distributor cap retaining screws, then remove the cap and position it clear of the distributor body **(see illustrations)**. Recover the seal from the cap.

3 Depress the retaining clip, and disconnect the wiring connector from the distributor. Disconnect the hose from the vacuum diaphragm unit **(see illustrations)**.

4 Check the cylinder head and distributor flange for signs of alignment marks. If no marks are visible, using a scriber or a marker pen, mark the relationship of the distributor body to the cylinder head. Slacken and remove the two mounting nuts and retaining plates, and withdraw the distributor from the cylinder head **(see illustration)**. Remove the O-ring from the end of the distributor body, and discard it; a new one must be used on refitting.

1905 cc models

5 Disconnect the battery negative terminal. If necessary, to improve access to the distributor, remove the airflow meter as described in Chapter 4.

6 Peel back the waterproof cover, slacken and remove the distributor cap retaining screws, then remove the cap and position it clear of the distributor body. Recover the seal from the cap.

7 Slacken and remove the two mounting bolts and washers, and withdraw the distributor from the cylinder head. Remove the O-ring from the end of the distributor body, and discard it; a new one must be used on refitting.

Refitting

8 Lubricate the new O-ring with a smear of engine oil, and fit it to the groove in the distributor body. Examine the distributor cap seal for wear or damage, and renew if necessary.

9 Align the distributor rotor shaft drive coupling key with the slots in the camshaft end, noting that the slots are offset to ensure that the distributor can only be fitted in one position. Carefully insert the distributor into the cylinder head, rotating the rotor arm slightly to ensure the coupling is correctly engaged.

1124 cc and 1360 cc models

10 Align the marks noted or made on removal, and install the distributor retaining plates and nuts, tightening them only lightly.

11 Ensure that the seal is correctly located in its groove, then refit the cap assembly to the distributor and tighten its retaining screws securely. Fold the waterproof cover back over the distributor cap, ensuring that it is correctly located.

12 Reconnect the vacuum hose to the diaphragm unit and the distributor wiring

connector. Where necessary, refit the ignition HT coil as described in Section 7, and the air intake duct as described in Chapter 4.

13 Check and, if necessary, adjust the ignition timing as described in Section 10, then fully tighten the distributor mounting nuts.

1905 cc models

14 Refit the distributor mounting bolts and washers and tighten the bolts.

15 Ensure that the seal is correctly located in its groove, then refit the cap assembly to the distributor and tighten its retaining screws securely. Fold the waterproof cover back over the distributor cap, ensuring that it is correctly located.

16 Where necessary, refit the airflow meter as described in the relevant Part of Chapter 4.

9 Ignition system amplifier unit(s) - removal and refitting

Removal

1 Disconnect the battery negative terminal.

1124 cc and 1360 cc models

2 The amplifier unit is mounted onto the side of the distributor body **(see illustration)**.

3 To improve access to the unit, disengage the hot-air intake hose from the control valve and manifold shroud, and remove it from the

8.3b . . . and the vacuum diaphragm hose . . .

8.4 . . . then undo the retaining nuts and remove the distributor

9.2 On 1124 cc and 1360 cc models, the ignition amplifier unit is secured to the side of the distributor by two screws

5

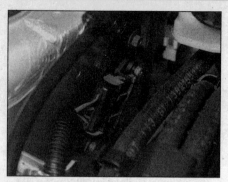

9.4 On 1905 cc models, the ignition amplifier unit is situated in the right-hand corner of the engine compartment

9.6 On 1998 cc 16-valve models, both ignition amplifier units are situated in the left-hand corner of the engine compartment

vehicle. Disconnect the wiring connector, undo the two retaining screws and remove the amplifier unit.

1905 cc models

4 The amplifier unit is situated in the right-hand rear corner of the engine compartment, mounted onto the wing valance **(see illustration)**.

5 To remove the unit, disconnect the wiring connector, undo the two retaining screws and remove the amplifier from its mounting bracket.

1998 cc 16-valve models

6 Both amplifier units are situated in the left-hand rear corner of the engine compartment, mounted onto the wing valance **(see illustration)**.

7 To remove either unit, disconnect the wiring connector, undo the two retaining screws and remove the amplifier unit from its mounting bracket.

Refitting

8 Refitting is a reverse of the removal procedure.

---

10 Ignition timing - checking and adjustment

1124 cc and 1360 cc models with a distributor

1 To check the ignition timing, a stroboscopic timing light will be required. It is also recommended that the flywheel timing mark is highlighted as follows.

2 Remove the plug from the aperture on the front of the transmission clutch housing. Using a socket and suitable extension bar on the crankshaft pulley bolt, slowly turn the engine over until the timing mark (a straight line) scribed on the edge of the flywheel appears in the aperture. Highlight the line with quick-drying white paint - typist's correction fluid is ideal **(see illustrations)**.

3 Start the engine, allow it to warm up to normal operating temperature, and then stop it.

4 Disconnect the vacuum hose from the distributor diaphragm, and plug the hose end.

5 Connect the timing light to No 1 cylinder spark plug lead (No 1 cylinder is at the transmission end of the engine) as described in the timing light manufacturer's instructions.

6 Start the engine, allowing it to idle at the specified speed, and point the timing light at the transmission housing aperture. The flywheel timing mark should be aligned with the appropriate notch on the timing plate (refer to the Specifications for the correct timing setting). The numbers on the plate indicate degrees Before Top Dead Centre (BTDC).

7 If adjustment is necessary, slacken the two distributor mounting nuts, then slowly rotate the distributor body as required until the flywheel mark and the timing plate notch are brought into alignment. Once the marks are correctly aligned, hold the distributor stationary and tighten its mounting nuts. Recheck that the timing marks are still correctly aligned and, if necessary, repeat the adjustment procedure.

8 When the timing is correctly set, increase the engine speed, and check that the pulley mark advances to beyond the beginning of the timing plate reference marks, returning to the specified mark when the engine is allowed to idle. This shows that the centrifugal advance mechanism is functioning; if a detailed check is thought necessary, this must be left to a Citroën dealer having the

necessary equipment. Reconnect the vacuum hose to the distributor, and repeat the check. The rate of advance should significantly increase if the vacuum diaphragm is functioning correctly, but again a detailed check must be left to a Citroën dealer.

9 When the ignition timing is correct, stop the engine and disconnect the timing light.

All other models (distributorless ignition system)

10 On models with static (distributorless) ignition systems, there are no timing marks on the flywheel or crankshaft pulley. The timing is constantly being monitored and adjusted by the engine management ECU, and nominal values cannot be given. Therefore, it is not possible for the home mechanic to check the ignition timing.

11 The only way in which the ignition timing can be checked is using special electronic test equipment, connected to the engine management system diagnostic connector (refer to Chapter 4 for further information).

12 On 1580 cc models and 1998 cc 8-valve models, with Magneti Marelli engine management systems, and 1761 cc models with the Bosch Motronic MP5.1 system, adjustment of the ignition timing is possible. However, adjustments can be made only by re-programming the ECU using the special test equipment.

13 On all other models, with Bosch engine management systems, no adjustment of the ignition timing is possible. Should the ignition timing be incorrect, then a fault must be present in the engine management system.

---

11 Charging system - testing

Note: *Refer to the warnings given in "Safety first!" and in Section 1 of this Chapter before starting work.*

1 If the ignition/no-charge warning light fails to illuminate when the ignition is switched on, first check the alternator wiring connections for security. If satisfactory, check that the warning light bulb has not blown, and that the

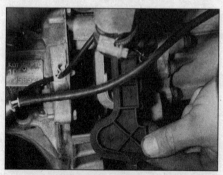

10.2a On 1124 cc and 1360 cc models with a distributor, remove the plug from the transmission housing . . .

10.2b . . . to reveal the timing plate and flywheel timing mark (arrowed)

13.3 Undo the retaining nuts and disconnect the wiring from the alternator - 1905 cc model shown

13.4a Slacken and remove the alternator upper mounting bolt . . .

13.4b . . . and lower bolt (arrowed), and manoeuvre out the alternator - 1998 cc 8-valve model shown

bulbholder is secure in its location in the instrument panel. If the light still fails to illuminate, check the continuity of the warning light feed wire from the alternator to the bulbholder. If all is satisfactory, the alternator is at fault, and should be renewed or taken to an auto-electrician for testing and repair.

2 If the ignition warning light illuminates when the engine is running, stop the engine. Check that the drivebelt is correctly tensioned (refer to Section 12) and that the alternator connections are secure. If all is so far satisfactory, check the alternator brushes and slip rings as described in Section 14. If the fault persists, the alternator should be renewed, or taken to an auto-electrician for testing and repair.

3 If the alternator output is suspect even though the warning light functions correctly, the regulated voltage may be checked as follows.

4 Connect a voltmeter across the battery terminals, and start the engine.

5 Increase the engine speed until the voltmeter reading remains steady; the reading should be approximately 12 to 13 volts, and no more than 14 volts.

6 Switch on as many electrical accessories (eg, the headlights, heated rear window and heater blower) as possible, and check that the alternator maintains the regulated voltage at around 13 to 14 volts.

7 If the regulated voltage is not as stated, the fault may be due to worn brushes, weak brush springs, a faulty voltage regulator, a faulty diode, a severed phase winding, or worn or

damaged slip rings. The brushes and slip rings may be checked (see Section 14), but if the fault persists, the alternator should be renewed, or taken to an auto-electrician for testing and repair.

12 Alternator drivebelt - removal, refitting and tensioning

1 Refer to the procedure given for the auxiliary drivebelt in Chapter 1.

13 Alternator - removal and refitting

Removal

1 Disconnect the battery negative lead.
2 Slacken the auxiliary drivebelt as described in Chapter 1, and disengage it from the alternator pulley.
3 Remove the rubber covers (where fitted) from the alternator terminals, then unscrew the retaining nuts and disconnect the wiring from the rear of the alternator **(see illustration)**.
4 Unscrew the nut and/or bolt securing the alternator to the upper mounting bracket. Unscrew the lower nut and/or mounting bolt, or undo the nut securing the adjuster bolt bracket to the alternator (as applicable). Note that, where a long through-bolt is used to secure the alternator in position, the bolt does not need to be fully removed; the alternator

can be disengaged from the bolt once it has been slackened sufficiently **(see illustrations)**. On some models, it may be necessary to remove the drivebelt idler/tensioner pulley to gain access to the alternator mounting nuts and bolts (depending on specification).
5 Manoeuvre the alternator away from its mounting brackets and out from the engine compartment.

Refitting

6 Refitting is a reversal of removal, tensioning the auxiliary drivebelt as described in Chapter 1, and ensuring that the alternator mountings are securely tightened.

14 Alternator brushes and regulator - inspection and renewal

1 Remove the alternator as described in Section 13.

Valeo alternator

2 Where applicable, scrape the sealing compound from the rear plastic cover, to expose the three rear cover retaining nuts **(see illustration)**.
3 Undo the retaining nuts and remove the rear cover **(see illustration)**.
4 If necessary, scrape the sealing compound from the rear of the alternator to expose the regulator/brush holder assembly fixings. The assembly is retained by two nuts and a single screw **(see illustration)**.

14.2 On the Valeo alternator, undo the three retaining nuts (arrowed) . . .

14.3 . . . and withdraw the rear cover

14.4 Alternator brush/regulator assembly retaining nuts (1) and screw (2) - Valeo alternator

14.5 Removing the cover from the armature shaft - Valeo alternator

14.6 Removing the brush/regulator assembly - Valeo alternator

14.9 Ensure the alternator slip-rings (arrowed) are clean and undamaged

5 Pull the plastic cover from the rear of the armature shaft **(see illustration)**.

6 Undo the retaining nuts and screw, and withdraw the regulator/brush holder assembly from the rear of the alternator **(see illustration)**.

7 Measure the protrusion of each brush from the its holder. No minimum dimension is specified by the manufacturers, but excessive wear should be self-evident. If either brush requires renewal, the complete regulator/brush holder assembly must be renewed. It is not possible to renew the brushes separately.

8 If the brushes are still serviceable, clean them with a petrol-moistened cloth. Check that the brush spring tension is equal for both brushes, and provides a reasonable pressure. The brushes must move freely in their holders.

9 Clean the alternator slip-rings with a petrol-moistened cloth **(see illustration)**. Check for signs of scoring, burning or severe pitting on the surface of the slip-rings. It may be possible to have the slip rings renovated by an electrical specialist.

10 Refit the regulator/brush holder assembly using a reverse of the removal procedure.

11 Refit the alternator as described in Section 13.

Bosch alternator

12 Unclip the cover from the rear of the alternator.

13 If necessary, scrape the sealing compound from the rear of the alternator, to expose the regulator/brush holder assembly retaining screws. Slacken and remove the two retaining screws, and remove the regulator/brush holder from the rear of the alternator.

14 Examine the alternator components as described above in paragraphs 7 to 9.

15 Refit the regulator/brush holder assembly, and securely tighten its retaining screws.

16 Clip the rear cover onto the alternator, and refit the alternator as described in Section 13.

Mitsubishi alternator

17 At the time of writing, no information on the Mitsubishi alternator was available.

Although the components differ in detail, the same basic principles outlined previously for the Valeo alternator are applicable.

15 Starting system - testing

Note: *Refer to the precautions given in "Safety first!" and in Section 1 of this Chapter before starting work.*

1 If the starter motor fails to operate when the ignition key is turned to the appropriate position, the following possible causes may be to blame.

(a) The battery is faulty.

(b) The electrical connections between the switch, solenoid, battery and starter motor are somewhere failing to pass the necessary current from the battery through the starter to earth.

(c) The solenoid is faulty.

(d) The starter motor is mechanically or electrically defective.

2 To check the battery, switch on the headlights. If they dim after a few seconds, this indicates that the battery is discharged - recharge (see Section 3) or renew the battery. If the headlights glow brightly, operate the ignition switch and observe the lights. If they dim, then this indicates that current is reaching the starter motor - therefore, the fault must lie in the starter motor. If the lights continue to glow brightly (and no clicking sound can be heard from the starter motor solenoid), this indicates that there is a fault in the circuit or solenoid - refer to the following paragraphs. If the starter motor turns slowly when operated, but the battery is in good condition, then this indicates that either the starter motor is faulty, or there is considerable resistance somewhere in the circuit.

3 If a fault in the circuit is suspected, disconnect the battery leads (including the earth connection to the body), the starter/solenoid wiring, and the engine/transmission earth strap. Thoroughly clean the connections, reconnect the leads and wiring, then use a voltmeter or test light to check that full battery voltage is available at

the battery positive lead connection to the solenoid, and that the earth is sound. Smear petroleum jelly around the battery terminals to prevent corrosion - corroded connections are among the most frequent causes of electrical system faults.

4 If the battery and all connections are in good condition, check the circuit by disconnecting the wire from the solenoid blade terminal. Connect a voltmeter or test light between the wire end and a good earth (such as the battery negative terminal), and check that the wire is live when the ignition switch is turned to the "start" position. If it is, then the circuit is sound - if not, the circuit wiring can be checked as described in Chapter 12, Section 2.

5 The solenoid contacts can be checked by connecting a voltmeter or test light between the battery positive feed connection on the starter side of the solenoid, and earth. When the ignition switch is turned to the "start" position, there should be a reading or lighted bulb, as applicable. If there is no reading or lighted bulb, the solenoid is faulty, and should be renewed.

6 If the circuit and solenoid are proved sound, the fault must lie in the starter motor. Begin checking the starter motor by removing it (see Section 16), and checking the brushes (see Section 17). If the fault does not lie in the brushes, the motor windings must be faulty. In this event, it may be possible to have the starter motor overhauled by a specialist, but check on the availability and cost of spares before proceeding, as it may prove more economical to obtain a new or exchange motor.

16 Starter motor - removal and refitting

Removal

1 Disconnect the battery negative lead.

2 On 1124 cc, 1360 cc models and 1998 cc 16-valve models, to improve access to the motor, remove the air cleaner housing and mounting bracket, as described in Chapter 4.

3 On all models, so that access to the motor can be gained both from above and below,

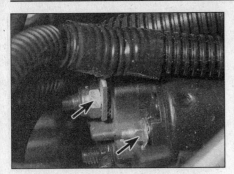

16.4 Unscrew the two retaining nuts (arrowed) and disconnect the wiring from the rear of the starter motor - 1905 cc model shown

16.5 Unscrew the starter motor securing bolts (1). Note the location of the bracket (2) - 1905 cc model shown

17.2 On the Valeo starter motor, remove the plastic cap from the end of the starter motor armature shaft . . .

firmly apply the handbrake, then jack up the front of the vehicle and support it on axle stands.

4 Slacken and remove the two retaining nuts, and disconnect the wiring from the rear of the starter motor **(see illustration)**. Recover the washers under the nuts.

5 Working at the rear of the starter motor, undo the three mounting bolts, supporting the motor as the bolts are withdrawn. Recover the washers from under the bolt heads, and note the locations of any wiring or hose brackets secured by the bolts **(see illustration)**. Note that on 1580 cc and larger-engined models, the top retaining bolt may foul the clutch release mechanism as it is withdrawn, but there is no need to withdraw it completely to remove the starter motor.

6 Manoeuvre the starter motor out from underneath the engine.

Refitting

7 Refitting is a reversal of removal, ensuring that any wiring or hose brackets are in place under the bolt heads, as noted prior to removal.

17 Starter motor - brush renewal

Valeo starter motor

1 No minimum brush length is specified by the manufacturers, but it should be self-evident if the brushes are worn to the extent

where renewal is required. With the motor removed as described in Section 16, proceed as follows.

2 Carefully prise the plastic cap from the end of the armature shaft, using a screwdriver or similar tool **(see illustration)**.

3 Prise the C-clip from the end of the armature shaft, and recover the shim **(see illustrations)**.

4 Unscrew the two through-bolts, then withdraw the end cover from the motor casing, and recover the shim from the armature shaft **(see illustrations)**. Do not mix up the shim with the one removed in the previous paragraph.

5 Carefully pull the brush plate from the end of the armature **(see illustration)**.

6 Using a suitable screwdriver, release the

17.3a . . . then prise off the C-clip . . .

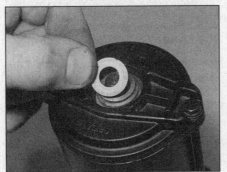

17.3b . . . and recover the shim

17.4a Remove the through-bolts . . .

17.4b . . . then withdraw the end cover, and recover the shim (arrowed)

17.5 Carefully pull the brush plate from the end of the armature . . .

17.6a . . . then, using a screwdriver . . .

5

17.6b . . . release the brush retainers . . .

17.6c . . . and withdraw the brushes from the brush holders

brush retainers, and withdraw the brushes from the brush holders **(see illustrations)**.

7 Unsolder the brush leads, or release them from the clips on the brush plate, as applicable.

8 Fit the new brushes. Solder the leads into position, or secure them to the brush plate by bending the securing clips into position, as applicable.

9 Fit the brush plate over the end of the armature shaft, leaving enough clearance to fit the brushes. Note that, when finally fitted, the lug on the brush plate must locate in the corresponding hole in the motor casing.

10 Push the brushes into their holders, so that they rest against the commutator on the armature shaft.

11 Carefully fit the brush retainers, complete with springs, and secure them to retain the brushes.

12 Check that the brushes are seated on the commutator, then slide the brush plate down the armature shaft until the lug on the brush plate engages with the hole in the motor casing.

13 Further refitting is a reversal of removal, ensuring that the shims are fitted to the armature shaft as noted before removal.

Bosch starter motor

14 At the time of writing, no specific information was available for the Bosch

20.2 Removing the oil level sensor from the cylinder block

starter motor. Although the components differ in detail, the same basic principles outlined previously for the Valeo starter motor are equally applicable.

18 Ignition switch - removal and refitting

1 The ignition switch is integral with the steering column lock, and can be removed as described in Chapter 10.

19 Oil pressure warning light switch - removal and refitting

Removal

Note: *If the switch was originally fitted using a sealing ring, a new sealing ring should be used on refitting.*

1 The switch is located at the front of the cylinder block, above the oil filter mounting. Note that on some models, access to the switch may be improved if the vehicle is jacked up and supported on axle stands, so that the switch can be reached from underneath.

2 Disconnect the battery negative lead.

3 Remove the protective sleeve from the

21.1 Oil temperature sensor is screwed into the rear of the sump

wiring plug (where applicable), then disconnect the wiring from the switch.

4 Unscrew the switch from the cylinder block, and recover the sealing ring, where applicable. Be prepared for oil spillage, and if the switch is to be left removed from the engine for any length of time, plug the hole in the cylinder block.

Refitting

5 Examine the sealing ring for signs of damage or deterioration, and if necessary, renew it. If no sealing ring was originally fitted, apply a smear of sealing compound to the threads of the switch prior to refitting.

6 Refit the switch, tightening it securely, and reconnect the wiring connector.

7 Lower the vehicle to the ground, then check and, if necessary, top-up the engine oil as described in Chapter 1.

20 Oil level sensor - removal and refitting

1 The sensor is located at the rear left-hand side of the cylinder block.

2 The removal and refitting procedure is as described for the oil pressure switch in Section 19 **(see illustration)**. Access is most easily obtained from underneath the vehicle.

21 Oil temperature sensor - removal and refitting

Removal

1 The oil temperature sensor is screwed into the rear of the sump **(see illustration)**.

2 To gain access to the sensor, firmly apply the handbrake, then jack up the front of the vehicle and support it on axle stands.

3 Drain the engine oil into a clean container, then refit and tighten the drain plug (see Chapter 1).

4 Undo the nut, and disconnect the wiring connector. Unscrew the sensor from the sump, and remove it from underneath the vehicle along with its sealing ring (where fitted).

Refitting

5 Examine the sealing ring for signs of damage or deterioration, and if necessary, renew it. If no sealing ring was originally fitted, apply a smear of sealing compound to the threads of the sensor prior to refitting.

6 Refit the sensor, tightening it securely, and reconnect the wiring connector, securely tightening its retaining nut.

7 Lower the vehicle to the ground, and refill the engine with oil as described in Chapter 1.

Chapter 6 Clutch

Contents

Clutch - adjustment 2
Clutch assembly - removal, inspection and refitting 5
Clutch cable - removal and refitting 3
Clutch pedal - removal and refitting 4
Clutch release mechanism - removal, inspection and refitting 6
General check . . . . See Chapter 1
General information 1

Degrees of difficulty

Easy, suitable for novice with little experience	**Fairly easy,** suitable for beginner with some experience	**Fairly difficult,** suitable for competent DIY mechanic 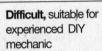	**Difficult,** suitable for experienced DIY mechanic	**Very difficult,** suitable for expert DIY or professional

Specifications

Type	Single dry plate with diaphragm spring, cable-operated
Clutch pedal travel	140 mm

Friction plate diameter

1124 cc and 1360 cc models:	
Valeo clutch	181.5 mm
Luk clutch	180 mm
1580 cc, 1761 cc and 1905 cc models	200 mm
1998 cc models	215 mm

Torque wrench settings	**Nm**	**lbf ft**
Pressure plate retaining bolts	20	15
Clutch pedal pivot bolt	25	18

1 General information

The clutch consists of a friction plate, a pressure plate assembly, a release bearing and the release mechanism; all of these components are contained in the large cast-aluminium alloy bellhousing, sandwiched between the engine and the transmission. The release mechanism is mechanical, being operated by a cable.

The friction plate is fitted between the engine flywheel and the clutch pressure plate, and is allowed to slide on the transmission input shaft splines. It consists of two circular facings of friction material riveted in position to provide the clutch bearing surface, and a spring-cushioned hub to damp out transmission shocks.

The pressure plate assembly is bolted to the engine flywheel, and is located by three dowel pins. When the engine is running, drive is transmitted from the crankshaft, via the flywheel, to the friction plate (these components being clamped securely together by the pressure plate assembly) and from the friction plate to the transmission input shaft.

To interrupt the drive, the spring pressure must be relaxed. On the models covered in this manual, two different types of clutch release mechanism are used. The first is a conventional "push-type" mechanism, where an independent clutch release bearing, fitted concentrically around the transmission input shaft, is pushed onto the pressure plate assembly. The second is a "pull-type" mechanism, where the clutch release bearing is an integral part of the pressure plate assembly, and is lifted away from the friction plate.

On models with the conventional "push-type" mechanism, at the transmission end of the clutch cable, the outer cable is retained by a fixed mounting bracket, and the inner cable is attached to the release fork lever. Depressing the clutch pedal pulls the control cable inner wire, and this in turn rotates the release fork by acting on the lever at the fork's upper end, above the bellhousing. The release fork then acts on the release bearing, pressing it against the fingers at the centre of the pressure plate diaphragm spring. Since the spring is held by rivets between two annular fulcrum rings, the pressure at its centre causes it to deform so that it flattens, and thus releases, the clamping force it exerts at its periphery, on the pressure plate.

On models with the "pull-type" mechanism, at the transmission end of the clutch cable, the inner cable is attached to a fixed mounting bracket, and the outer cable acts against the release fork lever. Depressing the clutch pedal pulls the outer cable towards the fixed end of the inner cable, and this in turn rotates the release fork by acting on the lever at the fork's upper end, above the bellhousing. The release fork then lifts the release bearing, which is attached to the pressure plate springs, away from the friction plate, and thus releases the clamping force exerted at the pressure plate periphery.

As the friction plate facings wear, the pressure plate moves towards the flywheel; this causes the diaphragm spring fingers to push against the release bearing, thus reducing the clearance which must be present in the mechanism. To ensure correct operation, the clutch cable must be regularly adjusted.

2 Clutch - adjustment

1 The clutch adjustment is checked by measuring the clutch pedal travel.
2 Ensure that there are no obstructions beneath the clutch pedal. Depress the clutch pedal fully to the floor, and measure the distance that the centre of the clutch pedal pad

2.2 To check clutch adjustment, measure the clutch pedal travel as described in text

2.4 Adjusting the clutch cable (air cleaner duct removed for clarity)

3.2a Slacken the clutch cable locknut and adjuster nut, then free the inner cable end fittings . . .

travels through, from the at-rest position to the floor (see illustration). If this is less than the distance given in the Specifications at the start of this Chapter, adjust the clutch as follows.

3 The clutch cable is adjusted by means of the adjuster nut on the transmission end of the cable. On some models, access to the locknut is limited and, if required, the air cleaner duct or housing component can be removed or disconnected to improve access. Refer to Chapter 4 for further information.

4 Working in the engine compartment, slacken the locknut from the end of the clutch cable. Adjust the position of the adjuster nut, then re-measure the clutch pedal travel. Repeat this procedure until the clutch pedal travel is as specified (see illustration).

5 Once the adjuster nut is correctly positioned, and the pedal travel is correctly set, securely tighten the cable locknut. Where necessary, refit any disturbed air cleaner duct/housing components as described in Chapter 4.

3 Clutch cable - removal and refitting

Removal

1 Working in the engine compartment, fully slacken the locknut and adjuster nut from the end of the clutch cable. On some models,

3.2b . . . and outer cable end fittings from the release lever and mounting bracket

access to these nuts is limited and, if required, the air cleaner duct or housing component can be removed or disconnected to improve access. Refer to Chapter 4 for further information.

2 Release the inner cable and outer cable fittings from the clutch release lever and mounting bracket, and free the cable from the transmission housing (see illustrations).

3 Working inside the vehicle, release the fasteners by turning them through a quarter of a turn, and remove the driver's side lower facia panel. Remove the heater duct which is situated behind the panel.

4 Release the facia felt undercover retaining clips, and peel back the material to gain access to the upper end of the clutch pedal.

5 Depress the metal retaining clip, and free the inner cable from the plastic retainer fitted to the upper end of the clutch pedal (see illustration).

6 Return to the engine compartment, and withdraw the cable forwards through the bulkhead, releasing it from any relevant retaining clips and guides. Note its correct routing, and remove it from the vehicle.

7 Examine the cable, looking for worn end

3.5 Depress the clutch pedal retainer clip (1) and release the inner cable end fitting (2) from the pedal

fittings or a damaged outer casing, and for signs of fraying of the inner wire. Check the cable's operation; the inner wire should move smoothly and easily through the outer casing.. Renew the cable if it shows signs of excessive wear or any damage.

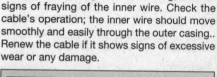

HAYNES HiNT *A cable that appears serviceable when tested off the car may well be much heavier in operation when in its working position*

Refitting

8 Apply a thin smear of multi-purpose grease to the cable end fittings, then pass the cable through the engine compartment bulkhead.

9 From inside the vehicle, engage the inner cable with the plastic retainer on the clutch pedal, and check that it is securely retained by the metal clip. Clip the felt undercover back into position, then refit the heater duct, ensuring it is correctly located at both ends, and install the lower facia panel.

10 Refit the plastic locating collar to the release lever, and ensure the rubber spacer is correctly located on the transmission end of the outer cable.

11 Ensuring that the cable is correctly routed and retained by all the relevant retaining clips and guides, pass the lower end through the release lever/mounting bracket (as applicable) and engage the inner cable. Refit the rubber spacer and flat washer to the end of the inner cable, and screw on the adjuster nut and locknut.

12 Adjust the clutch cable as described in Section 2.

4 Clutch pedal - removal and refitting

Removal

1 Remove the pedal bracket assembly from the vehicle, as described in Chapter 9.

2 With the pedal bracket assembly on the bench, slacken the nut, withdraw the clutch pedal pivot bolt, and separate the pedal and bracket. Slide the pivot bush and spring off the

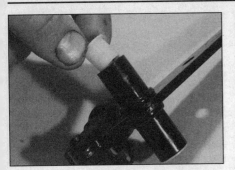

4.4a Press the pivot bushes into the pedal bore . . .

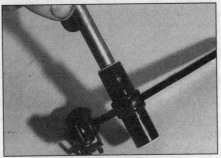

4.4b . . . then insert the spacer . . .

4.4c . . . and refit the pedal spring

4.5a Refit the pedal to the bracket, ensuring that the spring is correctly engaged in the bracket, and hooked over the pedal (arrowed)

4.5b Install the pedal pivot bolt, and tighten it to the specified torque

left-hand end of the pedal, and remove the spacer and pivot bushes from the pedal bore.

3 Carefully clean all components, and renew any that are worn or damaged; check the bearing surfaces of the pivot bushes and spacer with particular care; the bushes can be renewed separately if worn.

Refitting

4 Press the pivot bushes into the pedal bore, then apply a smear of multi-purpose grease to their bearing surfaces, and slide in the spacer. Install the spring and pivot bush on the end of the pedal pivot, ensuring that the inner end of the spring is correctly hooked over the pedal **(see illustrations)**.

5 Refit the pedal to the bracket, ensuring that the outer end of the pedal spring is correctly located in the slot on the pedal mounting bracket, and install the pivot bolt. Refit and tighten the pivot bolt nut **(see illustrations)**.

6 Check that the pedal pivots smoothly, then refit the pedal bracket assembly to the vehicle as described in Section 14 of Chapter 9.

5 Clutch assembly - removal, inspection and refitting

Warning: Dust created by clutch wear and deposited on the clutch components may contain asbestos, which is a health hazard. DO NOT blow it out with compressed air, or inhale any of it. DO NOT use petrol or petroleum-based solvents to clean off the dust. Brake system cleaner or methylated spirit should be used to flush the dust into a suitable receptacle. After the clutch components are wiped clean with rags, dispose of the contaminated rags and cleaner in a sealed, marked container.
Note: *Although some friction materials may no longer contain asbestos, it is safest to assume that they do, and to take precautions accordingly.*

Removal

1 Unless the complete engine/transmission unit is to be removed from the car and separated for major overhaul (see Chapter 2), the clutch can be reached by removing the transmission as described in Chapter 7, Part A.

2 Before disturbing the clutch, use chalk or a marker pen to mark the relationship of the pressure plate assembly to the flywheel.

3 Working in a diagonal sequence, slacken the pressure plate bolts by half a turn at a time, until spring pressure is released and the bolts can be unscrewed by hand.

4 Prise the pressure plate assembly off its locating dowels, and collect the friction plate, noting which way round the friction plate is fitted.

Inspection

Note: *Due to the amount of work necessary to remove and refit clutch* components, it is usually considered good practice to renew the clutch friction plate, pressure plate assembly and release bearing as a matched set, even if only one of these is actually worn enough to require renewal. It is also worth considering the renewal of the clutch components on a preventive basis if the engine and/or transmission have been removed for some other reason.

5 Remove the clutch assembly.

6 When cleaning clutch components, read first the warning at the beginning of this Section; remove dust using a clean, dry cloth, and working in a well-ventilated atmosphere.

7 Check the friction plate facings for signs of wear, damage or oil contamination. If the friction material is cracked, burnt, scored or damaged, or if it is contaminated with oil or grease (shown by shiny black patches), the friction plate must be renewed.

8 If the friction material is still serviceable, check that the centre boss splines are unworn, that the torsion springs are in good condition and securely fastened, and that all the rivets are tight. If any wear or damage is found, the friction plate must be renewed.

9 If the friction material is fouled with oil, this must be due to an oil leak from the crankshaft left-hand oil seal, from the sump-to-cylinder block joint, or from the transmission input shaft. Renew the seal or repair the joint, as appropriate, as described in Chapter 2 or 7, before installing the new friction plate.

10 Check the pressure plate assembly for obvious signs of wear or damage; shake it to check for loose rivets or worn or damaged fulcrum rings, and check that the drive straps securing the pressure plate to the cover do not show signs (such as a deep yellow or blue discoloration) of overheating. If the diaphragm spring is worn or damaged, or if its pressure is in any way suspect, the pressure plate assembly should be renewed.

11 Examine the machined bearing surfaces of the pressure plate and of the flywheel; they should be clean, completely flat, and free from scratches or scoring. If either is discoloured from excessive heat, or shows signs of cracks, it should be renewed - although minor damage of this nature can sometimes be polished away using emery paper.

12 Check that the release bearing contact surface rotates smoothly and easily, with no sign of noise or roughness. Also check that the surface itself is smooth and unworn, with no signs of cracks, pitting or scoring. If there is any doubt about its condition, the bearing must be renewed. On clutches with a "pull-type" release mechanism, this means that the complete pressure plate assembly must also be renewed.

6

5.14 Ensure the friction plate is fitted the correct way around, then install the pressure plate

5.18 Once the friction plate is centralised, tighten the pressure plate retaining bolts to the specified torque

6.7a Clip the lower pivot bush into position in the transmission housing . . .

Refitting

13 On reassembly, ensure that the bearing surfaces of the flywheel and pressure plate are completely clean, smooth, and free from oil or grease. Use solvent to remove any protective grease from new components.
14 Fit the friction plate so that its spring hub assembly faces away from the flywheel; there may also be a marking showing which way round the plate is to be refitted (see illustration).
15 Refit the pressure plate assembly, aligning the marks made on dismantling (if the original pressure plate is re-used), and locating the pressure plate on its three locating dowels. Fit the pressure plate bolts, but tighten them only finger-tight, so that the friction plate can still be moved.
16 The friction plate must now be centralised, so that when the transmission is refitted, its input shaft will pass through the splines at the centre of the friction plate.
17 Centralisation can be achieved by passing a screwdriver or other long bar through the friction plate and into the hole in the crankshaft; the friction plate can then be moved around until it is centred on the crankshaft hole.
18 When the friction plate is centralised,

tighten the pressure plate bolts evenly and in a diagonal sequence to the specified torque setting (see illustration).
19 Apply a thin smear of molybdenum disulphide grease to the splines of the friction plate and the transmission input shaft, and also to the release bearing bore and release fork shaft.
20 Refit the transmission as described in Chapter 7, Part A.

6 Clutch release mechanism - removal, inspection and refitting

Note: *Refer to the warning concerning the dangers of asbestos dust at the beginning of Section 5.*

Removal

1 Unless the complete engine/transmission unit is to be removed from the car and separated for major overhaul (see Chapter 2), the clutch release mechanism can be reached by removing the transmission only, as described in Chapter 7, Part A.
2 On models with a conventional "push-type" release mechanism, unhook the release bearing from the fork, and slide it off the input shaft. Drive out the roll pin, and remove the release lever from the top of the release fork shaft. Discard the roll pin - a new one must be used on refitting.
3 On both types of clutch, depress the retaining tabs, then slide the upper bush off the end of the release fork shaft. Disengage the shaft from its lower bush, and manoeuvre it out from the transmission. Depress the retaining tabs, and remove the lower pivot bush from the transmission housing.

Inspection

4 Check the release mechanism, renewing any component which is worn or damaged. Carefully check all bearing surfaces and points of contact.
5 When checking the release bearing itself, note that it is often considered worthwhile to renew it as a matter of course. Check that the contact surface rotates smoothly and easily, with no sign of noise or roughness, and that the surface itself is smooth and unworn, with no signs of cracks, pitting or scoring. If there is any doubt about its condition, the bearing

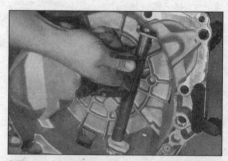

6.7b . . . locate the release fork shaft in the lower bush . . .

6.7c . . . and slide the upper pivot down the release fork shaft, and into position in the transmission housing - BE3 transmission shown

must be renewed. On models with a "pull-type" release mechanism, this means that the complete pressure plate assembly must be renewed, as described in Section 5.

Refitting

6 Apply a smear of molybdenum disulphide grease to the shaft pivot bushes and the contact surfaces of the release fork.
7 Locate the lower pivot bush in the transmission, ensuring it is securely retained by its locating tangs, and refit the release fork. Slide the upper bush down the shaft, and clip it into position in the transmission housing (see illustrations).
8 On models with a conventional "push-type" release mechanism, refit the release lever to the shaft. Align the lever with the shaft hole, and secure it in position by tapping a new roll pin fully into position. Slide the release bearing onto the input shaft, and engage it with the release fork.
9 Refit the transmission as described in Chapter 7, Part A.

A clutch-aligning tool can be used to eliminate the guesswork when fitting a friction plate; these can be obtained from most accessory shops). A home-made aligning tool can be fabricated from a length of metal rod or wooden dowel which fits closely inside the crankshaft hole, and has insulating tape wound around it to match the diameter of the friction plate splined hole.

Chapter 7 Part A: Manual transmission

Contents

Gearchange linkage - general information and adjustment 2
Gearchange linkage - removal and refitting 3
General information 1
Manual transmission - removal and refitting 7
Manual transmission oil level check . . . . See Chapter 1
Manual transmission oil renewal . . . . See Chapter 1
Manual transmission overhaul - general information 8
Oil seals - renewal 4
Reversing light switch - testing, removal and refitting 5
Speedometer drive - removal and refitting 6

7A

Degrees of difficulty

| Easy, suitable for novice with little experience | | Fairly easy, suitable for beginner with some experience | | Fairly difficult, suitable for competent DIY mechanic | | Difficult, suitable for experienced DIY mechanic | | Very difficult, suitable for expert DIY or professional | 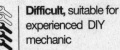 |

Specifications

General

Type	Manual, five forward speeds and reverse. Synchromesh on all forward speeds

Designation:
1124 cc and 1360 cc models	MA
1580 cc and larger-engined models	BE3

Lubrication

Recommended oil	See "Lubricants and fluids"
Recommended gearchange linkage grease	Esso Norva 275 or Total Multis G6

Torque wrench settings

	Nm	lbf ft
MA transmission - 1124 cc and 1360 cc models		
Gearchange selector rod pivot bolts	17	13
Selector lever mounting bracket nuts	17	13
Oil filler/level plug	25	18
Oil drain plug	25	18
Clutch release bearing guide sleeve bolts	12	9
Reversing light switch	25	18
Left-hand engine/transmission mounting:		
Mounting bracket-to-transmission nuts	18	13
Mounting bracket-to-body bolts	25	18
Centre nut	38	28
Engine-to-transmission unit fixing bolts	35	26
Roadwheel bolts	90	66
BE3 transmission - 1580 cc and larger-engined models		
Gearchange linkage bellcrank pivot bolt	28	21
Oil filler/level plug	22	16
Oil drain plug	35	26
Clutch release bearing guide sleeve bolts	12	9
Reversing light switch	25	18
Left-hand engine/transmission mounting:		
Mounting bracket-to-body bolts	25	18
Mounting stud	50	36
Centre nut	80	59
Engine-to-transmission unit fixing bolts	50	37
Clutch cable bracket retaining bolts ("pull-type" clutch only)	18	13
Roadwheel bolts	90	66

1 General information

1 The transmission is contained in a cast-aluminium alloy casing bolted to the engine's left-hand end, and consists of the gearbox and final drive differential - often called a transaxle.

2 Drive is transmitted from the crankshaft via the clutch to the input shaft, which has a splined extension to accept the clutch friction plate, and rotates in sealed ball-bearings. From the input shaft, drive is transmitted to the output shaft, which rotates in a roller bearing at its right-hand end, and a sealed ball-bearing at its left-hand end. From the output shaft, the drive is transmitted to the differential crownwheel, which rotates with the differential case and planetary gears, thus driving the sun gears and driveshafts. The rotation of the planetary gears on their shaft allows the inner roadwheel to rotate at a slower speed than the outer roadwheel when the car is cornering.

3 The input and output shafts are arranged side by side, parallel to the crankshaft and driveshafts, so that their gear pinion teeth are in constant mesh. In the neutral position, the output shaft gear pinions rotate freely, so that drive cannot be transmitted to the crownwheel (see illustration).

4 Gear selection is via a floor-mounted lever and selector rod mechanism. The selector rod causes the appropriate selector fork to move its respective synchro-sleeve along the shaft, to lock the gear pinion to the synchro-hub.

Since the synchro-hubs are splined to the output shaft, this locks the pinion to the shaft, so that drive can be transmitted. To ensure that gear-changing can be made quickly and quietly, a synchro-mesh system is fitted to all forward gears, consisting of baulk rings and spring-loaded fingers, as well as the gear pinions and synchro-hubs. The synchro-mesh cones are formed on the mating faces of the baulk rings and gear pinions.

5 Two different manual transmission units are used on the models covered in this manual; 1124 cc and 1360 cc models have the "MA" transmission, whereas 1580 cc and larger-engined models are fitted with the "BE3" unit.

1.1 Cutaway view of the BE3 manual transmission

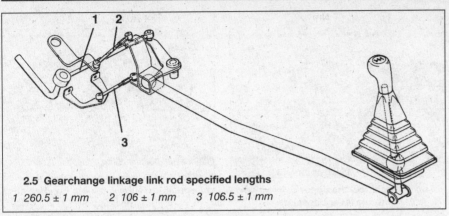
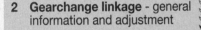

2.5 Gearchange linkage link rod specified lengths
1 260.5 ± 1 mm   2 106 ± 1 mm   3 106.5 ± 1 mm

3.2 Transmission selector lever arrangement - 1124 cc and 1360 cc models. Selector rod pivot bolt (arrowed)

2 Gearchange linkage - general information and adjustment

1 If a stiff, sloppy or imprecise gearchange leads you to suspect that a fault exists within the linkage, first dismantle it completely, and check it for wear or damage as described in Section 3. Reassemble it, applying a smear of the special grease to all bearing surfaces.

2 If this does not cure the fault, the car should be examined by an expert, as the fault must lie within the transmission itself. There is no adjustment as such in the linkage.

3 On 1580 cc and larger-engined models, note that, while the length of the link rods can be altered as described below, this is for initial setting-up only, and is not intended to provide a form of compensation for wear. If the link rods have been renewed, or if the length of the originals is incorrect, adjust them as follows.

Link rod adjustment - 1580 cc and larger-engined models

4 Firmly apply the handbrake, then jack up the front of the vehicle and support it on axle stands. Access to the link rods is poor, but they can be reached both from above and below the vehicle.

5 Working in (or under) the engine compartment, measure the length of each link rod, and compare this to the length specified

(see illustration). Note the measurements given are the distances between the centre points of the link rod balljoints, and not the total length of the rod.

6 If adjustment is necessary, slacken the locknut, then carefully lever the relevant link rod off its balljoint on the transmission unit. Turn the end of the rod until the specified distance between the link rod balljoint centres is obtained, then press the disconnected end of the rod firmly back onto its balljoint and securely tighten the link rod locknut.

7 Once all link rod lengths are correctly set, check that all gears can be selected, and that the gearchange lever returns properly to its correct at-rest (neutral) position.

3 Gearchange linkage - removal and refitting

Removal

1 Firmly apply the handbrake, then jack up the front of the vehicle and support it on axle stands.

1124 cc and 1360 cc models

2 Slacken and remove the nut and washer, then withdraw the pivot bolt from each end of the selector rod. Disengage the rod from gearchange lever and selector lever, and remove it from underneath the vehicle (see illustration).

3 Undo the two nuts securing the selector

lever mounting bracket to the transmission housing, then remove the bracket and lever assembly from the transmission.

4 Inspect all the linkage components for signs of wear or damage, paying particular attention to the selector lever balljoint, and renew worn components as necessary. If necessary, remove the gearchange lever as follows.

5 Where a leather gaiter is fitted to the lever, carefully prise the gearchange lever trim panel out from the centre console, then release the pop fastener and velcro strip, and remove the gaiter. Where a rubber gaiter is fitted, pull the knob from the gearchange lever. Prise the gearchange lever trim panel out from the centre console and remove the gaiter; alternatively, undo the two retaining screws securing the small centre console to the floor, and remove the gaiter and console assembly from the vehicle (as applicable). Undo the four retaining nuts, then lower the gearchange lever out of position and remove it from underneath the vehicle (see illustrations).

6 Peel back the lower gaiter from the base of the gearchange lever, then disengage the lever mounting plate, and slide the upper gaiter up the lever to gain access to the gearchange lever pivot ball. Examine the lever components for signs of wear or damage, paying particular attention to the rubber gaiters, and renew components as necessary. The lever can be separated from its baseplate after the retaining ring has been unclipped (see illustrations).

7A

3.5a Slacken and remove the four retaining nuts . . .

3.5b . . . then remove the gearchange lever from underneath the vehicle

3.6a Peel back the lower gaiter . . .

3.6b . . . then disengage the mounting plate . . .

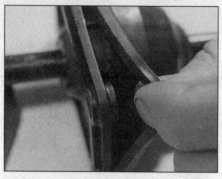

3.6c . . . and peel the upper gaiter away from the lever baseplate

3.6d The lever and baseplate can be separated once the retaining ring has been unclipped

1580 cc and larger-engined models

7 Slacken and remove the nut, and withdraw the pivot bolt securing the selector rod to the base of the gearchange lever.

8 Using a flat-bladed screwdriver, carefully lever the three link rods off their balljoints on the transmission **(see illustration)**. Disengage the selector rod from the bellcrank pivot, and remove it from underneath the vehicle.

9 Undo the two retaining screws, and unclip the heat shield from the top of the steering gear assembly.

10 Carefully prise the plastic cap off the bolt securing the gearchange linkage bellcrank to the subframe.

11 Slacken and remove the bellcrank pivot bolt and washer, then manoeuvre the bellcrank and link rod out from under the vehicle, and recover the spacer and pivot bushes from the centre of the bellcrank.

12 Inspect all the linkage components for signs of wear or damage, paying particular attention to the pivot bushes and link rod balljoints, and renew worn components as necessary. If necessary, the gearchange lever can be removed and inspected as described above in paragraphs 5 and 6.

Refitting

1124 cc and 1360 cc models

13 Refitting is a reversal of the removal procedure, noting the following points:
(a) Before refitting, apply a smear of the

3.8 On 1580 cc and larger-engined models, disconnect the three gearchange linkage link rods (arrowed) from their transmission balljoints

special grease (see Specifications) to the selector lever and rod pivots.
(b) Ensure the gearchange lever rubber gaiters are correctly seated before refitting the lever assembly to the vehicle.
(c) Tighten the selector rod pivot bolts and the selector lever bracket nuts to the specified torque.

1580 cc and larger-engined models

14 Refitting is a reversal of the removal procedure, noting the following points:
(a) Before refitting, check and if necessary adjust the link rod lengths as described in Section 2.
(b) Apply a smear of the special grease (see Specifications) to the gearchange lever pivot ball, the link rod balljoints and the bellcrank ball and pivot bushes.
(c) Ensure the gearchange lever rubber gaiters are correctly seated before refitting the lever assembly to the vehicle.
(d) Tighten the bellcrank pivot bolt to the specified torque, and ensure the link rods are securely pressed onto their balljoints.

4 Oil seals - renewal

Driveshaft oil seals

1 Chock the rear wheels, apply the handbrake, then jack up the front of the car

4.7 Use a large flat-bladed screwdriver to prise the driveshaft oil seals out of position

and support it on axle stands. Remove the appropriate front roadwheel.

2 Drain the transmission oil as described in Chapter 1.

3 Slacken and remove the three nuts securing the balljoint to the lower suspension arm, then withdraw the bolts and free the balljoint from the arm. Discard the nuts - new ones must be used on refitting.

Right-hand seal

4 Loosen the two intermediate bearing retaining bolt nuts, then rotate the bolts through 90° so that their offset heads are clear of the bearing outer race.

5 Carefully pull the swivel hub assembly outwards, and pull on the inner end of the driveshaft to free the intermediate bearing from its mounting bracket.

6 Once the driveshaft end is free from the transmission, slide the dust seal off the inner end of the shaft, noting which way around it is fitted, and support the inner end of the driveshaft to avoid damaging the constant velocity joints or gaiters.

7 Carefully prise the oil seal out of the transmission, using a large flat-bladed screwdriver **(see illustration)**.

8 Remove all traces of dirt from the area around the oil seal aperture, then apply a smear of grease to the outer lip of the new oil seal. Fit the new seal into its aperture, and drive it squarely into position using a suitable tubular drift (such as a socket) which bears only on the hard outer edge of the seal, until it

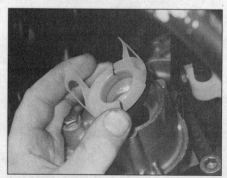

4.8a Fit the new seal to the transmission, noting the plastic seal protector . . .

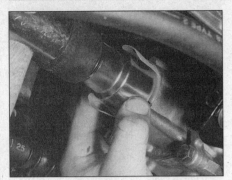

4.8b . . . and tap it into position using a tubular drift

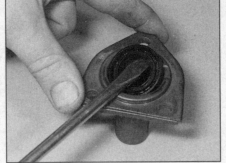

4.22 Removing the input shaft seal from the guide sleeve

4.25a Fit a new O-ring/gasket (as applicable) . . .

abuts its locating shoulder. If the seal was supplied with a plastic protector sleeve, leave this in position until the driveshaft has been refitted **(see illustrations)**.

9 Thoroughly clean the driveshaft splines, then apply a thin film of grease to the oil seal lips and to the driveshaft inner end splines.

10 Slide the dust seal into position on the end of the shaft, ensuring that its flat surface is facing the transmission.

11 Carefully locate the inner driveshaft splines with those of the differential sun gear, taking care not to damage the oil seal, then align the intermediate bearing with its mounting bracket, and push the driveshaft fully into position. If necessary, use a soft-faced mallet to tap the outer race of the bearing into position in the mounting bracket.

12 Ensure the intermediate bearing is correctly seated, then rotate its retaining bolts back through 90° so that their offset heads are resting against the bearing outer race, and tighten the retaining nuts to the specified torque. Remove the plastic seal protector (where supplied), and slide the dust seal tight up against the oil seal.

13 Align the balljoint with the lower arm, and fit the three retaining bolts. Fit new retaining nuts to the bolts, and tighten them to the specified torque setting.

14 Refit the roadwheel, then lower the vehicle to the ground and tighten the roadwheel bolts to the specified torque.

15 Refill the transmission with the specified type and amount of fluid/oil, and check the level using the information given in Chapter 1.

Left-hand seal

16 Pull the swivel hub assembly outwards and withdraw the driveshaft inner constant velocity joint from the transmission, taking care not to damage the driveshaft oil seal. Support the driveshaft, to avoid damaging the constant velocity joints or gaiters.

17 Renew the oil seal as described above in paragraphs 7 to 9.

18 Carefully locate the inner constant velocity joint splines with those of the differential sun gear, taking care not to damage the oil seal, and push the driveshaft fully into position. Where fitted, remove the plastic protector from the oil seal.

19 Carry out the operations described above in paragraphs 13 to 15.

Input shaft oil seal

20 Remove the transmission as described in Section 7.

21 Undo the three bolts securing the clutch release bearing guide sleeve in position, and slide the guide off the input shaft, along with its O-ring or gasket (as applicable). Recover any shims or thrustwashers which have stuck to the rear of the guide sleeve, and refit them to the input shaft.

22 Carefully lever the oil seal out of the guide using a suitable flat-bladed screwdriver **(see illustration)**.

23 Before fitting a new seal, check the input shaft's seal rubbing surface for signs of burrs, scratches or other damage, which may have caused the seal to fail in the first place. It may be possible to polish away minor faults of this sort using fine abrasive paper; however, more serious defects will require the renewal of the input shaft. Ensure that the input shaft is clean and greased, to protect the seal lips on refitting.

24 Dip the new seal in clean oil, and fit it to the guide sleeve.

25 Fit a new O-ring or gasket (as applicable) to the rear of the guide sleeve, then carefully slide the sleeve into position over the input shaft. Refit the retaining bolts and tighten them to the specified torque setting **(see illustrations)**.

26 Take the opportunity to inspect the clutch components if not already done (Chapter 6). Finally, refit the transmission as described in Section 7.

Selector shaft oil seal
1124 cc and 1360 cc models

27 On 1124 cc and 1360 cc models, to renew the selector shaft seal, the transmission must be dismantled. This task should therefore be entrusted to a Citroën dealer or transmission specialist.

1580 cc and larger-engined models

28 Park the car on level ground, apply the handbrake, then jack up the front of the vehicle and support it on axle stands. Remove the left-hand front roadwheel, and unclip the access cover from the centre of the wheel arch liner.

29 Using a large flat-bladed screwdriver, lever the link rod balljoint off the transmission selector shaft, and disconnect the link rod.

30 Carefully prise the selector shaft seal out of the housing, and slide it off the end of the shaft **(see illustrations)**.

31 Before fitting a new seal, check the selector shaft's seal rubbing surface for signs of burrs, scratches or other damage, which may have caused the seal to fail in the first place. It may be possible to polish away minor faults of this sort using fine abrasive paper; however, more serious defects will require the renewal of the selector shaft.

4.25b . . . refit the guide sleeve over the input shaft . . .

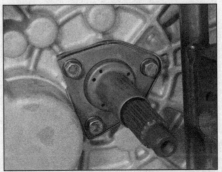

4.25c . . . and secure it in position with its three retaining bolts

7A

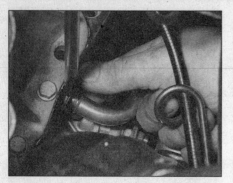

4.30a On 1580 cc and larger-engined models, use a large flat-bladed screwdriver to prise the selector shaft seal out of position . . .

32 Apply a smear of grease to the new seal's outer edge and sealing lip, then carefully slide the seal along the selector rod. Press the seal fully into position in the transmission housing.
33 Reconnect the link rod to the selector shaft, ensuring that its balljoint is pressed firmly onto the shaft. Lower the car to the ground.

5 Reversing light switch - testing, removal and refitting

Testing

1 The reversing light circuit is controlled by a plunger-type switch that is screwed into the top of the transmission casing. If a fault develops in the circuit, first ensure that the circuit fuse has not blown.
2 To test the switch, disconnect the wiring connector, and use a multimeter (set to the resistance function) or a battery-and-bulb test circuit to check that there is continuity between the switch terminals only when reverse gear is selected. If this is not the case, and there are no obvious breaks or other damage to the wires, the switch is faulty, and must be renewed.

Removal

3 On some 1580 cc and larger-engined models, to improve access to the switch, it

6.3a Slacken and remove the retaining bolt . . .

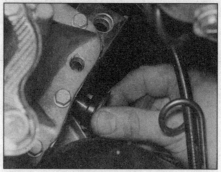

4.30b . . . then slide the seal off the shaft

may be necessary to remove the air intake duct(s) as described in the relevant Part of Chapter 4. It may also be necessary to remove the metal plate from the top of the transmission; the plate is retained by one of the transmission to engine unit bolts, and by a second bolt securing the plate to the top of the transmission housing.
4 Disconnect the wiring connector, then unscrew it from the transmission casing along with its sealing washer (see illustration).

Refitting

5 Fit a new sealing washer to the switch, then screw it back into position in the top of the transmission housing and tighten it to the specified torque setting. Reconnect the wiring connector, and test the operation of the circuit. Refit any components removed for access.

6 Speedometer drive - removal and refitting

Removal

1 Chock the rear wheels, firmly apply the handbrake, then jack up the front of the car and support it on axle stands. The speedometer drive is situated on the rear of the transmission housing, next to the inner end of the right-hand driveshaft.
2 Pull out the speedometer cable retaining

6.3b . . . then withdraw the speedometer drive from the transmission (transmission removed for clarity - type BE3 shown)

5.4 Disconnecting the wiring connector from the reversing light switch (arrowed)

pin, and disconnect the cable from the speedometer drive. Where necessary, disconnect the wiring connector from the speedometer drive.
3 Slacken and remove the retaining bolt, along with the heat shield (where fitted), and withdraw the speedometer drive and driven pinion assembly from the transmission housing, along with its O-ring (see illustrations).
4 If necessary, the pinion can be slid out of the housing, and the oil seal can be removed from the top of the housing. Examine the pinion for signs of damage, and renew if necessary. Renew the housing O-ring as a matter of course.
5 If the driven pinion is worn or damaged, also examine the drive pinion in the transmission housing for similar signs.
6 On 1124 cc and 1360 cc models, to renew the drive pinion, the transmission unit must be dismantled and the differential gear removed. This task should therefore be entrusted to a Citroën dealer or a transmission specialist.
7 On 1580 cc and larger-engined models, to remove the drive pinion, first disengage the right-hand driveshaft from the transmission, as described in paragraphs 1 to 7 of Section 4. Undo the three retaining bolts, and remove the speedometer drive housing from the transmission, along with its O-ring. Remove the drive pinion from the differential gear, and recover any adjustment shims from the gear (see illustrations).

6.7a On 1580 cc and larger-engined models (BE3 transmission), undo the three retaining bolts . . .

6.7b ... and remove the housing, O-ring and drive pinion from the transmission (shown with transmission removed for clarity)

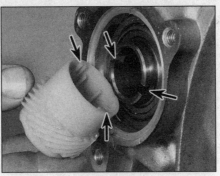

6.8 On refitting, ensure the drive pinion dogs are correctly engaged with the gear slots (arrowed)

7.3a Undo the four retaining bolts . . .

Refitting

8 On 1580 cc and larger-engined models, where the drive pinion has been removed, refit the adjustment shims to the differential gear, then locate the speedometer drive on the gear, ensuring it is correctly engaged in the gear slots **(see illustration)**. Fit a new O-ring to the rear of the speedometer drive housing, then refit the housing to the transmission and securely tighten its retaining bolts. Inspect the driveshaft oil seal for signs of wear, and renew if necessary. Refit the driveshaft to the transmission, using the information given in Section 4.

9 On all models, apply a smear of grease to the lips of the seal and to the driven pinion shaft, and slide the pinion into position in the speedometer drive.

10 Fit a new O-ring to the speedometer drive and refit it to the transmission, ensuring that the drive and driven pinions are correctly engaged.

11 Refit the retaining bolt and the heat shield (where fitted), and tighten the bolt. Where necessary, reconnect the wiring connector to the speedometer drive.

12 Apply a smear of oil to the speedometer cable O-rings, then reconnect the cable to the drive, and secure it in position with the rubber retaining pin. Lower the vehicle to the ground.

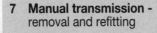

7 Manual transmission - removal and refitting

Removal

1 Chock the rear wheels, then firmly apply the handbrake. Jack up the front of the vehicle, and securely support it on axle stands. Remove both front roadwheels.

2 Drain the transmission oil as described in Chapter 1, then refit the drain and filler plugs, and tighten them to their specified torque settings.

3 Remove the battery and battery tray as described in Chapter 5. Slacken and remove the battery support tray retaining bolts, then free the wiring from its retaining clips on the edge of the tray, and remove the tray **(see illustrations)**.

4 Where necessary, to improve access to the top of the transmission unit remove the air cleaner housing and/or intake duct (as applicable) as described in Chapter 4.

5 Remove the starter motor as described in Chapter 5.

6 Fully slacken the clutch cable locknut and adjuster nut, then free the inner and outer cable end fittings from the mounting bracket

and release lever. Release the cable from any relevant retaining clips, and position it clear of the transmission.

7 Disconnect the wiring connector from the reversing light switch and, where necessary, the speedometer drive housing. Undo the retaining bolts, and disconnect the earth straps from the top of the transmission housing **(see illustration)**. Free the wiring from any relevant retaining clips, and position it clear of the transmission unit.

8 On 1124 cc and 1360 cc models, slacken and remove the nut and washer, then withdraw the pivot bolt and disconnect the selector rod from the transmission lever. Where necessary, undo the bolt securing the exhaust front pipe to its transmission mounting bracket.

9 On 1580 cc and larger-engined models, using a flat-bladed screwdriver, carefully lever the three gearchange mechanism link rods off their respective balljoints on the transmission **(see illustration)**. Position the rods clear of the transmission unit.

10 On models with power steering, undo the nuts securing the power steering pipe to the underside of the transmission, and free the pipe from its retaining studs **(see illustrations)**.

11 On 1580 cc and larger-engined models,

7A

7.3b ... and remove the battery support tray. Note the wiring retaining clip (arrowed)

7.7 Slacken and remove the bolts (arrowed) and disconnect the earth straps from the transmission - BE3 transmission shown

7.9 On 1580 cc and larger-engined models (BE3 transmission), carefully lever the gearchange link rods off their transmission balljoints using a large flat-bladed screwdriver

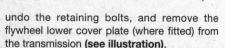
7.10a On models with power steering, undo the retaining nuts . . .

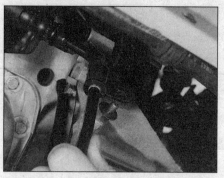
7.10b . . . and free the power steering pipe from its mountings on the underside of the transmission

7.11 On 1580 cc and larger-engined models, remove the flywheel lower cover plate

undo the retaining bolts, and remove the flywheel lower cover plate (where fitted) from the transmission (see illustration).

12 Withdraw the rubber retaining pin, disconnect the speedometer cable from the drive housing, and free it from any relevant retaining clips (see illustrations).

13 Slacken and remove the three nuts securing the balljoint to the left-hand lower suspension arm, then withdraw the bolts and free the balljoint from the arm. Discard the nuts - new ones must be used on refitting. Repeat the procedure on the right-hand side.

14 Release the inner end of the right-hand driveshaft from the transmission, as described in paragraphs 4 to 6 of Section 4.

15 To release the left-hand driveshaft inner constant velocity joint from the transmission, pull the swivel hub assembly outwards and withdraw the joint from transmission, taking great care not to damage the driveshaft oil seal. Support the driveshaft, to avoid damaging the constant velocity joints or gaiters.

16 Place a jack with a block of wood beneath the engine, to take the weight of the engine. Alternatively, attach a couple of lifting eyes to the engine, and fit a hoist or support bar to take the engine weight.

17 Place a jack and block of wood beneath the transmission, and raise the jack to take the weight of the transmission.

18 Slacken and remove the centre nut and washer from the left-hand engine/transmission mounting. Undo the two bolts securing the mounting bracket assembly to the vehicle body, and remove the mounting bracket assembly (see illustrations).

19 On 1124 cc and 1360 cc models, undo the three retaining nuts and remove the mounting plate from the top of the transmission.

20 On 1580 cc and larger-engined models, slide the spacer off the mounting stud, then unscrew the stud from the top of the transmission housing and remove it along with its washer. If the mounting stud is tight, a universal stud extractor can be used to unscrew it (see illustrations).

7.12a Withdraw the rubber retaining pin (arrowed) . . .

7.12b . . . and disconnect the speedometer cable from the transmission - BE3 transmission shown

7.18a Remove the centre nut and washer from the left-hand mounting . . .

7.18b . . . then undo the two retaining bolts and remove the mounting bracket assembly

7.20a On 1580 cc and larger-engined models, slide the spacer off the mounting stud . . .

7.20b . . . and unscrew the mounting stud. If the stud is tight, use a universal stud extractor to unscrew it

7.21a On models with a "pull-type" clutch, withdraw the retaining pin . . .

7.21b . . . then remove the clutch release lever . . .

7.21c . . . and make an alignment mark between the release fork shaft and transmission housing (arrowed)

21 On models with a "pull-type" clutch release mechanism (see Chapter 6), tap out the retaining pin or unscrew the retaining bolt (as applicable) and remove the clutch release lever from the top of the release fork shaft. This is necessary to allow the fork shaft to rotate freely, to disengage from the release bearing as the transmission is pulled away from the engine. Make an alignment mark across the centre of the clutch release fork shaft using a scriber, paint or similar, and mark its position relative to the transmission housing **(see illustrations)**. Undo the retaining bolts, and remove the clutch cable bracket from the top of the transmission housing.

22 With the jack positioned beneath the transmission taking the weight, slacken and remove the remaining bolts securing the transmission housing to the engine. Note the correct fitted positions of each bolt, and the necessary brackets, as they are removed, to use as a reference on refitting. Make a final check that all components have been disconnected, and are positioned clear of the transmission so that they will not hinder the removal procedure.

23 With the bolts removed, move the trolley jack and transmission to the left, to free it from its locating dowels.

24 Once the transmission is free, lower the jack and manoeuvre the unit out from under

the car **(see illustration)**. Remove the locating dowels from the transmission or engine if they are loose, and keep them in a safe place.

25 On models with a "pull-type" clutch, make a second alignment mark on the transmission housing, marking the relative position of the release fork mark after removal, noting the angle at which the release fork is positioned **(see illustration 7.26a)**. This mark can then be used to position the release fork before refitting, to ensure that the fork correctly engages with the clutch release bearing as the transmission is installed.

Refitting

26 The transmission is refitted by a reversal of the removal procedure, bearing in mind the following points:

(a) *Apply a little high-melting-point grease to the splines of the transmission input shaft. Do not apply too much, otherwise there is a possibility of the grease contaminating the clutch friction plate.*

(b) *Ensure the locating dowels are correctly positioned prior to installation.*

(c) *On models with a "pull-type" clutch, before refitting, position the clutch release bearing so that its HAUT mark is at the top, and the BAS mark is at the bottom, and align the release fork shaft mark with the second mark made on the transmission housing (see illustrations).*

*This will ensure that the release fork and bearing will engage correctly as the transmission is refitted to the engine. If the bearing and fork are correctly engaged, the mark on the shaft should be aligned with the original mark made on the transmission housing. **Ensure the release fork and bearing are correctly engaged before bolting the transmission onto the engine.***

(d) *On 1580 cc and larger-engined models, apply thread-locking fluid to the left-hand engine/transmission mounting stud threads, prior to refitting it to the transmission (see illustration). Tighten the stud to the specified torque.*

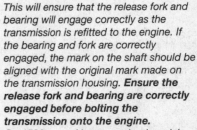

7.24 Removing the transmission from the vehicle

7A

7.26a On models with a "pull-type" clutch, prior to refitting the transmission, align the release fork mark with the second mark made on removal . . .

7.26b . . . and position the release bearing so that its HAUT mark is at the top, and the BAS mark at the bottom

7.26c On 1580 cc and larger-engined models, apply thread-locking fluid to the mounting stud threads

(e) *Tighten all nuts and bolts to the specified torque (where given).*

(f) *Renew the driveshaft oil seals and refit the driveshafts to the transmission, using the information given in Section 4.*

(g) *On completion, refill the transmission with the specified type and quantity of lubricant, as described in Chapter 1.*

8 Manual transmission overhaul - general information

Overhauling a manual transmission unit is a difficult and involved job for the DIY home mechanic. In addition to dismantling and reassembling many small parts, clearances must be precisely measured and, if necessary, changed by selecting shims and spacers. Internal transmission components are also often difficult to obtain, and in many instances, extremely expensive. Because of this, if the transmission develops a fault or becomes noisy, the best course of action is to have the unit overhauled by a specialist repairer, or to obtain an exchange reconditioned unit.

Nevertheless, it is not impossible for the more experienced mechanic to overhaul the transmission, provided the special tools are available, and the job is done in a deliberate step-by-step manner, so that nothing is overlooked.

The tools necessary for an overhaul include internal and external circlip pliers, bearing pullers, a slide hammer, a set of pin punches, a dial test indicator, and possibly a hydraulic press. In addition, a large, sturdy workbench and a vice will be required.

During dismantling of the transmission, make careful notes of how each component is fitted, to make reassembly easier and more accurate.

Before dismantling the transmission, it will help if you have some idea what area is malfunctioning. Certain problems can be closely related to specific areas in the transmission, which can make component examination and replacement easier. Refer to the Fault finding Section at the end of this manual for more information.

Chapter 7 Part B: Automatic transmission

Contents

Automatic transmission - removal and refitting 12
Automatic transmission fluid level check . . . . See Chapter 1
Automatic transmission fluid renewal . . . . See Chapter 1
Automatic transmission overhaul - general information 13
Fluid cooler - removal and refitting 9
General information 1
Kickdown cable - adjustment 5
Kickdown cable - renewal 6
Oil seals - renewal 8
Selector cable - adjustment 2
Selector cable - removal and refitting 3
Selector lever assembly - removal and refitting 4
Selector lever position display switch - removal, refitting and
  adjustment 11
Speedometer drive - removal and refitting 7
Starter inhibitor/reversing light switch - general
  information, removal and refitting 10

Degrees of difficulty

Easy, suitable for novice with little experience	Fairly easy, suitable for beginner with some experience	Fairly difficult, suitable for competent DIY mechanic	Difficult, suitable for experienced DIY mechanic	Very difficult, suitable for expert DIY or professional

Specifications

General

Type	Automatic, four forward speeds and reverse
Designation	4 HP 14
Transmission code:	
1580 cc models	GZ 56
1761 cc models	GZ 58
1905 cc models	GZ 55

Ratios

1st	2.415 : 1
2nd	1.370 : 1
3rd	1.000 : 1
4th	0.739 : 1
Reverse	2.833 : 1
Final drive:	
GZ 55 and 56	3.666 : 1
GZ 58	3.824 : 1

Lubrication

Recommended fluid	See "Lubricants and fluids"
Capacity (approximate):	
From dry	6.2 litres
Drain and refill	2.4 litres

Torque wrench settings

	Nm	lbf ft
Selector cable fixings:		
Outer cable locknuts	10	7
Mounting bracket-to-transmission bolts	20	15
Cable-to-mounting bracket screws	10	7
Selector lever retaining nuts	7	5
Transmission selector lever retaining nut	30	22
Fluid cooler centre bolt	50	36
Left-hand engine/transmission mounting:		
Mounting bracket-to-body bolts	25	18
Mounting stud	50	37
Centre nut	80	59
Engine-to-transmission unit securing bolts	40	30
Torque converter-to-driveplate bolts	35	26
Dipstick tube-to-sump union nut	45	33

7B

1 General information

Some models covered in this manual have a four-speed fully-automatic transmission, consisting of a torque converter, an epicyclic geartrain, and hydraulically-operated clutches and brakes **(see illustration)**.

The torque converter provides a fluid coupling between engine and transmission, which acts as an automatic clutch, and also provides a degree of torque multiplication when accelerating.

The epicyclic geartrain provides either of the four forward or one reverse gear ratios, according to which of its component parts are held stationary or allowed to turn. The components of the geartrain are held or released by brakes and clutches which are activated by a hydraulic control unit. A fluid pump within the transmission provides the necessary hydraulic pressure to operate the brakes and clutches.

Driver control of the transmission is by a seven-position selector lever. The transmission has a "drive" position, and a "hold" facility on the first three gear ratios. The "drive" position "A" provides automatic changing throughout the range of all four gear ratios, and is the one to select for normal driving. An automatic kickdown facility shifts the transmission down a gear if the accelerator pedal is fully depressed. The "hold" facility is very similar, but limits the number of gear ratios available - ie when the selector lever is in the "3" position, only the first three ratios can be selected; in the "2" position, only the first two can be selected, and so on. The lower ratio "hold" is useful for providing engine braking when travelling down steep gradients, or for preventing unwanted selection of top gear on twisty roads. Note, however, that the transmission should *never* be shifted down a position if the engine speed exceeds 4000 rpm.

Due to the complexity of the automatic transmission, any repair or overhaul work must be left to a Citroën dealer with the necessary special equipment for fault diagnosis and repair. The contents of the following Sections are therefore confined to supplying general information, and any service information and instructions that can be used by the owner.

2 Selector cable - adjustment

1 Position the selector lever firmly against its detent in the "N" position.
2 To improve access to the transmission end of the selector cable, remove the battery and battery tray as described in Chapter 5, then unbolt the support tray and remove it from the

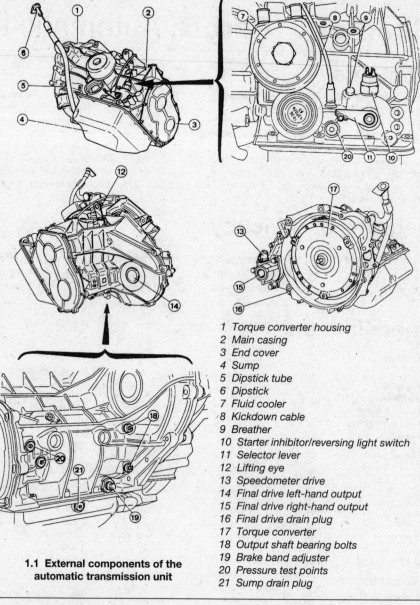

1 Torque converter housing
2 Main casing
3 End cover
4 Sump
5 Dipstick tube
6 Dipstick
7 Fluid cooler
8 Kickdown cable
9 Breather
10 Starter inhibitor/reversing light switch
11 Selector lever
12 Lifting eye
13 Speedometer drive
14 Final drive left-hand output
15 Final drive right-hand output
16 Final drive drain plug
17 Torque converter
18 Output shaft bearing bolts
19 Brake band adjuster
20 Pressure test points
21 Sump drain plug

1.1 External components of the automatic transmission unit

top of the transmission. On some models, it may also be necessary to remove the air intake duct(s) as described in the relevant Part of Chapter 4.
3 Using a large flat-bladed screwdriver, carefully lever the selector cable end fitting off the transmission selector lever balljoint, whilst ensuring that the lever does not move.
4 First ensure that the cable end fitting is screwed onto at least 5 mm of the inner cable thread.
5 With both the selector levers in the "N" (neutral) position, the selector cable end fitting should be correctly aligned with the transmission lever balljoint, so that the cable can be connected to the lever without the balljoint moving. If necessary, adjust the position of the end fitting by screwing or unscrewing it (as applicable) on the cable thread, bearing in mind

the point made above in paragraph 4. If this proves impossible, further adjustments can be made by slackening the locknuts securing the outer cable to its mounting bracket **(see illustration)**. Reposition the nuts as required until the end fitting and balljoint are correctly aligned, then tighten the nuts.
6 Once the end fitting is correctly positioned, press it firmly onto the balljoint, and check that it is securely retained.
7 Refit the battery support tray, and securely tighten its retaining bolts. Refit the battery tray and battery as described in Chapter 5. Also refit any disturbed air duct components as described in the relevant Part of Chapter 4.
8 Check the operation of the selector lever position display panel and, if necessary, adjust the switch using the information given in Section 11.

2.5 Selector cable transmission end fixings

1 Cable end fitting   3 Outer cable locknuts
2 Selector lever balljoint

3 Selector cable - removal and refitting

Removal

1 Firmly apply the handbrake, then jack up the front of the vehicle and support it on axle stands. Position the selector lever in the "N" position.
2 Remove the battery and battery tray as described in Chapter 5. Slacken and remove the battery support tray retaining bolts, then free the wiring from its retaining clip on the side of the tray, and remove the tray from the vehicle.
3 Remove the exhaust system as described in Chapter 4, and remove the heat shield(s) to gain access to the base of the selector lever assembly.
4 Working on the transmission end of the cable, undo the two screws securing the outer cable to its retaining bracket, and carefully lever the inner cable end fitting off its balljoint on the transmission selector lever. Note that the transmission selector lever must not be disturbed until the cable is refitted. As a precaution, mark the position of the lever in relation to the transmission housing.
5 Work back along the selector cable, releasing it from any relevant retaining clips, and noting its correct routing.
6 Working from inside the vehicle, carefully prise the selector lever trim panel out from the centre console, and fold the gaiter back over the selector lever.
7 Slacken and remove the four screws securing the handle to the shaft of the selector lever. Depress the selector lever handle detent knob, then rotate the handle through 90° anti-clockwise, lift the assembly up, and rotate it back 90° clockwise to release the detent button from the selector lever pushrod. With the handle removed, withdraw the detent button and spring from the handle.
8 Slide the gaiter off the selector lever shaft, then undo the four nuts securing the selector lever to the floor. Disengage the position display switch from the selector lever studs, and position it clear of the lever.

9 Working underneath the vehicle, disengage the selector lever assembly from the body, and remove the lever and cable assembly, noting the correct routing of the cable.
10 With the assembly on the bench, prise the rubber dust cover from the base of the lever, and slide it along the cable.
11 Slacken the outer cable retaining nut, then remove the retaining clip. Carefully prise the selector cable end fitting off its balljoint on the base of the selector lever, and separate the cable and lever assembly.
12 Examine the cable, looking for worn end fittings or a damaged outer casing, and for signs of fraying of the inner cable. Check the cable's operation; the inner cable should move smoothly and easily through the outer casing. Renew the cable if it shows any signs of excessive wear or any damage.

> **HAYNES HINT** A cable that appears serviceable when tested off the car may well be much heavier in operation when compressed into its working position

Refitting

13 Apply a smear of the special grease (Mobil Temp G9, available from your Citroën dealer) to the exposed sections of the inner cable and balljoints, and to the detent mechanism of the selector lever. In the absence of the specified grease, a good-quality molybdenum disulphide grease can be used.
14 Insert the selector cable into the selector lever housing, ensuring that the outer cable flange holes are correctly located on the pegs on the housing. Secure the cable in position with the retaining clip, ensuring that the outer ends of the clip are correctly located in the slots in the lever housing, and the inner ends are correctly hooked over the base of the housing. Tighten the outer cable retaining nut.
15 Press the inner cable end fitting firmly onto the lever balljoint. Check that the balljoint connection is securely made, then slide the rubber dust cover back into position over the selector lever base.
16 Ensuring that the cable is correctly routed, manoeuvre the lever and cable assembly back into position from underneath the vehicle.
17 From inside the vehicle, pull the lever up into position, and fit its two right-hand retaining nuts, tightening them finger-tight only at this stage.
18 Refit the position display switch onto the left-hand selector lever studs, ensuring that the switch lug is correctly engaged with the selector lever shaft. Refit the two left-hand nuts, then fully tighten all four selector lever retaining nuts.
19 Refit the gaiter to the selector lever.
20 Refit the spring and detent button to the selector lever handle, and press the button fully

into the handle. Keeping the button depressed, slide the handle assembly onto the lever then, exerting light downward pressure on the handle, rotate the handle through 90° clockwise, then back 90° anti-clockwise to engage the detent button with the lever pushrod. Release the detent button, then refit the four handle retaining screws and tighten them securely. Check the operation of the selector lever detent button before proceeding further.
21 From underneath the vehicle, work along the length of the selector cable, ensuring that it is retained by all the relevant clips. Align the outer cable bracket with its mounting bracket on the transmission, then refit and tighten its retaining bolts.
22 Ensure the selector lever is in the "N" position and the transmission selector lever is still in the neutral position, then adjust the cable and connect it to the transmission lever as described in paragraphs 4 to 6 of Section 2.
23 Refit the heat shield(s) and exhaust system as described in Chapter 4, then lower the vehicle to the ground.
24 Refit the battery support tray, and securely tighten its retaining bolts. Clip the wiring onto the side of the tray, and refit the battery tray and battery as described in Chapter 5.
25 Check and, if necessary, adjust the selector lever display switch using the information given in Section 11.

4 Selector lever assembly - removal and refitting

Removal

1 Firmly apply the handbrake, then jack up the front of the vehicle and support it on axle stands. Position the selector lever in the "N" position.
2 Remove the exhaust system as described in Chapter 4, and remove the heat shield(s) to gain access to the base of the selector lever assembly.
3 Carry out the procedures described in paragraphs 6 to 8 of Section 3.
4 Working again from underneath the vehicle, disengage the selector lever assembly from the body, and lower it out of position.
5 Prise the rubber dust cover from the base of the lever, and slide it along the cable.
6 Slacken the outer cable retaining nut, then remove the retaining clip. Carefully prise the selector cable end fitting off its balljoint on the base of the selector lever, and remove the lever assembly from underneath the vehicle.

Refitting

7 Carry out the operations described in paragraphs 13 to 20 of Section 3.
8 Refit the heat shield(s) and exhaust system as described in Chapter 4, then lower the vehicle to the ground.
9 On completion, check the selector cable adjustment as described in Section 2.

7B

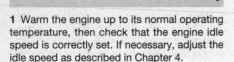

5 Kickdown cable - adjustment

1 Warm the engine up to its normal operating temperature, then check that the engine idle speed is correctly set. If necessary, adjust the idle speed as described in Chapter 4.

2 Detach the kickdown inner cable from the throttle body cam then, referring to Chapter 4, check that the accelerator cable is correctly adjusted.

3 Pull the kickdown inner cable fully out of its outer cable, and measure the distance between the end of the lug on the inner cable and the threaded end of the outer cable **(see illustration)**. This should be approximately 39 mm. If necessary, slacken the two outer cable locknuts, and position the nuts as required so that the distance is as specified.

4 Reconnect the kickdown cable to the throttle body cam, then check the clearance once more between the inner cable lug and the threaded end of the outer cable. Ensuring that the throttle body cam is fully against its stop, there should a gap of 0.5 to 1.0 mm **(see illustration)**. If not, adjust the gap by repositioning the outer cable locknuts as required. Once the outer cable is correctly positioned and the gap is as specified, securely tighten the cable locknuts.

6 Kickdown cable - renewal

1 Renewal of the kickdown cable is a complex task, which should be entrusted to a Citroën dealer. To detach the cable at the transmission end requires removal of the hydraulic valve block, which is a task that should not be undertaken by the home mechanic.

7 Speedometer drive - removal and refitting

Refer to Chapter 7A.

8 Oil seals - renewal

Driveshaft oil seals

1 Refer to Chapter 7A.

Selector shaft oil seal

2 Position the selector lever firmly against its detent mechanism in the "N" position.

3 To improve access to the transmission end of the selector cable, remove the battery and battery tray as described in Chapter 5, then unbolt the support tray and remove it from the top of the transmission. On some models, it may also be necessary to remove the air cleaner housing and/or intake duct as described in Chapter 4.

4 Undo the two screws securing the outer cable to its retaining bracket, and carefully lever the inner cable end fitting off its balljoint on the transmission selector lever. Note the transmission selector shaft must not be disturbed until the cable is refitted. As a precaution, mark the position of the lever in relation to the transmission housing.

5 Undo the retaining nut, and remove the lever from the transmission selector shaft.

6 Punch or drill two small holes opposite each other in the seal. Screw a self-tapping screw into each, and pull on the screws with pliers to extract the seal.

7 Clean the seal housing, and polish off any burrs or raised edges, which may have caused the seal to fail in the first place. Small imperfections can be removed using emery paper, but larger defects will require the renewal of the selector shaft.

8 Lubricate the lips of the new seal with clean engine oil, and carefully ease the seal into position over the end of the shaft, taking great care not to damage its sealing lip. Tap the seal into position until it is flush with the transmission casing, using a suitable tubular drift (such as a socket) which bears only on the hard outer edge of the seal. Note that the seal lips should face inwards.

9 Refit the selector lever to the shaft and tighten its retaining nut.

10 Align the outer cable bracket with its mounting bracket on the transmission, then refit and tighten its retaining bolts.

11 Ensure the selector lever is in the "N" position and the transmission selector lever is still in the neutral position, then adjust the cable and connect it to the transmission lever as described in paragraphs 4 to 8 of Section 2.

9 Fluid cooler - removal and refitting

Removal

1 The fluid cooler is mounted on the top of the transmission housing. To gain access to the fluid cooler, remove the air intake duct and, where necessary, the air cleaner housing as described in Chapter 4.

2 Using a hose clamp or similar, clamp both the fluid cooler coolant hoses to minimise coolant loss during subsequent operations **(see illustration)**.

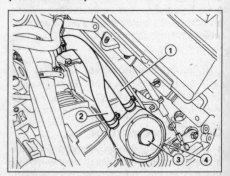

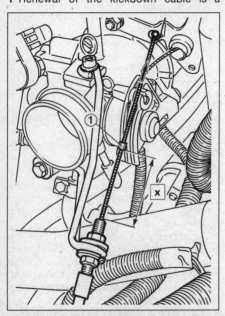

5.3 Fully extend the kickdown cable, and measure distance (X) between the cable lug (1) and the outer cable end

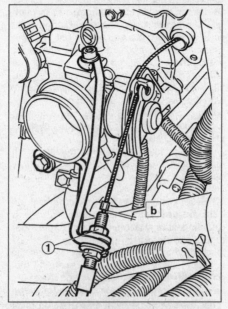

5.4 Reconnect the kickdown cable, and check that clearance (B) is as given in the text. If necessary, adjust by repositioning the locknuts (1)

9.2 Transmission fluid cooler details

1 Coolant hose   3 Centre bolt
2 Coolant hose   4 Fluid cooler

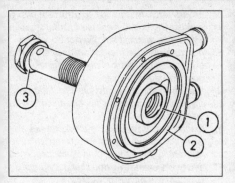

9.5 Transmission fluid cooler seals

1 Cooler inner seal   3 Centre bolt seal
2 Cooler outer seal

3 Slacken the retaining clips, and disconnect both coolant hoses from the fluid cooler - be prepared for some coolant spillage. Wash off any spilt coolant immediately with cold water, and dry the surrounding area before proceeding further.
4 Slacken and remove the fluid cooler centre bolt, and remove the cooler from the transmission. Remove the seal from the centre bolt, and the two seals fitted to the base of the cooler, and discard them; new ones must be used on refitting.

Refitting

5 Lubricate the new seals with clean automatic transmission fluid, then fit the two new seals to the base of the fluid cooler, and a new seal to the centre bolt **(see illustration)**.
6 Locate the fluid cooler on the top of transmission housing, ensuring its flat edge is parallel to the mating surface of the transmission/driveplate housing. Refit the centre bolt, and tighten it to the specified torque setting.
7 Reconnect the coolant hoses to the fluid cooler, and securely tighten their retaining clips. Remove the hose clamp.
8 Refit the disturbed intake duct/air cleaner housing components (as applicable) as described in Chapter 4.
9 On completion, top-up the cooling system and check the automatic transmission fluid level as described in Chapter 1.

10 Starter inhibitor/reversing light switch - general information, removal and refitting

General information

1 The starter inhibitor/reversing light switch is a dual-function switch which is screwed into the top of the transmission housing. The inhibitor function of the switch ensures that the engine can only be started with the selector lever in either the "N" or "P" positions, therefore preventing the engine

11.6 Adjusting the selector lever position display switch. Insert a screwdriver in the slot (1) and rotate the eccentric adjuster (2) so that the switch performs as described in the text

being started with the transmission in gear. This is achieved by the switch cutting the supply to the starter motor solenoid. If at any time it is noted that the engine can be started with the selector lever in any position other than "P" or "N", then it is likely that the inhibitor function of the switch is faulty. The switch also performs the function of the reversing light switch, illuminating the reversing lights whenever the selector lever is in the "R" position. If either function of the switch is faulty, the complete switch must be renewed as a unit.

Removal

2 To gain access to the switch, remove the battery and battery tray as described in Chapter 5, then unbolt the support tray from the top of the transmission.
3 Trace the wiring back from the switch, and disconnect it at the wiring connector.
4 Unscrew the switch, and remove it from the top of the transmission housing, along with its sealing ring.

Refitting

5 Fit a new sealing ring to the switch, screw it back into the transmission, and tighten it securely.
6 Reconnect the switch wiring, then refit the support tray and securely tighten its retaining bolts.
7 Refit the battery tray and battery as described in Chapter 5, and test the operation of the switch.

11 Selector lever position display switch - removal, refitting and adjustment

Removal

1 Working from inside the vehicle, carefully prise the selector lever trim panel out from the centre console, and fold the gaiter back over the selector lever.
2 Trace the wiring back from the switch, and disconnect it at its wiring connector.

3 Undo the two left-hand retaining nuts securing the selector lever to the floor, then disengage the position display switch from the selector lever studs and remove it from the vehicle.

Refitting and adjustment

4 Refit the position display switch onto the left-hand selector lever studs, ensuring that the switch lug is correctly engaged with the selector lever shaft. Refit the two left-hand selector lever retaining nuts, and tighten them to the specified torque.
5 Reconnect the wiring connector, then switch on the ignition and check the operation of the selector lever position display panel.
6 Move the selector lever throughout its range, and check that the corresponding position on the position display panel illuminates as each position is selected. If necessary, the switch can be adjusted by rotating the switch eccentric adjuster using a flat-bladed screwdriver **(see illustration)**.
7 Once the switch is correctly adjusted, fold the gaiter back down over the selector lever, and clip the trim panel back into position.

12 Automatic transmission - removal and refitting

Removal

1 Chock the rear wheels, apply the handbrake, and place the selector lever in the "N" (neutral) position. Jack up the front of the vehicle, and securely support it on axle stands. Remove both front roadwheels.
2 Drain the transmission fluid as described in Chapter 1, then refit the drain plugs, tightening them securely.
3 Remove the battery and battery tray as described in Chapter 5. Slacken and remove the support tray retaining bolts, then release the wiring from its retaining clip on the side of the tray, and remove the tray from the top of the transmission.
4 Remove the starter motor as described in Chapter 5.
5 Remove the air intake duct(s) as described in Chapter 4.
6 Undo the union nut securing the dipstick tube to the transmission sump, then undo the bolt securing the tube to the transmission housing, and remove the dipstick from the transmission unit.
7 Disconnect the wiring connector from the starter inhibitor/reversing light switch and, where necessary, the speedometer drive housing. Undo the retaining bolt(s) and disconnect the earth strap(s) from the top of the transmission housing.
8 Using a hose clamp or similar, clamp both the fluid cooler coolant hoses to minimise coolant loss. Slacken the retaining clips and disconnect both coolant hoses from the fluid cooler - be prepared for some coolant

7B

spillage. Wash off any spilt coolant immediately with cold water.

9 Undo the two screws securing the outer selector cable to its retaining bracket, and carefully lever the inner cable end fitting off its balljoint on the transmission selector lever. Note that the transmission selector lever must not be disturbed until the cable is refitted. As a precaution, mark the position of the lever in relation to the transmission housing. Work back along the selector cable, releasing it from any relevant retaining clips, and position it clear of the transmission unit.

10 Detach the kickdown inner cable from the throttle body cam, then slacken the outer cable locknuts and free the cable from its mounting bracket. Release the kickdown cable from any relevant retaining clips, so that it is free to be removed with the transmission unit.

11 On models with power steering, undo the nut securing the power steering pipe to the underside of the transmission, and free the pipe from its retaining stud.

12 Undo the retaining bolts and remove the lower driveplate cover plate from the transmission, to gain access to the torque converter retaining bolts. Slacken and remove the visible bolt then, using a socket and extension bar to rotate the crankshaft pulley, undo the remaining bolts securing the torque converter to the driveplate as they become accessible. There are three bolts in total.

13 To ensure that the torque converter does not fall out as the transmission is removed, secure it in position using a length of metal strip bolted to one of the starter motor bolt holes.

14 Withdraw the rubber retaining pin, disconnect the speedometer cable from the drive, and free it from any retaining clips.

15 Slacken and remove the three nuts securing the balljoint to the left-hand lower suspension arm, then withdraw the bolts and free the balljoint from the arm. Discard the nuts - new ones must be used on refitting. Repeat the procedure on the right-hand side.

16 Release the inner end of the right-hand driveshaft from the transmission, as described in Chapter 7A, Section 4, paragraphs 4 to 6.

17 Release the left-hand driveshaft inner constant velocity joint from the transmission by pulling the swivel hub assembly outwards. Withdraw the joint from the transmission, taking care not to damage the driveshaft oil seal. Support the driveshaft to avoid damaging the constant velocity joints or gaiters.

18 Place a jack with a block of wood beneath the engine, to take the weight of the engine. Alternatively, attach a couple of lifting eyes to the engine, and fit a hoist or support bar to take the weight of the engine.

19 Place a jack and block of wood beneath the transmission, and raise the jack to take the weight of the transmission.

20 Slacken and remove the centre nut and washer from the left-hand engine/transmission mounting. Undo the two bolts securing the mounting bracket assembly to the vehicle body, and remove the mounting bracket assembly, along with its spacer. Unscrew the mounting stud from the top of the transmission housing, and remove it, along with its washer.

21 With the jack positioned beneath the transmission taking the weight, slacken and remove the remaining bolts securing the transmission housing to the engine. Note the correct fitted positions of each bolt as it is removed, to use as a reference on refitting. Make a final check that all necessary components have been disconnected, and positioned clear of the transmission unit so that they will not hinder the removal procedure.

22 With the bolts removed, move the trolley jack and transmission to the left, to free it from its locating dowels.

23 Once the transmission is free, lower the jack and manoeuvre the unit out from under the car. If they are loose, remove the locating dowels from the transmission or engine unit, and keep them in a safe place.

Refitting

24 The transmission is refitted by a reversal of the removal procedure, bearing in mind the following points:

(a) Ensure the bush fitted to the centre of the crankshaft is in good condition, and apply a little Molykote G1 grease to the torque converter centring pin. Do not apply too much, otherwise there is a possibility of the grease contaminating the torque converter.

(b) Ensure the engine/transmission locating dowels are correctly positioned prior to installation.

(c) Once the transmission and engine are correctly joined, refit the securing bolts, tightening them to the specified torque setting, then remove the metal strip used to retain the torque converter.

(d) Apply thread-locking fluid to the left-hand engine/transmission mounting stud threads prior to refitting it to the transmission. Tighten the stud to the specified torque.

(e) Tighten all nuts and bolts to the specified torque (where given).

(f) Renew the driveshaft oil seals and refit the driveshafts to the transmission, using the information given in Section 4 of Chapter 7A.

(g) Adjust the selector cable and kickdown cable as described in Sections 2 and 5 of this Chapter.

(h) On completion, top-up the cooling system, then refill the transmission with the specified type and quantity of fluid as described in Chapter 1.

13 Automatic transmission overhaul - general information

In the event of a fault occurring with the transmission, it is first necessary to determine whether it is of an electrical, mechanical or hydraulic nature, and to do this, special test equipment is required. It is therefore essential to have the work carried out by a Citroën dealer if a transmission fault is suspected.

Do not remove the transmission from the car for possible repair before professional fault diagnosis has been carried out, since most tests require the transmission to be in the vehicle.

Chapter 8 Driveshafts

Contents

Driveshaft overhaul - general information 4
Driveshaft rubber gaiter and constant velocity (CV) joint
  check . . . . See Chapter 1
Driveshaft rubber gaiters - renewal 3
Driveshafts - removal and refitting 2
General information 1
Right-hand driveshaft intermediate bearing - renewal 5

Degrees of difficulty

Easy, suitable for novice with little experience	Fairly easy, suitable for beginner with some experience	Fairly difficult, suitable for competent DIY mechanic	Difficult, suitable for experienced DIY mechanic	Very difficult, suitable for expert DIY or professional

Specifications

Lubrication (overhaul only - see text)

Lubricant type/specification . . . . Use only special grease suppliedin sachets with gaiter kits - joints are otherwise pre-packed with grease and sealed

Torque wrench settings

	Nm	lbf ft
Driveshaft retaining nut:		
1124 cc and 1360 cc models	240	177
1580 cc and larger-engined models	320	236
Right-hand driveshaft intermediate bearing retaining bolt nuts	10	7
Lower suspension arm balljoint retaining nuts	45	33
Roadwheel bolts	90	66

1 General information

Drive is transmitted from the differential to the front wheels by means of two solid-steel driveshafts of unequal length.

Both driveshafts are splined at their outer ends, to accept the wheel hubs, and are threaded so that each hub can be fastened by a large nut. The inner end of each driveshaft is splined, to accept the differential sun gear.

Constant velocity (CV) joints are fitted to each end of the driveshafts, to ensure the smooth and efficient transmission of power at all suspension and steering angles. On 1124 cc and 1360 cc models, the outer constant velocity joints are of the spider-and-yoke type; on all 1580 cc and larger-engined models, they are of the ball-and-cage type. The inner constant velocity joints are of the tripod type on all models.

On the right-hand side, due to the length of the driveshaft, the inner constant velocity joint is situated approximately halfway along the shaft's length, and an intermediate support bearing is mounted in the engine/transmission rear mounting bracket. The inner end of the driveshaft passes through the bearing (which prevents any lateral movement of the driveshaft inner end) and the inner constant velocity joint outer member.

2 Driveshafts - removal and refitting

Removal

1 Chock the rear wheels of the car, firmly apply the handbrake, then jack up the front of the car and support it on axle stands. Remove the appropriate front roadwheel.
2 Drain the transmission oil or fluid as described in Chapter 1.
3 On models equipped with ABS, trace the wiring connector back from the wheel sensor, freeing it from its retaining clips, and disconnect it at its wiring connector.
4 On 1124 cc and 1360 cc models, using a hammer and a chisel or similar tool, tap up the staking securing the driveshaft retaining nut in position **(see illustration)**. Note that a new retaining must be used on refitting.
5 On all 1580 cc and larger-engined models, withdraw the R-clip and remove the locking cap from the driveshaft retaining nut.

6 Refit at least two roadwheel bolts to the front hub, and tighten them securely. Have an assistant firmly depress the brake pedal to prevent the front hub from rotating, then using a socket and a long extension bar, slacken and remove the driveshaft retaining nut. This nut is very tight; make sure that there is no risk of pulling the car off the axle stands. (If the roadwheel trim allows access to the driveshaft nut, the initial slackening can be done with the wheels chocked and on the ground.)

2.4 On 1124 cc and 1360 cc models, relieve the retaining nut staking with a suitable chisel-nosed tool

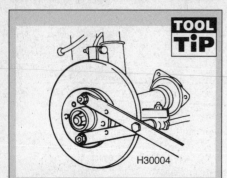

A tool to hold the front hub stationary can be fabricated from two lengths of steel strip (one long, one short) and a nut and bolt; the nut and bolt forming the pivot of a forked tool. Bolt the tool to the hub using two wheel bolts, and hold the tool to prevent the hub from rotating as the driveshaft retaining nut is undone.

7 Slacken and remove the three nuts securing the balljoint to the lower suspension arm, then withdraw the bolts and free the balljoint from the arm. Discard the nuts - new ones must be used on refitting.

Left-hand driveshaft

8 Carefully pull the swivel hub assembly outwards, and withdraw the driveshaft outer constant velocity joint from the hub assembly. If necessary, the shaft can be tapped out of the hub using a soft-faced mallet.
9 Support the driveshaft, then withdraw the inner constant velocity joint from the transmission, taking care not to damage the driveshaft oil seal. Remove the driveshaft from the vehicle.

Right-hand driveshaft

10 Loosen the two intermediate bearing retaining bolt nuts, then rotate the bolts through 90°, so that their offset heads are clear of the bearing outer race (see illustrations).
11 Carefully pull the swivel hub assembly outwards, and withdraw the driveshaft outer constant velocity joint from the hub assembly.

2.20 On 1124 cc and 1360 cc models, tighten the nut and stake it firmly into the driveshaft groove

2.10a On the right-hand driveshaft, slacken the two intermediate bearing retaining bolt nuts . . .

If necessary, the shaft can be tapped out of the hub using a soft-faced mallet.
12 Support the outer end of the driveshaft, then pull on the inner end of the shaft to free the intermediate bearing from its mounting bracket.
13 Once the driveshaft end is free from transmission, slide the dust seal off the inner end of the shaft, noting which way around it is fitted, and remove the driveshaft from the vehicle.

Refitting

14 Before installing the driveshaft, examine the driveshaft oil seal in the transmission for signs of damage or deterioration and, if necessary, renew it, referring to Chapter 7A for further information. (Having got this far it is worth renewing the seal as a matter of course.)
15 Thoroughly clean the driveshaft splines, and the apertures in the transmission and hub assembly. Apply a thin film of grease to the oil seal lips, and to the driveshaft splines and shoulders. Check that all gaiter clips are securely fastened.

Left-hand driveshaft

16 Offer up the driveshaft, and locate the joint splines with those of the differential sun gear, taking great care not to damage the oil seal. Push the joint fully into position.

2.21a On 1580 cc and larger-engined models, refit the locking cap . . .

2.10b . . . then rotate the bolts through 90° to disengage their offset heads (arrowed) from the bearing (shown with driveshaft removed)

17 Locate the outer constant velocity joint splines with those of the swivel hub, and slide the joint back into position in the hub.
18 Align the balljoint with the lower arm, and fit the three retaining bolts. Fit new retaining nuts to the bolts, and tighten them to the specified torque setting.
19 Lubricate the inner face and threads of the driveshaft retaining nut with clean engine oil, and refit it to the end of the driveshaft. Use the method employed on removal to prevent the hub from rotating, and tighten the driveshaft retaining nut to the specified torque. Check that the hub rotates freely.
20 On 1124 cc and 1360 cc models, stake the nut into the driveshaft grooves using a hammer and punch (see illustration).
21 On 1580 cc and larger-engined models, engage the locking cap with the driveshaft nut so that one of its cut-outs is aligned with the driveshaft hole. Secure the cap in position with the R-clip (see illustrations).
22 Where necessary, reconnect the ABS wheel sensor wiring connector, ensuring that the wiring is correctly routed and retained by all the necessary clips and ties.
23 Refit the roadwheel, then lower the vehicle to the ground and tighten the roadwheel bolts to the specified torque.
24 Refill the transmission with the specified type and amount of fluid/oil, and check the level using the information given in Chapter 1.

2.21b . . . and secure it in position with the R-clip

2.27a Manoeuvre the right-hand driveshaft into position . . .

2.27b . . . and locate the dust seal to its inner end, ensuring it is fitted the correct way round

2.29 Pull out the swivel hub assembly, and locate the outer constant velocity joint splines with those of the swivel hub

2.30 Secure the intermediate bearing in position, then slide the dust seal up tight against the driveshaft oil seal

Right-hand driveshaft

25 Check that the intermediate bearing rotates smoothly, without any sign of roughness or undue free play between its inner and outer races. If necessary, renew the bearing as described in Section 5. Examine the dust seal for signs of damage or deterioration, and renew if necessary.
26 Apply a smear of grease to the outer race of the intermediate bearing, and to the inner lip of the dust seal.
27 Pass the inner end of the shaft through the bearing mounting bracket, then carefully slide the dust seal into position on the driveshaft, ensuring that its flat surface is facing the transmission **(see illustrations)**.
28 Carefully locate the inner driveshaft splines with those of the differential sun gear, taking care not to damage the oil seal. Align the intermediate bearing with its mounting bracket, and push the driveshaft fully into position. If necessary, use a soft-faced mallet to tap the outer race of the bearing into position in the mounting bracket.
29 Locate the outer constant velocity joint splines with those of the swivel hub, and slide the joint back into position in the hub **(see illustration)**.
30 Ensure the intermediate bearing is correctly seated, then rotate its retaining bolts back through 90°, so that their offset heads are resting against the bearing outer race. Tighten the retaining nuts to the specified

torque. Ensure that the dust seal is tight against the driveshaft oil seal **(see illustration)**.
31 Carry out the operations described above in paragraphs 19 to 24.

3 Driveshaft rubber gaiters - renewal

Outer joint

1 Remove the driveshaft from the car as described in Section 2.

1124 cc and 1360 cc models

2 Remove the inner constant velocity joint and gaiter as described below in paragraphs 24 to 29. It is recommended that the inner gaiter is also renewed, regardless of its apparent condition.
3 Release the two outer gaiter retaining clips, then slide the gaiter off the inner end of the driveshaft.
4 Thoroughly clean the outer constant velocity joint using paraffin, or a suitable solvent, and dry it thoroughly. Carry out a visual inspection of the joint.
5 Check the driveshaft spider and outer member yoke for signs of wear, pitting or scuffing on their bearing surfaces. Also check that the outer member pivots smoothly and easily, with no traces of roughness.
6 If on inspection, the spider or outer member reveal signs of wear or damage, it will be necessary to renew the complete driveshaft as an assembly, since no components are available separately. If the joint components are in satisfactory condition, obtain a repair kit from your Citroën dealer, consisting of a new gaiter, retaining clips, and the correct type and quantity of grease.
7 Tape over the splines on the inner end of the driveshaft, then carefully slide the outer gaiter onto the shaft.
8 Pack the joint with the grease supplied in the repair kit. Work the grease well into the bearing tracks whilst twisting the joint, and fill the rubber gaiter with any excess.
9 Ease the gaiter over the joint, and ensure

that the gaiter lips are correctly located in the grooves on both the driveshaft and constant velocity joint. Lift the outer sealing lip of the gaiter, to equalise air pressure within the gaiter.
10 Fit the large metal retaining clip to the gaiter. Remove any slack in the gaiter retaining clip by carefully compressing the raised section of the clip. In the absence of the special tool, a pair of side cutters may be used. Secure the small retaining clip using the same procedure. Check that the constant velocity joint moves freely in all directions before proceeding further.
11 Refit the inner constant velocity joint as described in paragraphs 32 to 39.

1580 cc and larger-engined models

12 Secure the driveshaft in a vice equipped with soft jaws, and release the two rubber gaiter retaining clips. If necessary, the gaiter retaining clips can be cut to release them.
13 Slide the rubber gaiter down the shaft, to expose the outer constant velocity joint. Scoop out the excess grease.
14 Using a hammer and suitable soft metal drift, sharply strike the inner member of the outer joint to drive it off the end of the shaft. The joint is retained on the driveshaft by a circlip, and striking the joint in this manner forces the circlip into its groove, so allowing the joint to slide off.
15 Once the joint assembly has been removed, remove the circlip from the groove in the driveshaft splines, and discard it. A new circlip must be fitted on reassembly.
16 Withdraw the rubber gaiter from the driveshaft, and slide off the gaiter inner end plastic bush.
17 With the constant velocity joint removed from the driveshaft, thoroughly clean the joint using paraffin, or a suitable solvent, and dry it thoroughly. Carry out a visual inspection of the joint.
18 Move the inner splined driving member from side to side, to expose each ball in turn at the top of its track. Examine the balls for cracks, flat spots, or signs of surface pitting.
19 Inspect the ball tracks on the inner and outer members. If the tracks have widened, the balls will no longer be a tight fit. At the

8

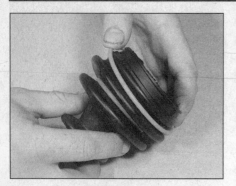

3.21a Fit the hard plastic rings to the outer CV joint gaiter . . .

3.21b . . . then slide on the new plastic bush (arrowed), and seat it in its recess in the shaft. Slide the gaiter onto the shaft . . .

3.21c . . . and seat the gaiter inner end on top of the plastic bush

same time, check the ball cage windows for wear or cracking between the windows.

20 If on inspection, any of the constant velocity joint components are found to be worn or damaged, it will be necessary to renew the complete joint assembly (where available), or even the complete driveshaft (where no joint components are available separately). Refer to your Citroën dealer for further information on parts availability. If the joint is in satisfactory condition, obtain a repair kit consisting of a new gaiter, circlip, retaining clips, and the correct type and quantity of grease.

21 To install the new gaiter, refer to the accompanying illustrations, and perform the operations shown (see illustrations 3.21a to 3.21k). Be sure to stay in order, and follow the

3.21d Fit the new circlip to its groove in the driveshaft splines . . .

3.21e . . . then locate the joint outer member on the splines, and slide it into position over the circlip. Ensure that the joint is securely retained by the circlip before proceeding

3.21f Pack the joint with the grease supplied, working it well into the ball tracks while twisting the joint, then locate the gaiter outer lip in its groove on the outer member

3.21g Fit the outer gaiter retaining clip and, using a hook fabricated out of welding rod and a pair of pliers, pull the clip tightly to remove all slack

3.21h Bend the clip end back over the buckle, then cut off the excess clip

3.21i Fold the clip end underneath the buckle . . .

3.21j . . . then fold the buckle firmly down onto the clip to secure the clip in position

3.21k Carefully lift the gaiter inner end to equalize air pressure in the gaiter, then secure the inner gaiter retaining clip in position using the same method

3.42a Release the inner gaiter retaining clips, and remove the joint outer member

3.42b Slide the gaiter off the end of the driveshaft . . .

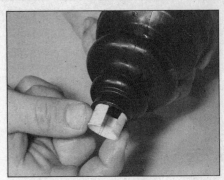

3.42c . . . and remove the plastic bush

captions carefully. Note that the hard plastic rings are not fitted to all gaiters, and the gaiter retaining clips supplied with the repair kit may be different to those shown in the sequence. To secure this other type of clip in position, lock the ends of the clip together, then remove any slack in the clip by carefully compressing the raised section of the clip using a pair of side cutters.

22 Check that the constant velocity joint moves freely in all directions, then refit the driveshaft to the car as described in Section 2.

Inner joint

23 Remove the driveshaft from the vehicle as described in Section 2.

1124 cc and 1360 cc models

24 Secure the driveshaft in a vice equipped with soft jaws then, using a suitable pair of pliers, carefully peel back the lip of the constant velocity joint outer member cover.

25 Once the lip of the cover is fully released, pull the joint outer member out from the cover, and recover the spring and thrust cap from the end of the shaft. Remove the O-ring from the outside of the outer member, and discard it.

26 Fold the gaiter back, and wipe away the excess grease from the tripod joint. If the rollers are not secured to the joint with circlips, wrap adhesive tape around the joint to hold them in position.

27 Using a dab of paint, or a hammer and punch, mark the relative position of the tripod joint in relation to the driveshaft. Using circlip pliers, extract the circlip securing the joint to the driveshaft.

28 The tripod joint can now be removed. If it is tight, draw the joint off the driveshaft end, using a two- or three-legged bearing puller. Ensure that the legs of the puller are located behind the joint inner member, and do not contact the joint rollers. Alternatively, support the inner member of the tripod joint, and press the shaft out of the joint using a hydraulic press, ensuring that no load is applied to the joint rollers.

29 With the tripod joint removed, slide the gaiter and inner retaining collar off the end of the driveshaft.

30 Thoroughly clean the constant velocity

joint components using paraffin, or a suitable solvent, and dry them thoroughly - take great care not to remove the alignment marks made on dismantling, especially if paint was used. Carry out a visual inspection of the joint.

31 Examine the tripod joint, rollers and outer member for any signs of scoring or wear, and for smoothness of movement of the rollers on the tripod stems. If any component is worn, the complete driveshaft assembly must be renewed; no joint components are available separately. If the joint components are in good condition, obtain a repair kit from your Citroën dealer, consisting of a new rubber gaiter and outer cover, circlip, thrust cap, spring, O-ring, and the correct quantity of the special grease.

32 Slide the gaiter into position inside the metal outer cover, then tape over the splines on the end of the driveshaft, and carefully slide the inner retaining collar and gaiter/cover assembly onto the shaft.

33 Remove the tape then, aligning the marks made on dismantling, engage the tripod joint with the driveshaft splines. Use a hammer and soft metal drift to tap the joint onto the shaft, taking great care not to damage the driveshaft splines or joint rollers.

34 Secure the tripod joint in position with the new circlip, ensuring that it is correctly located in the driveshaft groove.

35 Remove the tape (where fitted), and evenly distribute the special grease contained in the repair kit around the tripod joint and outer member. Pack the gaiter/cover with the remainder, then draw the cover over the tripod joint.

36 Fit the new O-ring, spring and thrust cap to the joint outer member.

37 Position the outer member assembly over the tripod joint, and locate the thrust cap against the end of the driveshaft. Push the outer member onto the shaft, compressing the spring, and locate it inside the outer cover. Secure the outer member in position by peening the end of the cover evenly over the joint outer edge.

38 Briefly lift the inner gaiter lip, using a blunt instrument such as a knitting needle, to equalise the air pressure within the gaiter. Secure the inner clip in position.

39 Check that the constant velocity joint moves freely in all directions, then refit the driveshaft to the car as described in Section 2.

1580 cc and larger-engined models

40 Remove the outer constant velocity joint as described above in paragraphs 1 to 5.

41 Tape over the splines on the driveshaft, and carefully remove the outer constant velocity joint rubber gaiter, and the gaiter inner end plastic bush. It is recommended that the outer joint gaiter is also renewed, regardless of its apparent condition.

42 Release the retaining clips, then slide the gaiter off the shaft, and remove its plastic bush. As the gaiter is released, the joint outer member will also be freed from the end of the shaft **(see illustrations)**.

43 Thoroughly clean the joint using paraffin, or a suitable solvent, and dry it thoroughly. Check the tripod joint bearings and joint outer member for signs of wear, pitting or scuffing on their bearing surfaces. Check that the bearing rollers rotate smoothly and easily around the tripod joint, with no traces of roughness.

44 If on inspection, the tripod joint or outer member reveal signs of wear or damage, it will be necessary to renew the complete driveshaft assembly, since the joint is not available separately. If the joint is in satisfactory condition, obtain a repair kit consisting of a new gaiter, retaining clips, and the correct type and quantity of grease. Although not strictly necessary, it is also recommended that the outer constant velocity joint gaiter is renewed, regardless of its apparent condition.

45 On reassembly, pack the inner joint with the grease supplied in the gaiter kit. Work the grease well into the bearing tracks and rollers, while twisting the joint.

46 Clean the shaft, using emery cloth to remove any rust or sharp edges which may damage the gaiter, then slide the plastic bush and inner joint gaiter along the driveshaft. Locate the plastic bush in its recess on the shaft, and seat the inner end of the gaiter on top of the bush.

47 Fit the outer member over the end of the

8

shaft, and locate the gaiter in the groove on the joint outer member. Push the outer member onto the joint, so that its spring-loaded plunger is compressed, then lift the outer edge of the gaiter to equalise air pressure in the gaiter. Fit both the inner and outer retaining clips, securing them in position using the information given in paragraph 21. Ensure the gaiter retaining clips are securely tightened, then check that the joint moves freely in all directions.

48 Refit the outer constant velocity joint components using the information given in paragraph 21.

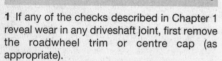

4 Driveshaft overhaul - general information

1 If any of the checks described in Chapter 1 reveal wear in any driveshaft joint, first remove the roadwheel trim or centre cap (as appropriate).

2 On 1124 cc and 1360 cc models, if the staking is still effective, the driveshaft nut should be correctly tightened; if in doubt, relieve the staking, then tighten the nut to the specified torque and restake it into the driveshaft grooves. Refit the roadwheel trim or centre cap (as applicable), and repeat the check on the remaining driveshaft nut.

3 On 1580 cc and larger-engined models, if the R-clip is fitted, the driveshaft nut should be correctly tightened; if in doubt, remove the R-clip and locking cap, and use a torque wrench to check that the nut is securely

fastened. Once tightened, refit the locking cap and R-clip, then refit the centre cap or trim. Repeat this check on the remaining driveshaft nut.

4 Road test the vehicle, and listen for a metallic clicking from the front as the vehicle is driven slowly in a circle on full-lock. If a clicking noise is heard, this indicates wear in the outer constant velocity joint. This means that the joint must be renewed; reconditioning is not possible.

5 If vibration, consistent with road speed, is felt through the car when accelerating, there is a possibility of wear in the inner constant velocity joints.

6 To check the joints for wear, remove the driveshafts, then dismantle them as described in Section 3; if any wear or free play is found, the affected joint must be renewed. In the case of the inner joints (and on some models, the outer joints), this means that the complete driveshaft assembly must be renewed, as the joints are not available separately. Refer to your Citroën dealer for information on the availability of driveshaft components.

5 Right-hand driveshaft intermediate bearing - renewal

Note: *A suitable bearing puller will be required, to draw the bearing and collar off the driveshaft end.*

1 Remove the right-hand driveshaft as described in Section 2 of this Chapter.

2 Check that the bearing outer race rotates

smoothly and easily, without any signs of roughness or undue free play between the inner and outer races. If necessary, renew the bearing as follows.

3 Using a long-reach universal bearing puller, carefully draw the collar and intermediate bearing off the driveshaft inner end **(see illustration)**. Apply a smear of grease to the inner race of the new bearing, then fit the bearing over the end of the driveshaft. Using a hammer and suitable piece of tubing which bears only on the bearing inner race, tap the new bearing into position on the driveshaft, until it abuts the constant velocity joint outer member. Once the bearing is correctly positioned, tap the bearing collar onto the shaft until it contacts the bearing inner race.

4 Check that the bearing rotates freely, then refit the driveshaft as described in Section 2.

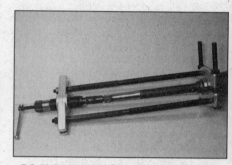

5.3 Using a long-reach bearing puller to remove the intermediate bearing from the right-hand driveshaft

Chapter 9 Braking system

Contents

Anti-lock Braking System (ABS) - general information 23
Anti-lock Braking System (ABS) components - removal and
   refitting 24
Brake pedal - removal and refitting 14
Front brake caliper - removal, overhaul and refitting 10
Front brake disc - inspection, removal and refitting 7
Front brake pad wear check . . . . See Chapter 1
Front brake pads - renewal 4
General information 1
Handbrake - adjustment 17
Handbrake cables - removal and refitting 19
Handbrake lever - removal and refitting 18
Hydraulic fluid level check . . . . See "Weekly checks"
Hydraulic fluid renewal . . . . See Chapter 1
Hydraulic pipes and hoses - renewal 3
Hydraulic system - bleeding 2
Master cylinder - removal, overhaul and refitting 13

Rear brake caliper - removal, overhaul and refitting 11
Rear brake disc - inspection, removal and refitting 8
Rear brake drum - removal, inspection and refitting 9
Rear brake pad wear check . . . . See Chapter 1
Rear brake pads - renewal 5
Rear brake pressure compensator (Estate models) - adjustment,
   removal and refitting 21
Rear brake pressure-regulating valves (models
   with rear disc brakes) - removal and refitting 20
Rear brake shoe wear check . . . . See Chapter 1
Rear brake shoes - renewal 6
Rear wheel cylinder - removal and refitting 12
Stop-light switch - removal, refitting and adjustment 22
Vacuum pump (16-valve models) - removal and refitting 25
Vacuum pump (16-valve models) - testing and overhaul 26
Vacuum servo unit - testing, removal and refitting 15
Vacuum servo unit check valve - removal, testing and refitting . . . 16

Degrees of difficulty

| Easy, suitable for novice with little experience | | Fairly easy, suitable for beginner with some experience | | Fairly difficult, suitable for competent DIY mechanic | | Difficult, suitable for experienced DIY mechanic | | Very difficult, suitable for expert DIY or professional | |

Specifications

Front brakes

Type	Disc, with single-piston sliding caliper
Disc diameter:	
16-valve models	266 mm
All other models	247 mm

	Solid disc	Ventilated disc
Disc thickness:		
New	10 mm	20.4 mm
Minimum thickness	8.0 mm	18.4 mm

Maximum disc run-out	0.2 mm
Brake pad minimum thickness	2.0 mm

Rear brakes

Type:	
Hatchback:	
Larger-engined models, and all models with ABS	Disc, with single-piston sliding caliper
All other non-ABS models	Single leading shoe drum
Estate:	
ABS and non-ABS models	Single leading shoe drum
Drum brakes:	
Drum diameter:	
Hatchback:	
New	180 mm
Maximum diameter after machining	182 mm
Estate:	
New	228.6 mm
Maximum diameter after machining	229.8 mm
Disc brakes:	
Disc diameter	247 mm
Disc thickness:	
New	8.0 mm
Minimum thickness	6.0 mm
Maximum disc run-out	0.2 mm
Brake pad minimum thickness	2.0 mm

9

ABS system

Wheel sensor-to-reluctor ring air gap . . . . 0.3 to 1.2 mm

Torque wrench settings	Nm	lbf ft
Front brake caliper:		
Guide pin bolts (Girling caliper)	35	26
Mounting bracket-to-swivel hub bolts	120	89
Rear brake caliper mounting bolts	120	89
Rear hub nut:		
Models with rear drum brakes	200	148
Models with rear disc brakes	180	133
Master cylinder-to-servo unit nuts	10	7
Brake pedal pivot bolt	25	18
Pedal bracket retaining nuts	5	4
Vacuum servo unit mounting nuts	20	15
ABS wheel sensor retaining bolts	9	7
Roadwheel bolts	90	66

1 General information

The braking system is of the servo-assisted, dual-circuit hydraulic type. The arrangement of the hydraulic system is such that each circuit operates one front and one rear brake from a tandem master cylinder. Under normal circumstances, both circuits operate in unison. However, in the event of hydraulic failure in one circuit, full braking force will still be available at two wheels.

Most large-capacity engine Hatchback models have disc brakes all round as standard; all other Hatchback models not equipped with the Anti-lock Braking System (ABS), and all Estate models, feature front disc brakes and rear drum brakes. ABS is fitted as standard to the 16-valve model, and was offered as an option on most other models. On Hatchback models equipped with ABS, disc brakes are fitted at both the front and rear, while on Estate models equipped with ABS, drum brakes are still retained at the rear.

The front disc brakes are actuated by single-piston sliding type calipers, which ensure that equal pressure is applied to each disc pad.

On models with rear drum brakes, the rear brakes incorporate leading and trailing shoes which are actuated by twin-piston wheel cylinders. The wheel cylinders on Hatchback models incorporate integral pressure regulating valves, which control the hydraulic pressure applied to the rear brakes. On Estate models a load-sensitive pressure compensator is used to control rear brake hydraulic pressure. The regulating valves and pressure compensator help to prevent rear wheel lock-up during emergency braking. A self-adjust mechanism is incorporated, to automatically compensate for brake shoe wear. As the brake shoe linings wear, the footbrake operation automatically operates the adjuster mechanism, which effectively lengthens the shoe strut and repositions the brake shoes, to remove the lining-to-drum clearance.

On models with rear disc brakes, the brakes are actuated by single-piston sliding calipers which incorporate mechanical handbrake mechanisms. A pressure-regulating valve is situated in the brake line to each rear caliper. The regulating valve is similar to that fitted to the rear wheel cylinders on drum brake models, and helps to prevent rear wheel lock-up during emergency braking.

On all models, the handbrake provides an independent mechanical means of rear brake application.

On 16-valve models, due to the ACAV intake system, there is insufficient vacuum in the inlet manifold to operate the braking system servo effectively at all times. To overcome this problem, a vacuum pump is fitted to the engine, to supplement the inlet manifold vacuum and ensure that sufficient vacuum is always present in the servo unit. The vacuum pump is mounted on the end of the cylinder head, and driven directly off the end of the inlet camshaft.

Note: *When servicing any part of the system, work carefully and methodically; also observe scrupulous cleanliness when overhauling any part of the hydraulic system. Always renew components (in axle sets, where applicable) if in doubt about their condition, and use only genuine Citroën replacement parts, or at least those of known good quality. Note the warnings given in "Safety first" and at relevant points in this Chapter concerning the dangers of asbestos dust and hydraulic fluid.*

2 Hydraulic system - bleeding

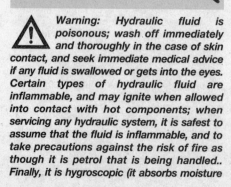

Warning: Hydraulic fluid is poisonous; wash off immediately and thoroughly in the case of skin contact, and seek immediate medical advice if any fluid is swallowed or gets into the eyes. Certain types of hydraulic fluid are inflammable, and may ignite when allowed into contact with hot components; when servicing any hydraulic system, it is safest to assume that the fluid is inflammable, and to take precautions against the risk of fire as though it is petrol that is being handled.. Finally, it is hygroscopic (it absorbs moisture from the air) - old fluid may be contaminated and unfit for further use. When topping-up or renewing the fluid, always use the recommended type, and ensure that it comes from a freshly-opened sealed container.

 Hydraulic fluid is an effective paint stripper, and will attack plastics; if any is spilt, it should be washed off immediately, using copious quantities of fresh water

General

1 The correct operation of any hydraulic system is only possible after removing all air from the components and circuit; this is achieved by bleeding the system.

2 During the bleeding procedure, add only clean, unused hydraulic fluid of the recommended type; never re-use fluid that has already been bled from the system. Ensure that sufficient fluid is available before starting work.

3 If there is any possibility of incorrect fluid being already in the system, the brake components and circuit must be flushed completely with uncontaminated, correct fluid, and new seals should be fitted to the various components.

4 If hydraulic fluid has been lost from the system, or air has entered because of a leak, ensure that the fault is cured before proceeding further.

5 Park the vehicle on level ground, switch off the engine and select first or reverse gear, then chock the wheels and release the handbrake.

6 Check that all pipes and hoses are secure, unions tight and bleed screws closed. Clean any dirt from around the bleed screws.

7 Unscrew the master cylinder reservoir cap, and top the master cylinder reservoir up to the "MAX" level line; refit the cap loosely, and remember to maintain the fluid level at least above the "MIN" level line throughout the procedure, or there is a risk of further air entering the system.

8 There are a number of one-man, do-it-yourself brake bleeding kits currently available from motor accessory shops. It is recommended that one of these kits is used whenever possible, as they greatly simplify the bleeding operation, and also reduce the risk of expelled air and fluid being drawn back into the system. If such a kit is not available, the basic (two-man) method must be used, which is described in detail below.

9 If a kit is to be used, prepare the vehicle as described previously, and follow the kit manufacturer's instructions, as the procedure may vary slightly according to the type being used; generally, they are as outlined below in the relevant sub-section.

10 Whichever method is used, the same sequence must be followed (paras 11 and 12) to ensure the removal of all air from the system.

Bleeding sequence

11 If the system has been only partially disconnected, and suitable precautions were taken to minimise fluid loss, it should be necessary only to bleed that part of the system (ie the primary or secondary circuit).

12 If the complete system is to be bled, then it should be done working in the following sequence:

Non-ABS models
(a) Left-hand rear brake.
(b) Right-hand front brake.
(c) Right-hand rear brake.
(d) Left-hand front brake.

ABS models
(a) Left-hand front brake.
(b) Right-hand front brake.
(c) Left-hand rear brake.
(d) Right-hand rear brake.

Note: If difficulty is experienced in bleeding the braking circuit on models with ABS, try bleeding the complete system working in the reverse of the specified sequence, starting with the right-hand rear brake and finishing with the left-hand front brake.

Bleeding - basic (two-man) method

13 Collect a clean glass jar, a suitable length of plastic or rubber tubing which is a tight fit over the bleed screw, and a ring spanner to fit the screw. The help of an assistant will also be required.

14 Remove the dust cap from the first screw in the sequence. Fit the spanner and tube to the screw, place the other end of the tube in the jar, and pour in sufficient fluid to cover the end of the tube.

15 Ensure that the master cylinder reservoir fluid level is maintained at least above the "MIN" level line throughout the procedure.

16 Have the assistant fully depress the brake pedal several times to build up pressure, then maintain it on the final downstroke.

17 While pedal pressure is maintained, unscrew the bleed screw (approximately one turn) and allow the compressed fluid and air to flow into the jar. The assistant should maintain pedal pressure, following it down to the floor if necessary, and should not release it until instructed to do so. When the flow stops,

tighten the bleed screw again, have the assistant release the pedal slowly, and recheck the reservoir fluid level.

18 Repeat the steps given in paragraphs 16 and 17 until the fluid emerging from the bleed screw is free from air bubbles. If the master cylinder has been drained and refilled, and air is being bled from the first screw in the sequence, allow approximately five seconds between cycles for the master cylinder passages to refill.

19 When no more air bubbles appear, tighten the bleed screw securely, remove the tube and spanner, and refit the dust cap. Do not overtighten the bleed screw.

20 Repeat the procedure on the remaining screws in the sequence, until all air is removed from the system and the brake pedal feels firm again.

Bleeding - using a one-way valve kit

21 As their name implies, these kits consist of a length of tubing with a one-way valve fitted, to prevent expelled air and fluid being drawn back into the system; some kits include a translucent container, which can be positioned so that the air bubbles can be more easily seen flowing from the end of the tube.

22 The kit is connected to the bleed screw, which is then opened. The user returns to the driver's seat, depresses the brake pedal with a smooth, steady stroke, and slowly releases it; this is repeated until the expelled fluid is clear of air bubbles **(see illustration)**.

23 Note that these kits simplify work so much that it is easy to forget the master cylinder reservoir fluid level; ensure that this is maintained at least above the "MIN" level line at all times.

Bleeding - using a pressure-bleeding kit

24 These kits are usually operated by the reservoir of pressurised air contained in the spare tyre. However, note that it will probably be necessary to reduce the pressure to a lower level than normal; refer to the instructions supplied with the kit.

25 By connecting a pressurised, fluid-filled container to the master cylinder reservoir, bleeding can be carried out simply by opening each screw in turn (in the specified sequence), and allowing the fluid to flow out until no more air bubbles can be seen in the expelled fluid.

26 This method has the advantage that the large reservoir of fluid provides an additional safeguard against air being drawn into the system during bleeding.

27 Pressure-bleeding is particularly effective when bleeding "difficult" systems, or when bleeding the complete system at the time of routine fluid renewal.

All methods of bleeding

28 When bleeding is complete, and firm pedal feel is restored, wash off any spilt fluid, tighten the bleed screws securely, and refit their dust caps.

2.22 Bleeding a rear brake caliper using a one-way valve kit

29 Check the hydraulic fluid level in the master cylinder reservoir, and top-up if necessary (Chapter 1).

30 Discard any hydraulic fluid that has been bled from the system; it will not be fit for re-use.

31 Check the feel of the brake pedal. If it feels at all spongy, air must still be present in the system, and further bleeding is required. Failure to bleed satisfactorily after a reasonable repetition of the bleeding procedure may be due to worn master cylinder seals.

---

3 Hydraulic pipes and hoses - renewal

Note: Before starting work, refer to the note at the beginning of Section 2 concerning the dangers of hydraulic fluid.

1 If any pipe or hose is to be renewed, minimise fluid loss by first removing the master cylinder reservoir cap, then tightening it down onto a piece of polythene to obtain an airtight seal. Alternatively, flexible hoses can be sealed, if required, using a proprietary brake hose clamp; metal brake pipe unions can be plugged (if care is taken not to allow dirt into the system) or capped immediately they are disconnected. Place a wad of rag under any union that is to be disconnected, to catch any spilt fluid.

2 If a flexible hose is to be disconnected, unscrew the brake pipe union nut before removing the spring clip which secures the hose to its mounting bracket **(see illustration)**.

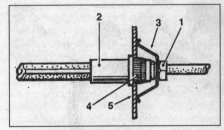

3.2 Hydraulic pipe-to-flexible hose connection

1 Union nut
2 Flexible hose
3 Spring clip support
4 Splined end fitting
5 Mounting bracket

4.2 Disconnecting the pad wear sensor wiring from its connector

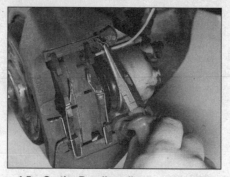

4.5a On the Bendix caliper, remove the spring clip . . .

4.5b . . . then slide out the retaining plate . . .

3 To unscrew the union nuts, it is preferable to obtain a brake pipe spanner of the correct size; these are available from most large motor accessory shops. Failing this, a close-fitting open-ended spanner will be required, though if the nuts are tight or corroded, their flats may be rounded-off if the spanner slips. In such a case, a self-locking wrench is often the only way to unscrew a stubborn union, but it follows that the pipe and the damaged nuts must be renewed on reassembly. Always clean a union and surrounding area before disconnecting it. If disconnecting a component with more than one union, make a careful note of the connections before disturbing any of them.

4 If a brake pipe is to be renewed, it can be obtained, cut to length and with the union nuts and end flares in place, from Citroën dealers. All that is then necessary is to bend it to shape, following the line of the original, before fitting it to the car. Alternatively, most motor accessory shops can make up brake pipes from kits, but this requires very careful measurement of the original, to ensure that the replacement is of the correct length. The safest answer is usually to take the original to the shop as a pattern.

5 On refitting, do not overtighten the union nuts. It is not necessary to exercise brute force to obtain a sound joint.

6 Ensure that the pipes and hoses are correctly routed, with no kinks, and that they are secured in the clips or brackets provided. After fitting, remove the polythene from the reservoir, and bleed the hydraulic system as

described in Section 2. Wash off any spilt fluid, and check carefully for fluid leaks.

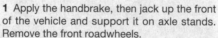

4 Front brake pads - renewal

⚠️ *Warning: Renew both sets of front brake pads at the same time - never renew the pads on only one wheel, as uneven braking may result. Note that the dust created by wear of the pads may contain asbestos, which is a health hazard. Never blow it out with compressed air, and don't inhale any of it. An approved filtering mask should be worn when working on the brakes. DO NOT use petrol or petroleum-based solvents to clean brake parts; use brake cleaner or methylated spirit only.*

1 Apply the handbrake, then jack up the front of the vehicle and support it on axle stands. Remove the front roadwheels.

2 Trace the brake pad wear sensor wiring back from the pads, and disconnect it from the wiring connector **(see illustration)**. Note the routing of the wiring, and free it from any relevant retaining clips.

3 Push the piston into its bore by pulling the caliper outwards.

4 There are two different types of front brake caliper fitted to the models covered in this manual. On 1124 cc and 1360 cc models, Bendix calipers are fitted, whereas on all 1580 cc and larger-engined models, Girling

calipers are used. Proceed as described under the relevant sub-heading.

Bendix caliper

5 Using pliers, extract the small spring clip from the pad retaining plate, and then slide the plate out of the caliper **(see illustrations)**.

6 Withdraw the pads from the caliper, then make a note of the correct fitted position of each anti-rattle spring, and remove the spring from each pad **(see illustration)**.

7 First measure the thickness of each brake pad's friction material. If either pad is worn at any point to the specified minimum thickness or less, all four pads must be renewed **(see illustration)**. Also, the pads should be renewed if any are fouled with oil or grease; there is no satisfactory way of degreasing friction material, once contaminated. If any of the brake pads are worn unevenly, or are fouled with oil or grease, trace and rectify the cause before reassembly. New brake pads and spring kits are available from Citroën dealers.

8 If the brake pads are still serviceable, carefully clean them using a clean, fine wire brush or similar, paying particular attention to the sides and back of the metal backing. Clean out the grooves in the friction material, and pick out any large embedded particles of dirt or debris. Carefully clean the pad locations in the caliper body/mounting bracket.

9 Prior to fitting the pads, check that the guide pins are free to slide easily in the caliper body/mounting bracket, and check that the rubber guide pin gaiters are undamaged **(see illustration)**. Brush the dust and dirt from the

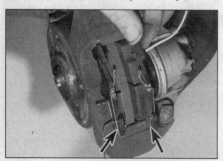

4.6 . . . and remove the pads. Note the correct fitted positions on pad springs (arrowed)

4.7 Measuring brake pad friction material thickness

4.9 While the caliper is removed, check the condition of the guide pins and gaiters - Girling caliper shown

caliper and piston, but *do not* inhale it, as it is injurious to health. Inspect the dust seal around the piston for damage, and the piston for evidence of fluid leaks, corrosion or damage. If attention to any of these components is necessary, refer to Section 10.

10 If new brake pads are to be fitted, the caliper piston must be pushed back into the cylinder to make room for them. Either use a G-clamp or similar tool, or use suitable pieces of wood as levers. Provided that the master cylinder reservoir has not been overfilled with hydraulic fluid, there should be no spillage, but keep a careful watch on the fluid level while retracting the piston. If the fluid level rises above the "MAX" level line at any time, the surplus should be syphoned off or ejected via a plastic tube connected to the bleed screw (see Section 2). **Note:** *Do not syphon the fluid by mouth, as it is poisonous; use a syringe or an old poultry baster.*

11 Fit the anti-rattle springs to the pads, so that when the pads are installed in the caliper, the spring end will be located at the opposite end of the pad in relation to the pad retaining plate.

12 Locate the pads in the caliper, ensuring that the friction material of each pad is against the brake disc, and check that the anti-rattle spring ends are at the opposite end of the pad to which the retaining plate is to be inserted. Note that if the pads are installed correctly, looking at the pads from the front of the vehicle, the innermost pad groove must be higher than the outer pad groove. Ensure the pads are fitted correctly before proceeding **(see illustration)**.

13 Slide the retaining plate into place, and install the new small spring clip at its inner end. It may be necessary to file an entry chamfer on the edge of the retaining plate, to enable it to be fitted without difficulty.

14 Reconnect the brake pad wear sensor wiring connectors, ensuring that the outer wire is correctly routed through the anti-rattle spring loops, and that both wires pass through the loop of the bleed screw cap.

15 Depress the brake pedal repeatedly, until the pads are pressed into firm contact with

the brake disc, and normal (non-assisted) pedal pressure is restored.

16 Repeat the above procedure on the remaining front brake caliper.

17 Refit the roadwheels, then lower the vehicle to the ground and tighten the roadwheel bolts to the specified torque setting.

18 Check the hydraulic fluid level as described in Chapter 1.

Girling caliper

19 Slacken and remove the upper and lower caliper guide pin bolts, using a slim open-ended spanner to prevent the guide pin itself from rotating **(see illustration)**. Where possible, new guide pin bolts should be used on refitting, otherwise clean the old ones thoroughly.

20 With the guide pin bolts removed, lift the caliper away from the brake pads and mounting bracket, and tie it to the suspension strut using a suitable piece of wire. Do not allow the caliper to hang unsupported on the flexible brake hose.

21 Withdraw the two brake pads from the caliper mounting bracket, and examine them as described above in paragraphs 7 to 10.

22 Install the pads in the caliper mounting bracket, ensuring that the friction material of each pad is against the brake disc **(see illustration)**.

23 Position the caliper over the pads, and pass the pad warning sensor wiring through the caliper aperture and underneath the retaining clip **(see illustration)**. If the threads of the guide pin bolts are not already coated with locking compound, apply a suitable thread-locking compound to them. Press the caliper into position, then install the guide pin bolts, tightening them to the specified torque setting while retaining the guide pins with an open-ended spanner.

24 Reconnect the brake pad wear sensor wiring connectors, ensuring that the wiring is correctly routed through the loop of the caliper bleed screw cap.

25 Depress the brake pedal repeatedly, until the pads are pressed into firm contact with the brake disc, and normal (non-assisted) pedal pressure is restored.

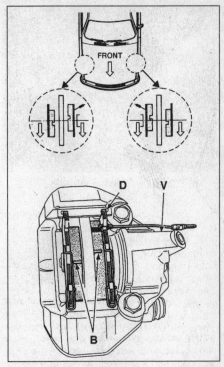

4.12 Correct fitting of brake pads - Bendix caliper

B Grooves
D Pad retaining plate spring clip
V Bleed screw

26 Repeat the above procedure on the remaining front brake caliper.

27 Refit the roadwheels, then lower the vehicle to the ground and tighten the roadwheel bolts to the specified torque setting.

28 Check the hydraulic fluid level as described in Chapter 1.

All calipers

29 New pads will not give full braking efficiency until they have bedded in. Be prepared for this, and avoid hard braking as far as possible for the first hundred miles or so after pad renewal.

4.19 On the Girling caliper, retain the guide pin with an open-ended spanner while slackening the guide pin bolt

4.22 Ensure that the brake pads are fitted the correct way around, with friction material facing the disc . . .

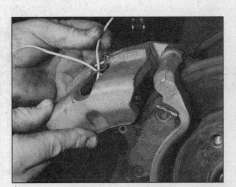

4.23 . . . then refit the caliper, feeding the pad wiring through the caliper aperture

9

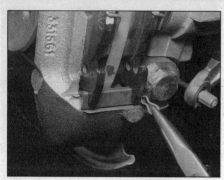

5.2a Extract the spring clip . . .

5.2b . . . then slide out the pad retaining plate . . .

5.3 . . . and withdraw the brake pads from the caliper

5 Rear brake pads - renewal

Warning: Renew both sets of rear brake pads at the same time - never renew the pads on only one wheel, as uneven braking may result. Note that the dust created by wear of the pads may contain asbestos, which is a health hazard. Never blow it out with compressed air, and don't inhale any of it. An approved filtering mask should be worn when working on the brakes. DO NOT use petrol or petroleum-based solvents to clean brake parts; use brake cleaner or methylated spirit only.

1 Chock the front wheels, then jack up the rear of the vehicle and support it on axle stands. Remove the rear wheels.
2 Extract the small spring clip from the pad retaining plate, and then slide the plate out of the caliper (see illustrations). Discard the spring clip - a new one must be used on refitting.
3 Using pliers if necessary, withdraw both the inner and outer pads from the caliper (see illustration). Make a note of the correct fitted position of the anti-rattle springs, and remove the springs from each pad.
4 First measure the thickness of the friction

material of each brake pad. If either pad is worn at any point to the specified minimum thickness or less, all four pads must be renewed. Also, the pads should be renewed if any are fouled with oil or grease; there is no satisfactory way of degreasing friction material, once contaminated. If any of the brake pads are worn unevenly, or fouled with oil or grease, trace and rectify the cause before reassembly. New brake pads and spring kits are available from Citroën dealers.
5 If the brake pads are still serviceable, carefully clean them using a clean, fine wire brush or similar, paying particular attention to the sides and back of the metal backing. Clean out the grooves in the friction material, and pick out any large embedded particles of dirt or debris. Carefully clean the pad locations in the caliper body/mounting bracket.
6 Prior to fitting the pads, check that the guide sleeves are free to slide easily in the caliper body, and check that the rubber guide sleeve gaiters are undamaged. Brush the dust and dirt from the caliper and piston, but **do not** inhale it, as it is injurious to health. Inspect the dust seal around the piston for damage, and the piston for evidence of fluid leaks, corrosion or damage. If attention to any of these components is necessary, refer to Section 11.
7 If new brake pads are to be fitted, it will be necessary to retract the piston fully into the

caliper bore, by rotating it in a clockwise direction. This can be achieved using a suitable square-section bar, such as the shaft of a screwdriver, which locates snugly in the caliper piston slots (see illustration). Provided that the master cylinder reservoir has not been overfilled with hydraulic fluid, there should be no spillage, but keep a careful watch on the fluid level while retracting the piston. If the fluid level rises above the "MAX" level line at any time, the surplus should be syphoned off, or ejected via a plastic tube connected to the bleed screw (see Section 2). **Note:** *Do not syphon the fluid by mouth, as it is poisonous; use a syringe or an old poultry baster.*
8 Position the caliper piston so that its piston slot is horizontal; this is necessary to ensure that the lug on the inner pad will locate with the caliper piston slot on installation (see illustration).
9 The brake pad with the lug on its backing plate is the inner pad. Refit the anti-rattle springs to the pads, so that when the pads are installed in the caliper, the spring end will be located at the opposite end of the pad, in relation to the pad retaining plate (see illustration).
10 Locate the outer brake pad in the caliper body, ensuring that its friction material is against the brake disc. Slide the inner pad into position in the caliper, ensuring that the lug on

5.7 Retract the piston using a square-section bar . . .

5.8 . . . and position the piston so that its slot (arrowed) is horizontal to the ground

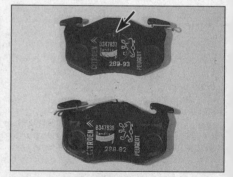

5.9 Inner brake pad can be identified by its locating lug (arrowed). Note the correct fitted positions of the anti-rattle springs

5.10 Install the inner pad, ensuring its locating lug is correctly engaged in the piston slot

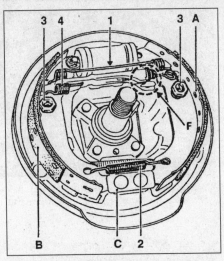

6.6a Correct fitted positions of the Bendix rear brake components

A Leading shoe
B Trailing shoe
C Lower pivot point
F Adjuster strut mechanism
1 Upper return spring
2 Lower return spring
3 Retaining pin, spring and spring cup
4 Adjuster strut-to-trailing shoe spring

6.6b Removing a shoe retainer spring cup

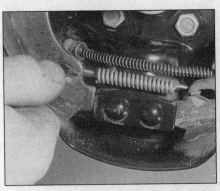

6.7 On Bendix rear brake shoes, ease the shoes out of the lower pivot point, and disconnect the lower return spring

its backing plate is aligned with the slot in the caliper piston (see illustration).

11 Ensure that the anti-rattle spring ends on both pads are correctly positioned, then slide the retaining plate into place, and secure it in position with a new spring clip. It may be necessary to file an entry chamfer on the edge of the retaining plate, to enable it to be fitted without difficulty.

12 Depress the brake pedal repeatedly until the pads are pressed into firm contact with the brake disc, and normal (non-assisted) pedal pressure is restored. Check that the inner pad lug is correctly engaged with one of the caliper piston slots.

13 Repeat the above procedure on the remaining rear brake caliper.

14 Check the handbrake cable adjustment as described in Section 17, then refit the roadwheels and lower the vehicle to the ground. Tighten the roadwheel bolts to the specified torque setting.

15 Check the hydraulic fluid level as described in Chapter 1.

16 Be prepared for reduced braking efficiency while the new pads bed in, as described at the end of the previous Section.

6 Rear brake shoes - renewal

⚠ **Warning: Brake shoes must be renewed on both rear wheels at the same time - never renew the shoes on only one wheel, as uneven braking may result. Also, the dust created by wear of the shoes may contain asbestos, which is a health hazard. Never blow it out with compressed air, and don't inhale any of it. An approved filtering mask should be worn when working on the brakes. DO NOT use petrol or petroleum-based solvents to clean brake parts; use brake cleaner or methylated spirit only.**

1 Remove the brake drum as described in Section 9.

2 Working carefully, and taking the necessary precautions, remove all traces of brake dust from the brake drum, backplate and shoes.

3 Measure the thickness of the friction material of each brake shoe at several points; if either shoe is worn at any point to the specified minimum thickness or less, all four shoes must be renewed as a set. The shoes should also be renewed if any are fouled with oil or grease; there is no satisfactory way of degreasing friction material, once contaminated.

4 If any of the brake shoes are worn unevenly, or fouled with oil or grease, trace and rectify the cause before reassembly.

5 To renew the brake shoes, proceed as described under the relevant sub-heading.

Bendix brake shoes - Hatchback models

6 Using a pair of pliers, remove the shoe retainer spring cups by depressing and turning them through 90° (see illustrations). With the cups removed, lift off the springs and withdraw the retainer pins.

7 Ease the shoes out one at a time from the lower pivot point, to release the tension of the return spring, then disconnect the lower return spring from both shoes (see illustration).

8 Ease the upper end of both shoes out from their wheel cylinder locations, taking care not to damage the wheel cylinder seals, and disconnect the handbrake cable from the trailing shoe. The brake shoe and adjuster strut assembly can then be manoeuvred out of position and away from the backplate. Do not depress the brake pedal until the brakes are reassembled; wrap a strong elastic band around the wheel cylinder pistons to retain them.

9 With the shoe and adjuster strut assembly on a bench, make a note of the correct fitted positions of the springs and adjuster strut, to use as a guide on reassembly. Release the handbrake lever stop-peg (if not already done), then carefully detach the adjuster strut bolt retaining spring from the leading shoe. Disconnect the upper return spring, then detach the leading shoe and return spring from the trailing shoe and strut assembly. Unhook the spring securing the adjuster strut to the trailing shoe, and separate the two.

10 If genuine Citroën brake shoes are being installed, it will be necessary to remove the handbrake lever from the original trailing shoe, and install it on the new shoe. Secure the lever in position with a new retaining clip. All return springs should be renewed, regardless of their apparent condition; spring kits are also available from Citroën dealers.

11 Withdraw the adjuster bolt from the strut, and carefully examine the assembly for signs of wear or damage. Pay particular attention to the threads of the adjuster bolt and the knurled adjuster wheel, and renew if necessary. Note that left-hand and right-hand struts are not interchangeable - they are marked "G" (gauche) and "D" (droit) respectively. Also note that the strut adjuster bolts are not interchangeable; the left-hand strut bolt has a left-handed thread, and the right-hand bolt a right-handed thread.

12 Ensure the components on the end of the strut are correctly positioned, then apply a little high-melting-point grease to the threads

6.12 Correct fitted position of Bendix adjuster strut components

6.16 Apply a little high-melting-point grease to the shoe contact points on the backplate

of the adjuster bolt (see illustration). Screw the adjuster wheel onto the bolt until only a small gap exists between the wheel and the head of the bolt, then install the bolt in the strut.

13 Fit the adjuster strut retaining spring to the trailing shoe, ensuring that the shorter hook of the spring is engaged with the shoe. Attach the adjuster strut to the spring end, then ease the strut into position in its slot in the trailing shoe.

14 Engage the upper return spring with the trailing shoe, then hook the leading shoe onto the other end of the spring, and lever the leading shoe down until the adjuster bolt head is correctly located in its groove. Once the bolt is correctly located, hook its retaining spring into the slot on the leading shoe.

15 Peel back the rubber protective caps, and check the wheel cylinder for fluid leaks or other damage; check that both cylinder pistons are free to move easily. Refer to Section 12, if necessary, for information on wheel cylinder renewal.

16 Prior to installation, clean the backplate, and apply a thin smear of high-temperature brake grease or anti-seize compound to all those surfaces of the backplate which bear on the shoes, particularly the wheel cylinder pistons and lower pivot point (see

illustration). Do not allow the lubricant to foul the friction material.

17 Ensure the handbrake lever stop-peg is correctly located against the edge of the trailing shoe, and remove the elastic band fitted to the wheel cylinder.

18 Manoeuvre the shoe and strut assembly into position on the vehicle, and locate the upper end of both shoes with the wheel cylinder pistons. Attach the handbrake cable to the trailing shoe lever. Fit the lower return spring to both shoes, and ease the shoes into position on the lower pivot point.

19 Tap the shoes to centralise them with the backplate, then refit the shoe retainer pins and springs, and secure them in position with the spring cups.

20 Using a screwdriver, turn the strut adjuster wheel to expand the shoes until the brake drum just slides over the shoes.

21 Refit the brake drum as described in Section 9.

22 Repeat the above procedure on the remaining rear brake.

23 Once both sets of rear shoes have been renewed, adjust the lining-to-drum clearance by repeatedly depressing the brake pedal. Whilst depressing the pedal, have an assistant listen to the rear drums, to check that the adjuster strut is functioning correctly; if so, a clicking sound will be emitted by the strut as the pedal is depressed.

24 Check and, if necessary, adjust the handbrake as described in Section 17.

25 On completion, check the hydraulic fluid level as described in "Weekly checks".

Bendix brake shoes - Estate models

26 Although of larger diameter, the Bendix rear drum brake assembly fitted to the Estate model is generally similar to that fitted to the Hatchback and a similar renewal procedure should be followed (see illustration).

27 To remove each shoe retainer spring, use a close fitting rod to slightly tilt the spring so that it disconnects from its retaining bracket (see illustration).

Girling brake shoes

28 Make a note of the correct fitted positions

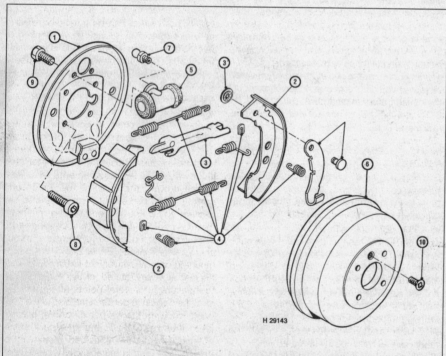

H 29143

6.26 Bendix rear drum brake assembly - Estate models

1	Brake plate	5	Wheel cylinder	8	Screw
2	Brake shoe	6	Brake drum	9	Bolt
3	Spacer	7	Bleed screw	10	Screw
4	Spring set				

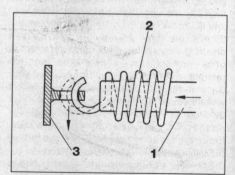

6.27 Use a close fitting rod (1) to slightly tilt each shoe retainer spring (2) so that it disconnects from its retaining bracket (3)

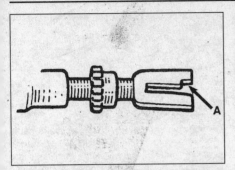

6.39 On Girling rear brake shoes, adjuster strut fork cut-out (A) must engage with leading shoe adjusting lever on refitting

7.3 Using a micrometer to measure disc thickness

7.4 Checking disc run-out using a dial gauge

of the springs and adjuster strut, to use as a guide on reassembly.

29 Carefully unhook both the upper and lower return springs, and remove them from the brake shoes.

30 Using a pair of pliers, remove the leading shoe retainer spring cup by depressing it and turning through 90°. With the cup removed, lift off the spring, then withdraw the retainer pin and remove the shoe from the backplate. Unhook the adjusting lever spring, and remove it from the leading shoe.

31 Detach the adjuster strut, and remove it from the trailing shoe.

32 Remove the trailing shoe retainer spring cup, spring and pin as described above, then detach the handbrake cable and remove the shoe from the vehicle. Do not depress the brake pedal until the brakes are reassembled; wrap a strong elastic band around the wheel cylinder pistons to retain them.

33 If genuine Citroën brake shoes are being installed, it will be necessary to remove the adjusting lever from the original leading shoe, and install it on the new shoe. All return springs should be renewed, regardless of their apparent condition; spring kits are also available from Citroën dealers.

34 Withdraw the forked end from the strut, and carefully examine the assembly for signs of wear or damage. Pay particular attention to the threads and the knurled adjuster wheel, and renew if necessary. Note that left-hand and right-hand struts are not interchangeable; the left-hand fork has a right-handed thread, and the right-hand fork a left-handed thread.

35 Peel back the rubber protective caps, and check the wheel cylinder for fluid leaks or other damage; check that both cylinder pistons are free to move easily. Refer to Section 12, if necessary, for information on wheel cylinder renewal.

36 Prior to installation, clean the backplate, and apply a thin smear of high-temperature brake grease or anti-seize compound to all those surfaces of the backplate which bear on the shoes, particularly the wheel cylinder pistons and lower pivot point. Do not allow the lubricant to foul the friction material.

37 Ensure the handbrake lever stop-peg is correctly located against the edge of the

trailing shoe, and remove the elastic band fitted to the wheel cylinder.

38 Locate the upper end of the trailing shoe in the wheel cylinder piston, then refit the retainer pin and spring, and secure it in position with the spring cup. Connect the handbrake cable to the lever.

39 Screw in the adjuster wheel until the minimum strut length is obtained, then hook the strut into position on the trailing shoe. Rotate the adjuster strut forked end, so that the cut-out of the fork will engage with the leading shoe adjusting lever once the shoe is installed **(see illustration)**.

40 Fit the spring to the leading shoe adjusting lever, so that the shorter hook of the spring engages with the lever.

41 Slide the leading shoe assembly into position, ensuring that it is correctly engaged with the adjuster strut fork, and that the fork cut-out is engaged with the adjusting lever. Ensure the upper end of the shoe is located in the wheel cylinder piston, then secure the shoe in position with the retainer pin, spring and spring cup.

42 Install the upper and lower return springs, then tap the shoes to centralise them with the backplate.

43 Using a screwdriver, turn the strut adjuster wheel to expand the shoes until the brake drum just slides over the shoes.

44 Refit the brake drum as described in Section 9.

45 Repeat the above procedure on the remaining rear brake.

46 Once both sets of rear shoes have been renewed, adjust the lining-to-drum clearance by repeatedly depressing the brake pedal. Whilst depressing the pedal, have an assistant listen to the rear drums, to check that the adjuster strut is functioning correctly; if so, a clicking sound will be emitted by the strut as the pedal is depressed.

47 Check and, if necessary, adjust the handbrake as described in Section 17.

48 On completion, check the hydraulic fluid level as described in Chapter 1.

All shoes

49 Be prepared for reduced braking efficiency while the new shoes bed in, as described at the end of Section 4.

7 Front brake disc - inspection, removal and refitting

Note: *Before starting work, refer to the note at the beginning of Section 4 concerning the dangers of asbestos dust.*

Inspection

Note: *If either disc requires renewal, BOTH should be renewed at the same time, to ensure even and consistent braking. New brake pads should also be fitted.*

1 Apply the handbrake, then jack up the front of the car and support it on axle stands. Remove the appropriate front roadwheel.

2 Slowly rotate the brake disc so that the full area of both sides can be checked; remove the brake pads if better access is required to the inboard surface. Light scoring is normal in the area swept by the brake pads, but if heavy scoring or cracks are found, the disc must be renewed.

3 It is normal to find a lip of rust and brake dust around the disc's perimeter; this can be scraped off if required. If, however, a lip has formed due to excessive wear of the brake pad swept area, then the disc's thickness must be measured using a micrometer **(see illustration)**. Take measurements at several places around the disc, at the inside and outside of the pad swept area; if the disc has worn at any point to the specified minimum thickness or less, the disc must be renewed.

4 If the disc is thought to be warped, it can be checked for run-out. Either use a dial gauge mounted on any convenient fixed point, while the disc is slowly rotated, or use feeler gauges to measure (at several points all around the disc) the clearance between the disc and a fixed point, such as the caliper mounting bracket **(see illustration)**. If the measure-ments obtained are at the specified maximum or beyond, the disc is excessively warped, and must be renewed; however, it is worth checking first that the hub bearing is in good condition (Chapters 1 and/or 10). Also try the effect of removing the disc and turning it through 180°, to reposition it on the hub; if the run-out is still excessive, the disc must be renewed.

7.7a Undo the two mounting bolts . . .

7.7b . . . then slide the caliper assembly off the disc . . .

7.7c . . . and tie it to the suspension strut, to avoid placing any strain on the flexible hose

5 Check the disc for cracks, especially around the wheel bolt holes, and any other wear or damage, and renew if necessary.

Removal

6 On 1124 cc and 1360 cc models, remove the brake pads as described in Section 4, paragraphs 1 to 6.

7 On all 1580 cc and larger-engined models, unscrew the two bolts securing the brake caliper to the swivel hub, and discard them - new bolts must be used on refitting. Slacken and remove the bolt securing the wiring retaining bracket to the swivel hub, then slide the caliper assembly off the disc. Using a piece of wire or string, tie the caliper to the front suspension coil spring, to avoid placing any strain on the hydraulic brake hose **(see illustrations)**.

8 Use chalk or paint to mark the relationship of the disc to the hub, then remove the screws securing the brake disc to the hub, and remove the disc **(see illustration)**. If it is tight, lightly tap its rear face with a hide or plastic mallet.

Refitting

9 Refitting is the reverse of the removal procedure, noting the following points:
(a) Ensure that the mating surfaces of the disc and hub are clean and flat.
(b) Align (if applicable) the marks made on removal, and securely tighten the disc retaining screws.

(c) If a new disc has been fitted, use a suitable solvent to wipe any preservative coating from the disc, before refitting the caliper.
(d) On 1580 cc and larger-engined models, if the threads of the newcaliper mounting bolts are not already pre-coated with locking compound, apply a suitable locking compound to them. Refit the caliper, and tighten the mounting bolts to the specified torque setting **(see illustration)**.
(e) On 1124 cc and 1360 cc models, refit the pads as described in paragraphs 12 to 18 of Section 4.
(f) Refit the roadwheel, then lower the vehicle to the ground and tighten the roadwheel bolts to the specified torque. On completion, repeatedly depress the brake pedal until normal (non-assisted) pedal pressure returns.

8 Rear brake disc -
inspection, removal and refitting

Note: Before starting work, refer to the note at the beginning of Section 5 concerning the dangers of asbestos dust.

Inspection

Note: If either disc requires renewal, BOTH should be renewed at the same time, to

ensure even and consistent braking. New brake pads should be fitted also.

1 Firmly chock the front wheels, then jack up the rear of the car and support it on axle stands. Remove the appropriate rear roadwheel.

2 Inspect the disc as described in Section 7.

Removal

3 Remove the brake pads as described in Section 5.

4 Use chalk or paint to mark the relationship of the disc to the hub, then remove the screw securing the brake disc to the hub, and remove the disc **(see illustration)**. If it is tight, lightly tap its rear face with a hide or plastic mallet.

Refitting

5 Refitting is the reverse of the removal procedure, noting the following points:
(a) Ensure that the mating surfaces of the disc and hub are clean and flat.
(b) Align (if applicable) the marks made on removal, and securely tighten the disc retaining screws.
(c) If a new disc has been fitted, use a suitable solvent to wipe any preservative coating from the disc, before refitting the caliper.
(d) Refit the brake pads as described in Section 5.
(e) Refit the roadwheel, then lower the vehicle to the ground and tighten the roadwheel bolts to the specified torque.

7.8 Undo the two retaining screws and remove the disc

7.9 On refitting, tighten the caliper mounting bolts to the specified torque setting

8.4 Removing the rear brake disc

9 Rear brake drum -
removal, inspection and
refitting

Note: *Before starting work, refer to the note at the beginning of Section 6 concerning the dangers of asbestos dust.*

Hatchback models
Removal

1 Chock the front wheels, then jack up the rear of the vehicle and support it on axle stands. Remove the appropriate rear wheel.

2 Using a hammer and a large flat-bladed screwdriver, carefully tap and prise the cap out of the centre of the brake drum. Discard the cap - a new one must be used on refitting. Using a hammer and chisel, tap up the staking securing the hub retaining nut to the groove in the stub axle.

3 Using a socket and long bar, slacken and remove the rear hub nut, and withdraw the thrustwasher. Discard the hub nut - a new nut must used on refitting.

4 It should now be possible to withdraw the brake drum and hub bearing assembly from the stub axle by hand. It may be difficult to remove the drum due to the tightness of the hub bearing on the stub axle, or due to the brake shoes binding on the inner circumference of the drum. If the bearing is tight, tap the periphery of

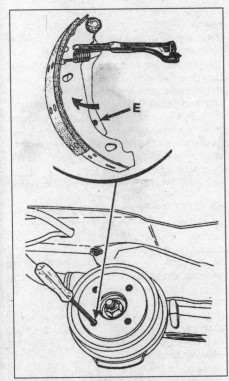

9.6a Using a screwdriver inserted through the brake drum to release the handbrake operating lever

E Handbrake operating lever stop-peg location

the drum using a hide or plastic mallet, or use a universal puller, secured to the drum with the wheel bolts, to pull it off. If the brake shoes are binding, first check that the handbrake is fully released, then proceed as follows.

5 Referring to Section 17 for further information, fully slacken the handbrake cable adjuster nut, to obtain maximum free play in the cable.

6 Insert a screwdriver through one of the wheel bolt holes in the brake drum, so that it contacts the handbrake operating lever on the trailing brake shoe. Push the lever until the stop-peg slips behind the brake shoe web, allowing the brake shoes to retract fully **(see illustrations)**. The brake drum can now be withdrawn, and the seal slid off the stub axle.

Inspection

Note: *If either drum requires renewal, BOTH should be renewed at the same time, to ensure even and consistent braking. New brake shoes should also be fitted.*

7 Working carefully, remove all traces of brake dust from the drum, but *avoid inhaling the dust, as it is injurious to health.*

8 Clean the outside of the drum, and check it for obvious signs of wear or damage, such as cracks around the roadwheel bolt holes; renew the drum if necessary.

9 Examine carefully the inside of the drum. Light scoring of the friction surface is normal, but if heavy scoring is found, the drum must be renewed. It is usual to find a lip on the drum's inboard edge which consists of a mixture of rust and brake dust; this should be scraped away, to leave a smooth surface which can be polished with fine (120- to 150-grade) emery paper. If, however, the lip is due to the friction surface being recessed by excessive wear, then the drum must be renewed.

10 If the drum is thought to be excessively worn, or oval, its internal diameter must be measured at several points using an internal micrometer. Take measurements in pairs, the second at right-angles to the first, and compare the two, to check for signs of ovality. Provided that it does not enlarge the drum to beyond the specified maximum diameter, it may be possible to have the drum refinished by skimming or grinding; if this is not possible,

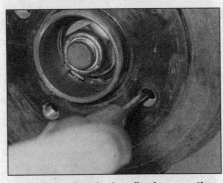

9.6b Releasing the handbrake operating lever

the drums on both sides must be renewed. Note that if the drum is to be skimmed, BOTH drums must be refinished, to maintain a consistent internal diameter on both sides.

Refitting

11 If a new brake drum is to be installed, use a suitable solvent to remove any preservative coating that may have been applied to its interior. Note that it may also be necessary to shorten the adjuster strut length, by rotating the strut wheel, to allow the drum to pass over the brake shoes.

12 Ensure that the handbrake lever stop-peg is correctly repositioned against the edge of the brake shoe web **(see illustration)**, then apply a smear of clean engine oil to the stub axle, and slide on the seal and brake drum.

13 Fit the thrustwasher and new hub nut, and tighten the hub nut to the specified torque. Stake the nut firmly into the groove on the stub axle, to secure it in position, then tap the new hub cap into place in the centre of the brake drum.

14 Depress the footbrake several times to operate the self-adjusting mechanism.

15 Repeat the above procedure on the remaining rear brake assembly (where necessary), then check and, if necessary, adjust the handbrake cable as described in Section 17.

16 On completion, refit the roadwheel(s), then lower the vehicle to the ground and tighten the wheel bolts to the specified torque.

Estate models
Removal

17 On Estate models, the rear brake drum can be removed independently of the rear hub. Chock the front wheels, then jack up the rear of the vehicle and support it on axle stands. Remove the appropriate rear wheel.

18 Undo the screw securing the drum to the rear hub and withdraw the drum. If it is not possible to withdraw the drum due to it binding on the brake shoes, first ensure that the handbrake is fully released, then carry out the procedure described in paragraphs 5 and 6.

Inspection

19 Refer to paragraphs 7 to 10.

9.12 Check that the handbrake lever stop-peg is correctly positioned against the shoe edge

9

Refitting

20 Refer to paragraphs 11 to 16 but ignore any references to stub axle, thrustwasher and hub nut; instead, secure the drum in position with the retaining screw.

10 Front brake caliper - removal, overhaul and refitting

Note: *Before starting work, refer to the note at the beginning of Section 2 concerning the dangers of hydraulic fluid, and to the warning at the beginning of Section 4 concerning the dangers of asbestos dust.*

Removal

1 Apply the handbrake, then jack up the front of the vehicle and support it on axle stands. Remove the appropriate roadwheel.
2 Minimise fluid loss by first removing the master cylinder reservoir cap, and then tightening it down onto a piece of polythene, to obtain an airtight seal. Alternatively, use a brake hose clamp, a G-clamp or a similar tool to clamp the flexible hose.

Bendix caliper - 1124 cc and 1360 cc models

3 Remove the brake pads as described in Section 4.
4 Clean the area around the union, then loosen the brake hose union nut.
5 Slacken the two bolts securing the caliper assembly to the swivel hub and remove them along with the mounting plate, noting which way around the plate is fitted. Lift the caliper assembly away from the brake disc, and unscrew it from the end of the brake hose.

Girling caliper - 1580 cc and larger-engined models

6 Clean the area around the union, then loosen the brake hose union nut. Disconnect the pad wear warning sensor wiring from the connector, and free it from any relevant retaining clips.
7 Slacken and remove the upper and lower caliper guide pin bolts, using a slim open-ended spanner to prevent the guide pin itself from rotating. Discard the guide pin bolts - new bolts must be used on refitting. With the guide pin bolts removed, lift the caliper away from the brake disc, then unscrew the caliper from the end of the brake hose. Note that the brake pads need not be disturbed, and can be left in position in the caliper mounting bracket.

Overhaul

8 With the caliper on the bench, wipe away all traces of dust and dirt, but *avoid inhaling the dust, as it is injurious to health.*
9 Where necessary, use a small flat-bladed screwdriver to carefully prise the dust seal retaining clip out of the caliper bore.
10 Withdraw the partially-ejected piston from the caliper body, and remove the dust seal. The piston can be withdrawn by hand, or if

necessary pushed out by applying compressed air to the brake hose union hole. Only low pressure should be required, such as is generated by a foot pump.
Caution: The piston may be ejected with some force.
11 Using a small screwdriver, extract the piston hydraulic seal, taking great care not to damage the caliper bore.
12 Withdraw the guide sleeves/pins from the caliper body/mounting bracket (as applicable), and remove the rubber gaiters.
13 Thoroughly clean all components, using only methylated spirit, isopropyl alcohol or clean hydraulic fluid as a cleaning medium. Never use mineral-based solvents such as petrol or paraffin, as they will attack the hydraulic system's rubber components. Dry the components immediately, using compressed air or a clean, lint-free cloth. Use compressed air to blow clear the fluid passages.
14 Check all components, and renew any that are worn or damaged. Check particularly the cylinder bore and piston; these should be renewed (note that this means the renewal of the complete body assembly) if they are scratched, worn or corroded in any way. Similarly check the condition of the guide sleeves/pins and their bores in the caliper body/mounting bracket (as applicable); both sleeves/pins should be undamaged and (when cleaned) a reasonably tight sliding fit in the body/mounting bracket bores. If there is any doubt about the condition of any component, renew it.
15 If the assembly is fit for further use, obtain the appropriate repair kit; the components are available from Citroën dealers in various combinations.
16 Renew all rubber seals, dust covers and caps disturbed on dismantling as a matter of course; these should never be re-used.
17 On reassembly, ensure that all components are absolutely clean and dry.
18 Soak the piston and the new piston (fluid) seal in clean hydraulic fluid. Smear clean fluid on the cylinder bore surface.
19 Fit the new piston (fluid) seal, using only your fingers (no tools) to manipulate it into the cylinder bore groove. Fit the new dust seal to the piston, and refit the piston to the cylinder bore using a twisting motion; ensure that the piston enters squarely into the bore. Press the piston fully into the bore, then press the dust seal into the caliper body.
20 Where fitted, install the dust seal retaining clip, ensuring that it is correctly seated in the caliper groove.
21 Apply the grease supplied in the repair kit, or a good quality high-temperature brake grease or anti-seize compound, to the guide sleeves/pins. Fit the guide sleeves/pins to the caliper body/mounting bracket, and fit the new rubber gaiters, ensuring that they are correctly located in the grooves on both the sleeve/pin and body/mounting bracket (as applicable).

Refitting

Bendix caliper - 1124 cc and 1360 cc models

22 Screw the caliper fully onto the flexible hose union, then position the caliper over the brake disc.
23 If the threads of the new caliper mounting bolts are not already pre-coated with locking compound, apply a suitable locking compound to them. Refit the bolts along with the mounting plate, ensuring that the plate is fitted so that its bend curves away from the caliper body. With the plate correctly positioned, tighten the caliper bolts to the specified torque.
24 Securely tighten the brake hose union nut, then refit the brake pads as described in Section 4.
25 Remove the brake hose clamp or polythene, as applicable, and bleed the hydraulic system as described in Section 2. Note that, providing the precautions described were taken to minimise brake fluid loss, it should only be necessary to bleed the relevant front brake.
26 Refit the roadwheel, then lower the vehicle to the ground and tighten the roadwheel bolts to the specified torque.

Girling caliper - 1580 cc and larger-engined models

27 Screw the caliper body fully onto the flexible hose union, then check that the brake pads are still correctly fitted in the caliper mounting bracket.
28 Position the caliper over the pads, and pass the pad warning sensor wiring through the caliper aperture. If the threads of the new guide pin bolts are not already pre-coated with locking compound, apply a suitable locking compound to them. Fit the new lower guide pin bolt, then press the caliper into position and fit the new upper guide pin bolt. Securely tighten both the guide pin bolts, while retaining the guide pin with an open-ended spanner.
29 Reconnect the brake pad wear sensor wiring connectors, ensuring that the wiring is correctly routed through the loop of the caliper bleed screw cap.
30 Tighten the brake hose union nut securely, then remove the brake hose clamp or polythene, where fitted, and bleed the hydraulic system as described in Section 2. Note that, providing the precautions described were taken to minimise brake fluid loss, it should only be necessary to bleed the relevant front brake.
31 Depress the brake pedal repeatedly, until the pads are pressed into firm contact with the brake disc, and normal (non-assisted) pedal pressure is restored.
32 Refit the roadwheel, then lower the vehicle to the ground and tighten the roadwheel bolts to the specified torque.

11.3a Disconnect the handbrake inner cable from the caliper lever . . .

11.3b . . . then tap the outer cable out from the caliper body

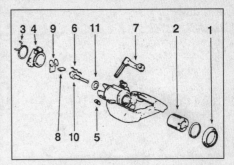

11.8 Exploded view of the rear brake caliper

1 Dust seal	6 Spring washers
2 Piston	7 Handbrake
3 Retaining clip	operating lever
4 Handbrake	8 Plunger cam
mechanism dust	9 Return spring
cover	10 Adjusting screw
5 Circlip	11 Thrustwasher

11 Rear brake caliper -
removal, overhaul and refitting

Note: *Before starting work, refer to the note at the beginning of Section 2 concerning the dangers of hydraulic fluid, and to the warning at the beginning of Section 5 concerning the dangers of asbestos dust.*

Removal

1 Chock the front wheels, then jack up the rear of the vehicle and support on axle stands. Remove the relevant rear wheel.
2 Remove the brake pads as described in Section 5.
3 Ensure the handbrake is fully released, then free the handbrake inner cable from the caliper handbrake operating lever. Tap the outer cable out of its bracket on the caliper body **(see illustrations)**.
4 Minimise fluid loss by first removing the master cylinder reservoir cap, and then tightening it down onto a piece of polythene, to obtain an airtight seal. Alternatively, use a brake hose clamp, a G-clamp or a similar tool

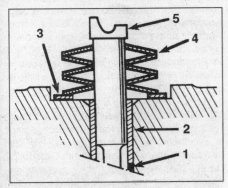

11.15 Correct fitted positions of the rear brake caliper handbrake mechanism adjuster screw and associated components

1 O-ring
2 Adjusting screw bush
3 Thrustwasher
4 Correct arrangement of spring washers
5 Adjusting screw

to clamp the flexible hose at the nearest convenient point to the brake caliper.
5 Wipe away all traces of dirt around the brake pipe union on the caliper, and slacken the union nut.
6 Slacken the two bolts securing the caliper assembly to the trailing arm, and remove them along with the mounting plate, noting which way around the plate is fitted. Lift the caliper assembly away from the brake disc, and unscrew it from the end of the brake hose. Discard the caliper mounting bolts - they should be renewed whenever they are disturbed.

Overhaul

7 With the caliper on the bench, wipe away all traces of dust and dirt, but *avoid inhaling the dust, as it is injurious to health.*
8 Using a small screwdriver, carefully prise out the dust seal from the caliper bore, taking care not to damage the piston **(see illustration)**.
9 Remove the piston from the caliper bore by rotating it in an anti-clockwise direction. This can be achieved using a suitable square-section bar, such as the shaft of a screwdriver, which locates snugly in the caliper piston slots. Once the piston turns freely but does not come out any further, the piston can be withdrawn by hand, or if necessary pushed out by applying compressed air to the union bolt hole. Only low pressure should be required, such as is generated by a foot pump.

Caution: The piston may be ejected with some force.

10 Using a small screwdriver, extract the piston hydraulic seal, taking care not to damage the caliper bore.
11 Withdraw the guide sleeves from the caliper body, and remove the guide sleeve gaiters.
12 Inspect all the caliper components as described in Section 10, paragraphs 13 to 17, and renew as necessary, noting that the inside of the caliper piston must **not** be dismantled. If necessary, the handbrake mechanism can be overhauled as described in the following paragraphs; if it is not wished

to overhaul the handbrake mechanism, proceed straight to paragraph 16.
13 Release the handbrake dust cover retaining clip, and peel the cover away from the rear of the caliper; make a note of the correct fitted positions of the relative components, to use as a guide on reassembly. Remove the circlip from the base of the operating lever shaft, then compress the adjusting screw spring washers, and withdraw the operating lever and dust cover from the caliper body. With the lever withdrawn, remove the return spring, plunger cam, adjusting screw and spring washers, and thrustwasher from the rear of the caliper body. Using a suitable pin punch, carefully tap the adjusting screw bush out of the caliper body, and remove the O-ring.
14 Clean all the handbrake components in methylated spirit, and examine them for wear. If there is any sign of wear or damage, the complete handbrake mechanism assembly should be renewed; a kit is available from your Citroën dealer. On reassembly, ensure that all components are absolutely clean and dry.
15 Install the O-ring, then press the adjusting screw bush into position in the rear of the caliper body until its outer edge is flush with the caliper body; if necessary, tap the bush into position using a tubular drift. Fit the thrustwasher, then install the adjusting screw and spring washers, ensuring that the washers are correctly positioned **(see illustration)**. Locate the plunger cam in the end of the adjusting screw, and position the return spring in the caliper housing. Fit the new dust cover to the operating lever, then compress the adjusting screw spring washers and insert the lever shaft through the caliper body, ensuring that it is correctly engaged with the return spring and plunger cam. Secure the operating lever in position with the circlip, then release the spring washers and check the operation of the handbrake mechanism. Apply a smear of high-melting-point grease to the operating lever shaft and

9

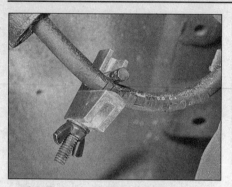

12.3 To minimise fluid loss, fit a brake hose clamp to the flexible hose

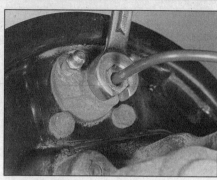

12.4 Using a brake pipe spanner to unscrew the wheel cylinder union nut

adjusting screw, then slide the dust cover over the caliper body, and secure it in position with a cable tie.

16 Soak the piston and the new piston (fluid) seal in clean hydraulic fluid. Smear clean fluid on the cylinder bore surface.

17 Fit the new piston (fluid) seal, using only the fingers to manipulate it into the cylinder bore groove, and refit the piston assembly. Turn the piston in a clockwise direction, using the method employed on dismantling, until it is fully retracted into the caliper bore.

18 Fit the dust seal to the caliper, ensuring that it is correctly located in the caliper and also the groove on the piston.

19 Apply the grease supplied in the repair kit, or a good quality high-temperature brake grease or anti-seize compound, to the guide sleeves. Fit the guide sleeves to the caliper body, and fit the new gaiters, ensuring that the gaiters are correctly located in the grooves on both the guide sleeve and caliper body.

Refitting

20 Screw the caliper fully onto the brake hose, then position the caliper over the brake disc. If the threads of the new caliper mounting bolts are not already pre-coated with locking compound, apply a suitable locking compound to them. Install the new caliper mounting bolts and the mounting plate, noting that the mounting plate must be fitted so that its bend curves away from the caliper body. With the plate correctly positioned, tighten the caliper bolts to the specified torque.

21 Tighten the brake hose union securely, then remove the clamp from the flexible brake hose, or the polythene from the master cylinder reservoir (as applicable).

22 Insert the handbrake cable through its bracket on the caliper, and tap the outer cable into position using a hammer and suitable pin punch. Reconnect the inner cable to the caliper operating lever.

23 Refit the brake pads as described in Section 5.

24 Bleed the hydraulic system as described in Section 2. Note that, providing the precautions described were taken to minimise brake fluid loss, it should only be necessary to bleed the relevant rear brake.

25 Repeatedly apply the brake pedal until normal (non-assisted) pedal pressure returns. Check and if necessary adjust the handbrake cable as described in Section 17.

26 Refit the roadwheel, then lower the vehicle to the ground and tighten the wheel bolts to the specified torque. On completion, check the hydraulic fluid level as described in Chapter 1.

12 Rear wheel cylinder - removal and refitting

Note: *Before starting work, refer to the note at the beginning of Section 2 concerning the dangers of hydraulic fluid, and to the warning at the beginning of Section 6 concerning the dangers of asbestos dust.*

Removal

1 Remove the brake drum as described in Section 9.

2 Using pliers, carefully unhook the upper brake shoe return spring, and remove it from both brake shoes. Pull the upper ends of the shoes away from the wheel cylinder to disengage them from the pistons.

3 Minimise fluid loss by first removing the master cylinder reservoir cap, and then tightening it down onto a piece of polythene, to obtain an airtight seal. Alternatively, use a brake hose clamp, a G-clamp or a similar tool to clamp the flexible hose at the nearest convenient point to the wheel cylinder **(see illustration)**.

4 Wipe away all traces of dirt around the brake pipe union at the rear of the wheel cylinder, and unscrew the union nut **(see illustration)**. Carefully ease the pipe out of the wheel cylinder, and plug or tape over its end to prevent dirt entry. Wipe off any spilt fluid immediately.

5 Unscrew the two wheel cylinder retaining bolts from the rear of the backplate, and remove the cylinder, taking great care not to allow surplus hydraulic fluid to contaminate the brake shoe linings.

6 Note that it is not possible to overhaul the cylinder, since no components are available separately. If faulty, the complete wheel cylinder assembly must be renewed.

Refitting

7 Ensure the backplate and wheel cylinder mating surfaces are clean, then spread the brake shoes and manoeuvre the wheel cylinder into position.

8 Engage the brake pipe, and screw in the union nut two or three turns to ensure that the thread has started.

9 Insert the two wheel cylinder retaining bolts, and tighten them securely. Now fully tighten the brake pipe union nut.

10 Remove the clamp from the flexible brake hose, or the polythene from the master cylinder reservoir (as applicable).

11 Ensure the brake shoes are correctly located in the cylinder pistons, then carefully refit the brake shoe upper return spring, using a screwdriver to stretch the spring into position.

12 Refit the brake drum as described in Section 9.

13 Bleed the brake hydraulic system as described in Section 2. Providing suitable precautions were taken to minimise loss of fluid, it should only be necessary to bleed the relevant rear brake.

13 Master cylinder - removal, overhaul and refitting

Note: *Before starting work, refer to the warning at the beginning of Section 2 concerning the dangers of hydraulic fluid.*

Removal

1 On left-hand-drive models, remove the battery and battery tray as described in Chapter 5.

2 On all models, remove the master cylinder reservoir cap, and syphon the hydraulic fluid from the reservoir. **Note:** *Do not syphon the fluid by mouth, as it is poisonous; use a syringe or an old poultry baster.* Alternatively, open any convenient bleed screw in the system, and gently pump the brake pedal to expel the fluid through a plastic tube connected to the screw (see Section 2). Disconnect the wiring connector from the brake fluid level sender unit **(see illustration)**.

13.2 Disconnecting the wiring connector from the master cylinder fluid level sender

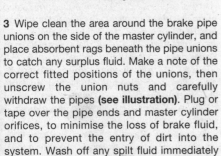

13.3 Using a brake pipe spanner to unscrew the master cylinder union nut

13.4 Master cylinder retaining nuts (arrowed)

14.5 Removing the pedal bracket assembly from the bulkhead

3 Wipe clean the area around the brake pipe unions on the side of the master cylinder, and place absorbent rags beneath the pipe unions to catch any surplus fluid. Make a note of the correct fitted positions of the unions, then unscrew the union nuts and carefully withdraw the pipes (see illustration). Plug or tape over the pipe ends and master cylinder orifices, to minimise the loss of brake fluid, and to prevent the entry of dirt into the system. Wash off any spilt fluid immediately with cold water.

4 Slacken and remove the two nuts securing the master cylinder to the vacuum servo unit, then withdraw the unit from the engine compartment (see illustration). Remove the O-ring from the rear of the master cylinder, and discard it.

Overhaul

5 Slacken the fluid reservoir retaining clamp screw, then unhook the clamp and remove the fluid reservoir and reservoir seals from the master cylinder body.

6 Using a wooden dowel, press the piston assembly into the master cylinder body, then extract the circlip from the end of the master cylinder bore.

7 Noting the order of removal, and the direction of fitting of each component, withdraw the washer, and the piston assemblies with their springs and seals, tapping the body on to a clean wooden surface to dislodge them. If necessary, clamp the master cylinder body in a vice (fitted with soft jaw covers) and use compressed air (applied through the secondary circuit fluid port) to assist the removal of the secondary piston assembly.

8 Thoroughly clean all components, using only methylated spirit, isopropyl alcohol or clean hydraulic fluid as a cleaning medium. Never use mineral-based solvents such as petrol or paraffin, as they will attack the hydraulic system's rubber components. Dry the components immediately, using compressed air or a clean, lint-free cloth.

9 Check all components, and renew any that are worn or damaged. Check particularly the cylinder bores and pistons; the complete assembly should be renewed if these are

scratched, worn or corroded. If there is any doubt about the condition of the assembly or of any of its components, renew it. Check that the body's fluid passages are clear.

10 If the assembly is fit for further use, obtain a repair kit from your Citroën dealer; the kit consists of both piston assemblies and springs, as well as a new circlip. Renew all seals and sealing O-rings disturbed on dismantling as a matter of course; these should never be re-used.

11 On reassembly, soak the pistons and the new seals in clean hydraulic fluid. Smear clean fluid into the cylinder bore.

12 Insert the pistons into the bore, using a twisting motion to avoid trapping the seal lips. Ensure that all components are refitted in the correct order and the right way round, then fit the washer to the end of the primary piston.

13 Press the piston assemblies fully into the bore using a clean wooden dowel, and secure them in position with the new circlip. Ensure the circlip is correctly located in the groove in the cylinder bore.

14 Fit the new mounting seals to the master cylinder body, then refit the reservoir. Clip the retaining clamp onto the reservoir, and securely tighten its clamp screw.

Refitting

15 Before refitting the master cylinder, clean the mounting faces, and check the distance between the tip of the master cylinder end of the pushrod and front of the servo unit, using the information given in Section 15, paragraph 9.

16 Remove all traces of dirt from the master cylinder and servo unit mating surfaces, and fit a new O-ring to the groove on the master cylinder body.

17 Fit the master cylinder to the servo unit, ensuring that the servo unit pushrod enters the master cylinder bore centrally. Refit the master cylinder mounting nuts, and tighten them to the specified torque.

18 Wipe clean the brake pipe unions, then refit them to the master cylinder ports and tighten them securely.

19 On left-hand-drive models, refit the battery tray and battery as described in Chapter 5.

20 On all models, refill the master cylinder

reservoir with new fluid, and bleed the complete hydraulic system as described in Section 2.

14 Brake pedal - removal and refitting

Removal

1 Remove the steering column as described in Chapter 10.

2 Remove the vacuum servo unit as described in Section 15.

3 On models with manual transmission, referring to Chapter 6 for further information, slacken the clutch cable adjuster nut to obtain maximum cable free play. From inside the vehicle, depress the metal retaining clip, and free the inner cable from the plastic retainer fitted to the upper end of the clutch pedal.

4 Disconnect the wiring connector from the stop-light switch.

5 Slacken and remove the six pedal bracket retaining nuts, then return to the engine compartment and manoeuvre the pedal bracket assembly out from the vehicle, noting its rubber seal (see illustration).

6 With the pedal bracket assembly on the bench, slacken the nut, then withdraw the pedal pivot pin, and separate the pedal from the bracket. Slide the spacer out from the centre of the pedal bore, and remove the pivot bushes (see illustrations).

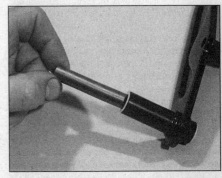

14.6a Withdraw the spacer from the brake pedal . . .

14.6b . . . and remove the pedal pivot bushes

14.9a Locate the pedal in the bracket, and insert the pivot bolt . . .

14.9b . . . then refit the nut, and tighten it to the specified torque setting

7 Carefully clean all components, and renew any that are worn or damaged; check the bearing surfaces of the pivot bushes and spacer with particular care; the bushes can be renewed separately if worn.

Refitting

8 Press the pivot bushes into the pedal bore, then apply a smear of multi-purpose grease to their bearing surfaces, and slide in the spacer.
9 Refit the pedal to the bracket, and install the pivot bolt. Refit the pivot bolt nut, and tighten it to the specified torque setting **(see illustrations)**. Check that the pedal pivots smoothly before proceeding further.
10 Ensure that the seal is correctly located, then manoeuvre the pedal bracket assembly back into position from the engine compartment. Refit the pedal bracket retaining nuts, and tighten them to the specified torque setting.
11 Where necessary, feed the clutch cable back through the bracket, and engage the inner cable with the plastic retainer on the clutch pedal. Check that it is securely retained by the metal clip. Adjust the clutch cable as described in Chapter 6.
12 Connect the wiring connector to the stop-light switch.
13 Refit the servo unit as described in Section 15.
14 Refit the steering column as described in Chapter 10. Prior to refitting the lower facia panel, check and, if necessary, adjust the stop-light switch as described in Section 22.

15 Vacuum servo unit - testing, removal and refitting

Testing

1 To test the operation of the servo unit, depress the footbrake several times to exhaust the vacuum, then start the engine whilst keeping the pedal firmly depressed. As the engine starts, there should be a noticeable "give" in the brake pedal as the vacuum builds up. Allow the engine to run for at least two minutes, then switch it off. If the brake pedal is now depressed it should feel normal, but further applications should result in the pedal feeling firmer, with the pedal stroke decreasing with each application.
2 If the servo does not operate as described, first inspect the servo unit check valve as described in Section 16. On 16-valve models, also check the operation of the vacuum pump as described in Section 26.
3 If the servo unit still fails to operate satisfactorily, the fault lies within the unit itself. Repairs to the unit are not possible - if faulty, the servo unit must be renewed.

Removal

Note: *On certain right-hand-drive models, to gain the clearance required to remove the servo unit, it may prove necessary to split the right-hand engine/transmission mounting and*

move the engine unit forward slightly; this is due to the lack of clearance between the servo unit and the rear of the engine. If this proves necessary, refer to the relevant Part of Chapter 2 for further information on supporting the engine unit and dismantling the mounting.
4 Remove the master cylinder as described in Section 13.
5 Slacken the retaining clip (where fitted) and disconnect the vacuum hose from the servo unit check valve.
6 From inside the vehicle, release the panel fasteners by rotating them through a quarter of a turn, and remove the driver's side lower facia panel. Release the heater duct, and remove the duct to improve access to the rear of the servo unit.
7 Prise off the spring clip, then withdraw the clevis pin securing the servo unit pushrod to the brake pedal **(see illustration)**.
8 Undo the four retaining nuts securing the servo unit to the pedal mounting bracket, then return to the engine compartment and manoeuvre the servo unit out of position, noting the gasket which is fitted to the rear of the unit **(see illustration)**.

Refitting

9 Prior to refitting, check the servo unit dimensions as follows. With the gasket removed, check that the pushrod protrusion from the rear of the unit, dimension "L", (measured from the rear of the servo unit to the centre of the pushrod clevis pin hole), and the distance between the tip of the master cylinder end of the pushrod and front of the unit, dimension "X", are as shown in **illustration 15.9a**. Where possible, dimension "L" can be altered by slackening the locknut and repositioning the pushrod clevis (C). Dimension "X" can be altered by repositioning the nut (P) **(see illustrations)**. After adjustment, ensure the clevis locknut is securely tightened. Note that on some servo units adjustment is not possible.
10 Check the servo unit check valve sealing grommet for signs of damage or deterioration, and renew if necessary.
11 Fit a new gasket to the rear of the servo

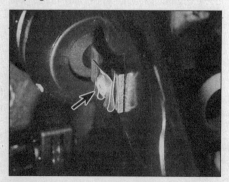

15.7 Servo unit pushrod clevis pin spring clip (arrowed)

15.8 Removing the servo unit

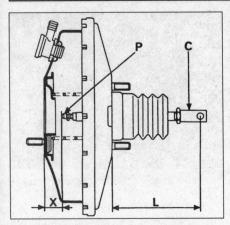

15.9a Vacuum servo unit adjustment dimensions

C Pushrod clevis
P Pushrod nut
L Non-ABS models: 22.3 ± 0.1 mm
   ABS models: 24.8 ± 0.1 mm
X Bendix servo unit: 88.0 + 0.5 mm
   Teves servo unit: 86.0 + 0.5 mm

unit, and reposition the unit in the engine compartment **(see illustration)**.

12 From inside the vehicle, ensure that the servo unit pushrod is correctly engaged with the brake pedal, then refit the servo unit mounting nuts and tighten them to the specified torque setting.

13 Refit the servo unit pushrod-to-brake pedal clevis pin, and secure it in position with the spring clip.

14 Refit the heater duct, ensuring it is

16.2 Servo unit check valve is a push fit in its sealing grommet (master cylinder removed for clarity)

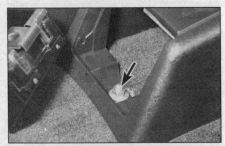

17.2a Remove the ashtray from the rear of the handbrake cover, then undo the retaining nut (arrowed) . . .

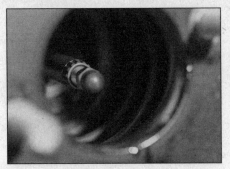

15.9b Servo unit pushrod adjustment nut

securely connected at either end, then refit the lower facia panel.

15 Reconnect the vacuum hose to the servo unit check valve and, where necessary, securely tighten its retaining clip.

16 Refit the master cylinder as described in Section 13 of this Chapter.

17 On completion, start the engine and check for air leaks at the vacuum hose-to-servo unit connection; check the operation of the braking system.

16 Vacuum servo unit check valve - removal, testing and refitting

Removal

1 Slacken the retaining clip (where fitted), and disconnect the vacuum hose from the servo unit check valve.

2 Withdraw the valve from its rubber sealing grommet, using a pulling and twisting motion. Remove the grommet from the servo **(see illustration)**.

Testing

3 Examine the check valve for signs of damage, and renew if necessary. The valve may be tested by blowing through it in both directions. Air should flow through the valve in one direction only - when blown through from the servo unit end of the valve. Renew the valve if this is not the case.

4 Examine the rubber sealing grommet and flexible vacuum hose for signs of damage or deterioration, and renew as necessary.

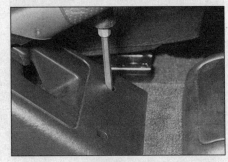

17.2b . . . and the two front retaining screws . . .

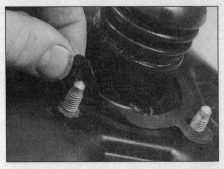

15.11 Prior to refitting, fit a new sealing gasket to the rear of the servo unit

Refitting

5 Fit the sealing grommet into position in the servo unit.

6 Carefully ease the check valve into position, taking great care not to displace or damage the grommet. Reconnect the vacuum hose to the valve and, where necessary, securely tighten its retaining clip.

7 On completion, start the engine and check the check valve-to-servo unit connection for signs of air leaks.

17 Handbrake - adjustment

1 To check the handbrake adjustment, first apply the footbrake firmly several times to establish correct shoe-to-drum/pad-to-disc clearance, then apply and release the handbrake several times to ensure the self-adjust mechanism is fully adjusted. Applying normal moderate pressure, pull the handbrake lever to the fully-applied position, counting the number of clicks emitted from the handbrake ratchet mechanism. If adjustment is correct, there should be between 4 and 7 clicks before the handbrake is fully applied. If this is not the case, adjust as follows.

2 Open up the rear ashtray, then depress the retaining tang and remove the ashtray from the handbrake lever cover panel. Slacken and remove the rear retaining nut and the two front retaining screws, then manoeuvre the cover panel off the handbrake lever **(see illustrations)**.

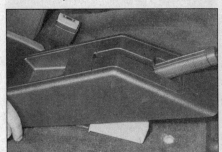

17.2c . . . and lift the cover off the handbrake lever

17.4 Adjusting the handbrake

18.4 Handbrake lever is retained by three nuts (arrowed)

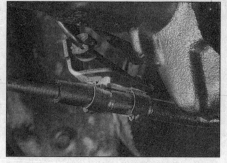

19.5 Handbrake cable trailing arm bracket

3 Chock the front wheels, then jack up the rear of the vehicle and support it on axle stands.
4 With the handbrake set on the first notch of the ratchet mechanism, rotate the adjusting nut until only a slight drag can be felt when the rear wheels/hubs are turned **(see illustration)**. Once this is so, fully release the handbrake lever, and check that the wheels/hubs rotate freely. Check the adjustment by applying the handbrake fully, counting the clicks emitted from the handbrake ratchet and, if necessary, re-adjust.
5 Refit the cover panel over the lever, and securely tighten its retaining screws and nut. Clip the rear ashtray back into position, then lower the vehicle to the ground.

18 Handbrake lever - removal and refitting

Removal

1 Remove the handbrake lever cover panel as described in paragraph 2 of Section 17.
2 Slacken the handbrake lever adjusting nut to obtain maximum free play in the cables, and disengage the inner cables from the handbrake lever plate.
3 On models with central locking, undo the nut and free the central locking control unit from the handbrake lever mounting studs.
4 Slacken and remove the three handbrake lever retaining nuts, and remove the lever from the vehicle **(see illustration)**.

Refitting

5 Refitting is a reversal of the removal. Prior to refitting the handbrake lever cover panel, adjust the handbrake as described in Section 17.

19 Handbrake cables - removal and refitting

Removal

1 Remove the handbrake lever cover panel as described in paragraph 2 of Section 17. The handbrake cable consists of two sections, a right- and a left-hand section, which are linked to the lever by an equalizer plate. Each section can be removed individually.
2 Slacken the handbrake lever adjusting nut to obtain maximum free play in the cable(s), and disengage the inner cables from the handbrake lever plate.
3 Firmly chock the front wheels, then jack up the rear of the vehicle and support it on axle stands.
4 Slacken and remove the retaining nuts, then release the exhaust system rear heat shield from the vehicle underbody, to gain access to the front of the relevant handbrake cable. Free the front end of the outer cable from the body, and withdraw the cable from its support guide.
5 Working back along the length of the cable, prise off the retaining clip and free it from its guide, then depress the retaining tangs and

free the cable from its trailing arm bracket **(see illustration)**.
6 On models with rear drum brakes, remove the rear brake shoes from the relevant side as described in Section 6. Using a hammer and pin punch, carefully tap the outer cable out from the brake backplate, and remove it from underneath the vehicle **(see illustration)**.
7 On models with rear disc brakes, disengage the inner cable from the caliper handbrake lever then, using a hammer and pin punch, tap the outer cable out of its mounting bracket on the caliper, and remove the cable from underneath the vehicle **(see illustration)**.

Refitting

8 Refitting is a reversal of the removal procedure, adjusting the handbrake as described in Section 17.

20 Rear brake pressure-regulating valves (models with rear disc brakes) - removal and refitting

Note: *Before starting work, refer to the warning at the beginning of Section 2 concerning the dangers of hydraulic fluid.*

Removal

1 Firmly chock the front wheels, then jack up the rear of the vehicle and support it on axle stands. The pressure-regulating valves are located just in front of the rear axle assembly; there are two valves, one for each rear brake caliper **(see illustration)**.

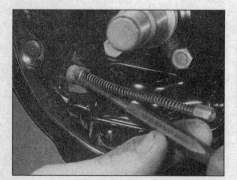

19.6 On drum brake models, drive the outer cable out from the brake backplate

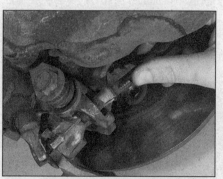

19.7 On disc brake models, disconnect the cable from the brake caliper

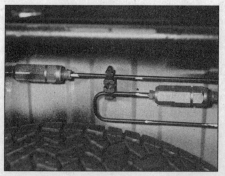

20.1 Rear disc brake pressure-regulating valves

21.1 Location of brake pressure compensator

2 Minimise fluid loss by first removing the master cylinder reservoir cap, and then tightening it down onto a piece of polythene, to obtain an airtight seal.

3 Wipe clean the area around the brake pipe unions on the relevant valve, and place absorbent rags beneath the pipe unions to catch any surplus fluid. Retain the relevant pressure-regulating valve with a suitable open-ended spanner, then slacken the union nuts, disconnect both brake pipes, and remove the valve from underneath the vehicle. Plug or tape over the pipe ends and valve orifices, to minimise the loss of brake fluid, and to prevent the entry of dirt into the system. Wash off any spilt fluid immediately with cold water.

Refitting

4 Refitting is a reverse of the removal procedure, ensuring that the pipe union nuts are securely tightened. On completion, bleed the complete braking system as described in Section 2.

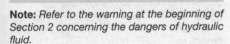

21 Rear brake pressure compensator (Estate models) - adjustment, removal and refitting

Note: *Refer to the warning at the beginning of Section 2 concerning the dangers of hydraulic fluid.*

Adjustment

1 The brake pressure compensator is located beneath the rear of the vehicle, adjacent to the right-hand suspension unit **(see illustration)**. Full access to the compensator can be obtained by removal of the spare wheel from its carrying rack.

2 To adjust the brake pressure compensator, it is first necessary to obtain Citroën tool nos. 9515-TM2, 9515-TM1, 4140-T and 2305-T. In view of the difficulty and expense connected with obtaining these tools and the fact that Citroën state that under no circumstances should the plastic adjusting nut on the end of the compensator be turned, we strongly advise that you entrust the adjustment procedure to your Citroën dealer.

Removal and refitting

3 Any attempt to fit a replacement compensator will result in it having to be adjusted, which will present the same difficulty as stated above. Again, we strongly advise that you entrust this procedure to your Citroën dealer.

22 Stop-light switch - removal, refitting and adjustment

Removal

1 The stop-light switch is located on the pedal bracket behind the facia.

2 To remove the switch, release the driver's side lower facia panel fasteners by rotating them through a quarter of a turn, and remove the panel. Release the heater duct, and remove the duct to gain access to the switch.

3 Disconnect the wiring connector, and unscrew the switch from its mounting bracket.

Refitting and adjustment

4 Screw the switch back into position in the mounting bracket, until the gap between the end of the main body of the switch and the lug on the brake pedal is approximately 2 to 3 mm.

5 Once the stop-light switch is correctly positioned, reconnect the wiring connector, and check the operation of the stop-lights. The stop-lights should illuminate after the brake pedal has travelled approximately 5 mm.

6 Refit the heater duct, ensuring it is securely connected at either end. Refit the lower facia panel, and secure it in position by rotating its fasteners through a quarter of a turn.

23 Anti-lock braking system (ABS) - general information

1 ABS is available as an option on all models covered in this manual. The system comprises a modulator block which contains the ABS computer, the hydraulic solenoid valves and accumulators, the electrically-driven return pump, and four roadwheel sensors; one fitted to each wheel. The purpose of the system is to prevent the wheel(s) locking during heavy braking. This is achieved by automatic release of the brake on the relevant wheel, followed by re-application of the brake.

2 The solenoids are controlled by the computer, which itself receives signals from the four wheel sensors (one fitted on each hub), which monitor the speed of rotation of each wheel. By comparing these speed signals from the four wheels, the computer can determine the speed at which the vehicle is travelling. It can then use this speed to determine when a wheel is decelerating at an abnormal rate, compared to the speed of the vehicle, and therefore predicts when a wheel is about to lock. During normal operation, the system functions in the same way as a non-ABS braking system **(see illustration)**.

3 If the computer senses that a wheel is about to lock, the ABS system enters the "pressure-maintain" phase **(see illustration overleaf)**. The computer operates the relevant solenoid valve in the modulator block, which then isolates the brake caliper on the wheel which is about to lock from the master cylinder, effectively sealing-in the hydraulic pressure.

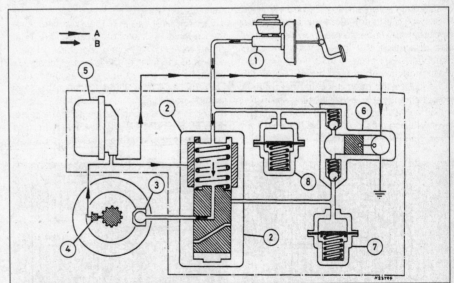

23.2 ABS system normal operation

1 Master cylinder	4 Wheel sensor and reluctor ring	6 Return pump
2 Solenoid valve	5 ABS computer	7 Accumulator
3 Brake caliper		8 Accumulator

A Flow of electrical signal
B Flow of hydraulic fluid

9•20 Braking system

4 If the speed of rotation of the wheel continues to decrease at an abnormal rate, the ABS system then enters the "pressure-decrease" phase (see illustration), where the electrically-driven return pump operates and pumps the hydraulic fluid back into the master cylinder, releasing pressure on the brake caliper so that the brake is released. Once the speed of rotation of the wheel returns to an acceptable rate, the pump stops; the solenoid valve opens, allowing the hydraulic master cylinder pressure to return to the caliper, which then re-applies the brake. This cycle can be carried out at up to 10 times a second.

5 The action of the solenoid valves and return pump creates pulses in the hydraulic circuit. When the ABS system is functioning, these pulses can be felt through the brake pedal.

6 The solenoid valves connected to the front calipers operate independently, but the valve connected to the rear calipers operates both calipers simultaneously. Since the braking circuit is split diagonally, a separate mechanical plunger valve in the modulator block divides the rear solenoid valve hydraulic outlet into two separate circuits; one for each rear brake.

7 The operation of the ABS system is entirely dependent on electrical signals. To prevent the system responding to any inaccurate signals, a built-in safety circuit monitors all signals received by the computer. If an inaccurate signal or low battery voltage is detected, the ABS system is automatically shut down, and the warning light on the instrument panel is illuminated, to inform the driver that the ABS system is not operational. Normal braking should still be available, however.

8 If a fault does develop in the ABS system, the vehicle must be taken to a Citroën dealer for fault diagnosis and repair.

24 Anti-lock braking system (ABS) components - removal and refitting

Modulator assembly

Note: *Before starting work, refer to the note at the beginning of Section 2 concerning the dangers of hydraulic fluid.*

Removal

1 Disconnect the battery negative terminal.
2 Undo the retaining screw, and remove the relay cover from the modulator assembly.
3 Disconnect the large 15-pin connector, the square 4-pin connector, and the return pump earth lead, from the modulator (see illustration).
4 Unscrew the master cylinder reservoir filler cap, then place a piece of polythene over the filler neck, and securely refit the cap. This will minimise brake fluid loss during subsequent operations. As a precaution, place absorbent rags beneath the modulator brake pipe unions.
5 Wipe clean the area around the modulator brake pipe unions, then make a note of how the pipes are arranged, to use as a reference on refitting; the four modulator outlet unions

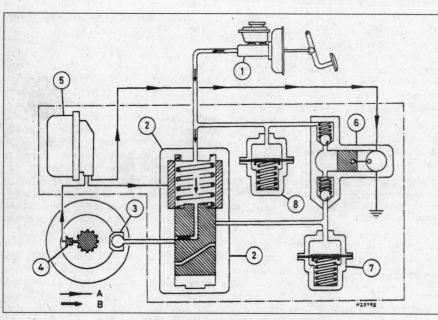

23.3 ABS system "pressure-maintain" phase

Refer to illustration 23.2 for key

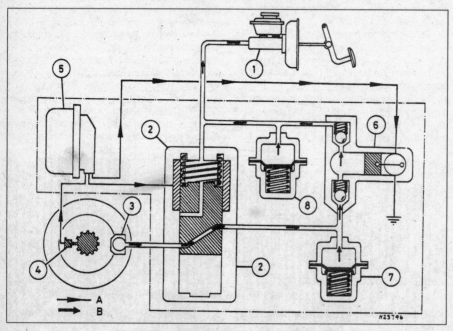

23.4 ABS system "pressure-decrease" phase

Refer to illustration 23.2 for key

24.3 Disconnecting the large wiring connector from ABS modulator computer (square connector arrowed)

24.5 ABS modulator block brake pipe unions (arrowed)

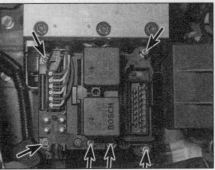

24.9 ABS modulator computer retaining screws (arrowed)

24.12 Remove the shield from the top of the front wheel sensor . . .

are marked, to aid refitting. Unscrew the union nuts, and carefully withdraw the pipes (see illustration). Plug or tape over the pipe ends and valve orifices, to minimise the loss of brake fluid, and to prevent the entry of dirt into the system. Wash off any spilt fluid immediately with cold water.

6 Slacken the mounting nuts, and remove the modulator assembly from the engine compartment. Note that the nuts do not need to be removed, since the mounting bracket bolt holes are slotted. Note: Do not attempt to dismantle the modulator block hydraulic assembly. Overhaul of the unit is a complex job, which if necessary should be entrusted to a Citroën dealer.

Refitting

7 Refitting is the reverse of the removal procedure, noting the following points:
(a) Tighten the modulator block mounting nuts securely.
(b) Refit the brake pipes to their respective unions, and securely tighten the union nuts.
(c) Ensure the wiring is correctly routed, and the connectors firmly pressed into position.
(d) On completion, and prior to refitting the battery, bleed the complete braking system as described in Section 2. Ensure the system is bled in the correct order, to prevent air entering the modulator return pump.

ABS computer
Removal

8 Disconnect the battery negative terminal, then slacken the retaining screw, and remove the relay cover from the modulator assembly.
9 Disconnect the three wiring connectors from the computer unit, then slacken and remove the six Torx retaining screws, and lift the computer away from the modulator assembly (see illustration).

Refitting

10 Refitting is a reversal of the removal procedure, ensuring that the computer retaining screws are securely tightened and the wiring connectors are firmly reconnected.

Front wheel sensor
Removal

11 Chock the rear wheels, then firmly apply the handbrake, jack up the front of the vehicle and support on axle stands. Remove the appropriate front roadwheel.
12 Slacken and remove the bolt securing the wiring retaining bracket to the top of the swivel hub assembly, then undo the retaining nut and remove the shield from the top of the sensor (see illustration).
13 Trace the wiring back from the sensor to the connector, freeing it from all the relevant retaining clips, and disconnect it from the main loom (see illustration).

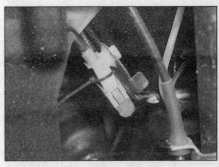

24.13 . . . then trace the sensor wiring back to its wiring connector, and disconnect it

14 Slacken and remove the bolt securing the sensor to the swivel hub, and remove the sensor and lead assembly from the vehicle (see illustrations).

Refitting

15 Prior to refitting, apply a thin coat of multi-purpose grease to the sensor tip.
16 Ensure that the sensor and swivel hub sealing faces are clean, then fit the sensor to the hub. Apply a few drops of locking fluid to the sensor bolt, then refit the bolt and tighten it to the specified torque.
17 Rotate the hub until one of the reluctor ring teeth is correctly aligned with the sensor tip. Using feeler gauges, measure the air gap between the tooth and sensor tip (see illustration). Rotate the hub, and repeat the

24.14a Slacken and remove the retaining bolt . . .

24.14b . . . and remove the sensor from the swivel hub

24.17 Checking the front wheel sensor air gap

9

24.21 Rear wheel sensor wiring connectors are located just in front of the rear axle

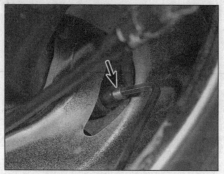

24.23a Undo the retaining bolt (arrowed) . . .

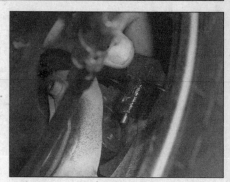

24.23b . . . and remove the rear wheel sensor from the trailing arm

procedure on several other teeth. If the air gap is not within the specified range given in the Specifications at the start of this Chapter, then the advice of a Citroën dealer must be sought.

18 Ensure the sensor wiring is correctly routed and retained by all the necessary clips, and reconnect it to its wiring connector.

19 Refit the roadwheel, then lower the vehicle to the ground and tighten the roadwheel bolts to the specified torque.

Rear wheel sensor
Removal

20 Chock the front wheels, then jack up the rear of the vehicle and support it on axle stands. Remove the appropriate roadwheel.

21 Trace the wiring back from the sensor to its wiring connector, which is situated just in front of the rear axle **(see illustration)**. Free the connector from its retaining clip, and disconnect the wiring from the main wiring loom.

22 Work back along the sensor wiring, and free it from any relevant retaining clips.

23 Slacken and remove the bolt securing the sensor unit to the trailing arm, and remove the sensor and lead assembly from the vehicle **(see illustrations)**.

Refitting

24 Prior to refitting, apply a thin coat of multi-purpose grease to the sensor tip.

25 Ensure that the sensor and trailing arm sealing faces are clean, then fit the sensor and tighten its retaining bolt to the specified torque.

26 Rotate the disc until one of the reluctor ring teeth is correctly aligned with sensor tip. Using feeler gauges, measure the air gap between the tooth and sensor tip. Note that this may prove difficult with the disc shield in position. Rotate the disc, and repeat the procedure on several other teeth. If the air gap is not within the specified range given in the Specifications at the start of this Chapter, then the advice of a Citroën dealer must be sought.

27 Ensure the sensor wiring is correctly routed and retained by all the necessary retaining clips, and reconnect it to the wiring connector.

28 Refit the roadwheel, then lower the vehicle to the ground and tighten the roadwheel bolts to the specified torque.

Front reluctor rings

29 The front reluctor rings are an integral part of the driveshaft outer constant velocity (CV) joints, and cannot be renewed separately. Examine the rings for damage such as chipped or missing teeth. If renewal is necessary, the complete outer constant velocity joint must be renewed as described in Chapter 8.

Rear reluctor rings

30 The rear reluctor rings are an integral part of the rear hub assembly, and cannot be renewed separately. Examine the rings for signs of damage such as chipped or missing teeth, and renew as necessary. If renewal is necessary, the rear hub assembly must be renewed as described in Chapter 10.

Relays

31 Both the solenoid relay and return pump relay are located in the modulator block assembly. To gain access to them, undo the relay cover retaining screw and lift off the cover. Either relay can then be simply pulled out of position **(see illustrations)**. Refer to Chapter 12 for further information on relays.

25 Vacuum pump (16-valve models) - removal and refitting

Removal

1 Release the retaining clip and disconnect the vacuum hose from the top of pump.

2 Slacken and remove the two bolts securing the pump to the left-hand end of the cylinder head, then remove the pump. Remove the pump O-ring (where fitted) and discard it - a new one must be used on refitting.

24.31a Undo the retaining screw . . .

24.31b . . . and lift the relay cover off the modulator block . . .

24.31c . . . to gain access to the ABS relays

Refitting

3 Where an O-ring was fitted, fit a new O-ring to the pump. Where no O-ring was fitted, apply a smear of suitable sealant to the pump mating surface.

4 Align the pump drive dog with the slot in the camshaft end, then refit the pump to the cylinder head. Refit the pump mounting bolts, and tighten them securely.

5 Reconnect the vacuum hose to the pump, and securely tighten its retaining clip.

26 Vacuum pump (16-valve models) - testing and overhaul

1 The operation of the braking system vacuum pump can be checked using a vacuum gauge.

2 Disconnect the vacuum pipe from the pump, and connect the gauge to the pump union using a suitable length of hose.

3 Start the engine and allow it to idle, then measure the vacuum created by the pump. As a guide, after one minute, a minimum of approximately 500 mm Hg should be recorded. If the vacuum registered is significantly less than this, it is likely that the pump is faulty. However, seek the advice of a Citroën dealer before condemning the pump.

4 Overhaul of the vacuum pump is not possible, since no components are available separately for it. If faulty, the complete pump assembly must be renewed.

9

Notes

Chapter 10 Suspension and steering

Contents

Front hub bearings - renewal 3
Front swivel hub assembly - removal and refitting 2
Front suspension and steering check .... See Chapter 1
Front suspension anti-roll bar - removal and refitting 8
Front suspension anti-roll bar connecting link - removal and refitting . 9
Front suspension lower arm balljoint - removal and refitting 7
Front suspension lower arm - removal, overhaul and refitting 6
Front suspension strut - overhaul 5
Front suspension strut - removal and refitting 4
Front suspension subframe - removal and refitting 10
General information 1
Ignition switch/steering column lock - removal and refitting 21
Power steering pump - removal and refitting 25
Power steering pump drivebelt check,
   adjustment and renewal .... See Chapter 1
Power steering fluid level check .... See "Weekly checks"
Power steering system - bleeding 24
Rear axle assembly - removal and refitting 17
Rear hub assembly - removal and refitting 11
Rear hub bearings - renewal 12
Rear shock absorber - removal, testing and refitting 13
Rear suspension anti-roll bar - removal and refitting 16
Rear suspension torsion bar - removal and refitting 14
Rear suspension trailing arm - removal and refitting 15
Steering column - removal, inspection and refitting 20
Steering gear assembly - removal, overhaul and refitting 22
Steering gear rubber gaiters - renewal 23
Steering wheel - removal and refitting 19
Track rod - removal and refitting 27
Track rod balljoint - removal and refitting 26
Vehicle ride height - checking and adjustment 18
Wheel alignment and steering angles - general information 28
Wheel and tyre maintenance and tyre pressure
   checks .... See "Weekly checks"

Degrees of difficulty

Easy, suitable for novice with little experience		**Fairly easy,** suitable for beginner with some experience		**Fairly difficult,** suitable for competent DIY mechanic		**Difficult,** suitable for experienced DIY mechanic		**Very difficult,** suitable for expert DIY or professional	

Specifications

Front suspension
Front ride height - fully-laden*:
   1124 cc and 1360 cc models .... 177 ± 10 mm
   1580 cc and 1761 cc models .... 185 ± 10 mm
   1905 cc and 1998 cc 8-valve models .... 167 ± 10 mm
   1998 cc 16-valve models .... 165 ± 10 mm
* Fully-laden - 4 occupants and 40 kg of luggage in the vehicle

Rear suspension
Rear ride height - fully-laden*:
   1124 cc and 1360 cc models .... 201 ± 10 mm
   1580 cc models:
      Three-door models .... 189 ± 10 mm
      Five-door models .... 209 ± 10 mm
   1761 cc models .... 189 ± 10 mm
   1905 cc and 1998 cc 8-valve models .... 200 ± 10 mm
   1998 cc 16-valve models .... 199 ± 10 mm
* Fully-laden - 4 occupants and 40 kg of luggage in the vehicle

Steering
Power steering fluid type .... See "Lubricants and fluids"

Roadwheels
Type .... Pressed-steel or aluminium alloy (depending on model)
Size .... 5B x 13, 5J x 13, 5.5J x 14 or 6J x 15 (depending on model)
Maximum run-out at rim .... 1.2 mm
Maximum eccentricity on tyre bead locating surface .... 0.8 mm

10

Wheel alignment and steering angles

Front wheel camber angle:
    Unladen . . . .   0° 30' ± 40'
    Fully-laden* . . . .   0° ± 40'
Castor angle:
    Unladen:
        Manual steering . . . .   0° 30' ± 40'
        Power-assisted steering . . . .   2° ± 40'
    Fully-laden*:
        Manual steering . . . .   1° 30' ± 40'
        Power-assisted steering . . . .   3° ± 40'
Steering axis inclination/kingpin inclination . . . .   10° 45' ± 40'
Front wheel toe setting:
    Unladen:
        Manual steering . . . .   0 to 2 mm (toe-out)
        Power-assisted steering . . . .   -2.5 to -4.5 mm (toe-in)
    Fully-laden*:
        Manual steering . . . .   1 to 3 mm (toe-out)
        Power-assisted steering . . . .   -1 to -3 mm (toe-in)
Rear wheel camber setting . . . .   -1° ± 40'
Rear wheel toe setting:
    Unladen . . . .   -2 to 2 mm (toe-in/toe-out)
    Fully-laden* . . . .   -2.5 to -6.0 mm (toe-in)
Fully-laden - 4 occupants and 40 kg of luggage in the vehicle

Torque wrench settings

	Nm	lbf ft
Front suspension		
Strut-to-swivel hub bolt (see text Section 2):		
Standard swivel hub	55	41
Modified swivel hub	45	33
Strut upper mounting bolts	20	15
Strut upper mounting retaining nut	45	33
Lower arm balljoint clamp bolt	40	30
Lower arm balljoint retaining nuts	45	33
Lower arm front pivot bolt	60	44
Lower arm rear pivot bush mounting bolts:		
8 mm bolt	27	20
10 mm bolt	55	41
Anti-roll bar (models with anti-roll bar connected to lower arm):		
Mounting clamp bolts	55	41
Bar-to-connecting link nuts	30	22
Connecting link-to-bracket bolt	40	30
Bracket-to-lower arm bolts	20	15
Anti-roll bar (models with anti-roll bar connected to strut):		
Mounting clamp bolts	55	41
Connecting link nuts	40	30
Subframe mounting bolts	84	62
Rear suspension		
Shock absorber upper mounting bolt	75	55
Shock absorber lower mounting bolt	70	52
Rear hub nut:		
Models with rear drum brakes	200	148
Models with rear disc brakes	180	133
Torsion bar Torx retaining screw	20	15
Anti-roll bar retaining bracket bolt	35	26
Brake backplate bolts (drum brakes only)	37	27
Rear axle mountings:		
Front mounting-to-body nuts	55	41
Front mounting-to-crossmember bolts	70	52
Rear mounting nuts	45	33
Track rod balljoint-to-swivel hub nut	35	26
Track rod-to-steering rack	50	37
Steering gear mounting bolts	40	30
Steering wheel nut	35	26
Steering column mounting nuts	17	13
Universal joint clamp bolt	25	18

Torque wrench settings (continued)

	Nm	lbf ft
Steering		
Power-assisted steering gear fluid unions:		
Feed pipe	25	18
Return pipe	20	15
Roadwheels		
Wheel bolts	90	66

1 General information

The independent front suspension is of the MacPherson strut type, incorporating coil springs and integral telescopic shock absorbers. The MacPherson struts are located by transverse lower suspension arms, which utilise rubber inner mounting bushes, and incorporate a balljoint at the outer ends. The front swivel hubs, which carry the wheel bearings, brake calipers and the hub/disc assemblies, are bolted to the MacPherson struts, and connected to the lower arms via the balljoints. A front anti-roll bar is fitted to all models. The anti-roll bar is rubber-mounted onto the subframe, and is either connected to both lower suspension arms or directly to the front suspension struts, depending on the model **(see illustration)**.

The rear suspension is of the independent trailing arm type, which consists of two trailing arms, linked by a tubular crossmember. Torsion bars linking the trailing arms are situated in front of and behind the crossmember, and an anti-roll bar linking the arms passes through the centre of the crossmember **(see illustration)**.

The complete rear axle assembly is mounted onto the vehicle underbody by four "self-steering" rubber mountings. These mountings are designed to move slightly under extreme cornering forces. This movement of the rear axle assembly has the effect of actually turning the rear wheels slightly, to help steer the vehicle in the required direction. This improves the handling of the vehicle when cornering at extreme speeds.

The steering column has a universal joint fitted in the centre of its length, which is connected to an intermediate shaft having a second universal joint at its lower end. The lower universal joint is clamped to the steering gear pinion by means of a clamp bolt **(see illustration)**.

The steering gear is mounted onto the front subframe, and is connected by two track rods, with balljoints at their outer ends, to the steering arms projecting rearwards from the swivel hubs. The track rod ends are threaded, to facilitate adjustment.

Power-assisted steering is fitted as standard on some models, and is available as an option on all others. The hydraulic steering system is powered by a belt-driven pump, which is driven off the crankshaft pulley.

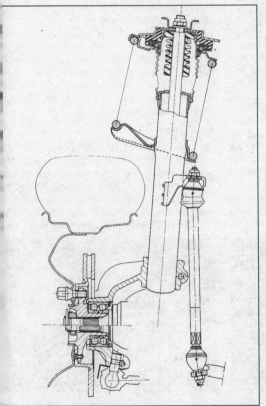

1.1 Cross-sectional view of the front suspension components

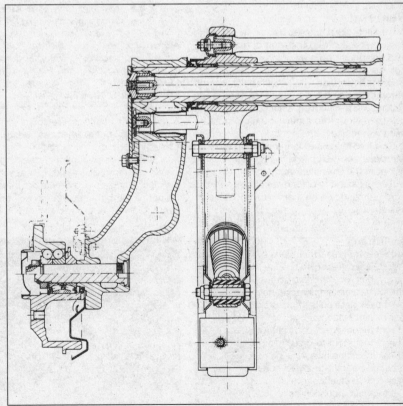

1.2 Cross-sectional view of the rear suspension components

10

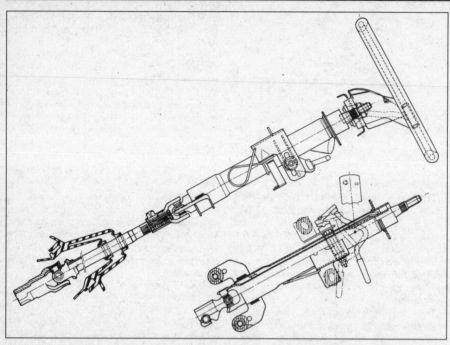

1.4 Cross-sectional view of the steering column and associated components

2.6 Slacken and remove the bolt securing the wiring retaining bracket to the swivel hub

---

2 Front swivel hub assembly - removal and refitting

Removal

1 Chock the rear wheels, then firmly apply the handbrake. Jack up the front of the vehicle, and support it on axle stands. Remove the appropriate front roadwheel.

2 On 1124 cc and 1360 cc models, using a hammer and a chisel-nosed tool, tap up the staking securing the driveshaft retaining nut in position. Note that a new retaining must be used on refitting.

3 On all 1580 cc and larger-engined models, withdraw the R-clip, and remove the locking cap from the driveshaft retaining nut.

4 Refit at least two roadwheel bolts to the front hub, and tighten them securely. Have an assistant firmly depress the brake pedal, to prevent the front hub from rotating, then using

a socket and extension bar, slacken and remove the driveshaft retaining nut.

> **TOOL TiP** *A tool to prevent the hub rotating can be fabricated from two lengths of steel strip (one long, one short) and a nut and bolt; the nut and bolt forming the pivot of a forked tool. Bolt the tool to the hub using two wheel bolts, and hold the tool to prevent the hub from rotating as the driveshaft nut is undone (see Chapter 8, Section 2).*

5 If the hub bearings are to be disturbed, remove the brake disc as described in Chapter 9. If not, unscrew the two bolts securing the brake caliper assembly to the swivel hub, and slide the caliper assembly off the disc. Using a piece of wire or string, tie the caliper to the front suspension coil spring, to avoid placing any strain on the hydraulic brake hose. Discard the caliper mounting

bolts - they must be renewed whenever they are disturbed.

6 Slacken and remove the bolt securing the wiring retaining bracket to the top of the swivel hub (see illustration).

7 On models with ABS, remove the wheel sensor as described in Chapter 9.

8 On all models, slacken and remove the nut securing the steering gear track rod balljoint to the swivel hub, and release the balljoint tapered shank using a universal balljoint separator.

9 Slacken and remove the three nuts securing the balljoint to the lower suspension arm, then withdraw the bolts and free the balljoint from the arm (see illustration).

10 Undo the nut and withdraw the swivel hub-to-suspension strut clamp bolt, noting which way around it is fitted.

11 Free the swivel hub assembly from the end of the strut, then release it from the outer constant velocity joint splines, and remove it from the vehicle. If the swivel hub is a tight fit on the strut, use a large flat-bladed screwdriver to carefully open up the clamp a little (see illustration).

Refitting

12 Note that all Nyloc nuts disturbed or removal must be renewed as a matter of course. These nuts have threads which are pre-coated with locking compound (this is only effective once), and include the track rod balljoint nut, lower suspension arm balljoint nuts, and the swivel hub clamp bolt nut.

2.9 Undo the three lower suspension arm balljoint retaining nuts

2.11 Removing the swivel hub assembly. Note the use of the screwdriver to open up the hub clamp

2.14a On refitting, ensure the swivel hub clamp is aligned with the lug (arrowed) on the strut prior to inserting the clamp bolt

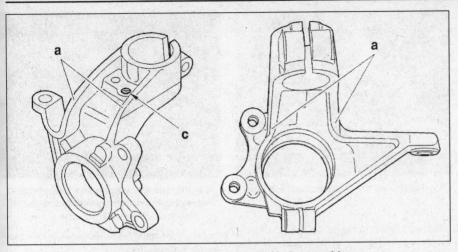

2.14b Standard type front swivel hub assembly

a H-shaped ribbing   c Wiring bracket mounting bolt hole

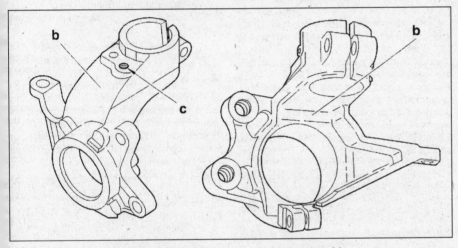

2.14c Modified type front swivel hub assembly

b Tubular shaped area   c Wiring bracket mounting bolt hole

13 Ensure the driveshaft outer constant velocity joint and hub splines are clean, then slide the hub fully onto the driveshaft splines.
14 Slide the hub assembly fully onto the suspension strut, aligning the split in the hub clamp with the lug on the base of the strut. Also ensure that the stop bosses on the strut are in contact with the top surface of the swivel hub. Insert the swivel hub-to-suspension strut clamp bolt from the rear side of the strut, then fit a new nut to the clamp bolt, and tighten it to the specified torque **(see illustration)**. Note that later models are fitted with a modified swivel hub assembly which can be identified by its tubular shape, and the lack of the H-shaped ribbing around the periphery **(see illustrations)**. If working on the modified assembly, note that the torque setting for the swivel hub-to-suspension strut clamp bolt has altered. Ensure that the correct torque setting is used according to swivel hub type.
15 Align the balljoint with the lower arm, and fit the three retaining bolts. Fit new retaining

nuts to the bolts, and tighten them to the specified torque.
16 Engage the track rod balljoint in the swivel hub, then fit a new retaining nut and tighten it to the specified torque.
17 Where necessary, refit the brake disc to the hub, referring to Chapter 9 for further information. If the threads of the new caliper mounting bolts are not already pre-coated with locking compound, apply a suitable locking compound to them. Slide the caliper assembly into position over the disc, then fit the mounting bolts and tighten them to the specified torque (see Chapter 9).
18 Where necessary, refit the ABS wheel sensor as described in Chapter 9.
19 Refit the wiring retaining bracket to the top of the swivel hub, and tighten its retaining bolt securely.
20 Lubricate the inner face and threads of the driveshaft retaining nut with clean engine oil, and refit it to the end of the driveshaft. Use the method employed on removal to prevent the hub from rotating, and tighten the

driveshaft retaining nut to the specified torque (see Chapter 8). Check that the hub rotates freely.
21 On 1124 cc and 1360 cc models, stake the nut firmly into the driveshaft grooves using a hammer and punch.
22 On 1580 cc and larger-engined models, engage the locking cap with the driveshaft nut so that one of its cut-outs is aligned with the driveshaft hole. Secure the cap with the R-clip.
23 Refit the roadwheel, then lower the vehicle to the ground and tighten the roadwheel bolts to the specified torque.

3 Front hub bearings - renewal

Note: *The bearing is a sealed, pre-adjusted and pre-lubricated, double-row roller type, and is intended to last the car's entire service life without maintenance or attention. Never overtighten the driveshaft nut beyond the specified torque wrench setting in an attempt to "adjust" the bearing.*
Note: *A press will be required to dismantle and rebuild the assembly; if such a tool is not available, a large bench vice and spacers (such as large sockets) will serve as an adequate substitute. The bearing's inner races are an interference fit on the hub; if the inner race remains on the hub when it is pressed out of the hub carrier, a knife-edged bearing puller will be required to remove it.*
1 Remove the swivel hub assembly as described in Section 2.
2 Support the swivel hub securely on blocks or in a vice. Using a tubular spacer which bears only on the inner end of the hub flange, press the hub flange out of the bearing. If the bearing's outboard inner race remains on the hub, remove it using a bearing puller (see note above).
3 Extract the bearing retaining circlip from the inner end of the swivel hub assembly **(see illustration)**.
4 Where necessary, refit the inner race back in position over the ball cage, and securely support the inner face of the swivel hub. Using a tubular spacer which bears only on

3.3 Front hub bearing retaining circlip

10

4.3 Where the anti-roll bar is linked to the strut, undo the retaining nut and free the connecting link from the strut body

4.6 Removing the front suspension strut

4.8 Tighten the suspension strut upper mounting bolts to the specified torque. Note upper mounting locating pin (arrowed)

the inner race, press the complete bearing assembly out of the swivel hub.

5 Thoroughly clean the hub and swivel hub, removing all traces of dirt and grease, and polish away any burrs or raised edges which might hinder reassembly. Check both for cracks or any other signs of wear or damage, and renew them if necessary. Renew the circlip, regardless of its apparent condition.

6 On reassembly, apply a light film of oil to the bearing outer race and hub flange shaft, to aid installation of the bearing.

7 Securely support the swivel hub, and locate the bearing in the hub. Press the bearing fully into position, ensuring that it enters the hub squarely, using a tubular spacer which bears only on the bearing outer race.

8 Once the bearing is correctly seated, secure the bearing in position with the new circlip, ensuring that it is correctly located in the groove in the swivel hub.

9 Securely support the outer face of the hub flange, and locate the swivel hub bearing inner race over the end of the hub flange. Press the bearing onto the hub, using a tubular spacer which bears only on the inner race of the hub bearing, until it seats against the hub shoulder. Check that the hub flange rotates freely, and wipe off any excess oil or grease.

10 Refit the swivel hub assembly as described in Section 2.

4 Front suspension strut - removal and refitting

Removal

1 Chock the rear wheels, apply the handbrake, then jack up the front of the vehicle and support on axle stands. Remove the appropriate roadwheel.

2 Unscrew the two bolts securing the brake caliper to the swivel hub, and discard them; new bolts must be used on refitting. Slacken and remove the bolt securing the wiring

retaining bracket to the swivel hub, then slide the caliper assembly off the disc. Using a piece of wire or string, tie the caliper to the front suspension lower arm, to avoid placing any strain on the hydraulic brake hose.

3 On models where the anti-roll bar is connected to the suspension strut body, undo the nut and washer securing the connecting link to the strut, and position the link clear of the strut (see illustration). Discard the nut - a new one must be used on refitting.

4 Undo the nut and withdraw the swivel hub-to-suspension strut clamp bolt, noting which way around it is fitted. Discard the nut - a new one must be used on refitting.

5 Slacken and remove the two suspension strut upper mounting bolts.

6 Release the strut from the swivel hub, and withdraw it from under the wheel arch. If the swivel hub is a tight fit on the strut, carefully open up the clamp a little using a large flat-bladed screwdriver (see illustration).

Refitting

7 Manoeuvre the strut assembly into position, ensuring that the top mounting plate locating pin is correctly located in its hole. Engage the lower end of the strut with the swivel hub, aligning the split in the hub clamp with the lug on the base of the strut.

8 Insert the two strut upper mounting bolts, and tighten them to the specified torque (see illustration).

9 Insert the swivel hub-to-suspension strut clamp bolt from the front side of the strut. Fit a new nut to the clamp bolt, and tighten it to the specified torque.

10 Where necessary, refit the anti-roll bar connecting link to the strut. Fit a new nut to the connecting link, and tighten it to the specified torque.

11 Slide the brake caliper into position over the disc. If the threads of the new caliper mounting bolts are not already pre-coated with locking compound, apply a suitable locking compound to them. Install the bolts and tighten them to the specified torque (see Chapter 9).

12 Refit the roadwheel, then lower the vehicle to the ground and tighten the roadwheel bolts to the specified torque.

5 Front suspension strut - overhaul

⚠️ **Warning: Before attempting to dismantle the front suspension strut, a suitable tool to hold the coil spring in compression must be obtained. Adjustable coil spring compressors are readily-available, and are recommended for this operation. Any attempt to dismantle the strut without such a tool is likely to result in damage or personal injury.**

1 With the strut removed from the car as described in Section 4, clean away all external dirt, then mount it upright in a vice.

2 Fit the spring compressor, and compress the coil spring until all tension is relieved from the upper mounting plate.

3 Remove the rubber cap, then slacken the upper mounting retaining nut whilst retaining the strut piston with an Allen key.

4 Remove the nut and washer, then lift off the collar, mounting plate, bearing, upper spring seat and flat washer. Remove the coil spring, then slide off the damper piston dust cover and rubber damper stop.

5 With the strut assembly now completely dismantled, examine all the components for wear, damage or deformation, and check the bearing for smoothness of operation. Renew any of the components as necessary.

6 Examine the strut for signs of fluid leakage. Check the strut piston for signs of pitting along its entire length, and check the strut body for signs of damage. While holding it in an upright position, test the operation of the strut by moving the piston through a full stroke, and then through short strokes of 50 to 100 mm. In both cases, the resistance felt should be smooth and continuous. If the resistance is jerky, or uneven, or if there is any visible sign of wear or damage to the strut, renewal is necessary.

7 If any doubt exists about the condition of the coil spring, carefully remove the spring

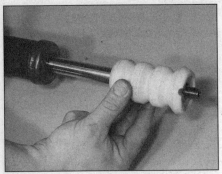

5.9a Ensure all components are clean and dry, then slide the rubber damper stop . . .

5.9b . . . and dust cover into position on the strut

5.9c Refit the coil spring, ensuring the spring end is correctly located against its stop on the lower seat (arrowed)

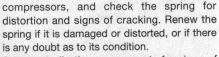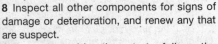

compressors, and check the spring for distortion and signs of cracking. Renew the spring if it is damaged or distorted, or if there is any doubt as to its condition.

8 Inspect all other components for signs of damage or deterioration, and renew any that are suspect.

9 To reassemble the strut, follow the accompanying photos, beginning with **illustration 5.9a**. Be sure to stay in order, and carefully read the caption underneath each (see illustrations).

10 Refit the rubber cap to the top of the strut piston, then refit the strut to the vehicle as described in Section 4.

5.9d Fit the flat washer to the top of the strut piston . . .

5.9e . . . then locate the upper spring seat on the spring, ensuring that the spring seat stop (arrowed) is correctly located against the spring end

5.9f Refit the bearing to the upper spring seat, ensuring that it is fitted the correct way around

5.9g Locate the upper mounting plate on the spring seat . . .

5.9h . . . and refit the collar to the mounting plate

5.9i Refit the washer and upper mounting retaining nut, and tighten the nut to the specified torque

5.9j Ensure that the spring ends are still correctly located against the seat stops, then release the spring compressors and remove them from the strut

5.9k With the compressors removed, push the rubber bump stop and gaiter upwards until they are correctly seated inside the upper mounting plate

10

6.3 Removing the lower suspension arm balljoint clamp bolt

6.4 Release the balljoint from the swivel hub, and remove the protector plate from the balljoint shank

6.5a Slacken and remove the lower suspension arm front pivot bolt . . .

6 Front suspension lower arm - removal, overhaul and refitting

Removal

1 Chock the rear wheels, firmly apply the handbrake, then jack up the front of the vehicle and support on axle stands. Remove the appropriate front roadwheel.

2 On models where the anti-roll bar is mounted onto the lower suspension arm, slacken and remove the two nuts securing the mounting bracket to the lower arm, then withdraw then retaining bolts and free the bracket from the arm. Discard the nuts - new ones must be used on refitting.

3 Slacken and remove the nut, then withdraw

6.5b . . . and the two rear mounting bush bolts (second bolt arrowed) . . .

6.5c . . . then remove the lower arm from the vehicle

the lower arm balljoint clamp bolt from the swivel hub (see illustration). Discard the nut - a new one must be used on refitting.

4 Lever the arm downwards to release the balljoint from the swivel hub, and remove the protector plate which is fitted to the balljoint shank (see illustration).

5 Slacken and remove the lower arm front pivot bolt and nut, then undo the two bolts securing the rear mounting bush to the subframe (the larger of which is also the anti-roll bar mounting clamp bolt), and recover the nut from the top of the subframe. Manoeuvre the lower arm assembly out from underneath the vehicle (see illustrations).

Overhaul

6 Thoroughly clean the lower arm and the area around the arm mountings, removing all traces of dirt and underseal if necessary, then check carefully for cracks, distortion or any other signs of wear or damage, paying particular attention to the pivot bushes, and renew components as necessary.

7 Check that the lower arm balljoint moves freely, without any sign of roughness; check also that the balljoint gaiter shows no sign of deterioration, and is free from cracks and splits. If renewal is necessary, slacken and remove its retaining bolts, and remove the balljoint from the arm. Fit the new balljoint, and insert its retaining bolts. Fit new retaining nuts to the bolts, and tighten them to the specified torque.

8 Examine the shank of the pivot bolt for signs of wear or scoring, and renew if necessary.

6.12 With the vehicle resting on its wheels, tighten the lower arm front pivot bolt to the specified torque setting

Refitting

9 Manoeuvre the lower arm assembly into position, and refit the front pivot bolt, tightening it finger-tight only. Refit the two rear pivot bush retaining bolts, and tighten both to their specified torque settings.

10 Refit the protector plate to the lower arm balljoint, then locate the balljoint shank in the swivel hub, ensuring that the lug on the protector plate is correctly located in the clamp split. Insert the balljoint clamp bolt, then fit the new retaining nut and tighten it to the specified torque.

11 Where necessary, align the anti-roll bar mounting bracket with the lower arm, and insert its retaining bolts. Fit new nuts to the bolts, and tighten them to the specified torque.

12 Refit the roadwheel, then lower the vehicle and tighten the roadwheel bolts to the specified torque. Rock the vehicle to settle the disturbed components in position, then tighten the lower arm front pivot bolt to the specified torque (see illustration).

7 Front suspension lower arm balljoint - removal and refitting

Removal

1 Release the balljoint from the swivel hub as described in Section 6, paragraphs 1 to 4.

2 Slacken and remove the three nuts, then withdraw the balljoint retaining bolts and remove the balljoint from the lower arm (see

7.2a Remove the three retaining bolts . . .

7.2b ... and remove the lower arm balljoint

illustrations). Discard the nuts - new ones must be used on refitting.

3 Check that the lower arm balljoint moves freely, without any sign of roughness. Check also that the balljoint gaiter shows no sign of deterioration, and is free from cracks and splits. Renew worn or damaged components as necessary.

Refitting

4 Locate the balljoint in the end of the suspension arm, and insert the three retaining bolts. Fit new nuts to the bolts, and tighten them to the specified torque.

5 Carry out the operations described in paragraphs 10 to 12 of Section 6.

8 Front suspension anti-roll bar - removal and refitting

Removal

1 Chock the rear wheels, firmly apply the handbrake, then jack up the front of the vehicle and support on axle stands. Remove both front roadwheels.

2 On models where the anti-roll bar is mounted onto the lower suspension arm, slacken and remove the two nuts and bolts securing the mounting bracket to the left-hand lower arm, then undo the nut securing the connecting link to the anti-roll bar, and remove the connecting link and bracket assembly. Repeat the procedure on the right-hand side.

3 On models where the anti-roll bar is connected to the suspension strut body, undo the nut and washer securing the left-hand connecting link to the anti-roll bar, and position the link clear of the bar. Repeat the procedure on the right-hand side.

4 On models with power steering, using brake hose clamps, clamp both the supply and return hoses near the power steering fluid reservoir. This will minimise fluid loss during subsequent operations. Mark the unions to ensure they are correctly positioned on reassembly, then unscrew the feed and return

pipe union nuts from the steering gear assembly; be prepared for fluid spillage, and position a suitable container beneath the pipes whilst unscrewing the union nuts. Disconnect both pipes, and plug the pipe ends and steering gear orifices, to prevent excessive fluid leakage and the entry of dirt into the hydraulic system.

5 On all models, using a hammer and punch, white paint or similar, mark the exact relationship between the steering intermediate shaft universal joint and the steering gear drive pinion. Slacken and remove the clamp bolt securing the joint to the pinion, and free the intermediate shaft from the steering gear.

6 Slacken and remove the nut securing the left-hand steering gear track rod balljoint to the swivel hub, and release the balljoint tapered shank using a universal balljoint separator. Repeat the procedure on the right-hand side.

7 On 1580 cc and larger-engined models with manual transmission, using a large screwdriver, carefully lever the three gearchange linkage link rods off their balljoints on the transmission unit.

8 Slacken and remove the engine/transmission rear mounting through-bolt and nut.

9 Slacken and remove the four front subframe mounting bolts which are situated at the rear of the subframe. Loosen the two front subframe mounting bolts by a few turns, until it is possible to lower the rear edge of the subframe approximately 65 mm. Wedge a block of wood between the rear of the subframe and the vehicle underbody, to hold the subframe in this position.

10 Slacken the two anti-roll bar mounting clamp retaining bolts, and recover the nuts from the top of the clamps (see illustration). Remove both clamps from the subframe.

11 Manoeuvre the anti-roll bar out from underneath the vehicle, and remove the mounting bushes from the bar.

12 Carefully examine the anti-roll bar components for signs of wear, damage or deterioration, paying particular attention to the mounting bushes. Renew worn components as necessary.

8.10 Slacken and remove the bolt and nut (arrowed) and remove the anti-roll bar mounting clamp

Refitting

13 Fit the rubber mounting bushes to the anti-roll bar, ensuring that the recess on the inside of each bush engages with the lugs on the anti-roll bar. Rotate each bush so that its marking is aligned with the paint mark on the anti-roll bar.

14 Offer up the anti-roll bar, and manoeuvre it into position on the subframe. Refit the mounting clamps, ensuring that their ends are correctly located in the hooks on the subframe, and refit the retaining bolts and nuts. Ensure that the bush markings are still aligned with the paint marks on the bars, then tighten the mounting clamp retaining bolts to the specified torque.

15 The remainder of the refitting is a reversal of the removal procedure, noting the following points:

(a) All Nyloc nuts disturbed on removal must be renewed as a matter of course. These nuts have threads which are pre-coated with locking compound (this is only effective once), and include the track rod balljoint nuts, connecting link nuts, engine mounting bolt nut, and the intermediate shaft clamp bolt nut. The intermediate shaft clamp bolt nut is retained by a metal cage; release the cage retaining tangs, then remove the old nut from inside the cage and install the new one. Refit the cage to the shaft, and secure it in position with the retaining tangs.

(b) Tighten all nuts and bolts to the specified torque settings (where given).

(c) Align the marks made on removal when reconnecting the intermediate shaft to the steering gear splines.

(d) On models with power steering, bleed the hydraulic system as described in Section 24.

(e) On completion check and, if necessary, adjust the front wheel alignment as described in Section 28.

9 Front suspension anti-roll bar connecting link - removal and refitting

Removal

1 Firmly apply the handbrake, then jack up the front of the car and support it on axle stands.

2 On models where the anti-roll bar is connected to the lower suspension arms, slacken and remove the nut and bolt securing the link to the lower arm bracket, then undo the nut and washer securing the link to the anti-roll bar. Disengage the connecting link from the end of the anti-roll bar, and remove it from the vehicle.

3 On models where the anti-roll bar is connected to the strut, slacken and remove the upper and lower connecting link retaining

9.3a Anti-roll bar connecting link lower retaining nut . . .

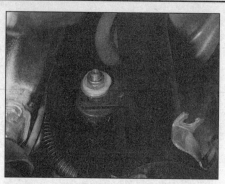

9.3b . . . and upper retaining nut - models with the anti-roll bar connected to the suspension strut body

Refitting

10 Refitting is a reversal of the removal procedure, noting the following points:

(a) All Nyloc nuts disturbed on removal must be renewed as a matter of course. These nuts have threads which are pre-coated with locking compound (this is only effective once), and include the connecting link nuts, lower arm balljoint nuts, engine mounting bolt nuts and steering gear bolt nuts.

(b) Tighten all nuts and bolts to the specified torque settings (where given).

(c) On completion check and, if necessary, adjust the front wheel alignment as described in Section 28.

nuts and washers, and remove the link from the vehicle **(see illustrations)**.

4 Examine the connecting link for signs of damage, paying particular attention to the mounting bushes or balljoints (as applicable), and renew if necessary. It is not possible to renew the bushes or balljoints separately. Note that the connecting link retaining nuts must be renewed as a matter of course.

Refitting

5 Refitting is a reversal of the removal procedure, using new retaining nuts and tightening them to the specified torque setting.

10 Front suspension subframe - removal and refitting

Removal

1 Chock the rear wheels, firmly apply the handbrake, then jack up the front of the vehicle and support it on axle stands. Remove both front roadwheels.

2 Remove the anti-roll bar connecting links as described in Section 9.

3 Slacken and remove the rear engine/transmission through-bolt and nut, then undo the nut and bolt securing the mounting bracket to the subframe and remove the bracket.

4 Slacken and remove the three nuts, then withdraw the balljoint retaining bolts and disengage the left-hand balljoint from the lower arm. Repeat the procedure on the right-hand side.

5 Slacken the steering gear mounting bolts, and recover the nuts. Withdraw the mounting bolts, and recover the spacers from the subframe apertures.

6 On 1580 cc and larger-engined models with manual transmission, using a large screwdriver, carefully lever the three gearchange linkage link rods off their balljoints on the transmission unit. Slacken and remove the pivot bolt securing the selector rod to the gearchange lever.

7 On models with power steering, undo the nut securing the steering gear pipe to its mounting bracket on the subframe, and free both pipes from any subframe retaining clips **(see illustration)**.

8 On right-hand-drive models, undo the nut securing the clutch cable retaining clip to the subframe, and disengage the cable from its retaining clips on either side of the subframe.

9 Slacken and remove the four rear front subframe mounting bolts and the two front mounting bolts, then carefully lower the subframe assembly out of position and remove it from underneath the vehicle **(see illustrations)**. On models with power steering, take great care to ensure the subframe assembly does not catch the power steering pipes as it is lowered out of position.

11 Rear hub assembly - removal and refitting

Rear drum brakes

1 On Hatchback models with rear drum brakes, the rear hub is an integral part of the brake drum. Refer to Chapter 9 for brake drum removal and refitting details. On Estate models, refer to Chapter 9 for brake drum removal and refitting details, then remove the hub assembly using the same procedure as for brake drum removal on Hatchback models.

Rear disc brakes

Note: Do not remove the hub assembly unless it is absolutely necessary. A puller will be required to draw the hub assembly off the stub axle, and the hub bearing will almost certainly be damaged by the removal procedure.

Removal

2 Remove the rear brake disc as described in Chapter 9.

3 Using a hammer and a large flat-bladed screwdriver, carefully tap and prise the cap out of the centre of the hub. Discard the cap - a new one must be used on refitting. Using a hammer and a chisel-nosed tool, tap up the

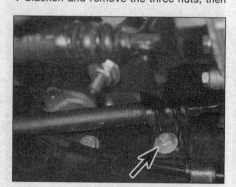

10.7 Power steering pipe-to-subframe retaining clip

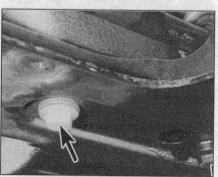

10.9a Front subframe left-hand rear mounting bolts (arrowed) . . .

10.9b . . . and front mounting bolt

11.3a Tap off the hub centre cap . . .

11.3b . . . then tap up the rear hub staking using a hammer and suitable punch

11.5 Use a puller to draw the hub assembly off the stub axle

staking securing the hub retaining nut to the groove in the stub axle (see illustrations).

4 Using a socket and long bar, slacken and remove the rear hub nut, and withdraw the thrustwasher. Discard the hub nut - a new nut must used on refitting.

5 Using a puller, draw the hub assembly off the stub axle, along with the outer bearing race (see illustration). With the hub removed, use the puller to draw the inner bearing race off the stub axle, then remove the hub spacer, noting which way around it is fitted.

6 Refit the races to the hub bearing, and check the hub bearing for signs of roughness. It is recommended that the bearing should be renewed as a matter of course, as it is likely to have been damaged during removal. This means that the complete hub assembly must be renewed, since it is not possible to obtain the bearing separately.

7 With the hub removed, examine the stub axle shaft for signs of wear or damage, and if necessary renew it. The stub axle is an interference fit in the trailing arm, and can either be tapped out of position, using a hammer and a soft-metal drift, or pushed out using a heavy-duty bearing puller. When installing the new stub axle, align its splines with those of the trailing arm, and drift or press it fully into position in the arm.

Refitting

8 Lubricate the stub axle shaft with clean engine oil, then slide on the spacer, ensuring it is fitted the correct way round.

9 Fit the new bearing inner race, and tap it fully onto the stub axle using a hammer and a tubular drift which bears only on the flat inside edge of the race.

10 Ensure that the bearing is packed with grease, then slide the hub assembly onto the stub axle. Fit the new outer bearing race, and tap it into position using the tubular drift.

11 Fit the thrustwasher and new hub nut, and tighten the hub nut to the specified torque. Stake the nut firmly into the groove on the stub axle to secure it in position, then tap the new hub cap into place in the centre of the hub (see illustrations).

12 Refit the rear brake disc as described in Chapter 9.

12 Rear hub bearings - renewal

Note: The bearing is intended to last the car's entire service life without maintenance or attention. Never overtighten the hub nut beyond the specified torque wrench setting, in an attempt to "adjust" the bearings.

11.11a Fit the thrustwasher and new hub nut . . .

11.11b . . . and tighten the nut to the specified torque

11.11c Using a hammer and punch . . .

11.11d . . . stake the hub nut firmly into the stub axle groove . . .

11.11e . . . then fit the new hub cap

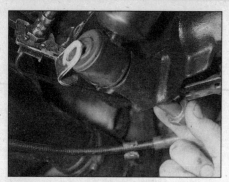

13.5a Withdraw the shock absorber lower mounting bolt . . .

13.5b . . . and the upper mounting bolt (arrowed) . . .

13.5c . . . and remove the shock absorber from underneath the vehicle

Rear drum brakes

1 Remove the rear brake drum as described in Chapter 9.

2 Using a flat-bladed screwdriver, lever the spacer out of the rear of the brake drum, noting which way around it is fitted.

3 Using circlip pliers, extract the bearing retaining circlip from the centre of the brake drum.

4 Securely support the drum hub, then press or drive the bearing out of position, using a tubular drift which bears on the bearing inner race.

5 Thoroughly clean the hub, removing all traces of dirt and grease, and polish away any burrs or raised edges which might hinder reassembly. Check the hub for cracks or any other signs of wear or damage, and renew them if necessary. The bearing and its circlip must be renewed whenever they are disturbed. Note that a replacement bearing kit, which consists of the bearing, circlip and spacer, is available from Citroën dealers.

6 Examine the stub axle shaft for signs of wear or damage, and if necessary renew it. The stub axle is an interference fit in the trailing arm, and can either be tapped out of position, using a hammer and a soft-metal drift, or pushed out using a heavy-duty bearing puller. When installing the new stub axle, align its splines with those of the trailing arm, and drive or press it fully into position in the arm.

7 On reassembly, apply a light film of clean engine oil to the bearing outer race, to aid installation of the bearing.

8 Securely support the drum, and locate the bearing in the hub. Press the bearing fully into position, ensuring that it enters the hub squarely, using a tubular spacer which bears only on the bearing outer race.

9 Ensure the bearing is correctly seated against the hub shoulder, and secure it in position with the new circlip. Ensure that the circlip is correctly seated in its hub groove.

10 Fit the new spacer to the drum, ensuring it is fitted the correct way around, and use a tubular spacer to press it into squarely into position.

11 Refit the brake drum as described in Chapter 9.

Rear disc brakes

12 On models with rear disc brakes, it is not possible to renew the rear hub bearing separately. If the bearing is worn, the complete rear hub assembly must be renewed. Refer to Section 11 for hub removal and refitting procedures.

13 Rear shock absorber - removal, testing and refitting

Removal

1 Chock the front wheels, then jack up the rear of the vehicle and support it on axle stands. Remove the relevant rear roadwheel.

2 On some models, note that if the left-hand shock absorber is to be removed, it will first be necessary to remove the exhaust tailpipe and tailpipe heatshield, in order to allow the shock absorber upper mounting bolt to be withdrawn. If this is the case, refer to Chapter 4 for information on exhaust system removal.

3 Using a trolley jack, raise the trailing arm until the shock absorber is slightly compressed.

4 Free the handbrake cable from its retaining clip on the bottom of the trailing arm. Slacken and remove the nuts and washers from both the upper and lower shock absorber mounting bolts, and free the brake hose mounting bracket from the lower mounting bolt.

5 Withdraw the mounting bolts, noting which way around they are fitted, and manoeuvre the shock absorber out from underneath the vehicle **(see illustrations)**.

Testing

6 Examine the shock absorber for signs of fluid leakage or damage. Test the operation of the shock absorber, while holding it in an upright position, by moving the piston through a full stroke and then through short strokes of 50 to 100 mm. In both cases, the resistance felt should be smooth and continuous. If the resistance is jerky, or uneven, or if there is any visible sign of wear or damage, renewal is necessary. Also check the rubber mounting bushes for damage and deterioration. Renew the complete unit if any damage or excessive wear is evident; the mounting bushes are not available separately. Inspect the shanks of the mounting bolts for signs of wear or damage, and renew as necessary.

Refitting

7 Prior to refitting the shock absorber, mount it upright in the vice, and operate it fully through several strokes in order to prime it. Apply a smear of multi-purpose grease to both the shock absorber mounting bolts.

8 Manoeuvre the shock absorber into position, and insert its mounting bolts; ensure that the upper bolt is inserted from the inside of the trailing arm, and the lower bolt from the outside.

9 Refit the nuts and washers to the mounting bolts, not forgetting to refit the brake hose bracket to the lower bolt, tightening them by hand only at this stage. Clip the handbrake cable onto the trailing arm bracket.

10 Refit the roadwheel, then lower the car to ground and tighten the roadwheel bolts to the specified torque.

11 With the car standing on its wheels, rock the car to settle the shock absorber in position, then tighten both the upper and lower mounting bolts to their specified torque settings.

12 Where necessary, refit the heat shield and tailpipe as described in the relevant part of Chapter 4.

14 Rear suspension torsion bar - removal and refitting

Note: *To ensure the trailing arm is correctly positioned prior to refitting the torsion bar, a special bracket is required. This bracket (special tool number 9501-T.G3) can be obtained from a Citroën dealer, or alternatively, a home-made substitute can be fabricated; the dimensions of the Citroën tool are shown in **illustration 14.0**. Note that the substitute bracket must be accurately fabricated to be of use.*

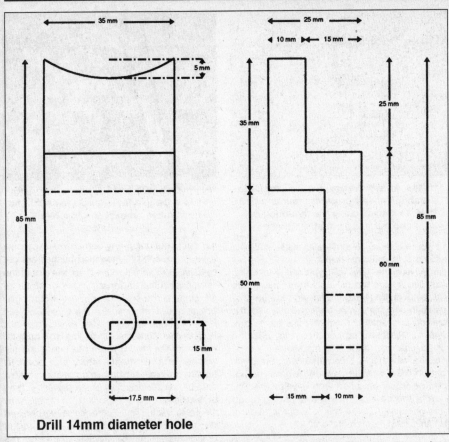

Drill 14mm diameter hole

14.0 Citroën trailing arm positioning bracket dimensions

A tool to hold the trailing arm in position can be fabricated from a length of threaded bar, and attached to the shock absorber mounting bolt holes.

5 Slacken and remove the Torx screw and washer from the right-hand end of the torsion bar. Using a punch or scriber, make alignment marks between the torsion bar and trailing arm. Unscrew the retaining nut from the left-hand end of the torsion bar, and remove the washer.
6 The torsion bar can now be withdrawn from the right-hand side, using a slide-hammer which is screwed into the 8 mm threaded hole in the end of the bar **(see illustration)**.

HAYNES HINT *It is possible to improvise torsion bar removal by screwing a long bolt with a flat washer into the bar, and placing the jaws of a spanner against the washer. Striking the spanner sharply with a hammer should free the torsion bar.*

7 Once the splines of the torsion bar are free, the bar can be withdrawn completely from its location. Note that the front and rear torsion bars are not interchangeable; the bars can be identified by the markings on their shafts. The front bar has one band painted around the left-hand end of its shaft, and the rear bar has two bands painted around its right-hand end.

Rear torsion bar
8 Remove the left-hand shock absorber as described in Section 13.
9 Carry out the operations described above in paragraphs 3 and 4.
10 Slacken and remove the bolt securing the anti-roll bar retaining bracket to the left-hand trailing arm, and unscrew the plastic plug from the centre of the bracket. Obtain a 12 x 1.5 mm bolt at least 70 mm long, lubricate its threads and screw it into the bracket. The bolt can then be used as a jacking bolt, to draw the bracket out of position **(see illustration)**. Once the bracket is free from the anti-roll bar splines, remove it from the trailing arm, along with its sealing rings. Discard the sealing rings - new ones should be used on refitting.

10

Removal
1 Chock the front wheels, then jack up the rear of the vehicle and support it on axle stands. Remove both rear roadwheels, then proceed as described under the relevant sub-heading.

Front torsion bar
2 Remove the right-hand shock absorber as described in Section 13.
3 With the trailing arm unsupported, measure the distance between the centres of the upper and lower shock absorber mounting bolt holes, on the side from which the shock absorber has been removed, and note this down; this measurement will be needed on refitting.
4 Position a trolley jack underneath the end of the trailing arm, and raise the jack until it is supporting the weight of the trailing arm. It is necessary to support the trailing arm, to prevent it moving as the torsion bar is removed. Excess trailing arm movement will place strain on the brake lines, which could cause them to fracture.

14.6 Using a slide-hammer to withdraw a torsion bar

14.10 Using a jacking bolt to draw the retaining bracket off the end of the anti-roll bar

11 Slacken and remove the Torx screw and washer from the left-hand end of the torsion bar. Using a punch or scriber, make alignment marks between the torsion bar and trailing arm. Unscrew the retaining nut from the right-hand end of the torsion bar, and remove the washer.

12 Withdraw the torsion bar from the left-hand side, using the information given above in paragraphs 6 and 7.

Refitting

Front torsion bar

13 Ensure that the trailing arm and torsion bar splines are clean and dry, then lubricate the splines with molybdenum disulphide grease. Where a new torsion bar is being installed, unscrew the threaded stud from the original bar, and screw it fully into the smaller-diameter end of the new bar.

14 Ensure the distance between the upper and lower shock absorber mounting bolt holes is still as measured prior to removal, and adjust as necessary. Attach the positioning bracket (see note above) to the shock absorber lower mounting bolt hole as shown in **illustration 14.14a**. Using feeler blades, check that the clearance between the inner edge of the bracket and the edge of the tubular crossmember is 0.05 mm. If necessary, adjust the position of the trailing arm by tapping it lightly with a soft-faced

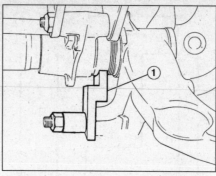

14.14a Attach the position bracket (1) to the shock absorber lower mounting bolt hole as shown, using the mounting bolt and nut and a suitable spacer

mallet until the 0.05 mm feeler blade is a light, sliding fit **(see illustrations)**.

15 Where the original torsion bar is being installed, rotate the bar until the marks made on removal are aligned, then slide the bar into position. The bar should engage freely with the trailing arm splines for the first 8 to 10 mm, and can then be tapped fully into position using a hammer and a soft metal drift.

16 If a new bar is being installed, rotate the bar until the position is found where the bar can be freely engaged with the first 8 to 10 mm of the trailing arm splines. Having found this position, tap the bar fully home using a hammer and a soft metal drift.

14.14b Using a feeler blade to check the positioning bracket-to-crossmember clearance

17 Once the torsion bar is fully home, refit the washer and Torx screw to the end of the torsion bar, and tighten it to the specified torque **(see illustrations)**.

18 Ensure the trailing arm is still correctly positioned, then unscrew the threaded stud from the opposite end of the torsion bar until its shoulder contacts the trailing arm cup; do not force the stud against the cup. Refit the washer and nut to the stud, and securely tighten the nut whilst retaining the stud with a small flat-bladed screwdriver **(see illustrations)**.

19 Refit the rear shock absorber as described in Section 13, then check and, if necessary, adjust the vehicle ride height as described in Section 18.

Rear torsion bar

20 Refit the torsion bar as described above in paragraphs 13 to 19.

21 Unscrew the plastic plug from the centre of the opposite anti-roll bar retaining bracket, and screw a short 8 mm bolt and washer into the end of the anti-roll bar. Securely tighten the bolt to hold the anti-roll bar in position.

22 Apply a smear of the special grease (Mobil Temp G9, available from your Citroën dealer) to the new sealing rings, and fit them to the anti-roll bar bracket. In the absence of the special grease, a good-quality molybdenum disulphide grease can be used.

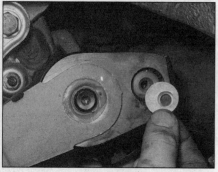

14.17a Refit the offset washer . . .

14.17b . . . and the retaining screw to the end of the torsion bar . . .

14.17c . . . and tighten the screw to the specified torque

14.18a Screw the threaded stud out from the end of the opposite end of the bar until it just contacts the cup

14.18b Refit the washer and retaining nut, and securely tighten the nut whilst retaining the stud with the screwdriver

23 Insert the retaining bracket into position in the trailing arm, aligning its retaining bolt hole with that of the trailing arm, and engage it with the anti-roll bar splines. Using a soft-faced mallet, tap the bracket into position until the clearance between the inside of the bracket and the trailing arm is 1.0 mm; this can be checked using a feeler blade. If the bracket is a tight fit on the anti-roll bar splines, screw a long 8 mm bolt, nut and washer into the end of the anti-roll bar. The bracket can then be drawn into position by tighten the nut **(see illustration 16.13b)**.

24 Once the bracket is correctly positioned, refit its retaining bolt, not forgetting to position the handbrake cable bracket underneath it, and tighten it to the specified torque setting. Unscrew the bolt(s) from the end(s) of the anti-roll bar, then wipe clean the threads of the retaining bracket holes. Apply a smear of sealant to the plugs, and refit them to the brackets.

25 Refit the rear shock absorber as described in Section 13, then check and, if necessary, adjust the vehicle ride height as described in Section 18.

15 Rear suspension trailing arm - removal and refitting

Note: *To ensure the trailing arm is correctly positioned on refitting, a special bracket is required. This bracket (special tool number 9501-T.G3) can be obtained from a Citroën dealer, or alternatively, a home-made substitute can be fabricated; the dimensions of the Citroën tool are shown in* **illustration 14.0**. *Note that the substitute bracket must be accurately fabricated to be of use.*

Removal

1 Chock the front wheels, then jack up the rear of the vehicle and support it on axle stands. Remove both rear roadwheels.
2 Remove the relevant shock absorber as described in Section 13.
3 Slacken and remove the bolt securing the anti-roll bar retaining bracket to the left-hand trailing arm, and unscrew the plastic plug from the centre of the bracket. Obtain a 12 x 1.5 mm bolt at least 70 mm long, lubricate its threads and screw it into the bracket. The bolt can then be used as a jacking bolt, to draw the bracket out of position. Once the bracket is free from the anti-roll bar splines, remove it from the trailing arm, along with its sealing rings. Discard the sealing rings - new ones should be used on refitting. Proceed as described under the relevant sub-heading.

Rear drum brakes

4 Remove the brake drum as described in Chapter 9.
5 Work back along the length of the brake pipe/hose, and remove any retaining clips securing it to the trailing arm. Note that on some models, it may be necessary to split the

brake hose at its union in order to free it from the trailing arm bracket; refer to Chapter 9 for further information.
6 Undo the four bolts and washers securing the brake backplate to the trailing arm. Carefully ease the backplate assembly over the end of the stub axle, and position it clear of the trailing arm. Tie the backplate assembly to the vehicle underbody, to prevent undue strain being placed on the brake pipe.
7 Remove the relevant torsion bar as described in Section 14.
8 The trailing arm can then be withdrawn from the crossmember, and removed from the vehicle.
9 Inspect the trailing arm bearings, axle tube tracks and crossmember outer sleeves for signs of wear and damage. If renewal is necessary, the task should be entrusted to a Citroën dealer. The bearing renewal procedure involves the use of numerous special tools to remove the original bearings and install the new ones. Attempting to install the bearings without these special tools will almost certainly lead to damage during fitting.

Rear disc brakes

10 Work back along the length of the brake hose/pipe, and remove any retaining clips securing it to the trailing arm. Note that on some models, it may be necessary to split the brake hose at its union in order to free it from the trailing arm bracket; refer to Chapter 9 for further information. On models with ABS, trace the wiring back from the wheel sensor, and disconnect it at the wiring connector.
11 Slacken the two bolts securing the caliper assembly to the trailing arm, and remove them along with the mounting plate, noting which way around the plate is fitted. Discard the caliper mounting bolts - they should be renewed whenever they are disturbed.
12 Slide the caliper assembly off the brake disc. Where the brake hose/pipe has not been split, tie the caliper to the vehicle underbody, to prevent any undue strain being placed on the brake hose.
13 Remove the relevant torsion bar as described in Section 14.
14 The trailing arm can then be withdrawn from the crossmember, and examined as described above in paragraph 9.

Refitting

15 Prior to refitting, inspect the trailing arm seal for signs of wear or damage, and renew if necessary. Ensure the new seal is installed the correct way around, and is pressed fully onto the trailing arm **(see illustration)**.
16 Coat the lips of the seal, and the bearing and bearing tracks, with a smear of the special grease (Total Multis G6, available from your Citroën dealer). In the absence of the special grease, a good-quality molybdenum disulphide grease can be used.
17 Slide the trailing arm into position in the crossmember, until its seal is against the crossmember sleeve. Support the trailing arm

so that the distance between the upper and lower mounting bolt holes is as noted prior to removal.
18 Refit the torsion bar as described in paragraphs 13 to 18 of Section 14.

Rear drum brakes

19 Ensure the mating surfaces of the brake backplate and trailing arm are clean and dry. Locate the backplate over the stub axle, then refit its retaining bolts and tighten them to the specified torque setting.
20 Refit the anti-roll bar retaining bracket as described in paragraphs 21 to 24 of Section 14.
21 Reconnect the brake pipe/hose (where split), and ensure the brake pipe/hose and handbrake cable are securely retained by all the necessary fasteners. Refit the brake drum, referring to the relevant Sections of Chapter 9.
22 Refit the rear shock absorber as described in Section 13, then check and, if necessary, adjust the vehicle ride height as described in Section 18.

Rear disc brakes

23 Slide the caliper into position over the brake disc.
24 If the threads of the new caliper mounting bolts are not already pre-coated with locking compound, apply a suitable locking compound to them. Install the new caliper mounting bolts and the mounting plate, noting that the mounting plate must be fitted so that its bend curves away from the caliper body. With the plate correctly positioned, tighten the caliper bolts to the specified torque setting (see Chapter 9).
25 Refit the anti-roll bar retaining bracket as described in paragraphs 21 to 24 of Section 14.
26 Reconnect the brake pipe/hose (where split), and ensure the brake hose/pipe and handbrake cable are securely retained by all the necessary fasteners. Where necessary, reconnect the ABS wheel sensor wiring connector, referring to Chapter 9 for further information.
27 Refit the rear shock absorber as described in Section 13. Check and, if necessary, adjust the vehicle ride height as described in Section 18.

10

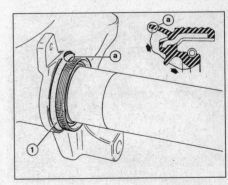

15.15 Ensure the seal (1) is fitted the correct way around, and is correctly located on the trailing arm shoulder (a)

16.5a Slide the inner . . .

16.5b . . . and outer sealing rings off the anti-roll bar

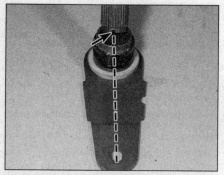
16.9a If a new anti-roll bar is being installed, align the cut-out (arrowed) with the bracket retaining bolt hole

16.9b Using a nut and bolt to draw the retaining bracket into position on the anti-roll bar

washer into the bar, and placing the jaws of a spanner against the washer. Striking the spanner sharply with a hammer should free the torsion bar. Alternatively, the bar can be tapped out of position, using a hammer and a soft-metal drift on the exposed right-hand end of the bar.

5 Remove the sealing rings from the left-hand end of the bar (see illustrations).

6 If it is wished, the anti-roll bar and left-hand retaining bracket can be separated using the jacking bolt (see paragraph 2). Prior to separation, make alignment marks between the bar and bracket.

7 Inspect the anti-roll bar and retaining brackets for signs of wear or damage, and renew if necessary. The sealing rings should be renewed as a matter of course.

Refitting

8 Ensure the splines of the anti-roll bar and retaining bracket(s) are clean and dry, then apply a smear of the special grease (Mobil Temp G9, available from your Citroën dealer) to them and the new sealing rings. In the absence of the special grease, a good-quality molybdenum disulphide grease can be used.

9 If the left-hand retaining bracket and anti-roll bar were separated, refit the bracket to the bar, aligning the marks made on removal. If a new bar or bracket is being fitted, align the bracket retaining bolt hole with the cut-out on the end of the anti-roll bar. Tap the bracket fully onto the splines using a soft-faced mallet. If the bracket is a tight fit on the anti-roll bar splines, screw a long 8 mm bolt, nut and washer into the end of the anti-roll bar. The bracket can then be drawn into position by tightening the nut (see illustrations).

10 Screw a short 8 mm bolt and washer into the left-hand end of the anti-roll bar, and tighten it securely (see illustration). This will ensure that the bar and bracket will stay correctly engaged during the refitting procedure.

11 Slide the new sealing rings onto the anti-roll bar, then slide the bar into position from the left-hand side of the vehicle. Refit the retaining bracket bolt, not forgetting to position the handbrake cable bracket underneath it, and tighten it to the specified torque setting (see illustrations).

16 Rear suspension anti-roll bar - removal and refitting

Removal

1 Chock the front wheels, then jack up the rear of the vehicle and support it on axle stands. Remove both rear roadwheels.

2 Slacken and remove the bolt securing the anti-roll bar retaining bracket to the right-hand trailing arm, and unscrew the plastic plug from the centre of the bracket. Obtain a 12 x 1.5 mm bolt at least 70 mm long, lubricate its threads and screw it into the bracket. The bolt

can then be used as a jacking bolt, to draw the bracket out of position. Once the bracket is free from the anti-roll bar splines, remove it from the trailing arm, along with its sealing rings. Discard the sealing rings - new ones should be used on refitting.

3 Slacken and remove the bolt securing the anti-roll bar retaining bracket to the left-hand trailing arm, and unscrew the plastic plug from the centre of the bracket.

4 The anti-roll bar and right-hand retaining bracket assembly can now be withdrawn from the left-hand side, using a slide-hammer which is screwed into the 8 mm threaded hole in the end of the anti-roll bar. It is possible to improvise by screwing a long bolt with a flat

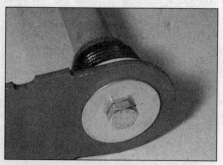
16.10 Secure the left-hand bracket in position with a short 8 mm bolt and washer before refitting the anti-roll bar to the vehicle

16.11a Refit the anti-roll bar and bracket assembly to the vehicle . . .

16.11b . . . then refit the retaining bracket bolt, and tighten it to the specified torque

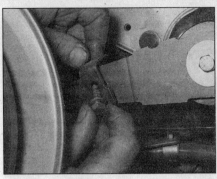

16.13a Fit the new sealing rings to the right-hand retaining bracket, then refit the bracket to the anti-roll bar

16.13b Using a nut and bolt arrangement to draw the right-hand bracket into position, whilst using a feeler blade to measure bracket-to-arm clearance

16.14a Refit the handbrake cable bracket to the trailing arm, then refit the retaining bracket bolt . . .

12 Fit the new sealing rings to the right-hand retaining bracket.

13 Insert the right-hand retaining bracket into position in the trailing arm, aligning its retaining bolt hole with that of the trailing arm, and engage it with the anti-roll bar splines. Using a soft-faced mallet, tap the bracket into position until the clearance between the inside of the bracket and the trailing arm is 1.0 mm; this can be checked using a feeler blade. If the bracket is a tight fit on the anti-roll bar splines, screw a long 8 mm bolt, nut and washer into the end of the anti-roll bar. The bracket can then be drawn into position by tightening the nut **(see illustrations)**.

14 Once the bracket is correctly positioned, refit its retaining bolt, not forgetting to position the handbrake cable bracket underneath it, and tighten it to the specified torque **(see illustrations)**.

15 Unscrew the bolt(s) from the end(s) of the anti-roll bar, then wipe clean the threads of the retaining bracket holes. Apply a smear of sealant to the threads of the plastic plugs, and refit them to the brackets **(see illustration)**.

16 Refit the roadwheels, then lower the car to ground and tighten the roadwheel bolts to the specified torque.

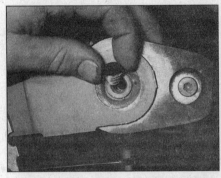

16.14b . . . and tighten it to the specified torque

16.15 Apply a smear of sealant to the threads of the plastic plugs, and refit them to the retaining brackets

17 Rear axle assembly - removal and refitting

Removal

1 Remove the rear seat assembly as described in Chapter 11.

2 Firmly chock the front wheels, then jack up the rear of the vehicle and support it on axle stands. Remove both rear roadwheels, then lower the spare wheel out from underneath the rear of the vehicle, and unhook the wheel carrier.

3 Remove the exhaust system and heat shield(s) as described in Chapter 4.

4 Remove the handbrake lever cover, and fully slacken the handbrake cable adjuster nut. Refer to Chapter 9 for further information.

5 On models with rear drum brakes,

disconnect both cables from the handbrake lever. From underneath the vehicle, work along the length of each cable, and free them from any retaining clips which secure them to the vehicle underbody.

6 On models with rear disc brakes, free the end of the handbrake inner cable from the caliper handbrake lever, then tap the outer cable out of the caliper using a hammer and punch. Where necessary, disconnect the ABS wheel sensors at the wiring connectors, and free them from any retaining clips.

7 Trace the brake pipes back from the caliper/backplate to their unions, which are situated just in front of the rear axle assembly. Slacken the union nuts, and disconnect the pipes. Plug the pipe ends, to minimise fluid loss and prevent the entry of dirt into the hydraulic system. Remove any retaining clips securing the rear section of the pipe to the vehicle underbody.

8 Make a final check that all necessary components have been disconnected and positioned so that they will not hinder the removal procedure, then position a trolley jack beneath the centre of the rear axle assembly. Raise the jack until it is supporting the weight of the axle.

9 Remove the luggage compartment lower side trim panels as described in Chapter 11. Lift up the rear luggage compartment carpet to gain access to the rear axle retaining nuts. Slacken and remove the two retaining nuts

and washers from each front mounting assembly, and the single nut and washer securing each rear mounting assembly to the vehicle.

10 Carefully lower the jack and axle assembly out of position, and remove it from underneath the vehicle.

11 Examine the rear axle mountings for signs or damage or deterioration of the mounting rubber, and renew if necessary. Note that all four mountings should be renewed as a set; do not renew the mountings individually.

Refitting

12 Refitting is a reversal of the removal procedure, bearing in mind the following points:

(a) Raise the rear axle assembly into position, and tighten the mounting retaining nuts to their specified torque settings.

(b) Ensure the brake pipes, handbrake cables and wiring (as applicable) are correctly routed, and retained by all the necessary retaining clips.

(c) Securely tighten the brake pipe union nuts.

(d) Adjust the handbrake cable as described in Chapter 9.

(e) On completion, lower the vehicle to the ground, and bleed the braking system hydraulic circuit as described in Chapter 9.

(f) Check and, if necessary, adjust the vehicle ride height as described in Section 18.

10

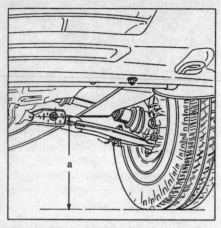

Front axle

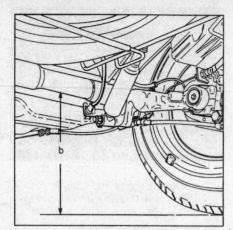

Rear axle

18.2 Vehicle front (a) and rear (b) ride height measurement points

18 Vehicle ride height -
checking and adjustment

Checking

1 Position the unladen vehicle on a level surface, with the tyres correctly inflated; roll the vehicle backwards and forwards, to relieve any stress in the suspension components. For the ride height measurements to be accurate, the vehicle must be loaded with the equivalent of 4 occupants and approximately 40 kg of luggage.

2 The front ride height is measured between the centre of the front lower suspension arm pivot and the ground; the rear ride height measurement is taken between the lower edge of the 58 mm section of the tubular crossmember and the ground **(see illustration)**.

3 Take three measurements on the right-hand side of the vehicle, then take the average of these three to be the correct right-hand height. Repeat the procedure on the left-hand side, to find the correct left-hand height. Note that the maximum permissible difference between the left- and right-hand side is 10 mm. Add both the left- and right-hand side averages together, and divide by two to obtain the correct vehicle ride height.

4 Compare the measurement obtained with those given in the Specifications at the start of this Chapter.

5 If the front ride height differs significantly from that specified, one of the suspension components must be worn or damaged; no adjustment is possible. Inspect all the front suspension components for signs of wear or damage, such as worn bushes, and renew components as necessary. If no sign of damage can be found, the vehicle should be taken to a Citroën dealer for a more detailed examination.

6 If the rear ride height differs from that specified, adjust it as follows.

Adjustment (rear ride height only)

7 Determine the amount of adjustment required. The rear suspension height can be adjusted in multiples of 3 mm, by rotating the rear torsion bars. If adjustment is necessary, determine the number of splines the torsion bar must be moved, noting that one spline is equal to roughly 3 mm of ride height. For example, if the ride height needs adjusting by 10 mm, the torsion bar should be moved by three splines. If the height difference between sides was excessive, compensate for this during the adjustment procedure.

8 Chock the front wheels, then jack up the rear of the vehicle and support it on axle stands. Remove both rear roadwheels.

9 Working first on the left-hand side, remove the rear torsion bar as described in Section 14.

10 Noting that a 2 mm change in distance between the rear shock absorber mounting bolt holes equals a 3 mm change in ride height, or one spline of torsion bar movement, raise or lower the trailing arm by the required amount. Note that increasing the distance between the bolt holes increases ride height,

and decreasing the distance lowers the ride height; if the ride needs lowering by 9 mm, decrease the distance between the shock absorber mounting bolt holes by 6 mm by raising the trailing arm.

11 Rotate the torsion bar by the required number of splines and in the required direction, and relocate it with the trailing arm splines. The bar should engage freely with the trailing arm splines for the first 8 to 10 mm, and can then be tapped into fully into position using a hammer and a soft metal drift.

12 Refit the anti-roll bar retaining bracket as described in Section 14.

13 Remove the front torsion bar as described in Section 14, and repeat the procedure described in paragraphs 10 and 11 on the right-hand side. Secure the bar in position as described in Section 14.

14 Refit the roadwheels, then lower the car to ground and tighten the roadwheel bolts to the specified torque.

15 With the car standing on its wheels, rock the car to settle the disturbed suspension components, then tighten the shock absorber mounting bolts to the specified torque settings.

16 Recheck the vehicle ride heights as described earlier in this Section and, if necessary, repeat the adjustment procedure. Note that it may be necessary to adjust the headlight beam alignment, referring to Chapter 12 for further information.

19 Steering wheel -
removal and refitting

Models without air bag
Removal

1 Set the front wheels in the straight-ahead position, and release the steering lock by inserting the ignition key.

2 Carefully ease off the steering wheel centre pad, then slacken and remove the steering wheel retaining nut **(see illustrations)**.

3 Mark the steering wheel and steering column shaft in relation to each other, then lift the steering wheel off the column splines. If it is tight, tap it up near the centre, using the palm of your hand, or twist it from side to side,

19.2a Remove the centre pad . . .

19.2b . . . then slacken and remove the steering wheel retaining nut

19.4a Indicator cancelling lug is secured to the base of the steering wheel by a circlip

19.4b Tighten the steering wheel retaining nut to the specified torque

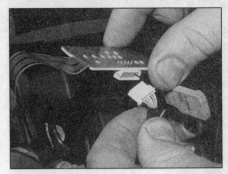

19.6 Disconnecting the wiring plug from the radio/cassette player remote control circuit board

whilst pulling upwards to release it from the shaft splines.

Refitting

4 Refitting is a reversal of removal, noting the following points:

(a) Check the indicator cancelling lug fitted to the rear of steering wheel is in good condition, and if necessary renew it. The lug is retained by a circlip (see illustration).

(b) Prior to refitting, ensure that the indicator switch stem is in its central position. Failure to do this could lead to the steering wheel lug breaking the switch tab as the steering wheel is refitted.

(c) On refitting, align the marks made on removal, and tighten the retaining nut to the specified torque (see illustration).

Models with air bag

Note: The air bag electronic control unit is integral with the steering wheel. Take care not to damage the unit during removal, and store the wheel carefully once removed.

Removal

5 Remove the air bag unit as described in Chapter 12.

6 Where applicable, disconnect the wiring plug from the radio/cassette player remote control circuit board located in the slot at the top of the steering wheel (see illustration).

7 Unclip the air bag wiring connector from the steering wheel, and separate the two

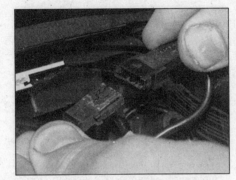

19.7 Disconnecting the air bag wiring connector

halves of the connector (see illustration).

8 Unscrew the steering wheel securing nut. Refer to paragraph 3 and withdraw the steering wheel (see illustration). Feed the wiring through the centre of the steering wheel as it is withdrawn.

9 Store the wheel carefully, taking care not to damage the air bag electronic control unit.

Refitting

10 Refitting is a reversal of removal, bearing in mind the following points:

(a) Make sure that the wiring is correctly routed through the wheel.

(b) Tighten the steering wheel securing nut to the specified torque.

(c) Refit the air bag unit as described in Chapter 12.

19.8 Unscrewing the steering wheel securing nut

20 Steering column - removal, inspection and refitting

Removal

1 Disconnect the battery negative terminal.

2 Remove the steering wheel as described in Section 19.

3 Release the panel fasteners by rotating them through a quarter of a turn, and remove the driver's side lower facia panel.

4 Slacken and remove the five screws which secure the two halves of the steering column shrouds together, then remove both the upper and lower shroud (see illustrations).

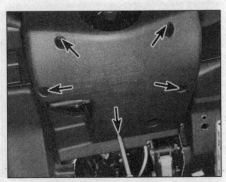

20.4a Undo the five steering column shroud retaining screws (arrowed) . . .

20.4b . . . then remove the both the lower . . .

20.4c . . . and upper shroud sections

10

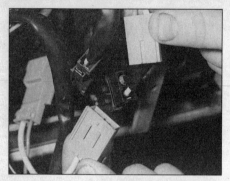

20.6 Disconnecting the ignition switch wiring connectors

20.8 Steering column lower mounting nuts (arrowed)

20.9a From inside the vehicle, slide the rubber gaiter off the intermediate shaft . . .

5 Release the facia felt undercover retaining clips, and peel back the material. Release the heater duct, and remove the duct to gain access to the steering column mountings.
6 Tilt the steering column fully downwards, and disconnect the wiring connectors from the steering column combination switches and the three wiring connectors from the ignition switch **(see illustration)**. Free the wiring from any relevant retaining clips.
7 Make alignment marks between the universal joint on the base of the steering column and the intermediate shaft, then slacken and remove the universal joint clamp bolt.
8 Slacken and remove the four steering column mounting nuts, then release the steering column from its mountings, and recover the column mounting spacers from the lower mounting studs **(see illustration)**. Disengage the universal joint from the intermediate shaft, and remove the steering column assembly from the vehicle.
9 To remove the intermediate shaft, firmly apply the handbrake, then jack up the front of the vehicle and support it on axle stands. Disengage the rubber gaiter from the floor, and slide it off the end of the shaft. Make alignment marks between the universal joint on the base of the intermediate shaft and steering gear pinion, then slacken and remove the universal joint clamp bolt **(see illustrations)**. Release the shaft from the pinion splines, and remove it from the vehicle.

Inspection

10 The steering column incorporates a telescopic safety feature. In the event of a front-end crash, the shaft collapses and prevents the steering wheel injuring the driver. Before refitting the steering column, examine the column and mountings for signs of damage and deformation, and renew as necessary.
11 Check the steering shaft for signs of free play in the column bushes, and check the universal joints for signs of damage or roughness in the joint bearings. If any damage or wear is found on the steering column universal joints or shaft bushes, the column

20.9b . . . then slacken and remove the universal joint clamp bolt, and free the shaft from the steering gear

must be renewed as an assembly. Inspect the column lower mounting rubbers for signs of damage or deterioration, and renew if necessary.
12 The steering column nuts (and, where disturbed, the intermediate shaft clamp bolt nuts) must be renewed as a matter of course. Each nut is retained by a metal cage; release the cage retaining tangs, then remove the old nut from inside the cage and install the new one. Refit the cage, and secure it in position with the retaining tangs **(see illustration)**.

Refitting

13 Where removed, refit the intermediate shaft, aligning the marks made prior to

20.12 Ensure the universal joint clamp bolt nut cage is securely held in position by its retaining tangs (arrowed)

removal, and engaging the universal joint with the steering gear drive pinion splines. Refit the shaft clamp bolt, and tighten it to the specified torque setting. Slide the rubber gaiter down the intermediate shaft, and locate it in the floorpan.
14 Manoeuvre the steering column assembly into position then, aligning the marks made prior to removal, engage the universal joint with the intermediate shaft splines.
15 Fit the column over its mounting studs, and refit the steering column mounting nuts, not forgetting the lower mounting stud spacers, and tighten them to the specified torque **(see illustrations)**.

20.15a Ensure the mounting rubbers and spacers are correctly positioned on the column lower mountings . . .

20.15b . . . then refit the steering column to the vehicle

20.16 Adjust the position of the steering shaft as described in text prior to tightening the universal joint clamp bolt

21.5 Ignition switch/steering column lock retaining screw (arrowed)

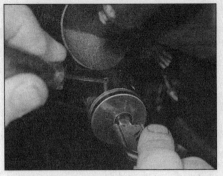

21.6a Insert the key, positioning it as described in the text, then depress the lock retaining lug . . .

16 Position the column universal joint on the intermediate shaft, so that the top of the steering shaft protrudes from the top of the steering column by 58 mm **(see illustration)**. Once correctly positioned, refit the clamp bolt and tighten it to the specified torque.

17 Ensuring that the wiring is correctly routed and retained by any necessary retaining clips, reconnect the wiring connectors to the combination switches and the ignition switch.

18 Refit the heater duct, ensuring that it is correctly seated at each end, and clip the undercover back into position.

19 Position the upper and lower column shrouds around the steering column, then refit the retaining screws and tighten them securely.

20 Refit the lower facia panel, and secure it in position by rotating the fasteners through a quarter of a turn.

21 Refit the steering wheel as described in Section 19.

22 Release the column tilt lever, check that the column moves freely, then lock the lever and check the column is securely held. If adjustment is necessary, working through the aperture in the lower shroud, slacken the lever locknut, then slacken the adjuster nut until the column moves freely with the lever released and locks securely with the lever locked. Note that on some models, a single Nyloc nut is used instead of the locknut and adjuster nut arrangement. Where necessary, hold the adjuster nut stationary and securely tighten the locknut. Check the operation of the lever and, if necessary, repeat the adjustment procedure. If a Nyloc nut is fitted, it may be necessary to renew it, to restore its effectiveness.

21 Ignition switch/steering column lock -
removal and refitting

Removal

1 Disconnect the battery negative terminal.

2 Working inside the car, release the panel fasteners by rotating them through a quarter of a turn, and remove the driver's side lower facia panel.

3 Slacken and remove the five screws which secure the two halves of the steering column shrouds together, then remove the lower shroud.

4 Tilt the steering column fully downwards, then trace the wiring back from the ignition switch, and disconnect its three wiring connectors from the main wiring loom.

5 Slacken and remove the lock retaining screw and washer from the side of the lock **(see illustration)**.

6 Insert the key, and rotate it so that is aligned with the mark positioned between the "A" and "S" marks on the barrel. Using a small flat-bladed screwdriver, depress the lock retaining lug, then withdraw the lock assembly from the steering column **(see illustrations)**.

Refitting

7 Refitting is a reversal of the removal procedure, ensuring that the lock assembly is securely held in position by its retaining lug. Prior to refitting the column shroud, remove the ignition key and check that the steering lock functions correctly.

22 Steering gear assembly -
removal, overhaul and refitting

Removal

1 Chock the rear wheels, firmly apply the handbrake, then jack up the front of the vehicle and support on axle stands. Remove both front roadwheels.

2 Slacken and remove the nuts securing the steering gear track rod balljoints to the swivel hubs, and release the balljoint tapered shanks using a universal balljoint separator.

3 Using a hammer and punch, white paint or similar, mark the exact relationship between

21.6b . . . and withdraw the lock assembly from the steering column

the intermediate shaft universal joint and the steering gear drive pinion. Slacken and remove the clamp bolt securing the joint to the pinion, and free the intermediate shaft from the steering gear **(see illustration)**.

4 Where necessary, undo the two retaining screws, then unclip the heat shield and remove it from the top of the steering gear assembly.

Manual steering gear

5 Slacken the steering gear mounting bolts, and recover the nuts. Withdraw the mounting bolts, and recover the spacers

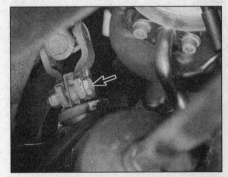

22.3 Intermediate shaft universal joint clamp bolt (arrowed) viewed from underneath

10

22.5a Slacken and remove the two steering gear retaining bolts (viewed underneath the front of the vehicle) . . .

22.5b . . . recover the nuts from the rear of the steering gear, and the spacers from the subframe apertures (arrowed)

from the subframe apertures (see illustrations).

6 The steering gear assembly can then be manoeuvred out from underneath the right-hand wheel arch. Note that on left-hand-drive 1580 cc and larger-engined models with manual transmission, it may be necessary to disconnect one or more of the gearchange linkage link rods from their balljoints on the transmission unit, to gain the necessary clearance required to withdraw the steering gear.

Power-assisted steering gear

7 Using brake hose clamps, clamp both the supply and return hoses near the power steering fluid reservoir. This will minimise fluid loss during subsequent operations.
8 Mark the unions to ensure they are correctly positioned on reassembly, then unscrew the feed and return pipe union nuts from the steering gear assembly; be prepared for fluid spillage, and position a suitable container beneath the pipes whilst unscrewing the union nuts. Disconnect both pipes, and plug the pipe ends and steering gear orifices, to prevent fluid leakage and to keep dirt out of the hydraulic system.
9 Free the power steering pipes from any retaining clips, and position them clear of the steering gear so that they will not hinder the removal procedure.
10 Remove the steering gear as described above in paragraphs 5 and 6.

Overhaul

11 Examine the steering gear assembly for signs of wear or damage, and check that the rack moves freely throughout the full length of its travel, with no signs of roughness or excessive free play between the steering gear pinion and rack. It is possible to overhaul the steering gear assembly housing components, but this task should be entrusted to a Citroën dealer. The only components which can be renewed easily by the home mechanic are the steering gear gaiters, the track rod balljoints and the track rods. Track rod, track rod balljoint and steering gear gaiter renewal procedures are covered in Sections 27, 26 and 23 respectively.

12 On models with power steering, inspect all the steering gear fluid unions for signs of leakage, and check that all union nuts are securely tightened. Also examine the steering gear hydraulic ram for signs of fluid leakage or damage, and if necessary renew it.

Refitting

13 Note that all Nyloc nuts disturbed on removal must be renewed as a matter of course. These nuts have threads which are pre-coated with locking compound (this is only effective once), and include the track rod balljoint nuts, steering gear mounting bolt nuts, and the intermediate shaft clamp bolt nut. The intermediate shaft clamp bolt nut is retained by a metal cage; release the cage retaining tangs, then remove the old nut from inside the cage and install the new one. Refit the cage to the shaft, and secure it in position with the retaining tangs (illustration 20.12).
14 Manoeuvre the steering gear assembly into position from the right-hand side of the vehicle.
15 Position the spacers in the subframe apertures, then insert the mounting bolts. Fit the new nuts onto the steering gear, then tighten the mounting bolts to the specified torque. Where necessary, clip the gearchange linkage link rods onto their balljoints.
16 Clip the heat shield (where fitted) onto the top of the steering gear, and securely tighten its two retaining screws.
17 Aligning the marks made prior to removal, engage the intermediate shaft universal joint with the steering gear pinion splines. Refit the clamp bolt with a new nut, and tighten it to the specified torque.
18 Engage the track rod balljoints in the swivel hubs, then fit a new retaining nut to each one. Tighten the nuts to the specified torque.
19 On models with power steering, wipe clean the feed and return pipe unions, then refit them to their respective positions on the steering gear, and tighten the union nuts to their specified torque settings. Ensure the pipes are correctly routed, and are securely held by all the necessary retaining clips.
20 On all models, refit the roadwheels, then lower the vehicle to the ground and

tighten the roadwheel bolts to the specified torque.
21 Where necessary, remove the hose clamps from the power steering hoses, then top-up the fluid reservoir and bleed the hydraulic system as described in Section 24.
22 On completion check and, if necessary, adjust the front wheel alignment as described in Section 28.

23 Steering gear rubber gaiters - renewal

Manual steering gear

1 Remove the track rod balljoint as described in Section 26.
2 Mark the correct fitted position of the gaiter on the track rod, then release the retaining clips and slide the gaiter off the steering gear housing and track rod end.
3 Thoroughly clean the track rod and the steering gear housing, using fine abrasive paper to polish off any corrosion, burrs or sharp edges, which might damage the new gaiter's sealing lips on installation. Scrape off all the grease from the old gaiter, and apply it to the track rod inner balljoint. (This assumes that grease has not been lost or contaminated as a result of damage to the old gaiter. Use fresh grease if in doubt.)
4 Carefully slide the new gaiter onto the track rod end, and locate it on the steering gear housing. Align the outer edge of the gaiter with the mark made on the track rod prior to removal, then secure it in position with new retaining clips.
5 Refit the track rod balljoint as described in Section 26.

Power-assisted steering gear

6 On power-assisted steering gear assemblies, it is only possible to renew the gaiter nearest the drive pinion, ie the right-hand gaiter on right-hand-drive models, and the left-hand gaiter on left-hand-drive models. This can be renewed as described above in paragraphs 1 to 5.
7 The task of renewing the opposite gaiter should be entrusted to a Citroën dealer. This is necessary since it is not possible to pass the gaiter over the steering rack stud to which the hydraulic ram is fixed. Therefore, the steering gear must be dismantled and the rack removed from the housing to allow the gaiter to be renewed.
8 The only task on this end of the assembly which can be carried out by the home mechanic is the renewal of the track rod inner balljoint dust cover. The dust cover can be renewed once the track rod balljoint has been removed as described in Section 26. On refitting, ensure the dust cover is correctly located on the track rod and steering rack, then refit the balljoint.

25.3 Undo the retaining nut (arrowed), and free the feed pipe from the rear of the power steering pump. Fluid supply hose retaining clip also arrowed

25.5a The two front power steering pump retaining bolts can be accessed through holes in the drive pulley

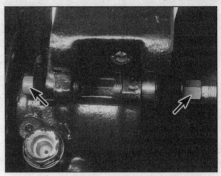

25.5b Power steering pump upper mounting bolts (viewed from above)

24 Power steering system - bleeding

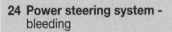

1 This procedure will only be necessary when any part of the hydraulic system has been disconnected.

2 Referring to Chapter 1, remove the fluid reservoir filler cap, and top-up with the specified fluid to the maximum level mark.

3 With the engine stopped, slowly move the steering from lock-to-lock several times to purge out the trapped air, then top-up the level in the fluid reservoir. Repeat this procedure until the fluid level in the reservoir does not drop any further.

4 Start the engine, then slowly move the steering from lock-to-lock several times to purge out any remaining air in the system. Repeat this procedure until bubbles cease to appear in the fluid reservoir.

5 If, when turning the steering, an abnormal noise is heard from the fluid lines, it indicates that there is still air in the system. Check this by turning the wheels to the straight-ahead position and switching off the engine. If the fluid level in the reservoir rises, then air is present in the system, and further bleeding is necessary.

6 Once all traces of air have been removed from the power steering hydraulic system, turn the engine off and allow the system to cool. Once cool, check that fluid level is up to the maximum mark on the power steering fluid reservoir, topping-up if necessary.

25 Power steering pump - removal and refitting

Removal

1 Release the drivebelt tension as described in Chapter 1, and unhook the drivebelt from the pump pulley. The power steering pump is either mounted directly above or directly below the alternator, depending on the engine type and the specification level of the vehicle.

2 Using brake hose clamps, clamp both the

supply and return hoses near the power steering fluid reservoir. This will minimise fluid loss during subsequent operations.

3 Undo the retaining nut, and free the power steering hose retaining clip from the rear of the pump, where necessary (see illustration).

4 Slacken the retaining clip, and disconnect the fluid supply hose from the rear of the pump. If the original Citroën clip is still fitted, cut the clip and discard it; replace it with a standard worm-drive hose clip on refitting. Slacken the union nut, and disconnect the feed pipe from the pump, along with its O-ring. Be prepared for some fluid spillage as the pipe and hose are disconnected, and plug the hose/pipe end and pump unions, to minimise fluid loss and prevent the entry of dirt into the system.

5 Slacken and remove the three bolts securing the power steering pump, and remove the pump from the engine compartment (see illustrations).

Refitting

6 Manoeuvre the pump into position, then refit its mounting bolts and tighten them securely.

7 Fit a new O-ring to the feed pipe union, then reconnect the pipe to the pump and securely tighten the union nut. Refit the supply pipe to the pump, and securely tighten its retaining clip. Remove the brake hose clamps used to minimise fluid loss.

8 Refit the fluid hose retaining clip to the rear

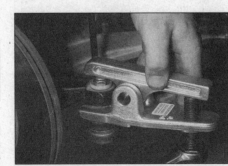

26.4 Using a universal balljoint separator to free the balljoint shank from the swivel hub

of the pump, and securely tighten its retaining nut.

9 Refit the drivebelt to the pump pulley, and tension it as described in Chapter 1.

10 On completion, bleed the hydraulic system as described in Section 24.

26 Track rod balljoint - removal and refitting

Removal

1 Apply the handbrake, then jack up the front of the vehicle and support it on axle stands. Remove the appropriate front roadwheel.

2 If the balljoint is to be re-used, use a straight-edge and a scriber, or similar, to mark its relationship to the track rod.

3 Hold the track rod, and unscrew the balljoint locknut by a quarter of a turn. Do not move the locknut from this position, as it will serve as a handy reference mark on refitting.

4 Slacken and remove the nut securing the track rod balljoint to the swivel hub, and release the balljoint tapered shank using a universal balljoint separator (see illustration). Discard the nut - a new one must be used when refitting.

5 Counting the **exact** number of turns necessary to do so, unscrew the balljoint from the track rod end.

6 Count the number of exposed threads between the end of the balljoint and the locknut, and record this figure. If a new balljoint is to be fitted, unscrew the locknut from the old balljoint.

7 Carefully clean the balljoint and the threads. Renew the balljoint if its movement is sloppy or too stiff, if excessively worn, or if damaged in any way; carefully check the stud taper and threads. If the balljoint gaiter is damaged, the complete balljoint assembly must be renewed; it is not possible to obtain the gaiter separately.

Refitting

8 If a new balljoint is to be fitted, screw the locknut onto its threads, and position it so

10

that the same number of exposed threads are visible, as was noted prior to removal.

9 Screw the balljoint into the track rod by the number of turns noted on removal. This should bring the balljoint locknut to within a quarter of a turn from the locknut, with the alignment marks that were made on removal (if applicable) lined up.

10 Refit the balljoint shank to the swivel hub, then fit a new retaining nut and tighten it to the specified torque.

11 Refit the roadwheel, then lower the vehicle to the ground and tighten the roadwheel bolts to the specified torque.

12 Check and, if necessary, adjust the front wheel toe setting as described in Section 28, then securely tighten the balljoint locknut.

27 Track rod - removal and refitting

Removal

1 Remove the track rod balljoint as described in Section 26.

2 Either release the retaining clips and slide the steering gear gaiter off the end of the track rod, or release the track rod balljoint dust cover from rack, and slide it off the track rod (as applicable). Refer to Section 23 for further information.

3 Unscrew the track rod inner balljoint from the steering rack end, preventing the steering rack from turning by holding the balljoint lock washer with a pair of grips. Take great care not to mark the surfaces of the rack and balljoint.

4 Remove the track rod assembly, and discard the lock washer - a new one must be used on refitting.

5 Examine the track rod inner balljoint for signs of slackness or tight spots, and check that the track rod itself is straight and free from damage. If necessary, renew the track rod; it is also recommended that the steering gear gaiter/dust cover is renewed.

Refitting

6 Locate the new lock washer assembly on the end of the steering rack, and apply a few drops of locking fluid to the track rod inner balljoint threads.

7 Screw the balljoint into the steering rack, and tighten it to the specified torque whilst retaining the lock washer with a pair of grips. Again, take great care not to damage or mark the track rod balljoint or steering rack.

8 Where a gaiter was removed, carefully slide on the new gaiter, and locate it on the steering gear housing. Turn the steering fully from lock-to-lock, to check that the gaiter is correctly positioned on the track rod, then secure it in position with new retaining clips.

9 Where a dust cover was removed, carefully slide on the new cover, and locate it in its grooves on the steering rack collar and track rod.

10 Refit the track rod balljoint as described in Section 26.

28 Wheel alignment and steering angles - general information

Definitions

1 A car's steering and suspension geometry is defined in four basic settings - all angles are expressed in degrees (toe settings are also expressed as a measurement); the steering axis is defined as an imaginary line drawn through the axis of the suspension strut, extended where necessary to contact the ground **(see illustration)**.

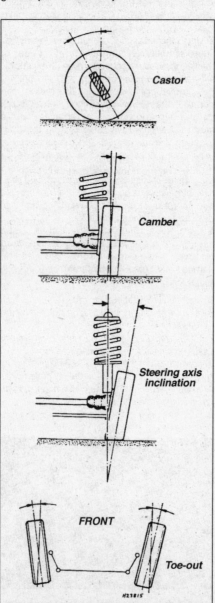

28.1 Wheel alignment and steering angle measurements

2 Camber is the angle between each roadwheel and a vertical line drawn through its centre and tyre contact patch, when viewed from the front or rear of the car. Positive camber is when the roadwheels are tilted outwards from the vertical at the top; negative camber is when they are tilted inwards.

3 Camber is not adjustable, and is given for reference only; while it can be checked using a camber checking gauge, if the figure obtained is significantly different from that specified, the vehicle must be taken for careful checking by a professional, as the fault can only be caused by wear or damage to the body or suspension components.

4 Castor is the angle between the steering axis and a vertical line drawn through each roadwheel's centre and tyre contact patch, when viewed from the side of the car. Positive castor is when the steering axis is tilted so that it contacts the ground ahead of the vertical; negative castor is when it contacts the ground behind the vertical.

5 Castor is not adjustable, and is given for reference only; while it can be checked using a castor checking gauge, if the figure obtained is significantly different from that specified, the vehicle must be taken for careful checking by a professional, as the fault can only be caused by wear or damage to the body or suspension components.

6 Steering axis inclination/SAI - also known as **kingpin inclination/KPI** - is the angle between the steering axis and a vertical line drawn through each roadwheel's centre and tyre contact patch, when viewed from the front or rear of the car.

7 SAI/KPI is not adjustable, and is given for reference only.

8 Toe is the difference, viewed from above, between lines drawn through the roadwheel centres and the car's centre-line. "Toe-in" is when the roadwheels point inwards, towards each other at the front, while "toe-out" is when they splay outwards from each other at the front.

9 The front wheel toe setting is adjusted by screwing the balljoints in or out of their track rods, to alter the effective length of the track rod assemblies.

10 Rear wheel toe setting is not adjustable, and is given for reference only. While it can be checked, if the figure obtained is significantly different from that specified, the vehicle must be taken for careful checking by a professional, as the fault can only be caused by wear or damage to the body or suspension components.

Checking - general

11 Due to the special measuring equipment necessary to check the wheel alignment, and the skill required to use it properly, the checking and adjustment of these settings is best left to a Citroën dealer or similar expert. Note that most tyre-fitting shops now possess sophisticated checking equipment.

12 For **accurate** checking, the vehicle **must** be at the kerb weight, ie unladen and with a full tank of fuel, and the ride height must be correct (see Section 18).

13 Before starting work, check first that the tyre sizes and types are as specified, then check the tyre pressures and tread wear, the roadwheel run-out, the condition of the hub bearings, the steering wheel free play, and the condition of the front suspension components (Chapter 1). Correct any faults found.

14 Park the vehicle on level ground, check that the front roadwheels are in the straight-ahead position, then rock the rear and front ends to settle the suspension. Release the handbrake, and roll the vehicle backwards 1 metre, then forwards again, to relieve any stresses in the steering and suspension components.

Toe setting - checking and adjusting

Front wheel toe setting

15 The front wheel toe setting is checked by measuring the distance between the front and rear inside edges of the roadwheel rims. Proprietary toe measurement gauges are available from motor accessory shops.

16 Prepare the vehicle as described in paragraphs 12 to 14 above.

17 Measure the distance between the front edges of the wheel rims and the rear edges of the rims. Subtract the rear measurement from the front measurement, and check that the result is within the specified range.

18 If adjustment is necessary, apply the handbrake, then jack up the front of the vehicle and support it securely on axle stands.

Turn the steering wheel onto full-left lock, and record the number of exposed threads on the right-hand track rod end. Now turn the steering onto full-right lock, and record the number of threads on the left-hand side. If there are the same number of threads visible on both sides, then subsequent adjustment should be made equally on both sides. If there are more threads visible on one side than the other, it will be necessary to compensate for this during adjustment. **Note:** *It is most important that after adjustment, the same number of threads are visible on each track rod end.*

19 First clean the track rod threads; if they are corroded, apply penetrating fluid before starting adjustment. Release the rubber gaiter outboard clips (where necessary), and peel back the gaiters; apply a smear of grease to the inside of the gaiters, so that both are free, and will not be twisted or strained as their respective track rods are rotated.

20 Use a straight-edge and a scriber or similar to mark the relationship of each track rod to its balljoint then, holding each track rod in turn, unscrew its locknut fully.

21 Alter the length of the track rods, bearing in mind the note made in paragraph 18. Screw them into or out of the balljoints, rotating the track rod using an open-ended spanner fitted to the flats provided on the track rod. Shortening the track rods (screwing them into their balljoints) will reduce toe-in/increase toe-out **(see illustration)**.

22 When the setting is correct, hold the track rods and securely tighten the balljoint locknuts. Check that the balljoints are seated correctly in their sockets, and count the

28.21 Adjusting the front wheel alignment

exposed threads to check the length of both track rods. If they are not the same, then the adjustment has not been made equally, and problems will be encountered with tyre scrubbing in turns; also, the steering wheel spokes will no longer be horizontal when the wheels are in the straight-ahead position.

23 If the track rod lengths are the same, lower the vehicle to the ground and re-check the toe setting; re-adjust if necessary. When the setting is correct, securely tighten the track rod balljoint locknuts. Ensure that the rubber gaiters are seated correctly, and are not twisted or strained, and secure them in position with new retaining clips (where necessary).

Rear wheel toe setting

24 The procedure for checking the rear toe setting is same as described for the front in paragraph 17. The setting is not adjustable - see paragraph 10.

Notes

Chapter 11 Bodywork and fittings

Contents

Body exterior fittings - removal and refitting 23
Bonnet - removal, refitting and adjustment 8
Bonnet lock - removal and refitting 10
Bonnet release cable - removal and refitting 9
Central locking components - removal and refitting 17
Centre console - removal and refitting 27
Door - removal, refitting and adjustment 11
Door inner trim panel - removal and refitting 12
Door handle and lock components - removal and refitting 13
Door window glass and regulator - removal and refitting 14
Electric window components - general information 18
Exterior mirrors and associated components - removal and refitting . 19
Facia panel assembly - removal and refitting 28
Front bumper - removal and refitting 6
General information 1
Interior trim - removal and refitting 26
Maintenance - bodywork and underframe 2
Maintenance - upholstery and carpets 3
Major body damage - repair 5
Minor body damage - repair 4
Rear bumper - removal and refitting 7
Rear quarter window (three-door models) - removal and refitting . . 21
Seat belt components - removal and refitting 25
Seats - removal and refitting 24
Sunroof - general information 22
Tailgate and support struts - removal and refitting 15
Tailgate lock components - removal and refitting 16
Underbody and general body check . . . . See Chapter 1
Windscreen, tailgate and fixed rear quarter window glass -
   general information 20

Degrees of difficulty

Easy, suitable for novice with little experience	**Fairly easy,** suitable for beginner with some experience	**Fairly difficult,** suitable for competent DIY mechanic	**Difficult,** suitable for experienced DIY mechanic	**Very difficult,** suitable for expert DIY or professional

1 General information

The bodyshell is made of pressed-steel sections, and is available in both three- and five-door Hatchback versions as well as in Estate form. Most components are welded together, but some use is made of structural adhesives; the front wings are bolted on.

The bonnet, door, and some other vulnerable panels are made of zinc-coated metal, and are further protected by being coated with an anti-chip primer prior to being sprayed.

Extensive use is made of plastic materials, mainly in the interior, but also in exterior components. The front and rear bumpers, front grille and tailgate assembly are injection-moulded from a synthetic material which is very strong and yet light. Plastic components such as wheel arch liners are fitted to the underside of the vehicle, to improve the body's resistance to corrosion.

2 Maintenance - bodywork and underframe

The general condition of a vehicle's bodywork is the one thing that significantly affects its value. Maintenance is easy, but needs to be regular. Neglect, particularly after minor damage, can lead quickly to further deterioration and costly repair bills. It is important also to keep watch on those parts of the vehicle not immediately visible, for instance the underside, inside all the wheel arches, and the lower part of the engine compartment.

The basic maintenance routine for the bodywork is washing - preferably with a lot of water, from a hose. This will remove all the loose solids which may have stuck to the vehicle. It is important to flush these off in such a way as to prevent grit from scratching the finish. The wheel arches and underframe need washing in the same way, to remove any accumulated mud, which will retain moisture and tend to encourage rust. Paradoxically enough, the best time to clean the underframe and wheel arches is in wet weather, when the mud is thoroughly wet and soft. In very wet weather, the underframe is usually cleaned of large accumulations automatically, and this is a good time for inspection.

Periodically, except on vehicles with a wax-based underbody protective coating, it is a good idea to have the whole of the underframe of the vehicle steam-cleaned, engine compartment included, so that a thorough inspection can be carried out to see what minor repairs and renovations are necessary. Steam-cleaning is available at many garages, and is necessary for the removal of the accumulation of oily grime, which sometimes is allowed to become thick in certain areas. If steam-cleaning facilities are not available, there are some excellent grease solvents available which can be brush-applied; the dirt can then be simply hosed off.

Note that these methods should not be used on vehicles with wax-based underbody protective coating, or the coating will be removed. Such vehicles should be inspected annually, preferably just prior to Winter, when the underbody should be washed down, and any damage to the wax coating repaired. Ideally, a completely fresh coat should be applied. It would also be worth considering the use of such wax-based protection for injection into door panels, sills, box sections, etc, as an additional safeguard against rust damage, where such protection is not provided by the vehicle manufacturer.

After washing paintwork, wipe off with a chamois leather to give an unspotted clear finish. A coat of clear protective wax polish will give added protection against chemical pollutants in the air. If the paintwork sheen has dulled or oxidised, use a cleaner/polisher combination to restore the brilliance of the shine. This requires a little effort, but such dulling is usually caused because regular washing has been neglected. Care needs to be taken with metallic paintwork, as special non-abrasive cleaner/polisher is required to avoid damage to the finish. Always check that the door and ventilator opening drain holes and pipes are completely clear, so that water can be drained out. Brightwork should be treated in the same way as paintwork. Windscreens and windows can be kept clear of the smeary film which often appears, by the use of proprietary glass cleaner. Never use any form of wax or other body or chromium polish on glass.

11

3 Maintenance - upholstery and carpets

Mats and carpets should be brushed or vacuum-cleaned regularly, to keep them free of grit. If they are badly stained, remove them from the vehicle for scrubbing or sponging, and make quite sure they are dry before refitting. Seats and interior trim panels can be kept clean by wiping with a damp cloth. If they do become stained (which can be more apparent on light-coloured upholstery), use a little liquid detergent and a soft nail brush to scour the grime out of the grain of the material. Do not forget to keep the headlining clean in the same way as the upholstery. When using liquid cleaners inside the vehicle, do not over-wet the surfaces being cleaned. Excessive damp could get into the seams and padded interior, causing stains, offensive odours or even rot.

 If the inside of the vehicle gets wet accidentally, it is worthwhile taking some trouble to dry it out properly, particularly where carpets are involved. Do not leave oil or electric heaters inside the vehicle for this purpose.

4 Minor body damage - repair

Note: *For more detailed information about bodywork repair, Haynes Publishing produce a book by Lindsay Porter called "The Car Bodywork Repair Manual". This incorporates information on such aspects as rust treatment, painting and glass-fibre repairs, as well as details on more ambitious repairs involving welding and panel beating.*

Repairs of minor scratches in bodywork

If the scratch is very superficial, and does not penetrate to the metal of the bodywork, repair is very simple. Lightly rub the area of the scratch with a paintwork renovator, or a very fine cutting paste, to remove loose paint from the scratch, and to clear the surrounding bodywork of wax polish. Rinse the area with clean water.

Apply touch-up paint to the scratch using a fine paint brush; continue to apply fine layers of paint until the surface of the paint in the scratch is level with the surrounding paintwork. Allow the new paint at least two weeks to harden, then blend it into the surrounding paintwork by rubbing the scratch area with a paintwork renovator or a very fine cutting paste. Finally, apply wax polish.

Where the scratch has penetrated right through to the metal of the bodywork, causing the metal to rust, a different repair technique is required. Remove any loose rust from the bottom of the scratch with a penknife, then apply rust-inhibiting paint to prevent the formation of rust in the future. Using a rubber or nylon applicator, fill the scratch with bodystopper paste. If required, this paste can be mixed with cellulose thinners to provide a very thin paste which is ideal for filling narrow scratches. Before the stopper-paste in the scratch hardens, wrap a piece of smooth cotton rag around the top of a finger. Dip the finger in cellulose thinners, and quickly sweep it across the surface of the stopper-paste in the scratch; this will ensure that the surface of the stopper-paste is slightly hollowed. The scratch can now be painted over as described earlier in this Section.

Repairs of dents in bodywork

When deep denting of the vehicle's bodywork has taken place, the first task is to pull the dent out, until the affected bodywork almost attains its original shape. There is little point in trying to restore the original shape completely, as the metal in the damaged area will have stretched on impact, and cannot be reshaped fully to its original contour. It is better to bring the level of the dent up to a point which is about 3 mm below the level of the surrounding bodywork. In cases where the dent is very shallow anyway, it is not worth trying to pull it out at all. If the underside of the dent is accessible, it can be hammered out gently from behind, using a mallet with a wooden or plastic head. Whilst doing this, hold a suitable block of wood firmly against the outside of the panel, to absorb the impact from the hammer blows and thus prevent a large area of the bodywork from being "belled-out".

Should the dent be in a section of the bodywork which has a double skin, or some other factor making it inaccessible from behind, a different technique is called for. Drill several small holes through the metal inside the area - particularly in the deeper section. Then screw long self-tapping screws into the holes, just sufficiently for them to gain a good purchase in the metal. Now the dent can be pulled out by pulling on the protruding heads of the screws with a pair of pliers.

The next stage of the repair is the removal of the paint from the damaged area, and from an inch or so of the surrounding "sound" bodywork. This is accomplished most easily by using a wire brush or abrasive pad on a power drill, although it can be done just as effectively by hand, using sheets of abrasive paper. To complete the preparation for filling, score the surface of the bare metal with a screwdriver or the tang of a file, or alternatively, drill small holes in the affected area. This will provide a really good "key" for the filler paste.

To complete the repair, see the Section on filling and respraying.

Repairs of rust holes or gashes in bodywork

Remove all paint from the affected area, and from an inch or so of the surrounding "sound" bodywork, using an abrasive pad or a wire brush on a power drill. If these are not available, a few sheets of abrasive paper will do the job most effectively. With the paint removed, you will be able to judge the severity of the corrosion, and therefore decide whether to renew the whole panel (if this is possible) or to repair the affected area. New body panels are not as expensive as most people think, and it is often quicker and more satisfactory to fit a new panel than to attempt to repair large areas of corrosion.

Remove all fittings from the affected area, except those which will act as a guide to the original shape of the damaged bodywork (eg headlight shells etc). Then, using tin snips or a hacksaw blade, remove all loose metal and any other metal badly affected by corrosion. Hammer the edges of the hole inwards, in order to create a slight depression for the filler paste.

Wire-brush the affected area to remove the powdery rust from the surface of the remaining metal. Paint the affected area with rust-inhibiting paint, if the back of the rusted area is accessible, treat this also.

Before filling can take place, it will be necessary to block the hole in some way. This can be achieved by the use of aluminium or plastic mesh, or aluminium tape.

Aluminium or plastic mesh, or glass-fibre matting, is probably the best material to use for a large hole. Cut a piece to the approximate size and shape of the hole to be filled, then position it in the hole so that its edges are below the level of the surrounding bodywork. It can be retained in position by several blobs of filler paste around its periphery.

Aluminium tape should be used for small or very narrow holes. Pull a piece off the roll, trim it to the approximate size and shape required, then pull off the backing paper (if used) and stick the tape over the hole; it can be overlapped if the thickness of one piece is insufficient. Burnish down the edges of the tape with the handle of a screwdriver or similar, to ensure that the tape is securely attached to the metal underneath.

Bodywork repairs - filling and respraying

Before using this Section, see the Sections on dent, deep scratch, rust holes and gash repairs.

Many types of bodyfiller are available, but generally speaking, those proprietary kits which contain a tin of filler paste and a tube of resin hardener are best for this type of repair. A wide, flexible plastic or nylon applicator will be found invaluable for imparting a smooth and well-contoured finish to the surface of the filler.

Mix up a little filler on a clean piece of card or board - measure the hardener carefully (follow the maker's instructions on the pack), otherwise the filler will set too rapidly or too slowly. Using the applicator, apply the filler paste to the prepared area; draw the applicator across the surface of the filler to achieve the correct contour and to level the surface. As soon as a contour that approximates to the correct one is achieved, stop working the paste - if you carry on too long, the paste will become sticky and begin to "pick-up" on the applicator. Continue to add thin layers of filler paste at 20-minute intervals, until the level of the filler is just proud of the surrounding bodywork.

Once the filler has hardened, the excess can be removed using a metal plane or file. From then on, progressively-finer grades of abrasive paper should be used, starting with a 40-grade production paper, and finishing with a 400-grade wet-and-dry paper. Always wrap the abrasive paper around a flat rubber, cork, or wooden block - otherwise the surface of the filler will not be completely flat. During the smoothing of the filler surface, the wet-and-dry paper should be periodically rinsed in water. This will ensure that a very smooth finish is imparted to the filler at the final stage.

At this stage, the "dent" should be surrounded by a ring of bare metal, which in turn should be encircled by the finely "feathered" edge of the good paintwork. Rinse the repair area with clean water, until all of the dust produced by the rubbing-down operation has gone.

Spray the whole area with a light coat of primer - this will show up any imperfections in the surface of the filler. Repair these imperfections with fresh filler paste or bodystopper, and once more smooth the surface with abrasive paper. Repeat this spray-and-repair procedure until you are satisfied that the surface of the filler, and the feathered edge of the paintwork, are perfect. Clean the repair area with clean water, and allow to dry fully.

 If bodystopper is used, it can be mixed with cellulose thinners, to form a really thin paste which is ideal for filling small holes.

The repair area is now ready for final spraying. Paint spraying must be carried out in a warm, dry, windless and dust-free atmosphere. This condition can be created artificially if you have access to a large indoor working area, but if you are forced to work in the open, you will have to pick your day very carefully. If you are working indoors, dousing the floor in the work area with water will help to settle the dust which would otherwise be in the atmosphere. If the repair area is confined to one body panel, mask off the surrounding panels; this will help to minimise the effects of a slight mis-match in paint colours. Bodywork

fittings (eg chrome strips, door handles etc) will also need to be masked off. Use genuine masking tape, and several thicknesses of newspaper, for the masking operations.

Before commencing to spray, agitate the aerosol can thoroughly, then spray a test area (an old tin, or similar) until the technique is mastered. Cover the repair area with a thick coat of primer; the thickness should be built up using several thin layers of paint, rather than one thick one. Using 400-grade wet-and-dry paper, rub down the surface of the primer until it is really smooth. While doing this, the work area should be thoroughly doused with water, and the wet-and-dry paper periodically rinsed in water. Allow to dry before spraying on more paint.

Spray on the top coat, again building up the thickness by using several thin layers of paint. Start spraying at one edge of the repair area, and then, using a side-to-side motion, work until the whole repair area and about 2 inches of the surrounding original paintwork is covered. Remove all masking material 10 to 15 minutes after spraying on the final coat of paint.

Allow the new paint at least two weeks to harden, then, using a paintwork renovator, or a very fine cutting paste, blend the edges of the paint into the existing paintwork. Finally, apply wax polish.

Plastic components

With the use of more and more plastic body components by the vehicle manufacturers (eg bumpers. spoilers, and in some cases major body panels), rectification of more serious damage to such items has become a matter of either entrusting repair work to a specialist in this field, or renewing complete components. Repair of such damage by the DIY owner is not really feasible, owing to the cost of the equipment and materials required for effecting such repairs. The basic technique involves making a groove along the line of the crack in the plastic, using a rotary burr in a power drill. The damaged part is then welded back together, using a hot-air gun to heat up and fuse a plastic filler rod into the groove. Any excess plastic is then removed, and the area rubbed down to a smooth finish. It is important that a filler rod of the correct plastic is used, as body components can be made of a variety of different types (eg polycarbonate, ABS, polypropylene).

Damage of a less serious nature (abrasions, minor cracks etc) can be repaired by the DIY owner using a two-part epoxy filler repair material. Once mixed in equal proportions, this is used in similar fashion to the bodywork filler used on metal panels. The filler is usually cured in twenty to thirty minutes, ready for sanding and painting.

If the owner is renewing a complete component himself, or if he has repaired it with epoxy filler, he will be left with the problem of finding a suitable paint for finishing which is compatible with the type of plastic used. At one time, the use of a universal paint was not possible, owing to the complex range of plastics

encountered in body component applications. Standard paints, generally speaking, will not bond to plastic or rubber satisfactorily. However, it is now possible to obtain a plastic body parts finishing kit which consists of a pre-primer treatment, a primer and coloured top coat. Full instructions are normally supplied with a kit, but basically, the method of use is to first apply the pre-primer to the component concerned, and allow it to dry for up to 30 minutes. Then the primer is applied, and left to dry for about an hour before finally applying the special-coloured top coat. The result is a correctly-coloured component, where the paint will flex with the plastic or rubber, a property that standard paint does not normally posses.

5 Major body damage - repair

Where serious damage has occurred, or large areas need renewal due to neglect, it means that complete new panels will need welding-in, and this is best left to professionals. If the damage is due to impact, it will also be necessary to check completely the alignment of the bodyshell, and this can only be carried out accurately by a Citroën dealer using special jigs. If the body is left misaligned, it is primarily dangerous, as the car will not handle properly, and secondly, uneven stresses will be imposed on the steering, suspension and possibly transmission, causing abnormal wear, or complete failure, particularly to such items as the tyres.

6 Front bumper - removal and refitting

Removal

1 Apply the handbrake, then jack up the front of the vehicle and support it on axle stands.
2 Remove both the right- and left-hand headlights as described in Chapter 12.
3 Working through the headlamp apertures, slacken and remove the four bolts (two on either side) securing the upper ends of the bumper to the vehicle.
4 Slacken and remove the five bolts securing the bottom edge of the bumper to the vehicle.
5 Working from underneath the vehicle, undo the two bolts (one on either end) securing the lower ends of the bumper to the vehicle. Where necessary, disconnect the wiring connectors from the front foglamps.
6 Release both the left- and right-hand ends of the bumper, and pull the bumper away from the vehicle in a forwards direction.

Refitting

7 Refitting is a reverse of the removal procedure, ensuring that the bumper mounting bolts are securely tightened.

11

7.2 Unscrew the wheel brace retaining clip from its mounting stud in the luggage compartment

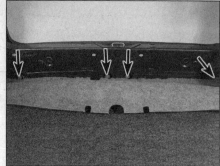

7.3 Peel back the carpet to gain access to the rear bumper retaining bolts (arrowed)

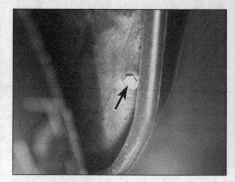

7.5 Slacken and remove the bolts securing the rear bumper to the wheel arch liners (arrowed) . . .

7 Rear bumper - removal and refitting

Removal

Hatchback models

1 Remove the luggage compartment rear trim panels (where fitted) as described in Section 26.

2 On five-door models, remove the wheel brace, and unscrew the wheel brace clip from the rear right-hand corner of the luggage compartment (see illustration). Remove the retaining nut and clip from the same position on the left-hand side.

3 Release the retaining clips and peel back

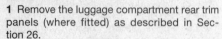

7.6a . . . and to the vehicle body . . .

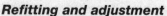

7.6b . . . then remove the bumper from the rear of the vehicle

the luggage compartment carpet, then slacken and remove the four bumper retaining bolts (see illustration).

4 Chock the front wheels, then jack up the rear of the vehicle and support it on axle stands.

5 Working from underneath the vehicle, undo the two bolts (one either side) securing the ends of the bumper to the wheel arch liner (see illustration).

6 Undo the two bolts securing the bumper to the underside of the vehicle, then release the left- and right-hand ends of the bumpers from their mountings, and pull the bumper away from the vehicle in a rearwards direction (see illustrations).

Estate models

7 Remove the luggage compartment rear trim panel to expose the two bumper securing screws. Remove these screws.

8 Chock the front wheels, then jack up the rear of the vehicle and support it on axle stands.

9 Working from underneath the vehicle, undo the two bolts (one either side) securing the ends of the bumper to the wheel arch liner.

10 Work along the lower edge of the bumper and remove the supporting screws.

11 Locate the plastic plugs which cover the four bumper securing nuts and prise them from position with the flat of a screwdriver.

12 With an assistant supporting the bumper, remove the four securing nuts and pull the bumper away from the vehicle in a rearwards direction.

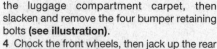

8.2a Slacken and remove the bonnet-to-hinge retaining bolts . . .

Refitting

13 Refitting is a reverse of the removal procedure, ensuring that all disturbed fasteners are securely tightened.

8 Bonnet - removal, refitting and adjustment

Removal

1 Open the bonnet and have an assistant support it. Using a pencil or felt tip pen, mark the outline of each bonnet hinge relative to the bonnet, to use as a guide on refitting.

2 Disconnect the windscreen washer supply pipe from its non-return valve on the right-hand side. Undo the bonnet retaining bolts and, with the help of an assistant, carefully lift the bonnet clear. Store the bonnet out of the way in a safe place (see illustrations).

3 Inspect the bonnet hinges for signs of wear and free play at the pivots, and if necessary renew. Each hinge is secured to the body by two pivot bolts. On refitting, apply a smear of multi-purpose grease to the shanks of the hinge pivot bolts, and tighten them securely.

Refitting and adjustment

4 With the aid of an assistant, offer up the bonnet and loosely fit the retaining bolts. Align

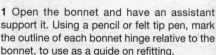
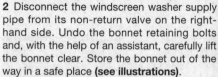

8.2b . . . then, with the aid of an assistant, lift off the bonnet

9.5 Removing the bonnet release lever retaining bolts

10.1 Undo the three retaining screws, and remove the plastic cover to gain access to the bonnet lock

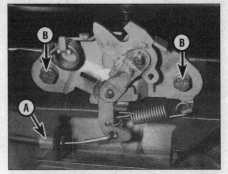

10.2 Unclip the release cable (A), then undo the retaining bolts (B) and remove the bonnet lock

the hinges with the marks made on removal, then tighten the retaining bolts securely, and reconnect the windscreen washer supply pipe.

5 Close the bonnet, and check for alignment with the adjacent panels. If necessary, slacken the hinge bolts and re-align the bonnet to suit. Once the bonnet is correctly aligned, tighten the hinge bolts to the specified torque.

6 Once the bonnet is correctly aligned, check that the bonnet fastens and releases in a satisfactory manner. If adjustment is necessary, slacken the bonnet lock retaining bolts, and adjust the position of the lock to suit. Once the lock is operating correctly, securely tighten its retaining bolts.

9 Bonnet release cable - removal and refitting

Removal

1 Open the bonnet. Undo the three retaining screws and remove the plastic cover to gain full access to the bonnet lock.

2 Unclip the bonnet release outer cable from the lock bracket, then release the inner cable from the lock lever.

3 Work back along the length of the cable, noting its correct routing, and free it from the retaining clips and ties. Tie a length of string to the end of the cable.

4 From inside the vehicle, release the panel fasteners by rotating them through a quarter of a turn, and remove the driver's side lower facia panel.

5 Slacken and remove the two retaining bolts, then free the bonnet release lever from its retaining bracket, and withdraw the cable (see illustration). Once the cable is free, untie the string and leave it in position in the vehicle; the string can then be used to draw the new cable back into position.

Refitting

6 Tie the inner end of the string to the end of

the cable, then use the string to draw the bonnet release cable through into the engine compartment. Once the cable is through, untie the string.

7 Manoeuvre the bonnet release lever back into position, and securely tighten its retaining bolts.

8 Ensure the cable is correctly routed, and secured to all the relevant retaining clips. Connect the end of the inner cable to the lock lever, then clip the outer cable into position in the lock bracket.

9 Operate the bonnet release lever, and check that the lock operates smoothly, without any sign of undue resistance. Check that the bonnet fastens and releases in a satisfactory manner. If adjustment is necessary, slacken the bonnet lock retaining bolts, and adjust the position of the lock to suit. Once the lock is operating correctly, securely tighten its retaining bolts and refit the lock cover.

10 Refit the lower facia panel, and secure it in position by rotating its fasteners through a quarter of a turn.

10 Bonnet lock - removal and refitting

Removal

1 Open the bonnet. Undo the three retaining screws and remove the plastic cover to gain full access to the bonnet lock (see illustration). Mark the outline of the bonnet lock on the body, to use as a guide on refitting.

2 Unclip the bonnet release outer cable from the lock bracket, then release the inner cable from the lock lever (see illustration).

3 Undo the two retaining bolts, and remove the lock assembly from the vehicle.

Refitting

4 Refit the lock to the vehicle, aligning it with the marks made on removal, and securely tighten its retaining bolts.

5 Connect the end of the inner cable to the lock lever, then clip the outer cable into position in the lock bracket.

6 Check that the bonnet fastens and releases in a satisfactory manner. If adjustment is necessary, slacken the bonnet lock retaining bolts, and adjust the position of the lock to suit. Once the lock is operating correctly, securely tighten its retaining bolts and refit the lock cover.

11 Door - removal, refitting and adjustment

Removal

1 Open the door, to gain access to the wiring connector which is fitted to the front edge of the door.

2 Where a circular wiring connector is used, unscrew the connector locking ring until its tab is located between the lugs on the connector, then disconnect the wiring connector from the door (see illustration). Where a rectangular connector is used, pull out the locking clip to release it, then disconnect the connector from the door.

3 Undo the two bolts securing the check link

11.2 On circular wiring connectors, unscrew the locking ring until its tab is located between the connector lugs (arrowed), then pull it away from the door

11.3 Undo the check link retaining bolts . . .

11.4 . . . slacken the hinge pin grub bolts (arrowed), and lift the door upwards and away from the vehicle

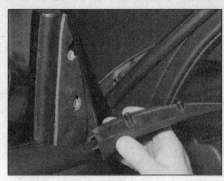

12.1 Unclip the exterior mirror inner trim panel from the door

to the pillar **(see illustration)**. On models where the bolts are not accessible, drive out the check link roll pin using a hammer and punch.

4 Loosen the two hinge pin grub bolts. With the aid of an assistant, lift the door to release it from the hinge pins, and remove it from the vehicle **(see illustration)**.

5 Examine the hinges for signs of wear or damage. The hinges are welded to the door and pillar; if renewal is necessary, the task should be entrusted to a Citroën dealer.

Refitting

6 Apply a smear of multi-purpose grease to the hinge pins, then, with the aid of an assistant, refit the door to the vehicle. Once the door is correctly positioned, securely tighten the grub bolts.

7 Align the check link with the door pillar, and securely tighten its retaining bolts. Where the check link roll pin was removed, align the link with its retaining bracket, and secure it in position by tapping in the roll pin.

8 Reconnect the wiring connector, and secure it in position by tightening its retaining ring, or by pressing in its retaining clip (as applicable).

Adjustment

9 Adjustment of the door position is not possible for the home mechanic. However, small adjustments can be made by bending the hinge pin slightly using a special Citroën service tool. This task should be entrusted to a Citroën dealer.

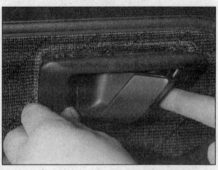

12.2 Lift the door inner handle, and remove the escutcheon from the door

12 Door inner trim panel - removal and refitting

Removal

Front door

1 Open the door. Carefully prise out and remove the exterior mirror inner trim panel **(see illustration)**.

2 Lift the door inner handle, then carefully prise the escutcheon out from the door panel and remove it **(see illustration)**.

3 On models with manual windows, pull the handle off the spindle, and remove the regulator escutcheon.

4 On models with electric windows, carefully prise the window switch out of the armrest,

12.4 On models with electric windows, remove the switch from the armrest

taking care not to mark the switch or armrest. Disconnect the wiring connector and remove the switch **(see illustration)**.

5 Lift up the inner door lock operating button, then, using a small flat-bladed screwdriver, depress the retaining tab, and slide off the button **(see illustration)**.

6 Slacken and remove the armrest retaining screws, and remove the armrest from the door **(see illustration)**.

7 Remove the speaker as described in Chapter 12.

8 Release the door trim panel studs, carefully levering between the panel and door with a flat-bladed screwdriver. Work around the outside of the panel, and when all the studs are released, slide the panel upwards and away from the door **(see illustration)**.

12.5 Depress the retaining tab, and slide the inner lock button off its link rod

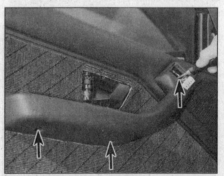

12.6 Undo the retaining screws (arrowed), and remove the armrest from the door

12.8 Removing the inner trim panel from the front door

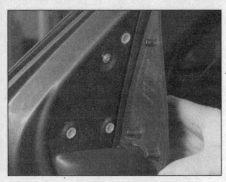

12.10 Removing the small inner trim panel from the rear door

12.11 Pull the window winder handle and trim collar off the regulator spindle

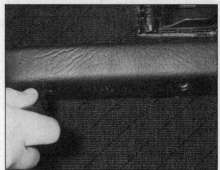

12.13 Undo the two retaining screws, and remove the armrest from the rear door

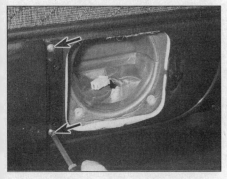

12.14 Undo the two retaining screws (arrowed) located behind the speaker grille

12.15 Unclip the inner trim panel, and remove it from the rear door

12.16 Refitting a door lock operating button. Note the locating tab (arrowed) engaged in the lower of the two button holes

Rear door

9 Lift the door inner handle, then carefully prise the escutcheon out from the door panel and remove it.

10 Carefully prise off the small inner trim panel from the rear of the door **(see illustration)**.

11 Pull the window winder handle off the spindle, and remove it, along with its trim collar **(see illustration)**.

12 Lift up the inner door lock operating button, then, using a small flat-bladed screwdriver, depress the retaining tab, and slide off the button **(see illustration 12.5)**.

13 Slacken and remove the armrest retaining screws, and remove the armrest from the door **(see illustration)**.

14 Prise off the speaker grille, and slacken and remove the two retaining screws securing the trim panel to the door **(see illustration)**.

15 Release the door trim panel studs, carefully levering between the panel and door with a flat-bladed screwdriver. Work around the outside of the panel, and when all the studs are released, lift the panel upwards and away from the door **(see illustration)**.

Refitting

16 Refitting of the trim panel is the reverse sequence of removal, noting the following points:

(a) *Before refitting, check whether any of the trim panel retaining studs were broken on removal, and renew them as necessary.*

(b) *To refit the inner door lock operating button, first lock the door, to ensure that*

the link rod is in its lowest position. Position the button locating tab in the lower of the its two holes, then firmly push the button onto the rod, until it clips into position and the retaining tab appears in the upper hole (see illustration).

13 Door handle and lock components - removal and refitting

Removal

1 Remove the door inner trim panel as described in Section 12, then proceed as described under the relevant sub-heading.

Interior door handle

2 Unclip the interior handle from the door, and disconnect it from the link rod.

Exterior door handle

3 Carefully cut the rubber insulating panel away from the rear of the door, to gain access to the rear of the handle.

4 Undo the three screws securing the lock assembly to the door, then drop the lock assembly slightly to disengage it from the handle.

5 On five-door models, working through the door aperture, slacken and remove the retaining nut, then free the handle from the lock assembly, and withdraw it from the door **(see illustrations)**.

13.5a On five-door models, undo the retaining nut from the inside of the door . . .

13.5b . . . then remove the exterior handle

11

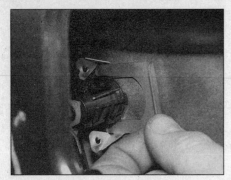

13.9a Slide out the retaining clip . . .

13.9b . . . then withdraw the lock cylinder, and disconnect it from its link rod

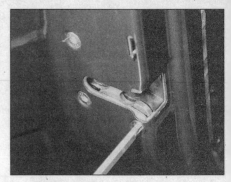

13.15a Undo the three retaining screws . . .

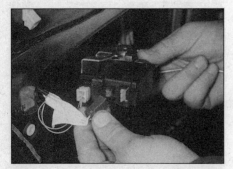

13.15b . . . manoeuvre the lock assembly out of the door, and (where necessary) disconnect the wiring connector from the servo unit

6 On three-door models, slacken and remove the two bolts securing the handle to the outside of the door, then free the handle from the lock assembly and remove it from the door.

Front door lock cylinder

7 Carefully cut the rubber insulating panel away from the rear of the door, to gain access to the rear of the lock cylinder.
8 Undo the three screws securing the lock assembly to the door, and drop the lock assembly slightly to improve access to the lock cylinder.
9 Using a pair of pliers, slide out the lock cylinder retaining clip, then withdraw the lock

cylinder from the outside of the door, and free it from its link rod **(see illustrations)**.

Front door lock

10 Remove the interior lock handle as described in paragraph 2.
11 Remove the lock cylinder as described in paragraphs 7 to 9.
12 Manoeuvre the lock and link rod assembly out through the door aperture. On models with central locking, it will be necessary to disconnect the wiring connector from the servo motor as the lock is removed.

Rear door lock

13 Remove the interior door handle as described in paragraphs 1 and 2.
14 Carefully cut the rubber insulating panel away from the rear of the door, to gain access to the rear of the lock assembly.
15 Slacken and remove the three lock retaining screws, then manoeuvre the lock and link rod assembly out through the door aperture. On models with central locking, it will be necessary to disconnect the wiring connector from the servo motor as the lock is removed **(see illustrations)**.

Refitting

16 Refitting is the reverse of the removal sequence, noting the following points:
(a) Ensure that all link rods are securely held in position by their retaining clips.
(b) Apply grease to all lock and link rod pivot points.

(c) Before installing the inner trim panel, thoroughly check the operation of all the door lock handles and, where applicable, the central locking system, and ensure that the rubber insulating panel is correctly positioned.

14 Door window glass and regulator - removal and refitting

Removal

1 Remove the door inner trim panel as described in Section 12.
2 Carefully cut the rubber insulating panel away from the edge of the door, remove the panel, then proceed as described under the relevant sub-heading **(see illustration)**.

Front door window glass

3 With the window in the fully-raised position, slacken and remove the upper and lower window guide retaining bolts, and remove the guide from the front of the door **(see illustrations)**.
4 Temporarily refit the handle (or reconnect the switch, as applicable), and lower the window glass approximately halfway.
5 Working from inside the door, release the clip securing the window glass to the

14.2 Removing the rubber insulating panel from the front door

14.3a Undo the two retaining bolts (arrowed) . . .

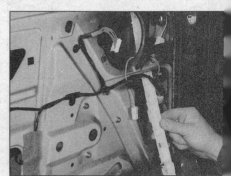

14.3b . . . and remove the window guide from the door

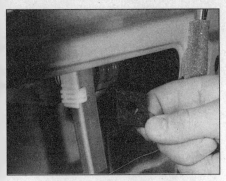

14.5 Remove the retaining clip as described in the text, and free the window glass from the regulator peg

14.6 Removing the window glass from the front door

14.7a Undo the retaining screw . . .

regulator peg by rotating it through 45°, then slide off the clip, and free the glass from the regulator mechanism (see illustration).
6 Fully lower the glass, and free the upper window guide from the rear of the sealing strip, then carefully manoeuvre the window glass out through the top of the door (see illustration).

Rear door window glass

7 Undo the retaining screw from the inside, then remove the small outer trim panel from the door (see illustrations).
8 Temporarily refit the handle, and lower the window glass.
9 Working around the edge of the strip, carefully ease the sealing strip out from the

door, and remove it from the vehicle (see illustration).
10 Release the window glass from the regulator mechanism as described above in paragraph 5, then carefully manoeuvre the glass out through the top of the door (see illustrations).

Window regulator

11 Remove the window glass as described above.
12 Slacken and remove the five regulator retaining nuts, then carefully manoeuvre the regulator assembly out through the largest door panel aperture. On models with electric windows, it will be necessary to disconnect the wiring connector from the regulator motor as it becomes accessible (see illustrations).

14.7b . . . and remove the trim panel from the outside of the rear door

14.9 Work around the edge of the sealing strip, freeing it from the door, and remove the strip

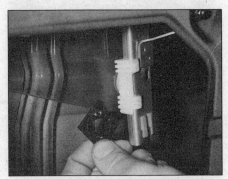

14.10a Remove the retaining clip, then free the window glass from the regulator . . .

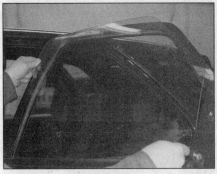

14.10b . . . and remove it from the top edge of the door

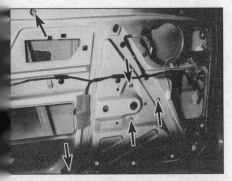

14.12a Undo the five regulator retaining nuts (arrowed) . . .

14.12b . . . and withdraw the regulator assembly through the largest door panel aperture

14.12c On models with electric windows, disconnect the wiring connector from the motor as the regulator is removed

11

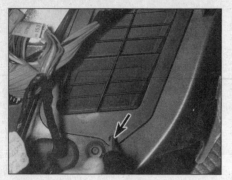

15.2a Undo the retaining screw (arrowed) and remove the vent grille . . .

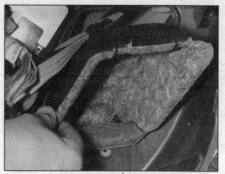

15.2b . . . and duct from each side of the luggage compartment

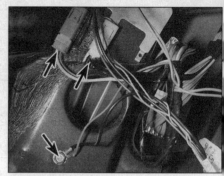

15.3a Disconnect the tailgate wiring connectors and earth lead connection (arrowed) - left-hand side shown . . .

Refitting

Front door window glass

13 Manoeuvre the window glass back into position through the top of the door.

14 Lower the window glass to the base of the door, and engage the upper guide with the rear of the sealing strip.

15 Raise the glass, and locate it on the regulator mechanism peg. Slide the retaining clip onto the regulator peg, and secure it in position by rotating it through 45°.

16 Fully raise the window glass, then refit the front window guide, tightening its retaining screws securely.

17 Check that the window glass can be raised and lowered smoothly, then refit the rubber insulating panel to the door.

18 Ensure the insulating panel is securely stuck to the door, and refit the inner trim panel as described in Section 12.

Rear door window glass

19 Manoeuvre the window glass back into position through the top of the door, and locate it on the regulator mechanism peg. Slide the retaining clip onto the regulator peg, and secure it in position by rotating it through 45°.

20 Engage the front edge of the sealing strip with the upper window glass guide, then work around the edge of the strip, and seat it back into position in the door. Refit the outer trim panel, and securely tighten its retaining screw.

21 Check that the window glass can be raised and lowered smoothly, then refit the rubber insulating panel to the door.

22 Ensure the insulating panel is securely stuck to the door, and refit the inner trim panel as described in Section 12.

Window regulator

23 Reconnect the wiring connector (where applicable), and manoeuvre the regulator assembly back into position in the door. Refit the five retaining nuts, and tighten them securely.

24 Refit the window glass as described above.

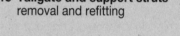

15 Tailgate and support struts - removal and refitting

Removal

Tailgate - Hatchback models

1 Remove both the left- and right-hand rear light units as described in Chapter 12.

2 Undo the retaining screw, and remove the vent grilles and ducts which are situated on the left- and right-hand sides of the luggage compartment **(see illustrations)**.

3 Disconnect the tailgate wiring connectors situated on the left- and right-hand sides from the main wiring loom, and unscrew the bolt securing the earth lead to the vehicle body. Withdraw the wiring connectors from the rear of the body, then work back along the length of each loom, and release them from underneath the outside of the tailgate sealing strip, and from any relevant retaining clips **(see illustrations)**.

4 Release the rear screen washer supply pipe from underneath the top of the tailgate sealing strip, and disconnect it at its non-return valve **(see illustration)**.

5 Have an assistant support the tailgate, then raise the spring clips and pull the support struts off their balljoint mountings on the tailgate. Carefully prise out the hinge pin retaining clips, then tap both hinge pins out of position, and remove the tailgate from the vehicle **(see illustrations)**.

6 Examine the hinge pins for signs of wear or damage, and renew if necessary.

15.3b . . . withdraw the wiring looms from the rear of the vehicle, and free them from underneath the tailgate sealing strip

15.4 Release the tailgate washer pipe from underneath the sealing strip, and disconnect it at its non-return valve

15.5a Remove the retaining clips . . .

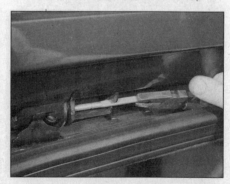

15.5b . . . and withdraw the tailgate hinge pins

Tailgate - Estate models

7 At the time of writing, no detailed information was available on removal and refitting of the tailgate assembly fitted to Estate models. However, each procedure may be assumed to be similar to Hatchback models. Work in a slow and methodical manner to avoid unnecessary mistakes.

Support struts

8 Support the tailgate in the open position, using a stout piece of wood, or with the help of an assistant.

9 Raise the spring clip, and pull the support strut off its balljoint mounting on the tailgate. Using a flat-bladed screwdriver, prise out the retaining clip, then carefully lever the strut off its balljoint, and remove it from the vehicle **(see illustrations)**.

Refitting

Tailgate

10 Refitting is a reversal of the removal procedure, noting the following points:

(a) Before refitting, apply a smear of multi-purpose grease to the hinge pins.

(b) Ensure that the hinge pins are securely retained by their retaining clips, and that the support struts are securely held in position by their spring clips.

(c) Ensure that the washer jet pipe and wiring looms are correctly located behind the tailgate sealing strip.

Support struts

11 Refitting is a reverse of the removal procedure, ensuring that the strut is securely retained by its spring clip and retaining clip.

16 Tailgate lock components - removal and refitting

Removal

Tailgate lock - Hatchback models

1 Open up the tailgate, then undo the two retaining bolts and remove the lock **(see illustrations)**.

15.9a Lift the spring clip (arrowed), and free the support strut from the tailgate . . .

Tailgate lock - Estate models

2 At the time of writing, no detailed information was available on removal and refitting of the tailgate lock assembly fitted to Estate models. However, each procedure may be assumed to be similar to Hatchback models.

Tailgate lock cylinder - Hatchback models

3 Remove the tailgate wiper motor as described in Chapter 12.

4 Using a pair of pliers, slide out the lock retaining clip, and withdraw the lock cylinder and handle from the tailgate **(see illustrations)**.

Refitting

5 Refitting is a reversal of the removal procedure.

16.1a Undo the two retaining bolts . . .

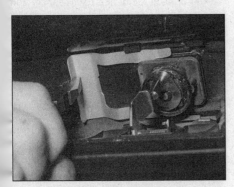
16.4a Slide out the retaining clip . . .

16.4b . . . then withdraw the lock cylinder and handle assembly from the tailgate

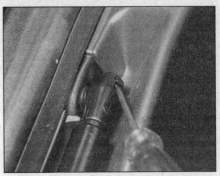
15.9b . . . then prise out the retaining clip, and free the strut from the body

17 Central locking components - removal and refitting

Electronic control unit

1 Open the rear ashtray, depress the retaining tang and remove the ashtray from the handbrake lever cover panel. Slacken and remove the rear retaining nut and the two front retaining screws, then manoeuvre the cover panel off the handbrake lever.

2 Undo the nut securing the control unit to the handbrake lever mounting stud. Disconnect the wiring connector and remove the unit from the vehicle **(see illustration)**.

3 Refitting is the reverse of removal.

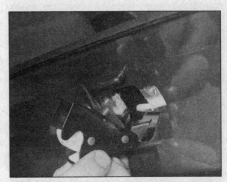
16.1b . . . and remove the lock from the base of the tailgate

17.2 Central locking electronic control unit is mounted onto one of the handbrake lever studs

17.5 Removing a central locking servo unit from a lock assembly

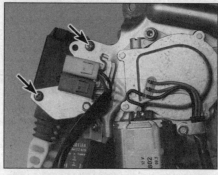

17.8 Tailgate lock servo motor is retained by two screws

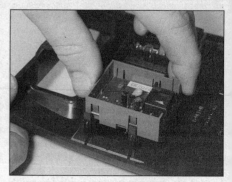

17.11 Removing the central locking receiver unit from the overhead console

17.13 Prise the two halves of the transmitter unit apart, and remove the batteries

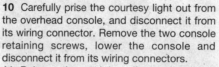

19.1 On manually-operated mirrors, prise off the inner trim panel . . .

Door lock servo unit

4 Remove the relevant door lock as described in Section 13.
5 The servo unit is a bayonet fit on the lock assembly. To remove it, twist it slightly to release it from the lock bracket, and disengage it from the lock peg **(see illustration)**.
6 On refitting, ensure that the servo unit is securely clipped in position, and that it is correctly engaged with the lock peg.

Tailgate lock servo unit

7 Remove the tailgate wiper motor as described in Chapter 12.
8 Undo the two retaining screws, and remove the servo unit from wiper motor bracket **(see illustration)**.

9 Refitting is the reverse of the removal procedure.

Remote receiver unit

10 Carefully prise the courtesy light out from the overhead console, and disconnect it from its wiring connector. Remove the two console retaining screws, lower the console and disconnect it from its wiring connectors.
11 Release the retaining clips, and remove the receiver unit from the top of the console **(see illustration)**.
12 Refitting is the reverse of removal.

Transmitter batteries

13 Using a small screwdriver, carefully prise the two halves of the transmitter apart, and remove the two batteries, noting which way around they are fitted **(see illustration)**.

14 Fit the two batteries, ensuring that they are fitted the correct way around; the battery and transmitter terminals are marked "+" and "-" to avoid confusion. Clip the transmitter back together.

18 Electric window components - general information

Window switches
1 Refer to Chapter 12.
Window winder motors
2 The window winder electric motor is an integral part of the regulator mechanism, and cannot be renewed separately. Refer to Section 14 for regulator removal and refitting details.

19 Exterior mirrors and associated components - removal and refitting

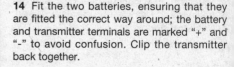

Removal
Manually-operated mirror
1 Carefully prise off the mirror interior trim panel **(see illustration)**.
2 Unscrew the two retaining screws, then slacken and remove the adjusting lever grub screw, and slide the retaining plate off the mirror adjusting lever **(see illustrations)**.

19.2a . . . then slacken and remove the two retaining screws . . .

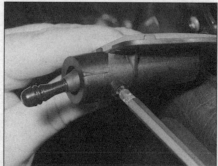

19.2b . . . and the adjusting lever grub screw . . .

19.2c . . . and remove the retaining plate from the adjusting lever

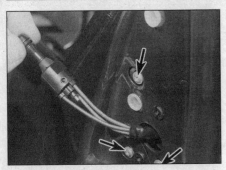

19.3 Undo the three retaining screws (arrowed), and remove the mirror assembly from the door

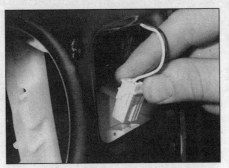

19.5 On electrically operated mirrors, remove the door inner trim panel to gain access to the mirror wiring connector

19.6a Peel back the rubber insulating foam . . .

3 Remove the rubber insulating foam, then slacken and remove the three retaining screws, and remove the mirror assembly from the door (see illustration).

Electrically-operated mirror

4 Remove the door inner trim panel as described in Section 12.
5 Carefully cut the rubber insulating panel away from the front edge of the door to gain access to the mirror wiring connector. Disconnect the connector from the main wiring loom (see illustration).
6 Remove the rubber insulating foam. Slacken and remove the three retaining screws and remove the mirror assembly from the door (see illustrations).

Mirror glass

7 The mirror glass is stuck onto the mirror assembly, and removal will almost certainly lead to the glass being broken. Therefore, the mirror glass should not be removed unless it is to be replaced.
8 To ease removal, gently warm the glass with a hairdryer, then carefully lever the glass out of position.

Mirror switch (electrically-operated mirror)

9 Refer to Chapter 12.

Refitting

Manually-operated mirror

10 Offer up the mirror, and securely tighten its three retaining screws.
11 Refit the insulating foam, then slide the retaining plate over the adjusting lever, and secure it in position with its two retaining screws. Refit the adjusting lever grub screw, and check the operation of the lever.
12 If all is well, refit the inner trim panel to door.

Electrically-operated mirror

13 Offer up the mirror, feeding its wiring connector through the door, and securely tighten its retaining screws.
14 Reconnect the mirror wiring connector, ensuring that the wiring loom is correctly routed.

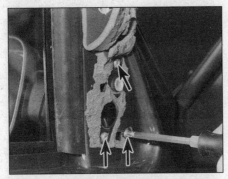

19.6b . . . then undo the three retaining screws (arrowed) . . .

15 Refit the insulating foam and panel to the door, and refit the inner trim panel as described in Section 12.

Mirror glass

16 Prior to fitting the new glass, use a solvent to remove all traces of old adhesive from the mounting plate. Remove the backing from the new mirror, then warm the adhesive gently, and press the glass firmly onto its mounting plate.

Mirror switch

17 Refitting is the reverse of removal.

20 Windscreen, tailgate and fixed rear quarter window - general information

These areas of glass are secured by the tight fit of the weatherstrip in the body aperture, and are bonded in position with a special adhesive. Renewal of such fixed glass is a difficult, messy and time-consuming task, which is beyond the scope of the home mechanic. It is difficult, unless one has plenty of practice, to obtain a secure, waterproof fit. Furthermore, the task carries a high risk of breakage; this applies especially to the laminated glass windscreen. In view of this, owners are strongly advised to have this sort of work carried out by one of the many specialist windscreen fitters.

19.6c . . . and remove the mirror assembly from the door

21 Rear quarter window (three-door models) - removal and refitting

At the time of writing, no information was available on removal and refitting of the rear quarter window on three-door models. Therefore, this task should be entrusted to a Citroën dealer.

22 Sunroof - general information

Due to the complexity of the sunroof mechanism, considerable expertise is needed to repair, replace or adjust the sunroof components successfully. Removal of the roof first requires the headlining to be removed, which is a complex and tedious operation, and not a task to be undertaken lightly (see Section 26). Therefore, any problems with the sunroof should be referred to a Citroën dealer.

On models with an electric sunroof, if the sunroof motor fails to operate, first check the relevant fuse. If the fault cannot be traced and rectified, the sunroof can be opened and closed manually using an Allen key to turn the motor spindle. (A suitable key is supplied with the vehicle, and should be located behind the driver's side lower facia panel, where it is clipped onto the fusebox.) To gain access to

11

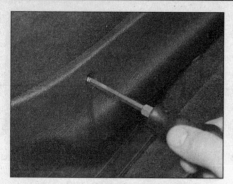

24.1a Undo the trim panel retaining screws . . .

24.1b . . . and peel back the trim panel to improve access to the front seat mounting bolts

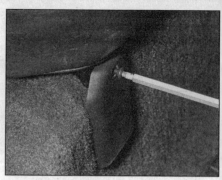

24.4a Undo the retaining screws . . .

the motor spindle, prise the courtesy light out of the overhead console, undo the two console retaining screws and lower the console assembly. Insert the Allen key in the motor spindle, and rotate the key to move the sunroof to the required position.

23 Body exterior fittings - removal and refitting

Wheel arch liners and body under-panels

1 The various plastic covers fitted to the underside of the vehicle are secured in position by a mixture of screws and retaining clips, and removal will be fairly obvious on inspection. Work methodically around the panel, removing its retaining screws and releasing its retaining clips until the panel is free and can be removed from the underside of the vehicle.

2 On refitting, renew any retaining clips that may have been broken on removal, and ensure that the panel is securely retained by all the relevant clips and screws.

Body trim strips and badges

3 The various body trim strips and badges are held in position with a special adhesive tape. Removal requires the trim/badge to be heated, to soften the adhesive, and then cut

away from the surface. Due to the high risk of damage to the vehicle's paintwork during this operation, it is recommended that this task should be entrusted to a Citroën dealer.

24 Seats - removal and refitting

Front seats

 Warning: On models with seat belt pre-tensioners, observe the following precautions before attempting to remove the seat:
(a) Remove the ignition key.
(b) Disconnect the battery negative lead, and wait for ten minutes before carrying out any further work.
(c) Disconnect the pre-tensioner wiring plug (located under the seat).
Do not tamper with the pre-tensioner unit in any way, and do not attempt to test the unit. Note that the unit is triggered if the mechanism is supplied with an electrical current (including via an ohmmeter), or if the assembly is subjected to a temperature of greater than 100ºC.

Removal

1 Slide the seat fully backwards, then undo the two Torx bolts securing the front of the seat slides to the floor. Where necessary, to

improve access to the bolts, undo the retaining screws, and prise the trim covers back from the base of the seat **(see illustrations)**.

2 Slide the seat fully forwards, then undo the two Torx bolts securing the rear of the seat slides to the floor, and remove the seat from the car.

Refitting

3 Refitting is a reverse of the removal procedure, ensuring that the seat mounting bolts are securely tightened.

Rear seat
Removal - fixed and sliding types

4 Undo the retaining screws, and remove the plastic trim covers from each of the three seat front mounting points. With the covers removed, slacken and remove the seat front retaining nuts **(see illustrations)**.

5 On models with a sliding rear seat assembly, slide the seat fully forwards, and remove the rear parcel shelf; unclip the trim cover from the base of the seat, to gain access to the rear mounting bolts **(see illustration)**. On models with a fixed rear seat assembly, remove the parcel shelf, then release the trim fasteners and peel back the carpet from the rear of the seat, to gain access to the rear mounting bolts.

6 Slacken and remove the three rear mounting bolts, and recover the spacers which are positioned beneath the seat mounting brackets **(see illustration)**.

7 Feed the rear seat belts back through the gap between the seat back and cushion, and

24.4b . . . and remove the trim covers to gain access to the rear seat front retaining nuts

24.5 On models with a sliding rear seat assembly, unclip the trim panel from the base of the seat, to gain access to the rear seat rear mounting bolts

24.6 Slacken and remove the rear mounting bolts, and recover the spacers (arrowed) from underneath the seat mounting brackets

manoeuvre the seat assembly out of the vehicle.

Removal - folding types

8 There are two types of folding rear seats fitted, the bench type or split type. On both types, pivot the seat base forwards so that it rests against the back of the front seats. Now pivot the back of the seat forwards to expose its retaining bar end covers. Remove these covers **(see illustration)**.

9 The back of the seat can now be removed by positioning it vertically and pulling it upwards so that the retaining bar clears its end slots in the vehicle bodywork.

10 Repositioning the seat base in its normal position will expose its hinged mounting points **(see illustration)**. To remove the base, remove each mounting point retaining nut then move the base forward to release it.

Refitting

11 Refitting is a reverse of the removal procedure, ensuring that all seat mounting bolts and nuts are securely tightened.

---

25 Seat belt components - removal and refitting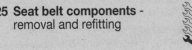

Note: *Take note of the positions of any washers and spacers on the seat belt anchors, and ensure that they are refitted in their original positions.*

Removal

Front seat belt - five-door models

1 Prise off the trim cap from the lower belt anchorage bolt, then slacken and remove the bolt and washers, and free the seat belt from its lower anchorage.

2 Prise the trim cover off the upper seat belt mounting bolt, then undo the bolt and release the seat belt.

3 Undo the two retaining screws from the base of the lower door pillar trim panel, then carefully prise the panel away from the pillar, and remove it from the vehicle.

4 Pull the knob off the seat belt upper mounting height adjuster lever. Slacken and remove the retaining screw, then unclip the

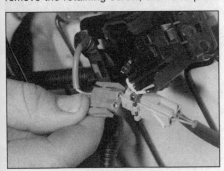

25.14 Disconnecting the front seat belt pre-tensioner wiring plug - seat tilted for clarity

24.8 Removing a folding rear seat retaining bar end cover

upper trim panel from the door pillar, and remove it from the vehicle.

5 Slacken and remove the inertia reel retaining bolt(s), and remove the seat belt from the vehicle.

Front seat belt - three-door models

6 Remove the centre door pillar upper trim panel, as described in paragraphs 45 to 48 of Section 26.

7 Carefully drill out the rivet securing the seat belt guide to the door pillar.

8 Slacken and remove the bolt and washers securing the lower seat belt mounting rail to the floor, and disengage the rail from the belt.

9 Slacken and remove the inertia reel retaining bolt(s), and remove the seat belt from the vehicle.

Front seat belt stalk - models without seat belt pre-tensioners

10 Remove the seat as described in Section 24.

11 Slacken and remove the bolt securing the stalk to the seat, and remove the stalk.

Front seat belt stalk - models with seat belt pre-tensioners

⚠ **Warning: Observe the following precautions before attempting to remove the seat belt stalk assembly:**

(a) Remove the ignition key.

(b) Disconnect the battery negative lead, and wait for ten minutes before carrying out any further work.

(c) Disconnect the pre-tensioner wiring plug (located under the seat).

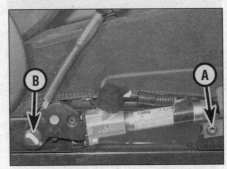

25.15 Seat belt pre-tensioner front securing screw (A) and rear securing bolt (B)

24.10 The central hinged mounting point of a split-type folding rear seat

Do not tamper with the pre-tensioner unit in any way, and do not attempt to test the unit. Note that the unit is triggered if the mechanism is supplied with an electrical current (including via an ohmmeter), or if the assembly is subjected to a temperature of greater than 100°C.

12 The seat belt stalk is an integral part of the seat belt tensioner mechanism.

13 Remove the securing screws or release the clips, as applicable, and remove the trim panel from the side of the seat.

14 Unclip the tensioner wiring harness from the bottom of the seat **(see illustration)**.

15 Slacken the front tensioner securing screw and remove the rear tensioner securing bolt **(see illustration)**.

16 Withdraw the tensioner mechanism from the seat.

⚠ **Warning: Do not hold the tensioner by the buckle or by the cable - only hold the unit around the tensioner body.**

Front seat belt pre-tensioner electronic control unit

17 This unit is located under the centre console.

18 Disconnect the battery negative lead, and wait for at least ten minutes before carrying out any further work.

19 Remove the centre console.

20 Disconnect the wiring connectors, noting the routing of the wiring.

21 Unscrew the four securing nuts, and withdraw the unit from the mounting bracket **(see illustration)**.

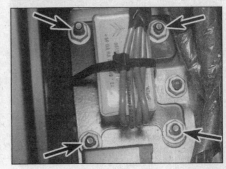

25.21 Front seat belt pre-tensioner electronic control unit securing nuts (arrowed)

11

25.23a Rear seat side belt inertia reel bolt, and upper belt mounting bolt (arrowed) - five-door model shown

25.23b Rear seat side belt lower mounting bolt

25.25 Rear seat centre belt/buckle retaining bolt

Rear seat side belt

22 Remove the lower and upper luggage compartment side trim panels as described in Section 26.

23 Slacken and remove the upper and lower seat belt mounting bolts and washers, if not already having done so, then undo the inertia reel retaining bolt and remove the seat belt from the vehicle (**see illustrations**).

Rear seat centre belt and buckles

24 On models with a sliding rear seat, slide the rear seat fully forwards then unclip the trim panel from the base of the rear of the seat. On models with a fixed rear seat, release the trim fasteners and peel back the carpet from the rear of the seat. On models with a folding rear seat, pivot the seat base forwards so that it rests against the back of the front seats.

25 Slacken and remove the bolt and washers securing the centre belt and/or buckle assembly to the floor, and remove it from the vehicle (**see illustration**).

Refitting

26 Refitting is a reversal of the removal procedure, ensuring that all the seat belt mounting bolts are securely tightened, and all disturbed trim panels are securely retained by all the relevant retaining clips.

27 On front seat belt stalks equipped with seat belt pre-tensioners, observe the following precautions:

(a) *Before refitting, ensure that the battery negative lead is disconnected and that the ignition is switched off.*
(b) *Do not touch the seat belt buckle when the ignition is first switched on.*

28 When refitting a front seat belt pre-tensioner electronic control unit, reverse the removal procedure but ensure that the unit wiring connectors are reconnected before reconnecting the battery negative lead.

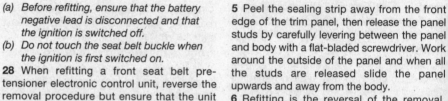

26 Interior trim - removal and refitting

Interior trim panels

Door trim panels

1 Refer to Section 12.

Rear seat side trim panels - three-door models

2 Remove the rear seat assembly as described in Section 24.

3 Unclip the speaker grille from the panel then undo the screws securing the speaker (where fitted) and panel to the vehicle. Where a speaker is fitted disconnect the wiring connectors and remove the speaker.

4 Slacken and remove the three other retaining screws (two at the base of the panel and one underneath the armrest) securing panel to the body (**see illustration**).

5 Peel the sealing strip away from the front edge of the trim panel, then release the panel studs by carefully levering between the panel and body with a flat-bladed screwdriver. Work around the outside of the panel and when all the studs are released slide the panel upwards and away from the body.

6 Refitting is the reversal of the removal, renewing any broken retaining clips prior to refitting the panel.

Luggage compartment rear trim panels - Hatchback models

7 Open the tailgate. Slacken and remove the bump-stop retaining screws, and remove both tailgate bump-stops (**see illustration**).

8 Undo the three retaining screws securing the right- or left-hand rear luggage compartment trim panel to the floor, noting the correct fitted positions of the luggage clips, and remove the panel (**see illustration**). If necessary, repeat the procedure and remove the remaining trim panel.

9 Refitting is a reversal of the removal procedure.

Luggage compartment lower side trim panel - Hatchback models

10 Slide the rear seat fully forwards (where possible), and fold down the rear seat backs.

11 Remove the appropriate half of the rear trim panel (where fitted) as described above. On three-door models, remove the rear seat side trim panel.

12 On five-door models, if the right-hand

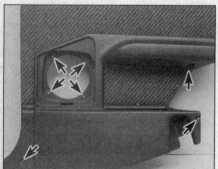

26.4 Three-door model rear seat side trim panel retaining screw locations (arrowed) - shown with panel removed

26.7 Removing a tailgate bump-stop from the rear of the vehicle

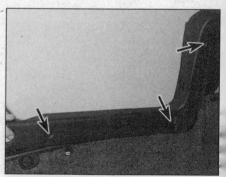

26.8 Removing a rear trim panel from the luggage compartment (retaining screw locations arrowed)

26.12 On five-door models, the wheel brace clip unscrews from the body

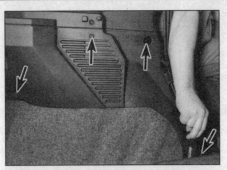

26.13 Removing the luggage compartment side trim panel retaining clip (retaining screw locations arrowed)

26.14 Removing a side trim panel from the luggage compartment

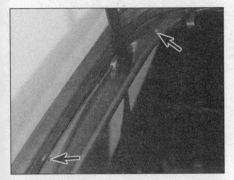

26.19a Slacken and remove the two upper retaining screws (arrowed) . . .

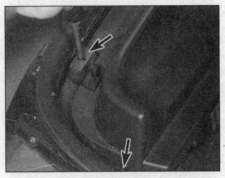

26.19b . . . and the two lower retaining screws (arrowed) . . .

26.19c . . . then remove the rear section of the upper trim panel

panel is being removed, remove the wheel brace, and unscrew the wheel brace clip from the rear right-hand corner of the luggage compartment (see illustration). If the left-hand panel is being removed, remove the retaining nut and clip from the same position on the left-hand side.

13 Slide the retaining clip, located just behind the base of the rear seat cushion, out of the trim panel (see illustration).

14 Slacken and remove the four trim panel retaining screws. Carefully release the edges of the panel from its surrounding components, then remove it from the vehicle (see illustration). If the left-hand panel is being removed, it will be necessary to disconnect the wiring connector from the luggage

compartment light as it becomes accessible.
15 Refitting is the reverse of removal, ensuring that all fasteners are securely tightened.

Luggage compartment upper side trim panel - Hatchback models

16 Remove the lower side trim panel as described above.
17 On three-door models, prise the trim cover off the rear seat belt upper mounting point, then slacken and remove the mounting bolts and washer(s), and free the belt from the panel. Also remove the centre pillar upper trim panel as described later in this Section.
18 Undo the two upper side trim panel lower retaining screws.

19 Slacken and remove the four retaining screws and rubber bump-stop from the rear section of the upper panel. Peel back the tailgate sealing strip from the side of the panel rear section, then remove the panel. Where necessary, disconnect the wiring connector from the luggage compartment light switch as it becomes accessible (see illustrations).
20 Undo the two retaining screws located behind the rear section of the trim panel, then free the panel from the side of the body (see illustrations). On five-door models, to remove the panel from the vehicle, slacken and remove the rear seat belt lower mounting bolt and washer, and feed the belt back through the slot in the panel.
21 Refitting is a reversal of the removal

26.20a Undo the upper retaining screw . . .

26.20b . . . and the lower retaining screw . . .

26.20c . . . and free the upper trim panel from the luggage compartment - five-door model shown

11

26.23 On refitting, ensure the windscreen trim pegs are correctly located in the facia (viewed through the windscreen)

26.46a On three-door models, remove the trim cover . . .

26.46b . . . then undo the mounting bolt, and free the seat belt from the body

procedure. Ensure that the tailgate wiring is correctly positioned beneath the sealing strip prior to pressing the sealing strip onto the vehicle.

Luggage compartment upper side trim panel - Estate models

22 Remove the back of the rear seat as described in Section 24.
23 Undo the six screws and remove the lower trim strip from the base of the tailgate aperture.
24 Undo the bolts and remove the tailgate bump stop and centring stop on the side concerned.
25 Undo the two screws on the inner face of the tailgate aperture side trim. Peel back the rubber sealing strip around the side of the tailgate aperture then remove the side trim.
26 Suitably support the tailgate, then raise the spring clips and pull the support strut off the balljoint mounting on the body. Undo the upper trim panel retaining screw adjacent to the support strut balljoint mounting.
27 Undo the two upper trim panel retaining screws above the luggage compartment storage box, and the two screws below the side window.
28 Undo the retaining screw at the extreme rear edge of the upper trim panel (exposed after removal of the side trim).
29 Undo the screws and remove the parcel shelf rear support.

30 Carefully release the retaining clips and withdraw the trim panel from its location.
31 Open the rear side door and peel back the rubber sealing strip from the rear of the door aperture.
32 Undo the screw at the base of the door aperture trim panel, release the clips and remove the panel.
33 Undo the now accessible seat belt lower mounting bolt and feed the belt through the opening in the upper side trim panel. The panel can now be removed from the luggage compartment.
34 Refitting is a reversal of the removal procedure.

Luggage compartment lower side trim panel - Estate models

35 Remove the upper side trim panel as described previously.
36 Undo the rear seat belt upper mounting and inertia reel mounting bolts and remove the seat belt.
37 Lift up the luggage tie-down rings and lift out the luggage compartment floor covering.
38 Carefully release the retaining clips and remove the lower side trim panel from the luggage compartment.
39 Refitting is a reversal of the removal procedure.

Windscreen pillar trim panel

40 Unclip the trim panel from the windscreen pillar and, where necessary, release the

alarm sensor from the clip on the top of the panel.
41 Prior to refitting, check the panel retaining clips, and renew any that are broken. Where necessary, ensure the alarm sensor wire is correctly routed, and refit the sensor to its retaining clip. Clip the panel back into position, ensuring that the pegs on the base of the panel are correctly located in the facia panel (see illustration).

Front footwell side trim panel

42 Undo the two retaining screws, and remove the trim panel from the side of the footwell.
43 Refitting is a reverse of the removal procedure.

Centre door pillar trim panels - five-door models

44 Refer to the information given in paragraphs 1 to 4 of Section 25.

Centre door pillar upper trim panel - three-door models

45 Remove the rear seat side trim panel as described earlier in this Section.
46 Prise the trim cover off the upper seat belt mounting bolt, then slacken and remove the bolt and washer(s), and release the seat belt (see illustrations).
47 Undo the retaining screw from the base of the upper trim panel (see illustration).
48 Peel back the sealing strip from the front edge of the panel, carefully prise the panel away from the pillar, and remove it from the vehicle (see illustration).
40 Refitting is a reversal of the removal procedure.

Glovebox

50 Remove the two retaining clips, and release the felt undercover from the underside of the glovebox.
51 Open the glovebox. Slacken and remove the four retaining screws situated along its upper edge, and the six retaining screws located along its lower edge, and slide the glovebox out of position.
52 Refitting is the reverse of the removal procedure, ensuring that the retaining screws are securely tightened.

26.47 Slacken and remove the retaining screw . . .

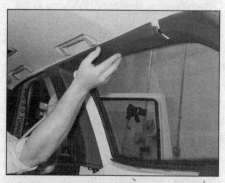

26.48 . . . free the door pillar trim panel from the sealing strip, and remove it from the vehicle

27.2 Removing the centre console left-hand front side panel - retaining screw location arrowed

27.3a On models with a leather gear lever gaiter, release the pop fastener and velcro strip . . .

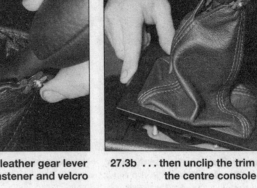

27.3b . . . then unclip the trim panel from the centre console

Carpets

53 The passenger compartment floor carpet is in one piece, and is secured at its edges by screws or clips - usually the same fasteners used to secure the various adjoining trim panels.

54 Carpet removal and refitting is reasonably straightforward but time-consuming, due to the fact that all adjoining trim panels must be removed first, as must components such as the seats, the centre console and seat belt lower anchorages.

Headlining

55 The headlining is clipped to the roof, and can be withdrawn only once all fittings such as the grab handles, sun visors, sunroof (if fitted), windscreen and rear quarter windows, and related trim panels, have been removed. The door, tailgate and sunroof aperture sealing strips will also have to be prised clear.

56 Note that headlining removal requires considerable skill and experience if it is to be carried out without damage, and is therefore best entrusted to an expert.

27 Centre console - removal and refitting

Removal

Low-specification models

1 Undo retaining the two retaining screws. Free the console from the gear lever gaiter and lift it over the lever.

High-specification models

2 Undo the left-hand front side panel retaining screw. Disengage the panel from the centre console and remove it from the vehicle (see illustration). Repeat the procedure and remove the right-hand panel.

3 On models with manual transmission, carefully prise the gear lever trim panel out from the centre console. Where a leather gaiter is fitted to the lever, release the pop fastener and velcro strip, and remove the

gaiter (see illustrations). Where a rubber gaiter is fitted, unscrew the knob from the gear lever, and remove the knob and gaiter assembly.

4 On models with automatic transmission, carefully prise the selector lever trim panel out from the centre console, and fold the gaiter back over the selector lever. Slacken and remove the four screws securing the handle to the shaft of the selector lever. Depress the selector lever handle detent knob, then rotate the handle through 90° anti-clockwise, lift the assembly up and rotate it back 90° clockwise, to release the detent button from the selector lever pushrod. With the handle removed, withdraw the detent button and spring from the handle.

27.5a Depress the retaining tang (arrowed), and slide out the ashtray . . .

27.6a Undo the rear retaining nut . . .

5 Depress the retaining tang, and slide the ashtray out from the centre facia panel, then slacken and remove the two front centre console retaining screws, located behind the ashtray (see illustrations).

6 Slacken and remove the retaining nut from the rear of the centre console, then manoeuvre the console over the gear lever, and remove it from the vehicle (see illustrations).

Refitting

Low-specification models

7 Locate the gaiter back in the console base, then refit the two retaining screws, tightening them securely.

27.5b . . . to gain access to the centre console front retaining screws (arrowed)

27.6b . . . then lift the centre console over the gear lever, and remove it from the vehicle

11

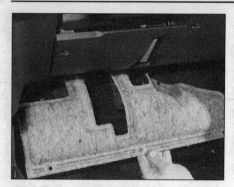

28.6 Removing the driver's side facia felt undercover

28.7a Unclip both the left-hand switch panel . . .

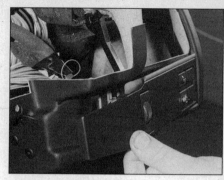

28.7b . . . and right-hand switch panel, and remove them from the facia (right-hand-drive model shown)

High-specification models

8 Manoeuvre the centre console back into position over the gear lever, ensuring that the heater ducts fitted to either side of the console are correctly located with the heater unit outlets at the front of the console.

9 Refit the two front retaining screws and the rear retaining nut, and tighten them securely. Slide the ashtray back into the centre facia panel.

10 On models with manual transmission, either screw the lever and gaiter back onto the gearchange lever, or locate the gaiter over the lever, and secure it in position with the velcro strip and pop fastener (as applicable). Clip the gaiter trim panel back into position in the centre console.

11 On models with automatic transmission, refit the spring and detent button to the selector lever handle, and press the button fully into the handle. Keeping the button depressed, slide the handle assembly onto the lever, then, exerting light downward pressure on the handle, rotate the handle through 90° clockwise, then back 90° anti-clockwise, to engage the detent button with the lever pushrod. Release the detent button, then refit the four handle retaining screws and tighten them securely. Check the operation of the selector lever detent button, then clip the

trim panel back into position in the centre console.

12 Refit the side panels to the front of the console, and secure them in position with their retaining screws.

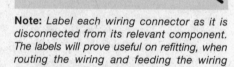

28 Facia panel assembly - removal and refitting

Note: *Label each wiring connector as it is disconnected from its relevant component. The labels will prove useful on refitting, when routing the wiring and feeding the wiring through the facia apertures.*

Removal

1 Disconnect the battery negative terminal.
2 Remove the instrument panel assembly and clock as described in Chapter 12.
3 Remove the steering column assembly as described in Chapter 10.
4 On high-specification models, remove the centre console as described in Section 27. On low-specification models where only a small centre console is fitted, undo the retaining screws and remove the heater duct cover (where fitted) from the centre of the facia assembly.

5 On carburettor models, remove the choke cable as described in Chapter 4A.
6 Unclip both the left- and right-hand felt undercovers from underneath the facia, and remove them from the vehicle **(see illustration)**.
7 Carefully prise the switch panels, located on either side of the instrument panel, out of the facia, taking care not to mark either the panel or facia. Disconnect the wiring connectors, and remove the panels **(see illustrations)**.
8 Where a radio/cassette player is fitted, remove it as described in Chapter 12, then undo the two retaining screws, and remove the mounting bracket from the radio aperture **(see illustrations)**. Where no radio/cassette player is fitted, carefully prise out the storage box from the centre of the facia panel.
9 Undo the four centre vent panel retaining screws (two located above the heater controls, and two directly below), then unclip the panel and withdraw it from the facia. Disconnect the wiring connectors from the cigarette lighter and ashtray illumination bulb, and remove the centre vent panel assembly from the vehicle **(see illustrations)**.
10 Undo the two heater control panel retaining screws, then release the lower panel retaining clip, and manoeuvre the panel out

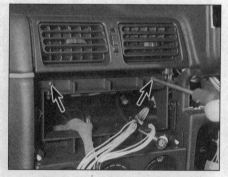

28.8a On models fitted with a radio/cassette player, undo the two retaining screws (arrowed) . . .

28.8b . . . and remove the mounting bracket

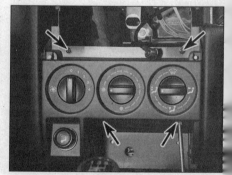

28.9a Undo the four retaining screws (arrowed) . . .

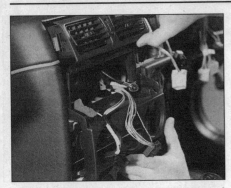
28.9b . . . then unclip the centre vent panel from the facia . . .

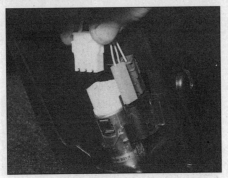
28.9c . . . and disconnect the wiring connectors from the cigarette lighter and bulb

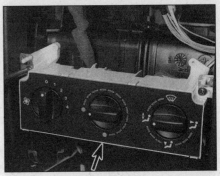
28.10a Undo the retaining screws, and release the heater control panel from the facia (retaining clip location arrowed) . . .

from the centre of the facia. Slacken and remove the facia mounting bolt and retaining screw which are located behind the heater control panel **(see illustrations)**.

11 Slacken and remove the retaining screw from each end of the facia panel **(see illustration)**.

12 Undo the two facia retaining nuts located on the lower edge of the instrument panel aperture **(see illustration)**.

13 Unscrew the retaining screw, located underneath the inner corner of the glovebox, securing the facia in position **(see illustration)**.

14 On right-hand-drive models, slacken and remove the retaining screw from the centre of the facia - accessed from underneath **(see illustration)**.

15 Where necessary, undo the nut and release the earth lead from the stud at the base of the centre of the facia **(see illustration)**.

16 Remove the windscreen wiper motor as described in Chapter 12.

17 With the wiper motor removed, slacken and remove the three retaining nuts and washers securing the facia panel to the bulkhead **(see illustration overleaf)**.

18 From inside the vehicle, unclip the trim panels from the front roof pillars. Where necessary, release the alarm sensors from the

28.10b . . . to gain access to the facia mounting bolt . . .

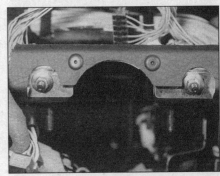
28.10c . . . and retaining screw located behind the panel

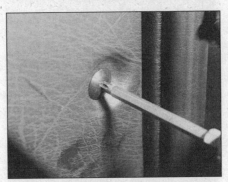
28.11 Removing a facia panel end retaining screw

28.12 Facia retaining nuts located beneath instrument panel aperture

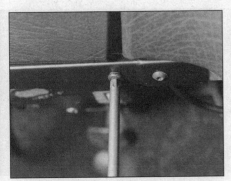
28.13 Removing the facia retaining screw situated underneath the glovebox

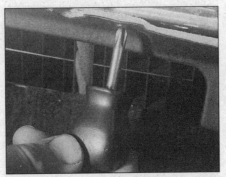
28.14 On right-hand-drive models, remove the retaining screw from beneath the centre of the facia panel

28.15 Undo the retaining nut, and free the earth strap from the base of the centre of the facia panel

11

28.17 Centre facia-to-bulkhead retaining nut and wiring bracket

28.19 Removing the facia assembly

clips on the top of each trim panel, and remove the panels.

19 The facia panel is now free to be removed.

Pull the panel away from the bulkhead to release it from its retaining pins, then remove the facia assembly, noting the correct routing

of the wiring harnesses, and feeding the wiring back through the facia apertures (see illustration).

Refitting

20 Refitting is a reversal of the removal procedure, noting the following points:

(a) Manoeuvre the facia into position and, using the labels stuck on during removal, ensure the wiring is correctly routed and fed through the relevant facia apertures.

(b) Clip the facia back into position, then refit all the facia fasteners, and tighten them securely.

(c) On completion, reconnect the battery and check that all the electrical components and switches function correctly. On carburettor models, check that the choke control is operating correctly.

Chapter 12 Body electrical systems

Contents

Air bag system components - removal and refitting 27
Air bag system - general information, precautions and system de-
   activation 26
Anti-theft alarm system - general information 24
Battery check and maintenance . . . .See "Weekly checks" and Chapter 1
Battery - removal and refitting . . . . See Chapter 5
Bulbs (exterior lights) - renewal 5
Bulbs (interior lights) - renewal 6
Cigarette lighter - removal and refitting 13
Clock - removal and refitting 11
"Dim-dip" lighting system (UK models only) - general information . . 25
Door-open warning display - general information 12
Electrical fault finding - general information 2
Exterior light units - removal and refitting 7
Fuses and relays - general information 3
General information and precautions 1
Headlight beam alignment - general information 8
Horn - removal and refitting 15
Instrument panel components - removal and refitting 10
Instrument panel - removal and refitting 9
"Lights-on" warning buzzer - general information 14
Loudspeakers - removal and refitting 22

Radio aerial - removal and refitting 23
Radio/cassette player - removal and refitting 21
Reversing light switch (models with manual
   transmission) - removal and refitting . . . . See Chapter 7A
Selector lever position display switch (models with automatic
   transmission) - removal, refitting and adjustment . . See Chapter 7B
Speedometer drive cable - removal and refitting 16
Starter inhibitor/reversing light switch (models with automatic
   transmission) - removal and refitting . . . . See Chapter 7B
Stop-light switch - removal, refitting and adjustment . . See Chapter 9
Switches - removal and refitting 4
Tailgate wiper motor - removal and refitting 19
Windscreen/headlight washer system check
   and adjustment . . . . .See "Weekly checks"
Windscreen/tailgate washer system components -
   removal and refitting 20
Windscreen/tailgate wiper blade check and
   renewal . . . . .See "Weekly checks"
Windscreen wiper motor and linkage - removal and refitting 18
Wiper arm - removal and refitting 17
Wiring diagrams - explanatory notes 28

Degrees of difficulty

Easy, suitable for novice with little experience	Fairly easy, suitable for beginner with some experience	Fairly difficult, suitable for competent DIY mechanic	Difficult, suitable for experienced DIY mechanic	Very difficult, suitable for expert DIY or professional

Specifications

System type . . . . 12-volt, negative earth

Facia fusebox fuses (1991 to 1992)

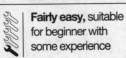

Fuse	Rating (amps)	Circuit(s) protected
F1	30	Headlamp washers, electric mirrors and heated seats
F2	30	Low fuel level, brake pad wear and battery charge warning lamps. Front and rear wipers. High pressure pump. Radio/cassette
F3	30	Heated rear window relay, electric front window relay, indicators
F4	25	Central locking
F5	30	Heated rear screen and heated exterior mirror
F6	10	Hazard warning lights
F7	10	Reversing lights, facia panel lights and instrument panel warning lights
F8	20	Radio/cassette, interior lights, cigarette lighter, luggage compartment light and clock
F9	30	Electric windows, sunroof and seat adjustment
F10	20	Horn
F11	5	High intensity rear foglight
F12	5	Right-hand front and rear sidelights, ashtray and cigarette lighter illumination, "lights-on" buzzer and switch illumination
F13	5	Left-hand front and rear sidelights, number plate light, interior lighting and side lamp warning light

Facia fusebox fuses (1992 to 1994)

Fuse	Rating (amps)	Circuit(s) protected
F1	30	Heater blower motor, headlamp washers, electric mirrors, air conditioning relay, headlamp washer timer and heated seats
F2	10	Radio/cassette, instrument panel, stop-lights, front and rear wash/wipe and "lights-on" buzzer
F3	30	Heated rear window relay, electric window relay, indicators and cooling fan relay(s)
F4	25	Central locking and anti-theft alarm
F5	25	Heated rear window and heated exterior mirror
F6	10	Hazard warning lights
F7	10	Reversing lights, facia panel lights and instrument panel warning lights
F8	20	Radio/cassette, interior lights, cigarette lighter, luggage compartment light, clock and remote central locking receiver
F9	30	Electric windows, sunroof, seat adjustment and map reading light
F10	20	Horn
F11	5	High intensity rear foglight
F12	5	Right-hand front and rear sidelights, ashtray and cigarette lighter illumination, "lights-on" buzzer and switch illumination
F13	5	Left-hand front and rear sidelights, number plate light

Facia fusebox fuses (1995-on)

Fuse	Rating (amps)	Circuit(s) protected
F1	30	Electric windows, sunroof and seat adjustment
F2	25	Heater blower controls and air conditioning switch
F3	25	Heated seat control, cooling fan relay(s), heated rear screen switch and timer, heated rear view mirrors
F4	25	Warning lamps for: battery charge, pad wear, low fuel. Lights on audible warning, control for sunroof and front windows, front and rear wash wipe.
F5	25	Heated rear window and heated exterior mirror
F6	10	Hazard warning lights, alarm switch and warning lamp, coded anti-theft keypad
F7	10	Dash lighting rheostat, tachometer, dash warning lamps, alarm unit, anti-theft keypad, cigar lighter relay, ABS, reverse lamp, reduced lighting
F8	30	Radio/cassette, interior lights, cigarette lighter, luggage compartment light, clock and remote central locking receiver, sunroof and window control, alarm and siren
F9	30	Headlamp wash, rear view mirror, indicators, STOP switch, Automatic display and map reading light
F10	20	Horn and cigar lighter
F11	5	High intensity rear foglight and warning lamp
F12	10	Right-hand front and rear sidelights, dash switch and radio illumination, ashtray illumination, "lights-on" buzzer, foglamp
F13	5	Left-hand front and rear sidelights, number plate light, side lamp warning light, alarm switch

Junction box fuses (two-fuse arrangement)

Fuse	Rating	Circuit
F1	-	Unused
F2	-	Unused
F3	5	Cooling fan relay
F4	30	Cooling fan

Junction box fuses (four-fuse arrangement)

Fuse	Rating	Circuit
F1	15	Front foglights
F2	30	Heater blower motor and air conditioning controls
F3	30	Supplementary cooling fan
F4	30	Cooling fan

Note: *Not all items fitted to all models*

Bulbs

	Fitting	Wattage
Headlights:		
Dip/main beam bulb	H4	60/55
Individual main beam (where fitted)	H1	55
Front foglights	H3	55
Front sidelights	Capless	5
Direction indicators	Bayonet	21
Direction indicator side repeaters	Capless	5

Bulbs (continued)

	Fitting	Wattage
Interior lights	Capless	5
Luggage boot light	Capless	5
Heater control panel illumination	Capless	1.2
Instrument panel warning lights/illumination	Integral with holder	1.2
Clock illumination	Integral with holder	1.2
Stop/tail lights	Bayonet	21/5
Rear foglight	Bayonet	21
Reversing lights	Bayonet	21

1 General information and precautions

⚠ **Warning: Before carrying out any work on the electrical system, read through the precautions given in "Safety first!" at the beginning of this manual, and in Chapter 5.**

The electrical system is of 12-volt negative earth type. Power for the lights and all electrical accessories is supplied by a lead/acid type battery, which is charged by the alternator.

This Chapter covers repair and service procedures for the various electrical components not associated with engine. Information on the battery, alternator and starter motor can be found in Chapter 5.

It should be noted that, prior to working on any component in the electrical system, the battery negative terminal should first be disconnected, to prevent the possibility of electrical short-circuits and/or fires.
Caution: If the radio/cassette player fitted to the vehicle is one with an anti-theft security code, as the standard unit is, refer to the information given in the preliminary Sections of this manual before disconnecting the battery.

2 Electrical fault finding - general information

Note: *Refer to the precautions given in "Safety first!" and in Section 1 of this Chapter before starting work. The following tests relate to testing of the main electrical circuits, and should not be used to test delicate electronic circuits (such as anti-lock braking systems), particularly where an electronic control module is used.*

General

1 A typical electrical circuit consists of an electrical component, any switches, relays, motors, fuses, fusible links or circuit breakers related to that component, and the wiring and connectors which link the component to both the battery and the chassis. To help to pinpoint a problem in an electrical circuit, wiring diagrams are included at the end of this manual.

2 Before attempting to diagnose an electrical fault, first study the appropriate wiring diagram, to obtain a more complete understanding of the components included in the particular circuit concerned. The possible sources of a fault can be narrowed down by noting whether other components related to the circuit are operating properly. If several components or circuits fail at one time, the problem is likely to be related to a shared fuse or earth connection.

3 Electrical problems usually stem from simple causes, such as loose or corroded connections, a faulty earth connection, a blown fuse, a melted fusible link, or a faulty relay (refer to Section 3 for details of testing relays). Visually inspect the condition of all fuses, wires and connections in a problem circuit before testing the components. Use the wiring diagrams to determine which terminal connections will need to be checked, in order to pinpoint the trouble-spot.

4 The basic tools required for electrical fault-finding include a circuit tester or voltmeter (a 12-volt bulb with a set of test leads can also be used for certain tests); a self-powered test light (sometimes known as a continuity tester); an ohmmeter (to measure resistance); a battery and set of test leads; and a jumper wire, preferably with a circuit breaker or fuse incorporated, which can be used to bypass suspect wires or electrical components. Before attempting to locate a problem with test instruments, use the wiring diagram to determine where to make the connections.

5 To find the source of an intermittent wiring fault (usually due to a poor or dirty connection, or damaged wiring insulation), a "wiggle" test can be performed on the wiring. This involves wiggling the wiring by hand, to see if the fault occurs as the wiring is moved. It should be possible to narrow down the source of the fault to a particular section of wiring. This method of testing can be used in conjunction with any of the tests described in the following sub-Sections.

6 Apart from problems due to poor connections, two basic types of fault can occur in an electrical circuit - open-circuit, or short-circuit.

7 Open-circuit faults are caused by a break somewhere in the circuit, which prevents current from flowing. An open-circuit fault will prevent a component from working, but will not cause the relevant circuit fuse to blow.

8 Short-circuit faults are caused by a "short" somewhere in the circuit, which allows the current flowing in the circuit to "escape" along an alternative route, usually to earth. Short-circuit faults are normally caused by a breakdown in wiring insulation, which allows a feed wire to touch either another wire, or an earthed component such as the bodyshell. A short-circuit fault will normally cause the relevant circuit fuse to blow.

Finding an open-circuit

9 To check for an open-circuit, connect one lead of a circuit tester or voltmeter to either the negative battery terminal or a known good earth.

10 Connect the other lead to a connector in the circuit being tested, preferably nearest to the battery or fuse.

11 Switch on the circuit, bearing in mind that some circuits are live only when the ignition switch is moved to a particular position.

12 If voltage is present (indicated either by the tester bulb lighting or a voltmeter reading, as applicable), this means that the section of the circuit between the relevant connector and the battery is problem-free.

13 Continue to check the remainder of the circuit in the same fashion.

14 When a point is reached at which no voltage is present, the problem must lie between that point and the previous test point with voltage. Most problems can be traced to a broken, corroded or loose connection.

Finding a short-circuit

15 To check for a short-circuit, first disconnect the load(s) from the circuit (loads are the components which draw current from a circuit, such as bulbs, motors, heating elements, etc).

16 Remove the relevant fuse from the circuit, and connect a circuit tester or voltmeter to the fuse connections.

17 Switch on the circuit, bearing in mind that some circuits are live only when the ignition switch is moved to a particular position.

18 If voltage is present (indicated either by the tester bulb lighting or a voltmeter reading, as applicable), this means that there is a short-circuit.

19 If no voltage is present, but the fuse still blows with the load(s) connected, this indicates an internal fault in the load(s).

Finding an earth fault

20 The battery negative terminal is connected to "earth" - the metal of the engine/transmission unit and the car body - and most systems are wired so that they only receive a positive feed, the current returning via the metal of the car body. This means that the component mounting and the body form part of that circuit. Loose or corroded mountings can therefore cause a range of electrical faults, ranging from

12

3.3 Using the plastic tweezers supplied to remove a fuse from the main fusebox

total failure of a circuit, to a puzzling partial fault. In particular, lights may shine dimly (especially when another circuit sharing the same earth point is in operation), motors (eg wiper motors or the radiator cooling fan motor) may run slowly, and the operation of one circuit may have an apparently-unrelated effect on another. Note that on many vehicles, earth straps are used between certain components, such as the engine/transmission and the body, usually where there is no metal-to-metal contact between components, due to flexible rubber mountings, etc.

21 To check whether a component is properly earthed, disconnect the battery, and connect one lead of an ohmmeter to a known good earth point. Connect the other lead to the wire or earth connection being tested. The resistance reading should be zero; if not, check the connection as follows.

22 If an earth connection is thought to be faulty, dismantle the connection, and clean back to bare metal both the bodyshell and the wire terminal or the component earth connection mating surface. Be careful to remove all traces of dirt and corrosion, then use a knife to trim away any paint, so that a clean metal-to-metal joint is made. On reassembly, tighten the joint fasteners securely; if a wire terminal is being refitted, use serrated washers between the terminal and the bodyshell, to ensure a clean and secure connection. When the connection is remade, prevent the onset of corrosion in the future by applying a coat of petroleum jelly or

silicone-based grease, or by spraying on (at regular intervals) a proprietary ignition sealer or a water-dispersant lubricant.

3 Fuses and relays - general information

Fuses

1 Most of the fuses are located behind the driver's side lower facia panel, with a few odd fuses on some models being located in the junction box on the left-hand side of the engine compartment.

2 To gain access to main fusebox, release the three fasteners by rotating them through 90°, then remove the driver's side lower facia panel. To gain access to those in the junction box, unclip the junction box lid, then release the retaining clip, and lift the small cover situated inside the box (see illustration 3.7a).

3 The fuse number is marked on the fusebox next to each fuse; a list of the circuits each fuse protects is given in the Specifications at the start of this Chapter. Plastic tweezers are also clipped into the fusebox, and can be used to remove and fit the fuses (see illustration).

4 To remove a fuse, first switch off the circuit concerned (or the ignition), then fit the tweezers and pull the fuse out of its terminals. Slide the fuse sideways from the tweezers. The wire within the fuse is clearly visible; if the fuse is blown, it will be broken or melted.

5 Always renew a fuse with one of an identical rating; never use a fuse with a different rating from the original, or substitute anything else. Never renew a fuse more than once without tracing the source of the trouble. The fuse rating is stamped on top of the fuse; note that the fuses are also colour-coded for easy recognition.

6 If a new fuse blows immediately, find the cause before renewing it again; a short to earth as a result of faulty insulation is most likely. Where a fuse protects more than one circuit, try to isolate the defect by switching on each circuit in turn (if possible) until the fuse blows again. Always carry a supply of spare fuses of each relevant rating in the vehicle.

Relays

7 The main relays are located to the rear of the fusebox, behind the facia on the driver's side. Other relays are in the junction box located on the left-hand side of the engine compartment (see illustration). The exceptions to this are as follows:

(a) Sunroof relay - located behind the overhead console
(b) Tailgate wiper motor relay - fitted to the wiper motor bracket
(c) Cooling fan relay(s) - in the rear of the fan shroud on models with twin fans, or at the side of the radiator where only one fan is fitted (see illustration).

8 The flasher relay is located to the rear of the fusebox, behind the facia trim panel on the driver's side (see illustrations 9.3a and 14.2). Refer to the appropriate Chapters for further information, and to the relevant wiring diagram for details of wiring connections.

9 If a circuit or system controlled by a relay develops a fault and the relay is suspect, operate the system; if the relay is functioning, it should be possible to hear it click as it is energized. If this is the case, the fault lies with the components or wiring of the system. If the relay is not being energized, then either the relay is not receiving a main supply or a switching voltage, or the relay itself is faulty. Testing is by the substitution of a known good unit, but be careful; while some relays are identical in appearance and in operation, others look similar but perform different functions.

10 To renew a relay, first ensure that the ignition switch is off. The relay can then simply be pulled out from the socket, and the new relay pressed in.

4 Switches - removal and refitting

Note: *Disconnect the battery negative lead before removing any switch, and reconnect the lead after refitting the switch.*

Ignition switch/steering column lock

1 Refer to Chapter 10, Section 21.

Steering column combination switches

2 Remove the steering wheel as described in Chapter 10.

3 Release the panel fasteners by rotating them through a quarter of a turn, and remove the driver's side lower facia panel.

4 Slacken and remove the five screws which secure the two halves of the steering column shrouds together, then remove both the upper and lower shroud.

5 Undo the three retaining screws, then disconnect the wiring connectors from the rear of the combination switches, and lift the switch assembly off the steering column (see illustrations).

3.7a Engine compartment junction box relays. Fuses are located beneath the small cover (arrowed)

3.7b On models with twin cooling fans, the fan relay(s) are located in the rear of the fan shroud

4.5a Undo the three retaining screws (arrowed) . . .

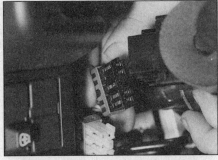

4.5b . . . then disconnect the wiring connectors, and slide off the combination switch assembly

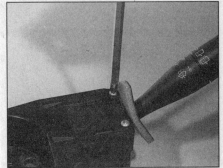

4.6a Undo the two retaining screws . . .

4.6b . . . and slide the relevant switch assembly out from the combination switch bracket

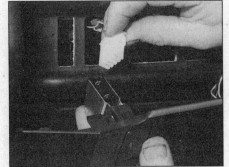

4.9 Removing the instrument panel dimmer switch

4.14 Removing an instrument shroud switch

6 Unscrew the two retaining screws, and slide the relevant switch assembly out of position (see illustrations).

7 Refitting is a reversal of the removal procedure.

Instrument panel dimmer switch, exterior mirror switch, alarm switch and air conditioning switch

8 Using a suitable flat-bladed screwdriver, carefully prise the relevant switch panel out of the facia, taking great care not to mark either the panel or facia.

9 Disconnect the wiring connector from the switch, then depress the retaining tangs, and slide the switch out of the panel (see illustration).

10 Slide the switch back into the panel until it

clicks into position. Reconnect the wiring connector, then clip the panel back into the facia.

Instrument shroud switches

11 Release the panel fasteners by rotating them through a quarter of a turn, and remove the driver's side lower facia panel.

12 Slacken and remove the five screws which secure the two halves of the steering column shrouds together, then remove both the upper and lower shroud.

13 Slacken and remove the four instrument panel shroud retaining screws, then remove the shroud, disconnecting the switch wiring connectors as they become accessible.

14 Depress the retaining tangs, and slide the relevant switch out of the shroud (see illustration).

15 Refitting is a reverse of the removal procedure.

Courtesy light switches

16 Open up the door, then prise the rubber gaiter from the courtesy switch.

17 Undo the retaining screw, then withdraw the switch from the pillar, disconnecting its wiring connector as it becomes accessible. Tie a piece of string to the wiring, to prevent it falling back into the door pillar.

18 Refitting is a reverse of the removal procedure, ensuring that the rubber gaiter is correctly seated on the switch.

Luggage compartment light switch

19 Open up the tailgate, then carefully prise

the switch out from the left-hand trim panel, and disconnect its wiring connector (see illustrations). Tie a piece of string to the wiring, to prevent it falling back behind the trim panel.

20 Reconnect the wiring connector, and clip the switch back into position in the trim panel.

Handbrake warning light switch

21 Open up the rear ashtray, then depress the retaining tang and remove the ashtray from the handbrake lever cover panel. Slacken and remove the rear retaining nut and the two front retaining screws, then manoeuvre the cover panel off the handbrake lever.

22 Disconnect the wiring connector from the handbrake switch, then undo the retaining screw and remove the switch from the side of the handbrake lever (see illustration).

4.19a Prise the luggage compartment light switch out of the trim panel . . .

4.19b . . . then withdraw the switch and disconnect its wiring connector

12

4.22 Handbrake warning light switch retaining screw (arrowed)

4.24b . . . and disconnect it from its wiring connector

23 Refitting is a reverse of the removal procedure.

Electric window switches

24 Carefully prise the window switch out of the armrest, taking great care not to mark the switch or the armrest, and disconnect the wiring connector (see illustrations).
25 On refitting, connect the wiring connector, and clip the switch back into position in the armrest.

Electric sunroof switch

26 Carefully prise the courtesy light out from the overhead console, and disconnect it from its wiring connector. Remove the two console retaining screws, then lower the console out of position, and disconnect it from its wiring connectors.

5.3a Disconnect the wiring connectors from the headlight bulb . . .

4.24a Carefully prise the window switch out of the armrest . . .

4.27 Depress the retaining tangs, and slide out the sunroof switch

27 Depress the retaining tangs, and slide the sunroof switch out of the console (see illustration).
28 Refitting is a reverse of the removal procedure.

5 Bulbs (exterior lights) - renewal

General

1 Whenever a bulb is renewed, note the following points:
(a) Disconnect the battery negative lead before starting work.
(b) Remember that, if the light has just been in use, the bulb may be extremely hot.

5.3b . . . then release the retaining clip . . .

(c) Always check the bulb contacts and holder, ensuring that there is clean metal-to-metal contact between the bulb and its live(s) and earth. Clean off any corrosion or dirt before fitting a new bulb.
(d) Wherever bayonet-type bulbs are fitted (see Specifications) ensure that the live contact(s) bear firmly against the bulb contact.
(e) Always ensure that the new bulb is of the correct rating, and that it is completely clean before fitting it; this applies particularly to headlight/foglight bulbs (see below).

Headlight

2 Working in the engine compartment, remove the relevant plastic cover from the rear of the headlight unit.
3 Disconnect the wiring connectors, then press together the ends of the bulb retaining clip, and release it from the rear of the light (see illustrations).
4 Withdraw the bulb (see illustration).
5 When handling the new bulb, use a tissue or clean cloth, to avoid touching the glass with the fingers; moisture and grease from the skin can cause blackening and rapid failure of this type of bulb.

> **HAYNES HiNT** *If the headllight glass is accidentally touched, wipe it clean using methylated spirit.*

6 Install the new bulb, ensuring that its locating tabs are correctly located in the light cut-outs. Secure the bulb in position with the retaining clip, and reconnect the wiring connectors.
7 Slide the plastic cover back into position, ensuring that it is correctly seated on the rear of the light unit.

Front sidelight

8 Working in the engine compartment, twist the bulbholder anti-clockwise, then withdraw it from the headlight unit (see illustration). Note that on some models, it will be necessary to displace the plastic cover from the rear of the unit to gain access to the bulbholder.

5.4 . . . and withdraw the bulb from the rear of the light unit

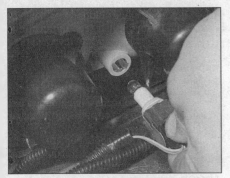

5.8 Removing the sidelight bulbholder from the rear of the headlight unit

5.11 Unhook the retaining spring from within the engine compartment . . .

5.12 . . . then withdraw the direction indicator from the front of the vehicle, and release its bulbholder

5.15 Push the direction indicator side repeater towards the rear of the vehicle, to release its retaining clips . . .

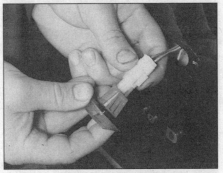

5.16a . . . then withdraw the light from the wing, and disengage it from its bulbholder

5.16b Side repeater bulb is of the capless type, being a push-fit in the holder

9 The bulb is of the capless (push-fit) type, and can be removed by simply pulling it out of the bulbholder.
10 Refitting is the reverse of the removal procedure, ensuring that the bulbholder seal is in good condition.

Front direction indicator

11 Working in the engine compartment, from behind the light, unhook the retaining spring and withdraw the light unit from the front of the vehicle (see illustration).
12 Twist the bulbholder in a clockwise direction to free it from the light, and remove the light unit (see illustration).
13 The bulb is a bayonet fit in the holder, and can be removed by pressing it and twisting in an anti-clockwise direction.

14 Refitting is a reverse of the removal procedure, ensuring that the light unit is correctly located and securely retained by its spring.

Front direction indicator side repeater

15 Push the light unit towards the rear of the vehicle, to free its retaining clips, then withdraw it from the wing (see illustration).
16 Pull the bulbholder out of the light unit, then pull the capless (push-fit) bulb out of its holder (see illustrations).
17 Refitting is a reverse of the removal procedure.

Front foglight

18 Undo the two retaining screws, and

withdraw the lens unit from the front of the light (see illustration).
19 Release the retaining clip, and withdraw the bulb from the rear of the unit. Unclip the plastic insulator cover, then disconnect the bulb wiring connector and remove the bulb (see illustrations).
20 When handling the new bulb, use a tissue or clean cloth, to avoid touching the glass with the fingers; moisture and grease from the skin can cause blackening and rapid failure of this type of bulb. If the glass is accidentally touched, wipe it clean using methylated spirit.
21 Connect the new bulb to the wiring connector, and refit the plastic insulator cover to the connector.
22 Install the bulb in the rear of the lens, ensuring that its locating tabs are correctly

5.18 Undo the two retaining screws, and withdraw the lens unit from the foglight

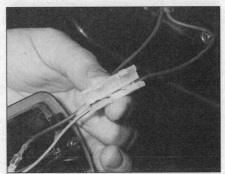

5.19a Unclip the plastic insulator cover . . .

5.19b . . . then disconnect the wiring connector and withdraw the foglight bulb

12

5.22 Prior to refitting the foglight lens, ensure that the plastic insulator (arrowed) is correctly positioned underneath the retaining clip

5.24a Rear light cluster lens is retained by two screws - Hatchback models

5.24b Removing a rear light cluster lens - Estate models

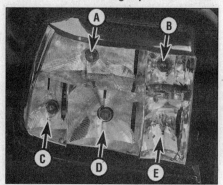

5.25a Rear light cluster bulbs - Hatchback models

A Direction indicator
B Reversing light
C Stop/tail light
D Sidelight
E Foglight (where fitted)

located in the cut-outs. Secure the bulb in position with the retaining clip, ensuring that the wiring insulator is correctly located underneath the clip **(see illustration)**.
23 Refit the lens to the light unit, taking great care not trap the wiring, and securely tighten its retaining screws.

Rear light cluster

24 Open up the tailgate, then undo the two retaining screws and remove the lens from the rear light cluster, noting its rubber seal **(see illustrations)**.

6.2a Prise the courtesy light out of position . . .

5.25b Removing a rear direction indicator bulb - Estate models

25 The relevant bulb can then be renewed - all bulbs have a bayonet fitting **(see illustrations)**. Note that the stop/tail light bulb has offset locating pins, to prevent it being installed incorrectly.
26 Refitting is the reverse of the removal sequence, noting that the rubber lens seal must be renewed if damaged.

Rear foglight - Estate models

27 Ease a thin blade between the side of the light unit and its housing in the bumper to depress the light retaining clip. With the clip depressed, pull the light from position.
28 Withdraw the bulb from the rear of the unit.
29 Push in the new bulb and push the light back into position.

Number plate light

30 Raise the tailgate slightly to improve access to the light, then carefully prise out the

6.2b . . . and twist the bulbholder anti-clockwise to release it from the rear of the light unit

5.31 Pulling a number plate light bulb from its holder - Estate models

light lens to gain access to the bulb.
31 The bulb is of the capless (push-fit) type, and is simply pulled out of position **(see illustration)**.
32 Push in the new bulb, and clip the lens back into position.

6 Bulbs (interior lights) - renewal

General

1 Refer to Section 5, paragraph 1.

Courtesy lights

2 Carefully prise the light unit out of position, then twist the bulbholder in an anti-clockwise direction, and remove it from the rear of the light unit **(see illustrations)**.
3 The bulb is of the capless (push-fit) type; pull the old bulb out of the holder, and press the new one into position.
4 Refit the bulbholder to the rear of the light unit, and clip the light unit back into position.

Luggage compartment light

5 Refer to the information given above in paragraphs 2 to 5 **(see illustration)**.

Map reading light

6 Carefully prise the map reading light unit out of the headlining, then disconnect the wiring connector and remove the light unit **(see illustrations)**.
7 Swivel the bulbholder unit fully away from

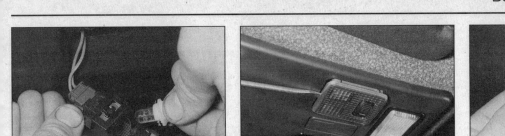

6.5 Removing the luggage compartment light bulbholder

6.6a Carefully prise the map reading light out of the overhead console . . .

6.6b . . . and disconnect it from its wiring connector

6.7 Align the bulbholder with the arrow (arrowed) on the light unit, and pull in the direction of the arrow to remove the bulbholder

6.8 The map reading light bulb is of the capless type

6.11 Removing an instrument panel bulb from the rear of the panel

the wiring connector, then pull the bulbholder lever in the direction of the arrow cast on the light unit, to disengage the holder from the light unit **(see illustration)**.

8 The bulb is of the capless (push-fit) type; pull the old bulb out of the holder, and press the new one into position **(see illustration)**.

9 Slide the bulbholder back onto its pivot in the light unit, then connect the wiring connector, and clip the light unit back into position in the headlining.

Instrument panel lights

10 Remove the instrument panel as described in Section 9.

11 Twist the relevant bulbholder anti-clockwise, and withdraw it from the rear of the panel **(see illustration)**.

12 All bulbs are integral with their holders. Be very careful to ensure that the new bulbs are of the correct rating, the same as those removed; this is especially important in the case of the alternator/no-charge warning light.

13 Refit the bulbholder to the rear of the instrument panel, then refit the instrument panel as described in Section 9.

Selector lever position display bulbs - models with automatic transmission

14 Remove the centre console as described in Chapter 11.

15 Twist the relevant bulbholder anti-

clockwise, and withdraw it from the rear of the panel.

16 The bulbs are of the capless (push-fit) type; pull the old bulb out of the holder, and press the new one into position.

17 Refit the bulbholder to the rear of the panel, then refit the centre console as described in Chapter 11.

Clock illumination bulb

18 Remove the clock as described in Section 11.

19 Twist the bulbholder anti-clockwise, and withdraw it from the rear of the clock **(see illustration)**. The bulb is integral with its holder.

20 Refit the bulbholder to the rear of the clock, then refit the clock as described in Section 11.

Cigarette light/ashtray illumination bulb

21 Remove the centre console as described in Chapter 11.

22 Where a radio/cassette player is fitted, remove it as described in Section 21, then undo the two retaining screws and remove the mounting bracket from the radio aperture. Where no radio/cassette player is fitted, carefully prise out the storage box from the centre of the facia panel.

23 Undo the four centre vent panel retaining screws (two located above the heater controls, and two directly below), then unclip the panel and withdraw it from the facia **(see illustrations 13.3a and 13.3b)**.

24 Slide the illumination bulbholder out of the panel, and renew the bulb **(see illustration)**.

6.19 Removing the clock illumination bulb

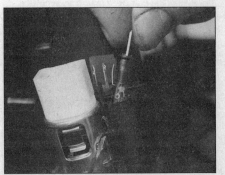

6.24 Removing the cigarette lighter/ashtray illumination bulb

12

6.28a Where required, unclip the heater vents from the centre facia panel . . .

6.28b . . . and use a screwdriver to disengage the retaining clip(s)

6.29a Carefully release the retaining lugs . . .

The bulbs is of the capless (push-fit) type; pull the old bulb out of the holder, and press the new one into position.

25 Slide the illumination bulbholder back into position, and refit the panel by reversing the removal procedure.

Heater control panel illumination bulb

26 Remove the centre console as described in Chapter 11, Section 27.

27 Carry out the operation described above in paragraphs 22 and 23.

28 If required, unclip the air vents from the top of the heater facia panel and release the retaining clips **(see illustrations)** to release the top of the panel.

29 Using a flat-bladed screwdriver, carefully unclip the heater control panel facia complete with control knobs from the heater control panel assembly **(see illustrations)**. Note the position of the heater control knobs for refitting.

30 The bulbs are of the capless (push-fit) type; pull the old bulb out of the holder, and press the new one into position **(see illustration)**.

31 Refitting is a reverse of the removal procedure.

Switch illumination bulbs

32 All of the switches are fitted with illuminating bulbs; some are also fitted with a bulb to show when the circuit concerned is operating. These bulbs are an integral part of the switch assembly, and cannot be obtained separately. Bulb replacement will therefore require the renewal of the complete switch assembly.

6.29b . . . and unclip the heater control facia, complete with the control knobs

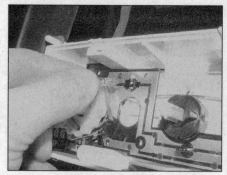

6.30 The capless bulbs can then be pulled from their holders

---

7 Exterior light units - removal and refitting

Note: *Disconnect the battery negative lead before removing any light unit, and reconnect the lead after refitting the light.*

Headlight

1 Open the bonnet, then slacken and remove the three retaining screws, and remove the plastic cover from the bonnet lock. Slacken the three retaining screws, and remove the radiator grille **(see illustration)**.

2 Remove the direction indicator light as described below.

3 Remove the plastic cover(s) from the rear of the headlight unit, and disconnect the wiring connectors from both the headlight and

sidelight bulbs (and, where fitted, from the headlight adjustment motor).

4 Using pliers, slide out the retaining clip from the top headlight mounting point (where fitted) **(see illustration)**.

5 Pull the headlight forwards, to release it from its two retaining spring clips, and remove the headlight from the vehicle **(see illustrations)**.

6 Refitting is a direct reversal of the removal procedure. On completion, check the headlight beam alignment, using the information given in Section 8.

Front direction indicator light

7 Open the bonnet, and from within the engine compartment, unhook the indicator light retaining spring from the vehicle body.

8 Withdraw the light unit from the front of the vehicle, and disconnect its wiring connector.

9 Refitting is the reverse of removal.

7.1 Radiator grille is retained by three screws (arrowed)

7.4 Using pliers remove the retaining clip from the top headlight mounting point

7.5a Pull the headlight forwards, to release it from its retaining spring clips . . .

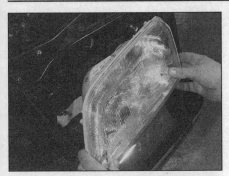

7.5b . . . and withdraw the headlight unit from the vehicle

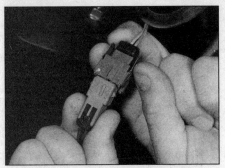

7.13 Disconnect the wiring connector . . .

7.14a . . . then slacken and remove the retaining nut . .

7.14b . . . and withdraw the foglight from the front of the bumper

7.17a Undo the retaining nut situated on the inside of the luggage compartment . . .

7.17b . . . then remove the rear light unit from the rear of the vehicle, and disconnect its wiring connector

Front direction side repeater light

10 Push the light unit towards the rear of the vehicle, to free its retaining clips, then withdraw it from the wing and disconnect its wiring connector.
11 On refitting, reconnect the wiring connector to the light, then clip it back into position on the wing.

Front foglight

12 Jack up the front of the vehicle, and support it on axle stands.
13 Trace the wiring back from the rear of the foglight, and disconnect it at the wiring connector (see illustration).
14 Slacken and remove the foglight retaining nut, and withdraw the light unit from the front of the bumper (see illustrations).
15 Refitting is the reverse of removal.

Rear light cluster

16 Remove the luggage compartment lower side trim panel as described in Chapter 11, Section 26.
17 Slacken and remove the rear light cluster retaining nut, then free the light cluster from the rear of the vehicle, and disconnect its wiring connector (see illustrations).
18 Refitting is a reversal of the removal procedure.

Rear foglight - Estate models

19 Ease a thin blade between the side of the light unit and its housing in the bumper to depress the light retaining clip. With the clip depressed, pull the light from position.
20 Refitting is a reversal of the removal

procedure. Ensure that the light is pushed fully back into position.

Number plate light

21 Raise the tailgate slightly to improve access to the light, then carefully prise out the light lens and disconnect its wiring connector.
22 On refitting, reconnect the wiring connector, and clip the light back into position.

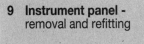

8 Headlight beam alignment - general information

1 Accurate adjustment of the headlight beam is only possible using optical beam-setting equipment, and this work should therefore be carried out by a Citroën dealer or suitably-equipped workshop.
2 For reference, the headlights can be adjusted using a suitable-sized Allen key to rotate the adjuster assemblies fitted to the top of each light unit. The outer adjuster alters the vertical height of the beam, whilst the inner adjuster alters the horizontal position of the beam. Prior to adjustment, ensure that the vehicle is unladen, and the adjuster units (see below) are both set to position "0".
3 Each headlight unit is equipped with a four-position adjuster unit - this can be used to adjust the headlight beam, to compensate for the relevant load which the vehicle is carrying. The adjuster units are incorporated into the vertical beam adjuster; access to them can be gained with the bonnet open. Position "0" is the standard position, positions "1" and "2"

for when the vehicle is partly-laden, and position "3" for when the vehicle is fully-laden. Ensure that both adjusters are set to the same position, and be sure to reset to position "0" once the load has been removed.

9 Instrument panel - removal and refitting

Removal

1 Disconnect the battery negative terminal.
2 Remove the steering wheel as described in Chapter 10.
3 Release the panel fasteners by rotating them through a quarter of a turn, and remove the driver's side lower facia panel. Release the heater duct, and remove it from behind the panel (see illustrations).

9.3a Remove the driver's side lower facia panel . . .

12

9.3b ... and remove the heater duct from behind the panel

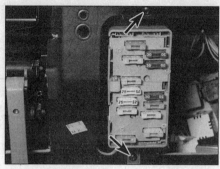

9.5 Fusebox retaining screws (arrowed)

9.6 Undo the two bonnet release lever retaining bolts, and free the lever from its bracket. Heater duct retaining screw is arrowed

9.7a Slacken and remove the instrument panel shroud retaining screws (arrowed) ...

9.7b ... then disconnect the switch wiring connectors and remove the shroud

9.9a Undo the retaining screws (arrowed) ...

4 Slacken and remove the five screws which secure the two halves of the steering column shrouds together, then remove both the upper and lower shroud. Release the steering column, and lock it in its lowest position.

9.9b ... then withdraw the instrument panel from the facia ...

5 Undo the two retaining screws, and free the fusebox from the facia panel **(see illustration)**.
6 Slacken and remove the two bolts securing the bonnet release lever to the facia, and free the release lever assembly from the facia. Undo the heater duct retaining screw, located directly beneath the bonnet release lever, then manoeuvre the heater duct out from the behind the facia **(see illustration)**.
7 Slacken and remove the four instrument panel shroud retaining screws, then remove the shroud, disconnecting the switch wiring connectors as they become accessible **(see illustrations)**.
8 Reaching in through the lower facia aperture, reach up behind the instrument panel, then depress the retaining tangs and detach the speedometer cable from the rear of the panel.
9 Undo the two lower retaining screws, then withdraw the instrument panel assembly from the facia. Disconnect the wiring connectors

from the rear of the panel, and remove the assembly from the vehicle **(see illustrations)**.

Refitting

10 Refitting is a reversal of the removal procedure. On completion, reconnect the battery and check the operation of all the panel warning lights and the instrument panel shroud switches, to ensure that they are functioning correctly.

10 Instrument panel components - removal and refitting

General

1 Remove the instrument panel as described in Section 9, then proceed as described under the relevant sub-heading.

Speedometer

2 Slacken and remove the three panel front cover retaining screws from the rear of the instrument panel. Carefully release the six retaining clips situated around the outside of the cover, then separate the cover and instrument panel **(see illustrations)**.
3 Undo the two retaining screws from the front of the speedometer face, then undo the two retaining bolts from the rear of the panel, and withdraw the speedometer **(see illustrations)**.
4 Refitting is a reverse of the removal procedure. Do not overtighten the instrument panel fasteners, as the plastic is easily cracked.

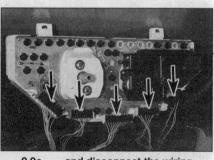

9.9c ... and disconnect the wiring connectors (arrowed) from the rear of the panel

10.2a Slacken and remove the three instrument panel cover retaining screws (arrowed) ...

10.2b ... then release the retaining clips, and separate the panel and cover

10.3a Instrument panel component front fasteners

A Speedometer screws
B Tachometer screws
C Temperature gauge screw
D Fuel gauge screw

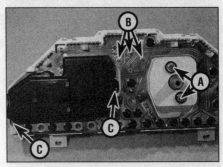

10.3b Instrument panel component rear fasteners

A Speedometer bolts   C Rear cover screws
B Fuel gauge nuts

Tachometer

5 Remove the panel front cover as described in paragraph 2.
6 Undo the two screws and remove the cover from the rear of panel, disconnecting its wiring connector as it becomes accessible **(see illustration)**.
7 Undo the four retaining nuts, and remove the circuit board from the rear of the tachometer **(see illustration)**.
8 Slacken and remove the three screws from the front face of the tachometer, and remove the tachometer from the case.
9 Refitting is a reverse of the removal procedure. Do not overtighten the instrument panel fasteners, as the plastic is easily cracked.

Temperature gauge

10 Remove the front cover and the rear cover, as described in paragraphs 2 and 6.
11 Undo the three retaining nuts from the

rear, and the single screw from the front, of the temperature gauge, and withdraw the gauge from the case **(see illustration)**.
12 Refitting is a reverse of the removal procedure. Do not overtighten the instrument panel fasteners, as the plastic is easily cracked.

Fuel gauge

13 Remove the front cover as described in paragraph 2.
14 Slacken and remove the three nuts from the rear, and undo the single retaining screw from the front face of the gauge, and withdraw the gauge from the case.
15 Refitting is a reverse of the removal procedure. Do not overtighten the instrument panel fasteners, as the plastic is easily cracked.

Printed circuit

16 Remove all the panel instruments as described above.
17 Remove all the bulbholders from the rear of the case, by twisting them in an anti-clockwise direction. Slacken and remove all the circuit retaining screws, then release the printed circuit from its retaining pins, and remove it from the rear of the case.
18 Refitting is a reversal of the removal procedure, ensuring that the printed circuit is correctly located on all the necessary retaining pins.

11 Clock - removal and refitting

Removal

1 Disconnect the battery negative terminal.
2 Using a flat-bladed screwdriver, carefully prise the clock out of the facia panel, taking great care not mark the clock or facia **(see illustration)**.
3 Disconnect the wiring connector, and remove the clock **(see illustration)**.

Refitting

4 Reconnect the wiring connector, then clip the clock into the position in the facia.
5 Reconnect the battery negative terminal, then reset the clock.

10.6 Instrument panel rear cover wiring connector

10.7 Tachometer rear retaining nuts and printed circuit board

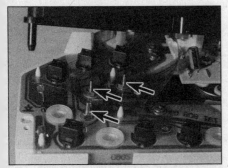

10.11 Temperature gauge retaining nuts (arrowed)

11.2 Carefully prise the clock out of the facia (note the use of padding under the screwdriver, to avoid damage) ...

11.3 ... and disconnect its wiring connector

12

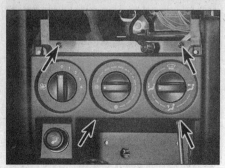

13.3a Undo the four retaining screws (arrowed) . . .

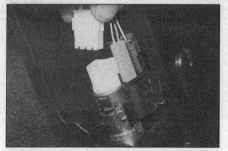

13.3b . . . then withdraw the centre vent panel, disconnecting the wiring connectors from the cigarette lighter

13.4a Release the retaining tangs, then withdraw the metal insert . . .

13.4b . . . followed by the plastic outer section of the cigarette lighter

12 Door-open warning display - general information

Some models covered in this manual are equipped with a door-open warning display in the instrument panel. If a door is not correctly shut, the relevant door on the warning panel will be illuminated.

The system consists of switches which are built into the door lock assemblies and the panel in the instrument cluster. The panel bulbs are the same as the other instrument panel bulbs, and can be renewed as described in Section 6. The switches are an integral part of each door lock assembly.

13 Cigarette lighter - removal and refitting

Removal

1 Remove the centre console as described in Chapter 11.
2 Where a radio/cassette player is fitted, remove it as described in Section 21, then undo the two retaining screws and remove the mounting bracket from the radio aperture. Where no radio/cassette player is fitted, carefully prise out the storage box from the centre of the facia panel.
3 Undo the four centre vent panel retaining screws (two located above the heater controls, and two directly below), then unclip

the panel and withdraw it from the facia. Disconnect the wiring connectors from the cigarette lighter and ashtray illumination bulb, and remove the centre vent panel assembly from the vehicle (see illustrations).
4 Remove the lighter element, release the retaining tangs and push out the metal insert, then remove the plastic outer section of the lighter (see illustrations).

Refitting

5 Refitting is a reversal of the removal procedure.

14 "Lights-on" warning system - general information

1 Most vehicles covered in this manual are equipped with a "lights-on" warning system. The purpose of the system is to inform the driver that the lights have been left on once the ignition switch has been turned off; the buzzer will sound when a door is opened. The system consists of a buzzer unit which is linked to the door courtesy light switches.
2 To gain access to the buzzer unit, release the three fasteners by rotating them through 90°, then remove the driver's side lower facia panel. The buzzer unit is situated in the relay panel located directly behind the fusebox. The buzzer unit is a push-fit in the panel, and can easily be identified by the slots in its cover (see illustration).
3 Refer to Section 4 for information on courtesy light switch removal.

15 Horn - removal and refitting

Removal

1 Jack up the front of the vehicle, and support it on axle stands.

Electric horn

2 Undo the nut securing the horn to its mounting bracket, then lower the horn out of position, and disconnect it from its wiring connector.

Air horn

3 Slacken and remove the nut and bolt securing the horn mounting bracket to the vehicle body, then remove the horn, disconnecting it from its air supply pipe (see illustrations).

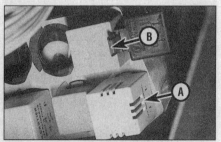

14.2 "Lights-on" warning buzzer (A) is situated behind the main fusebox

B   Flasher relay

15.3a Slacken and remove the retaining nut and bolt (arrowed) . . .

15.3b . . . then remove the horn, disconnecting it from its supply pipe

15.4a Disconnect the wiring connector . . .

15.4b . . . then undo the retaining nut and remove the air compressor

16.4 Unscrew the knurled retaining ring, and separate the upper and lower speedometer cable sections

4 Disconnect the wiring connector from the air compressor, then undo the retaining nut and withdraw the compressor from underneath the vehicle **(see illustrations)**. Recover the spacer from the compressor mounting bolt.

Refitting

5 Refitting is a reverse of the removal procedure.

16 Speedometer drive cable - removal and refitting

General

1 The drive cable is in two parts; the lower cable runs from the transmission to a point just in front of the left-hand end of the bulkhead, while the upper cable runs from that point to the rear of the instrument panel. Each section can be removed individually, as follows.

Upper cable

Removal

2 On left-hand-drive models, remove the instrument panel as described in Section 9.
3 On right-hand-drive models, remove the complete facia assembly (see Chapter 11).
4 Working in the engine compartment, slacken the knurled retaining ring, and separate the upper and lower cable sections **(see illustration)**. Tie a length of string to the end of the upper section of the cable.
5 From inside the vehicle, withdraw the cable from the bulkhead. Once the cable is free,

untie the string and leave it in position in the vehicle; the string can then be used to draw the new cable back into position.

Refitting

6 Tie the inner end of the string to the end of the cable, then use the string to draw the speedometer cable through into the engine compartment. Once the cable is through, untie the string.
7 On left-hand-drive models, position the cable so that approximately 145 mm of the cable protrudes into the engine compartment, then connect the end of the cable to the lower cable section, and securely tighten the retaining ring. Refit the instrument panel as described in Section 9.
8 On right-hand-drive models, position the cable so that approximately 100 mm of the cable protrudes into the engine compartment, then connect the end of the cable to the lower cable section, and securely tighten the retaining ring. Refit the facia assembly as described in Chapter 11.

Lower cable

Removal

9 Apply the handbrake, then jack up the front of the vehicle and support it on axle stands.
10 Working from underneath the vehicle, withdraw the rubber retaining pin, and detach the cable from the speedometer drive on the transmission.
11 Working in the engine compartment, slacken the knurled retaining ring, then detach the lower cable section from the upper section, and remove it from the vehicle.

Refitting

12 Examine the O-rings fitted to the cable lower-end fitting for signs of damage or deterioration, and renew if necessary. Apply a smear of clean engine oil to the O-rings, to aid installation.
13 Attach the lower cable to the upper cable, and securely tighten the retaining ring.
14 Ensuring that the cable is correctly routed, slide the lower end of the cable into position in the speedometer drive, and secure it in position with the rubber retaining pin. Lower the vehicle to the ground.

17 Wiper arm - removal and refitting

Removal

1 Operate the wiper motor, then switch it off so that the wiper arm returns to the at-rest position.

 HAYNES HiNT *Stick a piece of masking tape along the edge of the wiper blade, to use as an alignment aid on refitting.*

2 Lift up the wiper arm spindle nut cover, then slacken and remove the spindle nut. Lift the blade off the glass, and pull the wiper arm off its spindle **(see illustrations)**. If necessary, the arm can be levered off the spindle using a suitable flat-bladed screwdriver.

Refitting

3 Ensure that the wiper arm and spindle splines are clean and dry, then refit the arm to the spindle, aligning the wiper blade with the tape fitted on removal. Refit the spindle nut, tightening it securely, and clip the nut cover back in position.

18 Windscreen wiper motor and linkage - removal and refitting

12

17.2a Raise the spindle cover, then undo the retaining nut . . .

17.2b . . . and remove the wiper arm from the spindle

Removal

1 Disconnect the battery negative terminal.

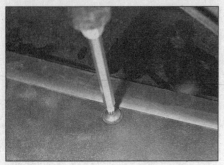

18.3a Undo the six retaining screws . . .

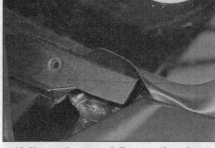

18.3b . . . then carefully ease the wiper motor/vent panel cover out from behind the windscreen sealing strip

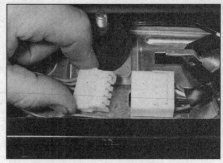

18.4 Disconnect the wiper motor wiring connector . . .

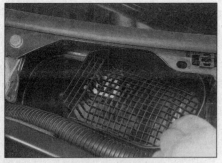

18.5 . . . and remove the plastic cover from the blower motor intake duct

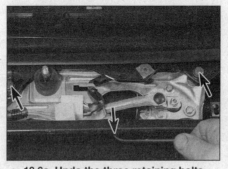

18.6a Undo the three retaining bolts (arrowed) . . .

18.6b . . . then remove the wiper motor from the vehicle

2 Remove the wiper arm as described in the previous Section.

3 Open the bonnet, and slacken and remove the six wiper motor cover/vent panel retaining screws. Carefully ease the cover out from behind the windscreen sealing strip, then disengage its front locating pegs, and manoeuvre the panel away from the vehicle **(see illustrations)**.

4 Disconnect the wiring connector from the front of the wiper motor **(see illustration)**.

5 Remove the plastic cover from the heater blower motor intake passage **(see illustration)**.

6 Undo the three wiper motor retaining bolts, then manoeuvre the wiper motor out of position, and remove it from the vehicle **(see illustrations)**.

7 If necessary, using a suitable flat-bladed screwdriver, carefully lever the wiper linkage off the motor spindle balljoint. Slacken and remove the three motor retaining bolts, and

separate the motor and linkage **(see illustration)**.

Refitting

8 Where necessary, assemble the motor and linkage, and securely tighten the motor retaining bolts. Clip the linkage onto the spindle balljoint, and check that it is securely retained.

9 Manoeuvre the motor assembly back into position, and refit the three retaining bolts, tightening them securely.

10 Reconnect the wiring connector to the motor, and refit the cover to the blower motor intake passage.

11 Manoeuvre the wiper motor/vent cover back into position, and engage its front locating pegs with their mounting rubbers **(see illustration)**. Starting at the centre and working outwards, carefully ease the top edge of the cover behind the windscreen sealing strip. Once the cover is correctly seated

behind the strip, secure it in position with its six retaining screws.

12 Refit the wiper arm as described in Section 17, and reconnect the battery negative terminal.

19 Tailgate wiper motor - removal and refitting

Removal

1 Remove the wiper arm as described in Section 17.

2 Unscrew the knurled retaining ring from the wiper spindle, and lift off the trim cover **(see illustrations)**.

3 Open up the tailgate. On Hatchback models, release the fasteners by rotating them through a quarter of a turn and remove the wiper motor cover from the centre of the

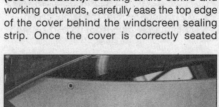

18.11 On refitting, ensure the wiper motor/vent cover locating pegs (arrowed) are correctly located

19.2a Unscrew the knurled retaining ring . . .

18.7 Windscreen wiper motor retaining bolts (arrowed)

Body electrical systems 12•17

tailgate **(see illustration)**. On Estate models, remove the tailgate inner trim panel complete.
4 Undo the three wiper motor retaining bolts, then withdraw the motor from the tailgate, disconnecting its wiring connectors as they become accessible **(see illustrations)**.

Refitting

5 Refitting is a reverse of the removal procedure. Ensure that the tailgate central locking servo motor (where fitted) is correctly engaged with the lock pin, prior to refitting the wiper motor retaining bolts.

20 Windscreen/tailgate washer system components - removal and refitting

Washer system reservoir

Note: *To minimise fluid spillage, it is recommended that the washer reservoir is at least half-empty prior to removal.*

1 Jack up the front of the vehicle, and support it on axle stands. Remove the right-hand front roadwheel.
2 Open the bonnet, and disconnect the windscreen washer supply pipe from its non-return valve, situated on the right-hand side of the bonnet **(see illustration)**.
3 Undo the retaining screw from the front edge of the wheel arch liner, then work around the liner carefully, prising out all its retaining clips, and remove the right-hand wheel arch liner and access cover from the vehicle **(see illustration)**.
4 Push the front direction indicator repeater light unit towards the rear of the vehicle, to free its retaining clips, then withdraw it from the wing.
5 Reach up behind the wing, and disconnect the wiring connector(s) from the washer pump(s).
6 Slacken and remove the two reservoir retaining bolts, then pull the top of the reservoir outwards, to release it from the reservoir filler neck **(see illustrations)**. Lower the reservoir out from underneath the wing, disconnecting the supply pipe(s) from the washer pump(s) as they become accessible.
7 Refitting is the reverse of removal, ensuring that the reservoir is correctly engaged with its filler neck.

19.2b . . . and remove the trim cover from the tailgate wiper motor spindle

19.4a Slacken and remove the three retaining bolts (arrowed) . . .

Washer pump(s)

Note: *Prior to removing the pump(s), empty the contents of the reservoir, or be prepared for fluid spillage.*

8 Jack up the front of the vehicle, and support it on axle stands. Remove the right-hand front roadwheel.

20.2 Disconnecting the windscreen washer supply pipe from its non-return valve

19.3 Removing the wiper motor cover from the rear of the tailgate

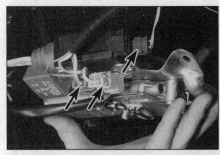

19.4b . . . then withdraw the motor, disconnecting the wiring connectors (arrowed) as they become accessible

9 Remove the wheel arch liner as described in paragraph 3.
10 Disconnect the wiring connector from the relevant pump, then carefully ease the pump out of its sealing grommet, and manoeuvre it out from behind the wing **(see illustrations)**. If necessary, to improve access to the pump,

20.3 Removing the right-hand wheel arch liner

20.6a Undo the two retaining bolts (arrowed) . . .

20.6b . . . and lower the washer reservoir out from behind the wing

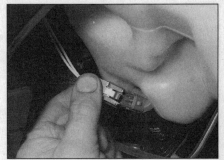

20.10a Disconnect the wiring connector . . .

12

20.10b . . . then ease the washer pump out from the reservoir

21.3a . . . and undo the two radio/cassette unit retaining screws

21.2 Remove the rubber plugs . . .

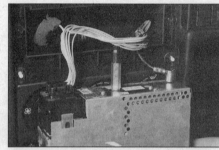

21.3b Slide the radio/cassette unit out of position, and disconnect the aerial connection and wiring connectors

undo the mounting bolts, and lower the reservoir slightly. Note that, on models with a dual pump arrangement, the upper pump is tailgate washer pump, and the lower one is the windscreen washer pump.
11 Refitting is a reversal of the removal procedure.

Windscreen washer jet

12 Open the bonnet, then unclip the washer jet from the underside of the bonnet, and disconnect it from its supply pipe.
13 On refitting, ensure that the jet is clipped securely in position. If necessary, the jet nozzles can be adjusted using a pin; aim the spray to a point slightly above the centre of the wiper swept area.

Tailgate washer jet

14 Carefully prise the washer jet out of the top of the tailgate, and disconnect it from its supply pipe. Whilst the jet is removed, tape

the supply pipe in position, to ensure that it does not fall back into the tailgate.
15 On refitting, ensure that the jet is clipped securely in position. If necessary, the jet nozzle can be adjusted using a pin; aim the spray to the centre of the wiper swept area.

Non-return valves

16 If trouble is experienced at any time with the flow to the tailgate or windscreen washer jets, check that the relevant non-return valve is not blocked. The windscreen washer valve is situated in the supply pipe, next to the right-hand bonnet hinge; the tailgate washer valve is situated at the rear of the vehicle, tucked away underneath the top of the tailgate sealing strip.
17 To remove a non-return valve, simply disconnect the hoses from either end of it.
18 On refitting, ensure that the valve is installed the correct way around, so that it allows fluid to flow only in the direction of the washer jet(s).

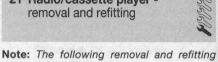

21 Radio/cassette player - removal and refitting

Note: *The following removal and refitting procedure is for the range of radio/cassette units which Citroën fit as standard equipment. Removal and refitting procedures for non-standard units may differ slightly.*

Removal

1 Disconnect the battery negative terminal.
2 Remove the two rubber plugs from the front of the unit, to gain access to the radio/cassette unit retaining screws (see illustration).
3 Undo the retaining screws, then withdraw the unit from the facia, and disconnect the wiring connectors and aerial from the rear of the unit (see illustrations).

Refitting

4 Refitting is the reverse of the removal procedure. On completion, reconnect the battery, and enter the radio security code using the information given in *"Radio/cassette unit anti-theft system"* at the start of this manual.

22 Loudspeakers - removal and refitting

Removal

1 The front speakers are located in the front door trim panels, in front of the door pull handles. On five-door models, the rear speakers are located at the bottom of the rear door trim panel; the rear speakers on three-door models are located in the rear seat side trim panels.
2 Carefully prise the speaker grille out from the trim panel (see illustration).
3 Slacken and remove the speaker retaining screws and, on the front speaker, remove the retaining clip from the mounting peg. Withdraw the speaker from the panel, disconnecting its wiring connector as it becomes accessible (see illustrations).

22.2 Remove the grille to gain access to the relevant speaker

22.3a Front speakers are retained by three screws and a retaining clip (arrowed)

22.3b Rear speakers are retained by four retaining screws

22.3c Remove the speaker from the panel, and disconnect it from its wiring connector

23.1a Undo the two retaining screws (arrowed) . . .

23.1b . . . then lower out the overhead console, and disconnect it from its wiring connectors

Refitting

4 Refitting is a reverse of the removal procedure.

23 Radio aerial - removal and refitting

Removal

Aerial

1 Carefully prise the courtesy light out from the overhead console, and disconnect it from its wiring connector. Remove the two console retaining screws, then lower the console out of position, and disconnect it from its wiring connectors (see illustrations).
2 Slacken and remove the nut from the base of the aerial, and disengage the aerial lead collar from its stud. The aerial can then be lifted away from the outside of the vehicle, noting the rubber seal which is fitted to its base (see illustrations).

Aerial lead upper section

3 Remove the aerial as described above.
4 Unclip the trim panel from the right-hand windscreen pillar, to gain access to the aerial connection (see illustration). Where necessary, release the alarm sensors from the clip on the top of the panel, and remove the panel. If the aerial connection is not situated behind the right-hand trim panel, remove the left-hand panel.
5 Disconnect the upper section of the lead, and tie a piece of string to it. Withdraw the aerial

lead through the overhead console aperture, and untie the string from its end. Leave the string in position - it can then be used to draw the lead back into position on refitting.

Aerial lead lower section

6 To remove the lower section of the aerial lead, linking the upper section to the rear of the radio/cassette unit, it is first necessary to remove the facia panel as described in Chapter 11. The lead can then be freed from all its relevant retaining clips, and removed from the vehicle.

Refitting

Aerial

7 Ensure that the rubber seal is in good condition, then refit it to the aerial base. Refit the aerial to the roof, ensuring that its locating pin is correctly located in its hole.
8 From inside the vehicle, locate the aerial lead collar on the aerial stud, and refit the retaining nut, tightening it securely.
9 Reconnect the wiring connectors to the overhead console, and locate the console in position in the headlining. Refit the two console retaining screws, and tighten them securely. Reconnect the courtesy light to its wiring connector, and clip the light back into position in the console.

Aerial lead upper section

10 Tie the string to the end of the aerial lead, and use the string to draw the lead back into position. Untie the string, and reconnect the lead to the lower aerial section.
11 Where necessary, ensure that the alarm

sensor wire is correctly routed, and refit the sensor to its retaining clip. Clip the panel back into position, ensuring that the pegs on the base of the panel are correctly located in the facia panel.
12 Refit the aerial as described above.

Aerial lead lower section

13 Refitting is a reversal of the removal procedure.

24 Anti-theft alarm system - general information

Note: *This information is applicable only to the anti-theft alarm system fitted by Citroën as standard equipment.*

Some models in the range are fitted with an anti-theft alarm system as standard equipment. The alarm is automatically armed and disarmed when the door locks are operated using the remote central locking transmitter.

Note that if the doors are operated using the key, the alarm will not be armed or disarmed (as applicable). If for some reason the remote central locking transmitter fails whilst the alarm is armed, the alarm can be disarmed using the key. To do this, open the door with the key, then enter the vehicle, noting that the alarm will sound as the door is opened, and switch on the ignition switch whilst depressing the small button on the alarm switch mounted in the facia. Note that the ignition switch must be turned on and the button depressed within 10 seconds of opening the door.

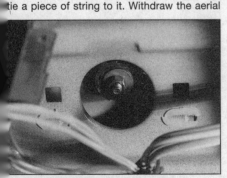

23.2a Undo the aerial lead retaining nut from inside the vehicle . . .

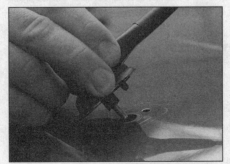

23.2b . . . then remove the aerial from the roof of the vehicle

23.4 Aerial lead upper-to-lower section connection is located behind the windscreen pillar trim panel

The alarm system has switches on the bonnet, tailgate and each of the doors. It also has ultrasonic sensing, which detects movement inside the vehicle, via the sensors mounted on the top of each windscreen pillar trim panel. If required, the ultrasonic sensing facility of the system can be switched off, whilst retaining the switched side of the system. To switch off the ultrasonic sensing, with the ignition switch off, depress the alarm switch on the facia for approximately 1 second, until the switch LED is continuously lit. Now, when the doors are locked using the remote central locking transmitter, and the alarm is armed, only the switched side of the alarm system is operational. This facility is useful, as it allows you to leave the windows/sunroof open, and still arm the alarm. If the windows/sunroof are left open with the ultrasonic sensing not switched off, the alarm may be falsely triggered by a gust of wind.

Should the alarm system become faulty, the vehicle should be taken to a Citroën dealer for examination.

25 "Dim-dip" lighting system (UK models only) - general information

1 To comply with UK regulations, a "dim-dip" lighting system is fitted to all UK models. The system is operates through a dim-dip relay, and a resistor unit situated at the front left-hand corner of the vehicle, above the horn assembly.
2 The dim-dip relay is supplied with current from the sidelight circuit, and energised by a feed from the ignition switch. When energised, the unit allows battery voltage to pass through the resistor unit to the headlight dipped-beam circuits; this lights the headlights with approximately one-sixth of their normal power, so that the car cannot be driven using sidelights alone.

26 Air bag system - general information, precautions and system de-activation

General information

Where fitted, the driver's side air bag is located in the steering wheel centre pad.

The air bag system is armed only when the ignition is switched on. However, a reserve power source maintains a power supply to the system in the event of a break in the main electrical supply. The system is activated by a "g" sensor (deceleration sensor) and is controlled by an electronic control unit which is integral with the steering wheel.

The air bag is inflated by a gas generator, which forces the bag out from its location in the steering wheel.

Precautions

 Warning: The following precautions must be observed when working on vehicles equipped with an air bag system, to prevent the possibility of personal injury.

General

The following precautions **must** be observed when carrying out work on a vehicle equipped with an air bag:
(a) Do not disconnect the battery with the engine running.
(b) Before carrying out any work in the vicinity of the air bag, removal of any of the air bag components, or any welding work on the vehicle, de-activate the system as described in the following sub-Section.
(c) Do not attempt to test any of the air bag system circuits using test meters or any other test equipment.
(d) If the air bag warning light comes on, or any fault in the system is suspected, consult a Citroën dealer without delay. **Do not** attempt to carry out fault diagnosis, or any dismantling of the components.

Handling the air bag unit

(a) Transport the unit by itself, bag upward.
(b) Do not put your arms around the unit.
(c) Carry the unit close to the body, bag outward.
(d) Do not drop the unit or expose it to impacts.
(e) Do not attempt to dismantle the unit.
(f) Do not connect any form of electrical equipment to any part of the air bag circuit.

Storing the air bag unit

(a) Store the unit in a cupboard with the air bag upward.
(b) Do not expose the unit to temperatures above 80°C.
(c) Do not expose the unit to naked flames.
(d) Do not attempt to dispose of the unit - consult a Citroën dealer.
(e) Never refit a unit which is known to be faulty or damaged.

De-activation of air bag system

The system must be de-activated before carrying out any work on the air bag components or surrounding area:
(a) Switch off the ignition.
(b) Remove the ignition key.
(c) Switch off all electrical equipment.
(d) Disconnect the battery negative lead.
(e) Insulate the battery negative terminal and the end of the battery negative lead to prevent any possibility of contact.
(f) Wait for at least ten minutes before carrying out any further work.

Activation of air bag system

To activate the system on completion of any work, proceed as follows:

(a) Ensure that the vehicle is unoccupied and that there are no loose objects around the vicinity of the steering wheel. Close the vehicle doors and windows.
(b) Ensure that the ignition is switched off, then reconnect the battery negative lead.
(c) Open the driver's door and switch on the ignition without reaching in front of the steering wheel. Check that the air bag warning light in the steering wheel illuminates for approximately 3 seconds and then extinguishes.
(d) Switch off the ignition.
(e) If the air bag warning light does not operate as described in paragraph (c), consult a Citroën dealer before driving the vehicle.

27 Air bag system components - removal and refitting

 Warning: Refer to the precautions given in Section 26 before attempting to carry out work on any of the air bag components.

General

1 The air bag system comprises the following.
(a) Air bag unit
(b) Warning light
(c) Firing unit
(d) Rotary switch
(e) Vehicle wiring and sensor
2 Any suspected faults with the system components should be referred to a Citroën dealer. Under no circumstances attempt to carry out any work other than removal and refitting of the air bag unit and/or the rotary switch, as described in the following paragraphs.

Firing unit

3 The air bag firing unit is integral with the steering wheel and cannot be removed independently. Refer to Chapter 10 for details of steering wheel removal.

Air bag unit

Removal

4 The air bag unit is an integral part of the steering wheel centre boss.
5 De-activate the air bag system as described in Section 26.
6 Move the steering wheel as necessary for access to the two air bag unit securing screws. The screws are located at the rear of the steering wheel boss.
7 Remove the two air bag unit securing screws (see illustration).
8 Unclip one edge of the air bag unit from the centre of the steering wheel and pivot away from the wheel, but do not pull it completely clear.

27.7 Removing an air bag unit securing screw

27.9 The air bag unit wiring connector (arrowed)

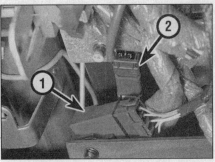

27.14 Disconnect the radio/cassette player remote control (1) and air bag unit (2) wiring connectors

9 Carefully disconnect the wiring connector from the rear of the unit, then withdraw the unit from the steering wheel **(see illustration)**.

10 If the air bag unit is to be stored for any length of time, refer to the storage precautions given in Section 26.

Refitting

11 Refitting is a reversal of removal, bearing in mind the following points:

(a) Do not strike the air bag unit, or expose it to impacts during refitting.

(b) On completion of refitting, activate the air bag system as described in Section 26.

Rotary switch

Removal

12 Remove the air bag unit as described previously in this Section.

13 Remove the steering wheel and steering column shrouds.

14 Locate the two rotary switch wiring connectors beneath the steering column, and separate the two halves of each connector **(see illustration)**.

15 Remove the switch securing clip by using a screwdriver. Alternatively, remove the two switch securing screws. Pull the unit from the steering column **(see illustrations)**.

16 Feed the wiring harnesses up through the housing (if necessary remove the right-hand stalk switch to allow the wiring to pass through the housing).

Refitting

17 Refitting is a reversal of removal. Refit the steering wheel with reference to Chapter 10 and refit the air bag unit as described previously in this Section.

28 Wiring diagrams - explanatory notes

The wiring diagrams in this manual represent typical examples of those available. To assist you in using the diagrams, here is an explanation of the various letters and their use, in conjunction with the wiring diagram keys **(see illustration)**.

(a) **Large numbers** - identify the various components.

(b) **Capital letters printed in the middle of a wire** - indicate which harness the wire is located in.

(c) **Small letters located at the connection points** - indicates the colour of either the wire itself, or of the marking on the wire. If the letter has a line drawn above it, then this shows it indicates the colour of the wire itself; if there is no line above the letter, it indicates the colour of the marking on the wire.

(d) **Connecting blocks** - the first number and letter(s) inside the box indicates the size and colour of the connecting block. The second letter (where applicable) and last number gives the exact location of the relevant wire in that connecting block; the letter indicates which row the wire is situated in, and the number denotes its location in that row. For example:

3 Bl 2 - shows that the wiring connector is blue in colour, and contains three wiring channels, the wire shown in the diagram being located in the second channel of the connector.

15 V A 2 - shows that the wiring connector is green in colour, and contains fifteen channels. The A shows that the wire shown in the diagram is in the upper row of the connector, and the 2 shows it to be in the second channel of that row.

27.15a Remove the rotary switch securing clip . . .

27.15b . . . and pull the switch from the steering column

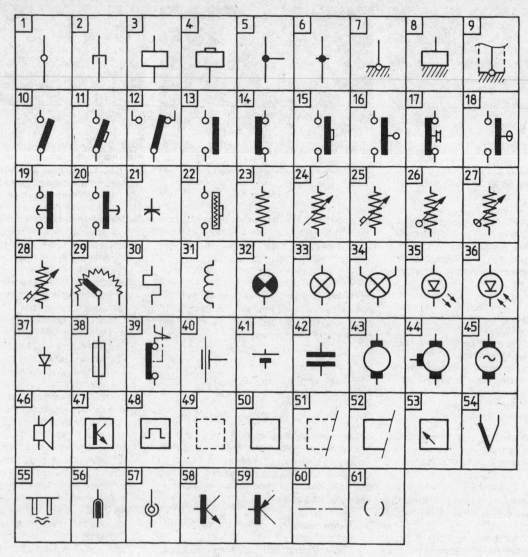

Symbols used in wiring diagrams

No.	Description	No.	Description	No.	Description
1	Socket connection	21	Friction contact switch	42	Suppressor
2	Pin connection	22	Manual contact switch (cigar lighter)	43	Motor
3	Connector connection		with resistance	44	Two-speed motor
4	Connector connection with index (for	23	Resistance	45	Alternative power generator
	differentiation)	24	Rheostat	46	Sound equipment (horn, loudspeaker)
5	Junction not to be dismantled (splice)	25	Manual rheostat	47	Electronic control unit
6	Junction not to be dismantled (with	26	Mechanical rheostat	48	Delay unit
	other connection possibilities)	27	Temperature rheostat (thermistor)	49	Part framing (with its circuit diagram)
7	Socket earthing	28	Pressure rheostat	50	Part framing (without its circuit
8	Connector earthing	29	Rheostat		diagram)
9	Part body earth connection	30	Shunt	51	Part extract
10	Switch (non-automatic return)	31	Coil (relay-solenoid)	52	Part extract
11	Manual switch	32	Warning light	53	Indicator
12	Selector switch	33	Light bulb	54	Thermocouple
13	Switch on at-rest (automatic return)	34	Double-filament light bulb	55	Electrodes
14	Swithc off at-rest (automatic return)	35	Light-emitting diode (LED)	56	Oxygen sensor
15	Manual contact switch	36	Photo-diode	57	Supply socket
16	Mechanical contact switch	37	Diode	58	NPN transistor
17	Pressure contact switch	38	Fuse	59	PNP transistor
18	Thermal switch	39	Thermal circuit breaker	60	Connection indicating line
19	Contact delayed on opening	40	Screening	61	No extremity
20	Contact delayed on closing	41	Battery cell		

Key to wiring diagrams

Not all items fitted to all models

No.	Description	No.	Description	No.	Description
5	Front cigar lighter	429	Fuel cut-off solenoid (stop solenoid)	715	LH headlight adjustment device motor
10	Ignition distributor	430	Canister discharge solenoid	716	RH headlight adjustment device motor
15	Alternator	431	Fast idling solenoid	720	Engine cooling fan (single, or LH of two)
20	LH horn	432	Idling actuator		
21	RH horn	434	Canister solenoid	721	RH engine cooling fan
35	Battery	437	Exhaust gas recirculation solenoid	742	Central interior light
40	Instrument cluster	441	Vacuum advance solenoid	743	Rear interior light
45	Ignition coil	443	Injection timing correction solenoid	750	LH front brake pads sensor
50	Supply connector box	480	LH rear light	751	RH front brake pads sensor
52	Junction box	481	RH rear light	755	Fuel pump
53	Water temperature control unit	482	LH front foglight	757	Windscreen washer pump
55	Central door locking control unit	483	RH front foglight	758	Rear screen washer pump
58	Remote control door locking receiver (PLIP)	484	LH rear foglight	765	Radio set
		485	RH rear foglight	770	Throttle spindle potentiometer
59	Pre-heater (glow plugs) control unit	486	LH dipped beams	772	Mixture adjustment potentiometer
62	Earth connection box	487	RH dipped beams	775	Pressure switch
100	Spark plugs	488	LH front direction indicator	779	TDC sensor plug (petrol) or Water temp. sensor (Diesel)
101	Glow plugs	489	RH front direction indicator		
130	Lights-on warning buzzer	490	LH rear direction indicator	781	ABS diagnostic socket
140	Anti-lock braking ECU	491	RH rear direction indicator	783	Injection diagnostic socket
141	Air conditioning ECU	492	LH sidelight	786	Headlight: LH main and dipped beams
142	Fuel injection ECU	493	RH sidelight	787	Headlight: RH main and dipped beams
144	Exhaust gas recirculation ECU	496	LH tail light	790	Air blower motor
152	Engine speed sensor	497	RH tail light	798	Injection timing cut-off relay
155	LH front wheel sensor (ABS)	498	LH reversing light	804	Air conditioning relay
156	RH front wheel sensor (ABS)	499	RH reversing light	805	Compressor cut-off relay (temperature)
157	LH rear wheel sensor (ABS)	500	LH direction indicator repeater	806	Front foglight relays
158	RH rear wheel sensor (ABS)	501	RH direction indicator repeater	807	Injection double relay
160	TDC sensor	502	LH headlight	809	Front window relay
170	Flasher unit	503	RH headlight	813	Engine cooling fan relay (fast speed)
180	Additional air control	504	LH stop-light	814	Engine cooling fan relay (slow speed)
183	Air blower control	505	RH stop-light	815	Engine cooling fan speed switchover relay
211	LH column switch (lights, indicators, horn)	550	LH front speaker		
		551	RH front speaker	819	Rear foglight relays
212	RH column switch (front and rear wipers)	554	LH rear speaker	820	Heated rear window relay
		555	RH rear speaker	822	Compressor cut-off relay (injection)
215	Exterior mirror switch	570	Injector	827	Dim-dip relay (UK only)
254	Air horn compressor	582	Refrigerated air switch	841	Window re-energising relay
255	Air con. compressor driving clutch	587	Front foglight switch	843	Air horn compressor relay
270	HT coil suppressor	588	Rear foglight switch	844	ABS main relay
300	Ignition switch	589	Hazard warning light switch	845	Hydraulic fluid motor relay
302	Boot light switch	590	Driver's window switch	849	Post-heating cut-off relay
305	Driver's door locking switch	591	Passenger's window switch (on driver's door)	857	Carburettor base heating resistance
306	Passenger's door locking switch			858	Dipped beams resistance (dim-dip)
307	LH rear door closing switch	592	Passenger's window switch (on passenger's door)	859	Air blower speed resistor
308	RH rear door closing switch			860	Coding resistance
310	LH front door pillar switch	597	Heated rear window switch	862	Injector additional resistance
311	RH front door pillar switch	608	Headlight adjustment device switch	876	RH rear view mirror
312	LH rear door pillar switch	650	Fuel gauge	880	Instrument lighting rheostat
313	RH rear door pillar switch	660	Map reading light	900	Oxygen sensor
314	Reversing light switch	671	Engine oil pressure switch	902	Engine oil level sensor
315	Handbrake switch	680	Ignition module	903	Injection air pressure sensor
317	Hydraulic fluid level switch	681	Air blower control module	904	Engine oil pressure sensor
318	Throttle butterfly switch	685	Digital clock	907	Injection air temperature sensor
319	Stop-light switch	694	Windscreen wiper motor	909	Injection water temperature sensor
322	Atmospheric pressure switch	695	Tailgate wiper motor	910	Water temp. sensor (control unit)
326	Starter motor switch	696	LH front window motor	912	Evaporator temperature sensor
330	Post-heater switch	697	RH front window motor	915	Water temperature switch sensor
340	Airflow meter	703	Driver's door locking motor	918	Engine oil temperature sensor
350	Starter motor	704	Passenger's door locking motor	962	Windscreen intermittent wipe timer
385	Front ashtray illumination	705	LH rear door locking motor	963	Tailgate intermittent wipe timer
389	Boot light	706	RH rear door locking motor	970	Coolant temp. warning thermal switch
391	Number plate LH light	708	Tailgate locking motor	971	Cooling fan thermal switch (radiator)
392	Number plate RH light	712	Idling control stepper motor	974	Water temperature switch
394	Air con. control illumination	714	ABS hydraulic pump motor	990	Heated rear window

12

Harness code

AB	ABS	PG	LH rear door
AV	Front	PJ	Headlight adjustment device
CL	Air conditioning	PL	Interior light
CN	Negative cable	PP	Passenger's door
CP	Positive cable	RD	RH rear
EF	Boot lighting	RG	LH rear
FR	Rear lights	RL	Direction indicator side repeater
HB	Interior	TJ	Headlight adjustment device switch
MT	Engine (and injection)	UD	RH brake pad wear
MV	Electric cooling fan	UG	LH brake pad wear
PB	Dashboard	VD	RH side tailgate
PC	Driver's door	VG	LH side tailgate
PD	RH rear door		

Colour code

B	White
Bl	Blue
G	Grey
Ic	Clear/transparent
J	Yellow
M	Brown
Mv	Purple
N	Black
Or	Orange
R	Red
Ro	Pink
V	Green
Vi	Lilac

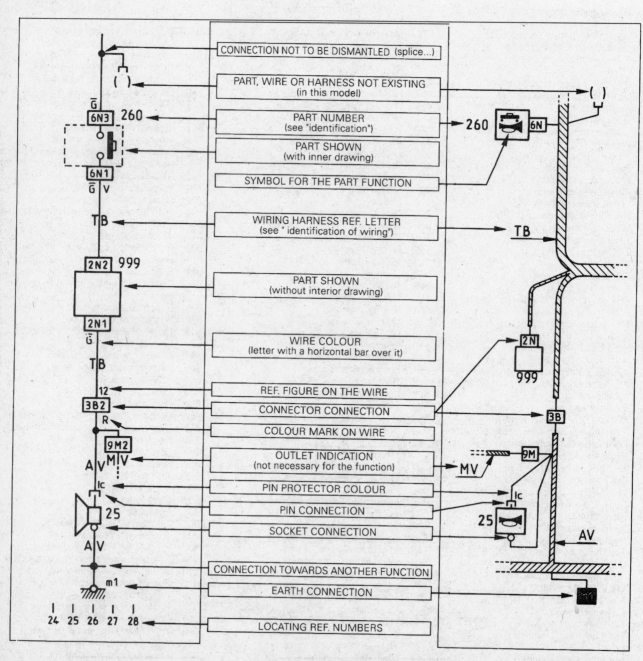

How to use the wiring diagrams

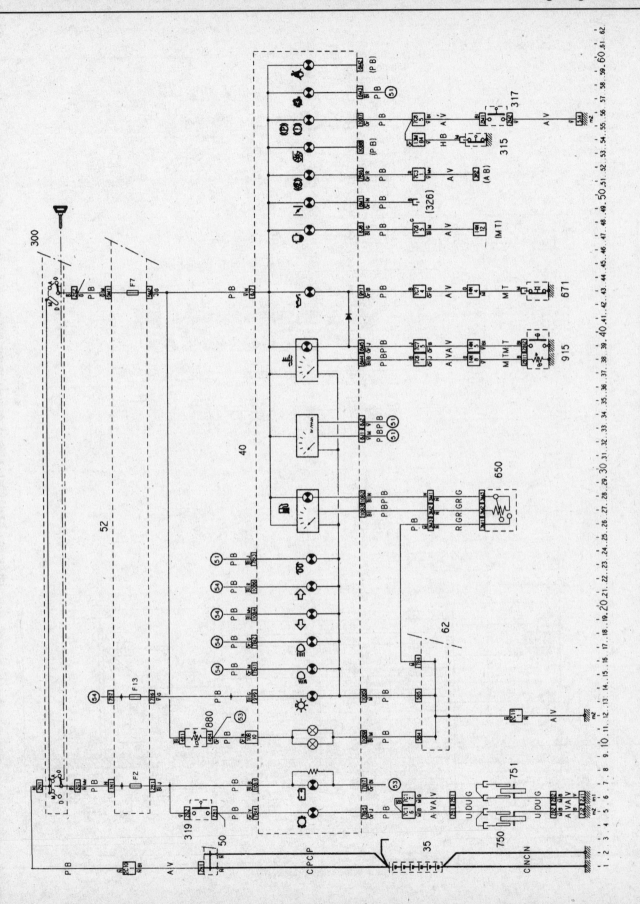

Instrument panel (low- to mid-specification models)

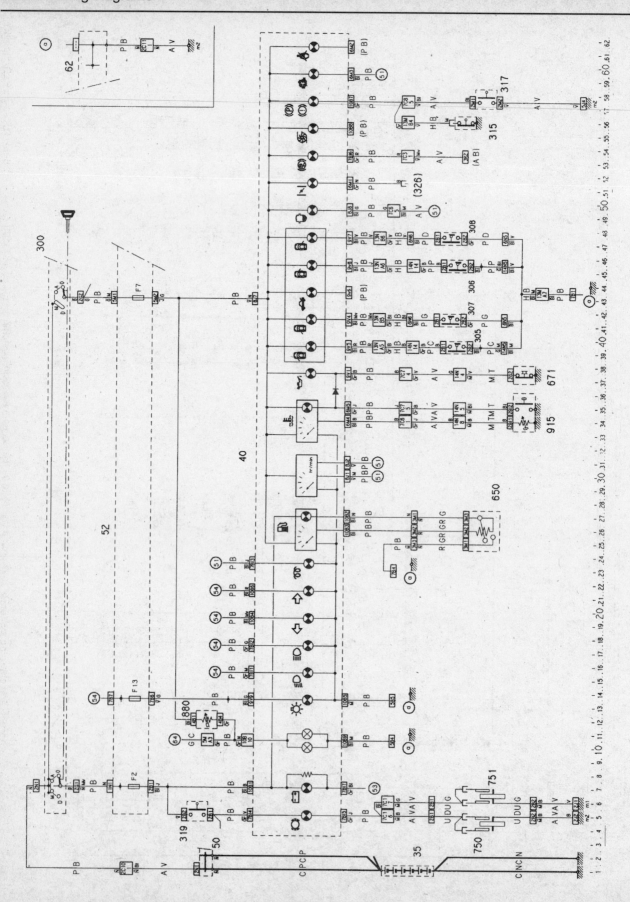

Instrument panel (mid-to high-specification models)

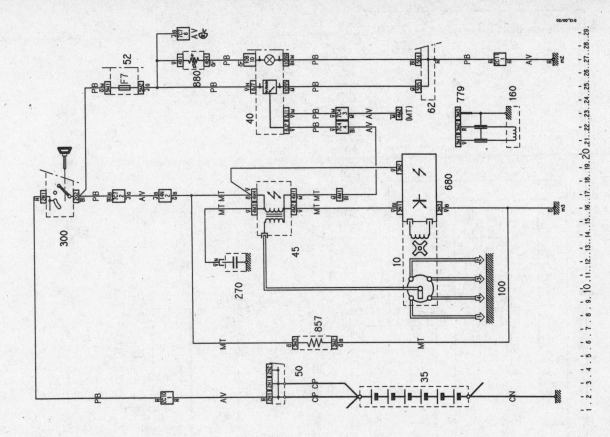

Engine electrical systems – 1124 cc and 1360 carburettor (H1A/TU1K and K2D/TU3 2K)

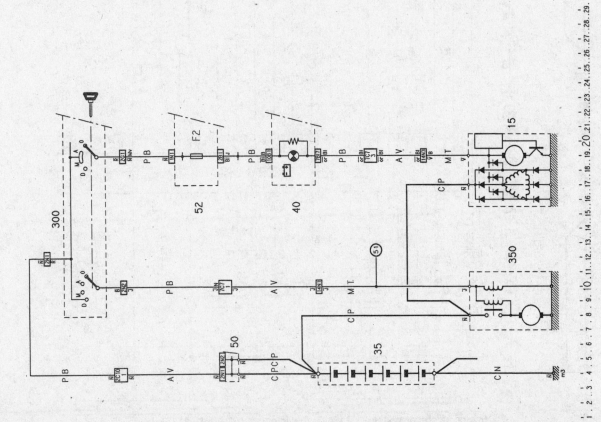

Starting and charging systems

12

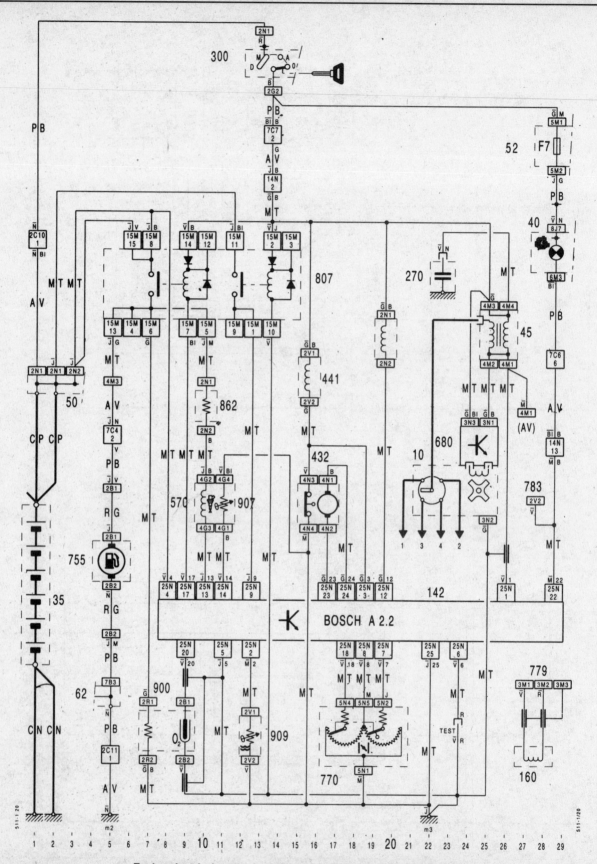

Engine electrical systems – 1124 cc fuel injection (HDZ/TU1M L/Z)

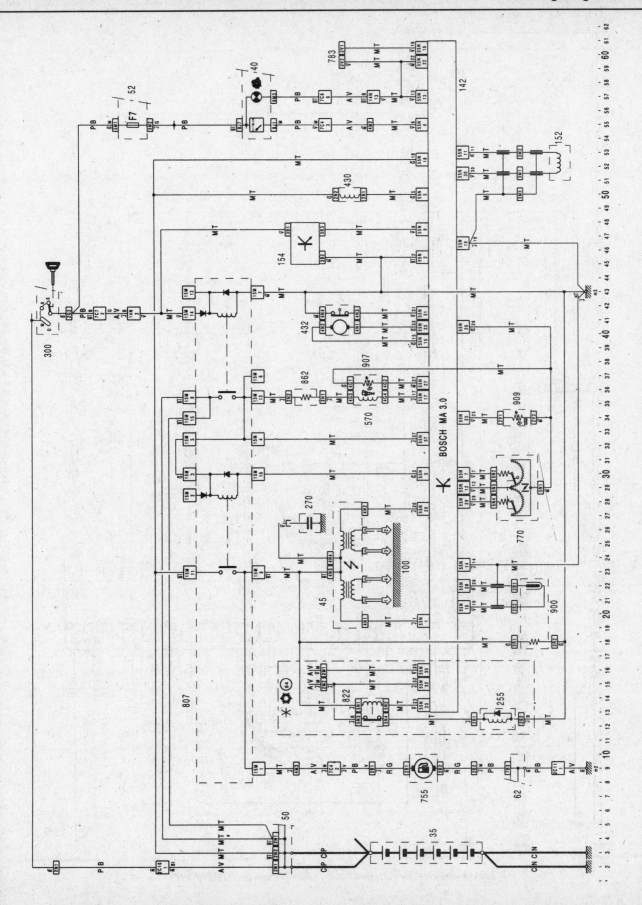

Engine electrical systems – 1360 cc fuel injection (KDX/TU3MC L/Z)

12

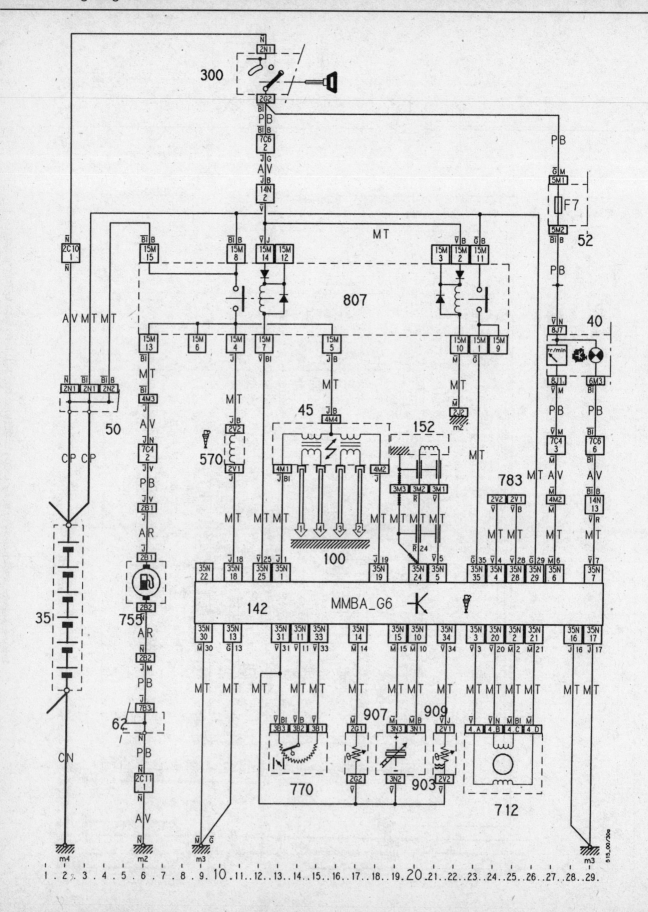

Engine electrical systems – 1580 cc cc non-catalyst (BA4/XU5M 3K and XU5M 4K)

515_00/30a

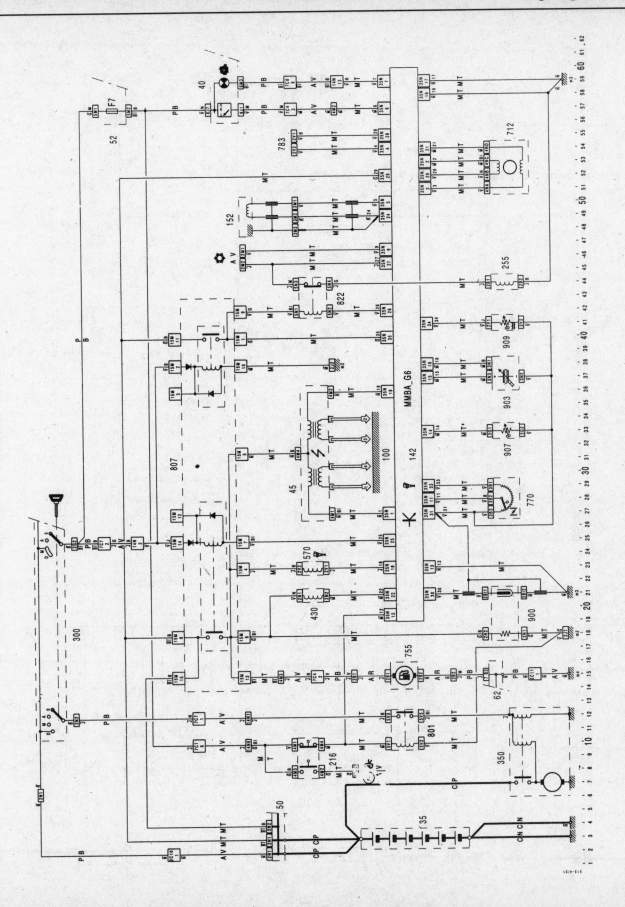

Engine electrical systems – 1580 cc catalyst (BDY/XU5M 3Z), automatic transmission

12

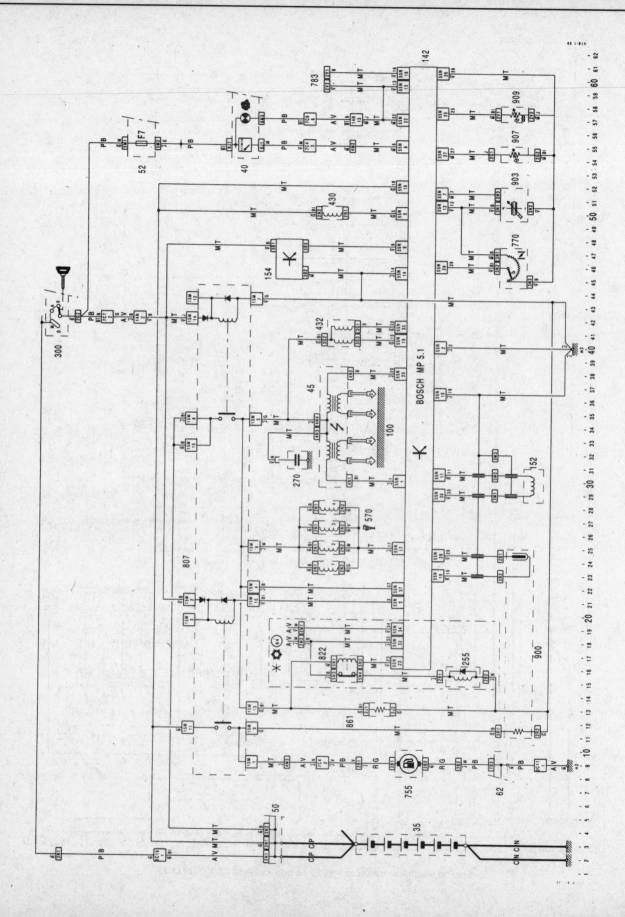

Engine electrical systems – 1761 cc (LFZ/XU7PJL/Z)

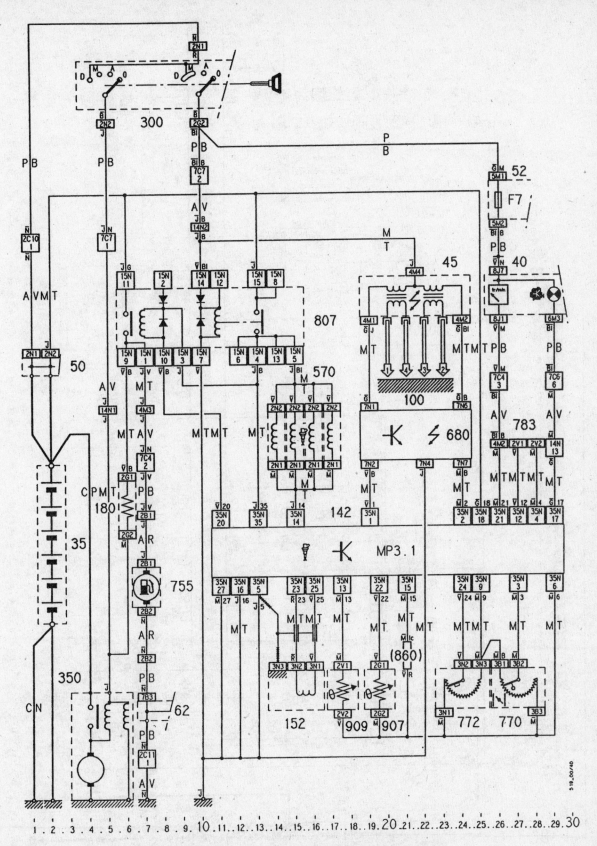

Engine electrical systems – 1905 cc non-catalyst (D6E/XU9JA K)

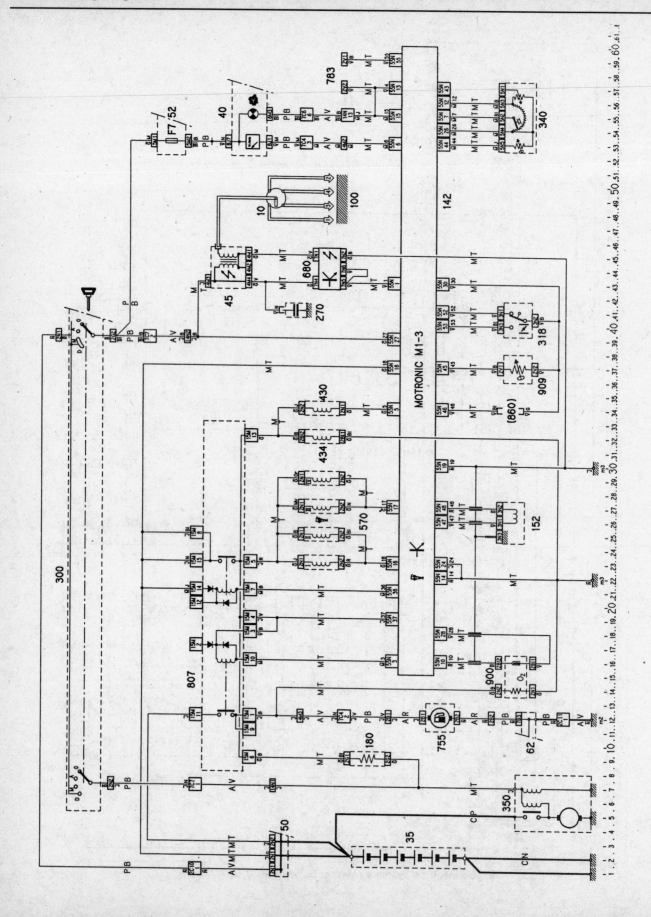

Engine electrical systems – 1905 cc catalyst (DKZ/XU9JA Z), manual transmission

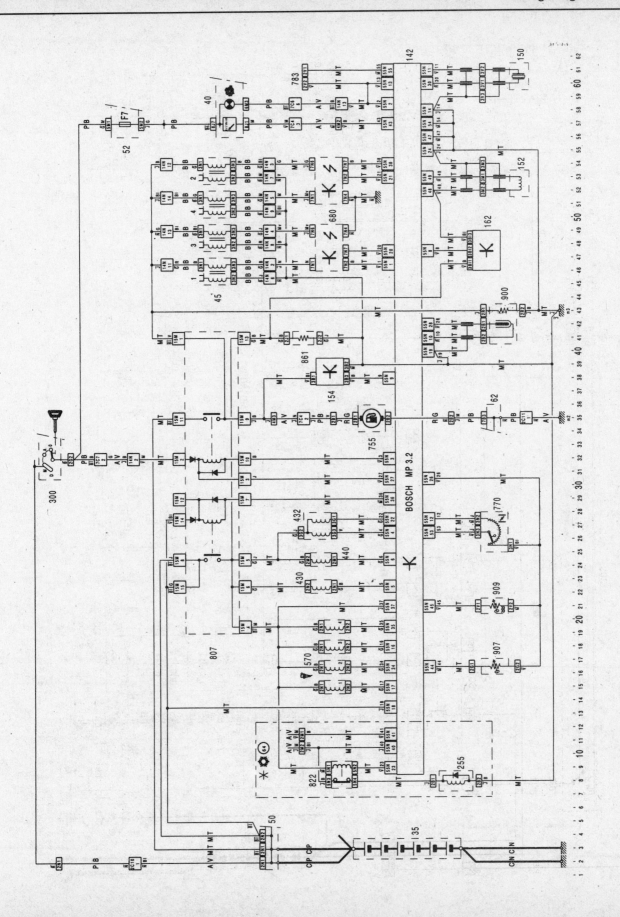

Engine electrical systems – 1998 cc 16-valve (RFY/XU10J4 LZ)

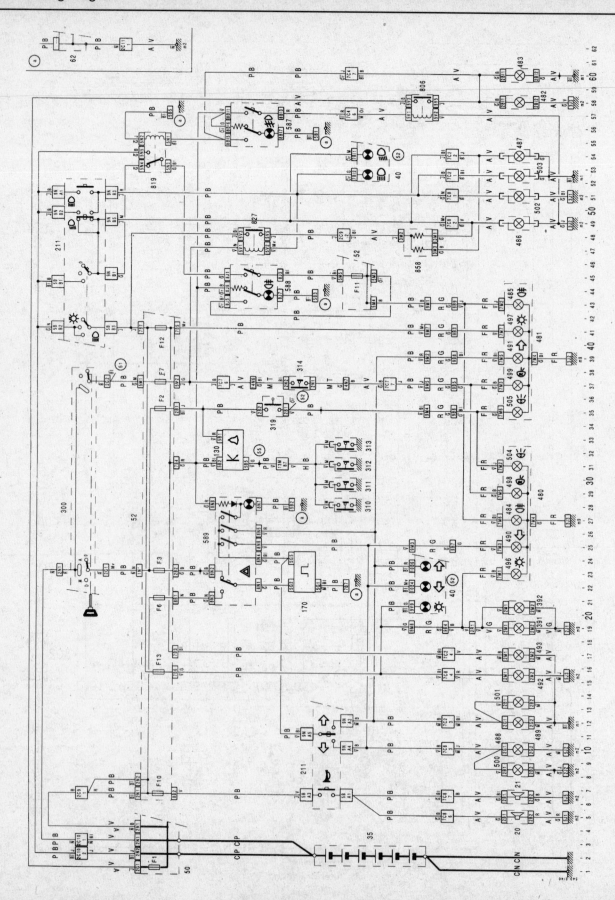

Exterior lighting

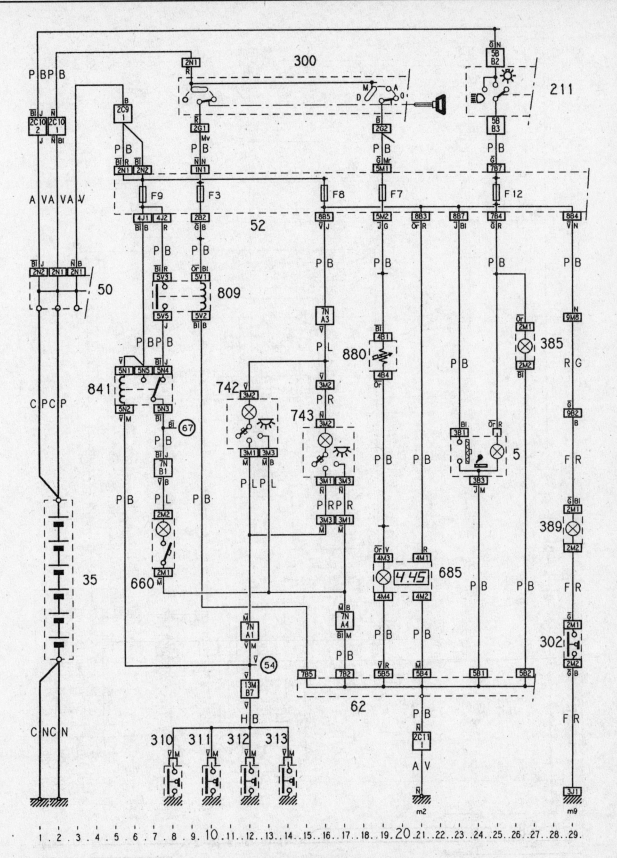

Interior lighting

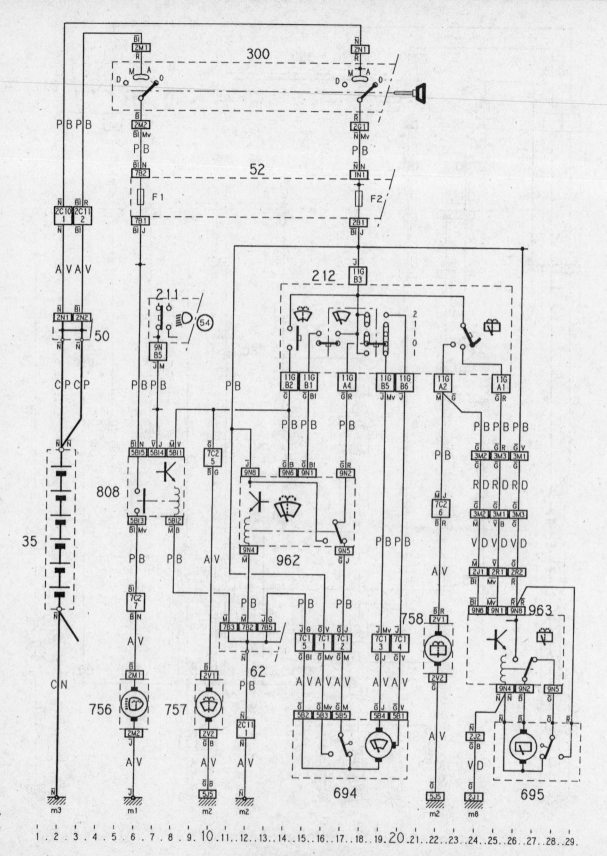

Wash/wipe systems

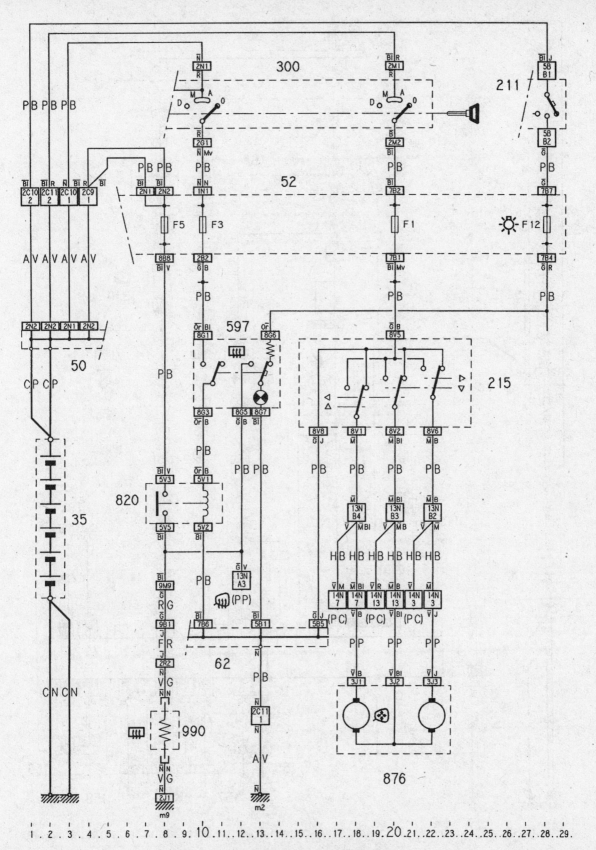

Heated rear window, electric mirror

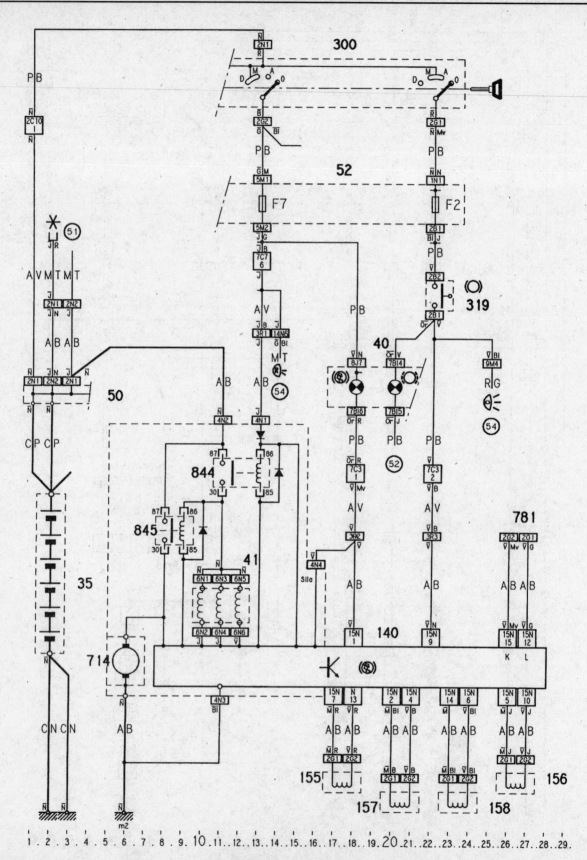

Anti-lock braking system

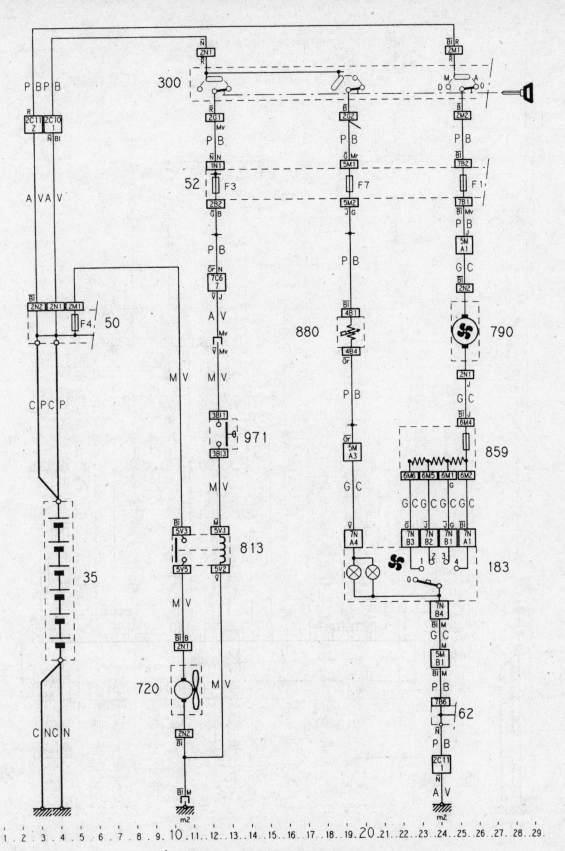

Engine cooling fan and heater blower

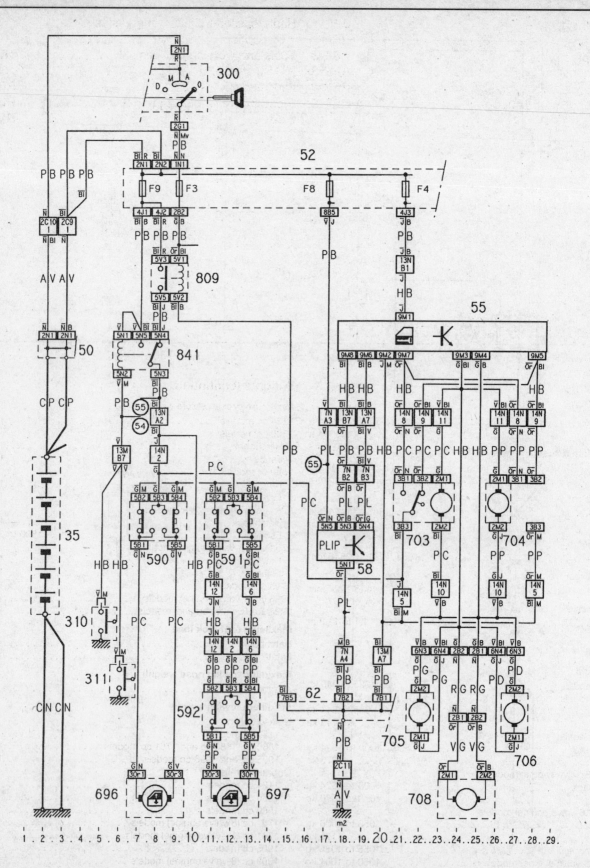

Electric windows and central locking

Dimensions and weights . . . . **REF•1**
Conversion factors . . . . **REF•2**
Buying spare parts . . . . **REF•3**
Vehicle identification . . . . **REF•3**
General repair procedures . . . . **REF•4**
Jacking and vehicle support . . . . **REF•5**

Radio/cassette unit anti-theft system -
  precaution . . . . **REF•5**
Tools and working facilities . . . . **REF•6**
MOT test checks . . . . **REF•8**
Fault finding . . . . **REF•12**
Glossary of technical terms . . . . **REF•19**
Index . . . . **REF•23**

Dimensions and weights

Note: *All figures are approximate, and may vary according to model. Refer to manufacturer's data for exact figures.*

Dimensions

Overall length
Hatchback . . . . .4070 to 4090 mm
Estate . . . . .4260 mm

Overall width (excluding mirrors)
Hatchback . . . . .1688 to 1710 mm
Estate . . . . .1705 mm

Overall height
Hatchback . . . . .1386 to 1404 mm
Estate . . . . .1460 mm

Wheelbase
All models . . . . .2540 mm

Front and rear track
All models . . . . .1414 to 1424 mm

Turning circle
All models . . . . .11.1 to 11.3 m

Weights

Kerb weight
1124 cc models . . . . .935 to 940 kg
1360 cc models:
  Hatchback . . . . .945 to 949 kg
  Estate . . . . .1015 kg
1580 cc models:
  Hatchback . . . . .1008 to 1024 kg
  Estate . . . . .1070 kg
1761 cc (8-valve engine) models:
  Hatchback . . . . .1008 to 1024 kg
  Estate . . . . .1070 to 1090 kg
1761 cc (16-valve engine) models:
  Hatchback . . . . .1058 to 1086 kg
  Estate . . . . .1105 kg
1905 cc models .1055 to 1085 kg
1998 cc (8-valve engine) models . . . . . . .1060 to 1091 kg
1998 cc (16-valve engine) models . . . . .1150 kg

Weights (continued)

Maximum gross vehicle weight
1124 cc models . . . . .1465 kg
1360 cc models:
  Hatchback . . . . .1490 kg
  Estate . . . . .1550 kg
1580 cc models:
  Hatchback . . . . .1550 kg
  Estate . . . . .1590 kg
1761 cc (8-valve engine) models:
  Hatchback . . . . .1550 kg
  Estate . . . . .1590 to 1610 kg
1761 cc (16-valve engine) models:
  Hatchback . . . . .1580 kg
  Estate . . . . .1630 kg
1905 cc models . . . . .1570 kg
1998 cc (8-valve engine) models . . . . .1600 kg
1998 cc (16-valve engine) models . . . . .1630 kg

Maximum roof rack load
Hatchback . . . . .75 kg
Estate . . . . .100 kg

Maximum towing nose weight
All models . . . . .70 kg

Maximum towing weight
Braked trailer:
  1124 cc models . . . . .900 kg
  1360 cc, 1580 cc and 1761 cc models . . . . .1000 kg
  1905 cc, and 1998 cc models . . . . .1100 kg
Unbraked trailer:
  1124 cc models . . . . .465 kg
  1360 cc models . . . . .470 kg
  1580 cc models . . . . .500 kg
  1761 cc (8-valve engine) models . . . . .500 kg
  1761 cc (16-valve engine) models . . . . .530 kg
  1905 cc models . . . . .510 kg
  1998 cc (8-valve engine) models . . . . .530 kg
  1998 cc (16-valve engine) models . . . . .575 kg

Conversion factors

Length (distance)

Inches (in)	x 25.4	= Millimetres (mm)	x 0.0394	= Inches (in)
Feet (ft)	x 0.305	= Metres (m)	x 3.281	= Feet (ft)
Miles	x 1.609	= Kilometres (km)	x 0.621	= Miles

Volume (capacity)

Cubic inches (cu in; in³)	x 16.387	= Cubic centimetres (cc; cm³)	x 0.061	= Cubic inches (cu in; in³)
Imperial pints (Imp pt)	x 0.568	= Litres (l)	x 1.76	= Imperial pints (Imp pt)
Imperial quarts (Imp qt)	x 1.137	= Litres (l)	x 0.88	= Imperial quarts (Imp qt)
Imperial quarts (Imp qt)	x 1.201	= US quarts (US qt)	x 0.833	= Imperial quarts (Imp qt)
US quarts (US qt)	x 0.946	= Litres (l)	x 1.057	= US quarts (US qt)
Imperial gallons (Imp gal)	x 4.546	= Litres (l)	x 0.22	= Imperial gallons (Imp gal)
Imperial gallons (Imp gal)	x 1.201	= US gallons (US gal)	x 0.833	= Imperial gallons (Imp gal)
US gallons (US gal)	x 3.785	= Litres (l)	x 0.264	= US gallons (US gal)

Mass (weight)

Ounces (oz)	x 28.35	= Grams (g)	x 0.035	= Ounces (oz)
Pounds (lb)	x 0.454	= Kilograms (kg)	x 2.205	= Pounds (lb)

Force

Ounces-force (ozf; oz)	x 0.278	= Newtons (N)	x 3.6	= Ounces-force (ozf; oz)
Pounds-force (lbf; lb)	x 4.448	= Newtons (N)	x 0.225	= Pounds-force (lbf; lb)
Newtons (N)	x 0.1	= Kilograms-force (kgf; kg)	x 9.81	= Newtons (N)

Pressure

Pounds-force per square inch (psi; lbf/in²; lb/in²)	x 0.070	= Kilograms-force per square centimetre (kgf/cm²; kg/cm²)	x 14.223	= Pounds-force per square inch (psi; lbf/in²; lb/in²)
Pounds-force per square inch (psi; lbf/in²; lb/in²)	x 0.068	= Atmospheres (atm)	x 14.696	= Pounds-force per square inch (psi; lbf/in²; lb/in²)
Pounds-force per square inch (psi; lbf/in²; lb/in²)	x 0.069	= Bars	x 14.5	= Pounds-force per square inch (psi; lbf/in²; lb/in²)
Pounds-force per square inch (psi; lbf/in²; lb/in²)	x 6.895	= Kilopascals (kPa)	x 0.145	= Pounds-force per square inch (psi; lbf/in²; lb/in²)
Kilopascals (kPa)	x 0.01	= Kilograms-force per square centimetre (kgf/cm²; kg/cm²)	x 98.1	= Kilopascals (kPa)
Millibar (mbar)	x 100	= Pascals (Pa)	x 0.01	= Millibar (mbar)
Millibar (mbar)	x 0.0145	= Pounds-force per square inch (psi; lbf/in²; lb/in²)	x 68.947	= Millibar (mbar)
Millibar (mbar)	x 0.75	= Millimetres of mercury (mmHg)	x 1.333	= Millibar (mbar)
Millibar (mbar)	x 0.401	= Inches of water (inH₂O)	x 2.491	= Millibar (mbar)
Millimetres of mercury (mmHg)	x 0.535	= Inches of water (inH₂O)	x 1.868	= Millimetres of mercury (mmHg)
Inches of water (inH₂O)	x 0.036	= Pounds-force per square inch (psi; lbf/in²; lb/in²)	x 27.68	= Inches of water (inH₂O)

Torque (moment of force)

Pounds-force inches (lbf in; lb in)	x 1.152	= Kilograms-force centimetre (kgf cm; kg cm)	x 0.868	= Pounds-force inches (lbf in; lb in)
Pounds-force inches (lbf in; lb in)	x 0.113	= Newton metres (Nm)	x 8.85	= Pounds-force inches (lbf in; lb in)
Pounds-force inches (lbf in; lb in)	x 0.083	= Pounds-force feet (lbf ft; lb ft)	x 12	= Pounds-force inches (lbf in; lb in)
Pounds-force feet (lbf ft; lb ft)	x 0.138	= Kilograms-force metres (kgf m; kg m)	x 7.233	= Pounds-force feet (lbf ft; lb ft)
Pounds-force feet (lbf ft; lb ft)	x 1.356	= Newton metres (Nm)	x 0.738	= Pounds-force feet (lbf ft; lb ft)
Newton metres (Nm)	x 0.102	= Kilograms-force metres (kgf m; kg m)	x 9.804	= Newton metres (Nm)

Power

Horsepower (hp)	x 745.7	= Watts (W)	x 0.0013	= Horsepower (hp)

Velocity (speed)

Miles per hour (miles/hr; mph)	x 1.609	= Kilometres per hour (km/hr; kph)	x 0.621	= Miles per hour (miles/hr; mph)

Fuel consumption*

Miles per gallon, Imperial (mpg)	x 0.354	= Kilometres per litre (km/l)	x 2.825	= Miles per gallon, Imperial (mpg)
Miles per gallon, US (mpg)	x 0.425	= Kilometres per litre (km/l)	x 2.352	= Miles per gallon, US (mpg)

Temperature

Degrees Fahrenheit = (°C x 1.8) + 32   Degrees Celsius (Degrees Centigrade; °C) = (°F - 32) x 0.56

* It is common practice to convert from miles per gallon (mpg) to litres/100 kilometres (l/100km), where mpg x l/100 km = 282

Spare parts are available from many sources, including maker's appointed garages, accessory shops, and motor factors. To be sure of obtaining the correct parts, it may sometimes be necessary to quote the vehicle identification number. If possible, it can also be useful to take the old parts along for positive identification. Items such as starter motors and alternators may be available under a service exchange scheme - any parts returned should always be clean.

Our advice regarding spare part sources is as follows:

Officially-appointed garages

This is the best source of parts which are peculiar to your car, and are not otherwise generally available (eg badges, interior trim, certain body panels, etc). It is also the only place at which you should buy parts if the vehicle is still under warranty.

Accessory shops

These are very good places to buy materials and components needed for the maintenance of your car (oil, air and fuel filters, spark plugs, light bulbs, drivebelts, oils and greases, brake pads, touch-up paint, etc). Parts like this sold by a reputable shop are of the same standard as those used by the car manufacturer.

Motor factors

Good factors will stock all the more important components which wear out comparatively quickly and can sometimes supply individual components needed for the overhaul of a larger assembly. They may also handle work such as cylinder block reboring, crankshaft regrinding and balancing, etc.

Tyre and exhaust specialists

These outlets may be independent or members of a local or national chain. They frequently offer competitive prices when compared with a main dealer or local garage, but it will pay to obtain several quotes before making a decision. Also ask what 'extras' may be added to the quote - for instance, fitting a new valve and balancing the wheel are both often charged on top of the price of a new tyre.

Other sources

Beware of parts of materials obtained from market stalls, car boot sales or similar outlets. Such items are not invariably sub-standard, but there is little chance of compensation if they do prove unsatisfactory. In the case of safety-critical components such as brake pads there is the risk not only of financial loss but also of an accident causing injury or death.

Second-hand components or assemblies obtained from a car breaker can be a good buy in some circumstances, but this sort of purchase is best made by the experienced DIY mechanic.

Vehicle identification

Modifications are a continuing and unpublicised process in vehicle manufacture, quite apart from major model changes. Spare parts manuals and lists are compiled upon a numerical basis, the individual vehicle identification numbers being essential to correct identification of the component concerned.

When ordering spare parts, always give as much information as possible. Quote the car model, year of manufacture, body and engine numbers as appropriate (**see illustrations**).

The *vehicle identification number* is stamped on a plate located under the bonnet on the right-hand wheel arch.

The *chassis number* is stamped on the body panel under the bonnet on the right-hand side of the bulkhead on models produced up to 1993, or on the right-hand wheel arch on models produced from 1993.

The *paint code number* is located on the body panel under the bonnet on the left-hand upper wheel arch.

The *engine number* is stamped on the front of the cylinder block.

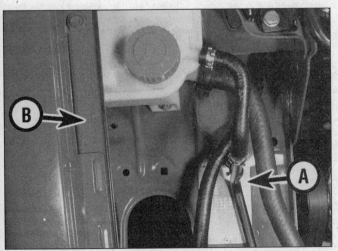

Vehicle identification plate (A) and chassis number (B

Engine number on front of cylinder block

Whenever servicing, repair or overhaul work is carried out on the car or its components, observe the following procedures and instructions. This will assist in carrying out the operation efficiently and to a professional standard of workmanship.

Joint mating faces and gaskets

When separating components at their mating faces, never insert screwdrivers or similar implements into the joint between the faces in order to prise them apart. This can cause severe damage which results in oil leaks, coolant leaks, etc upon reassembly. Separation is usually achieved by tapping along the joint with a soft-faced hammer in order to break the seal. However, note that this method may not be suitable where dowels are used for component location.

Where a gasket is used between the mating faces of two components, a new one must be fitted on reassembly; fit it dry unless otherwise stated in the repair procedure. Make sure that the mating faces are clean and dry, with all traces of old gasket removed. When cleaning a joint face, use a tool which is unlikely to score or damage the face, and remove any burrs or nicks with an oilstone or fine file.

Make sure that tapped holes are cleaned with a pipe cleaner, and keep them free of jointing compound, if this is being used, unless specifically instructed otherwise.

Ensure that all orifices, channels or pipes are clear, and blow through them, preferably using compressed air.

Oil seals

Oil seals can be removed by levering them out with a wide flat-bladed screwdriver or similar implement. Alternatively, a number of self-tapping screws may be screwed into the seal, and these used as a purchase for pliers or some similar device in order to pull the seal free.

Whenever an oil seal is removed from its working location, either individually or as part of an assembly, it should be renewed.

The very fine sealing lip of the seal is easily damaged, and will not seal if the surface it contacts is not completely clean and free from scratches, nicks or grooves. If the original sealing surface of the component cannot be restored, and the manufacturer has not made provision for slight relocation of the seal relative to the sealing surface, the component should be renewed.

Protect the lips of the seal from any surface which may damage them in the course of fitting. Use tape or a conical sleeve where possible. Lubricate the seal lips with oil before fitting and, on dual-lipped seals, fill the space between the lips with grease.

Unless otherwise stated, oil seals must be fitted with their sealing lips toward the lubricant to be sealed.

Use a tubular drift or block of wood of the appropriate size to install the seal and, if the seal housing is shouldered, drive the seal down to the shoulder. If the seal housing is unshouldered, the seal should be fitted with its face flush with the housing top face (unless otherwise instructed).

Screw threads and fastenings

Seized nuts, bolts and screws are quite a common occurrence where corrosion has set in, and the use of penetrating oil or releasing fluid will often overcome this problem if the offending item is soaked for a while before attempting to release it. The use of an impact driver may also provide a means of releasing such stubborn fastening devices, when used in conjunction with the appropriate screwdriver bit or socket. If none of these methods works, it may be necessary to resort to the careful application of heat, or the use of a hacksaw or nut splitter device.

Studs are usually removed by locking two nuts together on the threaded part, and then using a spanner on the lower nut to unscrew the stud. Studs or bolts which have broken off below the surface of the component in which they are mounted can sometimes be removed using a stud extractor. Always ensure that a blind tapped hole is completely free from oil, grease, water or other fluid before installing the bolt or stud. Failure to do this could cause the housing to crack due to the hydraulic action of the bolt or stud as it is screwed in.

When tightening a castellated nut to accept a split pin, tighten the nut to the specified torque, where applicable, and then tighten further to the next split pin hole. Never slacken the nut to align the split pin hole, unless stated in the repair procedure.

When checking or retightening a nut or bolt to a specified torque setting, slacken the nut or bolt by a quarter of a turn, and then retighten to the specified setting. However, this should not be attempted where angular tightening has been used.

For some screw fastenings, notably cylinder head bolts or nuts, torque wrench settings are no longer specified for the latter stages of tightening, "angle-tightening" being called up instead. Typically, a fairly low torque wrench setting will be applied to the bolts/nuts in the correct sequence, followed by one or more stages of tightening through specified angles.

Locknuts, locktabs and washers

Any fastening which will rotate against a component or housing during tightening should always have a washer between it and the relevant component or housing.

Spring or split washers should always be renewed when they are used to lock a critical component such as a big-end bearing retaining bolt or nut. Locktabs which are folded over to retain a nut or bolt should always be renewed.

Self-locking nuts can be re-used in non-critical areas, providing resistance can be felt when the locking portion passes over the bolt or stud thread. However, it should be noted that self-locking stiffnuts tend to lose their effectiveness after long periods of use, and should then be renewed as a matter of course.

Split pins must always be replaced with new ones of the correct size for the hole.

When thread-locking compound is found on the threads of a fastener which is to be re-used, it should be cleaned off with a wire brush and solvent, and fresh compound applied on reassembly.

Special tools

Some repair procedures in this manual entail the use of special tools such as a press, two or three-legged pullers, spring compressors, etc. Wherever possible, suitable readily-available alternatives to the manufacturer's special tools are described, and are shown in use. In some instances, where no alternative is possible, it has been necessary to resort to the use of a manufacturer's tool, and this has been done for reasons of safety as well as the efficient completion of the repair operation. Unless you are highly-skilled and have a thorough understanding of the procedures described, never attempt to bypass the use of any special tool when the procedure described specifies its use. Not only is there a very great risk of personal injury, but expensive damage could be caused to the components involved.

Environmental considerations

When disposing of used engine oil, brake fluid, antifreeze, etc, give due consideration to any detrimental environmental effects. Do not, for instance, pour any of the above liquids down drains into the general sewage system, or onto the ground to soak away. Many local council refuse tips provide a facility for waste oil disposal, as do some garages. If none of these facilities are available, consult your local Environmental Health Department, or the National Rivers Authority, for further advice.

With the universal tightening-up of legislation regarding the emission of environmentally-harmful substances from motor vehicles, most vehicles have tamperproof devices fitted to the main adjustment points of the fuel system. These devices are primarily designed to prevent unqualified persons from adjusting the fuel/air mixture, with the chance of a consequent increase in toxic emissions. If such devices are found during servicing or overhaul, they should, wherever possible, be renewed or refitted in accordance with the manufacturer's requirements or current legislation.

OIL CARE
FOLLOW THE CODE
OIL BANK LINE
0800 66 33 66
www.oilbankline.org.uk

Note: It is antisocial and illegal to dump oil down the drain. To find the location of your local oil recycling bank, call this number free.

The jack supplied with the vehicle tool kit should only be used for changing the roadwheels - see *"Wheel changing"* at the front of this manual. When using the jack, position it on firm ground and locate its head in the relevant vehicle jacking point **(see illustrations)**.

When carrying out any other kind of work, raise the vehicle using a hydraulic jack and always supplement the jack with axle stands positioned under the vehicle jacking points.

When using a hydraulic jack or axle stands, always position the jack head or axle stand head under one of the relevant jacking points. Note that the jacking points for use with a hydraulic jack and axle stands are different to those for use with the vehicle jack **(see illustration)**. Do not jack the vehicle under the sump or any of the steering or suspension components.

Note the following when using a hydraulic jack:

a) *When raising the side of the vehicle, ensure that the load is taken by the raised jacking plates on the sill panels. Do not jack under the body panel behind the sill panels.*

b) *When raising the front of the vehicle, use a suitable metal or strong wooden bar and wooden spacer blocks under the front suspension subframe.*

c) *When raising the rear of the vehicle, position the jack or axle stands under the rear suspension tubular crossmember.*

⚠️ **Warning: Never work under, around, or near a raised vehicle, unless it is adequately supported in at least two places.**

Locating jack head into vehicle jacking point

Raising vehicle with scissor jack

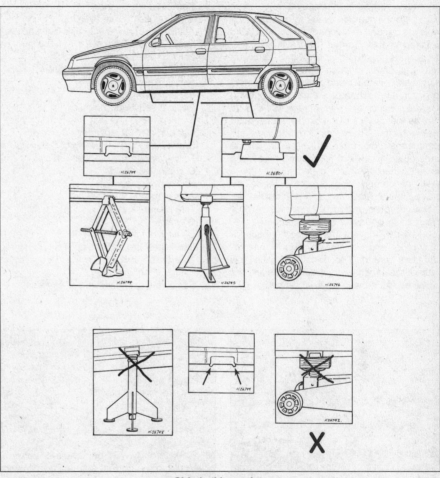

Side jacking points

Radio/cassette unit anti-theft system - precaution

The radio/cassette unit fitted as standard equipment by Citroën is equipped with a built-in security code to deter thieves. If the power source to the unit is cut, the anti-theft system will activate. Even if the power source is immediately reconnected, the radio/cassette unit will not function until the correct security code has been entered. Therefore, if you do not know the correct security code for the radio/cassette unit, do not disconnect either of the battery terminals or remove the radio/cassette unit from the vehicle.

To enter the security code, first switch the unit on - the display will show "Cod". The security code can then be entered using buttons 1 to 4 on the unit. Each button alters the corresponding digit of the code. Note that there is no facility on the radio display to show the number 0 for the first digit of the security code. For the first digit, 0 is indicated by a blank. Once the correct code is displayed, press the "up" section of the four-way tuning button to enter the code.

If an incorrect code is entered, the display will show three dashes, after which the radio will be locked for 10 seconds. On the first two attempts, after 10 seconds the radio display will show the "Cod" prompt again and allow you to enter the security code again.

However, if the correct security code is not entered on the third attempt, the unit will be locked for 1 hour. To make any further attempts, the unit must be switched on and left untouched for approximately 1 hour before the display shows the "Cod" prompt again and allows you to re-enter the security code. Note that after twenty attempts, the unit will become permanently locked.

If this happens, or if the security code is lost or forgotten, seek the advice of your Citroën dealer. On presentation of proof of ownership, a Citroën dealer will be able to unlock the unit and provide you with a new security code.

Introduction

A selection of good tools is a fundamental requirement for anyone contemplating the maintenance and repair of a motor vehicle. For the owner who does not possess any, their purchase will prove a considerable expense, offsetting some of the savings made by doing-it-yourself. However, provided that the tools purchased meet the relevant national safety standards and are of good quality, they will last for many years and prove an extremely worthwhile investment.

To help the average owner to decide which tools are needed to carry out the various tasks detailed in this manual, we have compiled three lists of tools under the following headings: *Maintenance and minor repair, Repair and overhaul*, and *Special*. Newcomers to practical mechanics should start off with the *Maintenance and minor repair* tool kit, and confine themselves to the simpler jobs around the vehicle. Then, as confidence and experience grow, more difficult tasks can be undertaken, with extra tools being purchased as, and when, they are needed. In this way, a *Maintenance and minor repair* tool kit can be built up into a *Repair and overhaul* tool kit over a considerable period of time, without any major cash outlays. The experienced do-it-yourselfer will have a tool kit good enough for most repair and overhaul procedures, and will add tools from the *Special* category when it is felt that the expense is justified by the amount of use to which these tools will be put.

Maintenance and minor repair tool kit

The tools given in this list should be considered as a minimum requirement if routine maintenance, servicing and minor repair operations are to be undertaken. We recommend the purchase of combination spanners (ring one end, open-ended the other); although more expensive than open-ended ones, they do give the advantages of both types of spanner.

☐ *Combination spanners:*
  Metric - 8 to 19 mm inclusive
☐ *Adjustable spanner - 35 mm jaw (approx.)*
☐ *Spark plug spanner (with rubber insert) - petrol models*
☐ *Spark plug gap adjustment tool - petrol models*
☐ *Set of feeler gauges*
☐ *Brake bleed nipple spanner*
☐ *Screwdrivers:*
  Flat blade - 100 mm long x 6 mm dia
  Cross blade - 100 mm long x 6 mm dia
  Torx - various sizes (not all vehicles)
☐ *Combination pliers*
☐ *Hacksaw (junior)*
☐ *Tyre pump*
☐ *Tyre pressure gauge*
☐ *Oil can*
☐ *Oil filter removal tool*
☐ *Fine emery cloth*
☐ *Wire brush (small)*
☐ *Funnel (medium size)*
☐ *Sump drain plug key (not all vehicles)*

Repair and overhaul tool kit

These tools are virtually essential for anyone undertaking any major repairs to a motor vehicle, and are additional to those given in the *Maintenance and minor repair* list. Included in this list is a comprehensive set of sockets. Although these are expensive, they will be found invaluable as they are so versatile - particularly if various drives are included in the set. We recommend the half-inch square-drive type, as this can be used with most proprietary torque wrenches.

The tools in this list will sometimes need to be supplemented by tools from the *Special* list:

☐ *Sockets (or box spanners) to cover range in previous list (including Torx sockets)*
☐ *Reversible ratchet drive (for use with sockets)*
☐ *Extension piece, 250 mm (for use with sockets)*
☐ *Universal joint (for use with sockets)*
☐ *Flexible handle or sliding T "breaker bar" (for use with sockets)*
☐ *Torque wrench (for use with sockets)*
☐ *Self-locking grips*
☐ *Ball pein hammer*
☐ *Soft-faced mallet (plastic or rubber)*
☐ *Screwdrivers:*
  Flat blade - long & sturdy, short (chubby), and narrow (electrician's) types
  Cross blade – long & sturdy, and short (chubby) types
☐ *Pliers:*
  Long-nosed
  Side cutters (electrician's)
  Circlip (internal and external)
☐ *Cold chisel - 25 mm*
☐ *Scriber*
☐ *Scraper*
☐ *Centre-punch*
☐ *Pin punch*
☐ *Hacksaw*
☐ *Brake hose clamp*
☐ *Brake/clutch bleeding kit*
☐ *Selection of twist drills*
☐ *Steel rule/straight-edge*
☐ *Allen keys (inc. splined/Torx type)*
☐ *Selection of files*
☐ *Wire brush*
☐ *Axle stands*
☐ *Jack (strong trolley or hydraulic type)*
☐ *Light with extension lead*
☐ *Universal electrical multi-meter*

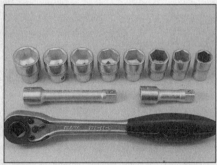

Sockets and reversible ratchet drive

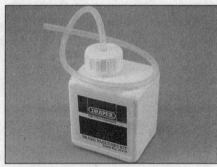

Brake bleeding kit

Torx key, socket and bit

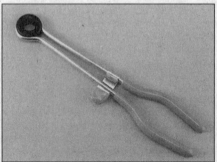

Hose clamp

Angular-tightening gauge

Special tools

The tools in this list are those which are not used regularly, are expensive to buy, or which need to be used in accordance with their manufacturers' instructions. Unless relatively difficult mechanical jobs are undertaken frequently, it will not be economic to buy many of these tools. Where this is the case, you could consider clubbing together with friends (or joining a motorists' club) to make a joint purchase, or borrowing the tools against a deposit from a local garage or tool hire specialist. It is worth noting that many of the larger DIY superstores now carry a large range of special tools for hire at modest rates.

The following list contains only those tools and instruments freely available to the public, and not those special tools produced by the vehicle manufacturer specifically for its dealer network. You will find occasional references to these manufacturers' special tools in the text of this manual. Generally, an alternative method of doing the job without the vehicle manufacturers' special tool is given. However, sometimes there is no alternative to using them. Where this is the case and the relevant tool cannot be bought or borrowed, you will have to entrust the work to a dealer.

- [ ] Angular-tightening gauge
- [ ] Valve spring compressor
- [ ] Valve grinding tool
- [ ] Piston ring compressor
- [ ] Piston ring removal/installation tool
- [ ] Cylinder bore hone
- [ ] Balljoint separator
- [ ] Coil spring compressors (where applicable)
- [ ] Two/three-legged hub and bearing puller
- [ ] Impact screwdriver
- [ ] Micrometer and/or vernier calipers
- [ ] Dial gauge
- [ ] Stroboscopic timing light
- [ ] Dwell angle meter/tachometer
- [ ] Fault code reader
- [ ] Cylinder compression gauge
- [ ] Hand-operated vacuum pump and gauge
- [ ] Clutch plate alignment set
- [ ] Brake shoe steady spring cup removal tool
- [ ] Bush and bearing removal/installation set
- [ ] Stud extractors
- [ ] Tap and die set
- [ ] Lifting tackle
- [ ] Trolley jack

Buying tools

Reputable motor accessory shops and superstores often offer excellent quality tools at discount prices, so it pays to shop around.

Remember, you don't have to buy the most expensive items on the shelf, but it is always advisable to steer clear of the very cheap tools. Beware of 'bargains' offered on market stalls or at car boot sales. There are plenty of good tools around at reasonable prices, but always aim to purchase items which meet the relevant national safety standards. If in doubt, ask the proprietor or manager of the shop for advice before making a purchase.

Care and maintenance of tools

Having purchased a reasonable tool kit, it is necessary to keep the tools in a clean and serviceable condition. After use, always wipe off any dirt, grease and metal particles using a clean, dry cloth, before putting the tools away. Never leave them lying around after they have been used. A simple tool rack on the garage or workshop wall for items such as screwdrivers and pliers is a good idea. Store all normal spanners and sockets in a metal box. Any measuring instruments, gauges, meters, etc, must be carefully stored where they cannot be damaged or become rusty.

Take a little care when tools are used. Hammer heads inevitably become marked, and screwdrivers lose the keen edge on their blades from time to time. A little timely attention with emery cloth or a file will soon restore items like this to a good finish.

Working facilities

Not to be forgotten when discussing tools is the workshop itself. If anything more than routine maintenance is to be carried out, a suitable working area becomes essential.

It is appreciated that many an owner-mechanic is forced by circumstances to remove an engine or similar item without the benefit of a garage or workshop. Having done this, any repairs should always be done under the cover of a roof.

Wherever possible, any dismantling should be done on a clean, flat workbench or table at a suitable working height.

Any workbench needs a vice; one with a jaw opening of 100 mm is suitable for most jobs. As mentioned previously, some clean dry storage space is also required for tools, as well as for any lubricants, cleaning fluids, touch-up paints etc, which become necessary.

Another item which may be required, and which has a much more general usage, is an electric drill with a chuck capacity of at least 8 mm. This, together with a good range of twist drills, is virtually essential for fitting accessories.

Last, but not least, always keep a supply of old newspapers and clean, lint-free rags available, and try to keep any working area as clean as possible.

Micrometers

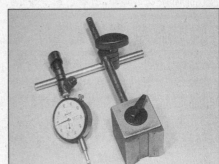

Dial test indicator ("dial gauge")

Strap wrench

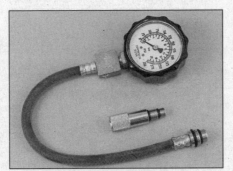

Compression tester

Fault code reader

This is a guide to getting your vehicle through the MOT test. Obviously it will not be possible to examine the vehicle to the same standard as the professional MOT tester. However, working through the following checks will enable you to identify any problem areas before submitting the vehicle for the test.

Where a testable component is in borderline condition, the tester has discretion in deciding whether to pass or fail it. The basis of such discretion is whether the tester would be happy for a close relative or friend to use the vehicle with the component in that condition. If the vehicle presented is clean and evidently well cared for, the tester may be more inclined to pass a borderline component than if the vehicle is scruffy and apparently neglected.

It has only been possible to summarise the test requirements here, based on the regulations in force at the time of printing. Test standards are becoming increasingly stringent, although there are some exemptions for older vehicles.

An assistant will be needed to help carry out some of these checks.

The checks have been sub-divided into four categories, as follows:

1 Checks carried out **FROM THE DRIVER'S SEAT**

2 Checks carried out **WITH THE VEHICLE ON THE GROUND**

3 Checks carried out **WITH THE VEHICLE RAISED AND THE WHEELS FREE TO TURN**

4 Checks carried out on **YOUR VEHICLE'S EXHAUST EMISSION SYSTEM**

---

1 Checks carried out **FROM THE DRIVER'S SEAT**

Handbrake

☐ Test the operation of the handbrake. Excessive travel (too many clicks) indicates incorrect brake or cable adjustment.
☐ Check that the handbrake cannot be released by tapping the lever sideways. Check the security of the lever mountings.

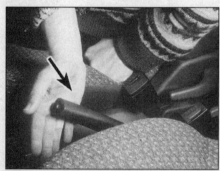

Footbrake

☐ Depress the brake pedal and check that it does not creep down to the floor, indicating a master cylinder fault. Release the pedal, wait a few seconds, then depress it again. If the pedal travels nearly to the floor before firm resistance is felt, brake adjustment or repair is necessary. If the pedal feels spongy, there is air in the hydraulic system which must be removed by bleeding.

☐ Check that the brake pedal is secure and in good condition. Check also for signs of fluid leaks on the pedal, floor or carpets, which would indicate failed seals in the brake master cylinder.
☐ Check the servo unit (when applicable) by operating the brake pedal several times, then keeping the pedal depressed and starting the engine. As the engine starts, the pedal will move down slightly. If not, the vacuum hose or the servo itself may be faulty.

Steering wheel and column

☐ Examine the steering wheel for fractures or looseness of the hub, spokes or rim.
☐ Move the steering wheel from side to side and then up and down. Check that the steering wheel is not loose on the column, indicating wear or a loose retaining nut. Continue moving the steering wheel as before, but also turn it slightly from left to right.
☐ Check that the steering wheel is not loose on the column, and that there is no abnormal

movement of the steering wheel, indicating wear in the column support bearings or couplings.

Windscreen, mirrors and sunvisor

☐ The windscreen must be free of cracks or other significant damage within the driver's field of view. (Small stone chips are acceptable.) Rear view mirrors must be secure, intact, and capable of being adjusted.

290mm

☐ The driver's sunvisor must be capable of being stored in the "up" position.

Seat belts and seats

Note: *The following checks are applicable to all seat belts, front and rear.*

☐ Examine the webbing of all the belts (including rear belts if fitted) for cuts, serious fraying or deterioration. Fasten and unfasten each belt to check the buckles. If applicable, check the retracting mechanism. Check the security of all seat belt mountings accessible from inside the vehicle.

☐ Seat belts with pre-tensioners, once activated, have a "flag" or similar showing on the seat belt stalk. This, in itself, is not a reason for test failure.

☐ The front seats themselves must be securely attached and the backrests must lock in the upright position.

Doors

☐ Both front doors must be able to be opened and closed from outside and inside, and must latch securely when closed.

2 Checks carried out WITH THE VEHICLE ON THE GROUND

Vehicle identification

☐ Number plates must be in good condition, secure and legible, with letters and numbers correctly spaced – spacing at (A) should be at least twice that at (B).

☐ The VIN plate and/or homologation plate must be legible.

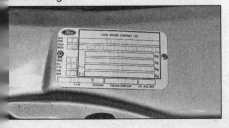

Electrical equipment

☐ Switch on the ignition and check the operation of the horn.

☐ Check the windscreen washers and wipers, examining the wiper blades; renew damaged or perished blades. Also check the operation of the stop-lights.

☐ Check the operation of the sidelights and number plate lights. The lenses and reflectors must be secure, clean and undamaged.

☐ Check the operation and alignment of the headlights. The headlight reflectors must not be tarnished and the lenses must be undamaged.

☐ Switch on the ignition and check the operation of the direction indicators (including the instrument panel tell-tale) and the hazard warning lights. Operation of the sidelights and stop-lights must not affect the indicators - if it does, the cause is usually a bad earth at the rear light cluster.

☐ Check the operation of the rear foglight(s), including the warning light on the instrument panel or in the switch.

☐ The ABS warning light must illuminate in accordance with the manufacturers' design. For most vehicles, the ABS warning light should illuminate when the ignition is switched on, and (if the system is operating properly) extinguish after a few seconds. Refer to the owner's handbook.

Footbrake

☐ Examine the master cylinder, brake pipes and servo unit for leaks, loose mountings, corrosion or other damage.

☐ The fluid reservoir must be secure and the fluid level must be between the upper (A) and lower (B) markings.

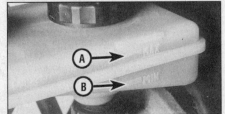

☐ Inspect both front brake flexible hoses for cracks or deterioration of the rubber. Turn the steering from lock to lock, and ensure that the hoses do not contact the wheel, tyre, or any part of the steering or suspension mechanism. With the brake pedal firmly depressed, check the hoses for bulges or leaks under pressure.

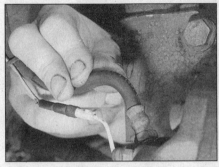

Steering and suspension

☐ Have your assistant turn the steering wheel from side to side slightly, up to the point where the steering gear just begins to transmit this movement to the roadwheels. Check for excessive free play between the steering wheel and the steering gear, indicating wear or insecurity of the steering column joints, the column-to-steering gear coupling, or the steering gear itself.

☐ Have your assistant turn the steering wheel more vigorously in each direction, so that the roadwheels just begin to turn. As this is done, examine all the steering joints, linkages, fittings and attachments. Renew any component that shows signs of wear or damage. On vehicles with power steering, check the security and condition of the steering pump, drivebelt and hoses.

☐ Check that the vehicle is standing level, and at approximately the correct ride height.

Shock absorbers

☐ Depress each corner of the vehicle in turn, then release it. The vehicle should rise and then settle in its normal position. If the vehicle continues to rise and fall, the shock absorber is defective. A shock absorber which has seized will also cause the vehicle to fail.

Exhaust system

☐ Start the engine. With your assistant holding a rag over the tailpipe, check the entire system for leaks. Repair or renew leaking sections.

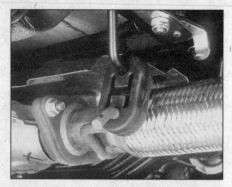

3 Checks carried out
WITH THE VEHICLE RAISED AND THE WHEELS FREE TO TURN

Jack up the front and rear of the vehicle, and securely support it on axle stands. Position the stands clear of the suspension assemblies. Ensure that the wheels are clear of the ground and that the steering can be turned from lock to lock.

Steering mechanism

☐ Have your assistant turn the steering from lock to lock. Check that the steering turns smoothly, and that no part of the steering mechanism, including a wheel or tyre, fouls any brake hose or pipe or any part of the body structure.
☐ Examine the steering rack rubber gaiters for damage or insecurity of the retaining clips. If power steering is fitted, check for signs of damage or leakage of the fluid hoses, pipes or connections. Also check for excessive stiffness or binding of the steering, a missing split pin or locking device, or severe corrosion of the body structure within 30 cm of any steering component attachment point.

Front and rear suspension and wheel bearings

☐ Starting at the front right-hand side, grasp the roadwheel at the 3 o'clock and 9 o'clock positions and rock gently but firmly. Check for free play or insecurity at the wheel bearings, suspension balljoints, or suspension mountings, pivots and attachments.
☐ Now grasp the wheel at the 12 o'clock and 6 o'clock positions and repeat the previous inspection. Spin the wheel, and check for roughness or tightness of the front wheel bearing.

☐ If excess free play is suspected at a component pivot point, this can be confirmed by using a large screwdriver or similar tool and levering between the mounting and the component attachment. This will confirm whether the wear is in the pivot bush, its retaining bolt, or in the mounting itself (the bolt holes can often become elongated).

☐ Carry out all the above checks at the other front wheel, and then at both rear wheels.

Springs and shock absorbers

☐ Examine the suspension struts (when applicable) for serious fluid leakage, corrosion, or damage to the casing. Also check the security of the mounting points.
☐ If coil springs are fitted, check that the spring ends locate in their seats, and that the spring is not corroded, cracked or broken.
☐ If leaf springs are fitted, check that all leaves are intact, that the axle is securely attached to each spring, and that there is no deterioration of the spring eye mountings, bushes, and shackles.

☐ The same general checks apply to vehicles fitted with other suspension types, such as torsion bars, hydraulic displacer units, etc. Ensure that all mountings and attachments are secure, that there are no signs of excessive wear, corrosion or damage, and (on hydraulic types) that there are no fluid leaks or damaged pipes.
☐ Inspect the shock absorbers for signs of serious fluid leakage. Check for wear of the mounting bushes or attachments, or damage to the body of the unit.

Driveshafts (fwd vehicles only)

☐ Rotate each front wheel in turn and inspect the constant velocity joint gaiters for splits or damage. Also check that each driveshaft is straight and undamaged.

Braking system

☐ If possible without dismantling, check brake pad wear and disc condition. Ensure that the friction lining material has not worn excessively, (A) and that the discs are not fractured, pitted, scored or badly worn (B).

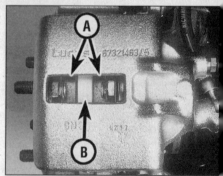

☐ Examine all the rigid brake pipes underneath the vehicle, and the flexible hose(s) at the rear. Look for corrosion, chafing or insecurity of the pipes, and for signs of bulging under pressure, chafing, splits or deterioration of the flexible hoses.
☐ Look for signs of fluid leaks at the brake calipers or on the brake backplates. Repair or renew leaking components.
☐ Slowly spin each wheel, while your assistant depresses and releases the footbrake. Ensure that each brake is operating and does not bind when the pedal is released.

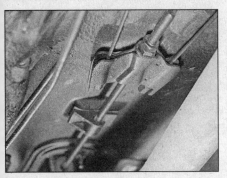

☐ Examine the handbrake mechanism, checking for frayed or broken cables, excessive corrosion, or wear or insecurity of the linkage. Check that the mechanism works on each relevant wheel, and releases fully, without binding.

☐ It is not possible to test brake efficiency without special equipment, but a road test can be carried out later to check that the vehicle pulls up in a straight line.

Fuel and exhaust systems

☐ Inspect the fuel tank (including the filler cap), fuel pipes, hoses, and unions. All components must be secure and free from leaks.

☐ Examine the exhaust system over its entire length, checking for any damaged, broken or missing mountings, security of the retaining clamps and rust or corrosion.

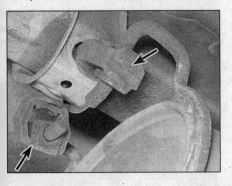

Wheels and tyres

☐ Examine the sidewalls and tread area of each tyre in turn. Check for cuts, tears, lumps, bulges, separation of the tread, and exposure of the ply or cord due to wear or damage. Check that the tyre bead is correctly seated on the wheel rim, that the valve is sound and properly seated, and that the wheel is not distorted or damaged.

☐ Check that the tyres are of the correct size for the vehicle, that they are of the same size and type on each axle, and that the pressures are correct.

☐ Check the tyre tread depth. The legal minimum at the time of writing is 1.6 mm over at least three-quarters of the tread width. Abnormal tread wear may indicate incorrect front wheel alignment.

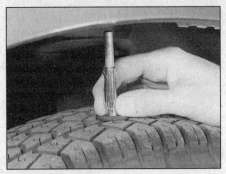

Body corrosion

☐ Check the condition of the entire vehicle structure for signs of corrosion in load-bearing areas. (These include chassis box sections, side sills, cross-members, pillars, and all suspension, steering, braking system and seat belt mountings and anchorages.) Any corrosion which has seriously reduced the thickness of a load-bearing area is likely to cause the vehicle to fail. In this case professional repairs are likely to be needed.

☐ Damage or corrosion which causes sharp or otherwise dangerous edges to be exposed will also cause the vehicle to fail.

4 Checks carried out on YOUR VEHICLE'S EXHAUST EMISSION SYSTEM

Petrol models

☐ Have the engine at normal operating temperature, and make sure that it is in good tune (ignition system in good order, air filter element clean, etc).

☐ Before any measurements are carried out, raise the engine speed to around 2500 rpm, and hold it at this speed for 20 seconds. Allow the engine speed to return to idle, and watch for smoke emissions from the exhaust tailpipe. If the idle speed is obviously much too high, or if dense blue or clearly-visible black smoke comes from the tailpipe for more than 5 seconds, the vehicle will fail. As a rule of thumb, blue smoke signifies oil being burnt (engine wear) while black smoke signifies unburnt fuel (dirty air cleaner element, or other carburettor or fuel system fault).

☐ An exhaust gas analyser capable of measuring carbon monoxide (CO) and hydrocarbons (HC) is now needed. If such an instrument cannot be hired or borrowed, a local garage may agree to perform the check for a small fee.

CO emissions (mixture)

☐ At the time of writing, for vehicles first used between 1st August 1975 and 31st July 1986 (P to C registration), the CO level must not exceed 4.5% by volume. For vehicles first used between 1st August 1986 and 31st July 1992 (D to J registration), the CO level must not exceed 3.5% by volume. Vehicles first

used after 1st August 1992 (K registration) must conform to the manufacturer's specification. The MOT tester has access to a DOT database or emissions handbook, which lists the CO and HC limits for each make and model of vehicle. The CO level is measured with the engine at idle speed, and at "fast idle". The following limits are given as a general guide:

> At idle speed -
>   CO level no more than 0.5%
> At "fast idle" (2500 to 3000 rpm) -
>   CO level no more than 0.3%
> (Minimum oil temperature 60°C)

☐ If the CO level cannot be reduced far enough to pass the test (and the fuel and ignition systems are otherwise in good condition) then the carburettor is badly worn, or there is some problem in the fuel injection system or catalytic converter (as applicable).

HC emissions

☐ With the CO within limits, HC emissions for vehicles first used between 1st August 1975 and 31st July 1992 (P to J registration) must not exceed 1200 ppm. Vehicles first used after 1st August 1992 (K registration) must conform to the manufacturer's specification. The MOT tester has access to a DOT database or emissions handbook, which lists the CO and HC limits for each make and model of vehicle. The HC level is measured with the engine at "fast idle". The following is given as a general guide:

> At "fast idle" (2500 to 3000 rpm) -
>   HC level no more than 200 ppm
> (Minimum oil temperature 60°C)

☐ Excessive HC emissions are caused by incomplete combustion, the causes of which can include oil being burnt, mechanical wear and ignition/fuel system malfunction.

Diesel models

☐ The only emission test applicable to Diesel engines is the measuring of exhaust smoke density. The test involves accelerating the engine several times to its maximum unloaded speed.

Note: *It is of the utmost importance that the engine timing belt is in good condition before the test is carried out.*

☐ The limits for Diesel engine exhaust smoke, introduced in September 1995 are:

Vehicles first used before 1st August 1979:
   Exempt from metered smoke testing, but must not emit "dense blue or clearly visible black smoke for a period of more than 5 seconds at idle" or "dense blue or clearly visible black smoke during acceleration which would obscure the view of other road users".

Non-turbocharged vehicles first used after 1st August 1979: 2.5m-1

Turbocharged vehicles first used after 1st August 1979: 3.0m-1

☐ Excessive smoke can be caused by a dirty air cleaner element. Otherwise, professional advice may be needed to find the cause.

Engine

- ☐ Engine fails to rotate when attempting to start
- ☐ Engine rotates, but will not start
- ☐ Engine difficult to start when cold
- ☐ Engine difficult to start when hot
- ☐ Starter motor noisy or excessively-rough in engagement
- ☐ Engine starts, but stops immediately
- ☐ Engine idles erratically
- ☐ Engine misfires at idle speed
- ☐ Engine misfires throughout the driving speed range
- ☐ Engine hesitates on acceleration
- ☐ Engine stalls
- ☐ Engine lacks power
- ☐ Engine backfires
- ☐ Oil pressure warning light on with engine running
- ☐ Engine runs-on after switching off
- ☐ Engine noises

Cooling system

- ☐ Overheating
- ☐ Overcooling
- ☐ External coolant leakage
- ☐ Internal coolant leakage
- ☐ Corrosion

Fuel and exhaust systems

- ☐ Excessive fuel consumption
- ☐ Fuel leakage and/or fuel odour
- ☐ Excessive noise or fumes from exhaust system

Clutch

- ☐ Pedal travels to floor - no pressure or very little resistance
- ☐ Clutch fails to disengage (unable to select gears)
- ☐ Clutch slips (engine speed rises, with no increase in vehicle speed)
- ☐ Judder as clutch is engaged
- ☐ Noise when depressing or releasing clutch pedal

Manual transmission

- ☐ Noisy in neutral with engine running
- ☐ Noisy in one particular gear
- ☐ Difficulty engaging gears
- ☐ Jumps out of gear
- ☐ Vibration
- ☐ Lubricant leaks

Automatic transmission

- ☐ Fluid leakage
- ☐ Transmission fluid brown, or has burned smell
- ☐ General gear selection problems
- ☐ Transmission will not downshift (kickdown) on full throttle
- ☐ Engine won't start in any gear, or starts in gears other than "P" or "N"
- ☐ Transmission slips, shifts roughly, is noisy, or has no drive in forward or reverse gears

Driveshafts

- ☐ Clicking or knocking noise on turns (at slow speed on full-lock)
- ☐ Vibration when accelerating or decelerating

Braking system

- ☐ Vehicle pulls to one side under braking
- ☐ Noise (grinding or high-pitched squeal) when brakes applied
- ☐ Excessive brake pedal travel
- ☐ Brake pedal feels spongy when depressed
- ☐ Excessive brake pedal effort required to stop vehicle
- ☐ Judder felt through brake pedal or steering wheel when braking
- ☐ Brakes binding
- ☐ Rear wheels locking under normal braking

Suspension and steering systems

- ☐ Vehicle pulls to one side
- ☐ Wheel wobble and vibration
- ☐ Excessive pitching and/or rolling around corners, or during braking
- ☐ Wandering or general instability
- ☐ Excessively-stiff steering
- ☐ Excessive play in steering
- ☐ Lack of power assistance
- ☐ Tyre wear excessive

Electrical system

- ☐ Battery will not hold a charge for more than a few days
- ☐ Ignition/no-charge warning light stays on with engine running
- ☐ Ignition/no-charge warning light fails to come on
- ☐ Lights inoperative
- ☐ Instrument readings inaccurate or erratic
- ☐ Horn inoperative, or unsatisfactory in operation
- ☐ Windscreen/tailgate wipers failed, or unsatisfactory in operation
- ☐ Windscreen/tailgate washers failed, or unsatisfactory in operation
- ☐ Electric windows inoperative, or unsatisfactory in operation
- ☐ Central locking system inoperative, or unsatisfactory in operation

Introduction

The vehicle owner who does his or her own maintenance according to the recommended service schedules should not have to use this section of the manual very often. Modern component reliability is such that, provided those items subject to wear or deterioration are inspected or renewed at the specified intervals, sudden failure is comparatively rare. Faults do not usually just happen as a result of sudden failure, but develop over a period of time. Major mechanical failures in particular are usually preceded by characteristic symptoms over hundreds or even thousands of miles. Those components which do occasionally fail without warning are often small and easily carried in the vehicle.

With any fault-finding, the first step is to decide where to begin investigations. This may be obvious, but some detective work may be necessary. The owner who makes half a dozen haphazard adjustments or replacements may be successful in curing a fault (or its symptoms), but will be none the wiser if the fault recurs, and ultimately may have spent more time and money than was necessary. A calm and logical approach will be found to be more satisfactory in the long run. Always take into account any warning signs that may have been noticed in the period preceding the fault - power loss, high or low gauge readings, unusual smells, etc - and remember - failure of components such as fuses or spark plugs may only be pointers to some underlying fault.

The pages which follow provide an easy-reference guide to the more common problems which may occur during the operation of the vehicle. These problems and their possible causes are grouped under headings denoting various components or systems, such as Engine, Cooling system, etc. The Chapter which deals with the problem is shown in brackets. Whatever the fault, certain basic principles apply. These are as follows:

Verify the fault. This is simply a matter of being sure that you know what the symptoms are before starting work. This is particularly important if you are investigating a fault for someone else, who may not have described it very accurately.

Don't overlook the obvious. For example, if the vehicle won't start, is there fuel in the tank? (Don't take anyone else's word on this particular point, and don't trust the fuel gauge either!) If an electrical fault is indicated, look for loose or broken wires before digging out the test gear.

Cure the disease, not the symptom. Substituting a flat battery with a fully-charged one will get you off the hard shoulder, but if the underlying cause is not attended to, the new battery will go the same way. Similarly, changing oil-fouled spark plugs for a new set will get you moving again, but remember that the reason for the fouling (if it wasn't simply an incorrect grade of plug) will have to be established and corrected.

Don't take anything for granted. Particularly, don't forget that a "new" component may itself be defective (especially if it's been rattling around in the boot for months), and don't leave components out of a fault diagnosis sequence just because they are new or recently-fitted. When you do finally diagnose a difficult fault, you'll probably realise that all the evidence was there from the start.

Engine

Engine fails to rotate when attempting to start

- ☐ Battery terminal connections loose or corroded ("Weekly checks").
- ☐ Battery discharged or faulty (Chapter 5).
- ☐ Broken, loose or disconnected wiring in the starting circuit (Chapter 5).
- ☐ Defective starter solenoid or switch (Chapter 5).
- ☐ Defective starter motor (Chapter 5).
- ☐ Starter pinion or flywheel ring gear teeth loose or broken (Chapters 2 and 5).
- ☐ Engine earth strap broken or disconnected (Chapter 5).

Engine rotates, but will not start

- ☐ Fuel tank empty.
- ☐ Battery discharged (engine rotates slowly) (Chapter 5).
- ☐ Battery terminal connections loose or corroded ("Weekly checks").
- ☐ Ignition components damp or damaged (Chapters 1 and 5).
- ☐ Broken, loose or disconnected wiring in the ignition circuit (Chapters 1 and 5).
- ☐ Worn, faulty or incorrectly-gapped spark plugs (Chapter 1).
- ☐ Choke mechanism incorrectly adjusted, worn or sticking - carburettor models (Chapter 4).
- ☐ Faulty fuel cut-off solenoid - carburettor models (Chapter 4).
- ☐ Fuel injection system fault - fuel-injected models (Chapter 4).
- ☐ Major mechanical failure (eg camshaft drive) (Chapter 2).

Engine difficult to start when cold

- ☐ Battery discharged (Chapter 5).
- ☐ Battery terminal connections loose or corroded ("Weekly checks").
- ☐ Worn, faulty or incorrectly-gapped spark plugs (Chapter 1).
- ☐ Choke mechanism incorrectly adjusted, worn or sticking - carburettor models (Chapter 4).
- ☐ Fuel injection system fault - fuel-injected models (Chapter 4).
- ☐ Other ignition system fault (Chapters 1 and 5).
- ☐ Low cylinder compressions (Chapter 2).

Engine difficult to start when hot

- ☐ Air filter element dirty or clogged (Chapter 1).
- ☐ Choke mechanism incorrectly adjusted, worn or sticking - carburettor models (Chapter 4).
- ☐ Fuel injection system fault - fuel-injected models (Chapter 4).
- ☐ Low cylinder compressions (Chapter 2).

Engine starts, but stops immediately

- ☐ Loose or faulty electrical connections in the ignition circuit (Chapters 1 and 5).
- ☐ Vacuum leak at the carburettor/throttle body or inlet manifold (Chapter 4).
- ☐ Blocked carburettor jet(s) or internal passages - carburettor models (Chapter 4).
- ☐ Blocked injector/fuel injection system fault - fuel-injected models (Chapter 4).

Starter motor noisy or excessively-rough in engagement

- ☐ Starter pinion or flywheel ring gear teeth loose or broken (Chapters 2 and 5).
- ☐ Starter motor mounting bolts loose or missing (Chapter 5).
- ☐ Starter motor internal components worn or damaged (Chapter 5).

Engine idles erratically

- ☐ Air filter element clogged (Chapter 1).
- ☐ Vacuum leak at the carburettor/throttle body, inlet manifold or associated hoses (Chapter 4).
- ☐ Worn, faulty or incorrectly-gapped spark plugs (Chapter 1).
- ☐ Uneven or low cylinder compressions (Chapter 2).
- ☐ Camshaft lobes worn (Chapter 2).
- ☐ Timing belt incorrectly tensioned (Chapter 2).
- ☐ Blocked carburettor jet(s) or internal passages - carburettor models (Chapter 4).
- ☐ Blocked injector/fuel injection system fault - fuel-injected models (Chapter 4).

Engine misfires at idle speed

- ☐ Worn, faulty or incorrectly-gapped spark plugs (Chapter 1).
- ☐ Faulty spark plug HT leads (Chapter 1).
- ☐ Vacuum leak at the carburettor/throttle body, inlet manifold or associated hoses (Chapter 4).
- ☐ Blocked carburettor jet(s) or internal passages - carburettor models (Chapter 4).
- ☐ Blocked injector/fuel injection system fault - fuel-injected models (Chapter 4).
- ☐ Distributor cap cracked or tracking internally (where applicable) (Chapter 1).
- ☐ Uneven or low cylinder compressions (Chapter 2).
- ☐ Disconnected, leaking, or perished crankcase ventilation hoses (Chapter 4).

Engine misfires throughout the driving speed range

- ☐ Fuel filter choked (Chapter 1).
- ☐ Fuel pump faulty, or delivery pressure low (Chapter 4).
- ☐ Fuel tank vent blocked, or fuel pipes restricted (Chapter 4).
- ☐ Vacuum leak at the carburettor/throttle body, inlet manifold or associated hoses (Chapter 4).
- ☐ Worn, faulty or incorrectly-gapped spark plugs (Chapter 1).
- ☐ Faulty spark plug HT leads (Chapter 1).
- ☐ Distributor cap cracked or tracking internally (where applicable) (Chapter 1).
- ☐ Faulty ignition coil (Chapter 5).
- ☐ Uneven or low cylinder compressions (Chapter 2).
- ☐ Blocked carburettor jet(s) or internal passages - carburettor models (Chapter 4).
- ☐ Blocked injector/fuel injection system fault - fuel-injected models (Chapter 4).

Engine (continued)

Engine hesitates on acceleration

- ☐ Worn, faulty or incorrectly-gapped spark plugs (Chapter 1).
- ☐ Vacuum leak at the carburettor/throttle body, inlet manifold or associated hoses (Chapter 4).
- ☐ Blocked carburettor jet(s) or internal passages - carburettor models (Chapter 4).
- ☐ Blocked injector/fuel injection system fault - fuel-injected models (Chapter 4).

Engine stalls

- ☐ Vacuum leak at the carburettor/throttle body, inlet manifold or associated hoses (Chapter 4).
- ☐ Fuel filter choked (Chapter 1).
- ☐ Fuel pump faulty, or delivery pressure low (Chapter 4).
- ☐ Fuel tank vent blocked, or fuel pipes restricted (Chapter 4).
- ☐ Blocked carburettor jet(s) or internal passages - carburettor models (Chapter 4).
- ☐ Blocked injector/fuel injection system fault - fuel-injected models (Chapter 4).

Engine lacks power

- ☐ Timing belt incorrectly fitted or tensioned (Chapter 2).
- ☐ Fuel filter choked (Chapter 1).
- ☐ Fuel pump faulty, or delivery pressure low (Chapter 4).
- ☐ Uneven or low cylinder compressions (Chapter 2).
- ☐ Worn, faulty or incorrectly-gapped spark plugs (Chapter 1).
- ☐ Vacuum leak at the carburettor/throttle body, inlet manifold or associated hoses (Chapter 4).
- ☐ Blocked carburettor jet(s) or internal passages - carburettor models (Chapter 4).
- ☐ Blocked injector/fuel injection system fault - fuel-injected models (Chapter 4).
- ☐ Brakes binding (Chapters 1 and 9).
- ☐ Clutch slipping (Chapter 6).

Engine backfires

- ☐ Timing belt incorrectly fitted or tensioned (Chapter 2).
- ☐ Vacuum leak at the carburettor/throttle body, inlet manifold or associated hoses (Chapter 4).
- ☐ Blocked carburettor jet(s) or internal passages - carburettor models (Chapter 4).
- ☐ Blocked injector/fuel injection system fault - fuel-injected models (Chapter 4).

Oil pressure warning light on with engine running

- ☐ Low oil level, or incorrect oil grade ("Weekly checks").

- ☐ Faulty oil pressure warning light switch (Chapter 5).
- ☐ Worn engine bearings and/or oil pump (Chapter 2).
- ☐ High engine operating temperature (Chapter 3).
- ☐ Oil pressure relief valve defective (Chapter 2).
- ☐ Oil pick-up strainer clogged (Chapter 2).

Engine runs-on after switching off

- ☐ Excessive carbon build-up in engine (Chapter 2).
- ☐ High engine operating temperature (Chapter 3).
- ☐ Faulty fuel cut-off solenoid - carburettor models (Chapter 4).
- ☐ Fuel injection system fault - fuel-injected models (Chapter 4).

Engine noises

Pre-ignition (pinking) or knocking during acceleration or under load

- ☐ Ignition timing incorrect/ignition system fault (Chapters 1 and 5).
- ☐ Incorrect grade of spark plug (Chapter 1).
- ☐ Incorrect grade of fuel (Chapter 1).
- ☐ Vacuum leak at the carburettor/throttle body, inlet manifold or associated hoses (Chapter 4).
- ☐ Excessive carbon build-up in engine (Chapter 2).
- ☐ Blocked carburettor jet(s) or internal passages - carburettor models (Chapter 4).
- ☐ Blocked injector/fuel injection system fault - fuel-injected models (Chapter 4).

Whistling or wheezing noises

- ☐ Leaking inlet manifold or carburettor/throttle body gasket (Chapter 4).
- ☐ Leaking exhaust manifold gasket or pipe-to-manifold joint (Chapter 4).
- ☐ Leaking vacuum hose (Chapters 4 and 9).
- ☐ Blowing cylinder head gasket (Chapter 2).

Tapping or rattling noises

- ☐ Worn valve gear or camshaft (Chapter 2).
- ☐ Ancillary component fault (coolant pump, alternator, etc) (Chapters 3, 5, etc).

Knocking or thumping noises

- ☐ Worn big-end bearings (regular heavy knocking, perhaps less under load) (Chapter 2).
- ☐ Worn main bearings (rumbling and knocking, perhaps worsening under load) (Chapter 2).
- ☐ Piston slap (most noticeable when cold) (Chapter 2).
- ☐ Ancillary component fault (coolant pump, alternator, etc) (Chapters 3, 5, etc).

Cooling system

Overheating

- ☐ Insufficient coolant in system ("Weekly checks").
- ☐ Thermostat faulty (Chapter 3).
- ☐ Radiator core blocked, or grille restricted (Chapter 3).
- ☐ Electric cooling fan or thermoswitch faulty (Chapter 3).
- ☐ Pressure cap faulty (Chapter 3).
- ☐ Ignition timing incorrect/ignition system fault (Chapters 1 and 5).
- ☐ Inaccurate temperature gauge sender unit (Chapter 3).
- ☐ Airlock in cooling system (Chapter 1).

Overcooling

- ☐ Thermostat faulty (Chapter 3).
- ☐ Inaccurate temperature gauge sender unit (Chapter 3).

External coolant leakage

- ☐ Deteriorated or damaged hoses or hose clips (Chapter 1).
- ☐ Radiator core or heater matrix leaking (Chapter 3).
- ☐ Pressure cap faulty (Chapter 3).
- ☐ Water pump seal leaking (Chapter 3).
- ☐ Boiling due to overheating (Chapter 3).
- ☐ Core plug leaking (Chapter 2).

Internal coolant leakage

- ☐ Leaking cylinder head gasket (Chapter 2).
- ☐ Cracked cylinder head or cylinder bore (Chapter 2).

Corrosion

- ☐ Infrequent draining and flushing (Chapter 1).
- ☐ Incorrect coolant mixture or inappropriate coolant type (Chapter 1).

Fuel and exhaust systems

Excessive fuel consumption

- [ ] Air filter element dirty or clogged (Chapter 1).
- [ ] Choke cable incorrectly adjusted, or choke sticking - carburettor models (Chapter 4).
- [ ] Fuel injection system fault - fuel injected models (Chapter 4).
- [ ] Ignition timing incorrect/ignition system fault (Chapters 1 and 5).
- [ ] Tyres under-inflated ("Weekly checks").
- [ ] Brakes binding (Chapters 1 and 9).

Fuel leakage and/or fuel odour

- [ ] Damaged or corroded fuel tank, pipes or connections (Chapters 1 and 4).
- [ ] Carburettor float chamber flooding (float height incorrect) - carburettor models (Chapter 4).

Excessive noise or fumes from exhaust system

- [ ] Leaking exhaust system or manifold joints (Chapters 1 and 4).
- [ ] Leaking, corroded or damaged silencers or pipe (Chapters 1 and 4).
- [ ] Broken mountings causing body or suspension contact (Chapters 1 and 4).

Clutch

Pedal travels to floor - no pressure or very little resistance

- [ ] Broken clutch cable (Chapter 6).
- [ ] Incorrect clutch cable adjustment (Chapter 6).
- [ ] Broken clutch release bearing or fork (Chapter 6).
- [ ] Broken diaphragm spring in clutch pressure plate (Chapter 6).

Clutch fails to disengage (unable to select gears)

- [ ] Incorrect clutch cable adjustment (Chapter 6).
- [ ] Clutch disc sticking on gearbox input shaft splines (Chapter 6).
- [ ] Clutch disc sticking to flywheel or pressure plate (Chapter 6).
- [ ] Faulty pressure plate assembly (Chapter 6).
- [ ] Clutch release mechanism worn or incorrectly assembled (Chapter 6).

Clutch slips (engine speed rises, with no increase in vehicle speed)

- [ ] Incorrect clutch cable adjustment (Chapter 6).

- [ ] Clutch disc linings excessively worn (Chapter 6).
- [ ] Clutch disc linings contaminated with oil or grease (Chapter 6).
- [ ] Faulty pressure plate or weak diaphragm spring (Chapter 6).

Judder as clutch is engaged

- [ ] Clutch disc linings contaminated with oil or grease (Chapter 6).
- [ ] Clutch disc linings excessively worn (Chapter 6).
- [ ] Clutch cable sticking or frayed (Chapter 6).
- [ ] Faulty or distorted pressure plate or diaphragm spring (Chapter 6).
- [ ] Worn or loose engine or gearbox mountings (Chapter 2).
- [ ] Clutch disc hub or gearbox input shaft splines worn (Chapter 6).

Noise when depressing or releasing clutch pedal

- [ ] Worn clutch release bearing (Chapter 6).
- [ ] Worn or dry clutch pedal bushes (Chapter 6).
- [ ] Faulty pressure plate assembly (Chapter 6).
- [ ] Pressure plate diaphragm spring broken (Chapter 6).
- [ ] Broken clutch disc cushioning springs (Chapter 6).

Manual transmission

Noisy in neutral with engine running

- [ ] Input shaft bearings worn (noise apparent with clutch pedal released, but not when depressed) (Chapter 7).*
- [ ] Clutch release bearing worn (noise apparent with clutch pedal depressed, possibly less when released) (Chapter 6).

Noisy in one particular gear

- [ ] Worn, damaged or chipped gear teeth (Chapter 7).*

Difficulty engaging gears

- [ ] Clutch fault (Chapter 6).
- [ ] Worn or damaged gear linkage (Chapter 7).
- [ ] Incorrectly-adjusted gear linkage (Chapter 7).
- [ ] Worn synchroniser units (Chapter 7).*

Jumps out of gear

- [ ] Worn or damaged gear linkage (Chapter 7).

- [ ] Incorrectly-adjusted gear linkage (Chapter 7).
- [ ] Worn synchroniser units (Chapter 7).*
- [ ] Worn selector forks (Chapter 7).*

Vibration

- [ ] Lack of oil (Chapter 1).
- [ ] Worn bearings (Chapter 7).*

Lubricant leaks

- [ ] Leaking differential output oil seal (Chapter 7).
- [ ] Leaking housing joint (Chapter 7).*
- [ ] Leaking input shaft oil seal (Chapter 7).*

*Although the corrective action necessary to remedy the symptoms described is beyond the scope of the home mechanic, the above information should be helpful in isolating the cause of the condition, so that the owner can communicate clearly with a professional mechanic.

Automatic transmission

Note: *Due to the complexity of the automatic transmission, it is difficult for the home mechanic to properly diagnose and service this unit. For problems other than the following, the vehicle should be taken to a dealer service department or automatic transmission specialist. Don't be in a hurry to remove the transmission if a fault is suspected, as most testing is carried out with the unit still fitted.*

Fluid leakage

☐ Automatic transmission fluid is usually dark in colour. Fluid leaks should not be confused with engine oil, which can easily be blown onto the transmission by airflow.
☐ To determine the source of a leak, first remove all built-up dirt and grime from the transmission housing and surrounding areas using a degreasing agent, or by steam-cleaning. Drive the vehicle at low speed, so airflow will not blow the leak far from its source. Raise and support the vehicle, and determine where the leak is coming from. The following are common areas of leakage:
a) *Fluid pan or "sump" (Chapter 1 and 7).*
b) *Dipstick tube (Chapter 1 and 7).*
c) *Transmission-to-fluid cooler pipes/unions (Chapter 7).*

Transmission fluid brown, or has burned smell

☐ Transmission fluid level low, or fluid in need of renewal (Chapter 1).

General gear selection problems

☐ Chapter 7B deals with checking and adjusting the selector cable

on automatic transmissions. The following are common problems which may be caused by a poorly-adjusted cable:
a) *Engine starting in gears other than Park or Neutral.*
b) *Indicator panel showing a gear other than that being used.*
c) *Vehicle moves when in Park or Neutral.*
d) *Poor gear shift quality or erratic gear changes.*
   Refer to Chapter 7 for the selector cable adjustment procedure.

Transmission will not downshift (kickdown) at full throttle

☐ Low transmission fluid level (Chapter 1).
☐ Incorrect selector cable adjustment (Chapter 7).

Engine won't start in any gear, or starts in gears other than Park or Neutral

☐ Incorrect starter/inhibitor switch adjustment (Chapter 7).
☐ Incorrect selector cable adjustment (Chapter 7).

Transmission slips, shifts roughly, is noisy, or has no drive in forward or reverse gears

☐ There are many probable causes for the above problems, but the home mechanic should be concerned with only one possibility - fluid level. Before taking the vehicle to a dealer or transmission specialist, check the fluid level and condition of the fluid as described in Chapter 1. Correct the fluid level as necessary, or change the fluid and filter. If the problem persists, professional help will be necessary.

Driveshafts

Clicking or knocking noise on turns (at slow speed on full-lock)

☐ Lack of constant velocity joint lubricant, possibly due to damaged gaiter (Chapter 8).
☐ Worn outer constant velocity joint (Chapter 8).

Vibration when accelerating or decelerating

☐ Worn inner constant velocity joint (Chapter 8).
☐ Bent or distorted driveshaft (Chapter 8).

Braking system

Note: *Before assuming that a brake problem exists, make sure that the tyres are in good condition and correctly inflated, that the front wheel alignment is correct, and that the vehicle is not loaded with weight in an unequal manner. Apart from checking the condition of all pipe and hose connections, any faults occurring on the anti-lock braking system should be referred to a Peugeot dealer for diagnosis.*

Vehicle pulls to one side under braking

☐ Worn, defective, damaged or contaminated brake pads/shoes on one side (Chapters 1 and 9).
☐ Seized or partially-seized front brake caliper/wheel cylinder piston (Chapters 1 and 9).
☐ A mixture of brake pad/shoe lining materials fitted between sides (Chapters 1 and 9).
☐ Brake caliper or backplate mounting bolts loose (Chapter 9).
☐ Worn or damaged steering or suspension components (Chapters 1 and 10).

Noise (grinding or high-pitched squeal) when brakes applied

☐ Brake pad or shoe friction lining material worn down to metal backing (Chapters 1 and 9).

☐ Excessive corrosion of brake disc or drum. May be apparent after the vehicle has been standing for some time (Chapters 1 and 9).
☐ Foreign object (stone chipping, etc) trapped between brake disc and shield (Chapters 1 and 9).

Excessive brake pedal travel

☐ Inoperative rear brake self-adjust mechanism - drum brakes (Chapters 1 and 9).
☐ Faulty master cylinder (Chapter 9).
☐ Air in hydraulic system (Chapters 1 and 9).
☐ Faulty vacuum servo unit (Chapter 9).

Excessive brake pedal effort required to stop vehicle

☐ Faulty vacuum servo unit (Chapter 9).
☐ Disconnected, damaged or insecure brake servo vacuum hose (Chapter 9).
☐ Primary or secondary hydraulic circuit failure (Chapter 9).
☐ Seized brake caliper or wheel cylinder piston(s) (Chapter 9).
☐ Brake pads or brake shoes incorrectly fitted (Chapters 1 and 9).
☐ Incorrect grade of brake pads or brake shoes fitted (Chapters 1 and 9).
☐ Brake pads or brake shoe linings contaminated (Chapters 1 and 9).

Braking system (continued)

Brake pedal feels spongy when depressed

- [ ] Air in hydraulic system (Chapters 1 and 9).
- [ ] Deteriorated flexible rubber brake hoses (Chapters 1 and 9).
- [ ] Master cylinder mounting nuts loose (Chapter 9).
- [ ] Faulty master cylinder (Chapter 9).

Judder felt through brake pedal or steering wheel when braking

- [ ] Excessive run-out or distortion of discs/drums (Chapters 1 and 9).
- [ ] Brake pad or brake shoe linings worn (Chapters 1 and 9).
- [ ] Brake caliper or brake backplate mounting bolts loose (Chapter 9).
- [ ] Wear in suspension or steering components or mountings (Chapters 1 and 10).

Brakes binding

- [ ] Seized brake caliper or wheel cylinder piston(s) (Chapter 9).
- [ ] Incorrectly-adjusted handbrake mechanism (Chapter 9).
- [ ] Faulty master cylinder (Chapter 9).

Rear wheels locking under normal braking

- [ ] Rear brake shoe linings contaminated (Chapters 1 and 9).
- [ ] Faulty brake pressure regulator (Chapter 9).

Suspension and steering

Note: *Before diagnosing suspension or steering faults, be sure that the trouble is not due to incorrect tyre pressures, mixtures of tyre types, or binding brakes.*

Vehicle pulls to one side

- [ ] Defective tyre (*"Weekly checks"*).
- [ ] Excessive wear in suspension or steering components (Chapters 1 and 10).
- [ ] Incorrect front wheel alignment (Chapter 10).
- [ ] Damage to steering or suspension components (Chapters 1 and 10).

Wheel wobble and vibration

- [ ] Front roadwheels out of balance (vibration felt mainly through the steering wheel) (Chapters 1 and 10).
- [ ] Rear roadwheels out of balance (vibration felt throughout the vehicle) (Chapters 1 and 10).
- [ ] Roadwheels damaged or distorted (*"Weekly checks"* and Chapter 10).
- [ ] Faulty or damaged tyre (*"Weekly checks"*).
- [ ] Worn steering or suspension joints, bushes or components (Chapters 1 and 10).
- [ ] Wheel bolts loose (Chapters 1 and 10).

Excessive pitching and/or rolling around corners, or during braking

- [ ] Defective shock absorbers (Chapters 1 and 10).
- [ ] Broken or weak spring and/or suspension part (Chapters 1 and 10).
- [ ] Worn or damaged anti-roll bar or mountings (Chapter 10).

Wandering or general instability

- [ ] Incorrect front wheel alignment (Chapter 10).
- [ ] Worn steering or suspension joints, bushes or components (Chapters 1 and 10).
- [ ] Roadwheels out of balance (*"Weekly checks"* and Chapter 1).
- [ ] Faulty or damaged tyre (*"Weekly checks"*).
- [ ] Wheel bolts loose (Chapters 1 and 10).
- [ ] Defective shock absorbers (Chapters 1 and 10).

Excessively-stiff steering

- [ ] Lack of steering gear lubricant (Chapter 10).
- [ ] Seized track rod end balljoint or suspension balljoint (Chapters 1 and 10).
- [ ] Broken or incorrectly-adjusted auxiliary drivebelt - power steering (Chapter 1).
- [ ] Incorrect front wheel alignment (Chapter 10).
- [ ] Steering rack or column bent or damaged (Chapter 10).

Excessive play in steering

- [ ] Worn steering column intermediate shaft universal joint (Chapter 10).
- [ ] Worn steering track rod end balljoints (Chapters 1 and 10).
- [ ] Worn rack-and-pinion steering gear (Chapter 10).
- [ ] Worn steering or suspension joints, bushes or components (Chapters 1 and 10).

Lack of power assistance

- [ ] Broken or incorrectly-adjusted auxiliary drivebelt (Chapter 1).
- [ ] Incorrect power steering fluid level (*"Weekly checks"*).
- [ ] Restriction in power steering fluid hoses (Chapter 1).
- [ ] Faulty power steering pump (Chapter 10).
- [ ] Faulty rack-and-pinion steering gear (Chapter 10).

Tyre wear excessive

Tyre treads exhibit feathered edges

- [ ] Incorrect toe setting (Chapter 10).

Tyres worn in centre of tread

- [ ] Tyres over-inflated (*"Weekly checks"*).

Tyres worn on inside and outside edges

- [ ] Tyres under-inflated (*"Weekly checks"*).

Tyres worn on inside or outside edges

- [ ] Incorrect camber/castor angles (wear on one edge only) (Chapter 10).
- [ ] Worn steering or suspension joints, bushes or components (Chapters 1 and 10).
- [ ] Excessively-hard cornering.
- [ ] Accident damage.

Tyres worn unevenly

- [ ] Tyres/wheels out of balance (*"Weekly checks"*).
- [ ] Excessive wheel or tyre run-out (Chapter 1).
- [ ] Worn shock absorbers (Chapters 1 and 10).
- [ ] Faulty tyre (*"Weekly checks"*).

Electrical system

Note: *For problems associated with the starting system, refer to the faults listed under "Engine" earlier in this Section.*

Battery won't hold a charge for more than a few days

- [ ] Battery defective internally (Chapter 5).
- [ ] Battery terminal connections loose or corroded (*"Weekly checks"*).
- [ ] Auxiliary drivebelt worn or incorrectly adjusted (Chapter 1).
- [ ] Alternator not charging at correct output (Chapter 5).
- [ ] Alternator or voltage regulator faulty (Chapter 5).
- [ ] Short-circuit causing continual battery drain (Chapters 5 and 12).

Ignition/no-charge warning light stays on with engine running

- [ ] Auxiliary drivebelt broken, worn, or incorrectly adjusted (Chapter 1).
- [ ] Alternator brushes worn, sticking, or dirty (Chapter 5).
- [ ] Alternator brush springs weak or broken (Chapter 5).
- [ ] Internal fault in alternator or voltage regulator (Chapter 5).
- [ ] Broken, disconnected, or loose wiring in charging circuit (Chapter 5).

Ignition/no-charge warning light fails to come on

- [ ] Warning light bulb blown (Chapter 12).
- [ ] Broken, disconnected, or loose wiring in warning light circuit (Chapter 12).
- [ ] Alternator faulty (Chapter 5).

Lights inoperative

- [ ] Bulb blown (Chapter 12).
- [ ] Corrosion of bulb or bulbholder contacts (Chapter 12).
- [ ] Blown fuse (Chapter 12).
- [ ] Faulty relay (Chapter 12).
- [ ] Broken, loose, or disconnected wiring (Chapter 12).
- [ ] Faulty switch (Chapter 12).

Instrument readings inaccurate or erratic

Instrument readings increase with engine speed

- [ ] Faulty voltage regulator (Chapter 12).

Fuel or temperature gauges give no reading

- [ ] Faulty gauge sender unit (Chapters 3 and 4).
- [ ] Wiring open-circuit (Chapter 12).
- [ ] Faulty gauge (Chapter 12).

Fuel or temperature gauges give continuous maximum reading

- [ ] Faulty gauge sender unit (Chapters 3 and 4).
- [ ] Wiring short-circuit (Chapter 12).
- [ ] Faulty gauge (Chapter 12).

Horn inoperative, or unsatisfactory in operation

Horn operates all the time

- [ ] Horn push either earthed or stuck down (Chapter 12).
- [ ] Horn cable-to-horn push earthed (Chapter 12).

Horn fails to operate

- [ ] Blown fuse (Chapter 12).
- [ ] Cable or connections loose, broken or disconnected (Chapter 12).
- [ ] Faulty horn (Chapter 12).

Horn emits intermittent or unsatisfactory sound

- [ ] Cable connections loose (Chapter 12).
- [ ] Horn mountings loose (Chapter 12).
- [ ] Faulty horn (Chapter 12).

Windscreen/tailgate wipers failed, or unsatisfactory in operation

Wipers fail to operate, or operate very slowly

- [ ] Wiper blades stuck to screen, or linkage seized or binding (Chapters 1 and 12).
- [ ] Blown fuse (Chapter 12).
- [ ] Cable or connections loose, broken or disconnected (Chapter 12).
- [ ] Faulty relay (Chapter 12).
- [ ] Faulty wiper motor (Chapter 12).

Wiper blades sweep over too large or too small an area of the glass

- [ ] Wiper arms incorrectly positioned on spindles (Chapter 1).
- [ ] Excessive wear of wiper linkage (Chapter 12).
- [ ] Wiper motor or linkage mountings loose or insecure (Chapter 12).

Wiper blades fail to clean the glass effectively

- [ ] Wiper blade rubbers worn or perished (*"Weekly checks"*).
- [ ] Wiper arm tension springs broken, or arm pivots seized (Chapter 12).
- [ ] Insufficient windscreen washer additive to adequately remove road film (*"Weekly checks"*).

Windscreen/tailgate washers failed, or unsatisfactory in operation

One or more washer jets inoperative

- [ ] Blocked washer jet (*"Weekly checks"*).
- [ ] Disconnected, kinked or restricted fluid hose (Chapter 12).
- [ ] Insufficient fluid in washer reservoir (*"Weekly checks"*).

Washer pump fails to operate

- [ ] Broken or disconnected wiring or connections (Chapter 12).
- [ ] Blown fuse (Chapter 12).
- [ ] Faulty washer switch (Chapter 12).
- [ ] Faulty washer pump (Chapter 12).

Washer pump runs for some time before fluid is emitted from jets

- [ ] Faulty one-way valve in fluid supply hose (Chapter 12).

Electric windows inoperative, or unsatisfactory in operation

Window glass will only move in one direction

- [ ] Faulty switch (Chapter 12).

Window glass slow to move

- [ ] Regulator seized or damaged, or in need of lubricant (Chapter 11).
- [ ] Door internal components or trim fouling regulator (Chapter 11).
- [ ] Faulty motor (Chapter 11).

Window glass fails to move

- [ ] Blown fuse (Chapter 12).
- [ ] Faulty relay (Chapter 12).
- [ ] Broken or disconnected wiring or connections (Chapter 12).
- [ ] Faulty motor (Chapter 11).

Central locking system inoperative, or unsatisfactory in operation

Complete system failure

- [ ] Blown fuse (Chapter 12).
- [ ] Faulty relay (Chapter 12).
- [ ] Broken or disconnected wiring or connections (Chapter 12).
- [ ] Faulty control unit (Chapter 11).

Latch locks but will not unlock, or unlocks but will not lock

- [ ] Faulty master switch (Chapter 12).
- [ ] Broken or disconnected latch operating rods or levers (Chapter 11).
- [ ] Faulty relay (Chapter 12).
- [ ] Faulty control unit (Chapter 11).

One solenoid/motor fails to operate

- [ ] Broken or disconnected wiring or connections (Chapter 12).
- [ ] Faulty solenoid/motor (Chapter 11).
- [ ] Broken, binding or disconnected latch operating rods or levers (Chapter 11).
- [ ] Fault in door latch (Chapter 11).

Glossary of technical terms REF•19

A

ABS (Anti-lock brake system) A system, usually electronically controlled, that senses incipient wheel lockup during braking and relieves hydraulic pressure at wheels that are about to skid.

Air bag An inflatable bag hidden in the steering wheel (driver's side) or the dash or glovebox (passenger side). In a head-on collision, the bags inflate, preventing the driver and front passenger from being thrown forward into the steering wheel or windscreen.

Air cleaner A metal or plastic housing, containing a filter element, which removes dust and dirt from the air being drawn into the engine.

Air filter element The actual filter in an air cleaner system, usually manufactured from pleated paper and requiring renewal at regular intervals.

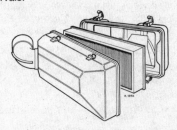
Air filter

Allen key A hexagonal wrench which fits into a recessed hexagonal hole.

Alligator clip A long-nosed spring-loaded metal clip with meshing teeth. Used to make temporary electrical connections.

Alternator A component in the electrical system which converts mechanical energy from a drivebelt into electrical energy to charge the battery and to operate the starting system, ignition system and electrical accessories.

Ampere (amp) A unit of measurement for the flow of electric current. One amp is the amount of current produced by one volt acting through a resistance of one ohm.

Anaerobic sealer A substance used to prevent bolts and screws from loosening. Anaerobic means that it does not require oxygen for activation. The Loctite brand is widely used.

Antifreeze A substance (usually ethylene glycol) mixed with water, and added to a vehicle's cooling system, to prevent freezing of the coolant in winter. Antifreeze also contains chemicals to inhibit corrosion and the formation of rust and other deposits that would tend to clog the radiator and coolant passages and reduce cooling efficiency.

Anti-seize compound A coating that reduces the risk of seizing on fasteners that are subjected to high temperatures, such as exhaust manifold bolts and nuts.

Asbestos A natural fibrous mineral with great heat resistance, commonly used in the composition of brake friction materials.

Asbestos is a health hazard and the dust created by brake systems should never be inhaled or ingested.

Axle A shaft on which a wheel revolves, or which revolves with a wheel. Also, a solid beam that connects the two wheels at one end of the vehicle. An axle which also transmits power to the wheels is known as a live axle.

Axleshaft A single rotating shaft, on either side of the differential, which delivers power from the final drive assembly to the drive wheels. Also called a driveshaft or a halfshaft.

B

Ball bearing An anti-friction bearing consisting of a hardened inner and outer race with hardened steel balls between two races.

Bearing The curved surface on a shaft or in a bore, or the part assembled into either, that permits relative motion between them with minimum wear and friction.

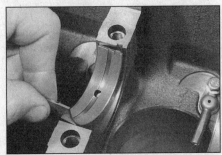
Bearing

Big-end bearing The bearing in the end of the connecting rod that's attached to the crankshaft.

Bleed nipple A valve on a brake wheel cylinder, caliper or other hydraulic component that is opened to purge the hydraulic system of air. Also called a bleed screw.

Brake bleeding Procedure for removing air from lines of a hydraulic brake system.

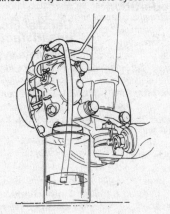
Brake bleeding

Brake disc The component of a disc brake that rotates with the wheels.

Brake drum The component of a drum brake that rotates with the wheels.

Brake linings The friction material which contacts the brake disc or drum to retard the vehicle's speed. The linings are bonded or riveted to the brake pads or shoes.

Brake pads The replaceable friction pads that pinch the brake disc when the brakes are applied. Brake pads consist of a friction material bonded or riveted to a rigid backing plate.

Brake shoe The crescent-shaped carrier to which the brake linings are mounted and which forces the lining against the rotating drum during braking.

Braking systems For more information on braking systems, consult the *Haynes Automotive Brake Manual*.

Breaker bar A long socket wrench handle providing greater leverage.

Bulkhead The insulated partition between the engine and the passenger compartment.

C

Caliper The non-rotating part of a disc-brake assembly that straddles the disc and carries the brake pads. The caliper also contains the hydraulic components that cause the pads to pinch the disc when the brakes are applied. A caliper is also a measuring tool that can be set to measure inside or outside dimensions of an object.

Camshaft A rotating shaft on which a series of cam lobes operate the valve mechanisms. The camshaft may be driven by gears, by sprockets and chain or by sprockets and a belt.

Canister A container in an evaporative emission control system; contains activated charcoal granules to trap vapours from the fuel system.

Canister

Carburettor A device which mixes fuel with air in the proper proportions to provide a desired power output from a spark ignition internal combustion engine.

Castellated Resembling the parapets along the top of a castle wall. For example, a castellated balljoint stud nut.

Castor In wheel alignment, the backward or forward tilt of the steering axis. Castor is positive when the steering axis is inclined rearward at the top.

Catalytic converter A silencer-like device in the exhaust system which converts certain pollutants in the exhaust gases into less harmful substances.

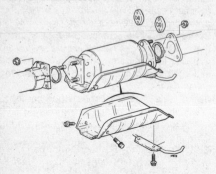

Catalytic converter

Circlip A ring-shaped clip used to prevent endwise movement of cylindrical parts and shafts. An internal circlip is installed in a groove in a housing; an external circlip fits into a groove on the outside of a cylindrical piece such as a shaft.

Clearance The amount of space between two parts. For example, between a piston and a cylinder, between a bearing and a journal, etc.

Coil spring A spiral of elastic steel found in various sizes throughout a vehicle, for example as a springing medium in the suspension and in the valve train.

Compression Reduction in volume, and increase in pressure and temperature, of a gas, caused by squeezing it into a smaller space.

Compression ratio The relationship between cylinder volume when the piston is at top dead centre and cylinder volume when the piston is at bottom dead centre.

Constant velocity (CV) joint A type of universal joint that cancels out vibrations caused by driving power being transmitted through an angle.

Core plug A disc or cup-shaped metal device inserted in a hole in a casting through which core was removed when the casting was formed. Also known as a freeze plug or expansion plug.

Crankcase The lower part of the engine block in which the crankshaft rotates.

Crankshaft The main rotating member, or shaft, running the length of the crankcase, with offset "throws" to which the connecting rods are attached.

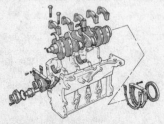

Crankshaft assembly

Crocodile clip See Alligator clip

D

Diagnostic code Code numbers obtained by accessing the diagnostic mode of an engine management computer. This code can be used to determine the area in the system where a malfunction may be located.

Disc brake A brake design incorporating a rotating disc onto which brake pads are squeezed. The resulting friction converts the energy of a moving vehicle into heat.

Double-overhead cam (DOHC) An engine that uses two overhead camshafts, usually one for the intake valves and one for the exhaust valves.

Drivebelt(s) The belt(s) used to drive accessories such as the alternator, water pump, power steering pump, air conditioning compressor, etc. off the crankshaft pulley.

Accessory drivebelts

Driveshaft Any shaft used to transmit motion. Commonly used when referring to the axleshafts on a front wheel drive vehicle.

Drum brake A type of brake using a drum-shaped metal cylinder attached to the inner surface of the wheel. When the brake pedal is pressed, curved brake shoes with friction linings press against the inside of the drum to slow or stop the vehicle.

E

EGR valve A valve used to introduce exhaust gases into the intake air stream.

Electronic control unit (ECU) A computer which controls (for instance) ignition and fuel injection systems, or an anti-lock braking system. For more information refer to the *Haynes Automotive Electrical and Electronic Systems Manual*.

Electronic Fuel Injection (EFI) A computer controlled fuel system that distributes fuel through an injector located in each intake port of the engine.

Emergency brake A braking system, independent of the main hydraulic system, that can be used to slow or stop the vehicle if the primary brakes fail, or to hold the vehicle stationary even though the brake pedal isn't depressed. It usually consists of a hand lever that actuates either front or rear brakes mechanically through a series of cables and linkages. Also known as a handbrake or parking brake.

Endfloat The amount of lengthwise movement between two parts. As applied to a crankshaft, the distance that the crankshaft can move forward and back in the cylinder block.

Engine management system (EMS) A computer controlled system which manages the fuel injection and the ignition systems in an integrated fashion.

Exhaust manifold A part with several passages through which exhaust gases leave the engine combustion chambers and enter the exhaust pipe.

F

Fan clutch A viscous (fluid) drive coupling device which permits variable engine fan speeds in relation to engine speeds.

Feeler blade A thin strip or blade of hardened steel, ground to an exact thickness, used to check or measure clearances between parts.

Feeler blade

Firing order The order in which the engine cylinders fire, or deliver their power strokes, beginning with the number one cylinder.

Flywheel A heavy spinning wheel in which energy is absorbed and stored by means of momentum. On cars, the flywheel is attached to the crankshaft to smooth out firing impulses.

Free play The amount of travel before any action takes place. The "looseness" in a linkage, or an assembly of parts, between the initial application of force and actual movement. For example, the distance the brake pedal moves before the pistons in the master cylinder are actuated.

Fuse An electrical device which protects a circuit against accidental overload. The typical fuse contains a soft piece of metal which is calibrated to melt at a predetermined current flow (expressed as amps) and break the circuit.

Fusible link A circuit protection device consisting of a conductor surrounded by heat-resistant insulation. The conductor is smaller than the wire it protects, so it acts as the weakest link in the circuit. Unlike a blown fuse, a failed fusible link must frequently be cut from the wire for replacement.

G

Gap The distance the spark must travel in jumping from the centre electrode to the side electrode in a spark plug. Also refers to the spacing between the points in a contact breaker assembly in a conventional points-type ignition, or to the distance between the reluctor or rotor and the pickup coil in an electronic ignition.

Adjusting spark plug gap

Gasket Any thin, soft material - usually cork, cardboard, asbestos or soft metal - installed between two metal surfaces to ensure a good seal. For instance, the cylinder head gasket seals the joint between the block and the cylinder head.

Gasket

Gauge An instrument panel display used to monitor engine conditions. A gauge with a movable pointer on a dial or a fixed scale is an analogue gauge. A gauge with a numerical readout is called a digital gauge.

H

Halfshaft A rotating shaft that transmits power from the final drive unit to a drive wheel, usually when referring to a live rear axle.

Harmonic balancer A device designed to reduce torsion or twisting vibration in the crankshaft. May be incorporated in the crankshaft pulley. Also known as a vibration damper.

Hone An abrasive tool for correcting small irregularities or differences in diameter in an engine cylinder, brake cylinder, etc.

Hydraulic tappet A tappet that utilises hydraulic pressure from the engine's lubrication system to maintain zero clearance (constant contact with both camshaft and valve stem). Automatically adjusts to variation in valve stem length. Hydraulic tappets also reduce valve noise.

I

Ignition timing The moment at which the spark plug fires, usually expressed in the number of crankshaft degrees before the piston reaches the top of its stroke.

Inlet manifold A tube or housing with passages through which flows the air-fuel mixture (carburettor vehicles and vehicles with throttle body injection) or air only (port fuel-injected vehicles) to the port openings in the cylinder head.

J

Jump start Starting the engine of a vehicle with a discharged or weak battery by attaching jump leads from the weak battery to a charged or helper battery.

L

Load Sensing Proportioning Valve (LSPV) A brake hydraulic system control valve that works like a proportioning valve, but also takes into consideration the amount of weight carried by the rear axle.

Locknut A nut used to lock an adjustment nut, or other threaded component, in place. For example, a locknut is employed to keep the adjusting nut on the rocker arm in position.

Lockwasher A form of washer designed to prevent an attaching nut from working loose.

M

MacPherson strut A type of front suspension system devised by Earle MacPherson at Ford of England. In its original form, a simple lateral link with the anti-roll bar creates the lower control arm. A long strut - an integral coil spring and shock absorber - is mounted between the body and the steering knuckle. Many modern so-called MacPherson strut systems use a conventional lower A-arm and don't rely on the anti-roll bar for location.

Multimeter An electrical test instrument with the capability to measure voltage, current and resistance.

N

NOx Oxides of Nitrogen. A common toxic pollutant emitted by petrol and diesel engines at higher temperatures.

O

Ohm The unit of electrical resistance. One volt applied to a resistance of one ohm will produce a current of one amp.

Ohmmeter An instrument for measuring electrical resistance.

O-ring A type of sealing ring made of a special rubber-like material; in use, the O-ring is compressed into a groove to provide the sealing action.

Overhead cam (ohc) engine An engine with the camshaft(s) located on top of the cylinder head(s).

Overhead valve (ohv) engine An engine with the valves located in the cylinder head, but with the camshaft located in the engine block.

Oxygen sensor A device installed in the engine exhaust manifold, which senses the oxygen content in the exhaust and converts this information into an electric current. Also called a Lambda sensor.

P

Phillips screw A type of screw head having a cross instead of a slot for a corresponding type of screwdriver.

Plastigage A thin strip of plastic thread, available in different sizes, used for measuring clearances. For example, a strip of Plastigage is laid across a bearing journal. The parts are assembled and dismantled; the width of the crushed strip indicates the clearance between journal and bearing.

Plastigage

Propeller shaft The long hollow tube with universal joints at both ends that carries power from the transmission to the differential on front-engined rear wheel drive vehicles.

Proportioning valve A hydraulic control valve which limits the amount of pressure to the rear brakes during panic stops to prevent wheel lock-up.

R

Rack-and-pinion steering A steering system with a pinion gear on the end of the steering shaft that mates with a rack (think of a geared wheel opened up and laid flat). When the steering wheel is turned, the pinion turns, moving the rack to the left or right. This movement is transmitted through the track rods to the steering arms at the wheels.

Radiator A liquid-to-air heat transfer device designed to reduce the temperature of the coolant in an internal combustion engine cooling system.

Refrigerant Any substance used as a heat transfer agent in an air-conditioning system. R-12 has been the principle refrigerant for many years; recently, however, manufacturers have begun using R-134a, a non-CFC substance that is considered less harmful to the ozone in the upper atmosphere.

Rocker arm A lever arm that rocks on a shaft or pivots on a stud. In an overhead valve engine, the rocker arm converts the upward movement of the pushrod into a downward movement to open a valve.

Rotor In a distributor, the rotating device inside the cap that connects the centre electrode and the outer terminals as it turns, distributing the high voltage from the coil secondary winding to the proper spark plug. Also, that part of an alternator which rotates inside the stator. Also, the rotating assembly of a turbocharger, including the compressor wheel, shaft and turbine wheel.

Runout The amount of wobble (in-and-out movement) of a gear or wheel as it's rotated. The amount a shaft rotates "out-of-true." The out-of-round condition of a rotating part.

S

Sealant A liquid or paste used to prevent leakage at a joint. Sometimes used in conjunction with a gasket.

Sealed beam lamp An older headlight design which integrates the reflector, lens and filaments into a hermetically-sealed one-piece unit. When a filament burns out or the lens cracks, the entire unit is simply replaced.

Serpentine drivebelt A single, long, wide accessory drivebelt that's used on some newer vehicles to drive all the accessories, instead of a series of smaller, shorter belts. Serpentine drivebelts are usually tensioned by an automatic tensioner.

Serpentine drivebelt

Shim Thin spacer, commonly used to adjust the clearance or relative positions between two parts. For example, shims inserted into or under bucket tappets control valve clearances. Clearance is adjusted by changing the thickness of the shim.

Slide hammer A special puller that screws into or hooks onto a component such as a shaft or bearing; a heavy sliding handle on the shaft bottoms against the end of the shaft to knock the component free.

Sprocket A tooth or projection on the periphery of a wheel, shaped to engage with a chain or drivebelt. Commonly used to refer to the sprocket wheel itself.

Starter inhibitor switch On vehicles with an automatic transmission, a switch that prevents starting if the vehicle is not in Neutral or Park.

Strut See MacPherson strut.

T

Tappet A cylindrical component which transmits motion from the cam to the valve stem, either directly or via a pushrod and rocker arm. Also called a cam follower.

Thermostat A heat-controlled valve that regulates the flow of coolant between the cylinder block and the radiator, so maintaining optimum engine operating temperature. A thermostat is also used in some air cleaners in which the temperature is regulated.

Thrust bearing The bearing in the clutch assembly that is moved in to the release levers by clutch pedal action to disengage the clutch. Also referred to as a release bearing.

Timing belt A toothed belt which drives the camshaft. Serious engine damage may result if it breaks in service.

Timing chain A chain which drives the camshaft.

Toe-in The amount the front wheels are closer together at the front than at the rear. On rear wheel drive vehicles, a slight amount of toe-in is usually specified to keep the front wheels running parallel on the road by offsetting other forces that tend to spread the wheels apart.

Toe-out The amount the front wheels are closer together at the rear than at the front. On front wheel drive vehicles, a slight amount of toe-out is usually specified.

Tools For full information on choosing and using tools, refer to the *Haynes Automotive Tools Manual.*

Tracer A stripe of a second colour applied to a wire insulator to distinguish that wire from another one with the same colour insulator.

Tune-up A process of accurate and careful adjustments and parts replacement to obtain the best possible engine performance.

Turbocharger A centrifugal device, driven by exhaust gases, that pressurises the intake air. Normally used to increase the power output from a given engine displacement, but can also be used primarily to reduce exhaust emissions (as on VW's "Umwelt" Diesel engine).

U

Universal joint or U-joint A double-pivoted connection for transmitting power from a driving to a driven shaft through an angle. A U-joint consists of two Y-shaped yokes and a cross-shaped member called the spider.

V

Valve A device through which the flow of liquid, gas, vacuum, or loose material in bulk may be started, stopped, or regulated by a movable part that opens, shuts, or partially obstructs one or more ports or passageways. A valve is also the movable part of such a device.

Valve clearance The clearance between the valve tip (the end of the valve stem) and the rocker arm or tappet. The valve clearance is measured when the valve is closed.

Vernier caliper A precision measuring instrument that measures inside and outside dimensions. Not quite as accurate as a micrometer, but more convenient.

Viscosity The thickness of a liquid or its resistance to flow.

Volt A unit for expressing electrical "pressure" in a circuit. One volt that will produce a current of one ampere through a resistance of one ohm.

W

Welding Various processes used to join metal items by heating the areas to be joined to a molten state and fusing them together. For more information refer to the *Haynes Automotive Welding Manual.*

Wiring diagram A drawing portraying the components and wires in a vehicle's electrical system, using standardised symbols. For more information refer to the *Haynes Automotive Electrical and Electronic Systems Manual.*

A

ACAV intake system
multi-point fuel injection models - 4C•18
Accelerator cable
carburettor engines - 4A•6
multi-point fuel injection models - 4C•3
single-point fuel injection models - 4B•3
Accelerator pedal
carburettor engines - 4A•6
multi-point fuel injection models - 4C•3
single-point fuel injection models - 4B•3
Acknowledgements - 0•4
Aerial - 12•19
Air bags - 0•5, 12•20
Air conditioning - 1•12, 1•17, 3•10
switch - 12•5
Air filter - 1•19
carburettor engines - 4A•2, 4A•3
multi-point fuel injection models - 4C•2
single-point fuel injection models - 4B•2
Air mixture temperature sensor
Magneti Marelli system - 4B•10
Air temperature control system
carburettor engines - 4A•3, 4A•4
single-point fuel injection models - 4B•3
Air temperature sensor
Bosch Monopoint system - 4B•8
Bosch Motronic M1.3 system - 4C•16
Bosch Motronic MP3.1 system - 4C•15
Bosch Motronic MP3.2 system - 4C•16
Bosch Motronic MP5.1 and MP5.2 system - 4C•12
Bosch Motronic MP5.1 and MP5.2 system - 4C•13
Magneti Marelli 1AP system - 4C•8
Magneti Marelli 8P and Sagem/Lucas 4GJ system - 4C•9
Magneti Marelli 8P and Sagem/Lucas 4GJ system - 4C•10
Airflow meter
Bosch Motronic M1.3 system - 4C•15
Alarm system - 12•19
switch - 12•5
Alternator - 5•8
Antifreeze - 0•15, 0•18, 1•24
Anti-lock braking system (ABS) - 9•19, 9•20
Anti-roll bar
front - 10•9
rear - 10•16

Asbestos - 0•5
Ashtray illumination bulb - 12•9
ATF - 0•18, 1•2, 1•10, 1•19
Automatic transmission - 2C•7, 7B•1 *et seq*
fault finding - REF•16
mountings - 2B•26
Automatic transmission fluid - 0•18, 1•2, 1•10, 1•19
Auxiliary air valve
Bosch Motronic M1.3 system - 4C•15
Bosch Motronic MP3.1 system - 4C•14
Auxiliary drivebelt - 1•16

B

Badges - 11•14
Battery - 0•5, 0•17, 5•3
Big-end bearings - 2C•16
running clearance check - 2C•22
Bitron temperature sensor - 3•6
Bleeding
brakes - 9•2
power steering - 10•23
Blower motor - 3•9
Body corrosion - REF•11
Body electrical systems - 12•1 *et seq*
Body under-panels - 11•14
Bodywork and fittings - 11•1 *et seq*
Bonnet - 11•4
lock - 11•5
release cable - 11•5
Bosch Monopoint system - 4B•7
Monopoint A2.2 system - 4B•3
Monopoint MA3.0 and MA3.1 systems - 4B•4
Bosch Motronic M1.3 system - 4C•4, 4C•15
Bosch Motronic MP3.1 system - 4C•4, 4C•13
Bosch Motronic MP3.2 system - 4C•5, 4C•16
Bosch Motronic MP5.1 and MP 5.2 systems - 4C•4, 4C•11
Brake fluid - 0•14, 0•18, 1•19
Braking system - 1•18, 9•1 *et seq*, REF•10
fault finding - REF•16
Bulbs
exterior lights - 12•6
interior lights - 12•8
Bumper
front - 11•3
rear - 11•4
Burning - 0•5

C

Cables
  accelerator
    carburettor engines - 4A•6
    multi-point fuel injection models - 4C•3
    single-point fuel injection models - 4B•3
  bonnet release - 11•5
  choke - 4A•6
  clutch - 6•2
  handbrake - 9•18
  heater/ventilation control - 3•8
  kickdown - 7B•4
  selector (automatic transmission) - 7B•3
  speedometer - 12•15
Calipers
  front - 9•12
  rear - 9•13
Camshaft oil seals
  TU series engine - 2A•8
  XU series engine - 2B•16
Camshaft position sensor
  Bosch Motronic MP3.2 system - 4C•16
Camshaft sprocket
  TU series engine - 2A•7, 2A•8
  XU series engine - 2B•13, 2B•14, 2B•15
Camshaft
  TU series engine - 2A•9, 2A•10
  XU series engine - 2B•16
Carburettor - 4A•7, 4A•8
  fault finding
    Solex 32 PBISA carburettor - 4A•9
    Solex 32-34 Z2 carburettor - 4A•10
Carpets - 11•2, 11•19
Cassette player - 12•18
Catalytic converter - 4D•2, 4D•3
  single-point fuel injection models - 4B•12
Central locking components - 11•11
Centre console - 11•19
Changing a wheel - 0•8
Charcoal canister - 4D•2
Charging - 5•3, 5•8
Choke cable
  carburettor engines - 4A•6
Choke pull-down setting
  Solex 32 PBISA carburettor - 4A•10
  Solex 32-34 Z2 carburettor - 4A•11
Cigarette lighter - 12•14
  illumination bulb - 12•9
Clock - 12•13
  illumination bulb - 12•9
Clutch - 1•10, 1•18, 6•1 *et seq*
  fault finding - REF•15
Coil(s) - 5•5
Compression test
  TU series engine - 2A•3
  XU series engine - 2B•5
Console - 11•19
Conversion factors - REF•2
Coolant - 0•15, 0•18, 1•2, 1•23
Coolant pump - 3•7
Coolant temperature gauge - 3•6
Coolant temperature sensor - 3•6
  Bosch Motronic M1.3 system - 4C•15
  Bosch Motronic MP3.1 system - 4C•15
  Bosch Motronic MP3.2 system - 4C•16
  Bosch Motronic MP5.1 and MP5.2 system - 4C•12, 4C•13

  Magneti Marelli 1AP system - 4C•8
  Magneti Marelli 8P and Sagem/Lucas 4GJ system - 4C•9, 4C•10
Coolant temperature warning light sender - 3•6
Cooling fan(s) - 3•5
  thermostatic switch - 3•5, 3•6
Cooling, heating and ventilation systems - 3•1 *et seq*
  electrical switches and sensors - 3•5
  fault finding - REF•14
  hoses - 3•2
Courtesy lights - 12•8
  switches - 12•5
Crankcase emission control - 4D•1, 4D•2
Crankshaft - 2C•12, 2C•16, 2C•18
Crankshaft oil seals
  TU series engine - 2A•13
  XU series engine - 2B•24
Crankshaft pulley
  XU series engine - 2B•8
Crankshaft sensor
  Bosch Monopoint system - 4B•9
  Bosch Motronic M1.3 system - 4C•16
  Bosch Motronic MP3.1 system - 4C•15
  Bosch Motronic MP3.2 system - 4C•17
  Bosch Motronic MP5.1 and MP5.2 system - 4C•12, 4C•13
  Magneti Marelli system - 4B•10
  Magneti Marelli 1AP system - 4C•8
  Magneti Marelli 8P and Sagem/Lucas 4GJ system - 4C•9, 4C•10
Crankshaft sprocket
  TU series engine - 2A•7, 2A•8
  XU series engine - 2B•13, 2B•14, 2B•15
Crushing - 0•5
CV joint - 1•11
Cylinder block/crankcase - 2C•13
Cylinder head - 2C•9, 2C•10, 2C•11
  TU series engine - 2A•10,
  XU series engine - 2B•19
Cylinder head cover
  TU series engine - 2A•4
  XU series engine - 2B•6

D

Dents in bodywork - 11•2
Depressurisation
  multi-point fuel injection models - 4C•5
  single-point fuel injection models - 4B•4
Dim-dip lighting system - 12•20
Dimensions and weights - REF•1
Direction indicator - 12•7, 12•10, 12•11
Discs
  front - 9•9
  rear - 9•10
Distributor - 5•6
Doors - 11•5, REF•9
  door-open warning display - 12•14
  handle and lock components - 11•7
  inner trim panel - 11•6
  window glass and regulator - 11•8
Drivebelt - 1•16
Driveplate
  XU series engine - 2B•25
Driveshafts - 8•1 *et seq*, REF•10
  fault finding - REF•16
  oil seals
    automatic transmission - 7B•4
    manual transmission - 7A•4
Drivetrain - 1•18
Drums - 9•11

E

Earth fault - 12•3
Electric cooling fan(s) - 3•5
  thermostatic switch - 3•5, 3•6
Electric shock - 0•5
Electric windows - 11•12
  switches - 12•6
Electrical equipment - 1•18, REF•9
Electrical systems - 0•17
  fault finding - 12•3, REF•18
Electronic control unit (ECU)
  Bosch Monopoint system - 4B•8
  Bosch Motronic M1.3 system - 4C•15
  Bosch Motronic MP3.1 system - 4C•14
  Bosch Motronic MP3.2 system - 4C•16
  Bosch Motronic MP5.1 and MP5.2 system - 4C•11, 4C•12
  Magneti Marelli system - 4B•10
  Magneti Marelli 1AP system - 4C•8
  Magneti Marelli 8P and Sagem/Lucas 4GJ system - 4C•9, 4C•10
Emission control systems - 1•16, 4D•1 *et seq*, REF•11
Engine electrical systems - 5•1 *et seq*
Engine fault finding - 5•5, REF•13
Engine oil - 0•13, 0•18, 1•1, 1•9
Engine removal and general overhaul procedures - 2C•1 *et seq*
Evaporative emission control - 4D•1, 4D•2
Exhaust emission control - 4D•1, 4D•2
Exhaust manifold
  carburettor engines - 4A•11
  multi-point fuel injection models - 4C•19
  single-point fuel injection models - 4B•11
Exhaust specialists - REF•3
Exhaust system - REF•10, REF•11
  carburettor engines - 4A•12
  multi-point fuel injection models - 4C•20
  single-point fuel injection models - 4B•11
Exterior light units - 12•10

F

Facia panel - 11•20
Facia vents - 3•10
Fan(s) - 3•5
  thermostatic switch - 3•5, 3•6
Fault finding - REF•12 *et seq*
  automatic transmission - REF•16
  braking system - REF•16
  clutch - REF•15
  cooling system - REF•14
  driveshafts - REF•16
  electrical system - 12•3, REF•18
  engine - 5•5, REF•13
  fuel and exhaust systems - REF•15
  manual transmission - REF•15
  Solex 32 PBISA carburettor - 4A•9
  Solex 32-34 Z2 carburettor - 4A•10
  suspension and steering systems - REF•17
Filling and respraying - 11•2
Filter
  air - 1•19
    carburettor engines - 4A•2, 4A•3
    multi-point fuel injection models - 4C•2
    single-point fuel injection models - 4B•2
  fuel
    carburettor models - 1•14
    fuel injected models - 1•22
  oil - 1•9

Fire - 0•5
Fixed rear quarter window - 11•13
Float height setting
  Solex 32 PBISA carburettor - 4A•10
  Solex 32-34 Z2 carburettor - 4A•11
Fluid cooler (automatic transmission) - 7B•4
Fluids - 0•18
Flywheel
  TU series engine - 2A•14
  XU series engine - 2B•25
Foglight
  front - 12•7, 12•11
  rear - 12•8, 12•11
Footbrake - REF•8, REF•9
Fuel and exhaust systems - carburettor engines - 4A•1 *et seq*
Fuel and exhaust systems - multi-point fuel injection models - 4C•1 *et seq*
Fuel and exhaust systems - single-point fuel injection models - 4B•1 *et seq*
Fuel and exhaust systems fault finding - REF•15
Fuel filter
  carburettor models - 1•14
  fuel injected models - 1•22
Fuel gauge - 12•13
  sender unit
    carburettor engines - 4A•4
    multi-point fuel injection models - 4C•5
    single-point fuel injection models - 4B•5
Fuel injection system
  multi-point fuel injection models - 4C•3, 4C•5
  single-point fuel injection models - 4B•3, 4B•6
Fuel injectors
  Bosch Monopoint system - 4B•7
  Magneti Marelli system - 4B•9
  Magneti Marelli 8P and Sagem/Lucas 4GJ system - 4C•9
Fuel pressure regulator
  Bosch Monopoint system - 4B•7
  Bosch Motronic M1.3 system - 4C•15
  Bosch Motronic MP3.1 system - 4C•13
  Bosch Motronic MP3.2 system - 4C•16
  Bosch Motronic MP5.1 and MP5.2 system - 4C•11
  Bosch Motronic MP5.1 and MP5.2 system - 4C•12
  Magneti Marelli system - 4B•9
  Magneti Marelli 1AP system - 4C•8
  Magneti Marelli 8P and Sagem/Lucas 4GJ system - 4C•9, 4C•10
Fuel pump
  carburettor engines - 4A•4
  multi-point fuel injection models - 4C•5
  single-point fuel injection models - 4B•5
Fuel rail and injectors
  Bosch Motronic M1.3 system - 4C•15
  Bosch Motronic MP3.1 system - 4C•13
  Bosch Motronic MP3.2 system - 4C•16
  Bosch Motronic MP5.1 and MP5.2 system - 4C•11, 4C•12
  Magneti Marelli 1AP system - 4C•8
  Magneti Marelli 8P and Sagem/Lucas 4GJ system - 4C•9
Fuel system - REF•11
Fuel tank
  carburettor engines - 4A•5
  multi-point fuel injection models - 4C•5
  single-point fuel injection models - 4B•5
Fuel/air mixture temperature sensor
  Magneti Marelli system - 4B•10
Fume or gas intoxication - 0•5
Fuses - 12•4

G

Gaiters
driveshaft - 1•11, 8•3
steering gear - 10•22
Gashes in bodywork - 11•2
Gearchange linkage (manual transmission) - 7A•3
General repair procedures - REF•4
Glossary of technical terms - REF•19 *et seq*
Glovebox - 11•18

H

Handbrake - 9•17, 9•18, REF•8
warning light switch - 12•5
Handles (door) - 11•7
Headlight - 12•6, 12•10
beam alignment - 12•11
washer fluid - 0•15
Headlining - 11•19
Heat shield(s)
carburettor engines - 4A•12
multi-point fuel injection models - 4C•20
single-point fuel injection models - 4B•12
Heating and ventilation system - 3•7, 3•8, 3•9, 3•10
control panel illumination bulb - 12•10
matrix hose connections - 3•3
Hinges and locks - 1•21
Horn - 12•14
HT coil(s) - 5•5
Hub assembly
front - 10•4
rear - 10•10
Hub bearings
front - 10•5
rear - 10•11
Hydraulic pipes and hoses - 9•3
Hydrofluoric acid - 0•5

I

Identifying leaks - 0•9
Idle control auxiliary air valve
Magneti Marelli system - 4B•9
Idle control stepper motor
Bosch Monopoint system - 4B•7
Magneti Marelli system - 4B•9
Idle speed and mixture - 1•14
Idle speed auxiliary air valve
Bosch Motronic MP3.2 system - 4C•16
Bosch Motronic MP5.1 and MP5.2 system - 4C•11
Idle speed control stepper motor
Bosch Motronic MP5.1 and MP5.2 system - 4C•12
Magneti Marelli 1AP system - 4C•8
Magneti Marelli 8P and Sagem/Lucas 4GJ system - 4C•9, 4C•10
Idle speed mixture adjustment potentiometer
Bosch Motronic MP3.1 system - 4C•14
Ignition switch/steering column lock - 10•21
Ignition system - 1•14, 5•4
amplifier unit(s) - 5•7
Ignition timing - 5•8
Indicators - 12•7, 12•10, 12•11
Injector resistor
Bosch Monopoint system - 4B•8

Inlet manifold
carburettor engines - 4A•11
multi-point fuel injection models - 4C•17
single-point fuel injection models - 4B•10
Input shaft oil seal (manual transmission) - 7A•5
Instrument panel - 12•11, 12•12
dimmer switch - 12•5
lights - 12•9
Instrument shroud switches - 12•5
Instruments and electrical equipment - 1•18
Intake air temperature sensor
Bosch Monopoint system - 4B•8
Bosch Motronic M1.3 system - 4C•16
Bosch Motronic MP3.1 system - 4C•15
Bosch Motronic MP3.2 system - 4C•16
Bosch Motronic MP5.1 and MP5.2 system - 4C•12, 4C•13
Magneti Marelli 8P and Sagem/Lucas 4GJ system - 4C•10
Intake ducts
multi-point fuel injection models - 4C•2
single-point fuel injection models - 4B•2
Intermediate bearing (driveshaft) - 8•6
Introduction to the Citroën ZX - 0•4

J

Jacking and vehicle support - REF•5
Jump starting - 0•7

K

Kickdown cable - 7B•4
Knock sensor
Bosch Motronic MP5.1 and MP5.2 system - 4C•13
Magneti Marelli 1AP system - 4C•8
Magneti Marelli 8P and Sagem/Lucas 4GJ system - 4C•11
multi-point fuel injection models - 4C•17

L

Lambda sensor - 4D•2
Magneti Marelli 1AP system - 4C•9
Leaks - 0•9, 1•10
Lights-on warning system - 12•14
Locks - 1•21
bonnet - 11•5
central locking - 11•11
door - 11•7
steering column - 10•21
tailgate - 11•11
Loudspeakers - 12•18
Lower arm - 10•8
Lubricants and fluids - 0•18
Luggage compartment light - 12•8
switch - 12•5

M

Magneti Marelli system - 4B•4, 4B•9, 4B•10
Magneti Marelli 1AP system - 4C•3, 4C•8
Magneti Marelli 8P and Sagem/Lucas 4GJ system - 4C•9, 4C•4
Main bearings - 2C•16
running clearance check - 2C•19

Manifold absolute pressure (MAP)
Magneti Marelli system - 4B•10
Manifold absolute pressure (MAP) sensor
Bosch Motronic M1.3 system - 4C•15
Bosch Motronic MP3.1 system - 4C•15
Bosch Motronic MP3.2 system - 4C•16
Bosch Motronic MP5.1 and MP5.2 system - 4C•11, 4C•13
Magneti Marelli 1AP system - 4C•8
Magneti Marelli 8P and Sagem/Lucas 4GJ system - 4C•9, 4C•10
Manifolds
carburettor engines - 4A•11
single-point fuel injection models - 4B•10, 4B•11
Manual transmission - 2C•4, 7A•1 *et seq*
fault finding - REF•15
mountings
TU series engine - 2A•14
XU series engine - 2B•26
Manual transmission oil - 0•18, 1•2, 1•21, 1•22
Map reading light - 12•8
Master cylinder - 9•14
Mirrors - 11•12, REF•8
switch - 12•5
Mixture - 1•14
Modulator assembly (ABS) - 9•20
MOT test checks - REF•8 *et seq*
Motor factors - REF•3
Mountings
TU series engine - 2A•14
XU series engine - 2B•26

N

Number plate light - 12•8, 12•11

O

Officially-appointed garages - REF•3
Oil cooler
XU series engine - 2B•24
Oil
engine - 0•13, 0•18, 1•1, 1•9
manual transmission - 0•18, 1•2, 1•21, 1•22
Oil filter - 1•9
Oil level sensor - 5•12
Oil pressure warning light switch - 5•12
Oil pump
TU series engine - 2A•13
XU series engine - 2B•23
Oil seals
camshaft
TU series engine - 2A•8
XU series engine - 2B•16
automatic transmission - 7B•4
crankshaft
TU series engine - 2A•13
XU series engine - 2B•24
manual transmission - 7A•4
Oil temperature sensor - 5•12
Open-circuit - 12•3

P

Pads - 1•18
front - 9•4
rear - 9•6

Pedal
accelerator
carburettor engines - 4A•6
multi-point fuel injection models - 4C•3
single-point fuel injection models - 4B•3
brake - 9•15
clutch - 6•2
Piston rings - 2C•17
Piston/connecting rod assembly - 2C•11, 2C•14, 2C•22
Plastic components - 11•3
Poisonous or irritant substances - 0•5
Power steering fluid - 0•13, 0•18, 1•2
Power steering pump - 10•23
Pressure compensator - 9•19
Pressure-regulating valves - 9•18
Printed circuit - 12•13
Purge valve(s) - 4D•2

Q

Quarter window - 11•13

R

Radiator - 3•4
bottom hose - 3•2
bypass hose connection - 3•3
Radio - 12•18
aerial - 12•19
anti-theft system - precaution - REF•5
Rear axle assembly - 10•17
Rear light cluster - 12•8, 12•10
Relays - 12•4
ABS - 9•22
Bosch Monopoint system - 4B•8
Bosch Motronic M1.3 system - 4C•16
Bosch Motronic MP3.1 system - 4C•15
Bosch Motronic MP3.2 system - 4C•17
Magneti Marelli system - 4B•10
Release mechanism (clutch) - 6•4
Reluctor rings (ABS) - 9•22
Respraying - 11•2
Reversing light switch
automatic transmission - 7B•5
manual transmission - 7A•6
Ride height - 10•18
Road test - 1•18
Roadside repairs - 0•6 *et seq*
Rocker arm
TU series engine - 2A•9, 2A•10
Routine maintenance and servicing - 1•1 *et seq*
bodywork and underframe - 11•1
upholstery and carpets - 11•2
Rubber gaiters
driveshaft - 1•11, 8•3
steering gear - 10•22
Rust holes or gashes in bodywork - 11•2

S

Safety first! - 0•5, 0•13, 0•14
Sagem/Lucas 4GJ systems - 4C•4
Scalding - 0•5
Scratches in bodywork - 11•2
Screen/headlamp washer fluid - 0•15

Seat belts - 11•15
Seats - 11•14
Selector cable (automatic transmission) - 7B•3
Selector lever (automatic transmission) - 7B•3
  display bulbs - 12•9
  display switch - 7B•5
Selector shaft oil seal
  automatic transmission - 7B•4
  manual transmission - 7A•5
Servo unit - 9•16, 9•17
Shock absorber - 1•11, 10•12, REF•9, REF•10
Shoes - 1•18, 9•7
Short-circuit - 12•3
Sidelight - 12•6
Solex 32 PBISA carburettor - 4A•7, 4A•10
  fault finding - 4A•9
Solex 32-34 Z2 carburettor - 4A•7, 4A•11
  fault finding - 4A•10
Spare parts - REF•3
Spark plugs - 1•12
Speed sensor
  Bosch Monopoint system - 4B•9
  Bosch Motronic MP5.1 and MP5.2 system - 4C•13
  Magneti Marelli 1AP system - 4C•9
  Magneti Marelli 8P and Sagem/Lucas 4GJ system - 4C•11
Speedometer - 12•12
  cable - 12•15
  drive
    automatic transmission - 7B•4
    manual transmission - 7A•6
Springs - REF•10
Starter inhibitor/reversing light switch (automatic transmission) - 7B•5
Starter motor - 5•10, 5•11
Starting system - 5•10
Start-up after overhaul - 2C•24
Steering - 1•11, 1•18, REF•9, REF•10
  angles - 10•24
  column - 10•19, REF•8
    combination switches - 12•4
    lock - 10•21
  gear assembly - 10•21
  gear rubber gaiters - 10•22
  wheel - 10•18, REF•8
Stop-light switch - 9•19
Strut (suspension) - 1•11, 10•6
Subframe - 10•10
Sump
  TU series engine - 2A•12
  XU series engine - 2B•23
Sunroof - 11•13
  switch - 12•6
Suspension - 1•11, 1•18, REF•9, REF•10
Suspension and steering - 10•1 et seq
  fault finding - REF•17
Switch illumination bulbs - 12•10
Switches - 12•4
  air conditioning - 12•5
  alarm - 12•5
  courtesy light - 12•5
  electric window - 12•6
  handbrake warning light - 12•5
  ignition - 10•21
  instrument panel dimmer - 12•5
  instrument shroud - 12•5
  luggage compartment light - 12•5
  mirror - 12•5
  reversing light (manual transmission) - 7A•6
  selector lever position display (automatic transmission) - 7B•5
  starter inhibitor/reversing light (automatic transmission) - 7B•5
  steering column - 12•4
  stop-light - 9•19
  sunroof - 12•6
Swivel hub assembly - 10•4

T

Tachometer - 12•13
Tailgate - 11•10, 11•13
  lock - 11•11
  washer jet - 12•18
  washer system - 12•17
  wiper motor - 12•16
TDC sensor
  Magneti Marelli 1AP system - 4C•8
Temperature gauge - 3•6, 12•13
Temperature sensor
  Bosch Monopoint system - 4B•8
  Bosch Motronic M1.3 system - 4C•15
  Bosch Motronic MP3.1 system - 4C•15
  Bosch Motronic MP3.2 system - 4C•16
  Bosch Motronic MP5.1 and MP5.2 system - 4C•12, 4C•13
  Magneti Marelli system - 4B•10
  Magneti Marelli 1AP system - 4C•8
  Magneti Marelli 8P and Sagem/Lucas 4GJ system - 4C•9, 4C•10
Temperature warning light sender - 3•6
Thermostat - 3•4
Throttle body
  single-point fuel injection models - 4B•5
Throttle housing heating element
  Bosch Motronic MP5.1 and MP5.2 system - 4C•12
  Magneti Marelli 1AP system - 4C•9
  Magneti Marelli 8P and Sagem/Lucas 4GJ system - 4C•9, 4C•10
  multi-point fuel injection models - 4C•17
Throttle housing
  multi-point fuel injection models - 4C•6
Throttle potentiometer
  Bosch Monopoint system - 4B•8
  Bosch Motronic MP3.1 system - 4C•14
  Bosch Motronic MP3.2 system - 4C•16
  Bosch Motronic MP5.1 and MP5.2 system - 4C•11, 4C•12
  Magneti Marelli system - 4B•10
  Magneti Marelli 1AP system - 4C•8
  Magneti Marelli 8P and Sagem/Lucas 4GJ system - 4C•9, 4C•10
Throttle switch
  Bosch Motronic M1.3 system - 4C•15
Throttle valve fast idle setting
  Solex 32 PBISA carburettor - 4A•10
  Solex 32-34 Z2 carburettor - 4A•11
Timing - 5•8
Timing belt
  TU series engine - 2A•6
  XU series engine - 2B•9
Timing belt covers
  TU series engine - 2A•5
  XU series engine - 2B•9
Timing belt tensioner and sprockets
  TU series engine - 2A•7, 2A•8
  XU series engine - 2B•13, 2B•14, 2B•15
Timing holes
  TU series engine - 2A•4
  XU series engine - 2B•5
Toe setting - 10•25
Tools and working facilities - REF•6 et seq
Torsion bar - 10•12

Towing - 0•9
Track rod - 10•23, 10•24
Trailing arm - 10•15
Trim panels - 11•6, 11•14, 11•16, 11•17, 11•18
TU series engine in-car repair procedures - 2A•1 *et seq*
Tyres - REF•11
    condition and pressure - 0•16
    pressures - 0•18
    specialists - REF•3

U

Underbonnet check points - 0•10 *et seq*
Underframe - 11•1
Unleaded petrol
    carburettor engines - 4A•7
    multi-point fuel injection models - 4C•3
    single-point fuel injection models - 4B•3
Upholstery - 11•2

V

Vacuum pump - 9•22, 9•23
Vacuum servo unit - 9•16, 9•17
Valve clearances - 1•12
    XU series engine - 2B•18
Valve timing holes
    TU series engine - 2A•4
    XU series engine - 2B•5
Valves - 2C•11
Vehicle identification - REF•3, REF•9
Vehicle ride height - 10•18
Vehicle speed sensor
    Bosch Monopoint system - 4B•9
    Bosch Motronic MP5.1 and MP5.2 system - 4C•13
    Magneti Marelli 1AP system - 4C•9
    Magneti Marelli 8P and Sagem/Lucas 4GJ system - 4C•11
    multi-point fuel injection models - 4C•17
Vehicle support - REF•5
Ventilation system - 3•7, 3•8
Vents - 3•10

W

Washer jet - 12•18
Washer pump(s) - 12•17
Washer system reservoir - 12•17
Weekly checks - 0•10 *et seq*
Weights - REF•1
Wheels - REF•11
    alignment and steering angles - 10•24
    bearings - REF•10
    changing - 0•8
    sensor (ABS) - 9•21, 9•22
Wheel arch liners and body under-panels - 11•14
Wheel cylinders - 9•14
Windows - 11•12
    glass and regulator - 11•8
    switches - 12•6
Windscreen - 11•13, REF•8
    washer jet - 12•18
    washer system - 12•17
    wiper motor and linkage - 12•15
Wiper arm - 12•15
Wiper blades - 0•14
Wiper motor and linkage - 12•15
Wiring diagrams - 12•21 *et seq*
Working facilities - REF•6 *et seq*

X

XU series engine in-car repair procedures - 2B•1 *et seq*

Haynes Manuals – The Complete List

Title	Book No.
ALFA ROMEO	
Alfa Romeo Alfasud/Sprint (74 - 88) up to F	0292
Alfa Romeo Alfetta (73 - 87) up to E	0531
AUDI	
Audi 80 (72 - Feb 79) up to T	0207
Audi 80, 90 (79 - Oct 86) up to D & Coupe (81 - Nov 88) up to F	0605
Audi 80, 90 (Oct 86 - 90) D to H & Coupe (Nov 88 - 90) F to H	1491
Audi 100 (Oct 82 - 90) up to H & 200 (Feb 84 - Oct 89) A to G	0907
Audi 100 & A6 Petrol & Diesel (May 91 - May 97) H to P	3504
Audi A4 (95 - Feb 00) M to V	3575
AUSTIN	
Austin A35 & A40 (56 - 67) *	0118
Austin Allegro 1100, 1300, 1.0, 1.1 & 1.3 (73 - 82)*	0164
Austin Healey 100/6 & 3000 (56 - 68) *	0049
Austin/MG/Rover Maestro 1.3 & 1.6 (83 - May 95) up to M	0922
Austin/MG Metro (80 - May 90) up to G	0718
Austin/Rover Montego 1.3 & 1.6 (84 - 94) A to L	1066
Austin/MG/Rover Montego 2.0 (84 - 95) A to M	1067
Mini (59 - 69) up to H	0527
Mini (69 - Oct 96) up to P	0646
Austin/Rover 2.0 litre Diesel Engine (86 - 93) C to L	1857
BEDFORD	
Bedford CF (69 - 87) up to E	0163
Bedford/Vauxhall Rascal & Suzuki Supercarry (86 - Oct 94) C to M	3015
BMW	
BMW 1500, 1502, 1600, 1602, 2000 & 2002 (59 - 77)*	0240
BMW 316, 320 & 320i (4-cyl) (75 - Feb 83) up to Y	0276
BMW 320, 320i, 323i & 325i (6-cyl) (Oct 77 - Sept 87) up to E	0815
BMW 3-Series (Apr 91 - 96) H to N	3210
BMW 3- & 5-Series (sohc) (81 - 91) up to J	1948
BMW 520i & 525e (Oct 81 - June 88) up to E	1560
BMW 525, 528 & 528i (73 - Sept 81) up to X	0632
CITROËN	
Citroën 2CV, Ami & Dyane (67 - 90) up to H	0196
Citroën AX Petrol & Diesel (87 - 97) D to P	3014
Citroën BX (83 - 94) A to L	0908
Citroën C15 Van Petrol & Diesel (89 - Oct 98) F to S	3509
Citroën CX (75 - 88) up to F	0528
Citroën Saxo Petrol & Diesel (96 - 01) N to X	3506
Citroën Visa (79 - 88) up to F	0620
Citroën Xantia Petrol & Diesel (93 - 98) K to S	3082
Citroën XM Petrol & Diesel (89 - 00) G to X	3451
Citroën Xsara Petrol & Diesel (97 - Sept 00) R to W	3751
Citroën ZX Diesel (91 - 98) J to S	1922
Citroën ZX Petrol (91 - 98) H to S	1881
Citroën 1.7 & 1.9 litre Diesel Engine (84 - 96) A to N	1379
FIAT	
Fiat 126 (73 - 87) *	0305
Fiat 500 (57 - 73) up to M	0090
Fiat Bravo & Brava (95 - 00) N to W	3572
Fiat Cinquecento (93 - 98) K to R	3501
Fiat Panda (81 - 95) up to M	0793
Fiat Punto Petrol & Diesel (94 - Oct 99) L to V	3251
Fiat Regata (84 - 88) A to F	1167
Fiat Tipo (88 - 91) E to J	1625
Fiat Uno (83 - 95) up to M	0923
Fiat X1/9 (74 - 89) up to G	0273
FORD	
Ford Anglia (59 - 68) *	0001
Ford Capri II (& III) 1.6 & 2.0 (74 - 87) up to E	0283

Title	Book No.
Ford Capri II (& III) 2.8 & 3.0 (74 - 87) up to E	1309
Ford Cortina Mk III 1300 & 1600 (70 - 76) *	0070
Ford Cortina Mk IV (& V) 1.6 & 2.0 (76 - 83) *	0343
Ford Cortina Mk IV (& V) 2.3 V6 (77 - 83) *	0426
Ford Escort Mk I 1100 & 1300 (68 - 74) *	0171
Ford Escort Mk I Mexico, RS 1600 & RS 2000 (70 - 74)*	0139
Ford Escort Mk II Mexico, RS 1800 & RS 2000 (75 - 80)*	0735
Ford Escort (75 - Aug 80) *	0280
Ford Escort (Sept 80 - Sept 90) up to H	0686
Ford Escort & Orion (Sept 90 - 00) H to X	1737
Ford Fiesta (76 - Aug 83) up to Y	0334
Ford Fiesta (Aug 83 - Feb 89) A to F	1030
Ford Fiesta (Feb 89 - Oct 95) F to N	1595
Ford Fiesta (Oct 95 - 01) N-reg. onwards	3397
Ford Focus (98 - 01) S to Y	3759
Ford Granada (Sept 77 - Feb 85) up to B	0481
Ford Granada & Scorpio (Mar 85 - 94) B to M	1245
Ford Ka (96 - 02) P-reg. onwards	3570
Ford Mondeo Petrol (93 - 99) K to T	1923
Ford Mondeo Diesel (93 - 96) L to N	3465
Ford Orion (83 - Sept 90) up to H	1009
Ford Sierra 4 cyl. (82 - 93) up to K	0903
Ford Sierra V6 (82 - 91) up to J	0904
Ford Transit Petrol (Mk 2) (78 - Jan 86) up to C	0719
Ford Transit Petrol (Mk 3) (Feb 86 - 89) C to G	1468
Ford Transit Diesel (Feb 86 - 99) C to T	3019
Ford 1.6 & 1.8 litre Diesel Engine (84 - 96) A to N	1172
Ford 2.1, 2.3 & 2.5 litre Diesel Engine (77 - 90) up to H	1606
FREIGHT ROVER	
Freight Rover Sherpa (74 - 87) up to E	0463
HILLMAN	
Hillman Avenger (70 - 82) up to Y	0037
Hillman Imp (63 - 76) *	0022
HONDA	
Honda Accord (76 - Feb 84) up to A	0351
Honda Civic (Feb 84 - Oct 87) A to E	1226
Honda Civic (Nov 91 - 96) J to N	3199
HYUNDAI	
Hyundai Pony (85 - 94) C to M	3398
JAGUAR	
Jaguar E Type (61 - 72) up to L	0140
Jaguar MkI & II, 240 & 340 (55 - 69) *	0098
Jaguar XJ6, XJ & Sovereign; Daimler Sovereign (68 - Oct 86) up to D	0242
Jaguar XJ6 & Sovereign (Oct 86 - Sept 94) D to M	3261
Jaguar XJ12, XJS & Sovereign; Daimler Double Six (72 - 88) up to F	0478
JEEP	
Jeep Cherokee Petrol (93 - 96) K to N	1943
LADA	
Lada 1200, 1300, 1500 & 1600 (74 - 91) up to J	0413
Lada Samara (87 - 91) D to J	1610
LAND ROVER	
Land Rover 90, 110 & Defender Diesel (83 -95) up to N	3017
Land Rover Discovery Petrol & Diesel (89 - 98) G to S	3016
Land Rover Series IIA & III Diesel (58 - 85) up to C	0529
Land Rover Series II, IIA & III Petrol (58 - 85) up to C	0314
MAZDA	
Mazda 323 (Mar 81 - Oct 89) up to G	1608
Mazda 323 (Oct 89 - 98) G to R	3455
Mazda 626 (May 83 - Sept 87) up to E	0929
Mazda B-1600, B-1800 & B-2000 Pick-up (72 - 88) up to F	0267
Mazda RX-7 (79 - 85) *	0460

Title	Book No.
MERCEDES-BENZ	
Mercedes-Benz 190, 190E & 190D Petrol & Diesel (83 - 93) A to L	3450
Mercedes-Benz 200, 240, 300 Diesel (Oct 76 - 85) up to C	1114
Mercedes-Benz 250 & 280 (68 - 72) up to L	0346
Mercedes-Benz 250 & 280 (123 Series) (Oct 76 - 84) up to B	0677
Mercedes-Benz 124 Series (85 - Aug 93) C to K	3253
Mercedes-Benz C-Class Petrol & Diesel (93 - Aug 00) L to W	3511
MG	
MGA (55 - 62) *	0475
MGB (62 - 80) up to W	0111
MG Midget & AH Sprite (58 - 80) up to W	0265
MITSUBISHI	
Mitsubishi Shogun & L200 Pick-Ups (83 - 94) up to M	1944
MORRIS	
Morris Ital 1.3 (80 - 84) up to B	0705
Morris Minor 1000 (56 - 71) up to K	0024
NISSAN	
Nissan Bluebird (May 84 - Mar 86) A to C	1223
Nissan Bluebird (Mar 86 - 90) C to H	1473
Nissan Cherry (Sept 82 - 86) up to D	1031
Nissan Micra (83 - Jan 93) up to K	0931
Nissan Micra (93 - 99) K to T	3254
Nissan Primera (90 - Aug 99) H to T	1851
Nissan Stanza (82 - 86) up to D	0824
Nissan Sunny (May 82 - Oct 86) up to D	0895
Nissan Sunny (Oct 86 - Mar 91) D to H	1378
Nissan Sunny (Apr 91 - 95) H to N	3219
OPEL	
Opel Ascona & Manta (B Series) (Sept 75 - 88) up to F	0316
Opel Ascona (81 - 88) (Not available in UK see Vauxhall Cavalier 0812)	3215
Opel Astra (Oct 91 - Feb 98) (Not available in UK see Vauxhall Astra 1832)	3156
Opel Astra & Zafira Diesel (Feb 98 - Sept 00) (See Astra & Zafira Diesel Book No. 3797)	
Opel Astra & Zafira Petrol (Feb 98 - Sept 00) (See Vauxhall/Opel Astra & Zafira Petrol Book No. 3758)	
Opel Calibra (90 - 98) (See Vauxhall/Opel Calibra Book No. 3502)	
Opel Corsa (83 - Mar 93) (Not available in UK see Vauxhall Nova 0909)	3160
Opel Corsa (Mar 93 - 97) (Not available in UK see Vauxhall Corsa 1985)	3159
Opel Frontera Petrol & Diesel (91 - 98) (See Vauxhall/Opel Frontera Book No. 3454)	
Opel Kadett (Nov 79 - Oct 84) up to B	0634
Opel Kadett (Oct 84 - Oct 91) (Not available in UK see Vauxhall Astra & Belmont 1136)	3196
Opel Omega & Senator (86 - 94) (Not available in UK see Vauxhall Carlton & Senator 1469)	3157
Opel Omega (94 - 99) (See Vauxhall/Opel Omega Book No. 3510)	
Opel Rekord (Feb 78 - Oct 86) up to D	0543
Opel Vectra (Oct 88 - Oct 95) (Not available in UK see Vauxhall Cavalier 1570)	3158
Opel Vectra Petrol & Diesel (95 - 98) (Not available in UK see Vauxhall Vectra 3396)	3523
PEUGEOT	
Peugeot 106 Petrol & Diesel (91 - 01) J to X	1882
Peugeot 205 Petrol (83 - 97) A to P	0932
Peugeot 206 Petrol and Diesel (98 - 01) S to X	3757
Peugeot 305 (78 - 89) up to G	0538

* Classic reprint

Title	Book No.
Peugeot 306 Petrol & Diesel (93 - 99) K to T	3073
Peugeot 309 (86 - 93) C to K	1266
Peugeot 405 Petrol (88 - 97) E to P	1559
Peugeot 405 Diesel (88 - 97) E to P	3198
Peugeot 406 Petrol & Diesel (96 - 97) N to R	3394
Peugeot 505 (79 - 89) up to G	0762
Peugeot 1.7/1.8 & 1.9 litre Diesel Engine (82 - 96) up to N	0950
Peugeot 2.0, 2.1, 2.3 & 2.5 litre Diesel Engines (74 - 90) up to H	1607

PORSCHE

Title	Book No.
Porsche 911 (65 - 85) up to C	0264
Porsche 924 & 924 Turbo (76 - 85) up to C	0397

PROTON

Title	Book No.
Proton (89 - 97) F to P	3255

RANGE ROVER

Title	Book No.
Range Rover V8 (70 - Oct 92) up to K	0606

RELIANT

Title	Book No.
Reliant Robin & Kitten (73 - 83) up to A	0436

RENAULT

Title	Book No.
Renault 4 (61 - 86) *	0072
Renault 5 (Feb 85 - 96) B to N	1219
Renault 9 & 11 (82 - 89) up to F	0822
Renault 18 (79 - 86) up to D	0598
Renault 19 Petrol (89 - 94) F to M	1646
Renault 19 Diesel (89 - 96) F to N	1946
Renault 21 (86 - 94) C to M	1397
Renault 25 (84 - 92) B to K	1228
Renault Clio Petrol (91 - May 98) H to R	1853
Renault Clio Diesel (91 - June 96) H to N	3031
Renault Clio Petrol & Diesel (May 98 - May 01) R to Y	3906
Renault Espace Petrol & Diesel (85 - 96) C to N	3197
Renault Fuego (80 - 86) *	0764
Renault Laguna Petrol & Diesel (94 - 00) L to W	3252
Renault Mégane & Scénic Petrol & Diesel (96 - 98) N to R	3395
Renault Mégane & Scénic (Apr 99 - 02) T-reg onwards	3916

ROVER

Title	Book No.
Rover 213 & 216 (84 - 89) A to G	1116
Rover 214 & 414 (89 - 96) G to N	1689
Rover 216 & 416 (89 - 96) G to N	1830
Rover 211, 214, 216, 218 & 220 Petrol & Diesel (Dec 95 - 98) N to R	3399
Rover 414, 416 & 420 Petrol & Diesel (May 95 - 98) M to R	3453
Rover 618, 620 & 623 (93 - 97) K to P	3257
Rover 820, 825 & 827 (86 - 95) D to N	1380
Rover 3500 (76 - 87) up to E	0365
Rover Metro, 111 & 114 (May 90 - 98) G to S	1711

SAAB

Title	Book No.
Saab 90, 99 & 900 (79 - Oct 93) up to L	0765
Saab 95 & 96 (66 - 76) *	0198
Saab 99 (69 - 79) *	0247
Saab 900 (Oct 93 - 98) L to R	3512
Saab 9000 (4-cyl) (85 - 98) C to S	1686

SEAT

Title	Book No.
Seat Ibiza & Cordoba Petrol & Diesel (Oct 93 - Oct 99) L to V	3571
Seat Ibiza & Malaga (85 - 92) B to K	1609

SKODA

Title	Book No.
Skoda Estelle (77 - 89) up to G	0604
Skoda Favorit (89 - 96) F to N	1801
Skoda Felicia Petrol & Diesel (95 - 01) M to X	3505

SUBARU

Title	Book No.
Subaru 1600 & 1800 (Nov 79 - 90) up to H	0995

SUNBEAM

Title	Book No.
Sunbeam Alpine, Rapier & H120 (67 - 76) *	0051

SUZUKI

Title	Book No.
Suzuki SJ Series, Samurai & Vitara (4-cyl) (82 - 97) up to P	1942
Suzuki Supercarry & Bedford/Vauxhall Rascal (86 - Oct 94) C to M	3015

TALBOT

Title	Book No.
Talbot Alpine, Solara, Minx & Rapier (75 - 86) up to D	0337
Talbot Horizon (78 - 86) up to D	0473
Talbot Samba (82 - 86) up to D	0823

TOYOTA

Title	Book No.
Toyota Carina E (May 92 - 97) J to P	3256
Toyota Corolla (Sept 83 - Sept 87) A to E	1024
Toyota Corolla (80 - 85) up to C	0683
Toyota Corolla (Sept 87 - Aug 92) E to K	1683
Toyota Corolla (Aug 92 - 97) K to P	3259
Toyota Hi-Ace & Hi-Lux (69 - Oct 83) up to A	0304

TRIUMPH

Title	Book No.
Triumph Acclaim (81 - 84) *	0792
Triumph GT6 & Vitesse (62 - 74) *	0112
Triumph Herald (59 - 71) *	0010
Triumph Spitfire (62 - 81) up to X	0113
Triumph Stag (70 - 78) up to T	0441
Triumph TR2, TR3, TR3A, TR4 & TR4A (52 - 67)*	0028
Triumph TR5 & 6 (67 - 75) *	0031
Triumph TR7 (75 - 82) *	0322

VAUXHALL

Title	Book No.
Vauxhall Astra (80 - Oct 84) up to B	0635
Vauxhall Astra & Belmont (Oct 84 - Oct 91) B to J	1136
Vauxhall Astra (Oct 91 - Feb 98) J to R	1832
Vauxhall/Opel Astra & Zafira Diesel (Feb 98 - Sept 00) R to W	3797
Vauxhall/Opel Astra & Zafira Petrol (Feb 98 - Sept 00) R to W	3758
Vauxhall/Opel Calibra (90 - 98) G to S	3502
Vauxhall Carlton (Oct 78 - Oct 86) up to D	0480
Vauxhall Carlton & Senator (Nov 86 - 94) D to L	1469
Vauxhall Cavalier 1300 (77 - July 81) *	0461
Vauxhall Cavalier 1600, 1900 & 2000 (75 - July 81) up to W	0315
Vauxhall Cavalier (81 - Oct 88) up to F	0812
Vauxhall Cavalier (Oct 88 - 95) F to N	1570
Vauxhall Chevette (75 - 84) up to B	0285
Vauxhall Corsa (Mar 93 - 97) K to R	1985
Vauxhall/Opel Corsa (Apr 97 - Oct 00) P to X	3921
Vauxhall/Opel Frontera Petrol & Diesel (91 - Sept 98) J to S	3454
Vauxhall Nova (83 - 93) up to K	0909
Vauxhall/Opel Omega (94 - 99) L to T	3510
Vauxhall Vectra Petrol & Diesel (95 - 98) N to R	3396
Vauxhall/Opel 1.5, 1.6 & 1.7 litre Diesel Engine (82 - 96) up to N	1222

VOLKSWAGEN

Title	Book No.
Volkswagen 411 & 412 (68 - 75) *	0091
Volkswagen Beetle 1200 (54 - 77) up to S	0036
Volkswagen Beetle 1300 & 1500 (65 - 75) up to P	0039
Volkswagen Beetle 1302 & 1302S (70 - 72) up to L	0110
Volkswagen Beetle 1303, 1303S & GT (72 - 75) up to P	0159
Volkswagen Beetle Petrol & Diesel (Apr 99 - 01) T reg onwards	3798
Volkswagen Golf & Bora Petrol & Diesel (April 98 - 00) R to X	3727

Title	Book No.
Volkswagen Golf & Jetta Mk 1 1.1 & 1.3 (74 - 84) up to A	0716
Volkswagen Golf, Jetta & Scirocco Mk 1 1.5, 1.6 & 1.8 (74 - 84) up to A	0726
Volkswagen Golf & Jetta Mk 1 Diesel (78 - 84) up to A	0451
Volkswagen Golf & Jetta Mk 2 (Mar 84 - Feb 92) A to J	1081
Volkswagen Golf & Vento Petrol & Diesel (Feb 92 - 96) J to N	3097
Volkswagen LT vans & light trucks (76 - 87) up to E	0637
Volkswagen Passat & Santana (Sept 81 - May 88) up to E	0814
Volkswagen Passat Petrol & Diesel (May 88 - 96) E to P	3498
Volkswagen Passat 4-cyl Petrol & Diesel (Dec 96 - Nov 00) P to X	3917
Volkswagen Polo & Derby (76 - Jan 82) up to X	0335
Volkswagen Polo (82 - Oct 90) up to H	0813
Volkswagen Polo (Nov 90 - Aug 94) H to L	3245
Volkswagen Polo Hatchback Petrol & Diesel (94 - 99) M to S	3500
Volkswagen Scirocco (82 - 90) up to H	1224
Volkswagen Transporter 1600 (68 - 79) up to V	0082
Volkswagen Transporter 1700, 1800 & 2000 (72 - 79) up to V	0226
Volkswagen Transporter (air-cooled) (79 - 82) up to Y	0638
Volkswagen Transporter (water-cooled) (82 - 90) up to H	3452
Volkswagen Type 3 (63 - 73) *	0084

VOLVO

Title	Book No.
Volvo 120 & 130 Series (& P1800) (61 - 73) *	0203
Volvo 142, 144 & 145 (66 - 74) up to N	0129
Volvo 240 Series (74 - 93) up to K	0270
Volvo 262, 264 & 260/265 (75 - 85) *	0400
Volvo 340, 343, 345 & 360 (76 - 91) up to J	0715
Volvo 440, 460 & 480 (87 - 97) D to P	1691
Volvo 740 & 760 (82 - 91) up to J	1258
Volvo 850 (92 - 96) J to P	3260
Volvo 940 (90 - 96) H to N	3249
Volvo S40 & V40 (96 - 99) N to V	3569
Volvo S70, V70 & C70 (96 - 99) P to V	3573

AUTOMOTIVE TECHBOOKS

Title	Book No.
Automotive Air Conditioning Systems	3740
Automotive Brake Manual	3050
Automotive Carburettor Manual	3288
Automotive Diagnostic Fault Codes Manual	3472
Automotive Diesel Engine Service Guide	3286
Automotive Electrical and Electronic Systems Manual	3049
Automotive Engine Management and Fuel Injection Systems Manual	3344
Automotive Gearbox Overhaul Manual	3473
Automotive Service Summaries Manual	3475
Automotive Timing Belts Manual – Austin/Rover	3549
Automotive Timing Belts Manual – Ford	3474
Automotive Timing Belts Manual – Peugeot/Citroën	3568
Automotive Timing Belts Manual – Vauxhall/Opel	3577
Automotive Welding Manual	3053
In-Car Entertainment Manual (3rd Edition)	3363

* Classic reprint

CL13.4/02

Preserving Our Motoring Heritage

< The Model J Duesenberg Derham Tourster. Only eight of these magnificent cars were ever built – this is the only example to be found outside the United States of America

Almost every car you've ever loved, loathed or desired is gathered under one roof at the Haynes Motor Museum. Over 300 immaculately presented cars and motorbikes represent every aspect of our motoring heritage, from elegant reminders of bygone days, such as the superb Model J Duesenberg to curiosities like the bug-eyed BMW Isetta. There are also many old friends and flames. Perhaps you remember the 1959 Ford Popular that you did your courting in? The magnificent 'Red Collection' is a spectacle of classic sports cars including AC, Alfa Romeo, Austin Healey, Ferrari, Lamborghini, Maserati, MG, Riley, Porsche and Triumph.

A Perfect Day Out

Each and every vehicle at the Haynes Motor Museum has played its part in the history and culture of Motoring. Today, they make a wonderful spectacle and a great day out for all the family. Bring the kids, bring Mum and Dad, but above all bring your camera to capture those golden memories for ever. You will also find an impressive array of motoring memorabilia, a comfortable 70 seat video cinema and one of the most extensive transport book shops in Britain. The Pit Stop Cafe serves everything from a cup of tea to wholesome, home-made meals or, if you prefer, you can enjoy the large picnic area nestled in the beautiful rural surroundings of Somerset.

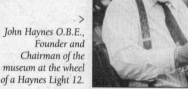

John Haynes O.B.E., Founder and Chairman of the museum at the wheel of a Haynes Light 12.

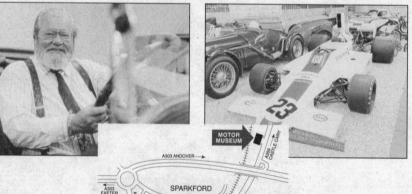

< Graham Hill's Lola Cosworth Formula 1 car next to a 1934 Riley Sports.

The Museum is situated on the A359 Yeovil to Frome road at Sparkford, just off the A303 in Somerset. It is about 40 miles south of Bristol, and 25 minutes drive from the M5 intersection at Taunton.
Open 9.30am - 5.30pm (10.00am - 4.00pm Winter) 7 days a week, *except Christmas Day, Boxing Day and New Years Day*
Special rates available for schools, coach parties and outings Charitable Trust No. 292048